LEADERSHIP
FOR HEALTH PROFESSIONALS

Theory, Skills, and Applications

Gerald (Jerry) R. Ledlow, PhD, MHA, FACHE
Associate Professor
Jiann-Ping Hsu College of Public Health
Georgia Southern University
Statesboro, Georgia

M. Nicholas Coppola, PhD, MHA, FACHE
Program Director and Associate Professor
School of Allied Health Sciences
Texas Tech University Health Sciences Center
Lubbock, Texas

JONES & BARTLETT
LEARNING

World Headquarters
Jones & Bartlett Learning
40 Tall Pine Drive
Sudbury, MA 01776
978-443-5000
info@jblearning.com
www.jblearning.com

Jones & Bartlett Learning
Canada
6339 Ormindale Way
Mississauga, Ontario L5V 1J2
Canada

Jones & Bartlett Learning
International
Barb House, Barb Mews
London W6 7PA
United Kingdom

Jones & Bartlett Learning books and products are available through most bookstores and online booksellers. To contact Jones & Bartlett Learning directly, call 800-832-0034, fax 978-443-8000, or visit our website, www.jblearning.com.

Substantial discounts on bulk quantities of Jones & Bartlett Learning publications are available to corporations, professional associations, and other qualified organizations. For details and specific discount information, contact the special sales department at Jones & Bartlett Learning via the above contact information or send an email to specialsales@jblearning.com.

This publication is designed to provide accurate and authoritative information in regard to the Subject Matter covered. It is sold with the understanding that the publisher is not engaged in rendering legal, accounting, or other professional service. If legal advice or other expert assistance is required, the service of a competent professional person should be sought.

Production Credits
Publisher: David Cella
Associate Editor: Maro Gartside
Editorial Assistant: Teresa Reilly
Production Manager: Julie Champagne Bolduc
Associate Production Editor: Jill Morton
Marketing Manager: Grace Richards
Assistant Photo Researcher: Rebecca Ritter
Manufacturing and Inventory Control Supervisor: Amy Bacus
Composition: DataStream Content Solutions, LLC
Cover Design: Kristin E. Parker
Cover Image: © Adam Jastrzębowski/Dreamstime.com
Printing and Binding: Malloy, Inc.
Cover Printing: John P. Pow Company

Library of Congress Cataloging-in-Publication Data
Ledlow, Gerald R.
  Leadership for health professionals : theory, skills, and applications / by Gerald R. Ledlow and M. Nicholas Coppola.
    p. ; cm.
  Includes bibliographical references and index.
  ISBN-13: 978-0-7637-8151-4
  1. Health services administration. 2. Leadership. I. Coppola, M. Nicholas. II. Title.
  [DNLM: 1. Health Services Administration. 2. Leadership. W 84.1 L473L 2011]
  RA971.L3686 2011
  362.1068—dc22
                                                                    2010011837

6048

Printed in the United States of America
15 14 13 12   10 9 8 7 6 5 4 3

Contents

Foreword

It is a privilege to write a foreword for this new book by Dr. Gerald Ledlow and Dr. Nicholas Coppola, for two reasons. First, the topic of leadership is something that has been central to my 20-plus years in academia, either in the books and articles I have written or in the courses I have taught. Second, I have known both Jerry and Nick for many years as trusted friends and respected colleagues. Both have excelled in their own careers within and outside of academia. They themselves are leaders who have become scholars of leadership theory and practice. Their book, *Leadership for Health Professionals: Theory, Skills, and Applications*, represents the culmination of many years of leadership engagement and scholarship in health organizations throughout the world and across all sectors of society, including public, private, and nonprofit agencies.

While reading an advance copy of this book, I was reminded of an interview I did as editor of the *Journal of Healthcare Management*. The interview was with Warren Bennis, noted as one of the top 10 leadership scholars and authors in history. In response to one of my questions about the essence of leadership, Dr. Bennis described the leader as "one who manifests direction, integrity, hardiness, and courage in a consistent pattern of behavior that inspires trust, motivation, and responsibility on the part of the followers who in turn become leaders themselves" (Johnson, 1998). I have never seen a more succinct and comprehensive description of the leader. However, in the book you are about to read, you will indeed gain a comprehensive understanding of leadership that captures the deep and rich meaning I was able to hear firsthand in that interview.

Leadership for Health Professionals: Theory, Skills, and Applications addresses the full scope of leadership, with its many challenges and its special significance in healthcare environments. Furthermore, the book provides the breadth of knowledge and range of skills an individual needs to improve his or her own leadership abilities and effectiveness. As I have advocated in my own writings, leaders of today and tomorrow are compelled to adopt principles and practices that create sustainable organizations. In particular, there must be a focus on the co-equal and vital mandates of financial viability, social responsiveness, and environmental responsibility (Johnson, 2009). The book you are about to read will provide you with a substantial and timely understanding of the art and science of leadership that will help you shape the world in meaningful and productive ways. Enjoy and learn.

James A. Johnson, PhD
Medical Social Scientist and Professor
Central Michigan University

REFERENCES

1. Johnson, J. A. (1998, July/August). Interview with Warren Bennis. *Journal of Healthcare Management, 43*(4), 293.
2. Johnson, J. A. (2009). *Health organizations: Theory, behavior, and development.* Sudbury, MA: Jones and Bartlett.

Preface

As the authors of this book, we want to thank you for purchasing and using this textbook for professional development, instruction, and education. We believe that the title of this book says it all: *Leadership for Health Professionals: Theory, Skills, and Applications.* Up to this point, there has not been a development-focused textbook, specific to health organizations and health professionals, that combines the classical knowledge of leadership theory in the literature with the time-honored best practices and outcomes associated with the skills and applications practiced by industry leaders. Until the publication of this book, students, educators, and professionals were placed in the position of having to buy two (or more) texts, or supplement their readings with multiple journal articles, to achieve the compilation of knowledge presented in these pages.

This textbook captures our collective hope of enabling and encouraging ever-improving leadership practice, continuous leadership development, and ultimately a more effective, efficient, and efficacious health industry. From our own practical experience, academic study, and facilitation of leadership instruction over the past 25 years, we fervently posit that great leadership practice is one of a few critical factors necessary to ensure quality healthcare delivery, good health status in our communities, and high levels of productivity in our society. As part of our ongoing effort to improve leadership practice, we developed this book and the associated materials for your use as a learning system.

The foundation of this health leadership learning system is informed by the following definition: **Leadership** is the *dynamic* and *active* creation and maintenance of an organizational *culture* and *strategic systems* that focus the collective energy of both *leading people and managing resources* toward *meeting the needs of the external environment* utilizing the most efficient, effective, and, most importantly, efficacious methods possible by moral means. As a system, the text is based on the hierarchical learning stages of Bloom's Taxonomy of the Cognitive Domain. It takes advantage of our experiences in facilitating leadership instruction to graduate students from all walks of life and with varying levels of practical health experience for more than a decade. Put simply, the material, concepts, theories, models, applications, and skills integrated within this system greatly facilitate learning. A graduate student, reviewing this work from a student's perspective, wrote the following.

> As a student, I have learned that the material taught in a course is often not as valuable as the way in which it is taught. Drs. Ledlow and Coppola have succeeded in integrating the content of leadership practice with learning how to lead in their text, *Leadership for Health Professionals: Theory, Skills, and Applications.* Students will be eager, as was I, to learn the methods employed within this

rich text. The health industry is a dynamic and engaging environment where the only constant is change. This text allows the student to become engaged in the material and extrapolate the roles, obligations, and responsibilities of leaders and managers. Drs. Ledlow and Coppola have spent years instructing health leaders and have simplified the exercise of learning into a concise, easy-to-follow format that can be straightforwardly adapted into today's ever-changing leadership environment. The reiteration of material sets a foundation, expands upon the context, and then places the information into a health context. This repetition makes it easy to learn and maximize what a student gains from a course. This text illustrates how to address continuity and stabilization in an environment ripe with change and uncertainty.

Compiled into four parts, the text begins by establishing the fundamentals of leadership (Part 1: Leadership Foundations). The thorough analysis of leadership's history establishes the underpinnings of organization and practice (Part 2: Leadership in Practice). By studying the practice of leadership, the rudimentary components of organizational structure emerge and define organizational leadership (Part 3: Leadership in Health Organizations). These building blocks establish the core theme that people are led and resources are managed (Part 4: Leading People and Managing Resources into the Future). This system facilitates learning. The knowledge is applicable and blends well into the dynamic environment of the health industry. The recurrent theme of leading people and managing resources is laced within Bloom's Taxonomy, offering a comfortable fit to any student. This is an exemplary offering to any student with the capacity to learn and grow as a leader in the health industry.

From a content perspective, themes of leadership principles, applications, and constructs such as organizational culture, cultural competency, ethical frameworks and moral practice, scientific methodology, leader competencies, external and internal assessment and evaluation, communication, planning, decision making, employee enhancement, and knowledge management are woven through the entire text and the supplemental materials. These themes are presented in multiple contexts throughout the book, and echoed in multiple chapters. To wit, the most important constructs and concepts are presented in an early chapter, further expanded and explored in a middle chapter, and then used in a context in a later chapter. The reiteration of key leader systems, actions, and behaviors provides additional opportunities for learning within a leadership course. Many times, students have not been exposed much to the material presented in a leadership course, so multiple interactions with critical content material are both efficacious and pedagogically sound. In practice, students learn more with construct and content reiteration in a time-limited semester or term.

Collectively, the authors of this book have more than 50 years of professional leadership experience that spans the continuum of health care from ambulatory clinics, to large multisite and multidisciplinary health entities, to academia. In this text, we combine our practitioner knowledge and experience and our academic experience to elucidate the competencies and learning outcomes required for graduate programs. In combining both practitioner knowledge and industry best practices in graduate education, it is our desire that you will find the studying, learning, and/or instructing of health leadership more effective, efficient, and efficacious and will enjoy a competitive advantage in your own career. It is our expectation that through studying this text, your leadership will bring about a better health organization, community, industry, and society through your application of the theories, skills, and concepts presented in this textbook.

In closing, we believe strongly that learning is a lifelong process that requires continuous exposure to, thinking about, and reflection on new information that can be turned into knowledge that is "actionable" in your leadership practice. Although this book went through a rigorous peer review process, we actively encourage feedback on its content from students, educators, and professional executives in the field. If any part of this book requires additions or omissions, please contact us. We also encourage active contribution to this text for future editions. Should you or your colleagues desire to share for consideration any cases, models, exercises, or written text for inclusion in future editions, please do not hesitate to contact us with your ideas and suggestions. If applicable and possible, your contributions may be included in future versions of this text.

Thank you for allowing us to take part in your leadership development and practice!

Acknowledgments

As in any major project, teamwork, collaboration, compromise, and dedication are required for a successful outcome when writing a book. God, first and foremost, has nurtured, loved, and cared for me and my family to enable all that I am. My beautiful wife, Silke, and my wonderful daughters, Sarah, Rebecca, and Miriam, supported and encouraged my work for this textbook: Thank you, and I love you all very much. Heidi Hulsey, a doctoral candidate and my assistant, worked tirelessly to assist in reviewing and refining the manuscript and supporting materials; her work is greatly appreciated. Nick Coppola, my partner in this project, provided a superb collegial environment while working intelligently and diligently on the many aspects of this textbook and supporting materials: Thank you for your collaborative spirit and dedication. Lastly, I greatly appreciate and empathize with the myriad of health leaders—those now on the stage and those waiting in the wings—who provide the organizational nourishment, direction, and moral fiber for the health industry on a daily basis. I am greatly encouraged by those health leaders who "lead people and manage resources" in our dynamic world.

Gerald (Jerry) R. Ledlow, PhD, MHA, FACHE

Becoming a leader is a process that cannot be accomplished alone. Although the names would be too numerous to mention, dozens of mentors and role models over the decades have provided guidance, encouragement, and wisdom that I now share with the readers of this text. I thank all of them for allowing me to share their knowledge with you. My heartfelt thanks also go out to my spouse (and better half), Susannah, and my three wonderful children, Nicholas, Holly, and GiGi. My family supported me during more than one late night and weekend visit to the office while writing this text. Thank you for your love and support. I also want to thank the students in my leadership classes who aided in the development of this effort. Furthermore, I extend my gratitude to my graduate assistants for conducting research and literature reviews for this book: Major Jake Bustoz, Jeanette Krajca, and Corey Morrell. Special thanks are extended to my friend and colleague, Dr. Jerry Ledlow. Without his generous invitation to partner on this leadership journey with him, I would not be a co-author on this text. Finally, thank you to all the health leaders currently working in the industry today who make the U.S. healthcare system the most respected in the world!

M. Nicholas Coppola, PhD, MHA, FACHE

Author Biographies

GERALD (JERRY) R. LEDLOW, PHD, MHA, FACHE

 Dr. Gerald (Jerry) R. Ledlow, as a board-certified healthcare executive and Fellow in the American College of Healthcare Executives, has led team members and managed resources in health organizations for more than 25 years, including 15 years as a practitioner and a decade as an academically based teacher–scholar. He has successfully held a variety of positions: (1) executive-level positions in corporate and military health systems in the areas of clinical operations, managed care, supply chain and logistics, information systems, and facility management; (2) management positions in health services, medical materials, and the supply chain; and (3) various academic leadership positions as the director of doctoral programs at two universities, director of academic affairs, director of student services, and director of the center for survey research and health information, as well as holding tenured faculty positions at two doctoral research universities. Dr. Ledlow earned his PhD in organizational leadership from the University of Oklahoma, a master of health administration degree from Baylor University, and a bachelor of arts degree in economics from the Virginia Military Institute. He has held tenured graduate faculty positions at Central Michigan University and currently is a tenured associate professor and graduate faculty member at Georgia Southern University.

Dr. Ledlow has taught 24 different graduate-level courses, including teaching doctoral- and master's-level students in the topic of health leadership. "Dr. Jerry" (as his students call him) has made presentations on health-related topics and health leadership models and applications across the globe; he has presented to a myriad of audiences internationally, nationally, and locally. He has published in many venues (e.g., journals, book chapters) and has been author, contributing author, editor, and reviewer for several books.

Dr. Ledlow is married to his beautiful wife, Silke, and has three fantastic daughters, Sarah, Rebecca, and Miriam. He is a regional editor for the *Journal of Global Business and Technology,* is on several publication review teams, and participates as a member of various task forces and committees internationally, nationally, and at the state level. Years ago, Dr. Jerry was a National Registry–certified emergency management technician as a volunteer and was deployed to combat zones as a commissioned officer in the U.S. Army Medical Service Corps. He received the Federal Sector Managed Care Executive of the Year Award in 1998 and the American College of Healthcare Executives' Regent's Award in 1997 and in 2003. His interests are health industry oriented and focus on the areas of leadership, management, decision sciences, supply chain and logistics, community preparedness for terrorism and disasters, socioeconomic constructs of health and community health status, and any project that has the potential to improve the health of communities through moral, effective, efficient, and efficacious health leadership and management practices.

M. NICHOLAS COPPOLA, PHD, MHA, FACHE

Dr. M. Nicholas Coppola is the Program Director for the Healthcare Master of Science in Clinical Practice Management program at Texas Tech University Health Sciences Center. He is also the (elected) American College of Healthcare Executives (ACHE) Regent for the West Texas Region. In this capacity, he represents the interests of nearly 500 senior healthcare executives in West Texas and New Mexico.

Dr. Coppola retired from the U.S. Army in 2008 after more than 26 years of officer and enlisted service. He served in progressive leadership positions in engineer, infantry, and medical units. Dr. Coppola is also the past ACHE Regent for the Army. In this capacity, he represented the interests of Army healthcare executives worldwide. Dr. Coppola is the Founding Associate Dean of the Army Medical Department's Graduate School, and was the Founding Program Director of the Army–Baylor Graduate Program in Health and Business Administration (MHA/MBA joint degree). He is an ACHE Fellow, and a Past Fellow of the U.S. Medicine Institute.

Dr. Coppola earned a master of science degree in administration from Central Michigan University, and a master of health administration degree from Baylor University, Texas. He has a PhD in health service organizations and research from the Medical College of Virginia Campus, Virginia Commonwealth University.

Dr. Coppola is the author of more than 100 scholarly publications and presentations, and has lectured globally on healthcare leadership and healthcare administration. He is the proud recipient of numerous leadership awards, including the 9A Proficiency Designator award from the Surgeon General (which identifies the top 1 percent of Army medical personnel), four ACHE Leader-to-Leader awards, one ACHE Governor's Award, and awards of leadership and recognition from every university from which he has earned a degree. Prior to his military retirement, officers worldwide nominated and elected him as the Medical Service Corps' Mentor of the Year. Dr. Coppola is listed in two national *Who's Who* publications, and is a member of three national honor societies in allied health, business, and healthcare administration.

Dr. Coppola and his wife, Susannah, have three wonderful children together: Nicholas, Holly, and GiGi.

Contributors

Donald M. Bradshaw
Senior Partner, Martin, Blanck & Associates
Falls Church, Virginia

Michael Sack
President and CEO, Hallmark Health
Melrose, Massachusetts

Susan Reisinger Smith, DHA, MSN, RN
Chief Executive Officer, Regency Hospital of
    Central Georgia
Macon, Georgia

James H. Stephens, FACHE
Assistant Professor and Distinguished Fellow in
    Healthcare Leadership
MHA Director
Jiann-Ping Hsu College of Public Health
Georgia Southern University
Statesboro, Georgia

Reviewers

Jean E. Beatson, EdD, RN
Research Assistant Professor
University of Vermont
Burlington, Vermont

Pauline A. Cawley, PharmD
Assistant Professor
School of Pharmacy
Pacific University–Oregon
Forest Grove, Oregon

Cynthia Clark, RN, PhD, ANEF
Professor
Boise State University
Boise, Idaho

Colonel Lawrence V. Fulton, United States Army,
    PhD, MSStat, MHA, MS, MMAS, MSSl
Professor
Baylor University
Waco, Texas

Ahmad Hakemi, MD
Program Director
Central Michigan University
Mount Pleasant, Michigan
Medical Director
Baxter Healthcare Corporation
Deerfield, Illinois

Marcy Halterman-Cox, DC, JD, MSPH
Clinical Assistant Professor
Texas A&M Health Science Center
    College of Medicine
College Station, Texas

Jeffrey P. Harrison, PhD, MBA, MHA, FACHE
Associate Professor
University of North Florida
Jacksonville, Florida

Heidi Hulsey
Doctoral Candidate and Graduate Assistant
Jiann-Ping Hsu College of Public Health
Georgia Southern University
Statesboro, Georgia

Michael H. Kennedy, PhD, MHA, FACHE
Associate Professor
East Carolina University
Greenville, North Carolina

Anthony A. Miller, MEd, PA-C
Professor and Director, Division of Physician
    Assistant Studies
Shenandoah University
Winchester, Virginia

Tony Palmer, RPh, MBA
Coordinator, OUPTCH Pharmacy Services
Clinical Associate Professor
University of Oklahoma College of Pharmacy
Tulsa, Oklahoma

Lisa Tekell, MS, OTR/L, OTD
Academic Fieldwork Coordinator,
  Assistant Professor
University of Tennessee Health Science Center
Memphis, Tennessee

Jesse C. Vivian, JD
Professor
Wayne State University
Detroit, Michigan

1

Leadership Foundations

1

Leadership Thought

The leader is a stimulus, but he is also a response.
Edward C. Lindeman, *Social Discovery*

Leadership has been important to human endeavor for thousands of years. Debates about leadership and the ways in which leaders came into power have been prevalent for centuries. Some leaders are born with instinctive leadership skills, charisma, and insights into human motivation. Even so, all great leaders must devote time, energy, and study to various aspects of leadership to master the discipline while developing superior competencies in situational assessment, motivation, communication, and understanding dynamic group behavior. Whatever the case, health professionals should consider the discipline of leadership as one of the more important aspects of personal and professional education. Leadership in the health industry is required to navigate and successfully solve problems of cost, quality, and access to care across the continuum of care in our society.

LEARNING OBJECTIVES

1. Outline why the study of leadership is important to professionals in the health industry and what the challenges in the industry requiring quality leadership are.
2. Explain and give examples of leadership as compared with management, and state why health organizations need both leaders and managers.
3. Relate and discuss the application of a prescriptive leadership model compared to a descriptive leadership model.
4. Distinguish the phases of leadership thought from ancient to modern times, and identify unique characteristics associated with each of these phases.
5. Relate the phases of leadership thought to modern leadership practices and research.
6. Evaluate the health industry's need for leadership today and into the next decade.

INTRODUCTION

People are led and resources are managed! Knowing this critical and sometimes subtle difference is the beginning of leadership wisdom. Leadership wisdom is an essential component to being successful in a fast-paced, ever-changing, and highly complex health environment.[1] Today, "evidence-based leadership" is a common phrase, as are "evidence-based management" and "evidence-based medicine." "Evidence-based" means that the practice of leadership, management, and medicine is informed by empirical evidence from the structure, process, and—especially—outcomes of practice. This text provides foundations, principles, and strategies for leadership that are also informed by quantitative and qualitative evidence.

This chapter presents some of the basic definitions and distinctions of leadership. Specific emphasis is placed on defining the importance of leadership study in the healthcare environment and its appropriate place in the field of both academics and professional practice. Leadership is differentiated from management; although there are certainly differences between these two skills, health organizations need leaders and managers who are consistently focused on the direction of the enterprise. Emphasis is placed on both descriptive (tells about "leadership") and prescriptive (gives direction and guidance) notions of leadership before the basic goals of leadership—and the text—are presented to readers. In summary, this chapter provides an overview of the complex and exciting topic of leadership.

Within the realms of graduate education, business practice, and organizational analysis, there is no topic more important than the study of leadership. The contemporary study of leadership is a century-old, enormously complex discipline; however, fewer topics inspire more interest and have more stakeholder consequences than leadership in any organization in any industry. In the highly complex health industry, the role of leadership is further pronounced, and adept leadership is clearly necessary for success. Furthermore, no great leaders of our time have become successful and prosperous without first understanding the principles of leadership. This book encapsulates the best practices in the health and business environment for the edification of early careerists, students, and experienced health leaders alike, so as to enhance their knowledge, skills, and abilities.[2, 3]

As scholars, future practitioners, and current practitioners, our role as professionals is to perform at least two roles—that is, to "wear two hats." One of these "hats" is that of the practitioner, who is directly in touch with the delivery of human services in health systems and leadership change for process improvement. In this role, you work closely with individuals, families, and other groups, organizations, and communities as a helping professional; from this perspective, you are positioned to observe the issues and emerging trends that most challenge those persons you serve in living healthy and fulfilling lives. The other "hat" you wear is that of scholar. In other words, early careerists must be capable of becoming a critical consumer of leadership research by personal study. Leaders *must* be aware of both the practices and habits of successful leaders, as well as the recognized traits and skills that are commensurate with leadership success as documented in the literature over the years.[4, 5] For example, when as a working health executive, suppose you encounter an issue with outside stakeholders that you are not familiar with. It is to your benefit to turn to the archived literature and search out articles and research that can help you gain deeper understanding of the problem facing you. Because of your training in leadership gained from this text, as well as from your mentors and educators, you can approach this literature with a basic understanding of the foundations of leadership and select the most appropriate course of action based on both your burgeoning experience and the successful practices documented in the literature of best practices.

Leadership is holistic. This means that leadership means leading laterally or collaboratively, and not just from upper echelons in a top-down approach. Leadership entails leading the people, the structure, and the processes of the organization. In addition to the many definitions of this concept, there is an abundance of literature on leadership in general, leadership principles, and topics related to leadership. As a topic, leadership is of immense interest to international militaries, governments, businesses, and health organizations. Leadership and attributed outcomes in schools are commonly taught but likewise encompass varying approaches and lines of thought.[6]

THE PURPOSE OF THIS LEADERSHIP TEXT

The purpose of this text is to provide you with a foundation for not only the study of leadership practice and theory, but also the broader concept of leading people and health organizations across multiple and interconnected disciplines. A second goal is to bridge theory and the abstract concepts of leadership with the practical or concrete operational behaviors and action of leaders. This goal is integrated with the discussion of the popular evidence-based leadership of today. We meet these goals by utilizing a four-tier strategy that walks students, early careerists, and practicing health leaders through the foundations of leadership, leadership principles and practices, and the complexity of leadership in health care, and finally into the world of leading people and managing resources into the future. Comprising four parts, this text is geared toward building readers' leadership knowledge, skills, and abilities.

Although the discipline of leadership, with its myriad of related topics, theories, and models, is rather large and extensive in the literature and knowledge base, the authors' perspective focuses on the most pertinent leadership content, theories, models, principles, and strategies that produce results in the health industry. The authors have put many of these theories and models into practice during the course of our successful practitioner careers. Of course, the health industry differs in many ways from other services and products industries: Many times efficacy is more important than efficiency, patient outcomes are more important than profits/margin, the "rational man" theory of economics is set aside when certain injuries or illnesses invade our families such that chaos or irrational economic decisions prevail, and society holds the health industry to an extremely high standard of perfection. Moreover, health organizations are extremely complex, run continuously, and are highly regulated and scrutinized. These realities create a distinctive leadership niche—that of the health leader. This text is intended specifically for the person filling that role.

This textbook combines both the scholarship of the academy of leadership and the practicalities involved in leading people and managing resources in the real world. With more than 50 years of combined experience leading people in complex organizations, the authors hope to impart that experience to the next generation of health leaders in a way that is both meaningful and useful to scholars and practicing health professionals.

People are led and resources are managed! This text has multiple objectives. This text was created to provide you with an understanding of leadership principles; an ability to apply leadership principles through actions, behaviors, and processes in a dynamic world; a capacity to synthesize leadership theories and models to create a personalized leadership model; and the ability to evaluate leadership theories, models, principles, and ideas in a sound manner. Most importantly, the intent of this text is to develop an increasingly competent and confident cadre of leaders for the health industry so that complex health systems, population health status, and a multidisciplinary health workforce can be improved, enhanced, and strengthened to successfully overcome the significant challenges that society faces now and in the future. Six key trends in the health industry, identified in 2009, clearly highlight the need for quality, competent, and enthusiastic leadership:

1. "Quality and performance reporting will shift from value-add to essential.
2. Asset rightsizing will provide new levers to fund strategic growth.
3. Departmental autonomy will fade as technology enables an enterprise view.
4. Care architecture will drive smarter facility design.
5. Effective leaders will be part policymaker, part entrepreneur.
6. Managing clinical staff will require new thinking and methods."[7]

To achieve success in the health industry, an organization must have focused and intelligent effort. Leaders are the catalysts for organizational, group, and individual greatness. This book seeks to make you a better leader who can lead a group or organization to accomplish great achievements; the ultimate goal is for you to have a fulfilling health career. The authors applaud your enthusiasm to become a better leader!

This text serves as your road map to start your leadership journey, a multidisciplinary journey. In essence, this text is a catalyst to begin or continue your leadership development. Later in this chapter, a summary of the text is provided to introduce the spectrum of content covered in each chapter. Each chapter was carefully conceptualized, written, refined, and integrated into a whole text to better serve you, the future leader. At the end of the text, you will be able to develop your personal leadership system for practical application. Along the way, you should strive to become a better leader who is poised to morally conquer challenges, improve our communities, and serve others.

Why Study Leadership?

Leaders of any organization encounter issues and decision-making challenges in everyday life. Some decisions are easily solved, whereas others may call for a critical analysis of the situation, a split-second judgment, an assessment made by one individual, or decisions made by a group. Whatever the circumstances, the decisions that are made will have consequences for human resources and the organization itself. It is, therefore, necessary for individuals to be trained in leadership and to become well equipped to make the right decision at the right time.[8]

The concept and discussion of leadership is ancient; the discipline of leadership study can be consistently traced back to Machiavelli in 1530, with first documentation of leadership dating back to 2300 B.C. However, leadership theory and research is a relatively modern discipline. Indeed, the first relevant theories were not proposed until the mid-1800s. From approximately 1840 to 1880, "great man" theorists Carlyle, Galton, and James studied great men from history who exhibited certain traits and suggested those traits led to successful leadership.[9] This theory was later abandoned for more valid and reliable theories of leadership based on best practice and sound discovery. Many of these theories will be addressed later in this text. For now, simply recognize that for nearly 125 years some of the greatest minds have attempted to catalogue and archive best practices in leadership for the benefit of the next generation of leaders and the current chief executives in the field. Although this area is a relatively modern topic of study, numerous qualitative and quantitative experiments continue to fill the stacks of journal articles each year. Clearly, the study of leadership is complex and ongoing, and the current and newer theories of leadership vary with its definitions as defined by the authors.[10] The authors of this book welcome you to the world of the study of leadership research and practice, and encourage you to join the many generations who came before in search of continuing education and new tools for your leadership toolkit.

Leadership is one of the few academic disciplines that is difficult for early careerists to embrace without both didactic training and real-world experience. While some leaders may possess natural predispositions allowing them to become successful in small circles in colloquial events, successful leader practitioners will agree that as their ever-increasing circles of influence grow, it becomes necessary to develop and hone natural predispositions while simultaneously cultivating new skills necessary to bring them to the next level of leadership. Leadership skills and traits that enable a person to become successful within one circle with one group of individuals with particular skill sets and academic disciplines may not allow the same person to become successful in the increasingly more complex concentric circles.[11, 12] All leaders along the continuum of care must engage in lifelong learning to be successful.

Many early careerists find that the transition from being a follower and an employee to one who leads others and takes responsibility can be difficult. Mistakes must be made and experience accumulated at lower supervisory levels to gain a perspective on which kind of leader each individual can become. However, without knowing the best practices of leaders, the strategies leaders employ for success, and the natural predispositions emulated by leaders, it will be difficult for early careerists to become successful.[13] Also, the health environment is continually changing. For example, recent literature suggests the need for new models of nurse leadership to deal with dynamic change but also to serve as the bridge between clinical and administrative practice in health organizations.[14]

This text provides an overview of many of the facets of leadership in which early careerists will become engaged over their career. For example, leadership diagnostics are included to help you identify your natural predispositions toward introversion or extroversion. While these traits may already be well known to you, formally diagnosing them provides a road map to developing those skills lacking in many persons who are determined to be leaders while also identifying current strengths to build upon. If an early careerist is already leaning toward extroversion, he or she may already be comfortable in delivering clear goals and sharing vision statements with future groups of employees. For those on the other side of the spectrum, developmental opportunities are suggested such as joining professional organizations and speaking groups where it may be possible to "practice" developing extrovert tendencies.

Leadership is a "universal phenomenon."[15] As long as people are part of the equation of health systems as workforce members and patients, leadership will be a critical component of successful organizations. "Since the effectiveness of the leader has frequently determined the survival or demise of a group, organization, or an entire nation, it has been of concern to some of the foremost thinkers in history, like Plato, Machiavelli, and von Clausewitz. If leadership were easy to understand, we would have had all the answers long before now."[16] Today, leadership far too often focuses more on *coping* strategies than on *leading* strategies. As scholars and experienced leadership practitioners in the health industry, the authors believe that leadership needs to be dramatically improved to enhance today's systems and deal with the challenges our society faces. It is not acceptable to merely perpetuate the status quo.

The coping strategy nature of leadership has been a concern for at least the past two decades, if not longer. In 1989, Warren Bennis talked about this issue in *Why Leaders Can't Lead: The Unconscious Conspiracy Continues,* in which he discussed the restrictions leaders place on themselves. More recently, Jo Manion, in 1998's *From Management to Leadership: Interpersonal Skills for Success in Health Care,* discussed the critical decline of skills and the overall lack of leadership in the healthcare industry. Hints of self-protection and self-promotion have begun to taint the noble profession of health leadership. It seems that there is a significant lack of morality, knowledge, skills, and abilities at the individual leader level.

In the last decade, nurse managers have learned that they must rely on more "leadership" capabilities than on "nurse" capabilities to be successful.[17] In 2000, Ian Morrison posited several leadership challenges for different sectors of the health industry:

> "Political organizations must: 1) create a political consensus that sweeping changes are necessary (possibly using public outrage over the uninsured as fuel); 2) reduce party (Republican and Democrat) indifference of each other and work together to develop and implement long-term strategies for the country; and 3) [reform] Medicare to more closely resemble the Federal Employees Health Benefits Program (defined contribution). Managed care must: 1) reassert preeminence as leaders in innovation for both quality and value; 2) find a sustainable business strategy to deliver on the promise of truly managing care; and 3) overcome their negative image with the public and physicians. Hospitals and health systems must: 1) reconcile the difference between improving the health of communities with delivering sick care; and 2) unite on certain public policy positions despite the diversity between hospitals, and the communities they serve. Physicians must: 1) nominate physician leaders and follow the solutions proposed by those leaders; 2) move beyond the vision of returning to the "good old days"; and 3) "take a stand" and help to develop models of organization and reimbursement. Pharmaceutical and the medical technology industry must: 1) deal with high out-of-pocket costs before voters (elderly [voters], in particular, have begun this) force the government to legislate more reforms; and 2) keep focus on what they do best (research and development to produce new drugs). Lastly, public health leaders and workers must: 1) decide to participate in the mainstream of medical care (as opposed to remaining off to the side as a critic); 2) decide how to incorporate the ideas of public health into the mainstream political agenda without sounding too much like socialism for the average American (socialism and fiscally irresponsible social justice ideology will not "play well" in mainstream America); and 3) [recognize that] the public health community can be incredibly self-righteous about having a monopoly on compassion for the poor[18]; this social expression is perceived by others as arrogance, so toning down the rhetoric must occur so that public health can become more inclusive across health disciplines.[19]

To tackle these challenges, leadership is required. Those who wish to lead must be competent; competence starts with knowing what you know and what you do not know.

There are four states of knowing:

- Unconscious incompetence, where "we do not know that we do not know"
- Conscious incompetence, where "we know that we do not know"
- Conscious competence, where "we know how to perform a skill but must consciously think about it"
- Unconscious competence, where performance of a skill is second nature[20]

Moving from one state of knowing to another takes considerable effort. Becoming a "conscious leader" takes study, effort, trial, error, and evaluation. Clearly, the most successful health leaders are not lucky, but rather are competent at leading people to do important and tremendous tasks and achieve great success. Successful leaders have discipline, persistence, and humility while continuously working to improve their capabilities.

Studying, learning, and applying leadership knowledge, skills, and abilities are crucial to being a successful leader in the health industry. Regardless of where and at what level you lead—as a laboratory chief, physical therapy director, clinical office administrator, or health system chief executive officer—leadership knowledge, skills, and abilities are important to you, your organization, and the communities you serve. The health industry in the United States is destined for renewal; leadership will be essential to the health industry throughout this period of change.[21]

Regardless of cultural identity, all leaders of health organizations lead people and manage resources. Their work involves focusing the collective energy of both leading people and managing resources toward meeting the needs of the external environment in the most efficient, effective, and—most importantly—efficacious approach possible (that is, focusing on the mission of the organization). It is important for leaders to understand that the individuals who make up the health workforce are people with vastly different education, training, and experience. These same individuals also have vastly different roles within the organization—and no leader can ever hope to understand the complexity of all aspects of jobs within the system. As a result, the good leader's job is to successfully motivate individuals within the organization toward goal-directed behavior that supports the leader's vision and organization's mission.

The last important job of leaders is the management of nonhuman resources in the system. The role of a healthcare administrator, healthcare executive, public health leader, or healthcare manager is to merge the complexity of leading people and the complexity of managing resources into a culture that serves communities by maintaining and improving the health of individuals in those communities. This is done by influencing the people and distributing the resources under their stewardship to serve those individuals who come to health organizations for assistance, to build strong and effective relationships with their communities, and, especially, to build working relationships with the public health infrastructure in their communities.

INTRODUCTION OF LEADERSHIP IN ACADEMICS AND PRACTICE

Leadership has never been defined based on any one experience, theory, or historical study. Rather, leadership is the product of several cumulative factors from several different cultural disciplines. Cultural leadership is discussed in more detail later in this text. For now, it is important to know that the education and development of a leader require a broader perspective that emphasizes leadership as both a process and a set of scientific/technical and artistic/relational skills and abilities in need of development.[22]

History is replete with stories and examples of fearless, selfless leaders—people who have risked their lives and fought on against seemingly insurmountable odds or who have been able to motivate those around them to go beyond what they believed they were capable of accomplishing. For example, anthropology, archeology, social anthropology, political science, psychology, business, communication, and numerous other disciplines have all contributed to the foundations of leadership theory and practice. Leadership has been observed and documented for centuries: "leaders as prophets, priests, chiefs and kings served as symbols, representatives, and models for their people in the Old and New Testaments, in the Upanishads, in the Greek and Latin classics, and in the Icelandic sagas."[23] Initiated by necessity, leadership in practice was observed and documented by scholars of the era, and the connection between leadership practice and academic understanding of leadership began. Four thousand and three hundred years ago, in the Instruction of Ptahhotep (2300 B.C.), three qualities were attributed to the Pharoah's leadership.[24] In many ways, the documentation, study, synthesis and evaluation of leadership has been a key basis of humans' historical record.

Most modern studies and research have been U.S. or "Western" based, although recently a little more effort has been devoted to international applications of leadership. This has not always been the case: In ancient times, "the subject of leadership was not limited to the classics of Western literature. It was of as much interest to Asoka and Confucius as to Plato and Aristotle."[25] However, much of our current literature on leadership is greatly influenced by Western culture and the documentation of history through the leaders' exploits such as during the time of the Roman Empire. Remnants of the Roman Empire attest to the power of leadership in society as illustrated in the next figures.

Until recently (the 1930s–1940s), emphasis on leadership has focused on trait theories and the "great man" theory. Trait theory assumes that individuals possess certain traits or attributes that serve as the catalyst to leadership and securing leadership roles. Behavior theory gained acceptance in the 1940s; this research phase focused on which styles or behaviors leaders used and how those styles contributed to subordinate satisfaction, perfor-

FIGURE 1–1   Ancient Ruins of the Roman Forum
Early "leadership" documentation can be attributed to ancient Egyptian, Greek, Roman, Chinese, and Persian societies.

FIGURE 1–2   The Ruins of the Ancient Roman Senate

TABLE 1–1   Leadership Theory and Model Categorization Through Time

Great Man and Trait Phase (Circa 450 B.C.–1940s)	Behavior Phase (1940s–1960s)	Situational Phase (1970s–Present)
Attempted to determine which specific traits make a person an effective leader	Attempted to determine which particular behaviors/styles leaders utilize to cause others to follow them	Attempts to explain effective leadership within the context of the larger work situation

mance, and quality. The behavior research first acknowledged that leadership and leading could be a learned skill. Very recently (considering the more than 4,300 years of leadership information and knowledge), situational leadership has gained favor. This line of research suggests that successful leaders must assess the situation and then choose the appropriate leadership style to make the greatest positive impact on subordinate effort; it assumes that leaders have a full "toolbox" of capabilities. All phases of leadership research build on each other and are interwoven into various models of leadership.

Is there "truth" in all three phases of research? What can you take away from each phase of study and information? Hundreds of leadership theories have been proposed, although only a dozen or so really show promise. Using the three phases (summarized in **Table 1–1**), this text provides a framework to make sense of the enormity of leadership foundational research. The next few chapters cover a moderate amount of leadership research; the remainder of the book then focuses on application of leadership, the processes and skills of leadership, and ethical and moral issues related to leadership.

FIGURE 1–3   Sign of Leadership Power and Influence in Ancient Rome

Even with more than 4,300 years of leadership practice, observation, and scholarly synthesis and evaluation, what we know about leadership continues to elude mastery. When examining the major leadership theories commonly accepted by practitioners and theorists, the similarities of the theories may be rather intuitive for many leaders, *but the lessons have often not been learned.* "For example, the following components are shared across theories: (1) vision, (2) inspiration, (3) role modeling, (4) intellectual stimulation, (5) meaning-making, (6) appeals to higher order needs, (7) empowerment, (8) setting of high expectations, and (9) fostering collective identity . . . models basically share similar beliefs about the role of vision in providing direction and meaning."[26]

Thinking About Leadership

Leadership is both an art and a science (**Table 1–2**).[27] Fundamentally, the leadership art encompasses relationships, interpersonal skills, timing and tempo, power, and intuition. The science of leadership embodies technical acumen, skills, and principles along with expertise of the business of health.

From this very broad thought process, five important foundations must be in place for true leadership success, even as the individual strives to better balance the *science* and the *art* of leadership. First, communication knowledge, skills, and abilities need to be in place, which means that the individual leader knows how, what, and when to communicate to important constituencies, and how to become known as authentic and genuine. A keen sense of communication means that the leader understands, interprets, and utilizes nonverbal and symbolic communication as well as verbal means. Second, consistency of behavior and temperament are highly prized, both by subordinates and those to whom the leader is accountable. Third, emotional intelligence is a valued foundation for the leader, as it connotes the ability to monitor self and social settings, and then to govern behavior accordingly. Fourth, the effective leader understands the powerful relationship between trust and understanding; increased trust leads to greater understanding, and increased understanding in turn leads to greater trust.

Finally, the role of integrity cannot be overstated. In many ways, the previous four foundations are part of what is considered integrity in leadership. That is, a leader with integrity communicates in a fair and balanced manner; is consistent in living a life of integrity, on and off the job; and is trustworthy and understood, because the leader values trusting and understanding others. Integrity in leadership, however, includes many more elements. Leadership integrity means sometimes being alone to act in a moral fashion. It means doing the right thing for the organization while not forgetting the rights and sensibilities of individuals. It means putting the interests of others before and above one's own. Integrity, coupled with competence, forms the necessary foundation for a successful health leader.

TABLE 1–2   Leadership as a Science Compared to an Art

Science	Art
Technical skills orientation: forecasting, budgeting	Relationship oriented: networking, interpersonal relationships
Decisions are based more on analysis	Decisions are based more on perceptions of people
Developing systems is important to organizations	Developing relationships and networks are important to organizations
Expert systems	Experts as people
Cost control and evaluation of value are important	Image and customer relationships are important

Source: Ledlow, G., & Cwiek, M. (2005). The process of leading: Assessment and comparison of leadership team style, operating climate and expectation of the external environment. *Proceedings of Global Business and Technology Association,* Lisbon, Portugal.

Many leadership theories and models contain elements of both the science and artistry of leadership, either directly or by implication. Consider the model by Chambers of the six agencies of leadership: (1) communication; (2) participation; (3) preparation; (4) identification of options; (5) closure (move beyond past conflicts, negativity, and inequity); and (6) celebration.[28] Of these six agencies, some are artistic, some are scientific, and others could work both ways. The science is embodied in processes and tasks associated in evaluating, planning, decision making, and training. The artistry of leadership is embodied in processes and tasks associated in relationship building, communicating, persuading, coaching, and evaluating or establishing context. The scientist-leader and the artist-leader both envision, create and develop, and implement. The key is to produce the best possible results through solid leadership, to do that which must be done to balance science and art. Where the scientist and the artist converge is in the creation, implementation, refinement, and maintenance of communication systems, strategic planning, decision-making systems, employee enhancement mechanisms, organizational learning, and knowledge management.

While leaders are gifted in different ways, with different personalities and varying skill sets, all leaders can grow, become more skillful, and become more competent so that they can achieve greater effectiveness. The common factors shared by those who succeed in becoming great leaders in the health industry are the desire to learn more about themselves, the motivation to learn and practice new skill sets, and the need to become more tomorrow than what they are today. This is not the easiest path, but it is the path that optimizes the likelihood of leadership effectiveness and success.

Defining Leadership

Numerous studies have demonstrated that leaders—and more specifically, the characteristics, styles, and traits that leaders exhibit—influence organizational performance and success. Thus definitions of leadership and development of definitions and applications for leadership in the health environment are very important. Different perceptions and paradigms exist across the literature. Perception is how people see something within a context; paradigm is how they understand something in a context. Perceptions and paradigms may be "right" or "wrong."[29] There are five characteristics of paradigms, according to Harris and Nelson:

- Paradigms mitigate uncertainty.
- Uncertainty leads to unpredictability, so individuals are driven to find a paradigm to make sense of the situation.
- Past successes lead individuals to use the same paradigm, thereby causing them to neglect situation-based or other solutions.
- Paradigms are imitated when homogeneous groups lead paradigm solutions.
- As long as they are logically optimal, paradigms continue to be used even though they may be flawed.[30]

Different perceptions and paradigms create different definitions of leadership. The complexity of leading and the complexity of the industry or organization where leadership occurs increase the ambiguity.

The definition of leadership found in a typical dictionary—in this case, *Webster's Dictionary*—is somewhat tautological. The first two entries in *Webster's* state that "leadership is the position of office of the leader" and "leadership is the capacity or ability to lead." Further review of the term "leader" is similarly tautological, with definitions stating a leader is "one who leads." Perhaps scholarly researchers of leadership theory do not know how or where to apply leadership theory within the environment. After a thorough review of the literature over a 50-year period, Yukl has suggested that there are as many definitions of leadership as there are researchers attempting to study it. Additionally, new definitions associated with leadership continue to be introduced into the literature every year.

When the famed Native American and cavalry fighter Geronimo was asked what made him a good leader, he replied, "The ability to ride a strong horse." General Douglas MacArthur said during World War II that a leader's only mission was to win wars.[31] According to Indian leader Mahatma Gandhi, leadership was about getting along with people, whereas U.S. General Colin Powell suggested leadership was about solving problems. Management guru Peter Drucker countered this philosophical trend, suggesting that leadership was not about being liked, but rather about obtaining results. Finally, President Dwight Eisenhower stated that "Leadership is the art of getting someone else to do something you want done because he wants to do it."[32] The lack of a clear, parsimonious, accepted, and applied model of leadership is a fundamental weakness within the literature. Additionally, few leadership studies actually define leadership before researching variables associated with it.

Within the refereed literature, leadership is said to be as much an art as a science. Leadership is also a cultural phenomenon, allowing for different traits and characteristics to emerge as successful parables across society. Lastly, leadership is a dynamic and evolving paradigm that takes on different literal and figurative definitions over the centuries. With so many available and partisan positions on leadership, it is easy to understand why there continues to be vehement debate on defining, testing, framing, and understanding this concept.

Conservative leadership empiricists suggest the understanding of leadership is founded in traditional research methods and may be discerned through the development of testable hypotheses and the operationalization of demonstrable unit variables that are derived from latent constructs. Liberal leadership enthusiasts advocate acceptance of leadership as an art; like beauty itself, its definition may lie in the eye of the beholder. One person's leader may be another's despot. Additionally, framing leadership is not culture free; one's understanding of this concept lives in a sea of bias (or differing perceptions and paradigms). Techniques and activities developed in one society may need to be adapted to be effective in another. American society recognizes leadership regardless of age or gender, whereas Asian and Middle Eastern societies place heavy emphasis on gender and age as precursors to leader recognition.

Akin to cultural awareness is the perspective of time. For more than two millennia, many leaders were selected to fill their positions owing to their associations with feudal guilds, religious associations, or tribal rituals. In early Greek and Roman societies, leaders were often recognized and rose through the ranks into important senate and military positions through associations with other men of power. Finally, leadership recognition was often a matter of genetics and bloodlines, similar to the situation found in European and Asian monarchies.

With such a broad base and so many potential starting points for leadership, is it possible that the terms "leader" and "leadership" may have been misunderstood and leadership constructs misapplied? Early geographic, anthropological, and scientific literature is often flawed and full of assumptions and opinions often presumed to be fact until something better comes along. A whimsical example is the "flat earth theory," which was largely abandoned after the invention of the telescope and the circumnavigation of the globe by early mariners. Other scientific research is less amusing and produces harmful consequences.

Organizational literature is likewise peppered with misnomers and reevaluated ideas. Older theories, such as Fredric Taylor's scientific management, management by objectives (MBO), and even participatory management, are rarely used and applied as theoretical frameworks within modern literature. These earlier theories suggested micromanagement, a high degree of structure, or consensus making were cornerstones to management success. Contemporary literature suggests treating employees like objects, restricting their freedom, and allowing too much creativity are counterproductive to organizational goals. Managers must possess some of the skills of the leader to be successful in the practice of management, but management is separate from the leadership discipline itself. That is, leadership is just one of the many assets a successful manager must possess. Care must be taken in distinguishing between the two concepts. The main aim of a manager is to maximize the output of the organization through administrative implementation.

Some authors have suggested that the terms "leader" and "leadership" are culturally confounded with alternative and non-equivalent positions. For example, these terms are culturally confounded with the terms associated with "manager," "supervisor," "public figure," and several other non-leadership or non-leader designations. This misapplication has had an adverse impact on health policy and planning, as the wrong caliber of individual is made responsible for areas of responsibility over and above his or her level of competence. The simple truth is that people are led and resources are managed.

A basic definition of leadership, as identified by Peters and Waterman, might suggest that leadership is "the process of influencing others to accomplish the mission by providing purpose, direction, and motivation."[33] These authors may have defined this term best when they suggested the following:

> Leadership is many things. It is patient, usually boring coalition building. It is the purposeful seeding of cabal that one hopes will result in the appropriate ferment in the bowels of the organization. It is meticulously shifting the attention of the institution through the mundane language of management systems. It is altering agendas so that new priorities get enough attention. It is being visible when things are going awry and invisible when they are working well. It's listening carefully

much of the time, frequently speaking with encouragement, and reinforcing words with believable action. It's being tough when necessary, and it's the occasional naked use of power.

Numerous definitions and variants of definitions can be found in the literature. A few definitions of leadership are provided here:

■ In 1961, Tannenbaum, Weschler, and Massarik defined leadership as *interpersonal influence*, exercised in a situation, and *directed* through the *communication* process, toward the attainment of a specified *goal or goals.*[35]

■ In 1974, Stogdill stated that leadership is the initiation and maintenance of *structure* in expectation and *interaction.*[35]

■ In 1982, in their bestselling book *In Search of Excellence*, Peters and Waterman defined leadership as guiding an organization toward success.[34]

■ In 1984, Rauch and Behling suggested that leadership is the process of *influencing* the activities of an organized *group* toward *goal* achievement.[35]

■ In 1990, Jacobs and Jacques stated that leadership is a process of *giving purpose* (meaningful direction) to *collective effort*, and causing *willing effort* to be expended to achieve purpose.[35]

■ In 1994, Yukl noted that most definitions of leadership reflect the assumption that it involves a social influence process whereby intentional influence is exerted by one person over other people to structure the activities and relationships in a group or organization."[35]

■ In 1999, it was suggested that leader is "the unique and important function of leadership, contrasted with management or administration; is the conceptualization, creation and management of *organizational culture.*"[36]

■ In 2000, Blanchard and Hersey suggested that leadership is the ability to foster and succeed in obtaining good outcomes and noted that leadership is the result of training, not just the consequence of an accident or good fortune.[37]

■ In 1990, Covey stated that leaders catalyze commitment to and vigorous pursuit of a clear and compelling vision while at the same time inspiring and leading the group to achieve high performance standards.[38]

■ In 2005, Gupta suggested that leadership is a discipline and that the ability to effectively discipline an organization's structure and habits consistently is a positive technique.[39]

■ In 2008, Ling and colleagues suggested that leadership requires an individual's ability to motivate and instill pride in followers so that followers operate beyond self-interest and do what is necessary for the good of the organization.[40]

■ In 2009, Ledlow and Coppola defined leadership as the ability to assess, develop, maintain, and change the organizational culture and strategic systems to optimally meet the needs and expectations of the external environment.[41]

Schein's well-established paradigm of leadership is an excellent example of implied scientific and artistic elementalism. That is, the unique and important function of leadership, contrasted with management or administration, is defined as the conceptualization, creation, and management of *organizational culture.*[42] Culture is a learned system of knowledge, behavior, attitudes, beliefs, values, and norms that is shared by a group of people.

> Leaders go beyond a narrow focus on power and control in periods of organizational change. They create commitment and energy among stakeholders to make the change work. They create a sense of direction, then nurture and support others who can make the new organization a success."[43]

Other important elements of leadership (including leadership teams) include the cultural impact of leadership. An important consideration in this realm is the cultural impact of communication on leadership effectiveness. The need to be skillful with regard to cultural differences illustrates not just the global challenges of leadership, but also the richness of different styles of leadership, individually and as a leadership team. The areas of greatest interest include individualism versus collectivism, time perception, and high versus low communication contexts.

For health leaders in particular—and for leaders in general, for that matter—the definition of leadership used in this book comes from integrating ideas, study, and research from many scholars and practitioners that came before. *Leadership* is the *dynamic* and *active* creation and maintenance of an organizational *culture* and *strategic systems* that focus the collective energy of both *leading people and managing resources* toward *meeting the needs of the external environment* utilizing the most efficient, effective, and efficacious methods possible by moral means.

There is, however, a distinction between what is considered *management* and what is considered *leadership*. A manager tends to be more reactive and stays more closely coupled to organizational policies, standards, guidelines, and established processes. A health leader tends to be more proactive and more involved in developing the organizational culture and strategic systems (such as the supply chain, human resources, revenue management, financial, and clinical operational systems of the core organizational functions) necessary to maximize the efficiency, effectiveness, and efficacy of the organization within the external environment.

Leadership is one of the most widely debated and broadly defined organization theories within the realm of organization behavior. Strong partisan opinions abound, such that leaders are differentiated by disciplines or positions. The study of leadership has occupied hundreds of pages and decades of debate within the refereed literature, with little agreement on discussion and results to show for these efforts.[44] A review of searchable databases at the Library of Congress in Washington, D.C., while employing a series of partially overlapping searches using the terms "leader," "leadership," "manager," "executive," "supervisor," and "director," covering printed material from 1945 to 1995, suggests the common media (comprising television, radio, and newspapers) has popularized the term "leadership" above the other terms.

The discussions of leadership and leaders have transcended traditional boundaries in recent decades, with these terms being used synonymously and extended to describe behavior and phenomena in management, supervisory positions, coaching, education, role models, celebrities, political representatives, inspirational personnel, sports figures, and subject matter experts, among others. Despite well-respected literature that distinctly separates leadership from other identifiers, the term "leadership" continues to be used to describe a plethora of activities in society.[45]

Because of this misapplication, the terms "leader" and "leadership" have dominated the fashionable connotations associated with non-equivalent positions, resulting in a popularly accepted hierarchy. Being a leader is perceived as better than being just a manager, supervisor, or subject matter expert. Being designated a leader rather than a manager (or something else) results in an artificial perception of status, which translates into a "feel good" perception for the individual.

Perhaps this evolution is, in part, associated with the increasing competition for the best employees and other cultural changes that occurred within society in the last century. A review of want ads in *The Washington Post* finds few vacancies for "secretaries," but identifies several requests for "administrative assistants." Janitorial positions are advertised as "custodial engineers." The American College of Healthcare Executives contains a directory of search firms that suggests few hospitals are hiring "medical doctors." Instead, the current spin appears to be searching for "physician leaders."

As a result of these ever-broader applications, the term "leadership" has become ubiquitous within the literature and society. Consequently, leadership constructs are no longer viewed as distinct and mutually exclusive. A review of the literature, in fact, suggests there is no single construct unique to leadership theory. Researchers of leadership theory are often forced to borrow from the plethora of micro-organizational theories in the discipline to explain phenomena associated with leadership theory.

What is your definition of leadership? What is your definition of management?" Are your definitions different?

Defining Management

There is a definite difference between leaders and managers. For example, one researcher has suggested that managers think incrementally, whereas leaders think radically. Moreover, Predpall states that "Managers do things right, while leaders do the right things."[46] Another distinction is that leaders do not manage daily operations, but rather they create vision and motivation; in contrast, managers implement objectives and programs.[47]

Several authors have suggested that leaders must have good managerial skills to organize and delegate tasks; however, not all managers have the ability to direct complex health organizations and guide vision and strategy.

As Maxwell has suggested, an individual is either a follower or a leader: There is no in between—you are either a reactor or an imitator, not both.[48]

As a final distinction, leaders must let vision, strategies, goals, and values become the guideposts for their action and behavior rather than attempting to merely control others. This is starkly different from the managerial function itself, which has almost by definition an inherent obligation to know the daily duties and productivity of the persons under the manager's supervisory control.[49]

As a reading of the body of leadership literature quickly reveals, many researchers over the decades have blurred the lines between leadership and management. Today, much of this fuzziness still exists. Within this "gray area," you should decide what makes an excellent manager and what defines an excellent leader for yourself. Leadership and management are compared in **Table 1–3**.

A further distinction can be seen in the values associated with team building and relationship nurturing. For example, managers may be involved with evaluating outcomes of employees, whereas leaders are responsible for selecting the original talent in the organization. Another example might suggest that managers oversee the daily accountability to a fiscal budget, whereas leaders direct the strategy dictating where elements of resources will be allocated. Finally, managers may act as facilitators between employees and the upper leadership team, whereas the leadership team itself instills and builds trust through maintaining a healthy, surviving, and prosperous organization where employees' job security, benefits, and livelihoods are maintained.[50]

In the simplest terms, *management* is the *process* of *getting activities completed* efficiently and effectively with and *through other people.*[51] Management functions and sets of knowledge, skills, and abilities have been researched for several decades. The most widely accepted approach for classifying managerial skills is in terms of a categorization system (called a "taxonomy"). Those skills are defined as follows:

■ *Technical skills*: knowledge about methods, processes, procedures, and techniques for conducting specialized activity; the ability to use those tools and equipment relevant to the activity.

■ *Interpersonal skills*: knowledge about human behavior and interpersonal processes; the ability to understand the feelings, attitudes, and motives of others; the ability to communicate effectively; the ability to establish effective relationships.

■ *Conceptual skills*: general analytical ability; logical thinking; proficiency in concept formation and conceptualization of complex and ambiguous relationships; creativity in idea generation and problem solving; the

TABLE 1–3   Comparison of Leadership and Management

Leadership	Management
Longer time horizon	Shorter time horizon
Vision, then mission oriented	Mission oriented
Organizational validity (Are we doing the right things?): environmental scanning and intuition	Organizational reliability (Are we doing things correctly and consistently?): compliance with rules and policies, and rule development
Does the organization have the correct components (people, resources, expertise) to meet future as well as current needs?	How can current components work best now?
Developing and refining organizational culture to meet external environment needs	Maintaining organizational climate to ensure performance
Timing and tempo of initiatives and projects	Scheduling of initiatives and projects

Source: Ledlow, G., & Cwiek, M. (2005). The process of leading: Assessment and comparison of leadership team style, operating climate and expectation of the external environment. *Proceedings of Global Business and Technology Association,* Lisbon, Portugal.

ability to analyze events and perceive trends, anticipate changes, and recognize opportunities and potential problems (inductive and deductive reasoning).

- *Administrative skills*: the ability to perform a particular type of managerial function or behavior (planning, organizing, delegating, negotiating, coaching, conducting meetings).[52, 53]

Indeed, leadership and management research, literature, and practice have intermingled to a high degree. A leader can be a manager, and a manager can be a leader. Many times, depending on your job role and responsibilities, you have to be both leader and manager. Typically, the higher a person moves up the career ladder, the more extensively leadership thinking, behaviors, and actions are used. Successful organizations have both effective leaders and managers. The key to success is the consistency and focus on the organization's mission across the leadership and management team. Both leaders and managers are on the same health organizational team, focused on similar outcomes, but performing their responsibilities differently to ensure successful results.

In summary, the difference between management and leadership is based on experience and potential. For example, managers are usually employees who have experience in the field and discipline within the area of work and production with which the organization is associated. They are generally individuals who have worked their way up through the ranks of a company from "mailroom"-type activities to a position where their knowledge of policies, practices, and procedures creates a stable environment of institutionalism such that daily operations are consistent and operations of daily reoccurring work remain relatively constant. Managers will know each layer of work under them—and in many cases, be able to perform the duties of the subordinates under them. In stark contrast is the leader, who may be a new arrival to the organization, yet whose careful risk taking, vision, wisdom, and ideas are capable of breaking down barriers and propelling the organization toward new levels of productivity and performance.[54]

Organizations Need Leaders and Managers

Leaders are essential to organization achievement and success. Managers are essential to organization achievement and success. Both leaders and managers must work in concert to develop an effective system with which to administer an organization. Henry Mintzberg, a prominent management researcher, scholar, and author, describes management in terms of roles. As you read through the descriptions of these managerial roles, consider the leader and manager comparison presented earlier in this chapter and determine whether a leader or a manager, or both, would perform roles defined by Mintzberg.

In Mintzberg's work, chief executive officers were observed. During this process, managerial work was categorized as encompassing 10 roles: three that involved mainly *interpersonal contact* (figurehead, leader, and liaison); three that involved *information processing* (monitor, disseminator, and spokesperson); and four that related to *decision making* (entrepreneur, disturbance handler, resource allocator, and negotiator). Managerial roles can be independent of situations that rely on traits and behavioral theories, although this line of research has proved more valid with the situational approach where managers move from role to role depending on the situation. The Mintzberg roles for managers are as follows:

- *Figurehead*: based on formal authority; symbolic duties of a legal and social nature.
- *Leader*: responsible for making the organization function as an integrated whole in pursuit of the mission/goals of the organization.
- *Liaison*: behavior intended to establish and maintain a web of relationships internal and external to the organization.
- *Monitor*: continually seeking information from a variety of sources (situational analysis, environmental "scanning").
- *Disseminator*: special access to information not available to subordinates; passing on of information to subordinates and, in some degree, to peers and superiors.
- *Spokesperson*: obligation to transmit information and express value statements to people outside of the organization.

- *Entrepreneur*: initiator and designer of controlled change; exploiting change to improve the current situation or position for future risk.

- *Disturbance handler*: dealing with sudden crises that cannot be ignored (conflict, for example). Typically, the manager gives this role priority over others.

- *Resource allocator*: authority to allocate scarce resources (power).

- *Negotiator*: negotiations requiring substantial commitment of resources are facilitated by the manager having the authority to make commitments.[55]

Leaders and managers have different perspectives on the health organization and their personal roles within that organization. Both need to be "on the same page" to meet the organization's mission and vision. Again, an administrator or executive can be both a leader and a manager depending on the situation, job position, and immediate role required at the time. As long as the health industry remains dynamic, both leaders and managers are essential to the organization's success and survival; coordination and consistency of their efforts are keys to determine how well the strategic leadership/management system performs over time.

LEADERS AND SYSTEMS: INDIVIDUAL, GROUP, ORGANIZATION, AND INDUSTRY SUCCESS

Leadership requires a predetermined vision of an individual, group, organization, and industry as a whole. The complexity of the leader's actions and behaviors increases as one moves from individual to group, to organization, and so on. As complexity increases, the need for a predetermined vision, consistency, development of a strategic leadership and management system, and development of an improved culture intensifies as well. Leaders use strategic systems to direct the organization—but people are still led and resources are managed. In health organizations, a number of systems are integrated (or should be integrated) to provide tools for leaders to lead, including strategic human resources management systems, strategic supply chain systems, financial and revenue management systems, information and decision support systems, a strategic planning system, and a strategic network of internal and external stakeholders.

A significant system used by leaders is that of the leadership and management team. The members of this team, when aligned with the mission and vision of the organization, are the developers of organizational culture; strategic decision makers; directional, competitive, and adaptive strategists; and prime movers in the organization. The more knowledge, skills, abilities, and propensities the leadership team brings to the collective table, the better able the organization is to be successful in dynamic or changing times.

Leadership at the health industry level is difficult due to the industry's enormous size, unaligned motivations, differing incentives, scarcity of resources and, especially, lack of a unifying and widely accepted (consensus of all stakeholders) common vision. However, there is a desperate need for a unified leadership effort at the industry level. Maybe you are the leader who will fill that gap.

BRIDGING THEORY AND PRACTICE OF LEADERSHIP IN HEALTH CARE: APPLYING LEADERSHIP THEORY

In this text, the intention is to build a bridge between theory and practice. Simply put, how can the academic world of the abstract link to the concrete operational world of practice and the leadership practitioner? In reading through this book, think of examples and ways to apply the leadership theories and models presented here to your own experience and reality. Chapter 3 will assist you greatly by expanding your ability to link theory to practice. Of special note is the difference between descriptive and prescriptive leadership theories and models.

Descriptive and Prescriptive Theories

Leadership theories and models can be descriptive, prescriptive, or both descriptive and prescriptive. Descriptive theories and models illustrate, define, and capture the description of leadership phenomenon but do not recommend or prescribe actions, behaviors, or processes to employ. Prescriptive theories and models provide recommendations to the leader practitioner with regard to actions, behaviors, or processes to use to be a successful leader. Some leadership theories and models both describe and prescribe.

The Study of Leadership: What's in It for Me?

All disciplines across the spectrum of education discuss leadership in one form or another. Whether they are chemists or musicians, successful individuals must know how to motivate people toward goal-directed behavior. The study of leadership provides the tools needed to accomplish this outcome—and make you successful in your own endeavors in achieving success.

Being a leader is a special privilege. To have power, influence, and control over the lives of employees is a special responsibility. Of course, with that responsibility come special rewards, similar to those associated with being a parent. It is a special privilege to guide, nurture, and coach a group of employees toward an organizational objective and then share in the pride of accomplishing that objective. It is a joy to celebrate the success of those whom you lead. It is rewarding to mentor and develop the next generation of leaders and managers under your guidance as they look to you to provide them with the examples, tools, skills, insights, and judgments needed to be successful. And similar to the gift of parenthood, when your own employees assume positions of responsibility of their own one day, and later call to say "thank you" for helping them be successful, you can share in that special pride and reward that all leaders experience when they have successfully passed the reins of responsibility on to one of their protégées.[56, 57]

What's in it for you? To be the best leader and have the best career in serving others that you can achieve. As you study leadership in this text, you should focus on several goals. You may add your own goals to the following list:

1. Define, describe, and categorize leadership knowledge, skills, and abilities.
2. Understand leadership principles that contribute to successful groups and organizations.
3. Apply leadership principles in thought, in writing, and then in practice.
4. Analyze, compare, and deconstruct the leadership theories, models, and skills presented in the text.
5. Combine elements from the text and from personal study to develop, refine, and defend a personal model of leadership that you can use in practice.
6. Compare and contrast several leadership theories, models, and skills and summarize the expected outcomes of the various leadership elements.
7. Mentor, coach, and guide others in the health professions to be better leaders.

IN THIS TEXT

This text is intended to build foundational leadership knowledge and bridge the gap between theory and practice so as to enhance the skills and abilities of the reader and student of leadership in health organizations. These goals are accomplished in the book's four parts, each of which consists of four chapters. A summary of the four parts provides a good overview of the content of this textbook.

Part 1: Leadership Foundations. Part 1 is divided into four chapters. Chapter 1 defines leadership from historical, cultural, and contemporary perspectives. Chapter 2 assesses individual leadership styles and allows the student to relate his or her style to the various leadership theories and case studies presented in the text. Chapter 3 describes what a theory is and explains how leadership theories can be measured and assessed once theory is broken down into its fundamental parts. Chapter 4 provides a classical and historical review of leadership theories as they have evolved over the last several hundred years, especially since the 1930s.

Part 2: Leadership in Practice. Part 2 focuses on leadership in action and the knowledge, skills, and abilities required of a health leader. Chapter 5 outlines the personal responsibilities leaders have to maintain relevancy in skills, tools, abilities, and education. Chapter 6 focuses on applying those skills, tools, abilities, and education to communication, planning, decision making, managing knowledge, and training. Chapter 7 provides the health leader with a road map to success in personal leadership development by using the leader "crawl, walk, and run" methodology. Chapter 8 looks at some new methods in practice that help guide and hone leader skills; emphasis is placed on "leading people and managing resources" in the health organization.

Part 3: *Leadership in Health Organizations.* The third major module in this textbook focuses specifically on the complexity of health organizations. Chapter 9 begins by exploring the complex world of health and describing how leaders can identify and manage horizontal, vertical, institutional, and resource-dependent environments. It is followed by Chapter 10, which offers a sound review of ethics and morality in health and discusses a leader's responsibility to manage and maintain an ethical framework that fosters a moral environment. Chapter 11 is a unique chapter on measuring and defining outcomes of health leadership initiatives that apply the model building techniques discussed in Chapter 2. Part 3 concludes with Chapter 12's special analysis of the unique and interdisciplinary roles of health leaders, focusing specifically on physicians, nurses, administrators, and department heads.

Part 4: *Leading People and Managing Resources into the Future.* Chapter 13 offers suggestions for leaders in the next decade, with a specific emphasis on globalization and an understanding that many discussions in this book focus on Western philosophies of leadership; other worldviews of leadership are presented. Next, Chapter 14 impresses on the reader that—as in the practice of medicine—a constant practice of leadership must be fostered and nurtured for health leaders to mature and stay relevant. Chapter 15 outlines the responsibilities of leaders in the management of nonperforming employees. Tips, strategies, and best practices are introduced throughout this part of the textbook. The textbook closes with Chapter 16's discussion of mentoring and succession planning.

SUMMARY

This chapter focused on the basic definitions and distinctions of leadership. Specific emphasis was placed on defining the importance of leadership study in the healthcare environment and its appropriate place in the field of both academics and professional practice. Leadership was differentiated from management, and a distinction between managers and leaders was presented. Final emphasis was placed on descriptive (tells about "leadership") and prescriptive (gives direction and guidance) theories and models before the basic goals of leadership study, and the text overview, were presented to readers.

DISCUSSION QUESTIONS

1. Why is the study of leadership important to early careerists in the health industry? What are the challenges in the industry that require quality leadership?

2. Can you explain and give examples of leadership as compared with management? Why might health organizations need both leaders and managers?

3. Compare the application of a prescriptive leadership model to the application of a descriptive leadership model: What is the difference?

4. What distinguishes the phases of leadership thought from ancient to modern times, and what are the differences of each of the phases?

5. Can you relate the phases of leadership thought to modern leadership practices and research and provide examples?

6. What is your evaluation of the health industry's need for leadership today and into the next decade? Which specific leadership knowledge, skills, and abilities are particularly important today?

EXERCISES

1. What is leadership, and why is leadership vital to successful health organizations? Write a paragraph that supports your definition and another paragraph explaining why health organizations need leadership.

2. Distinguish between leadership and management. How are leadership and management similar? How are they different? Answer this question in three to four paragraphs.

3. Construct a list of leadership principles based on actions and behaviors of a leader (preferably a health leader) you observe or have observed. Why are those principles successful or not successful in leading the organization? List and relate observed principles to outcomes in two to three paragraphs.

4. Upon considering the trait, behavior, and situational leadership phases of research, which phase seems most relevant today in the health industry? Are there underlying constructs from each phase that can work together to form a coherent leadership model that explains leadership and can predict organizational outcomes? Break down each phase and relate the underlying constructs to leadership in health organizations today, paying particular attention to organizational outcomes.

5. Which attributes do you (or would you) look for in a manager? Which attributes do you look for in a leader? In your answers to these questions, is there a theoretical link in your response? (Can you reference this chapter, another reading, or a lecture that forms a connection to your responses?) Compile a list of manager attributes and a list of leader attributes. Categorize each manager and leader attribute as a "trait," a "behavior," or a "situational" attribute and summarize the major themes of your lists in one to two paragraphs.

6. Critique one of the following articles, or an article provided by your instructor, in four to five paragraphs. Relate the critiqued article to the content in this chapter in two to three paragraphs.

   a. Boehnke, K., DiStefano, A. C., DiStefano, J. J., & Bontis, N. (1997). Leadership for extraordinary performance. *Business Quarterly, 61*(4), 56–63.

   b. Gerstner, C. R., & Day, D. V. (1997). Meta-analytic review of leader–member exchange theory: Correlates and construct issues. *Journal of Applied Psychology, 82*(6), 827–844.

   c. Jelinek, M., & Litterer, J. A. (1995). Toward entrepreneurial organizations: Meeting ambiguity with engagement. *Entrepreneurship: Theory and Practice, 19*(3), 137–169.

   d. Mintzberg, H. (1996). Musings on management. *Harvard Business Review, 74*(4), 61–67.

   e. Calhoun, J. G., Dollett, L., Sinioris, M. E., Wainio, J. A., Butler, P. W., Griffith, J. R., & Warden, G. L. (2008). Development of an interprofessional competency model for healthcare leadership. *Journal of Healthcare Management, 53*(6), 375–389.

REFERENCES

1. Adams, A. (2007). Developing leadership wisdom. *International Journal of Leadership in Public Services, 3*(2), 39–50.
2. Pounder, J. (2008). Transformational leadership: Practicing what we teach in the management classroom. *Journal of Education for Business, 84*(1), 2–6.
3. Marques, J. F. (2006). Awakened leadership. *Performance Improvement, 45*(7), 35–38.
4. Pounder, note 2.
5. Marques, note 3.
6. Evers, C., & Katyal, K. (2007). Paradoxes of leadership: Contingencies and critical learning. *South African Journal of Education, 27*(3), 377–390.
7. Vachon, M. (2009). Six trends for your next strategy session agenda. *GE Healthcare Performance Solutions* [booklet], p. 2. www.gehealthcare.com.
8. Rowold, J., & Rohmann, A. (2008). Relationships between leadership styles and followers' emotional experience and effectiveness in the voluntary sector. *Nonprofit and Voluntary Sector Quarterly, 38*(2), 270–286.
9. Ledlow, G. R., & Coppola, M. N. (2009). Leadership theory and influence (167–191). In J. A. Johnson, *Health organizations: Theory, behavior, and development.* Sudbury, MA: Jones and Bartlett.
10. Turnock, B. (2004). *Healthcare leadership: What it is and how it works.* Sudbury, MA: Jones and Bartlett.

11. Dreachslin, J. L. (2007). The role of leadership in creating a diversity-sensitive organization. *Journal of Healthcare Management, 52*(3), 151–155.
12. Cook, M. J., & Leathard, H. L. (2004). Learning for clinical leadership, *Journal of Nursing Management, 12,* 436–444.
13. Dreachslin, J. L. (2007). Diversity management and cultural competence: Research practice and the business case. *Journal of Healthcare Management, 52*(2), 79–86.
14. Hurley, J., & Linsley, P. (2007). Leadership challenges to move nurses toward collaborative individualism within a neo-corporate bureaucratic environment. *Journal of Nursing Management, 15*(7), 749–755.
15. Bass, B. M. (1990). *Bass & Stogdill's handbook of leadership.* New York: Free Press, p. 4.
16. Fiedler, F. E. (1996). Research on leadership selection and training: One view of the future. *Administrative Science Quarterly, 41*(2), 242.
17. Surakka, T. (2008). The nurse manager's work in the hospital environment during the 1990s and 2000s: Responsibility, accountability and expertise in nursing leadership. *Journal of Nursing Management, 16*(5), 525–534.
18. Morrison, I. (2000). *Health care in the new millennium.* San Francisco, CA: Jossey-Bass, p. 30.
19. Morrison, note 18, pp. 16–38.
20. Beebe, S. A., & Masterson, J. T. (1997). *Communicating in small groups: Principles and practices* (5th ed.). New York: Addison-Wesley Educational Publishers.
21. Morrison, note 18.
22. Kolenda, C. (2001). *Leadership: The warrior's art.* Carlisle, PA: Army War College Press.
23. Bass, note 15, p. 3.
24. Lichtheim, M. (1973). *Ancient Egyptian literature. Vol. 1: The Old and Middle Kingdoms.* Los Angeles, CA: University of California Press.
25. Bass, note 15, p. 3.
26. Conger, J. A. (1999). Charismatic and transformational leadership in organizations: An insider's perspective on these developing streams of research. *Leadership Quarterly, 10*(2), 156–157.
27. Lynn, L. E. Jr. (1994). Public management research: The triumph of art over science. *Journal of Policy Analysis and Management, 13*(2), 231–287.
28. Chambers, H. E. (1999). The agencies of leadership. *Executive Excellence, 16*(8), 12.
29. Harris, T. E., & Nelson, M. D. (2008). *Applied organizational communication: Theory and practice in a global environment* (3rd ed.). New York: Lawrence Erlbaum Associates, Chapter 2.
30. Harris & Nelson, note 29.
31. Puryear, E. (1971). *Nineteen stars: A study in military character and leadership.* Novato, CA: Presidio Press.
32. Brainey Quote. Retrieved June 20, 2009, from http://www.brainyquote.com/quotes/keywords/leadership.html.
33. Peters, T. J., & Waterman, R. H. (1982). *In search of excellence.* New York: Harper and Row.
34. Peters & Waterman, note 33.
35. Yukl, G. (1994). *Leadership in organizations* (3rd ed.). Englewood Cliffs, NJ: Prentice Hall, p. 3.
36. Schein, E. H. (1999). *The corporate culture survival guide: Sense and nonsense about culture change.* San Francisco, CA: Jossey-Bass.
37. Blanchard, K., Hersey, P., & Johnson, D. E. (2000). *Management of organizational behavior: Leading human resources* (8th ed.). Upper Saddle River, NJ: Prentice Hall.
38. Covey, S. (1990). *Principle-centered leadership.* Provo, UT: Institute for Principle-Centered Leadership.
39. Gupta, A. (2005). Leadership in a fast-paced world: An interview with Ken Blanchard. *American Journal of Business, 20*(1), 7–11.
40. Ling, Y., Simsek, Z., Lubatkin, M. H., & Veiga, J., (2008). The impact of transformational CEOs on the performance of small- to medium-sized firms: Does organizational context matter? *Journal of Applied Psychology, 93*(4), 923–934.
41. Ledlow & Coppola, note 9.
42. Schein, note 36.
43. Kent, T., Johnson, J. A., & Graber, D. A. (1996). Leadership in the formation of new health care environments. *Health Care Supervisor, 15*(2), 28–29.
44. Zaleznik, A. (1990). Managers and leaders: Are they different? *Harvard Business Review,* March/April, 126–135.
45. Ledlow & Coppola, note 9.
46. Predpall, D. F. (1994, May/June). Developing quality improvement processes in consulting engineering firms. *Journal of Management in Engineering,* pp. 30–31.
47. Maxwell, J. C. (1993). *Developing the leader within you.* Nashville, TN: Nelson.
48. Maxwell, J. C. (2002). *Leadership 101: What every leader needs to know.* Nashville, TN: Nelson.
49. Predpall, note 46.
50. Maccoby, M. (2000). Understanding the difference between management and leadership. *Research Technology Management, 43*(1), 57–59.
51. Development of Management Thought. Retrieved May 8, 2009, from http://choo.fis.utoronto.ca/FIS/Courses/LIS1230/LIS1230sharma/history4.htm.

52. Katz, R. L. (1955, January–February). Skills of an effective administrator. *Harvard Business Review*, pp. 33–42.

53. Mann, F. C. (1965). Toward an understanding of the leadership role in formal organizations (68–103). In R. Dubin, G. C. Homans, F. C. Mann, & D. C. Miller (Eds.), *Leadership and productivity*. San Francisco, CA: Chandler.

54. University of Edinburgh School of Engineering. (2009). Retrieved June 18, 2009, from http://www.see.ed.ac.uk/~gerard/MENG/ME96.

55. Mintzberg, H, (1973). *The nature of managerial work*. New York: Harper and Row.

56. Prather, J. (2009, Winter). Soldiering on. *Baylor Line*.

57. Rubenstein, H. (2005). The evolution of leadership in the workplace. *Journal of Business Perspective*, *9*(2), 41–49.

2

Determining Your Own Leadership Style

> *Personally I am always ready to learn, although I do not always like being taught.*
> Sir Winston Churchill

This chapter introduces the influence of personality and physiology on leadership dynamics. Students are introduced to various leadership and personality assessment tests. After completing the assessment tests, students are asked to write a summary essay integrating findings of their own leader and personality outcomes. This summary, and the tests that precede it, assist students in identifying a penchant for certain leadership styles presented later in the text. The assessments will assist students in understanding and relating to theories, models, and evolutionary trends discussed later in this text and in the literature.

LEARNING OBJECTIVES

1. Name and describe at least four assessments related to leadership.
2. Explain your personality type, leadership style, principles, and foundational skills as informed by leadership and leadership-related assessment instruments.
3. Produce results of at least four leadership related assessments and prepare and apply those results to your leadership persona.
4. Identify and distinguish your leadership style, principles, and foundational skills (both strengths and weaknesses) based on the results obtained from leadership-related assessment instruments.
5. Based on self-assessments of your personality type, leadership style, principles, and foundational skills, devise a plan to improve your weaknesses while leveraging or enhancing your strengths.
6. Critique and interpret your unique leadership persona and relate your leadership persona with examples from your life experiences.

INTRODUCTION

The first step in improving your ability to lead people in health organizations is to understand yourself. To take that first step, gaining an understanding of your personality type, leadership style, and associated leadership skills is paramount. It matters what you know, who you know, and, perhaps most importantly, what you know about yourself![1] This chapter starts the journey to understand yourself. As part of this effort, by identifying your strengths, weaknesses, and propensities, you can work to become a better leader by adding knowledge, skills, and abilities to your leadership "toolbox." This is a lifelong endeavor. Just as you have a dominant personality (the personality you naturally have), so you also have a dominant leadership style, a dominant conflict management style, and so forth. Even so, you can learn, practice, and master other styles, which then become part of your repertoire to lead people and manage resources.

To begin your journey to understanding yourself, this chapter introduces a variety of assessment-related topics: the Myers–Briggs personality indicator, "introvertedness" and "extrovertedness" (Type A/B personality indicators), creative and empirical thinkers (left- and right-brain thinkers), and the propensity to lead and learn through visual, auditory, reading, or kinesthetic (VARK) constructs. Prior to completing the leadership-related assessments, students are asked to complete the enneagram diagnostic to discern whether their personal motivational objectives mirror those of traditional leaders. The supplement to this text, available at http://www.jblearning.com/catalog/9780763781514/, provides additional assessments as well.

The final assessments focus on the test taker's propensity and affiliation in relationship to traditional leadership or traditional managerial roles. Other assessments provide diagnostics that evaluate risk taking, charisma, vision, and empirical leadership characteristics. This chapter also discusses the constant battle a leader experiences between his or her natural predispositions and the precepts taught in leadership training and mechanical execution. While we do not present these tests as a panacea for leadership diagnosis, we do suggest that certain ability–job fit characteristics may become clearer after completing these self-assessments.

KNOW THYSELF: WHAT KIND OF LEADER ARE YOU?

Newt Gingrich, the former Republican Speaker of the U.S. House of Representative, once said of former Democratic President Bill Clinton that he did not like to talk with Clinton for too long a period of time, because after a while he began to agree with him.[2] Although former White House Press Secretary George Stephanopoulos may have made this comment jovially in his book *All Too Human,* the statement was fundamentally accurate in more ways than one. President Clinton was widely admired for his *natural charisma,* political savvy, and social skills that inspired followership and easy friendship. The same might not be true of his spouse, Secretary of State Hillary Clinton,[3] who has grown and matured in political creditability through nearly two decades of on-the-job leader training coupled with personal and professional self-development. What one leader possesses intrinsically and naturally, the other honed through application of best practices and understanding of leadership styles, principles, and skills. In other words, some leaders have natural abilities, while others must work to learn those abilities.

All leaders—regardless of their natural abilities, experience, education, and training—must be aware of their own personal areas for improvement so that they can grow and become more successful. As a result, we ask you to consider the following questions:

■ What kind of leader are you?
■ What are your strengths and weaknesses?
■ Are you aware of how those strengths and weaknesses support or fail to support your leadership style?

Traits of Leaders

There is an ongoing debate, within both the literature and professional practice, over whether leaders are born or made. This argument centers on the premise that those qualities that make leaders successful cannot be taught. Such qualities might include ambition, motivation, and a strong work ethic.

There is a general agreement in the literature that these qualities are inherent within individuals who emerge as leaders in the organizational workplace. Certainly, many great leaders of our time have possessed these qualities. However, qualities—or *traits*—of motivation, ambition, and work ethic are difficult to measure by themselves. Most often, proxy outcomes are assigned to these qualities as justification for the presence of these traits. Such proxy variables might include education (if the individual is motivated, he or she might pursue higher education for an advanced degree), number of hours worked, or number of jobs held at one time, all of which might lead outside agents to conclude that the individual possesses a strong work ethic. While motivation and ambition are certainly good qualities for leaders to possess, they are not by themselves precursors to successful leader outcomes.

Take, for example, the "Ponzi scheme" created by former tycoon Bernard Madoff.[4] Well known as an extremely ambitious and motivated individual, Madoff became the architect of the greatest financial scam in U.S. history.[5] Clearly, ambition and motivation are not by themselves traits of leadership.

Another example might be Adolf Hitler. Using basic leadership theories of followership and transformation, Hitler might effectively be designated a leader through the example of his successful rebuilding of Germany after World War I. Nevertheless, to refer to Hitler as a leader—after considering the totality of his "work"—is insulting to the profession of leadership. No, Hitler does not occupy a position in the highly regarded field of leaders. He was, at best, a despot and a dictator.[6] Leaders must be moral actors.

We will discuss this definition of leadership later in this text. For now, we point out that new leader models have emerged in the field of leadership that screen out dictators and despots from the honored study of those individuals who have earned the designation of *leader*.

Personality Profiling in Action

From 2004 through 2007, the Program Director of Baylor University's joint master's degree in health administration (MHA) and master's degree in business administration (MBA) program conducted a series of personality assessments on members of the entering graduate class.[7] One of the personality self-assessments was the VARK test.[8] This self-completed survey provides users with a profile of their unique learning preferences. The scores profile an individual as having a predisposition for learning through visual, auditory, reading/writing, and kinesthetic (i.e., doing) constructs or modalities.

In the past, it has been suggested that those individuals who score low in the auditory predisposition on the VARK test may have difficulty in the graduate and post-graduate setting, as oral lectures are the preferred method of delivering information in the traditional classroom. To test this hypothesis, 165 graduate students in Baylor's MHA/MBA program (approximately 41 in each class) were followed through four years of classroom dynamics. **Table 2–1** profiles the outcomes for these graduate students.

Table 2–1 suggests some common traits are associated with graduate students selected to attend a traditional full-time university. While discrepancies are common, and reasonable variance is assumed between scores within the bounded rationality of standard personality diagnosis, in 2006, only two students identified themselves as having a preferred learning modality associated with listening to lectures (auditory). In the other years, the number of auditory learners was consistent and steady over time, which suggested this learning style preference might be a shared trait among graduate classes in traditional academia. Furthermore, the percentage of students who preferred the reading/writing and visual styles stayed relatively consistent over the years.

TABLE 2–1 VARK Learning Outcomes at Baylor University's MHA/MBA Program (*n* = 164)

VARK Test 2004		VARK Test 2005		VARK Test 2006		VARK Test 2007	
Aural	9	Aural	2	Aural	9	Aural	9
Kinesthetic (doing)	8	Kinesthetic (doing)	22	Kinesthetic (doing)	12	Kinesthetic (doing)	10
Read/write	8	Read/write	10	Read/write	8	Read/write	8
Visual	18	Visual	9	Visual	11	Visual	12

The data recorded in 2005 were unique insofar as the class had no stabilizers for auditory learning. As a result, the class as a whole often became frustrated and irascible when faced with the prospect of long lectures. The feedback received on end of course evaluations for professors who refused to change or modify their teaching methods from lecture to case study was extremely poor ($n = 2.8$ on a 5-point scale). As the program director, Dr. Coppola would continually make recommendations to the faculty to modify teaching styles for the benefit of the class. Those faculty members who did modify their teaching practices for the second term received significantly higher end-of-course evaluations ($n = 3.8$ on a 5-point scale). Those faculty members who did not modify their teaching practice continued to receive poor feedback for their entire teaching year with those students. Knowing how the students learned was helpful to the professors—and it made them better educators. Health leaders can apply the same information to their leadership styles and adapt their message delivery to their subordinates' propensities.

This small example demonstrates two points. First, personality profiling does provide insights into leading people that can result in positive outcomes. Second, those professors who were savvy and aware of how their teaching practice (i.e., their leadership style) was affecting the students were able to adapt and modify situations to create win-win opportunities for both themselves and the students.

The Importance of Understanding Personalities in the Workforce

The average worker will change jobs seven to nine times over the course of his or her career. The decision to depart a current place of employment may be based on advancement opportunities or dissatisfaction with the current work environment. Whatever the specific reason given, the pursuit of new leadership opportunities is often driven by the seeker's interest in matching his or her educational and work history against published criteria about a new job. However, matching only past experience and educational accomplishments will not produce a positive outcome when seeking to match skills with available openings.[9]

Personality dynamics influence success in the workplace in many ways. Performance, personal satisfaction, and outcomes are all enhanced when the employee and the work environment are in alignment—that is, when there is synchronization with personality. Synchronization is a process that includes many dimensions of an individual's abilities, such as education and experience, ability to learn, mental "hard-wiring," personality archetypes, leadership dynamics, and physical abilities.[10] Understanding the personalities of subordinates, peers, and superiors in the health organization is important for health leaders. This understanding informs the health leader as to others' expectations and provides insights into motivation, competitiveness, team building, coalition building, and interpersonal relationships and communication.

Leadership and Personality Self-Assessment

This section identifies some of the more popularly available personality and leadership self-assessments available on the Internet (World Wide Web). These sites provide free leadership and personality self-assessments that are highly commensurate with many of the private and for-profit assessments that can be purchased. In fact, for many large for-profit organizations, personality screening is a necessary precursor to being offered a position in the company. Many large-scale organizations have found that a basic interview and reference checking are just small parts of a larger interview process. Personality assessment via computerized testing is becoming more common, as organizations have realized that most all references provided by candidates result in positive narratives. Additionally, a favorable half-day interview may not provide the organization with a complete picture of the individual's predisposition for participatory, autocratic, and authoritarian leadership styles or level of mastery of critical leadership skills such as communication.

Many organizations are weary of the litigation potential when an individual is hired, only to then be terminated for failing to get along with coworkers or adapt to existing workplace dynamics. As a result, personality self-assessment has become a piece of the overall picture of the job candidate developed by organizations prior to making a final offer of employment. As such, it is incumbent on early careerists to not only become aware of their own personality archetype, but also to gain some experience with personality assessment prior to any real-world screening process so that nervousness and second guessing does not present itself during the actual corporate screening process.

Upon completing each one of these personality diagnostics, the test taker is supplied with a free assessment of his or her scores by the hosting Web site. While there are often no right or wrong answers, and all tests are subject to issues of reliability and validity, many of these assessments, if taken consistently over the period of several weeks or months, will provide similar responses over time.

Drs. Ledlow and Coppola suggest that for use in the university course setting, four to six self-assessments should be completed, based on the learning outcomes of the course. Upon completing these assessments, you should write a two- to three-page integrated self-assessment based on the diagnostic outcomes. This essay should list professional strengths for the career field that the test taker is about to enter, as well as areas of potential professional development where weaknesses are identified. One last note: Everyone—leader and follower alike—has weaknesses and areas of career and professional performance that can be improved.

The following section is exciting and fun, but can also be scary and anxiety provoking. The goal is to "know thyself" as a health leader, and to learn to identify and leverage your strengths while shoring up your weaknesses to create more potential for great leadership—your great leadership—in the health industry. The assessments can be found at the reference attached to each section's heading.

LEADER AND PERSONALITY ASSESSMENTS

Emotional Intelligence[11]

Emotional intelligence (EI) is one of the more difficult concepts for individuals to understand, improve, and master. It is based on a variety of non-intellectual factors that can influence behavior. Some leaders are unaware of how their emotional intelligence affects their superiors and subordinates. In fact, many individuals will reassign negative outcomes and behaviors to those around them and be completely unaware of their personal effect on others' actions.[12, 13]

Emotional intelligence is a relatively new concept in leadership, having only been studied since the early 1980s.[14] Many definitions of EI can be found in the literature. Notably, the Institute for Health and Human potential defines EI as the ability or capacity to perceive, assess, and manage the emotions of oneself and of others. EI might also be thought of as having "street smarts." Street smarts are those characteristics most often possessed by highly charismatic leaders that allow them to exercise savvy and poise in controlling relationships among outside agents and stakeholders. Executives possessing this ability have a better understanding of how to manage the complex relationships in teams and foster positive relationships with rivals while attaining control and collegiality among organizational members. Fostering EI in organizations and teams is an essential factor in successful organizations and should not be overlooked.[15]

Emotional intelligence might also be defined as having a high locus of control. Those individuals with a high locus of control are able to process, receive, and transmit information absent of emotional content, and believe that they control their own destiny and future. For example, an individual having worked very hard on a business case analysis (BCA) that is not approved by his or her boss during a large staff meeting should refrain from an emotional outburst in front of other staff members. Likewise, leaders with high EI levels would refrain from displaying a threatening demeanor when asked to support positions of contention in an organization with subordinate employees of a differing opinion. The four salient constructs of the emotional intelligence model are (1) self-awareness, (2) self-management, (3) social awareness, and (4) social skills.[16] These constructs are slanted toward the relational or "art" aspect of leadership. At the same time, these constructs can and should merge to form a secondary level of "intelligence" that is ever present and that monitors the technical and relationship orientations of the leader. Conscious engagement and mastery leads to subconscious implementation; this is the internal gyroscope that many successful leaders learn to depend upon. "Those who use the emotional intelligence framework to guide their thoughts and actions may find it easier to create trust in relationships, harness energy under pressure, and sharpen their ability to make sound decisions—in other words, they increase their potential for success in the workplace."[17] The dynamic culture leader connects the four emotional intelligence constructs together with this "internal gyroscope" to analyze himself or herself and the organization, and to merge the appropriate levels of science and art in creating an organizational culture that can withstand ever-changing environmental challenges.[18]

Hemisphere Dominance[19]

The hemisphere dominance personality assessment indicates the brain hemisphere (right or left) that dominates in the test taker. Most professionals are aware there is a dominant side of the brain; however, these same professionals are often unaware of the influence this hard-wiring has on the day-to-day activities of professional performance. For example, "right-brained" individuals tend to be more creative. Professionals with dominant right brains may be best suited for creating new product and service lines, developing long-range strategic plans, and forecasting threats on the environmental horizon. In contrast, "left-brained" individuals are more detail oriented, methodical, and calculating. They prefer implementing strategic plans over developing them. While it is difficult to change one's predisposition for creativeness versus detail orientation, creative thinkers can make specific adjustments in their daily business of work to become more organized, while more concrete thinkers can exercise creative elements of their brain by engaging in more creative arts such as writing, music, or art.

Jungian Assessments[20]

Scholars have suggested that all individuals are born with a personality archetype. Over the years, family, society, and the environment all exert influences on this archetype. Working professionals should be aware of their natural predispositions (as measured by Jungian assessments) so that certain characteristics can be leveraged, or weaknesses avoided. The most popular assessment of this kind is the Myers–Briggs Type Indicator (MBTI), which has been a reliable source of documenting personality since World War II. The MBTI focuses on four dimensions of personality: extraversion or introversion, sensing or intuition, thinking or feeling, and judging or perceiving.[21–23] (Two preferences are identified in each dimension.) The MBTI results indicate the test taker's preferred style and remain fairly stable throughout a person's career.

Extroverts prefer the company and collaboration of teams, while *introverts* prefer comfort zones that involve the interaction of just a few people. Extroverts tend to be "charged" by other people and interaction with others, whereas introverts tend to be "charged" by quiet reflection and isolated activities. Extroverts can be alone and function very well, just as introverts can be with other people for long periods and function very well. Extroverts tend to be more assertive, while introverts have refined listening skills.

Sensing individuals seek empirical affirmation from the environment—that is, reassurance that history plays a critical role in today's decision and will impact tomorrow. *Intuitive* personality types prefer more latent cues from the environment for decision making and, at the extreme, ignore the past.

Thinking individuals tend to be very strong at execution, while the strength of *feeling* individuals resides with interaction. Logic and cause-and-effect reasoning are valued by the thinking profile, whereas emotion and the impact of decisions on the organization are important to the feeling-oriented individual.

Judging people carefully weigh all of the options and alternatives. They tend to be more structured in their approaches to implementation. In contrast, *perceiving* individuals find confidence in their own heuristics (rules of thumb with which to make decisions) and prior knowledge for decision making. Perceiving individuals tend to be more spontaneous.

Type A and B Personality Indicators[24]

In the 1940s and 1950s, when personality archetypes and behavior theories were emerging as seminal fields of study to add to the trait theory literature, it was posited that people were hard-wired to fit into one of three neat, clear-cut clean predispositions for the purposes of personality classification—namely, Type A, Type B, and Type A/B individuals.[25]

Type A individuals are competitive, inquisitive, and easily bored with routine; they have a "short fuse," often feel impatient, and may be aggressive. These individuals may also have a difficult time relaxing, staying focused on details, and maintaining stability in any one place for long periods of time. Type B people are the direct opposite: They can relax easily, tend to maintain focus on activities and projects, see stability as comforting, and can be perceived as more social and easygoing.[26]

Type A/B individuals may present characteristics of both personality traits and present characteristics in either dimension depending on environment, circumstance, and mood. Type A/B personalities are said to be balanced personalities and can find comfort in a variety of situations.

While there is no direct evidence that any of the personal predispositions aids in leadership development and success, a growing body of work suggests that Type A individuals have higher burnout and mortality rates.[27] There is general agreement in the literature that individuals are predisposed to present behaviors in either the Type A or B modality. Even so, it may be possible for individuals to switch over and mimic personality characteristics and behaviors of the other dynamic based on their education, work stimulus, and coping skills.

Knowing which archetype best defines an individual creates leverage in the workplace. Successful Type B individuals will know when to "turn on" and become excited and committed to projects and ventures. This posture can be mimicked until the work is completed. Likewise, Type A individuals can present a high locus of control and know when to mitigate their own emotions and instincts to perform more cooperatively in groupwork and interdisciplinary team dynamics.

The VARK Test[28]

As mentioned earlier in this chapter, a VARK assessment provides an insight into an individual's predisposition toward a particular learning style. Most people have a dominant learning style, a secondary style, a tertiary style, and a least preferred style. Some individuals may also have high abilities in more than one style. While the VARK test may seem somewhat oriented to university education, all organizations have a set of continuing education and professional development competencies that must be achieved for an individual to advance or maintain employment in the workplace. By knowing which specific modality fosters a higher learning outcome for himself or herself, an individual can maximize use of his or her discretionary time to focus on those events that promote the greatest transfer of information. Such examples of different professional development activities might include on-site conferences, webinars, distance learning, traditional education, and personal self-development through reading, listening to audio books, or working on computer-based problems or games.

While learning styles change over time, prudent early careerists will conduct a personal self-assessment of their own preferred learning modality. It is important for young leaders to know that potential organizations may or may not appreciate individual learning styles. For example, if an individual is an auditory learner in an organization that emphasizes verbal communication, the probability for successful synchronization between that individual and the organization should be enhanced. Conversely, an auditory learner in an environment where mass reading of policy and procedure statements is necessary may not fare as well. Thus health leaders should be aware of their preferred methods of learning—that is, whether they emphasize visual, aural, reading, or kinesthetic traits. Other assessments use the terms "visual verbal" (reading), "visual nonverbal" ("visual" referring to pictures, figures, and graphs), "auditory" (aural), and "learning by doing" (kinesthetic) to describe the learning style preferences. Collectively, these characteristics are referred to as VARK.[29]

Visual learners prefer graphs, pictures, and flowcharts to help them understand complex phenomena. These learners feel most comfortable surrounded by blueprints and matrixes, but may be distracted by debates and decision discussions.

Aural learners are stimulated by conversation and debate. These learners may often be more interested in the discussion of decision making than decision making itself. They "think out loud" and may often use other employees as sounding boards for new ideas.

Reading and writing (R/W) learning preference is a common characteristic among healthcare executives. These individuals prefer cross-referencing written material, writing summaries, and e-mailing thoughts. They do well with complex tasks and multitasking.

Kinesthetic learners require practical exercises, a hands-on approach, or meticulous simulation to learn efficiently. These learners prefer learning through experience over alternative preparatory methods. However, they are rapid processors of information in an on-the-job environment. Kinesthetic learners are also more comfortable with ambiguity.

The New Enneagram Test[30]

Enneagrams are said to be natural encodings in neural tissue in everyone's brain that provide a physical predisposition to behave a certain way based on environmental stimulus. Similar to left- and right-brain dominance, the way in which the brain forms relationships within itself to process information is unique.[31] As a result, it is incumbent on health leaders to be aware of these visceral tendencies to see if there is any opportunity for professional development or self-awareness.

Enneagrams identify the test taker's natural inclination toward behavior. The results can be classified into nine primary constructs or types: Reformer, Helper, Motivator, Romantic, Thinker, Skeptic, Adventurers, Leader, and Peacemaker.[32-35]

The *Reformer* is the perfectionist and obedient child who must do everything right. Individuals with this tendency prefer that others get along with them and prefer to dictate terms in groups and interdisciplinary teams. This behavior stands in contrast to that of the *Helper*, who will seek to engage in supportive relationships with others so as to gain favor and acceptance.

The *Motivator* is the high achiever who seeks to pull those around him or her toward success. This individual may not try to conform those around him or her to the Motivator's own standards of excellence; rather, the Motivator will pull those in his or her inner circle toward goals and objectives.

The *Romantic* strives for warm and collegial connections with those in the workplace. Words of approbation are very important to the Romantic, as individuals with this tendency do not thrive in a critical atmosphere. The Romantic may work well in small groups of known colleagues, but may have difficulty in new environments.

The *Thinker* sees the world as "over-stimulating" and confusing, and will need privacy to contemplate actions in the environment. Type B personalities are most often thinkers. Thinkers will often be plain-spoken and direct, and they sometimes communicate without tact. However, they are often detail oriented and factually accurate. They leave little room for discrepancy or speculation. When a Thinker finally speaks, there often is little room for alternative positions and opinions.

The *Skeptic* is eager to investigate life and propositions. Skeptics, sometimes called challengers, have a great lust for life and a keen intellectual curiosity. They are most often Type A archetypes, challenge institutionalism, and may demonstrate creative and right-brain thinking. At the same time, they have a need for social integration and can be tactful and wary of irritating relationships.

The *Adventurer* wants excitement, pleasure, and fun. Individuals in this category see work as a game; however, they can have difficulty organizing activities and projects themselves. They prefer stimulating conversation over the labor of work, and they prefer to be the center of attention without taking responsibility. The Adventurer is an odd mix of a charismatic personality coupled with a degree of avoidance behavior. He or she may be the "idea person" in the organization who wants someone else to produce the concepts that he or she has suggested. A difficult archetype to pin down, the Adventurer may succeed best when surrounded by talented subordinate personnel.

The *Leader* archetype is not always presented in some assessments, as researchers believe that the leadership construct is a composite of several modalities coupled with environmental opportunities. However, in many enneagram tests, the Leader may not be the individual who inspires followership or who occupies a director role in project management; rather, the Leader in this case may be called the "Asserter." Asserters have strong personalities and are direct, self-reliant, and seemingly unfettered by the opinions of those around them. At the same time, the Leader can be supportive of those close to him or her.

Peacemakers do not want to be part of the spotlight, nor do they think of themselves as important or special to the group dynamic. They tend to avoid prominent leadership roles and prefer to "hide in plain sight" by neither confronting antagonists nor supporting commonly agreed-upon direction. Far from being lazy, the Peacemaker can provide a neutral sense of direction between competing priorities and introduce new ones if carefully coddled and treated well within the group dynamic.

Dynamic Culture Leadership Alignment Assessment[36]

Individual assessment is important, as is a leadership team evaluation. An accurate assessment can yield many positive results, including the ability of the team to better align itself to bring real diversity of style, skills, experience, and abilities into the health organization. In this model, which is discussed later in this text, cultural and individual diversity are valued because they enable the organization to better respond to dynamic organizational and external environments. A diverse leadership team brings robustness to solving organizational problems as long as focus and adherence to team goals are maintained.

An assessment that looks at leadership as a team, across organizational levels, operating environments, and external environment needs, is especially valuable.[37] This assessment intends to evaluate the leadership styles and propensities of the leadership group of an organization, the organization's operating style, and the perceived external environment expectations of the organization. It can also be used as an individual assessment for leadership, management, technical (science) and art (relationships) propensities, communication, planning, decision alignment, employee enhancement, and knowledge management constructs.

Figures 2–1 and **2–2** illustrate the use of such an assessment tool for a leadership team of a hospital. Two continua are defined: leadership–management and science–art. The leadership–management continuum distinctions were presented in Chapter 1. The science–art continuum assesses leaders in terms of their preferences for technical skills and abilities (science) such as forecasting, analysis, budgeting, decision making, and related capabilities, by comparing them to relational skills and abilities (art) such as interpersonal relationships, team building, and related capabilities.

The reliability of the assessment tool and model are moderately strong in Figures 2–1 and 2–2, which illustrate the results with a sample size of 85 leaders from four different hospitals, two different university colleges, and a U.S. Army Medical Department Regional Command (Department of Defense). Graduate students—a total of 58—have taken this assessment as well. Thus the total number taking this assessment for purposes of internal reliability is $n = 143$. Although this is not a very large number, early results with this tool appear promising. The preliminary internal reliability and internal consistency measures are near or above reasonable levels; for example, Cronbach's coefficient alpha measures were between .68 and .89 (where .7 is reasonable for the social sciences and .77 is strong or good) for the constructs of the model.

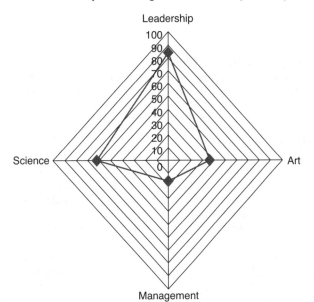

Leadership and Management Team Composite Style

FIGURE 2–1   Dynamic Culture Leadership Assessment: Community Hospital Leadership Team Style
Source: Ledlow, G., & Cwiek, M. (2005). The process of leading: Assessment and comparison of leadership team style, operating climate and expectation of the external environment. *Proceedings of Global Business and Technology Association*, Lisbon, Portugal.

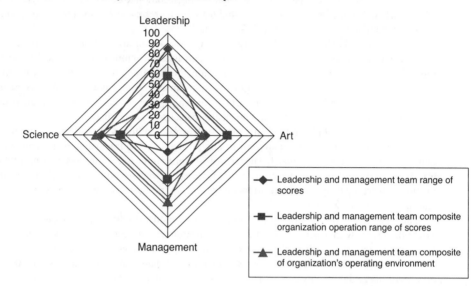

Comparison of Team Style, Actual Organization Operation Style, and Required Environment Style

FIGURE 2–2 **Dynamic Culture Leadership Assessment: Comparison of Leadership Team Style, Operating Style, and External Environment Requirements for a Community Hospital**
Source: Ledlow, G., & Cwiek, M. (2005). The process of leading: Assessment and comparison of leadership team style, operating climate and expectation of the external environment. *Proceedings of Global Business and Technology Association*, Lisbon, Portugal.

Studer Group[38]

The Studer Group is a leadership and organizational consulting firm with a large hospital clientele. The "Leader as Coach" assessment is a quick evaluation of the test taker's coaching propensity. The instrument groups the assessment outcomes into one of three categories: high, middle, or low coaching capability.

Other Leadership Assessments

Many other leadership and leadership-related assessments are available on the World Wide Web. However, health leaders must be able to separate research-based assessments from those that are not empirically based. Does the assessment discuss or reveal internal consistency or reliability measures such as Cronbach's coefficient alpha (where .7 is reasonable, .77 is good, .8 to .89 is very good, and .9 and higher is excellent) or other measures of the assessment's credibility? Does the assessment have ecological validity or does it make sense or justify the real world?

Another way to look at the value of an assessment tool is in terms of its usefulness. An assessment's usefulness is in question if decisions, increased knowledge, or increased self-awareness cannot be achieved through use of the assessment. Of course, some assessments are wonderful as "ice breakers" to get subordinates, peers, superiors, and multilevel groups to talk about themselves and learn about others with whom they work in the health organization. Some assessments are great ways to encourage people to open up at meetings where they do not know one another very well, for early stages of team building, and other group activities where people must "gel" to accomplish a task or a set of tasks.

Can you distinguish research-based assessments and useful assessments from fun or "ice breaker" assessments? The following assessments are presented for your review.

Leadership Diagnostics[39]

This assessment is more speculative in nature. It evaluates a leader's potential to be a "twenty-first-century leader" based on several constructs such as team building.

Anthony J. Mayo[40]

This assessment determines whether the test taker is one of three leadership types: the entrepreneur, the manager, or the charismatic. Based on a book about brilliant leaders, it compares the test taker to successful contemporary leaders from several industries.

Dale Kurow[41]

This assessment evaluates leadership skills from a direct superior-to-subordinate basis. Also, individual leadership questions support the evaluation for this dichotomous assessment.

Price Group[42]

Are you more of a leader or a manager? This assessment tries to answer this question based on a series of skills- and actions-based questions.

THE RELATIONSHIP BETWEEN PERSONALITY ARCHETYPE AND LEADERSHIP

The research is in agreement that personality archetypes do affect leadership style, success, and outcomes in the workplace.[43–45] While difficult to manage without a high degree of self-awareness, the first step in any leadership development process is to recognize potential weaknesses or areas for improvement. Some of this understanding will come with experience. Other professional development areas will present themselves with personal self-recognition. This chapter has provided some tools for the latter kind of diagnosis.

By the time many students get to college, they have already established certain predispositions toward one or more of the personality archetypes presented in this book. Simple predispositions may be perceived as habits at first, such as reading alone or studying to music. These habits, or preferred predispositions, may provide clues to early discovery of mental hard-wiring. Social networking and competing in sports and intramurals may suggest a tendency toward Type A behavior, whereas preferring the company of small groups of intimate friends and social clubs may suggest a predisposition for Type B behaviors.

If an individual aspires to become a CEO of a large and munificent healthcare organization and is predisposed to Type B personality traits, he or she must either reconsider entering into a career field where high external presence is mandatory or gradually exercise those areas of the individual's personality that may be lying dormant, but are open to cultivation. Remember—leadership styles, knowledge, skills, and abilities can be learned as well as enhanced. Malcolm Gladwell, in his book *Outliers: The Story of Success,* suggests that 10,000 hours of practice, experience, trial and error, and self-discovery are required to become a master or an expert in anything, with rare exception to this standard.[46] Gladwell also states that the average graduate student has an intelligence quotient (IQ) of 115 or higher[47]; this point suggests that you are intellectually poised to learn and master health leadership whether you are innately gifted or just willing to learn.

STRATEGIES TO MAXIMIZE YOUR NATURE-VERSUS-NURTURE LEADERSHIP STATE OF BEING

Numerous strategies are available to early careerists to help them cultivate dormant personality capabilities. For example, joining professional organizations is critical for success, as they provide opportunities for exercising leadership skills in closed and friendly environments that may not have direct visibility in the workplace. For instance, if an individual is predisposed to be a Skeptic, volunteering to support a continuing health education event with a local professional organization can provide the opportunity to be a follower without the pressure of being scrutinized in terms of professional outcomes that may end up in a performance appraisal in the workplace. The classroom setting is uniquely suited for trial and error; mistakes are used to learn and improve rather than having negative career implications. Take advantage of the classroom environment to practice leadership by volunteering for group leader roles, community service project leadership, and similar opportunities. Find ways to lead people in a useful endeavor and find ways to manage resources in useful endeavors; build up your experience to achieve the 10,000 hours of practice!

Within the workplace, early careerists can seek out professional mentors not in their direct supervisory chain who can provide both education and candid professional development advice from a non-performance appraisal perspective. While joining a professional organization may provide an opportunity for mentorship, many large organizations now have formal mentor programs where mentees can be paired up with volunteer mentors in a structured environment.

Self-development and self-directed learning may be the easiest method for individuals to gain a perspective on how to develop and cultivate dormant leader traits. Many professional development books include self-diagnostic scales that provide tools and strategies to augment leader skills.

Finally, the value of self-awareness and acceptance cannot be underscored in this chapter. While none of the assessments in this chapter are by themselves 100 percent valid and reliable predictors of personality traits and leadership skills, they should be considered one part in your personal puzzle. The synthesis of these assessments should form an initial picture of your current situation—a situation you can improve and develop into a great health leader. To ignore these assessments because you are not pleased with the outcome is essentially paramount to ignoring your own potential.

SUMMARY

This chapter provided a small sample of minimal diagnostic self-examinations that provide usable information for professional development in a course setting. While the authors do not recommend taking all of these assessments, when completed under the supervision of your course director, these evaluations will support the learning outcomes of your program.

Following successful completion of several of these assessments, students should conduct an analysis and look for trends and patterns that may reveal areas of personality dominance or personality void. You might then write a paper integrating your personal findings into one composite essay. The final essay should include a personal plan to hone existing traits while also cultivating knowledge, skills, and abilities that may present themselves for development later. Ideally, the course director, executive in residence, or professional community leader will then sit down with each student and provide a mentoring session aimed at leadership and career success.

Strong personalities with high levels of education dominate the health environment. As a person progresses up the corporate ladder, he or she will encounter new and different personality types at all levels. Leaders will most likely have to develop different personality skill sets to foster and cultivate relationships in the various environments in which they work. Knowing oneself will provide an edge for success and a platform for improvement and mastery of leadership.

DISCUSSION QUESTIONS

1. Describe four leadership, leadership-related, or personality assessments that were most informative for you. Did other students select the same assessments? Why or why not?

2. Distinguish the various typologies (categories) used in personality assessments and personality archetype assessments and explain the differences associated with the various "types."

3. Relate two or more assessments from this chapter to your personal situation: Were the assessment results complementary or contradictory? Why do you think these results occurred?

4. From the assessments (two or more), identify the health leader most appealing to you (a real leader or a fictitious one whom you create). Using the assessments' constructs and typologies, why is that health leader appealing?

5. Compile and categorize your assessment results, summarize the results, and tell the group your plan for leadership mastery.

6. Appraise the empirical strength of the various assessment instruments, critique two or more assessments, and justify your critique.

EXERCISES

1. Name and describe at least four assessments related to leadership you used, in two pages or less.

2. Explain your leadership style, principles, and foundational skills as related to leadership assessment instruments, using at least four assessments, in a three-page essay.

3. Produce results of at least four leadership-related assessments, apply those results to your leadership persona, and attach the results to your three-page essay from Exercise 2.

4. Identify and distinguish your leadership style, principles, and foundational skills strengths and weaknesses based on your leadership-related assessments' results, in a two-page document attached to your essay and results document.

5. Based on self-assessments of your personality style, leadership style, principles, and foundational skills, devise a plan to improve your weaknesses while leveraging or enhancing your strengths. Add this work to your essay, results, and strengths and weaknesses document.

6. Critique and interpret your unique leadership persona, and relate your leadership persona to examples from your life experiences in a two- to three-page document. Attach this work to your previous work. Return and read this document once a month until you have achieved your goals for improving your leadership capabilities.

REFERENCES

1. Ledlow, G., & Cwiek, M. (2005, July). The process of leading: Assessment and comparison of leadership team style, operating climate and expectation of the external environment. *Proceedings of the Global Business and Technology Association*, Lisbon, Portugal.

2. Stephanopoulos, G. (1999). *All too human: A political education*. Boston: Little, Brown.

3. Kellerman, G. (2008). Leadership lessons from Hillary Clinton's election results. *Conversation Starter*, Harvard Business Publishing. Retrieved June 22, 2009, from http://conversationstarter.hbsp.com/2008/02/leadership_lessons_from_hillar.html.

4. Healy, J. (2009, June 29). Madoff sentenced to 150 years for Ponzi scheme. *The New York Times*. Retrieved June 29, 2009, from http://www.nytimes.com/2009/06/30/business/30madoff.html?_r=1&hp.

5. Lambiet, J. (2008, December 12). Bernie Madoff's arrest sent tremors into Palm Beach, *Palm Beach Daily*. Retrieved December 12, 2008, from http://www.palmbeachdailynews.com/news/content/news/2008/12/12/ponzi1212.html.

6. Coppola, M. N. (2004). A propositional perspective of leadership: Is the wrong head on the model? *Journal of International Research in Business Disciplines, Business Research Yearbook, International Academy of Business Disciplines*, *11*, 620–625.

7. Coppola, M. N. (2008). Observations and outcomes of graduate students based on VARK profiling. White paper, Fort Sam Houston, San Antonio, TX.

8. Fleming, N. D., & Mills, C. (1992). Not another inventory, rather a catalyst for reflection, to improve the Academy. *Academy of Management Journal*, *11*, 137.

9. Coppola, M. N., & Carini, G. (2006, March/April). Ability job–fit self-assessment. Healthcare Executive, pp. 60–63.

10. Coppola & Carini, note 9.

11. Retrieved July 20, 2009, from http://www.queendom.com/tests/access_page/index.htm?idRegTest=1121.

12. Kluemper, D. H. (2008). Trait emotional intelligence: The impact of core-self evaluations and social desirability. *Personality and Individual Differences*, *44*(6), 1402–1412.

13. Smith, L., Ciarrochi, J., & Heaven, P. C. L. (2008). The stability and change of trait emotional intelligence, conflict communication patterns, and relationship satisfaction: A one-year longitudinal study. *Personality and Individual Differences*, *45*, 738–743.

14. Gardner, H. (1983). *Frames of mind*. New York: Basic Books.

15. Cherniss, C., & Adler, M. (2000). *Promoting emotional intelligence in organizations*. Washington, DC: American Society for Training and Development.

16. Lanser, E. G. (2000). Why you should care about your emotional intelligence: strategies for honing important emotional competencies. *Healthcare Executive*, *15*(6), 7– 9.

17. Lanser, note 17, p. 9.

18. Ledlow & Cwiek, note 1.

19. Retrieved July 20, 2009, from http://www.mindmedia.com/brainworks/profiler.

20. Carl Jung was a notable Swiss psychiatrist and influential scholar for his work in personalities in the late 19th and 20th centuries. Retrieved July 20, 2009, from http://www.humanmetrics.com/cgi-win/JTypes2.asp.

21. McCrae, R. R., & Costa, P. T. (1989). Reinterpreting the Myers–Briggs Type Indicator from the perspective of the five-factor model of personality. *Journal of Personality*, *57*, 17–40.

22. Boyle, G. J. (1995). Myers–Briggs Type Indicator (MBTI): Some psychometric limitations. *Australian Psychologist*, *30*, 71–74.

23. Harvey, R. J. (1996). Reliability and validity. In A. L. Hammer (Ed.), *MBTI applications* (pp. 5–29). Palo Alto, CA: Consulting Psychologists Press.

24. Retrieved July 29, 2009, from http://www.psych.uncc.edu/pagoolka/TypeAB.html.

25. Jenkins, C. D., Zyzanski, S. J., & Roseman, R. H. (1971). Progress towards validation of a computer-scored test for the Type A coronary-prone behaviour pattern. *Psychosomatic Medicine*, *33*, 193–202.

26. Kuiper, N. A., & Martin, R. A. (1989). Type A behavior: A social cognition motivational perspective. In Gordon H. Bower (Ed.), *The psychology of learning and motivation: Advances in research and theory* (Vol. 24, pp. 311–341). New York: Academic Press.

27. Friedman, M., & Rosenman, R. H. (1974). *Type A behavior and your heart*. New York: Knopf.

28. Retrieved July 20, 2009, from http://www.vark-learn.com/english/page.asp?p=questionnaire.

29. Fleming, N. D. (2001). *Teaching and learning styles: VARK strategies*. Honolulu Community College.

30. Retrieved July 20, 2009, from http://www.9types.com/newtest/homepage.actual.html.

31. Riso, D. R., & Hudson, R. (1996). *Personality types: Using the enneagram for self-discovery*. Boston, MA: Houghton Mifflin.

32. Palmer, H. (1995). *The pocket enneagram: Understanding the 9 types of people*. San Francisco, CA: Harper Press.

33. Putnoi, J. (2000). *Senses wide open*. Berkeley, CA: Ulysses Press.

34. The nine types. Retrieved June 26, 2009, from http://www.9types.com/index.php.

35. Introduction to engrams. Retrieved June 26, 2009, from http://www.eclecticenergies.com/enneagram/introduction.php.

36. http://www.jblearning.com/catalog/9780763781514/ or contact Dr. Gerald Ledlow at gledlow@georgiasouthern.edu.

37. Conger, J., & Toegel, G. (2002). A story of missed opportunities: Qualitative methods for leadership research and practice. In K. W. Parry & J. R. Meindl (Eds.), *Grounding leadership theory and research: Issues, perspectives, and methods* (pp. 175–197). Greenwich, CT: Information Age Publishing.

38. Retrieved July 8, 2009, from http://www.studergroup.com/tools_andknowledge/tools/index.dot.

39. Retrieved July 20, 2009, from http://www.coachingandmentoring.com/Quiz/21stmanager.html.

40. Retrieved July 20, 2009, from http://www.fastcompany.com/articles/2005/08/quiz.html.

41. Retrieved July 20, 2009, from http://www.dalekurow.com/leadership_quiz.

42. Retrieved July 20, 2009, from http://www.pricegroupleadership.com/tl_quiz.shtml.

43. Judge, T. A., & Bono, J. E. (2000). Five-factor model of personality and transformational leadership. *Journal of Applied Psychology*, *85*, 751–765.

44. Chemers, M. M., Watson, C. B., & May, S. T. (2000). Dispositional Affect and leadership effectiveness: A comparison of self-esteem, optimism, and efficacy. *Personality and Social Psychology Bulletin*, *26*, 267–277.

45. Rychlak, J. F. (1963). Personality correlates of leadership among first level managers. *Psychological Reports*, *12*, 43–52.

46. Gladwell, M. (2008). *Outliers: The story of success*. New York: Little, Brown.

47. Gladwell, note 46.

3

Understanding Leadership as a Theory

Opinion is that exercise of the human will which helps us to make a decision without information.

John Erskine, *The Complete Life*

This chapter presents students and early career executives with a sound understanding of theory. Theory is explored in terms of both anatomy (parts of the whole) and physiology (relationships with each other) so as to better understand the complexity of theory itself before applying it to the study of leadership. It is difficult for students of leadership to fully embrace all the nuances of leadership study if they first do not understand what a theory is—and how the study of leadership theory fits in with the general dynamics of applying specific leadership theories to the practical world.

LEARNING OBJECTIVES

1. Describe why the study of theory is important in the study of leadership in health organizations.
2. Define and distinguish the basic elements and relationships of a theory.
3. Demonstrate the utility of theory in the study of leadership, leadership principles, and leadership applications.
4. Describe and compare two or more conceptual models, and discuss how the models relate to theory and support the discussion of leadership.
5. Design a simple model of leadership principles or applications (from constructs and concepts in this chapter or other literature) and summarize the relationships between the model's theoretical elements and the application of leadership principles.
6. Justify and defend the constructs in a simple model of leadership.

WHY STUDY THEORY?

While the study of theory may seem nonessential and without practicality in a leadership course, students should ask themselves two simple questions: First, what is a theory? Second, what is leadership? If you can answer the second question without answering the first, there may be a gap in your understanding of the complexities of the art and science of leadership—and how leadership theory supports the development processes of early career executives.

The authors of this text have more than 50 years of combined experience in health leadership positions in civilian and military health organizations and in academia. We have been educated academically and trained practically in the understanding, application, synthesis, and evaluation of leadership. As a result, we feel that it may not be possible to fully embrace all the fundamentals of leadership and leadership theories without first understanding the complex relationships in theory structure and processes. Failing to understand theory may result in students of leadership not understanding what they are reading. More importantly, lack of theoretical methods knowledge could lead to misinterpretation, resulting in an inability to apply leadership knowledge, skills, and abilities in the organizational world.

As a small prologue to some of the discussions that appear later in this text, consider one of the early leadership theories posited by scholars in the mid-1800s—something called the "great man" theory. In essence, this theory suggested that to be a "great man," one had to emulate the specific "traits" of the acknowledged leaders of the time. There is overlap between "great man" and "trait" theories of leadership. What is missing is an understanding of what "great" means and how the specific "traits" define the word "great" for us to study. In reality, the "great man" theories of the early 1800s offered us no benchmark for success and no road map for others to follow. Essentially, the words "great" and "trait" were not universally understood or applied. As a result, the theory offered no utility for education or application. Simply put, behavior of great leaders and their traits were observed and emulated without any attempt to understand the foundations of behaviors or influence of traits.

Another example we will discuss later in this book is the transformational leadership theory, which was introduced in 1978.[1] This theory suggests that leaders can inspire followership by raising subordinate goals toward higher levels of motivation through developing a spirit of trust, respect, and loyalty. For example, John F. Kennedy's presidency is often characterized as inspiring the civil rights movement and a manifest destiny toward U.S. exploration of space. In support of this proposition, a janitor at NASA was once asked what he was doing cleaning a building after hours when he was not authorized to receive overtime pay for the work. His reply: "I am helping to put a man on the moon." President Kennedy was successful in transforming the perceptions of the janitor to view his job not only as a task, but as one part of a greater vision—the U.S. quest for space exploration. Kennedy was an astute student of leadership. As a result, he was able to recognize the core values necessary to change individual behavior and form followership among the masses.[2]

Scholars of leadership theory can deconstruct Kennedy's natural abilities and provide tools, skills, and a road map for young scholars and early careerists to follow. Deconstructing "transformational theory" provides developmental insights that young executives can build on until their natural abilities associated with maturity and experience develop over time. Deconstructing theory and methods of theory building can greatly assist in this effort.

WHAT IS A THEORY?

Theory is the primordial soup from which complex questions can be modeled and discussed in bounded rationality where like-minded executives can agree on issues and causality. It is important to know that there is no one accepted definition of "theory" within the organization behavior literature. In layperson's terms, a theory is an advanced form of an idea or an opinion that has some basis in the empirical world. Regardless of the definition selected, a theory must be capable of support by qualitative measures or quantitative data. If a theory is incapable of initial development based on qualitative or quantitative properties, the burgeoning theory may not have evolved past the opinion or idea phase, and it may not be valuable to the profession or the advancement of knowledge.

The term "theory" is derived from an ancient Greek word meaning to contemplate, to contemplate the divine, or to speculate. Simply put, a theory is a way to capture and represent a set of ideas, constructs, variables, and observations within a context to demonstrate how a part of the world works, or could work better. A theory intends to evaluate variables that are operationally defined and measured in a dynamic world. Theories are analytical structures that seek to illustrate how linked ideas, domains, constructs and variables perform under various conditions by using quantitative, qualitative, or combined methods. "A particular feature of science (including social science) is that it is continually evolving as a result of the scientific method which calls for a constant testing of ideas and observations of scientific facts, theories, and models."[3] Theories start out as models that have been developed using empirical thinking. Qualitative information and analysis (also known as theory building methods) such as observation and literature review start this empirical process. Quantitative analysis (also known as theory testing methodology) tests models as hypotheses to determine if the model represents the world better than what was known before. This empirical hypothesis testing can be performed as qualitative research alone in certain cases, but may also be carried out in combination with quantitative methods (a process called triangulation).

Definitions of the term "theory" support the notion that a theory provides for an integration of ideas within a context of a phenomenon. "A theory is a set of interrelated principles and definitions that present a systematic view of phenomena by specifying relationships among variables with the purpose of explaining natural phenomena."[4, 5] Another definition suggests that a theory is "Any set of hypotheses or principles linked by logical or mathematical arguments which is advanced to explain an area of empirical reality or type of phenomenon."[6, 7] As discussed previously, the terms "model" and "hypothesis" nudge their way into the discussion; this is especially true in the study of leadership.

Theory as a Conceptual Model

In this unit we will learn to visualize theory as a conceptual model. A conceptual model is a "conceptual description" of something abstract. It is not uncommon in business practices for executives to develop *models* to represent certain ideas and concepts. The model itself, like a photograph, breaks down barriers of communication, thereby making it easier for individuals to view the model and understand complex relationships. Models serve as representations of the world or phenomenon around us; they are particularly useful for understanding, analyzing, and evaluating how the world works around us.

Figure 3–1 shows an example of a conceptual model for a hospital. In this basic model, hospital performance is achieved as a result of an organization's inputs and outputs. In this case, the inputs are constructs (to

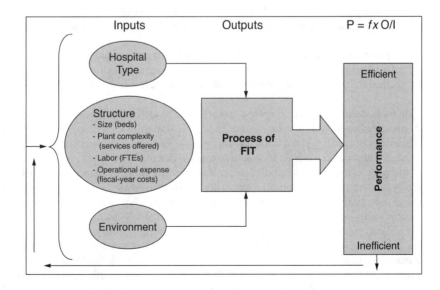

FIGURE 3–1   Conceptual Model

be discussed later) of hospital types, structural units, and the environment. The outputs in this model are the result of the previous three constructs combining together to form some sort of recognized output. Finally, the performance of the hospital is based on the efficiency of those outputs being earmarked as high or low. If the output is high, there is no need for leadership to take action. If the output is low, the conceptual model guides leaders back to the relationship between constructs so that additional action can be taken.

The basic conceptual model shown in Figure 3–1 helps us to evaluate hospital efficiency in a manner that is complex, yet easily understood by outside agents and stakeholders. Understanding that many of the leadership theories in this book are displayed as conceptual models will make it easy for students to understand what they are looking at in the following pages.

OVERVIEW OF THEORY

This section presents a brief overview of theory and explores how a theory can be deconstructed into constructs, variables, and measures. Readers are instructed on how to use visual and graphical tools to create a conceptual model that measures a specific outcome of leadership principals. Model building is a necessary precursor to performance-based management development, health system examination, policy formulation, and conducting quantitative analysis—to name only a few of its potential uses. Nevertheless, understanding the process of building empirically measurable healthcare and leadership models may be one of the more underrated aspects of leader development in today's healthcare system. This chapter places specific emphasis on creating conceptual models of leadership that can be used to measure the outcomes of the theories presented later in this text.

Differentiating Between Theories and Models

The terms "theory" and "model" are used interchangeably in much of the literature. A theory is a hypothesis that has undergone scientific and practical scrutiny, albeit at various levels of intensity, to determine its value, truth, and validity. A model is a simplified abstraction of reality; it has not yet met a level of academic and practical scrutiny for scientific validation, so its value is yet to be determined. Both theories and models require ecological validity to represent and present reality well, so that scholars and practitioners can study and use them. In the leadership discipline, it is more difficult to prove value, truth, and validity than it is in a basic science such as chemistry or physics. Consequently, one could argue that leadership theories and models are really hypotheses—that is, speculations about how a phenomenon actually behaves or works:

> A [social] scientific theory is a synthesis of well-tested and verified hypotheses about some aspect of the world around us. When a [social] scientific hypothesis has been confirmed repeatedly by experiment, it may become known as a [social] scientific law or scientific principle.[8]

In the leadership literature, the terms "theory" and "model" are much more prevalent than the terms "law" and "principle," mostly due to the social requirement and nature of leadership: People's beliefs, values, attitudes, and behaviors often change, and situations are dynamic. Going back to the structure of theory, constructs, and variables, an example can explain this social sciences–based methodology.

Many leadership theories include *interpersonal relationships* as a category within their theories. Within the category of interpersonal relationships, one of the constructs is *communication*. As a construct, communication is broad and has many possible variables that can be measured. For example, *conflict management style* may be a variable within the construct of communication. Conflict management style, as a variable, can be measured using a survey to determine the leader's dominant style from six previously identified conflict management styles. Because a theory, to be useful, needs to adjust and work well in a dynamic world, recommending a conflict management style based on a particular situation would be more helpful than just relying on chance to pick the correct conflict management style out of six possibilities. Thus, in this example, a situational variable (observations from the situation) can interact with a variable from the interpersonal relationships category and communication construct, and specifically the conflict management style variable, to provide a recommended conflict management style. From a social sciences and academic perspective, this approach serves as a structure to facilitate studying, teaching, and learning about leadership. From an application viewpoint, however, the leadership theory in practice would be transformed into knowledge, skills, and abilities.

Continuing with the same example, the practicing leader understands that interpersonal relationships are important and can describe and explain why this subject is important in general, but also based on the constructs included under this category. This is an example of *knowledge*. Focusing on the communication construct and the conflict management style variable, the practicing leader can identify the type of situation at hand and apply observations from the environment to the leadership theory to reveal a recommendation for the appropriate conflict management style to use in this situation. This is an example of *ability*. Even though the recommended conflict management style may not be the leader's dominant or preferred style, the leader uses the recommended style in this particular situation. This is an example of a *skill*. If the leader can use any of the six conflict management styles dictated by the situation as appropriate, he or she would be more skillful or have more skill than a leader who can use just two or three conflict management styles.

To increase the value of studying leadership, building your knowledge of theories and models is critical. Developing an ability to take apart leadership theories and models and separate them into their component domains, constructs, and variables is vital. Also, developing the ability to assess the situation or environment of leadership is important. Lastly, developing, refining, and maintaining skills associated with analyzing and using constructs and variables of leadership theories and models are paramount. As you study and master the knowledge and practice the abilities and skills presented in this text through discussions of the various theories and models, your leadership acumen will improve.

THEORIES, MODELS, CONSTRUCTS, VARIABLES, AND MEASUREMENTS

History has recorded leaders' exploits for thousands of years. Anthropology, archeology, social anthropology, political science, business, communication, and other disciplines have all made valuable contributions to the basic foundations of leadership theory and practice. The health professions place leadership foundational theories and models and the practice of leadership into the complex environment of promoting health, preventing disease and injury, diagnosing and treating disease and injury, rehabilitating human bodies and functions, and facilitating dignity at the end of life. In this arena, leadership, as a complex topic, is coupled with a complex environment, the health industry, that creates a multilayered and integrative system in which the health leader must perform. To use leadership theories and models, it is important to understand the scholarly building blocks of these foundations and to extend or bridge scholarly and theoretical perspectives to the applied or practical use of leadership knowledge, skills, and abilities.

Leadership is an interdisciplinary field of study of the social sciences. Leadership is a social phenomenon: It involves individuals, groups, and populations, and focuses on how those people interact given the multitude of beliefs, values, attitudes, and behaviors in society. Leadership can be simple or very complex depending on how complicated the social environment appears to both the leaders and the led. As a science (in this case, a social science), leadership is explained, taught, learned, and documented in the literature. Within this knowledge base, theories and models combine domains, constructs, and variables that can be measured to describe, prescribe, or both describe and prescribe how to think about, practice, and evaluate leadership. Given that leadership knowledge comes from several disciplines, it is important to use social sciences–based methods to provide clarity to the study of leadership. That clarity is provided through a structure that uses theories, models, constructs, variables, and measurement as a common language and guide to leadership inquiry, practice, and evaluation.

Anatomy of Theory

The anatomy of theory can be broken down into specific units of analysis—namely, the theory itself, followed by subordinate constructs, variables, and operationalized measures. Surrounding these elements is the environment of discussion, an enclosure called bounded rationality. When discussing theoretical constructs, variables, and measures, it is first necessary to frame these elements within a plausible discussion group. By framing constructs, variables, and measures in a bounded rationality, an "out of bounds" area is revealed that helps researchers stay within certain parameters of discussion.

Contained within this bounded rationality is the physiology of theory (discussed in the next subsection). The physiology of theory describes the interaction among constructs, variables, measures, and other elements. In this regard, the interaction of constructs within theory is helpful for developing propositional statements. This consideration is important in the early stages of qualifying theoretical relationships before quantitative data become available for testing or disconfirmation of the theory. Forming more concrete and testable relationships within the theory are the relationships between variables known as hypotheses. Propositional and hypothetical relationships are discussed in greater detail later in this chapter.

Also contained within the bounded rationality of theory are contextual factors and confounders. Contextual factors are generally known elements that exist in the same environment as constructs, variables, and measures. The interaction of contextual factors on certain constructs and variables may be known in advance and can be controlled for through awareness and intervention. Confounders are properties in the environment that are generally not known in advance and may interact with theory to produce unanticipated effects.

Figure 3–2 depicts theory as a conceptual model for visual representation and understanding. A conceptual model is a "conceptual description" of the key elements of a phenomenon under study. The conceptual model should be parsimonious (simple) and offer graphic representations of theoretical elements that help outsiders understand the issue(s) being investigated at a glance. A conceptual model may include the actual theory, as well as constructs, variables, measures, confounders, and contextual factors. Some conceptual models, however, consider only specific constructs as well as certain elements specific to the unit of analysis under study. Many of the models presented in this text will include a discussion of the actual theory itself, whereas other models may simply present constructs for discussion.

Physiology of Theory

The physiology of theory can be described in terms of the relationships within the theoretical model. Two of these relationships are expressed in terms of hypotheses and propositions (**Figure 3–3**). A proposition is a statement of opinion, based on some degree of preliminary study or heuristics that is offered as a true or valid statement. While the statement may not always be true or valid, it is offered as such until evidence of disconfirmation

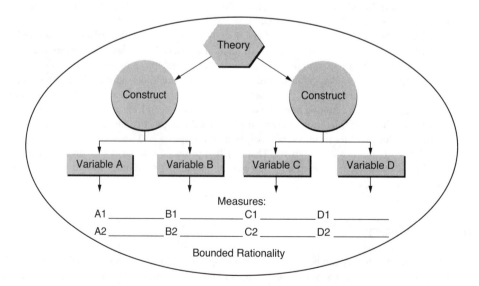

FIGURE 3–2   Anatomy and Physiology of a Theory

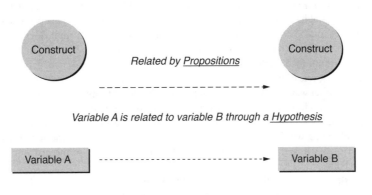

FIGURE 3–3   Conceptual Model of Theory Physiology

is provided. The apomorphism "time is endless" is an example of a propositional statement between constructs. Another classic example of a propositional statement combining constructs is "the right to bear arms." This propositional statement is offered as a statement of fact as is if it were true; however, the interpretive nature of this proposition continues to be repeatedly addressed in the United States.

A hypothesis is a testable relationship between two variables. The purpose of hypothesis testing is to discover casual relationships or associations between variables. Hypothesis statements are the foundation for all social sciences research and form the basis for the advancement of knowledge.

> The words *model*, *hypothesis*, and *theory* are each used quite differently in science. Their use in science is also quite different that in everyday language. To scientists the phrase "the *theory* of . . ." signals a particularly well-tested idea. A *hypothesis* is an idea or suggestion that has been put forward to explain a set of observations. It may be expressed in terms of a mathematical *model*. The *model* makes a number of predictions that can be tested in experiments. After many tests have been made, if the *model* can be refined to correctly describe the outcome of all experiments, it begins to have a greater status than a mere suggestion. Scientist do not use the term "the *theory* of . . ." except for those ideas that have been so thoroughly tested and developed that we know there is indeed some range of phenomena for which they give correct predictions every time. (But, language being flexible, scientists may use "a *theory*" as a synonym for "a *hypothesis*," so listen carefully.) Today, any set of scientific ideas referred to as "the *theory* of . . ." is a well-tested and well-established understanding of an underlying mechanism or process. Such a *theory* can never be proved to be complete and final—that is why we no longer call it a "law." However, it is the same kind of well-tested set of rules, with an established area of applicability, as the older ideas called "laws."[9]

In essence, a theory is a representation of the world that has been confirmed to be reasonably true, valuable, and valid. Some theories (and some models) are better than others; some are very specific to particular situations, whereas others are broad or even universal. Theories and "those hoping to be theories" (i.e., models) represent an aspect of our world or a methodology to improve our world through a structured process grounded in language and approaches of the scientific method used by scholars and theorists. At the next lower level, theories (as well as models) integrate and combine constructs.

CONSTRUCTS

The building blocks of theory are constructs. Throughout this text, students will encounter dozens of constructs. For this reason, it is critical to the study of organization behavior to have a clear understanding of what a construct is. Failing to have a clear understanding of constructs will result in an inability to understand many of the concepts presented in subsequent chapters of this book.

By definition, a construct is a latent variable that lacks empiricism (taste, touch, see, smell, hear). Elements that are empirical have tangible, physical properties. For example, an apple possesses empiricism insofar that it can be tasted, touched, seen, and smelled. It does not matter that the apple does not make *noise*. Because an apple possesses attributes related to four of the five empirical senses, we can say that an apple is not a construct because it can be rationalized through empirical properties. Any physical element or property that can be described through at least one of the five senses does not qualify technically as a construct.

Said another way, a construct is an organizing device that captures a topic, subject area, or smaller and specific theory or model within a larger theory or model. For example, communication is a construct within a larger leadership theory. Constructs organize and combine multiple variables that are closely linked into one grouping or subheading within the structure of the theory or model. The critical feature of constructs derives from the term "closely linked." Constructs must make sense in relation to the real world; thus they must have ecological validity.

Constructs, then, are the basic building blocks for grouping variables within a model or theory. It is commonplace to see the term "concept" associated with constructs. A concept is a method of organizing or categorizing an abstract topic or reality under a construct. A concept should be linked logically to the construct. A group of concepts under a construct must have cohesion that is logical or holds true to reality (ecological validity). Concepts, in essence, are either variables or constants. Variables and constants are located at the lowest level within the organization of the construct.

Another classic example of a construct is the term "quality." Quality is a construct that cannot be discussed without identifying it through other measurable properties or variables. The well-known statement, "Quality is in the eye of the beholder," generalizes the difficult problem we have describing quality. The discussion of other latent variables, such as efficiency, effectiveness, performance, satisfaction, organizational survival, leadership, success, and motivation, emphasizes that they are all examples of constructs. Many of these constructs are discussed in this book. They cannot be universally discussed without first assigning empirical properties to them. The empirical properties used to describe constructs comprise variables.

Variables

Flowing from constructs are variables. A variable is "a property associated with a concept that varies when measured."[10] Variables are empirical units that can be identified through one of the five senses. Accordingly, a variable is an element that has precise meaning in the physical world. Generally, variables are universally understood and easily described. *Weight* is a good example of a variable. When discussing weight with peers or colleagues, universally understood concepts of pounds, ounces, or tons are immediately recognized as valid descriptors of weight. If a variable is incapable of being defined with a generalized descriptor, it may cause problems in describing theory. However, if the builder of the theoretical concept makes a careful argument for the use of certain variables—and defines them appropriately—those variables may have utility in helping frame the model.

The notion of "something that can be measured, and whose measurement can vary or change," is the essence of a variable. An example would be *height*. If the concept is "body type," then a characteristic of body type would be height. Height can be measured, yet varies by person. A constant is a property that "does not vary"[11]; it is an unchanging constant. Variables are essential to theory confirmation through model and hypothesis testing because they are the properties or items that are tested to see whether the theory is confirmed. The importance of variables is that they vary; they change so that empirical testing can be accomplished. If the model is full of constants that do not vary, how could you test whether the model is true to reality? Moreover, how could such a model help someone to be a better leader if everything stayed the same?

Constants

Constants are those concepts that do not vary. However, depending on what you are studying, a concept may be either a constant or a variable. An example would be the study of prostate cancer: Would gender be a variable or a constant in this study? Although gender is important, only males get prostate cancer. Given that gender would not vary, it is a constant in this example. High-risk pregnancy would be another example where gender would not vary, as only females would be included in the study. In contrast, in a population-based heart disease study, gender could vary, as each observation could be either male or female; thus gender would be a variable in this situation. The variable—gender in this case—would be a nominal mutually exclusive and categorically exhaustive (you can be either male or female, but not both, and you have to be one or the other) variable that could vary. Many times the situation or context dictates whether a concept is a variable or a constant.

Operationalization

Each variable has an operational definition and an operational process for measurement. An operational definition is the exact description of the conceptual property—the variable—under empirical study:

> An operational definition identifies one or more specific observable conditions [or characteristics] or events and then tells the researcher how to measure that event. Typically, there are several operational definition possibilities for variables and values. The operation chosen will often have an immediate impact on the course of the research, especially the findings.[12]

The operational process for measurement is important because it lists the steps in the measurement of the variable as it is operationally defined. Some variables are observed and measured with a tape measure or ruler (such as height); some are categorized (such as shirt size being small, medium, or large); still others use survey measurement (such as conflict management styles). This brings us to the important construct of measurement.

Measures

Derived from variables are operationalized measures—that is, operationalized descriptions of variables that must be capable of numerical identification. Operationalizing is the process of quantifying a variable using appropriate, numerical, descriptive terms. Additionally, measures must be universally understood and are classically categorized as continuous (1 to *n*, with *n* equal to infinity), dichotomous or binary (e.g., yes or no; on or off), or categorical (e.g., Caucasian, African American, Latino). If measures are incapable of being operationalized through continuous, dichotomous, or categorical identification, the measure may not have enough precise significance to be valid in describing or testing the theoretical model under study.

Another aspect of measurement is numbering taxonomy. Measurements can be categorized into four distinct types (a taxonomy): nominal, ordinal, interval, and ratio (discussed later in this section). Each type of number has distinct properties associated with it. For example, if you asked a health leader how many subordinates he or she leads, you could get four different answers based on the numbering taxonomy employed; all four answers would be true and correct. If you asked, "Do you have more than 10 subordinates?" you could get a yes or no answer. If you asked, "Which group best describes your number of subordinates: 5 or fewer, 6 to 10, 11 to 15, 16 to 20, and so on," you would get a categorical answer. If you asked, "How many subordinates do you lead exactly?" you could get an answer of 17. Depending on the number taxonomy used, data can be changed. With an answer of 17 subordinates, you would group the data (16 to 20) or categorize the answer into the "yes, greater than 10" grouping. However, you cannot manipulate the data from a yes or no answer into a hierarchical group or a pure number.

Why not always use exact numbers? There are two reasons:

- Some variables are not exact, but rather are inherently hierarchically grouped (e.g., place in a race) or categorical (e.g., gender).
- It tends to cost more in resources, time, money, attention, and materials to obtain precision or higher-order data such as interval or ratio taxonomical data.

The four types of number taxonomy data are nominal, ordinal, interval, and ratio.[13, 14] Interval and ratio data are frequently identified as "continuous" data in the literature. Of note, ratio data can be transformed into interval, ordinal, or nominal data; interval data can be transformed into ordinal or nominal data; and ordinal data can be transformed into nominal data. Nominal data, however, cannot be transformed. A researcher can transform data down the taxonomy (ratio down to nominal) but never up the taxonomy. **Table 3–1** presents the distinction of each type of numbering taxonomy.

Variables should be capable of several different methods of operationalization. For example, the variable *age* can be operationalized as a continuous, categorical, or binary variable depending on how the researcher chooses to define and measure this variable. The following section discusses this process in more detail.

Operationalizing Measures

To operationalize the variable *age*, we first must associate the variable with a specific unit of analysis (such as an organization, team, or individual). Next, we create a brief definition of the variable *age* that supports the unit of analysis under study. For example, we may say that *age* is defined as the number of years associated with a human individual's life. This statement includes two important features. First, it qualifies *age* in terms of years. Second, it provides a reference group for *age*, where a potential range for a life span is universally understood. Given this information, it becomes possible to operationalize *age* in several different ways: (1) as a continuous variable (interval or ratio data); (2) as a binary (nominal) variable; and (3) as a hierarchical group variable (ordinal), as illustrated in **Table 3–2**.

In Table 3–2, we arbitrarily established cutoff points for categorical and dichotomous variables that help support the issue under study. The categorical description of age could have also been classified using quarter-century marks or five-year increments. The selection of a category is up to the executive analyzing the data. Finally, if the executive is interested in partitioning age-eligible Medicare recipients from non-Medicare recipients, setting a break point at age 65 provides opportunity to analyze the two different groups.

TABLE 3–1   Number Taxonomy Measures

Type	Definition	Scale Transformation
Nominal	Codes are assigned as labels to observations and are mutually exclusive and categorically exhaustive, such as gender (male = 1, female = 2). Also known as categorical or binary variables.	One-to-one, where each observation assigned a label code must be recoded as a group.
Ordinal	Numbers coded to observations are in rank or sequential order, such as the result of a race (e.g., first, second, third place).	Monotonic increasing or decreasing as long as order is maintained.
Interval	A quantitative score is given to an observation where the interval between scores holds meaning (e.g., observation B is 2 times as much as observation A, observation C is 3¼ less than observation D). Examples include height in meters or temperature on a Celsius scale.	Positive linear.
Ratio	Observations are given a quantitative score as in the interval scale number, but an absolute zero is possible (e.g., on the Kelvin temperature scale).	Positive similarities such as multiplication.

TABLE 3–2   Operationalized Variable: Age

Age is defined as the number of years associated with a human individual's life.

Continuous (interval or ratio data): 1 to *n* (e.g., 105)

Hierarchical group or category (ordinal data): 0 to 10, 11–20, 21–30, 31–40, 41–50, 51–60, 61–70, 71–80, 81–90, 91–100, *n* > 101

Binary (nominal data): Medicare age eligible? Yes or No (Medicare eligibility = 65 years of age or older)

Measurement is vital to empirical assessment and evaluation, and measurements taken must be both reliable and valid. *Reliability* is the "consistency of an operationalized measure."[15] This concept applies to both the measurement apparatus or method and the person or machine doing the measuring. *Validity* focuses on the notion of measuring what is intended to be measured. An unreliable measure is also invalid, whereas an invalid measure can still be reliable—that is, you can measure the wrong thing correctly with repetitive and consistent results. Within the concept of validity, specific kinds of validity are distinguished:

1. "Face validity refers to whether a measure, on its face, seems to be related to the concept that is presumably being measured.

2. Predictive validity refers to whether a new measure of something has the same predictive relationship with something else that the old measure had.

3. Convergent validity refers to whether two different measures of presumably the same thing are consistent with each other—whether they converge to give the same measurement.

4. Criterion validity is a test of a measure when the measure has several different parts or indicators in it—compound measures. Each part, or criterion, of the measure should have a relationship with all the parts in the measure for the variable to which the first measure is related in a hypothesis.

5. Content validity—does the measure have sufficient content [does it cover or contain enough measurement of the property or characteristic] in it to be acceptable."[16]

Not all variables lend themselves to operationalized measures through all three metrics. For example, the variable *racial category* does not lend itself to a continuous measure. The most appropriate nomenclature for race is a category, where the researcher selects racial categories of interest in the study for analysis.

The process of operationalizing measures is critically important in the business world and in the health industry. A requirement to gather, manage, and measure outcomes from data implies a continuous process. Before data can be collected and analyzed, however, they must be operationalized in a consistent and logical manner. The Balanced Score Card developed by Kaplan and Norton is an example of a quality-oriented tool that requires executives to select and define not only constructs of interest to measure, but also valid and reliable variables capable of identification through operationalized measures that provide meaningful data for trend analysis.[17]

The last step in operationalizing variables is the construction of a code sheet. Whenever variables are tested in a hypothetical relationship, it is not the variables themselves that are actually tested, but rather the operationalized units of the variables. This step is a necessary precursor to loading data into a statistical software program such as SPSS, SAS, Mini-tab, or Excel. When we operationalize data for statistical software manipulation, we create code sheets and coding methodology.

A code sheet is a very simple explanation of how operationalized units of a variable will be used in the study. The researcher must keep in mind the assumptions of the test when building a code sheet. For example, parametric and nonparametric tests require different assumptions, which should be incorporated in the code sheet. While numerous examples of building code sheets are available that demonstrate how data may be operationalized in a study, **Table 3–3** provides one proven example of success—in this case, a code sheet is created for the variable "education."

TABLE 3–3   Example Code Sheet for Variable "Education"

Label	Description	Operationalized
Education	Highest education degree obtained by member	*Taxonomy = Ordinal*
		1 = high school degree
		2 = associate's degree
		3 = bachelor's degree
		4 = master's degree
		5 = JD
		6 = MD
		7 = PhD

KEY RELATIONSHIPS: LEADERSHIP MODELS TO THEORIES TO ACCEPTED THEORIES

As noted earlier in this chapter, a theory has undergone scientific and practical scrutiny, albeit at various levels of intensity, to determine its value, truth, and validity. A model has not yet met a level of academic and practical scrutiny for scientific validation, so its value has yet to be determined. Both theories and models require ecological validity—that is, the ability to represent and present reality well—for scholars and practitioners to study and utilize them. Once a leadership model achieves the designation of a theory, however, how is the theory justified and placed within the greater context of leadership studies and understanding? There is no perfect answer to this question, although the system of evaluation presented here is ecologically valid:

The word "criteria" is the plural of the term "criterion." A criterion is a standard of judgment such as an examination score of 85% is a grade of 'B' or 95% is a grade of 'A.' Here are five criteria that are generally used when comparing theories and a new theory satisfying these will then replace a previously accepted theory.

1. The previously accepted theory gives an acceptable explanation of something so the new theory must give the same results;

2. New theory explains something that the previously accepted theory either got wrong or, more commonly, did not apply;

3. The new theory makes a prediction that is later verified;

4. The new theory is elegant, has aesthetic quality, is simple, [is] powerful, and includes universal symmetries that are simple, easy to remember or apply, and/or are expressed as some symmetry of nature, and/or are powerful enough to be used in many applications; and

5. Provide a deeper insight or link to another branch of knowledge.[18]

DESCRIPTIVE AND PRESCRIPTIVE LEADERSHIP MODELS REVISITED: A CONCEPTUAL MODEL OF A LEADERSHIP THEORY ON MOTIVATION

Leadership theories and models can be descriptive, prescriptive, or both descriptive and prescriptive. Descriptive theories and models illustrate, define, and capture the description of leadership phenomenon but do not recommend or prescribe actions, behaviors, or processes to employ. Prescriptive theories and models provide recommendations to the leader practitioner with regard to actions, behaviors, or processes to use to be a successful leader. Some leadership theories and models both describe and prescribe.

As an example, let's explore an application of a leadership theory—in this case, a motivational theory introduced by Edwin Locke—to measure organizational outcomes such as satisfaction and performance and investigate this theory's connection to other motivational theories. As you read about Locke's theory, try to list the constructs, concepts, and variables from this leadership motivational theory.

Goal setting theory[19] was first introduced by Edwin A. Locke in 1968, where he published the classic article "Toward a Theory of Task Motivation and Incentives" in the journal *Organizational Behavior and Human Performance.* Since the late 1960s, considerable attention has been given to applying goal setting theory in industry and management situations. Locke, along with other contributors such as Latham, performed laboratory and field experiments; the most widely publicized were the field studies in the 1970s conducted in conjunction with the logging industry.[20] During the past few decades, Locke's emphasis has focused on the area of applied goal setting theory with regard to improved performance in complex business tasks. In 1992, Locke and others studied the relationship between goal setting and expectancy theory.[21] Studies over the past 30 or more years were performed in an effort to learn more about the potential for improving performance by using goal setting as a motivational technique.

This theory can be disassembled into constructs, concepts, and variables (try to list or draw the elements of this theory out on your own). First, Locke's basic assumptions and ideas are important to understand.

Goals are the aim of an action or behavior. Goals can be set for any verifiable or measurable outcome. Locke's basic assumption is that goals are immediate regulators of human action.[22] An individual synthesizes *direction, effort, and persistence* to accomplish goals. To maximize goal setting, *specific and challenging goals are set to focus action and effort over time* to accomplish tasks. From 1968 to 1980, 90 percent of studies showed that specific, well-defined, and challenging goals led to greater improved performance than did vague and easy goals.[23–28] Individuals must commit to set goals to produce results; the more difficult (challenging yet reasonable) the goal, the better the individual will perform. Individuals need management support (feedback, reward mechanisms, and required resources [time, training, and material goods]) to maximize performance when applying goal setting.[29] To apply this theory, Locke suggests seven steps[30] to follow to optimize goal setting:

1. Specify objectives or tasks to be done.
2. Specify how performance will be measured.
3. Specify the standard to be reached.
4. Specify the time frame involved.
5. Prioritize goals.
6. Rate goals as to difficulty and importance.
7. Determine the coordination requirements.

Managers must ensure that they set goals that do not conflict with each other or conflict with organizational goals. For groups, every group member should have verifiable specific goals, as well as a group goal to counter the tendency toward "social loafing." Smaller groups (three to eight people) are more effective than larger ones. Potential negative issues related to this theory include excessive risk taking, excessive competition, and goal failure, all of which can diminish members' confidence and create unwanted stress. A graphic illustration, like that shown in **Figure 3–4**, should assist in understanding this theory.

Can you list the constructs, variables, and process of goal setting theory? How would you operationalize the variables? How would you measure them if you conducted a study to see how goal setting works in a health organization?

Goal setting theory is readily integrated with other motivational theories as well. Although goal setting is a principal attribute of many motivational and performance theories, recent research has largely focused on locus of control theory influences and expectancy theory relationships. Locus of control theory suggests that people acquire motivation either through an internal catalyst (internalizers) or via an external catalyst (externalizers). Integration of goal setting theory with locus of control theory has revealed that internalizers tend to have better performance than externalizers.[31] Both of these theories also relate very well to expectancy theory, in that the goals we set are based on the outcomes we hope to achieve.

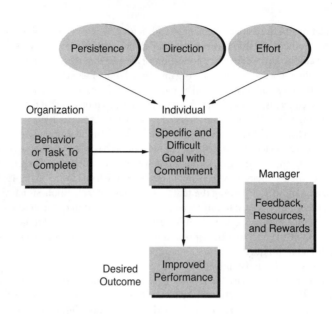

FIGURE 3–4   Goal Setting Theory

Considering another motivational theory, expectancy theory may be integrated with goal setting theory in that goal setting is negatively related to valence (setting low goals does not satisfy individuals as well as setting high goals) and instrumentality is positively related to goal setting (achieving difficult goals gives the individual a greater sense of achievement, self-efficacy, and skill improvement than achieving easy goals).[32] To illustrate the connection of goal setting theory to expectancy theory, a summary is provided. Can you see how the constructs relate?

Expectancy theory was developed by Victor Vroom in 1964. This theory combines motivation and the process of leadership.[33] With expectancy theory, subordinate behavior and action are seen as the result of the subordinate making conscious choices among alternatives such as a reward or no reward. Constructs of this theory are valence, expectancy, and instrumentality. Valence concerns the affective/emotional orientations that subordinates have regarding rewards based on outcomes; this construct focuses on the extent to which the subordinate has extrinsic motivation (see Herzberg's two-factor theory or hygiene theory; extrinsic motivation refers to money, promotion, time off, or some other external reward) or intrinsic motivation (e.g., satisfaction, self-esteem, self-efficacy). Leaders must understand which type of reward will best motivate the subordinate, given his or her wants and needs. Expectancy is the subordinate's expectations, confidence, knowledge, skills, and abilities to perform a task or action. Leaders should remove barriers and enhance resources appropriately to allow the subordinate to perform to his or her maximum ability. Instrumentality is the perception of the subordinate concerning receiving the reward for the task or action performed based on the resulting outcome. Leaders should fulfill promises to subordinates; that is, leaders should reward subordinates for their performance outcomes.

A formula for this theory would be

$$\text{Motivation} = \text{Valence} \times \text{Expectancy (Instrumentality)}$$

Expectancy theory is closely tied to social exchange theory and the transactional leadership model. **Figure 3–5** illustrates its major precepts.

Which constructs make up goal setting theory? Clearly, persistence, direction or focus, effort, and performance are constructs. Also, managerial feedback, resources and rewards, and organizational behaviors and tasks

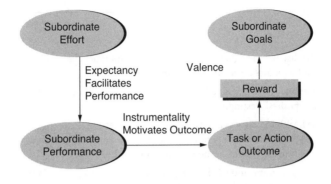

FIGURE 3–5   Expectancy Theory

are constructs. Concepts from each construct may be identified, such as time on task and attention, and then operationally defined as variables. Because each variable observation changes or varies, the total model is evaluated against performance. Can you operationally define the variables that make up the concepts of the constructs of goal setting theory? How would you operationally define the variables of this theory? Could you operationally define the variables of goal setting theory and expectancy theory so as to merge these theories into a larger model?

SUMMARY

This chapter presented the underlying fundamentals of theory. A brief overview and definition of theory was presented, following by a dissection of a theory into its components—constructs, concepts, variables and constants, and measures. Measurement, reliability, validity, and number taxonomy were discussed as well. Visual and graphical tools were used to illustrate how a conceptual model and a theory measure specific outcomes based on leadership principles. Understanding the process of building empirically measurable healthcare and leadership theories and models may be one of the more underrated aspects of leader development in the health system today. The knowledge and ability needed to build conceptual models of leadership and evaluate existing leadership theories and models based on measurement of outcomes of those theories will prove valuable as more theories and models are presented later in this text.

DISCUSSION QUESTIONS

1. Why is the study of theory important in the study of leadership in health organizations?
2. Which examples can you give in relation to health or leadership to define and distinguish the basic elements and relationships of a theory that can be applied to this field?
3. How would you apply goal setting theory's constructs and variables in an organizational setting? How would you apply operational variables to your answer? How about expectancy theory?
4. Distinguish conceptual models from theory.
5. How could you design a simple model of leadership principles or applications? Summarize the relationships between the model's theoretical elements and the application of leadership principles.
6. Critique the social sciences' use of theory within the context of leadership as a discipline.

EXERCISES

1. Review the discussion of goal setting theory and expectancy theory in this chapter, and list the theories, constructs, and variables associated with those theories.

2. Summarize the social sciences hierarchy of a theory or model, and explain how this hierarchy works in terms of hypothesis testing.

3. Using the health industry as a context, modify goal setting theory by incorporating an additional construct with at least two variables, operationally define the variables and show how you would measure the variables, including the type of number taxonomy used.

4. Break down, diagram, and label your modified goal setting model. Write a paragraph explaining how your model differs from the original theory proposed by Locke and Latham.

5. Select two of the articles listed below, or those provided by your instructor. Categorize each construct and variable studied and/or discussed in that article. Next, reorganize the constructs and variables into one model, and operationally define each variable and how it is to be measured.

   a. Calhoun, J. G., Dollett, L., Sinioris, M. E., Wainio, J. A., Butler, P. W., Griffith, J. R., & Warden, G. L. (2008). Development of an interprofessional competency model for healthcare leadership. *Journal of Healthcare Management, 53*(6), 375–389.

   b. Bartling, C. (1996). Leadership for the information age. *Association Management, 46*(8), 61–66.

   c. Church, A. H., & Waclawski, J. (1998). The relationship between individual personality orientation and executive leadership behavior. *Journal of Occupational & Organizational Psychology, 71*(part 2), 99–125.

   d. Chambers, H. (1999). The agencies of leadership. *Executive Excellence, 16*(8), 12.

   e. Dering, N. (1998). Leadership in quality organizations. *Journal of Quality and Participation, 21*(1), 32–35.

   f. Kent, T., Johnson, J. A., & Graber, D. A. (1996). Leadership in the formation of new health care environments. *Health Care Supervisor, 15*(2), 27–34.

6. Appraise, conclude, and justify how the variables in your model from Exercise 5 will vary, and hypothesize what will cause the variables to vary or change.

REFERENCES

1. Bass, B. (1990). *Bass & Stogdill's handbook of leadership: Theory, research and managerial applications* (3rd ed.). New York: Free Press.

2. Stevens, D. (2009). Man on the moon. Retrieved November 2, 2009, from http://dcstevens1.wordpress.com/2009/10/21/man-on-the-moon/.

3. Retrieved May 4, 2009, from http://aether.lbl.gov/www/classes/p10/theory.html.

4. Kerlinger, F. N. (1986). *Foundations of behavioral research* (3rd ed.). New York: Holt, Rinehart, and Winston.

5. Kerlinger, F. N. (1979). *Behavioral research: A conceptual approach.* New York: Holt, Rinehart, and Winston.

6. Jary, D., & Jary, J. (1995). The transformations of Anthony Giddens: The continuing story of structuration theory. *Theory, Culture & Society, 12*(2), 141–160.

7. Jary, D., & Jary, J. (1995). *Dictionary of sociology.* Glasgow/New York: HarperCollins Publishers.

8. Retrieved May 4, 2009, from http://aether.lbl.gov/www/classes/p10/theory.html.

9. SLAC, National Accelerator Laboratory, Stanford University, U.S. Department of Energy. Retrieved May 4, 2009, from http://www2.slac.stanford.edu/vvc/theory/modeltheory.html.

10. Retrieved May 6, 2009, from http://www.usca.edu/polisci/apls301/concepts.htm.

11. Retrieved May 6, 2009, from http://www.usca.edu/polisci/apls301/concepts.htm.

12. Retrieved May 6, 2009, from http://web.utk.edu/~wrobinso/540_lec_opdefs.html.

13. Stevens, S. (1951). Mathematics, measurement and psychophysics. In S. Stevens (Ed.), *Handbook of experimental psychology* (pp. 1–49). New York: Wiley Publishers.

14. Stevens, S. (1946). On the theory of scales of measurement. *Science, 103*, 677–680.

15. Retrieved May 6, 2009, from http://www.usca.edu/polisci/apls301/concepts.htm.

16. Retrieved May 6, 2009, from http://www.usca.edu/polisci/apls301/concepts.htm.

17. Kaplan, R. S., & Norton, D. P. (1992). The Balanced Scorecard: Measures that drive performance. *Harvard Business Review, 70*(1), 71–79.

18. Retrieved May 4, 2009, from http://aether.lbl.gov/www/classes/p10/theory.html.

19. Locke, E. A. (1968, May). Toward a theory of task motivation and incentives. *Organizational Behavior and Human Performance*, pp. 157–189.

20. Latham, G. P., & Locke, E. A. (1979). Goal-setting: A motivational technique that works. *Organizational Dynamics, 8*(2), 68–80.

21. Mento, A. J., Locke, E. A., & Klein, H. J. (1992). Relationship of goal level to valence and instrumentality. *Journal of Applied Psychology, 77*(4), 395–405.

22. Locke, note 19.

23. Ivancevich, J. M., & Matteson, M. T. (1993). *Organizational behavior and management.* Burr Ridge, IL: Richard D. Irwin.

24. Locke, E. A., Shaw, K. N., Saari, L. M., & Latham, G. P. (1981). Goal setting and task performance: 1969–1980. *Psychological Bulletin, 90*(1), 125–152.

25. Locke, E. A., Gist, M. E., & Taylor, M. S. (1987). Organizational behavior: Group structure, process, and effectiveness. *Journal of Management, 13*(2), 237–257.

26. Locke, E. A., & Chesney, A. A. (1991). Relationships among goal difficulty, business strategies, and performance on a complex management simulation task. *Academy of Management Journal, 34*(2), 400–424.

27. Locke, E. A. (1986). *Generalizing from laboratory to field settings.* Lexington, MA: Lexington Books.

28. Locke, E. A., & Latham, G. P. (1984). *Goal setting: A motivational technique that works!* Englewood Cliffs, NJ: Prentice-Hall.

29. Locke & Latham, note 28.

30. Locke & Latham, note 28.

31. Locke et al., note 24.

32. Mento et al., note 21.

33. Retrieved July 11, 2009, from http://www.12manage.com/methods_vroom_expectancy_theory.html.

C H A P T E R

4

Chronology of Leadership Study and Practice

One's feelings waste themselves in use of words; they ought all to be distilled into actions and into actions which bring results.

Florence Nightingale

This chapter provides a historical summary and overview of leadership theory as it has evolved over the ages. Major theories and models are presented. Early documents (2300 B.C.) outlining leadership principles and definitions (400 B.C.) are addressed, with the discussion then proceeding through the contemporary and accepted models of the twentieth and twenty-first centuries. This chapter presents the theories and models in the original light that the creating authors intended. Strengths and weaknesses of each theory, as well as applications and strategies for use, are integrated into each theoretical overview.

LEARNING OBJECTIVES

1. Describe the progression of leadership thought as portrayed in theories and models from the "great man" and trait phase, to the behavioral phase, to the situational or contingency phase.

2. Distinguish constructs of a trait theory or model, a behavioral theory or model, and a situational or contingency theory or model of leadership, and interpret those constructs' value in the present day.

3. Apply a behavioral theory or model and a situational or contingency theory or model of leadership, and demonstrate the application in an example based on a definition of leadership.

4. Compare and contrast, through use of illustrative diagrams, two or more behavioral or situational/contingency theories or models of leadership.

5. From the progression of leadership thought, design, create, and explain a personal leadership model applicable to leading health organizations today.

6. Appraise and relate constructs and variables from the progression of leadership thought to your personal leadership model for leading health organizations today.

INTRODUCTION

The study of historical leadership is important for both graduate students and early careerists for several reasons. First, as with the study of any historical theory grounded in the literature, it is important to know where the study of the discipline began so that leaders do not repeat mistakes of the past or spend effort on advocating philosophies no longer considered relevant in the study of leadership. Second, early careerists will recognize opportunities and best practices discovered by predecessors that, if applied properly, can aid them in developing competencies in their own leadership practice. Third, leadership theories and models have built upon one another over time; contemporary leadership theories, models, and practices have a lineage stretching back for decades—if not centuries—that have paved the way and informed modern leadership thought.

These are the most salient reasons to study the history of leadership thought. In reality, hours-long discussions could be sustained pondering many other reasons to explore the history of the discipline. For practical purposes, better-known theories and models are presented in this chapter; a thorough discussion of leadership theories and models could easily run to thousands of pages of text.

The progression of leadership thought is a constructivist approach over time; that is, early theories and models form the foundations or stepping stones for the next theories or models proposed. As you read about the theories and models, list the constructs and variables associated with each theory or model under the various phases of leadership thought and begin to identify which constructs and approaches are salient to health leadership in today's environment. As you study the leadership progression of thought and research, think about which theories and models are descriptive, prescriptive, or both. Ultimately, you should begin to identify leadership constructs and approaches that resonate with your own philosophy, thereby enabling you to build a preliminary personal leadership model that you can utilize in your career.

There are three distinct phases of leadership thought: (1) "great man" and trait theories and models; (2) behavioral theories and models; and (3) situational or contingency theories and models (**Table 4–1**). A fourth phase may now be in an early stage of development; this potential phase incorporates organizational culture into situational leadership practice.

Some theories and models from earlier phases did overlap somewhat with part of another phase of leadership though. Nevertheless, in general, the theories and models presented in this chapter can be classified into a specific phase based on the constructs and variables they incorporate rather than the chronological time period in which they emerged. When leaders' traits—for example, height or eye color—are utilized to distinguish them or measure success or select another leader, traits are the overriding factor of the theory or model. Likewise, when an individual "great" leader is identified and characterized, such as Alexander the Great or George Washington, for purposes of measuring success, identifying another leader, or role modeling, the basis of the theory or model is considered a "great man" phase approach. Upon reflection, "great man" and trait theories and models are very similar and, therefore, tend to be grouped together. Behavioral theories are behavior or action based.

TABLE 4–1   Progression of Leadership Thought by Phase

"Great Man" and Trait Phase (Circa 450 B.C.–1940s)	Behavioral Phase (1940s–1960s)	Situational or Contingency Phase (1970s–Present)
Attempted to determine which specific traits make a person an effective leader. Great leaders are the focus of trait identification.	Attempted to determine which particular behaviors and styles leaders use to cause others to follow them. Which behaviors and styles were successful was a focus of the theories.	Attempts to explain effective leadership within the context of the larger work situation and environment where the leader adapts styles, strategies, and applications to best fit the situation or by selecting a leader who best fits the situation based on the leader's style and strategies.

In other words, successful leaders perform some action of behavior or a set of actions or behaviors, such as showing concern for people by rounding (i.e., walking around the workplace talking with subordinates purposefully). Situational (or contingency) theories and models incorporate the context or situation or environment into the leadership approach to identify avenues for success that can be attributed to the leader. Situational leadership requires leaders to be flexible, and to build and develop the competencies, knowledge, skills, and abilities (especially situational assessment) needed to adapt styles and practices to the current situation. The "toolbox" of leadership—that is, the capability to use several styles, practices, or "tools"—is most important in situational leadership theories and models.

"GREAT MAN" AND TRAIT LEADERSHIP PHASE

"Great man" and trait theories and models concentrated on individual leaders who were considered "great," with those leaders' characteristics or traits being identified as reasons for their success. Other models focused simply on traits without identifying a "great man." "Great women" were also identified, such as Joan of Arc, but to a lesser degree due to social norms and cultures that prevailed prior to the 1900s. Many "great leaders"—both women and men—could serve as the focus of a "great man" theory or model. The cultural norm through the early twentieth century was encapsulated by Dowd in 1936, who argued that there is no such thing as leadership by the masses. According to his view, the individuals in every society possess different degrees of intelligence, energy, and moral force, and in whatever direction the masses may be influenced to go, they are always led by the superior few.[1]

Although pure trait theory has fell into obsolescence, traits of leadership are still very important to the subject of leadership.[2] Based more heavily on description, these theories and models propose emulation of what great leaders do and which traits they possess; prescription is indirect and "universal," in that situational context and behavior adaption are not incorporated into this genre of leadership thought. Some of the more accepted (for their time) theories and models of this phase are presented here.

Xenophon: An Early Leader Theory (400 B.C.)

As early as 400 B.C., Xenophon (**Figure 4–1**) first defined leadership and its impact on organizations; later, Bennis stated the converse notion—namely, that the most important (and underlying) issue is lack of leadership.[3]

FIGURE 4–1   Xenophon

FIGURE 4–2   Niccolo Machiavelli

Today, leaders in a variety of organizations must understand the role and importance of effective leadership, leadership development, and succession planning in achieving organizational success. Unfortunately, leadership and leadership development do not confine themselves to a single "checklist," comprehensive model, or flow-chart. Xenophon wrote *Anabasis,* which served as a guide to Alexander the Great during his conquests. Restated in modern terms, Xenophon's key idea was that leaders guide their people (their army) to success by demon-strating courage and modeling "leadership." A key characteristic of a leader, from Xenophon's perspective, was horsemanship; being a great horseman was critical to role-modeling leadership. In the warfare of the time, horses were essential and mastery of horsemanship was a valuable leader attribute.

Xenophon's writings included *On the Cavalry Commander,*[4] which described the successful military leader. The strength of this body of work was its focus on military leadership and its value as a unique source of wis-dom for future leaders such as Alexander the Great. Weaknesses were its focus on characteristics and skills in-directly linked to subordinates' performance or motivation.

Machiavelli: Narcissist Theory (1530)

While leadership has been discussed from the earliest times, one of the first formal documents written about lead-ership and organizational structure was Niccolo Machiavelli's (1527) *The Prince.* Machiavelli (**Figure 4–2**) sug-gested that the qualities of a good leader were to be malevolent and feared. The major theme of Machiavelli's work was "The end justifies the means." Although behavioral discussions are presented in Machiavelli's work, the over-tones of trait and "great man" approaches are clear throughout his book. At the same time, the lack of consider-ation of consequences and the inherent immorality of his strategies should be apparent. Strengths of this work are its pragmatic approach, which served as fodder for political science thought; its weaknesses are the cynical na-ture of the discussions. Also, the focus on leaders' use of fear as a motivational tool is clearly suspect.

Carlyle, Galton, and James's "Great Man" Theory (1840–1880)

From approximately 1840 to 1880, "great man" theorists Carlyle, Galton, and James studied great men from history who exhibited certain behaviors and possessed certain characteristics. They documented successful outcomes of these "great" leaders, such as prosperity, political standing, or affluence. Based on the study of these characteristics, the theorists suggested that to be a good leader, a person would have to emulate the characteristics of these men. Such characteristics often centered on an individual's race and gender. Not surprisingly, many of the "great men" identified in the early chronicles were Anglican, male, and Caucasian (such as George Washington, depicted in **Figure 4–3**). In the past, some authors advocating this theory combined "great man" and trait theories into a common field of study; others did not.

In the early study of "great man" theories, an inordinate amount of weight was placed on certain immutable variables such as gender, race, height, and oration. Mutable variables, such as social class, education, and religion, factored heavily into the early "great man" theories as well. As the study of historical figures evolved, scholars began to exam commonalities among great historical figures and develop a finite list of traits associated with leadership. The primary focus on traits eventually evolved into a distinct discipline called "trait theory." This niche concept suggested that leaders are defined by various characteristics, such as intelligence,

FIGURE 4–3   George Washington: A "Great Man" Theory Icon

extraversion, experience, education, confidence, and initiative. Possession of these traits were said to distinguish a leader from a follower in early trait-based theories.[5]

Lewin, Lippitt, and White's Trait Theory (1938–1939)

The emphasis on traits was solidified as an acceptable practice in 1938 and 1939 when Lewin, Lippitt, and White's research emerged as the benchmark studies of their time.[6, 7] These scholars studied the leadership styles of two groups of 10- and 11-year-olds in mask-making clubs. During the experiment, they noted that the two groups demonstrated two distinct leadership behavior types: authoritarian or democratic. The study led to the subsequent examination of the effects of these leadership styles on production, group tension, cooperation, and feelings of "we'ness" versus "I'ness." Lewin, Lippitt, and White's early work has since become some of the more often-cited and highly quoted leadership and social psychology studies of the modern era. This work aided in the migration to the behavioral phase. Accordingly, much of the modern research in leadership theory traces its roots back to these early studies. Unfortunately, the failure of Lewin, Lippitt, and White's theory to identify any single trait or behavior, or set of traits or behaviors, that could systematically explain leadership success across various situations promoted a paradigm shift in leadership study, such that researchers began to analyze the effects of situations on leader behavior.

Stogdill's Leader Traits and Skills

Stogdill performed reviews of trait theory research well after the "great man" and trait phase of leadership had ended. From this analysis, he compiled a list of traits and skills of the successful leader from that literature. "However, Stogdill makes it clear that recognition of the relevance of leader traits is not a return to the original trait approach."[8] **Table 4–2** lists the traits and skills Stogdill found consistently in the trait literature.

TABLE 4–2   Stogdill's Leader Traits and Skills

Traits	Skills
Adaptable to situations	Clever (intelligence)
Alert to social environment	Conceptually skilled (abstract to operational)
Ambitious and achievement oriented	Creative
Assertive	Diplomatic and tactful
Cooperative	Fluent in speaking
Decisive	Knowledgeable about group tasks
Dependable	Organized
Dominant	Persuasive
Energetic	Socially skilled
Persistent	
Self-confident	
Willing to assume responsibility	
Tolerant of stress	

Source: Yukl, G. (1994). *Leadership in organizations* (3rd ed.). Englewood Cliffs, NJ: Prentice Hall, p. 256.

BEHAVIORAL LEADERSHIP PHASE

The behavioral phase of leadership study and thought emerged in the middle of the twentieth century, once theorists realized that the traits and "great man" arguments were unable to totally explain the phenomenon of leadership. In particular, the question of which actions and behaviors facilitated leadership success lay at the heart of leadership research of this period. An important assumption of this behavioral phase was the notion that leadership could be learned or nurtured. Earlier theories and models accepted the idea that leadership was inherited, genetic, based on nature. Although it seems less dramatic now, this shift in thought from only nature being at work to a combination of nature and nurture being recognized as part of leadership marked a huge step in research and leadership practice (**Figure 4–4**). Leadership could be learned! More prescription is assumed in these theories and models as compared to the earlier phase of leadership. Even so, the behavioral phase was built upon the "great man" and trait phase of leadership thought.

McGregor's Theory X and Theory Y (1950)

At the sunset of the trait phase and the dawning of the behavior phase of leadership research, the concept of Theory X and Theory Y emerged. In the 1950s, McGregor hypothesized that leaders generally hold one of two contrasting sets of assumptions about people. He additionally suggested that these two dichotomous sets of assumptions would influence leadership behavior. For example, if managers/leaders assumed that their followers were lazy, indifferent, and uncooperative, then they would be treated accordingly (Theory X). Conversely, if they viewed their subordinates as energetic, bright, and friendly, they would treat them quite differently (Theory Y). These leadership attitudes toward followers would soon condition the leader to behave in a certain manner. In essence, this theory exemplifies a self-fulfilling prophecy.

Those leaders who hold Theory X assumptions would be autocratic and very directive and those who hold Theory Y would be democratic and consensus-building oriented. A Theory X leader would view a subordinate who was late as irresponsible and would require stricter control over his or her behavior, whereas a Theory Y leader might speculate that this same subordinate found his or her job boring and might need additional opportunities to stimulate the person and improve performance (and behavior). The real contribution of McGregor's work was the suggestion that a manager/leader influenced a leadership situation by these two dichotomous assumptions about people.

- *Theory X*: People are lazy, extrinsically motivated, not capable of self-discipline, and want security and no responsibility in their jobs.

- *Theory Y*: People do not inherently dislike work, are intrinsically motivated, exert self-control, and seek responsibility.

Theory Y leaders assess themselves (internal modifiers) in areas such as preferred leadership style, motives and limitations, past experiences, and external modifiers such as characteristics of the task, time constraints,

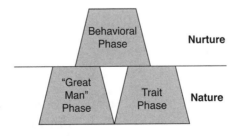

FIGURE 4–4   Leadership Thought Progression

organizational norms, structure and climate, past history with group, economic and legal limits, and degree of stability of the organization. Once the assessment is complete, the Theory Y leader chooses a leadership style (which may include an autocratic style depending on the situation). A Theory X leader has one leadership style—autocratic—and has a limited view of the world; that is, he or she does not consider internal and external modifiers. There is also a hint of situational or contingency leadership research in McGregor's theory. The weakness of this model is its dichotomous nature.

Stogdill and Coons's Ohio Leadership Studies (1950)

In 1947, under the direction of Stogdill, the Ohio State Leadership Studies[9] were conducted. The goal of these studies was to determine whether a relationship exists between effective leader behavior and subordinates' satisfaction and performance. Two dimensions of leader behavior that emerged from these studies were consideration and initiating structure. The consideration focused on psychological closeness between the leader and followers, whereas the initiating structure dealt with concern for actively directing subordinates toward job completion or goal attainment.

Surprisingly, some people who rated highly on both constructs of "consideration" and "initiating structure" were not always the most effective leaders. Further research along these lines indicated that *both* of these dimensions were needed for effective leadership. It was found to be more important for a leader to strike a balance in terms of what is appropriate for the situation than to consistently display high consideration and high structure at all times (**Table 4–3**).

The following summaries delineate the conclusions of how effective leader behavior relates to follower satisfaction and performance[10]:

Consideration

1. Employee satisfaction with a leader depends on the degree of consideration displayed by the leader.

2. Leader consideration affects employee satisfaction more when jobs are unpleasant and stressful than when they are pleasant and have low stress.

3. A leader who rates high on consideration can exercise more initiating structure without a decline in employee satisfaction.

4. Consideration given in response to good performance will increase the likelihood of future good performance.

TABLE 4–3   Initiating Structure and Consideration

		Manager's Initiating Structure	
		High	Low
Manager's Consideration	High	High performance	Low performance
		Low grievance rate	Low grievance rate
		Low turnover	Low turnover
	Low	High performance	Low performance
		High grievance rate	High grievance rate
		High turnover	High turnover

Source: Gordon, J. (1991). *A diagnostic approach to organizational behavior* (3rd ed.). Englewood Cliffs, NJ: Prentice Hall.

Initiating Structure

1. Initiating structure by a leader that adds to role clarity will increase employee satisfaction.

2. Initiating structure by a leader will decrease employee satisfaction when structure is already adequate.

3. Initiating structure by a leader will increase performance when a task is unclear.

4. Initiating structure by a leader will not affect performance when a task is clear.

The major drawback to the Ohio State Studies was the limited consideration given to situational differences that may influence leader effectiveness. From this point, you can see the development of research (future studies) leaning toward situational leadership.

University of Michigan Leadership Studies (1950)

Conducted around the same time as the Ohio State Studies, the University of Michigan leadership studies sought answers to many of the same research questions as their Ohio State counterparts. Not surprisingly, the Michigan study results were similar to those conducted at Ohio State, thus supporting some convergent validity assumptions. Like the Ohio State Studies, the Michigan studies suggested that leaders could be grouped into one of two classifications: employee oriented or production oriented. The research suggested that highly productive supervisors spent more time planning departmental work and supervising their employees. The same supervisors spent less time working alongside and performing the same tasks as subordinates. The successful supervisors accorded their subordinates more freedom in specific task performance and tended to be employee oriented. In contrast, the employee-focused leader spent his or her time on forging relationships and in maintaining harmony in the work environment. Such a leader was less interested in written policies and formalized delegation of responsibilities.[11] In the end, leaders with both an employee orientation and a production orientation were the most successful.

Katz's Skills Theory (1955)

In 1955, Robert Katz proposed three categories of skills leaders should have: technical skills, human skills, and conceptual skills. Technical skills relate to knowledge and capabilities the leader needs to be competent and proficient in certain activities. Human skills are nearly self-evident: They are the skills leaders need to relate to and to interact with other people. Such skills would include excellent communication skills, the ability to work with groups and teams, and the social skills to get each member of the team to perform at his or her maximum potential. Conceptual skills are a bit more difficult to define: They are the many skills that allow the leader to understand what needs to be done, how it should be done, and when to do it. Leaders need to be able to conceptualize ideas to be able to see the "big picture."

Katz identified the level of importance that each of these three areas has for each level of management. The most important skills for top-level management are human and conceptual; the most important skills for mid-level management are human; and the most important skills for supervisory management are technical and human. Mid-level managers also need a fair degree of technical and conceptual skills, while technical skills are not as important for top-level leadership and conceptual skills are not as important for supervisory management.[12, 13] A summary of the skills follows:

- *Technical skills*: knowledge about approaches, methods, processes, procedures, and techniques for conducting specialized work; and the ability to use those tools and equipment relevant to the activity.

- *Interpersonal skills*: knowledge about human behavior and interpersonal relationships; the ability to understand the feelings, attitudes, and motivations of others; the ability to communicate and deal with conflict effectively; and the ability to build effective relationships.

- *Conceptual skills*: analytical ability; logical thinking; proficiency in concept development and the capability to make sense of complex and ambiguous relationships; creativity in idea generation and problem-solving;

and the ability to analyze events and perceive trends, anticipate changes, and recognize opportunities and problems (inductive and deductive reasoning).

■ *Administrative skills* (added as a fourth category by later researchers): the ability to perform particular types of managerial functions or behaviors (e.g., hiring, planning, organizing, budgeting, delegating, negotiating, coaching, mentoring, and conducting meetings).

Argyris's Personality and Organization Theory (1957)

In 1957, Argyris published a seminal work called *Personality and Organization.* It was one of the first publications to relate organizational learning and success with a leader's ability to achieve synchronization between his or her vision and goals with the subordinate's or employee's perception or tolerance of the vision and goals. To demonstrate this theory, Argyris posited two sets of organizational values he called "theories in use" and "theories in action."

Theories in use suggest that, given a basic scenario dealing with organizational norms, cultures, or values in a stable environment, an individual's outcome can be forecasted and predicted. The theory suggests that there is an implicit acknowledgment of what we should do as leaders and managers. That is, the person's predicted answers are conducive to the behavior and effort expected in the organization.

Theories in action are those activities that occur in the organization that are dissimilar from the predicted theories in use. For example, if organizational norms and behaviors call for a multicultural workforce and the personnel hired reflect only one gender or race, there could be a disconnect between organizational goals and organizational outcomes. In this case, the two may not be in synchrony.[14–16]

This early leader theory on managing and leader organizations acknowledges that organizations are part and parcel of the humans who work in them. Sufficient training, branding, and communication of institutional norms, values, and objectives are the leader's responsibilities.

Training and culture shifts can increase the effectiveness of a leader's ability to ensure that the actions and thoughts executed come from the same (desired) agenda.[17] For example, multicultural sensitivity training can provide an opportunity for personnel in organizations to become more tolerant of different races and demographic characteristics. Extreme methods of applying this theory may include organizational reengineering where personnel in the organization who are incapable of unlearning irrelevant predispositions and do not support the organization are moved to different parts of the organization or "right-sized" out of a job.

Blake and Mouton's Managerial Grid (1964)

In 1964, Blake and Mouton offered what was then a very unique approach to leadership. Their managerial grid is a behavioral leadership model based on four constructs: concern for production, concern for people, motivation, and leadership style. Motivation can be negative (motivate by fear) or positive (motivate through desire and encouragement). Motivation is rarely shown (perhaps due to the difficulty in determining motivation type and amount).

Essentially, Blake and Mouton identified five different managerial styles based on the priority the individual leader assigns to product versus people: Country Club, Team Leader, Impoverished, Produce or Perish, and Middle of the Road. The first two styles place far more importance on people than on product, the second two emphasize product, and the last one rides the fence, emphasizing neither product/production nor the person or people/subordinates. **Figure 4–5** depicts the managerial grid.

In the Mouton–Blake managerial grid, the least effective leadership style is the Impoverished style, because such a person does not really care about either product or people. The most effective is Team Leader, because such an individual places a high priority both on the product and the people and will look for win-win solutions that will satisfy the needs of all. This leader is not naive; he or she does realize that in some situations it is not possible to reach a solution that will satisfy everyone. Another key facet of the Mouton–Blake managerial grid is that each leadership approach is understood to be important and useful given certain circumstances and in certain situations. There are clear connections between Blake and Mouton's work on the managerial grid to

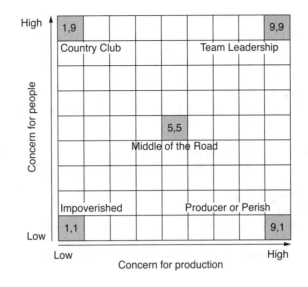

FIGURE 4–5   Blake and Mouton's Managerial Grid

Hersey and Blanchard's 1977 situational leadership model. Although the managerial grid is taught in most graduate management and leadership programs, there is no research validating its efficacy.[18, 19]

SITUATIONAL OR CONTINGENCY LEADERSHIP PHASE

We turn now to more recent research in leadership theory. Situational leadership theories and models—also called contingency models, because the leader model should change contingent (based) on the situation at hand—are more applicable to health organizations today because the healthcare environment is dynamic and stakeholder relationships are multifaceted and complex. Contingency or situational theories and models assert that no one way of leading works well in all situations. Instead, leaders need the ability to change styles and select those skills that best deal with the organizational situation at hand. Effective leaders diagnose the situation, identify an appropriate leadership style, and then determine whether its implementation is possible. At least four dimensions must be evaluated when assessing situational or contingent leadership research:

- Subordinate: expertise, experience, resources, motivation, task load, and knowledge of the job
- Supervisor/leader/manager: values, attitudes, level of influence, and level of authority
- Task characteristics: complexity, time, risk, autonomy, ambiguity, uncertainty, and workload
- Organizational culture: coupling, communication environment, ambiguity and uncertainty tolerance, balance of work, social and personal life, planning emphasis, decision-making alignment, employee enhancement, and level of knowledge management and learning orientation

The other significant element in situational leadership is the emergence of organizational culture within the situational context. Simply stated, culture is a group's unique view of the world. Every organization—whether a family or a health system conglomerate—has an overriding organizational culture and various sets of subcultures. Leaders must attend to cultural issues to be successful.

Some researchers have suggested that leadership strategies in any setting have strong underlying similarities, but must change as the setting changes over time. Even if the health organization remains essentially the same, change in the environment, such as the recent changes in healthcare delivery, may require leaders to change their strategy/style to be effective. Culture comes into the discussion of leadership as an influence on leadership style selection; organizational culture has grown in importance over the last decade in that leaders can actually develop culture—not merely assess and adapt to it. This realization may be leading into another phase of leadership thought; this idea is discussed briefly in the next section of this chapter.

To provide a simple example of situational leadership in action, suppose that subordinates have the expertise and competence needed to perform an organizational task. In such a case, an employee-oriented leadership style will be more effective than a task-oriented leadership style. In contrast, if leader and follower both have the same attitudes, then followers may be more willing to accept a task- or production-oriented leadership style.

This phase of leadership—the phase currently in vogue—immerses behaviors into the context of the leadership situation and environment. Situational assessment skills are critical to this body of knowledge on leadership. Thus leaders can be "made" through nature, can be nurtured, and now must consider situational factors and adapt to those situations to be successful. Leaders must also adapt! This phase has more potential for prescription and not just description of theories and models. As illustrated in **Figure 4–6**, leadership models are a progression wherein later approaches build on the knowledge of the past. A number of different models of leadership fit under the general category of contingency. Given that this phase constitutes the most widely accepted set of theories and models today, several approaches falling under this rubric are highlighted in this section.

Exchange Theory

Exchange theory focuses on a vertical dyad linkage approach that comprises the connection between the leader and the led. This approach emphasizes the interaction of the leader with the subordinate group. The leader exchanges resources, such as increased rewards, increased job latitude, influence on decision making, and open communication, for members' commitment to higher involvement in organizational functioning. This line of research embraces social exchange theory, which suggests that leaders must offer something in exchange (e.g., bonus, increased status) for improved or additional performance by subordinates. It is the precursor of modern transactional leadership theory.

According to exchange theory, the leader categorizes followers into two groups: (1) the cadre or in-group and (2) the hired hands or out-group. With the in-group, the leader allows greater latitude, which in turn yields higher performance ratings, lower propensity to quit, greater supervisory relationships, and greater job satisfaction. The out-group receives less latitude and, therefore, demonstrates poorer performance outcomes.

This approach has been criticized because it relies on narrow information and situations, does not study the organizational outcomes associated with this exchange relationship, and utilizes exchanges in diverse and inconsistent ways.[20] The important point is that social exchange is a viable way of regarding leadership and is directly linked to transactional leadership theory.

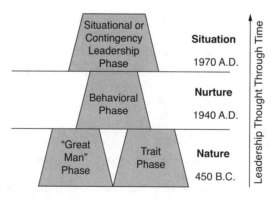

FIGURE 4–6　Leadership Thought Progression Revisited

Fiedler's Contingency Model (1964)

In the mid-1960s, Fiedler introduced a contingency model of leadership.[21] In this model, Fiedler proposed that the performance of any group depends on the leader's style in terms of motivation and relationship to the subordinates and the favorability of the situation. De Jonge[22] explains that Fiedler was the first to discuss this approach, and it is Fiedler's approach that has been researched most often. Fiedler identified three variables related to the context: group atmosphere, task structure, and leader's power position. For this researcher, the performance of any group depended on two other factors, which became known as "leadership style" and" situational favorableness"; these two factors determine how effective the leader will be.[23] The term "leadership style" is a leader's manner of behaving and acting in a work environment, is strongly dependent upon his or her personality, and is relatively stable.

Fiedler identified three situational factors that are present in any situation: (1) leader–member relations; (2) task structure; and (3) position power of the leader. A leader utilizing a *task-oriented style* (notice the progression from the Ohio State and University of Michigan studies) will most likely be successful when subordinates have enough of the following attributes:

- *Leader–member relations*: the amount the group trusts and respects the leader and is willing to follow his or her directions.
- *Task structure*: the amount in which the task is clearly specified and defined or structured.
- *Position power*: the leader's amount of official power—that is, the ability to influence others due to the leader's position in the organization (also known as "legitimate power" in French and Raven's power taxonomy).

The antithetic leader style is indicated when a lack of enough leader–member relations, task structure, and position power would suggest the leader use a relationship-oriented style. Fiedler's theory defines leadership effectiveness in terms of work group performance. Group performance is *contingent* upon the situational constructs and match between (1) a person's leadership style and (2) the "favorableness" of the leadership situation where the following relationship holds:

Group Performance = Leadership Style + Situational Favorableness

According to Yukl, to determine a person's leadership style, Fiedler developed a measure called the least preferred coworker (LPC) scale.[24] This instrument describes the one person with whom the leader worked least well among all the workers he or she has supervised. Such an evaluation classifies people into three types:

- Those who are relationship oriented—who see good interpersonal relationships as a requirement for task accomplishment and find satisfaction from these close relations
- Those who are task oriented—who focus on task completion and worry about interpersonal relationships afterward
- The middle-LPC people—who are flexible and not overly constrained with either relationship or task completion

Situational favorableness refers to the extent a particular situation enables a leader to influence a group of subordinates. Three factors are used to measure this aspect of the model:

- *Leader–member relations*: the quality of the relationship between the leader and followers (the most important construct because it directly contributes to the influence the leader will have over subordinates)
- *Task structure*: step-by-step clarity of a task (the higher the degree of task structure, the more influence the leader will have)
- *Position power*: the ability for the leader to reward and punish subordinates by hiring, firing, and promoting them

Several important issues exist regarding Fiedler's model of leadership. First, evidence suggests that other situational variables, such as training and experience, contribute to leader effectiveness. Second, there is some doubt as to whether the LPC scale is a true measure of leadership style; critics contend its interpretation is speculative and inadequately supported.[25] Some researchers argue that the reliability of the measurement of leadership style using the LPC is low and the range and appropriateness of the three situational components are narrow.

Erikson's Psychoanalytic Theory (1964)

Psychoanalytic theory was a derivative of the early Freudian studies of personality and development. The factors that were originally thought by Freud to affect only an individual's relationship with the environment and close family members have now been extended to consider their influence on teams and organizations. Psychoanalytic theory has become an interesting tool used over the last 50 years to study the various influences on followership, leadership, and group and organizational dynamics in both large organizations and smaller groups built on interpersonal relationships.[26–28]

In 1964, Erikson posited psychoanalytic theory as a study of attachment and childhood development.[29] Over time, however, psychoanalytic theory became recognized as an opportunity to research "intrigue" in the leadership literature. For example, Erikson's initial theory posited that a variety of unconscious factors stimulate and motivate behavior. For some individuals, followership may be stimulated by a need of a subordinate to replace a father figure with a person of authority in the workplace. Consequently, a father's mentoring and emotional attachment for children within the family dynamic may extend to the need to display those tendencies by subordinates in the workplace. All this occurs through an unconscious need to follow or lead others.[30]

In many cases, a charismatic leader may be viewed as a father figure by followers in the organization.[31, 32] The charismatic leader may display those qualities that are desired or sought after by subordinates in the workplace who are seeking to have as their guide a leader who will exhibit patriarchal behaviors. In a pure tribal sense, a natural pecking order (informal chain of command) is established that may (or may not) establish legitimate lines of authority in the workplace.

While natural predispositions to follow and obey may present themselves in the workplace, the same might be said of the opposite tendencies—in other words, the inclination to rebel and disobey.[33] Predispositions in the environment toward certain traits may evoke (unconsciously or otherwise) certain outcomes, leading to negative results.[34, 35] For example, if a new leader in an organization has a more rigid philosophy of leadership that emphasizes adherence to an 8 A.M. to 5 P.M. workday, as opposed to the more flexible self-directed and autonomous philosophy espoused by that leader's predecessor, the employees may present as "organizational disrupters" and noncompliant. In this case, the employees may not be rebelling against the new leader as much as demonstrating their predisposed feeling to rebel against the rigid schedule and the perception of authoritative leadership. The resistance may derive from the employee's unconscious being, related to a sense of negative control and directorship experienced in adolescence.

A leader's awareness of his or her predisposition to lead or follow is crucial in any self-diagnosis and application. Those who are predisposed to be followers may be uncomfortable in filling the leader role and may perform better with fewer leaders over them to provide praise and structure. Similarly, those predisposed to lead and mentor others in a personal and predisposed manner may be uncomfortable in environments characterized by stricter organizational norms and reporting mechanisms.

House's Path-Goal Theory (1971)

Path–goal theory, which was developed by Robert House in 1971, suggests that a leader can affect subordinates' performance, satisfaction, and motivation by (1) offering rewards for achieving performance goals; (2) clarifying paths toward these goals; and (3) removing obstacles to performance.[36] This theory adds the elements of clarity (step-by-step instructions, for example) and explicit effort by the leader to remove barriers blocking goal achievement for the subordinate to the leadership discussion. The ability and effects of the leader's efforts are influenced and moderated by the subordinate's personality (e.g., the subordinate's locus of control [as described by Rotter, either internalizer or externalizer], self-perceived ability, and self-efficacy) and characteristics of the environment (e.g., the amount of task structure, organizational coupling, and team orientation).

Victor Vroom was very active in developing theories that fall within this realm, including expectancy theory (a motivational approach that was described in Chapter 3). Vroom's 1964 theory is significantly connected

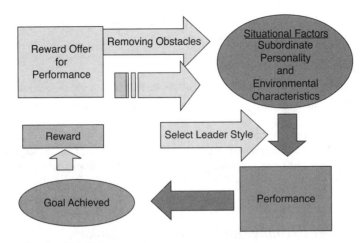

Leadership Styles
Directive: leader gives specific guidance to subordinates.
Supportive: leader is friendly and shows concern for subordinates.
Participative: leader consults with and considers recommendations by subordinates.
Achievement oriented: leader sets high goals and expects subordinates to achieve them.

FIGURE 4–7   Path–Goal Theory

to House's path–goal theory of leadership and the situational leadership theory introduced by Hersey and Blanchard. The constructs of leadership styles in the path–goal theory have similarity to those found in situational leadership theory. The path–goal theory began with just two options for a leader's behavior: supportive or directive. This model was then subsequently expanded to incorporate McClelland's achievement orientation and participation. According to House, the leader can influence employee performance by "offering rewards for achieving performance goals; clarifying paths towards goals, removing obstacles to performance."[37]

Path–goal theory now encompasses four leadership behavior options: directive, supportive, achievement oriented, and participative (**Figure 4–7**). Each approach has its time and place. When a task is not structured, when it is complex, or when employees lack the skills to adequately perform the task, the leader needs to use the directive approach. When the task is boring and routine, the leader needs to be supportive. When a task is unstructured but could be challenging for the worker, the leader might be more achievement oriented, offering encouragement to build employee confidence. When the task is totally unstructured, the leader might be more effective by using a participative approach.

Vroom, Yetton, and Jago's Normative Decision-Making Model (1973)

Vroom, Yetton, and Jago's normative decision-making model was intended to help leaders make more effective decisions while at the same time garnering support for those decisions from their subordinates. These researchers identified five styles of decision making, ranging from very autocratic to consultative. Because it incorporates the idea that leaders make decisions differently based on different situations, their model falls under the very broad umbrella of contingency models. Vroom, Yetton, and Jago suggested that four major categories of decision-making styles exist, with two subcategories appearing under three of the major categories:[38]

Autocratic Type 1: The leader uses information that is easily available and makes the decision alone.

Autocratic Type 2: The leader collects information from followers, makes the decision alone, and then informs others.

Consultative Type 1: The leaders share the problem individually with those persons whom he or she considers to be relevant, asks for ideas and suggestions, and then makes the decision.

Consultative Type 2: The leader shares problems with relevant others as a group, asks for ideas and suggestions, and then makes the decision alone.

Group-Based Type 1: The leader brings one other person into the decision-making process for the purposes of sharing information and making the decision.

Group-Based Type 2: The group makes the decision with the leader, with consensus being the priority.[39, 40]

Delegative: The leader gives the responsibility and authority to make the decision to someone else.

The strengths of this model include (1) its incorporation of the reality that decisions are made in situational context; (2) the broad range of decision-making styles; and (3) its inclusion of leader and group dynamics in the decision-making process. Weaknesses include (1) the lack of understanding of decision load, technology, and leader and subordinate attention and (2) the lack of acknowledgment of irrational decision making.

Graen's Leader–Member Exchange and Vertical Dyad Linkage Theories (1975)

The leader–member exchange theory (LMX) was proposed in 1975 by Graen and Cashman. This model suggests that leaders accomplish work through various personal relationships with different members of the subordinate group. Leaders give tasks that are more positive to members whom they feel support them. LMX suggests behavior is not consistent across subordinates. As a result, leaders classify subordinates into two groups: an in-group and an out-group (similar to the classifications used in Fiedler's contingency theory). Subsequently, the leader adapts his or her behavior to account for individual subordinate needs for direction, contact, and supervision. This creates a unique relationship with every different member of the group, called a "dyad." Graen and Cashman later coined the term *vertical dyad linkage* (VDL) to describe the situation in which leader–group interactions, judgments, and opinions are formed by the leader and the members of each dyad. With this theoretical model of leader behavior, the emphasis is on the interaction of the leader with the supervised group. For example, the leader exchanges resources, such as increased job latitude, influence on decision making, and open communication, for members' commitment to higher involvement in organizational functioning.

This line of research embraces the social exchange theory, which suggests that leaders must offer an exchange (e.g., bonus, increased status) if they hope to obtain improved or additional performance by subordinates. The LMX approach has been criticized because it does not study the organizational outcomes associated with the exchange relationship, and because it links exchanges in diverse and inconsistent ways. Nevertheless, the obvious reality is that many leaders do treat employees differently based on personal relationships, suggesting that LMX theory merits additional attention.

LMX theory emphasizes "the two-way relationship between supervisors and subordinates [and] aims to maximize organization success by establishing positive interactions between the two."[41] Research has shown there is a significant relationship between an employee's performance and commitment and the quality of the relationship between leader and follower. LMX is said to increase employee commitment and loyalty to the company, and the research consistently concludes that "committed employees are associated with better organizational performance, have a lower turnover rate, and have lower absenteeism."[42]

Graen and colleagues originally called this relationship a vertical dyad linkage, only later referring to it as the leader–member exchange theory. Miner also points out that Graen et al.'s theory has commonalities with Vroom's normative decision-making model.[43] Graen and colleagues are basically saying that the relationship between manager and subordinate must be positive and of high quality. The quality of this linkage will have a direct impact on performance and job satisfaction.

Two types of dyadic relationships are of great importance in LMX, which Graen referred to as "relationships with informal assistants and ordinary members . . . leadership and supervisory relationships and in-group and out-group relationships or high- and low-quality relationships."[44] Each is a dyad. The most important dyadic relationship remains that between the manager and the subordinate. As leaders form higher-quality relationships with employees, those employees begin to feel as though they are part of the in-group. The in-group will always have more responsibilities and more influence in decision making as well as greater job satisfaction compared to the out-group. A low-quality relationship between the leader and an employee leads to a feeling of being in the out-group.[45] Leaders use a more participative approach with in-group employees and a more directive style with out-group employees.

Hersey and Blanchard's Situational Leadership Theory (1977)

In the late 1970s, Hersey and Blanchard discussed situational leadership.[46] They initially called their model the "life-cycle theory of leadership," but later renamed it "situational leadership theory (SLT)." Initially, Hersey and Blanchard identified four possible styles of leadership: telling, selling, participating, and delegating. Notice how similar these styles are to those identified by other theorists. While SLT also falls under the broad umbrella of contingency theory, it is different from the other theories found within this realm.[47]

In Hersey and Blanchard's model, the leader must determine what these researchers refer to as the "maturity of the follower." This determination dictates the degree of supervision that employees need. Employees with low maturity are those with low motivation or those with few or no skills in the task activities. Telling or directing is the leadership style most appropriate with such workers. Low to moderately mature employees need a combination of telling and personal attention. Moderate to highly mature employees require attention as well as sharing in decision making, and highly mature employees need freedom to make their own decisions.[48] This is really a very sensible approach: The less motivated and/or less skilled employees require more direction (more telling). As employees become more mature, more motivated, and more highly skilled, they need little or no direction or even encouragement.

From 1969 through 1977, Hersey and Blanchard developed SLT,[49] which they formally defined as a leadership style driven by the situation at hand. This model specifies the readiness of followers, defined as the ability and willingness to accomplish a specific task, as the major contingency that influences appropriate leadership style. SLT is based on the relationships among three components:

- Directive behavior (task behavior) the leader provides followers
- The amount of supportive behavior (relational behavior) a leader provides
- The development level (maturity) of the follower, which is derived from the amount of competence and commitment demonstrated while performing a specific task

In the last component, *competence* is the degree of knowledge or skills gained from education, training, or experience needed to do the task, and *commitment* is defined as the combination of confidence and motivation displayed by the follower in reference to doing the task. A follower can be competent but not committed to do a task; consequently, he or she may need support to regain the devotion to accomplish the task.

SLT also suggests that the individual leadership style demonstrated should match the maturity of the subordinates who are being led.[50] Thus, according to this theory, there is no one best style of leadership. Instead, people in leadership and management positions become more effective when they select a leadership style that is appropriate to the development level of the individual or group they want to influence. Maturity is assessed in relation to a specific task and the psychological maturity and job experience of the follower. The leader may then exercise various levels of delegating, participating, selling, and telling to coax employees to complete their assigned tasks and achieve the desired goals. Application of the correct leadership style based on the developmental level of the follower or group is the key ingredient in the SLT model; however, sometimes situational variables that may affect the leadership style—for example, time constraints, supervisory demands, and job demands. Each style varies the leadership approach based on the aforementioned situational factors. The most recently described leadership approaches include additional dimensions of leadership, such as whether the leader utilizes a transactional or transformational style.

As summarized in **Figure 4–8**, SLT posits that leaders must utilize different styles depending on the situation: telling and directing (S1); selling and coaching (S2); participating and supporting (S3), or delegating (S4). Subordinate competence and commitment moderate the leader's style.

While contingency and normative decision-making approaches are types of situational theory, Hersey and Blanchard's approach is more centric, as it depends on the amount of tasks and people that the leader adopts in reference to the level of subordinates' commitment and competence. In Figure 4–8, notice how subordinate development level D1 relates to S1 (directing) leader behavior, D2 relates to S2 (coaching) leader behavior, and so

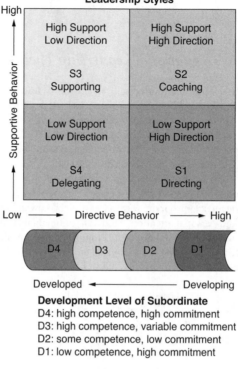

FIGURE 4–8   Situational Leadership

on. The greater the subordinates' level of commitment and competence, the less the leader has to provide task-based and relation-based leadership. SLT holds that successful leadership is achieved by selecting the correct leadership style based on the readiness of the followers. In critiquing the SLT, some researchers have questioned its conceptual clarity, validity, robustness, and utility, as well as the instruments used to measure leadership style. Of course, others have supported the utility of the model.

House's Charismatic Leadership Model (1977)

Based on the earlier suggestion of Max Weber, who posited the dimension of charismatic leadership that he called *charismatic domination* in the early 1920s, House revisited the construct of charisma. Building on the earlier theories, he proposed a theory specifically called charismatic leadership in 1977.[51] Recent studies have extended this theoretical base to examine the degree of employee's or subordinate's identification with a team or work group as a function of charismatic leadership.[52]

Charismatic leadership inspires followership through intangibles in personality that cannot be measured directly in an individual. Making the dynamic even more complex, charisma may be identified in a leader by subordinates, but cannot be directly operationalized as any one set of traits or skill sets. Similar to the old adage "Beauty is in the eye of the beholder," charisma is in the eye of the beholder; however, levels of acceptance and acknowledgment cannot be uniformly communicated by the members of the organization. Charisma, like the definition of any construct itself, cannot be measured directly by any tangible property in a universal way.

Charismatic leaders inspire trust, faith, and confidence in nonmechanical ways. They have a natural predisposition to be self-assured and comfortable "in their own skin." They rarely second-guess themselves and are generally extroverts. Charismatic leaders are always "turned on" in one dimension or another—that is, they may be the individual at a social gathering everyone wants to talk to, or they may be the voice of direction and order in an otherwise panicked and disordered atmosphere.

It is very difficult for those without natural charisma to mimic those who possess this natural ability on a long-term basis. Environmental change and culture shifts will make the mechanical charismatic leader unable to function for long periods of time in work or social situations; fatigue and apathy will set in. Being charismatic cannot be "acted."

For those leaders with natural charismatic qualities, opportunities exist to leverage these inherent capabilities in the organization. Consider a leader with a natural predisposition to inspire and befriend who can combine this ability with learned executive skills and competencies in organizational dynamics; this blending can lead to success for the adept leader. For example, a CEO negotiating policy change in a legal market may know little about the financial structure of the merger's initial public offering valuation; however, the CEO may excel in maintaining a positive dialogue with stakeholders that will maintain calm during times of unfamiliarity that allow the change to occur.[53–55]

Despite the many positives associated with charismatic leadership, there are disadvantages to use of this leadership style as well. Charismatic leaders may be prone to avoiding professional discourse and could be challenged on ideas. They may surround themselves with "yes men" during long stints of leadership that result in organizational institutionalism and stagnation. In the worst-case scenarios, charismatic leaders may be prone to narcissism and feel superior to those persons who are not within their immediate circle of influence.[56, 57]

Burns's Transformational Leadership Model (1978)

Two of the more recent theories of leadership discussed a great deal are transactional and transformational leadership theories. Transactional leadership was first described by Max Weber in 1947 and was resurfaced in 1981 by Benjamin Bass, who hypothesized that transactional leaders believe workers are motivated by rewards. That is similar to McGregor's Theory X description of one type of subordinate. The transformational leadership model is a situation-influenced theory that suggests the situation influences the leader to adapt a style most fitting to the specific circumstances at hand. This style may be transactional or transformational, or some combination of the two. In practice, a combination of these approaches is the most practical leadership strategy to undertake in health organizations. The knowledge, skills, and abilities of a health leader to use transformation and transactional leadership is critical for success in today's environment.

The descriptors applied to transactional leadership are "working to achieve specific goals, rewarding employees, [responding] to employees and [their] self-interests."[58] Because a trade—an exchange of work and effort for rewards—occurs, transactional leadership is perceived as an economic model of leadership.[59] A potential negative outcome with this model is that employees may not be motivated to accomplish certain tasks if there is no reward attached to performance and positive outcomes.

It was James MacGregor Burns, who, around 1978, distinguished between transactional and transformational leadership styles. Burns based his theories on other sources, such as Maslow's hierarchy of needs and Kohlberg's theories of moral development.[60] Burns believed the transactional leader lived in keeping with certain values, such as fairness, responsibility, and integrity. Transformational leadership is sometimes viewed as the opposite end of the pole from transactional leadership, though in reality that perception is inaccurate. Transformational leaders are charismatic; they have vision, empathy, self-assurance, commitment, and the ability to assure others of their own competence; and they are willing to take risks.[61, 62] "Transformational leadership refers to the process of building commitment to the organization's objectives and empowering followers to accomplish these objectives."[63]

> Burns compared and contrasted transactional with transformational leadership. Transactional leadership involves values, but they are values relevant to the exchange process such as honesty, fairness, responsibility, and reciprocity and bureaucratic organizations enforce the use of legitimate

power and respect for rules and tradition rather than influence based on inspiration. For Burns, leadership is a process, not a set of discrete acts. Burns (1978) described leadership as "a stream of evolving interrelationships in which leaders are continuously evoking motivational responses from followers and modifying their behavior as they meet responsiveness or resistance, in a ceaseless process of flow and counter-flow." At the macro-level of analysis, transformational leadership involves shaping, expressing, and mediating conflict among groups of people in addition to motivating individuals.[64]

Building on Burns's work, Bernard Bass argued that rather than the two leadership styles being polar opposites, there was a linear progression from transactional to transformational leadership. Bass also believed that transformational leadership should be measured in terms of how it affects employees, such as how much they trust and respect the leader. According to Bass, transformational leadership must be grounded in moral foundations that include inspirational motivation, individualized consideration, intellectual stimulation, and idealized influence. These concepts position the transformational leader in a place similar to that identified in servant-leader models such as the model proposed by Greenleaf.[65]

From this discourse, Bass (1985) proposed a theory of transformational leadership that is measured in terms of the leader's influence on subordinates or followers. Subordinates or followers "connect" to the transformational leader through trust, admiration, a sense of loyalty, and respect for the leader. Transformational leaders, in turn, create an environment that propels subordinates and followers to greater performance and greater deeds[66] than previously expected, in three ways: (1) by making followers aware of the importance of their performance and task outcomes; (2) by replacing their own self-interest with the good of the group, team, and organization; and (3) by energizing and motivating followers' higher-order needs.[67] In more recent research, transformational leadership has been identified as the most important predictor of individual success and active involvement in healthcare delivery teams (multidisciplinary teams).[68]

In summary, transformational leadership focuses on four constructs. Bass's original theory included three behaviors of transformational leaders, while the fourth was added later to transformational behaviors:

- *Charisma*: The leader influences followers by arousing strong emotions and identification with the leader.
- *Intellectual stimulation*: The leader increases follower awareness of problems and influences followers to view problems from a new perspective.
- *Individualized consideration*: The leader provides support, encouragement, and developmental experiences for followers.
- *Inspirational motivation*: The leader communicates an appealing vision using symbols to focus subordinate effort and to model appropriate behavior (role modeling; Bandera's social learning theory).[69, 70]

In support of this theory, Fairholm, in an assessment of empowering leadership techniques that closely resemble transformational leadership, suggests that leaders fulfill the following responsibilities:

- Utilize goal setting
- Delegate to followers
- Encourage participation
- Encourage self-reliance
- Challenge followers
- Focus on followers
- Specify followers' roles[71]

Transformational leadership can be measured by an instrument called the Multi-factor Leadership Questionnaire (MLQ). Using this tool, global attributes, specific traits, and combinations of assessments have been applied to validate forecasts of retrospective and concurrent transformational leadership through measurement.[72] Several different approaches have been used to confirm the reliability and validity of MLQ assessments. According to Bass, promising predictors (variables categorized by construct) include those listed in **Table 4–4**.

TABLE 4–4 **Transformational Leadership Variables: Possible Predictors**

Construct	Charisma	Inspiration	Motivation	Intellectual Stimulation	Individualized Consideration
Variables	Ascendancy	Confidence	Ascendancy	Ascendancy	Ascendancy
	Sociability	Personal adjustment	Sociability	Internal locus of control	Sociability
	Less thinking than feeling	Pragmatism	Sensing		Extroversion
	Internal locus of control	Nurturance	Internal locus of control		Feeling
	Self-acceptance	Femininity			Self-acceptance
		Less aggression			

Source: Bass, B. (1998). *Transformational leadership: Industrial, military, and educational impact*. Mahwah, NJ: Lawrence Erlbaum Associates.

Under situational or contingency theory, transformational leadership and transactional leadership are viewed as encompassing a range of viable styles that a leader can select from depending on the situation. Like Burns, Bass considers transactional leadership to entail an exchange of rewards for compliance. Transactional behaviors include the following:

- *Contingent reward*: clarification of work required to obtain rewards.

- *Active management by exception*: monitoring subordinates and corrective action to ensure that the work is effectively accomplished.

- *Passive management by exception*: use of contingent punishments and other corrective action in response to obvious deviations from acceptable performance standards.[73, 74]

> Bass regards theories such as Leader–Member Exchange Theory and Path–Goal Theory as descriptions of transactional leadership. He views transformational and transactional leadership as distinct but not mutually exclusive processes; the same leader may use both types of leadership at different times in different situations.[75]

The strengths of transformational leadership are its pragmatic approach, intuitiveness, flexibility, attention to individual and groups of subordinates, and motivation orientation. Its weaknesses hinge on validation and testing: Much of the research in this area has been descriptive and qualitative, and few quantitative data exist. Qualitative research focuses on "theory building," using such methods as biographies, observation activities, informal interviews, and the like. In contrast, quantitative research is a "theory testing" methodology that tries to prove causality: This causes that to happen. This approach is normally associated with statistical applications such as the general linear model (*t*-tests, analysis of variance [ANOVA], analysis of covariance [ANCOVA], regression) or relationships (such as correlations).

In the qualitative research that has been done on transformational leadership, this model shows real promise. For example, Bennis and Nanus conducted a multiyear study of transformational, dynamic, innovative leaders that included 65 top-level corporate leaders and 30 leaders of public-sector organizations. They collected data through unstructured interviews (3–4 hours each) and supplemented interviews with observation. Several themes were associated with successful transformational leaders:

- *Ability to meet external expectations to develop an effective vision* that is right for the times, right for the organization, and right for the people who are in the organization

- *Ability to develop a clear and appealing vision* to focus collective organizational energy toward a consistent set of strategies, goals, and objectives

- *Ability to inspire* others by leveraging the basic human need to feel and be important and valuable
- *Ability to facilitate decision making, take initiative, and delegate decision making* so as to extend authority and discretion to all levels appropriately (empowerment)
- *Ability to develop commitment and trust across all stakeholders* by communicating vision and embedding it in the culture of the organization
- *Ability to develop systems of internal and external environmental scanning, monitoring, analysis, and forecasting*
- *Ability to be a great facilitator of organizational learning and developer of knowledge management systems,* using experimentation to encourage innovation and to test new products, services, and procedures[76]

In the healthcare arena, transformational leadership is a critical health leader style associated with success. "Transformational leaders motivate others to do more than they originally intended and often even more than they thought possible."[77]

In summary, transformational Leaders tend to have the following characteristics:

- Idealized:
  - Followers seek to identify with and emulate their leader
  - The leader puts the needs of others over his or her own
  - The leader uses power only when needed
- Inspiring:
  - Commitment to goals
  - Arouse team spirit
- Intellectually stimulating:
  - Expands the use of the followers' abilities
  - Creativity is encouraged
  - Try new approaches to problems
  - Followers' ideas are not criticized
- Individually considerate:
  - Supporting, mentoring, and coaching
  - New learning opportunities are created in a supportive environment
  - "Management by walking around"
  - Delegation of tasks[78]

Transactional leaders tend to have the following characteristics:

- Contingently rewarding:
  - Followers are rewarded for satisfactory completion of assignments
- Active in managing by exception:
  - Monitors standards, mistakes, and errors
  - Takes corrective action
- Nontransactional passive leaders:
  - Laissez-faire attitude
  - Avoidance or absence of leadership[79]

Transformational leaders may choose to use a transactional leadership style based on the situation; it is not a "this or that" decision. In reality, *successful health leaders use both transformational and transactional leadership styles,* many times simultaneously. However, the laissez-faire and avoidance or absent style is not recommended to be used often. It is important to remember that "the performance of the organization is the ultimate measure of a leader."[80]

Bennis's Competency-Based Leadership (1985–1993)

Building on earlier work by Burns, Bennis proposed his competency-based model of leadership.[81, 82] The competency-based model has been widely embraced by professional organizations and executives alike. This model suggests that the skills and tools necessary to lead organizations must be learned—whether through incremental on-the-job training (OJT), formal education, or years of professional development. Bennis interviewed some 90 executives from various sectors and identified four areas of competency:

- Creating attention through vision
- Creating meaning through communication
- Becoming a person of trust
- Self-development

The competency-based model suggests strongly that leaders are made and not simply born (the antithesis of the "great man" leadership theory). That is, in any complex and dynamic organization, there are certain educational requirements that require years of exposure to and specific training to achieve parity with peers in similar positions. Becoming a chief of a department of surgery is one example—one cannot successfully hold such a position without years of medical education and a successful practice of medicine.

Kouzes and Posner's Leadership Framework (1995)

In 1995, Kouzes and Posner[83] developed a twist on earlier leadership frameworks, in which they suggested that leadership is successful only if a shared vision can be communicated to followers that changes their values, thereby resulting in goal-directed behavior and positive work-related outcomes.[84] To achieve this vision, the leader must be aware of the intangibles that exist in the ideals that motivate those employees around them. According to Covey (as cited by Kouzes & Posner, 1995)[85]:

> Leaders "ignite" subordinates' passions and serve as a compass by which to guide followers. They define leadership as "the art of mobilizing others to want to struggle for shared aspirations." The emphasis lies in the follower's desire to contribute and the leader's ability to motivate others to action. Leaders respond to customers, create vision, energize employees, and thrive in fast-paced "chaotic" environments. Leadership is about articulating visions, embodying values, and creating the environment within which things can be accomplished.

To achieve this positive outcome, Kouzes and Posner developed five constructs of action: Challenging the Process, Inspiring a Shared Vision, Enabling Others to Act, Modeling the Way, and Encouraging the Heart.[86]

Challenging the Process
Leaders must be capable of not only creating a vision, but also helping others to understand why certain workplace architectures or policies must be unlearned, and new structures developed in their place; those new structures are created from learning or doing new things. As a metaphor, the old adage that "Better the devil you know than the devil you don't" is valid here. Many persons, once they are trained and become comfortable with one process of accomplishing missions, must be convinced that an alternative process can result in better outcomes or future benefit to (preferably) the organization and/or the individual. In this respect, the leader is more effective when not just implementing new ideas and programs, but also identifying the weaknesses and lack of legitimacy of current programs and policies. Articulating these necessary changes to subordinates is paramount.

Inspiring a Shared Vision
Once processes are challenged and problems with these processes are successfully communicated, there must be an effort to communicate the vision to followers in a manner that results in the desired behavior changes. This

goal is difficult to accomplish and may be threatened by barriers of age, subcultures, incentives, and education. For example, communicating a vision to transform Medicare may be difficult to translate to persons younger than age 30, who are a lifetime away from collecting benefits themselves. Similarly, complex issues involving deficits and fiscal responsibility can be difficult to communicate even to those with advanced degrees. As an example, an effective political talking point might be that "'Homeowners could see their taxes increase by $64 per year if we cannot expand our tax revenue by creating new jobs," as opposed to stating "We need to create 400 new jobs so that the county can increase its annual tax revenues by $3,064,000."[87] Inspiring a shared vision requires personal communication and frequent communication with an appealing aspiration that connects to subordinates in a personal way.

Enabling Others to Act

Words without resources will not yield any return on investment. If calling community members to volunteer for action is requested by leaders, then infrastructure must be in place to ensure that those volunteers are able to produce some form of usable output. The dominant political parties in the United States, for example, realize this reality, which explains why both the Democratic and Republican parties place preaddressed and unsigned letters to various Congressional and Senatorial leaders on their Web sites. These letters may lobby in favor of a certain position or request a certain vote be made in an upcoming hearing. Through such tactics, the leaders of each party may challenge the process and provide a vision, and then follow up by providing a concrete opportunity for the person's voice to be heard.

Modeling the Way

In a daily example of leadership, the leader demonstrates a "Do as I do" philosophy. Sometimes seen as a trait of leadership theory on its own, modeling can be an effective methodology of living by example the values that others then seek to emulate; this social learning theory–based model was originally developed by Albert Bandura. For example, during President Jimmy Carter's administration, the United States experienced an energy crisis; in a television address to the nation, Carter urged viewers to conserve energy by turning down their thermostats and keeping their houses cooler during winter months. Carter led the country in this modeling effort by ordering White House thermostats set to 65 degrees Fahrenheit.[88] Although the effort had little effect on the energy crisis of the day, the President's effort to model conservation through behavior remains one of his most widely cited White House exploits.

Encouraging the Heart

In this final construct of leadership strategy, Kouzes and Posner suggest that no followership will occur without an emotional connection from leader to follower that is derived from simple leader encouragement. This construct was so highly regarded when it was proposed in 1995 that the authors eventually introduced it as a leadership theory of its own in 1999.[89] In this relatively simple leadership theory, the authors suggested that becoming a leader who is recognized as someone who cares and understands people results in engenderment and loyalty that cannot be duplicated with other artificial means. The authors of this book prefer to think of this concept as an updated version of the *Pygmalion effect*.

Pygmalion, a character in Greek mythology, sculpted a statue of such beauty in ivory that he eventually fell in love with his own creation. He named the statue Galatea and later prayed to the gods that she be brought to life, which eventually happened. This Greek myth later became generalized in the sciences as the "Pygmalion effect." This model has been suggested as a means through which leaders can believe in and encourage their employees over a constant period of time with the hopes that they will "come to life" and emulate the expectations leaders have for them. Unfortunately, the model has a notable weakness, known as the "halo effect." That is, if a leader has a preconceived notion that, for example, women are lower achievers than men, then the leader may interpret outcomes incorrectly as well. Although some constructs of this model remain the subject of debate, leaders can never go wrong with appropriate simple praise and acknowledgment of employee accomplishments and efforts!

The following story highlights the tenets of Kouzes and Posner's leadership model by viewing this framework in the light of ongoing efforts to enact healthcare reform.

Challenging The Process: Events That Changed History

During the latter part of the 1980s and prior to the 1990 U.S. election cycles, less than 10 percent of the U.S. public ranked health care among the nation's most important problems in any public survey conducted at that time. By 1992, however, when the Presidential debates took place between candidates Bill Clinton and George H. W. Bush, Americans ranked health care as the second biggest problem facing the nation, just behind the economy. What happened in those two years to dramatically increase the importance of health care to the American public? Roberts (1994) explains that emphasizing this issue started out as a risky political move by a democratic Senatorial candidate in 1990, and was then capitalized on by (then) Governor Bill Clinton during the 1992 Presidential election.

In 1990, Senatorial candidate Harris Wofford of Pennsylvania became the first candidate in U.S. history to become elected to political office based solely on a platform of reforming health care. For decades, the U.S. healthcare system had been considered too difficult to fix or too challenging for the common worker to understand. As a result, politicians and candidates for office steered away from this issue. Indeed, this may have remained the case in the 1992 Presidential election as well—at least until Wofford was able to capitalize on the misunderstandings and frustration associated with the healthcare system by the citizens of Pennsylvania and win the election.

In preparing for the 1992 Democratic Presidential nomination, Bill Clinton changed his platform priorities from crime and the U.S. deficit to healthcare reform. If the strategy had been successful for a Senator from Pennsylvania, his election team reasoned, then Clinton might potentially use this avenue to propel him to the Presidency.

The attack on the mismanagement of health care in the United States came largely as a surprise to Presidential incumbent George H. W. Bush. Only two years earlier (in 1990), Bush had received the largest popular support of any sitting president since Theodore Roosevelt for actions he had taken during the Gulf War. Bush, who was widely viewed as a master of foreign policy but had a notable history of underestimating political crises at home, seemed almost bored with the topic of health care during one 1992 Presidential debate. Frequently throughout the discussion, Bush could be shown on camera checking his watch, waiting for the debate to end.

According to most healthcare historians, it was during this period that the U.S. public embraced health care as a national issue because of what later become known as the "Wofford factor." Before 1990 and 1992, healthcare debates may have been witnessed only in graduate classrooms and hospital faculty meetings. From a retrospective point of view, Clinton's and Wofford's campaigns served as the crucible for a debate that continues to shape the political landscape today.

Sources: Roberts, M. J. (1994). *Your money or your life: The health care crisis explained.* New York: Main Street Books; Dreyfuss, R. (1993). "America's healthcare crisis: A case of media malpractice." Retrieved July 22, 2009, from http://www.fair.org/index.php?page=1532.

Buckingham and Clifton's Managerial and Strategic Leadership (2001)

Buckingham and Clifton[90] suggest that leadership is a process of focusing on follower strengths rather than trying to eliminate weaknesses. Understanding the "hard-wiring" people possess, through nature and nurture, is a tool to accomplish this goal.[91]

It is imperative for leaders to conduct a self-assessment (as suggested in Chapter 2) and really understand themselves, their organizational direction, and the strengths and weaknesses of their subordinates prior to trying to change the behavior of others. After all, leaders cannot develop the strengths of anyone in the workplace if they do not know how to find, name, and develop their own talents. Thus, according to this philosophy, the best strategy is to identify the individual's total strengths and, based on that understanding, to capitalize on these existing strengths. At the same time, it is also important to improve those areas in which the individual is weak.

In 2003, Wise noted that this model was particularly helpful in the nursing profession.[92] One of the "strengths" found to be of particular interest in nurses was empowerment. Nurses, who are often caught between several stakeholders (patient, provider, administrator, counselor, advocate, and supply chain/logistician), have a greater need to be empowered by their leaders than many other patient care and stakeholder authorities. Responding to this fact of life, leaders who recognize this need in nurses for empowerment can nurture, support, and grow this intrinsic need while learning to give up some power to improve the care process in the organization.

Ulrich, Zenger, and Smallwood's (1999) and Nohria, Joyce, and Roberson's Results-Based Leadership

Results-based leadership[93] may have its roots in the path–goal theory methodology proposed by House. However, in this modern-millennium twist, results are tied to desired outcomes, which may themselves be tied to competencies. Competencies act as goals for leaders to achieve in strategy and training; likewise, employees are wedded to those competencies through achieved attributes such as education, training, and certifications. For example, if a hospital executive desires to improve patient outcomes in his or her facility by lowering morbidity and mortality rates, the end results might be achieved through hiring and directing personnel who are knowledgeable in achieving those outcomes by learning the competencies associated with those results. Several articles have been written linking such quality outcomes to leadership, as well as linking competencies to training as opposed to demographic variables or other influences.[94–96]

Nohria, Joyce, and Roberson[97] also suggest that the key to achieving excellence for leaders is to focus on the organizational strategy. They insist that if a strategy is communicated clearly (and competency-based communication is the key to achieving that feat), then customers, employees, and shareholders will receive this communication in a uniform way that results in similar and desired outcomes.

The Army Leadership Model (2007) and the Ministry L-Model (1995)

Closing out this review of the evolution of seminal leadership theories, two lesser-known models of leadership are presented here; these models are rarely cited or quoted in academic texts and scholarly journals. These models are the Army Leadership Model[98] and the Ministry L-model.[99]

Academic and scholarly journals tend to disregard military and religious models of leadership, as part of a "good intentions" bias that is meant to avoid offending those who may be less tolerant of military or religious affiliations. This view may be short-sighted, however. More than 1 million people currently serve on active duty in the U.S. military, and there are an additional 8 million retired military people and their families in the United States. Many have been exposed to the fundamentals of the Military Leadership Model. As a result, this model is ripe for scholarly review.

A similar argument can be made for the Ministry Model proposed by Rick Warren. Warren's seminal thesis on spiritual leadership has inspired millions. His presence as a national leadership and spiritual leader was so highly regarded by President Barack Obama that Warren was chosen as the person to delivery his invocation during the 2008 Presidential inauguration.[100] Tens of millions of people are members of religious organizations and institutions in the United States.

The Army Leadership Model makes a distinction from previous models in that it incorporates a definition of leadership into its conceptual model. In this model, leadership is defined as "influencing people by providing purpose, direction, and motivation while operating to accomplish the mission and improving the organization." Defined constructs are character, knowledge and application—more commonly summarized as "be, know, and do."

Be–know–do emphasizes the philosophy that one must lead by example. Leading by example means that a leader will do what he or she says, and says what he or she will do. Such a model implies a high value is placed on morality, and posits that a leader is the organization's role model. Concomitantly, the leader must be both the legitimate leader of the organization and the individual most highly versed in the technical and strategic skills of the organization.

Variables derived from the be–know–do philosophy include values, attributes, skills, and actions. The Army Leadership Model differs somewhat from traditional applications, however. A key premise in this model is the notion that leadership is a process that requires experience. Additional, didactic education and training are a must. It is not uncommon for officers in the military to return to school for periods of weeks, months, or years between major rotational assignments (i.e., those that occur every 3 to 4 years). Upon an officer's retirement from active duty after 20 years, it may be feasible that the individual spent 5 years (or more) of his or her 20-year career in classrooms and training centers. In this regard, the military model of leadership is also dissimilar to previous theories in which education and experience are seen as falling outside the model's discussion. **Figure 4–9** shows a conceptual view of this model.

Finally, the ministry model of leadership, sometimes referred to as the L-model, suggests a *leadership by behavior* construct (role modeling). In this regard, values and institutional beliefs act as guidelines for daily life. These values can be summed up in one simple expression: Follow the golden rule of "Do unto others as you would have others do unto you."

Seminal constructs in the ministry model are discipleship, servanthood, gifting, traits, skills, organizational management, and transformational leadership. The ministry model also suggests an overriding higher-order principle as the cornerstone of moral living. While rarely used outside religious practices and spiritual family units, the religious model of leadership has been the most distinctly applied and followed model by citizens in the United States for the latter part of the twentieth century.[101]

The Army Leadership Model and Ministry L-model are two examples of lesser-known leadership models. However, these models may enjoy a higher level of practical application and individual internalization than many other academically derived leadership models.

Leadership as Managing Organizational Culture

There is a growing trend to incorporate organizational culture into leadership theories and models. This is a rather new emphasis, but a critically important one. Leaders build culture in everything they do—from role

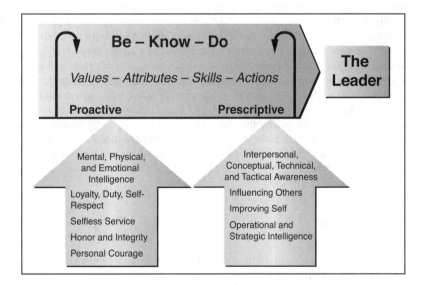

FIGURE 4–9   U.S. Army Conceptual Leadership Model
Source: Adapted from Department of the Army. (2007). *Field manual M-22-100: Army leadership.*

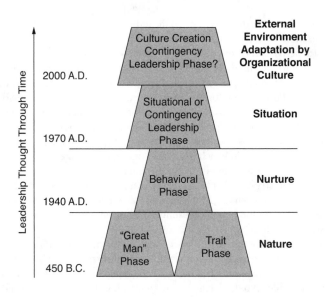

FIGURE 4–10   A Possible Progression of Leadership Thought

modeling, to assigning responsibilities, to communicating with others, including how they communicate and what they do not do or do not say. Models with an organizational culture emphasis require leaders to determine, develop, and maintain an organizational culture that can best meet the expectations—if not thrive—in the external environment. This perspective envisions a more important and dramatic role for organizational culture as a construct—a leadership role—compared to that assigned under the situational leadership philosophy. Leaders must now create culture!

The next leadership phase may very well be the *culture creation contingency leadership* (CCCL) phase, which combines situational or contingency leadership with organizational culture creation, refinement, and enhancement (**Figure 4–10**). In facilitation of the CCCL movement, organizational culture and leadership models with this emphasis are presented later in this text; organizational culture is presented in the context of leadership in that leaders predetermine the organizational culture that best meets the needs of the external environment and fosters success in the health organization (or any organization). In this phase of leadership thought, leaders are proactive (culture developers, creators, modifiers) rather than reactive (culture is considered to determine a leadership style or actions), as is assumed in the situational leadership phase; this is the greatest difference between the two lines of thought. Even so, the CCCL phase builds on the past. Notably, Edgar Schein's work on organizational culture, and specifically on mechanisms of organizational culture, lies at the heart of this discussion. Developing models such as the dynamic culture leadership model, which incorporates transformational, transactional, and team leadership into an organizational culture development process, would be considered a synthesis of leadership and organizational culture concepts; this model, as well as several other emerging models, is profiled later in this text.

SUMMARY

This chapter provided a historical summary and overview of leadership theory as it has evolved over the ages. The theories and models of leadership have evolved dramatically over the centuries, with later theories and models building on their predecessors. For example, early documents (dating back to 2300 B.C.) of leadership principles and definitions (such as Xenophon's definition of leadership from 400 B.C.) served as key resources for later philosophers who developed the contemporary and accepted models of the twentieth and twenty-first centuries. This chapter presented the theories and models in the original light that their creators intended. Strengths and weaknesses of each theory, as well as applications and strategies for use, were explored within each theoretical overview.

In simple terms, the progression of leadership thought builds from a "nature" perspective to weave the idea of "nurture" (learning and experience) into the discussion, then incorporates situational adaption to facilitate success, and finally adds organizational culture development into the formula for leader success. A health leader focused on success will understand and hone leadership capabilities from nature, build capabilities through nurture (learning, study, and experience), adapt styles and practices to dynamic situations, and develop or create organizational culture based on external expectations to be successful. This effort of building leadership capabilities and practicing leadership must be performed in a moral and efficacious manner. In essence, leadership success could be formulized across all leadership thought phases (see **Table 4–5**).

Leader Success = Individual (Nature + Nurture) × Situational Adaptation
× Organization Culture Creation × Personal + Subordinate Accountability

DISCUSSION QUESTIONS

1. Describe the progression of leadership thought as portrayed in theories and models from the "great man" and trait phase, to the behavioral phase, to the situational or contingency phase.

2. Distinguish constructs of a trait theory or model, a behavioral theory or model, and a situational or contingency theory or model of leadership and interpret those constructs' value in the present day. Does the culture creation contingency leadership phase emerge as a new phase based on your interpretation? Why or why not?

3. Apply a behavioral theory or model of leadership and a situational or contingency theory of model of leadership; demonstrate these applications using examples based on a definition of leadership you produce. Were you drawn more to descriptive or prescriptive theories and models?

4. Compare and contrast, with illustrating diagrams, two or more behavioral or situational/contingency theories or models of leadership.

5. Referring to the progression of leadership thought, design, create, and explain a personal leadership model applicable to leading health organizations today.

6. Appraise and relate constructs and variables from the progression of leadership thought to your personal leadership model applicable to leading health organizations today.

EXERCISES

1. Describe a trait, behavioral, and situational/contingency theory or model of leadership in one paragraph each.

2. Distinguish situational leadership theory from transactional leadership and from transformational leadership. What is similar and what is different for each theory of leadership?

3. Prepare a personal definition of leadership and construct a personal application-based model of leadership geared toward health organizations today from the theories and models of the situational or contingency phase of leadership, categorizing the descriptive and prescriptive elements. Your paper should be two to three pages long.

4. Analyze the strengths and weaknesses of your personal application-based leadership model from Exercise 3 and modify your personal application-based leadership model to overcome the weaknesses you identify in a one- to two-page paper.

TABLE 4-5　Summary of Leadership Theories and Models

Theory	Goal	Antecedent Framework	Constructs	Variables	Relationship	Utility for Greater Understanding in Practice
Carlyle, Galton, and James's "Great Man" Theory (1840–1880)	Identify immutable traits of past leaders so future leaders can be identified	Most likely Machiavelli	Physical characteristics	Immutable physical characteristics	Possession of characteristics is leadership	Evolved into trait theory over time
Lewin, Lippitt, and White's Trait Theory (1938–1939)	Identify mutable traits of past leaders so that future leaders can be identified	"Great man" theory	Intelligence, extraversion, physical stature	Outcomes of intelligence, extraversion, physical stature	Those with "leadership" traits should be good leaders	Incorporated into broader leadership models such as behavioral and situational theories
McGregor's Theory X and Theory Y (1950)	Identify lazy and self-motivating personnel	Early trait theories	Laziness and motivation	Various	Laziness equals failure and motivation equals success	Suggests motivated leaders can achieve more than lazy leaders
Stogdill and Coons's Ohio Leadership Studies (1950)	Identify individual dimensions of behavior	Early trait theories	Initiating structure and consideration	Work-related variables and satisfaction	Leaders who set high standards while respecting employees achieve high outcomes	Organizational management design
Michigan Leadership Studies (1950)	Identify leader objectives associated with performance effectiveness	Early trait theories	Employee oriented and production oriented	Satisfaction and goal attainment	Focus is on employee task performance	Task organization and employee workload
Katz's Skills Theory (1955)	Identify individual dimensions of behavior	Early trait theories	Technical, conceptual and human abilities	Various traits and outcomes	Must have all three to be successful	Production outcomes
Argyris's Personality and Organization Theory (1957)	Organizational learning	Fledgling humanistic theories	Organizations, learning, and employee mental maps	Governing, action, and consequences	Institutional norms and cultures	Measurement of organizational outcomes affected by the leader

Blake and Mouton's Managerial Grid (1964)	Focus is on attitudes	Early trait theories, motivation and management research in practice	Concern for results and concerns for people	Satisfaction, outcomes, and productivity	Those with high ratings for both people and results are most effective	Team building and consensus making
Erikson's Psychoanalytic Theory (1964)	Psychoanalysis theory	Early studies of Freud (1913) and Fromm (1941)	Father figure role, mentoring, and love	Pleasing and fear proposition: My subordinates are my children; they must respect me	Inter-subjective object, relational context	Early behavior studies on loyalty and engendering
Fiedler's Contingency Model (1964)	Identify variables affecting group performance	Motivation and management	Situation favorableness/ preferred coworker scale	Task and relationship orientation	The more favorable the relationship (or perceived relationship) between the leader and the follower, the higher degree of task orientation	Psychology, management teams
House's Path–Goal Model (1971)	Predict leadership effectiveness based on communication of leader intent; expectancy motivation theory	Earlier works in expectancy, motivation, and satisfaction Vroom's expectancy theory	Perception of work, self-development, and path to goals Communications: directive, supportive, participative, and achievement oriented	Rewards, goals, accomplishment, personal characteristics, environment	Leader behavior will be motivational to the extent it assists subordinates to accomplish assigned goals	Management communication

(continues)

TABLE 4-5 Summary of Leadership Theories and Models (*Continued*)

Theory	Goal	Antecedent Framework	Constructs	Variables	Relationship	Utility for Greater Understanding in Practice
Vroom–Yetton–Jago's Normative Decision-Making Model (1973)	No one decision-making model is appropriate	Earlier work in decision making	Quality or rationality of the decision, the acceptance, or the commitment on the part of subordinates to execute the decision effectively, and the amount of time required to make the decision	Various	Better decision making is achieved through balancing construct dimensions	Decision making
Graen's Leader–Member Exchange and Vertical Dyad Linkage (1975)	Tasks are accomplished based on personal relationships	Katz and Kahn's (1966) work on motivation, equity, and organizational citizenship behavior	Vertical dyad linkage	In-group and out-group	Satisfaction will be higher with the in-group, leading those individuals toward goal attainment	Motivation, satisfaction, delegation
Hersey and Blanchard's Situational Leadership Model (1977)	Four leader choices: tell, sell, participate, or delegate	Graen's leader–member exchange theory, vertical dyad linkage, and other antecedent theories	Directive behavior, supportive behavior, development level	Structure variables of time, supervisory demands, and job demands	Optimizing the leadership choice based on the environmental constraints maximizes outcomes	Delegation and decision making
House's Charismatic Leadership Model (1977)	Influence and followership	Max Weber, early theories on charisma	Dominance, influence, confidence, and values	Success, culture, and change	Followership is achieved through some divine personality trait that cannot be measured	Various organizational and individual trait outcomes

Model						
Burns's Transformational Leadership Model (1978)	Leaders and followers raise each other to higher levels of motivation	Max Weber's charismatic leadership theory	Charisma, intellectual stimulation, environment	Rewards	Followers of a transformational leader feel: • Trust • Admiration • Loyalty • Respect	Motivation and satisfaction
Bennis's Competency-Based Leadership (1985–1993)	Learned skills specific to the organizational dynamic can make leaders successful	Transformational leadership	Creating attention by vision; creating meaning by communication; being a person of trust; self-development	Education, skills, and training	Education and experience lead to success	Professional development
Kouzes and Posner's Leadership Framework (1995)	Eliminate institutionalism through inspired change	Burns's transformational leadership	Challenging the Process, Inspiring a Shared Vision, Enabling Others to Act, Modeling the Way, Encouraging the Heart	Organizational outcomes	Eliminating institutionalism and inspiring change results in different outcomes	Culture change
Warren's Ministry L-Model (1995)	Leadership by behavior	Spiritual teachings	Discipleship, servanthood, gifting, traits, skills, organizational management, transformational leadership	Outcomes	Modeling behavior results in the reflection of that behavior by others	Applying the omnibus leadership model

(continues)

TABLE 4–5 **Summary of Leadership Theories and Models** (*Continued*)

Theory	Goal	Antecedent Framework	Constructs	Variables	Relationship	Utility for Greater Understanding in Practice
Buckingham and Clifton's Managerial and Strategic Leadership Model (2001)	Leverage personality	Trait theories	Personality and Enneagrams	Verbal and non-verbal communication characteristics	Weakness are hard to change; focus on developing strengths	Personality assessment to drive organizational outcomes
Ulrich, Zenger & Smallwood's (1999); Nohria, Joyce & Roberson's (2003) Results-Based Leadership	Achieve desired results	House's path–goal theory	Performance	Outcomes	Outcomes are tied to goals	Organizational strategy
Military Leadership Model (2007)	Leading by example	Earlier trait and transformational leader theories	Be, know, and do	Organizational outcomes	The leader is both the legitimate authority and the organizational expert	Determining educational/training factors that influence organization and team outcomes

5. Summarize at least four of the following articles from the literature on transformational and transactional leadership models in a three- to four-page paper:

   a. Avolio, B., Bass, B., & Jung, D. (1999). Re-examining the components of transformational and transactional leadership using the Multifactor Leadership Questionnaire. *Journal of Occupational and Organizational Psychology, 72*, 441–462.

   b. Bass, B. (1999). Ethics, character, and authentic transformational leadership behavior, *Leadership Quarterly, 10*(2), 181–217.

   c. Conger, J. A. (1999). Charismatic and transformational leadership in organizations: An insider's perspective on these developing streams of research. *Leadership Quarterly, 10*(2), 145–179.

   d. Yukl, G. (1999). An evaluation of conceptual weaknesses in transformational and charismatic leadership theories. *Leadership Quarterly, 10*(2), 285–305.

   e. Barling, J., Weber, T., & Kelloway, E. K. (1996). Effects of transformational leadership training on attitudinal and financial outcomes: A field experiment. *Journal of Applied Psychology, 81*(6), 827–832.

6. Interpret, critique, defend, and support a position based on your appraisal of the situational leadership theory by reading the following *scholarly debate* literature:

   Additional Source for the Situational Leadership Theory (use if needed):

   Hersey, P., & Blanchard H. (1993). *Management of organizational behavior: Utilizing human resources* (6th ed.). Englewood Cliffs, NJ: Prentice Hall, Chapters 8–17.

   Scholarly Debate Regarding the Situational Leadership Theory:

   Vecchio, R. P. (1987). Situational leadership theory: An examination of a prescriptive theory. *Journal of Applied Psychology, 72*, 444–451.

   Graeff, C. L. (1983). The situational leadership theory: A critical view. *Academy of Management Review, 8*, 285–291.

   Lueder, D. C. (1985). Don't be misled by LEAD," *Journal of Applied Behavioral Science, 21*, 143–151.

   Lueder, D. C. (1985). A rejoinder to Dr. Hersey. *Journal of Applied Behavioral Science, 21*, 154.

   Hersey, P. (1985). A letter to the author of "Don't be misled by LEAD." *Journal of Applied Behavioral Science, 21*, 152–153.

REFERENCES

1. Dowd, J. (1936). *Control in human societies.* New York: Appleton-Century.
2. Bass, B. (1990). *Bass & Stogdill's handbook of leadership: Theory, research and managerial applications* (3rd ed.). New York: Free Press, p. 38.
3. Nanus, B. (1992). *Visionary leadership.* San Francisco: Jossey-Bass.
4. Retrieved July 10, 2009, from http://classics.mit.edu/Browse/browse-Xenophon.html.
5. Ledlow, J. R., & Coppola, M. N. (2009). Leadership theory and influence. In J. A. Johnson (Ed.), *Health organizations: Theory, behavior, and development.* Sudbury, MA: Jones and Bartlett, pp. 167–191.
6. Lewin, K., & Lippitt, R. (1938). An experimental approach to the study of autocracy and democracy: A preliminary note. *Sociometry, 1*, 292–300.
7. Lewin, K., Lippitt R., & White, R. (1939). Patterns of aggressive behavior in experimentally created social climates. *Journal of Social Psychology, 10*, 271–301.
8. Yukl, G. (1994). *Leadership in organizations* (3rd ed.). Englewood Cliffs, NJ: Prentice Hall, p. 256.
9. Gordon, J. (1991). *A diagnostic approach to organizational behavior* (3rd ed.). Englewood Cliffs, NJ: Prentice Hall.
10. Filley, A. C. (1978). *The complete manager.* Champaign, IL: Research Press, pp. 57–60.
11. Ledlow & Coppola, note 5.
12. Valenzuela, K. (2009). The leadership skills approach. Retrieved June 11, 2009, from BeALeader.Net http://www.bealeader.net/the-leadership-skills-approach/.
13. Yukl, note 8, p. 256.
14. Argyris, C. (1957). *Personality and organization.* New York: Harper Collins.

15. Argyris, C. (1962). *Interpersonal competence and organizational effectiveness.* Homewood, IL: Dorsey Press.

16. Argyris, C. (1964). *Integrating the individual and the organization.* New York: Wiley.

17. Argyris, C. (1993). *Knowledge for action: A guide to overcoming barriers to organizational change.* San Francisco: Jossey-Bass.

18. Leadership Champs. (2008). Vroom–Yetton–Jago normative leadership decision model, Retrieved June 12, 2009, from http://leadershipchamps.wordpress.com/2008/11/06/vroom-yetton-jago-normative-leadership-decision-model/.

19. Boje, D. M. (2009). Traditional situation leadership theories. New Mexico State University. Retrieved June 11, 2009, from http://cbae.nmsu.edu/~dboje/388/2009_book/pdf/Chapter%2023%20Traditional%20Situation%20Leadership%20Theories.pdf.

20. Yukl, note 8.

21. Blair, G. M. (1997, February 7). Contingency models. Science and Engineering, University of Edinburgh. Retrieved June 10, 2009, from http://www.see.ed.ac.uk/~gerard/MENG/ME96/Documents/Styles/conti.html.

22. De Jonge, J. (Ed.). (2009). Contingency theory. Retrieved June 10, 2009, from http://www.12manage.com/methods_contingency_theory.html.

23. De Jonge, note 22.

24. Yukl, note 8.

25. Yukl, note 8.

26. Shapiro, R. L. (1991). Psychoanalytic theory of groups and organizations. *Journal of the American Psychoanalytic Association, 39,* 759–781.

27. Kernberg, O. F. (2004). *Contemporary controversies in psychoanalytic theory, technique, and their applications.* New Haven, CT: Yale University Press.

28. Winer, J. A., Jobe, T., & Ferrono, C. (1984). Toward a psychoanalytic theory of the charismatic. *Annals of Psychoanalysis, 12,* 155–175.

29. Erikson, E.H. (1964). *Insight and Responsibility.* New York: Norton.

30. Kernberg, note 27.

31. Winer et al., note 28.

32. Towler, A. (2005). Charismatic leadership development: Role of parental attachment style and parental psychological control. *Journal of Leadership & Organizational Studies, 11*(3), 247–258.

33. Rubinstein, B. B. (1975). On the clinical psychoanalytic theory and its role in the inference and confirmation of particular clinical hypotheses. *Psychoanalytic Contemporary Science, 4*(3), 57.

34. Ray, J. J. (1990). The old-fashioned personality. *Human Relations, 43,* 997–1015.

35. Ray, J. J. (1988). Why the F scale predicts racism: A critical review. *Political Psychology, 9*(4), 671–679.

36. Retrieved July 11, 2009, from http://www.12manage.com/methods_path_goal_theory.html.

37. Woolard, D. (2009). Path–goal theory of leadership. Campbell University. Retrieved June 11, 2009, from http://www.drwoolard.com/miscellaneous/path_goal_theory.htm.

38. Boje, note 19.

39. Boje, note 19.

40. Leadership Champs, note 18.

41. Truckenbrodt, Y. B. (2000, Summer). The relationship between leader–member exchange and commitment and organizational citizenship behavior. *Acquisition Review Quarterly.* Retrieved June 15, 2009, from http://findarticles.com/p/articles/mi_m0JZX/is_3_7/ai_78360115/.

42. Truckenbrodt, note 41.

43. Miner, J. B. (2005). *Organizational behavior 1: Essential theories of motivation and leadership.* Armonk, NY: M. E. Sharpe.

44. Miner, note 43.

45. Boje, note 19.

46. Hersey, P., & Blanchard, K. (1974). *So you want to know your leadership style?* Englewood Cliffs, NJ: Prentice-Hall.

47. Hersey, P., & Blanchard, K. (1993). *Management of organizational behavior* (6th ed.). Englewood Cliffs, NJ: Prentice-Hall.

48. Bass, B. M. (1990). From transactional to transformational leadership: Learning to share the vision. *Organizational Dynamics, 18*(3), 19–30.

49. Hersey, P., & Blanchard, K. (1969). *Management of organizational behavior: Utilizing human resources* (1st ed.). Englewood Cliffs, NJ: Prentice-Hall.

50. Hersey & Blanchard, note 49.

51. House, R. J. (1977). A 1976 theory of charismatic leadership. In J. G. Hunt & L. L. Larson (Eds.), *Leadership: The cutting edge* (pp. 189–207). Carbondale, IL: Southern Illinois University Press.

52. Cicero, L., & Pierro, A. (2007). Charismatic leadership and organizational outcomes: The mediating role of employee's work group identification. *International Journal of Psychology, 42*(5), 297–306.

53. Towler, A. (2005). Charismatic leadership development: Role of parental attachment style and parental psychological control. *Journal of Leadership & Organizational Studies, 11*(3), pp. 15–25.

54. Crandall, D. (2006). *Leadership lessons from West Point*. New York: John Wiley and Sons.
55. Waldman, D. A., & Yammarino, F. J. (1999). CEO charismatic leadership: Levels of management and levels of analysis effects. *Academy of Management Review, 24*, 266–285.
56. Crandall, note 54.
57. Waldman & Yammarino, note 55.
58. Bryant, S. E. (2003, Spring). The role of transformational and transactional leadership in creating, sharing and exploiting organizational knowledge. *Journal of Leadership & Organizational Studies, 9*(4), 32–45.
59. Bryant, note 58.
60. Burns, J. (1978). *Leadership*. New York: Harper & Row.
61. Tucker, B. A., & Russell, R. F. (2004, March 22). The influence of transformational leadership. *Journal of Leadership & Organizational Studies*. Retrieved June 16, 2009, from http://goliath.ecnext.com/coms2/summary_0199-2375126_ITM.
62. Bass, note 2.
63. Yukl, note 8, p. 350.
64. Yukl, note 8, p. 351.
65. Retrieved July 11, 2009, from http://www.12manage.com/methods_greenleaf_servant_leadership.html.
66. Bass, note 2.
67. Yukl, note 8.
68. Savic, B. S., & Pagon, M. (2008). Individual involvement in health care organizations: Differences between professional groups, leaders, and employees. *Stress & Health: Journal of the International Society for the Investigation of Stress, 24*(1), 71–84.
69. Yukl, note 8.
70. Bass, note 2.
71. Fairholm, G. (2003). *The techniques of inner leadership: Making inner leadership work*. Westport, CT: Praeger.
72. Bass, B. (1998). *Transformational leadership: Industrial, military, and educational impact*. Mahwah, NJ: Lawrence Erlbaum Associates.
73. Yukl, note 8.
74. Bass, note 2.
75. Yukl, note 8, p. 352.
76. Bennis, W. G., & Nanus, B. (1985). *Leaders: The strategies for taking charge*. New York: Harper and Row.
77. Avolio, B. J., & Bass, B. M. (2002). *Developing potential across a full range of leadership: Cases on transactional and transformational leadership*. Mahwah, NJ: Lawrence Erlbaum Associates, p. 1.
78. Avolio & Bass, note 77.
79. Avolio & Bass, note 77.
80. Avolio & Bass, note 77, p. 19.
81. Bennis & Nanus, note 76.
82. Bennis, W. (1989). *On becoming a leader*. Wilmington, MA: Perseus.
83. Kouzes, J. M., & Posner, B. Z. (2007). *The leadership challenge* (4th ed.). New York: John Wiley and Sons.
84. Boulais, N. A. (2002). Leadership in children's literature: Qualitative analysis from a study based on the Kouzes and Posner leadership framework. *Journal of Leadership Studies, 5*, pp. 54–63.
85. Covey, S. R. (2004). *The 8th habit: From effectiveness to greatness*. New York: Free Press.
86. Kouzes, J. M., & Posner, B. Z. (2003). *The leadership challenge* (3rd ed.). San Francisco: Jossey-Bass.
87. Lubbock County Democratic Talking Points, Lubbock, TX (July 2009).
88. Koncius, J. (2009, June 6). Former Chief Usher of White House offers rare glimpse of first families. *The Washington Post*. Retrieved July 22, 2009, from http://www.columbiamissourian.com/stories/2009/06/08/former-head-usher-white-house-saw-first-families-most-vulnerable/.
89. Kouzes, J. M., & Posner, B. Z. (1999). *Encouraging the heart: A leader's guide to rewarding and recognizing others*. San Francisco, CA: Jossey-Bass.
90. Buckingham, M., & Clifton, D. O. (2001). *Now, discover your strengths*. New York: Free Press.
91. Coppola, M. N., & Carini, G. (2006, March/April). Ability job-fit self-assessment. *Healthcare Executive*, pp. 60–63.
92. Wise, P. S. (2003). *Leading and managing in nursing*. St. Louis, MI: Elsevier Health Sciences.
93. Ulrich, D., Zenger, J. H., Zenger, J., & Smallwood, W. M. (1999). *Results-based leadership*. Boston: Harvard Business Press.
94. Harrison, J. P., & Coppola, M. N. (2007). Is the quality of hospital care a function of leadership? *Health Care Manager, 26*(3), 1–10.
95. Harrison, J., & Coppola, M. N. (2008). Is the quality of hospital care a function of leadership? Poster presentation, Annual Research Meeting sponsored by the Academy of Health, Washington, DC, June 8, 2008.
96. Coppola, M. N., Lafrance, K. G., & Carretta, H. J. (2002, November/December). The female infantryman: Testing the possibility. *Journal of Military Review, 6*, 55–60.

97. Nohria, N., Joyce, W., & Roberson, B. (2003). What really works. *Harvard Business Review, 79*(11), 85–96.

98. Department of the Army. (2007, January 1). *Field manual M-22-100: Army leadership.* Washington, DC.

99. Warren, R. (1995). *The purpose driven church.* Zondervan Publishers, Trinity Western University; Trinity Western Seminary; Associated Canadian Theological Schools of Trinity Western University. http://www.saffold.com/leadership/resources/lmodel/lmodel10.htm.

100. Rick Warren and Barack Obama's inaugural address. (2008, December 22). *USA Today.* http://content.usatoday.com/communities/religion/post/2008/12/60306978/1.

101. Warren, note 99.

Leadership in Practice

Leadership Competence I: Personal Responsibilities

Men are conquered only by love and kindness, by quiet, discreet example, which does not humiliate them and does not constrain them to give it. They dislike to be attacked by a man who has no other desire but to overcome them.
Giosue Borsi, *A Soldier's Confidences with God*

This chapter discusses the personal responsibility a leader has to maintain—if not advance—relevancy in his or her environment. It also discusses leadership competencies and the ability–job fit a leader has with his or her organizational environment. Emphasis is placed on the understanding that health leaders work in a highly complex environment with a very educated and interdisciplinary workforce. Leadership success is often based on the leader's capabilities in terms of motivation, influence, interpersonal relationships, communication, situational assessment, and inspiring teams.

LEARNING OBJECTIVES

1. Describe the complexity of the health industry in terms of workforce, environment, and societal expectations, and explain how a health leader's mastery of competencies, situational assessment, influence processes, motivation, interpersonal relationships, and communication capabilities is necessary to successfully navigate that complexity.

2. Explain how the complexity of the health workforce may lead to communication failure and conflict, and summarize the use of quality communication and conflict management skills to successfully motivate subordinates, build interdisciplinary teams, and lead a health organization based on commitment rather than compliance or resistance.

3. Predict the outcomes of continuous use of the avoiding and competing strategies, as compared to the compromising, accommodating, and problem-solving strategies, in a health organization; predict the outcomes of face-to-face communication as compared to use of the memoranda communication channel and media to disseminate ambiguous and urgent messages.

4. Analyze the health leader competencies in terms of the knowledge, skills and abilities discussed in this chapter, differentiating the competencies described here with those not discussed; support your assessment.

5. By combining several theories and models, design an influence and motivation leadership model for use in health organizations focused on subordinate commitment; modify this model for use with an interdisciplinary health team or group, and explain why this modification was necessary.

6. Evaluate competencies (knowledge, skills, and abilities) found in leadership practice concerning situational assessment, interpersonal relationships, influence processes, motivation, and communication necessary to successfully lead health organizations; support your evaluation.

THE COMPLEX AND DYNAMIC HEALTH ENVIRONMENT

The health industry exists in a very dynamic environment. If the environment were static (i.e., not changing), the workforce homogenous and consistent, and the technology of health simple, the need for and the value of leaders would be much lower than they are in reality. In effect, the real dynamic and complex environment of health necessitates competent and motivated leaders. Because the environment, workforce, technology, and systems are complex and dynamic, leadership in the health realm is essential. Also, societal expectations for health organizations and health professionals are very high; in truth, these expectations are for these organizations and professionals to be error free or flawless. How long would a pharmacy director keep his or her job if even 5 percent, or 3 percent, of that section's work was erroneous? How successful would a physical therapy director or branch chief of the clinic be if new therapies and technologies were adopted 5 or 10 years after a competitor had adopted them? Would the director of the supply chain for a hospital be successful if that person did not keep up with the new medical and surgical items needed for the hospital to meet the professional or national standard of care? Of course, the responses in these scenarios would not be favorable; in fact, failure in these areas would be career minimizing for these hypothetical individuals. Clearly, the dynamic environment of the health industry requires competent leaders throughout the organization, from chief executive officer to section or branch director.

In today's health industry, the need for professionalization and competence are especially important. *Competence* means recognizing and having the ability to utilize the capabilities associated with leadership. It requires mastery of the special skills and learning from experiences that are required to become a "professional." Many organizations in the United States focus on increasing the competence of professionals of health organizations. Many of these organizations or associations are populated by executives in the profession who are committing their time and resources for the causes that are important to them. Without this kind of interdisciplinary exchange, increasing competence levels of the industry, one leader at a time, might not be achievable.

Situational Assessment and Environmental Scanning

All health leaders must be able to assess the situation currently facing their organization, which would incorporate an assessment of both internal and external environments. A situational assessment must be an objective and honest look at the diverse factors that could affect the health organization's success in achieving its vision, mission, strategies, and goals. One tool commonly used for the internal assessment is SWOT analysis, which investigates internal strengths and weaknesses and external opportunities and threats.[1]

SWOT analysis offers insight into both the internal and external factors that might affect the organization's performance and success. Every organization needs more information about the environment than just its potential opportunities and threats. Choo reports that it is important to obtain information about relationships, trends, and information in the external environment; health leaders need to know which influences are acting on the industry and even the economy.[2] A focused environmental scan is one that concentrates on specific information, such as how many consumers bought this particular product or that service in the last year. External scanning, whether focused or more general, is essential for planning and forecasting the organization's performance into the future.

Situational assessment and continuous environmental scanning are crucial if organizations hope to survive in the dynamic health industry. A leader's and leadership team's responsibility is to remain current about and relevant to situational and environmental change that can or will affect the organization. Forces that contribute to the health industry's rapid and dynamic environment are varied but are cumulative; as a consequence, they have a cumulative impact on the industry. "Technology, demography, economics and politics drive change, not only as individual factors but interacting to make the rate of change faster."[3]

Another approach is to look at the dynamic environment as comprising macro-environmental forces and health micro-environmental forces. In an approach that has been validated over the last two decades, Rakich, Longest, and Darr in 1992 outlined a series of categories that leaders can scan (environmental scanning) to keep current and relevant in the industry:

1. Macro-Environmental Forces
   a. Legal, [regulatory, executive orders, and case law] and Ethical forces;
   b. Political (including government policy) forces;
   c. Cultural and Sociological (including values [beliefs and attitudes]) forces;
   d. Public Expectations (including community, interest groups, and media);
   e. Economic forces; and
   f. Ecological forces.

2. Health Care Environmental Forces [also called Micro-Environmental Forces]
   a. Planning and Public Policy (regulation, licensure, and accreditation) forces;
   b. Competitive forces;
   c. Health Care Financing (third-party payers, public and private, and financial risk);
   d. Technology (equipment, material, and supply entities) forces;
   e. Health Research and Education;
   f. Health Status and Health Promotion (wellness and disease); and
   g. [Integration with other health disciplines and organizations] Public Health (sanitation, environmental protection, etc…) forces.[4]

The Rand Corporation suggests that the immense pressure exerted by cost-containment efforts and the rapid speed of change are the major factors influencing the health industry at this time.[5] Multiple forces have cumulatively contributed to change in the health industry in recent decades. Compare the health organization of the 1960s or 1970s to those of today: There is a vast difference between two temporal organizations. The speed of that change in a mere 30 to 40 years is astonishing, as are the gains in the ability of healthcare delivery systems to diagnose, treat, and rehabilitate patients who present with health needs.

For example, consider the life expectancy of people living in the 1960s compared to today. "Between 1961 and 1999, average life expectancy in the [United States] increased from 66.9 to 74.1 years for men and from 73.5 to 79.6 for women."[6] Trends in aging are also tied to life expectancy but have profound implications for health services.[7]

This dynamic whirlwind, often called "whitewater change," frames a picture of the world that the health leader must navigate. Although there have been tremendous successes in this industry, health leaders must continue to recognize the dynamic nature of the industry and challenge their organizations, groups, teams, and individuals to become more efficient, effective, and efficacious, while functioning under significant cost-containment pressure. From a practical viewpoint, Kotter suggests eight steps to transform organizations in dynamic situations (*italics* added):

1. *Establish a Sense of Urgency* by examining market and competitive realities and identifying and discussing crises, potential crises or major opportunities;

2. *Form a Powerful Guiding Coalition* by assembling a group with enough power to lead the change effect [from an level of the organization] and encourage the group to work together as a team;

3. *Create a Vision* to help direct the change effort and develop strategies for achieving that vision;

4. *Communicate the Vision* by using every vehicle possible to communicate the new vision and strategies and by teaching new behaviors by the example of the guiding coalition [at lower levels of the organization, the leader translates the senior leadership's vision for his or her section, branch, or unit into understandable and actionable tasks for that level and situation];

5. *Empower Others to Act on the Vision* by getting rid of obstacles to change, changing systems or structures that seriously undermine the vision, and encouraging risk taking and nontraditional ideas, activities, and actions;

6. *Plan for and Create Short-Term Wins* by planning for visible performance improvements, creating those improvements, and recognizing and rewarding employees involved in the improvements;

7. *Consolidate Improvements and Produce Still More Change* by using increased credibility to change systems, structures, and policies that don't fit the vision; hiring, promoting, and developing employees who can implement the vision; and reinvigorating the process with new projects, themes, and change agents; and

8. *Institutionalize New Approaches* by articulating the connections between the new behaviors and corporate [organizational] success and developing the means to ensure leadership development and succession.[8]

Kotter's eight steps are a sequence of leader actions and are cybernetic; that is, a feedback loop goes from the last step back to the first step. Leaders of health organizations should consider the changes in the macro and micro environments by assessing them against the *cost, quality,* and *access* health assessment constructs for those community members whom they serve. This analysis, for the segment of the continuum of care (from self-care and health promotion and prevention to primary, secondary, and tertiary care to long-term care and hospice care) in which the leaders are responsible, should be integrated into the holistic aspect of health and the health infrastructure available (or needed) in the community.

The leader must stay attuned to the macro and micro forces of change; professional associations and societies can assist greatly in this continuous effort. Professional associations, societies, and educational accrediting bodies are discussed later in this chapter. As leadership is all about "leading people," the discussion here now turns to the complexity of the health workforce, the leader's development, and the subordinate's development.

The Complex and Highly Educated World of the Health Workforce

The health workforce is a complex assortment of individuals characterized by different backgrounds, educational experiences, certifications, specialties, and work locations. Reviewing the workforce reports from the federal government's Health Resources and Services Administration, Bureau of Health Professions[9] division, provides some appreciation of the diversity and heterogeneity of the health workforce. As a whole, the health workforce accounts for nearly 12 percent of the total U.S. workforce.[10]

Leaders in the health sector must be able to foster a culture that is conducive to change and growth as well as develop the full potential of their staff members and volunteers. Understanding culture is a big part of this effort. Put simply, a major component of culture is the human element. Culture includes the sum total of knowledge, beliefs, art, morals, laws, customs, and shared patterns of behaviors, interactions, cognitive constructs, and affective understanding that are acquired by a particular society through socialization.[11] These shared patterns distinguish the members of one group from the members of another group. Studies have found that the values that vary from one culture to another significantly influence the constitutional effectiveness of the organization. Each of these groups has its own specialized training, norms, beliefs, and values, which may differ from those espoused by other groups.

In stable times, such individual dynamics may be masked and subgroups submissive; in contrast, in turbulent times, these internal groups may seek some degree of autonomy. Moreover, the training, education, and experience of health administrators, doctors, nurses, allied health professionals and other paraprofessionals may result in the presentation of certain cultural concepts that are unique and may be expressed in different ways, such as aggressive needs for autonomy or increased advocacy for patient care versus financial survivability of the healthcare organization.[12]

Mechanisms that reinforce norms and behaviors arise when the leader focuses attention on specific, high-priority goals and objectives. These characteristics are taught by the leaders and, in turn, adopted by the staff and the supporters of the organization. In a reciprocal relationship, the culture influences leadership as much as leadership influences culture. The adroit leader in a health organization has a direct impact on the culture, which can affect how decisions are made with respect to fundraising, volunteers, and placement within the organization.[13] Organizational culture is discussed more thoroughly later in this text.

For a leader in this complex world, the important issues are threefold: (1) the leader's ability to focus a diverse group of individuals toward the mission, vision, and tasks of the organization; (2) the leader's ability to determine which individuals, with their unique sets of knowledge, skills, and abilities, should be employed where and how they should be utilized to the greatest value of the organization; and (3) the leader's use of the skills of communication and motivation, as well as culture development and maintenance to create systems and processes that are effective, efficient, and efficacious so that the organization can be successful within the environment in which it performs its mission. These leadership challenges are salient for leaders throughout the industry regardless of their level in a specific organization. As leaders progress upward in responsibility and accountability in a health organization, the complexity widens and deepens. Those are rather large leadership tasks!

The myriad of specialties in the health workforce underline the advancement and specialization of the application of knowledge, skills, abilities, and technologies of the industry. Multidisciplinary teams, whether in clinical, administrative, or allied health, are becoming more prevalent in the delivery of care, administration of health organizations, and improvement of health status of communities. Understanding the different knowledge, skills, abilities, and perspectives each health professional brings to an issue, opportunity, or challenge that the organization faces is important for leaders. Effective handling of this need is essential so that the proper mix of professionals can be formed into a team, proper resources can be provided, and appropriate expectations can be set for the multidisciplinary team. Learning about each discipline and knowing which capability each type of health professional can competently perform will allow the leader to make the most efficient use of the most valuable resource—people.

Table 5–1 presents a simple summary of a current snapshot of the health workforce.

TABLE 5–1   Health Workforce Specialty Categories and Disciplines

Category	Specialties		
Medicine	Physicians of medicine (MD) and physicians of allopathic medicine (DO)	Many specialties, such as neurology, pathology, radiology, psychiatry, and surgery (e.g., thoracic, cardiac, orthopedic)	Many specialties, such as pediatrics, family medicine, obstetrics and gynecology, internal medicine, ophthalmology, and cardiology
Nursing	Registered nurses (RN)	Advance practice nurses (NP or APN)	Licensed practical and vocational nurses (LPN)
Dentistry	Dentists of surgery (DDS) and dentists of medical dentistry (DMD)	Dental hygienist	Dental assistants
Non-physician clinicians	Physician assistants (PA), and podiatrists (DPM)	Chiropractors	Optometrists and opticians
Pharmacy	Doctors of pharmacy (PharmD)	Pharmacists	Pharmacy technicians and aides
Mental health	Psychologists	Social workers	Counselors
Allied health	Physical therapy, occupational therapy, speech-language pathology and audiology, and respiratory therapy	Various technicians and technologists (laboratory, emergency medical, radiology), paramedics, medical and clinical technologists, and nuclear medicine technologists	Medical records and health information technologists and technicians, dieticians and nutritionists, home health aides and nursing aides, orderlies and attendants
Health administration	Health system and hospital administration, nursing home/long-term care administration, home health administration, health insurance, and integrated system administration	Medical practice administration, clinical practice administration, and technical area administration	Public health administration as a whole and/or, for examples, in environmental health science, epidemiology, community and social behavior, health policy, maternal women and children, and biostatistics

These various specialties and disciplines all have different education, licensure, credentialing and licensure maintenance requirements. As such, different professional associations and societies, and credentialing and accreditation associations, have been developed to provide a set of standards for each distinct profession. These associations and societies also provide valuable connections and updates concerning the macro- and micro-environmental forces that are changing the health industry.

A recent collaboration of five professional associations has created five domains that encompass a total of 300 competencies for the health leader and manager. An extract of competencies, focusing on leadership and management from Domain 2: Leadership, are summarized in **Table 5–2**. Although this table focuses on the Leadership domain, leaders should possess the competencies identified in each domain. A file for all domains can be found at http://www.jblearning.com/catalog/9780763781514/ in the supporting Web site for this text.

The professional associations involved in the collaboration to create this list of competencies are essential to leaders and managers in the health industry. The associations' mission or charter (a reason to exist, a purpose), taken as a whole, is to keep their membership—that is, the leaders, managers, and stakeholders of the health industry—current on changing environmental forces. One of the many ways they perform this mission is to maintain close relationships with the legislative, judicial, and political entities of U.S. society.

Health industry leaders should seek membership in these associations and certification as appropriate to their career track and personal career goals. This is a sincere and strong recommendation. **Table 5–3** lists some of these associations, as well as providing contact information for the National Center for Healthcare Leadership and the Association of University Programs in Health Administration.

Health leaders should become members and earn the appropriate certification from a professional association of the health industry. The associations and societies listed in Table 5–3 are the best known in the industry for leadership careers. For example, the National Center for Healthcare Leadership (NCHL) provides essential services and information for the health leader. The Association of University Programs in Health Administration (AUPHA) and Commission on Accreditation of Healthcare Management Education (CAHME) provide instructors of health industry leadership and management students with the standards and specialty certification for their programs. In addition, specialty associations exist to serve women, Asian, and African American health leaders and managers. Of note, recognized universities may be regionally accredited as institutions of higher learning, whereas specific colleges and specific programs are specialty accredited, such as with health administration regarding CAHME. Other specialty accrediting bodies for health industry leadership and management programs include the Council on Education for Public Health (CEPH)[23] and the Association to Advance Collegiate Schools of Business (AACSB).[24]

Many leaders come from clinical or technical programs, backgrounds, and practical experiences. These leaders, for example, include physicians, physical therapists, pharmacists, occupational therapists, audiologists and speech pathologists, optometrists, and nurses. For would-be health leaders, maintaining membership and certification for your clinical or technical specialty is important, but securing membership in one of the professional leadership and management health associations—the one that provides the best fit for you—is also important for your personal growth, professional development, and upward career mobility. Not only are your leadership knowledge, skills, and abilities important, and not only is the environmental scanning support important, but the broader network of similar leaders that you will develop can also assist you and your organization greatly throughout your career.

Industry segment associations are valuable assets not just to the health industry as a whole, but also to your organization. These associations include the American Hospital Association, American Medical Association, American Dental Association, and American Nurses Association, among many others. Maintaining connections and good relationships with these organizations will assist your organization in environmental scanning and situational assessment activities as well.

As a health leader, you are responsible for maintaining your competence and your subordinate team's competence, and for striving for and achieving organizational success. Leaders should regularly seek out continuing education—much of which is provided by the health professional associations—not just for themselves but also for their subordinates. Most certifications you earn as a health leader, or as a clinician or technician for that matter, require regular continuing education credits or units. The next section expands on the topic of learning and competence.

TABLE 5–2 Leadership Domain: Health Professional Associations Collaborative Competency Directory

Domain	Knowledge/Skill	Competency	Skill Area	Key Words	Core/Specialty	Core and Specialty Competencies Relevant to the Professionals Represented by the HLA Organizations (X indicates relevancy)				
						ACHE	ACMPE	AONE	HFMA	HIMSS
Domain 2: Leadership	Knowledge of	Leadership styles/techniques		Methods, models	Core	X	X	X	X	X
Domain 2: Leadership	Knowledge of	Personal journey disciplines		Methods, models	Specialty			X		
Domain 2: Leadership	Skill	Gain physician buy-in to accept risk and support new business ventures	Facilitate	Decision making	Core	X	X	X	X	X
Domain 2: Leadership	Skill	Adhere to legal and regulatory standards	Be accountable	Regulation	Core	X	X	X	X	X
Domain 2: Leadership	Skill	Advocate and participate in healthcare policy initiatives (e.g., uninsured crisis; medical malpractice; access to health care; patient safety)	Advocate	External factors	Core	X	X	X	X	X
Domain 2: Leadership	Skill	Anticipate and plan strategies for overcoming obstacles	Think strategically	Problem solving	Core	X	X	X	X	X
Domain 2: Leadership	Skill	Anticipate the need for resources to carry out initiatives	Think strategically	Needs	Core	X	X	X	X	X
Domain 2: Leadership	Skill	Assess the organization including corporate values and culture; business processes and impact of systems on operations	Analyze	Organization	Core	X	X	X	X	X
Domain 2: Leadership	Skill	Champion solutions and encourage decision making	Promote	Decision making	Core	X	X	X	X	X

(continues)

TABLE 5–2   Leadership Domain: Health Professional Associations Collaborative Competency Directory *(Continued)*

Domain	Knowledge/ Skill	Competency	Skill Area	Key Words	Core/ Specialty	Core and Specialty Competencies Relevant to the Professionals Represented by the HLA Organizations (X indicates relevancy)				
						ACHE	ACMPE	AONE	HFMA	HIMSS
Domain 2: Leadership	Skill	Create an organizational climate that encourages teamwork	Develop	Culture	Core	X	X	X	X	X
Domain 2: Leadership	Skill	Create an organizational climate that facilitates individual motivation	Develop	Culture	Core	X	X	X	X	X
Domain 2: Leadership	Skill	Develop external relationships	Develop	External relations	Core	X	X	X	X	X
Domain 2: Leadership	Skill	Encourage a high level of commitment to the purpose and values of the organization	Promote	Vision, goals	Core	X	X	X	X	X
Domain 2: Leadership	Skill	Establish a compelling organizational vision and goals	Develop	Vision, goals	Core	X	X	X	X	X
Domain 2: Leadership	Skill	Establish an organizational culture that values and supports diversity	Develop	Culture	Core	X	X	X	X	X
Domain 2: Leadership	Skill	Explore opportunities for the growth and development of the organization on a continuous basis	Develop	Organization	Core	X	X	X	X	X
Domain 2: Leadership	Skill	Foster an environment of mutual trust	Develop	Culture	Core	X	X	X	X	X

						ACHE	ACMPE	AONE	HFMA	HIMSS	HLA
Domain 2: Leadership	Skill	Hold self and others accountable for organizational goal attainment	Be accountable	Vision, goals	Core	X	X	X	X	X	X
Domain 2: Leadership	Skill	Incorporate and apply management techniques and theories into leadership activities	Integrate	Methods, models	Core	X	X	X	X	X	X
Domain 2: Leadership	Skill	Plan for leadership succession	Develop	Staff	Core	X	X	X	X	X	X
Domain 2: Leadership	Skill	Promote and manage change	Manage	Decision making	Core	X	X	X	X	X	X
Domain 2: Leadership	Skill	Promote continuous organizational learning/improvement	Develop	Organization	Core	X	X	X	X	X	X
Domain 2: Leadership	Skill	Represent physician interests in negotiating and managing relationship with hospitals, insurance companies, and others (e.g., fair market value of services; on-call coverage of specialists)	Advocate	Physicians	Core	X	X	X	X	X	X
Domain 2: Leadership	Skill	Support and mentor high-potential talent within the organization	Develop	Staff	Core	X	X	X	X	X	X

ACHE: American College of Healthcare Executives; ACMPE: American College of Medical Practice Executives; AONE: American Organization of Nurse Executives; HFMA: Healthcare Financial Management Association; HIMSS: Healthcare Information and Management Systems Society; HLA: Health Leader Attributes.

TABLE 5–3 **Professional Associations Geared Toward Health Leaders and Managers**

Health Professional Association (Web Address/URL)	Mission
American College of Healthcare Executives (ACHE) http://www.ache.org/	ACHE is an international professional society of more than 30,000 health executives who lead hospitals, healthcare systems, and other healthcare organizations. ACHE is known for its prestigious FACHE credential, signifying board certification in healthcare management, and its educational programs, including the annual Congress on Healthcare Leadership, which draws more than 4,000 participants each year. ACHE's established network of more than 80 chapters provides access to networking, education and career development at the local level.[14]
Medical Group Management Association (MGMA) http://www.mgma.com/index.aspx	The mission of MGMA is to continually improve the performance of medical group practice professionals and the organizations they represent. MGMA serves 22,500 members who lead and manage more than 13,700 organizations in which almost 275,000 physicians practice. Its diverse membership comprises administrators, chief executive officers (CEO)s, physicians in management, board members, office managers, and many other management professionals. They work in medical practices and ambulatory care organizations of all sizes and types, including integrated systems and hospital- and medical school–affiliated practices. Three related organizations, and their boards of directors and committees, help MGMA fulfill its commitment to members. • **American College of Medical Practice Executives (ACMPE):** the standard-setting and certification organization for group practice professionals. • **MGMA Center for Research:** the research and development companion to MGMA that conducts quantitative and qualitative research to advance the art and science of medical group management. • **MGMA Services Inc.:** a wholly owned, for-profit subsidiary of MGMA that was established to further the provision of high-quality medical management services and assist medical group practices in delivering efficient and effective health care.[15]
American Organization of Nurse Executives (AONE) http://www.aone.org/aone/about/home.html	AONE is the national organization of nurses who design, facilitate, and manage care. With more than 6,500 members, AONE is the voice of nursing leadership in health care. Since 1967, this organization has provided leadership, professional development, advocacy, and research to advance nursing practice and patient care, promote nursing leadership excellence, and shape public policy for health care. AONE's 48 affiliated state and metropolitan chapters and its alliances with state hospital associations give the organization's initiatives both regional and local presences. AONE is a subsidiary of the American Hospital Association.[16]
Healthcare Financial Management Association (HFMA) http://www.hfma.org/about/	HFMA is the United States' leading membership organization for healthcare financial management executives and leaders. Its more than 35,000 members—ranging from CFOs to controllers to accountants—consider HFMA a respected thought leader on top trends and issues facing the healthcare industry. HFMA members can be found in all areas of the healthcare system, including hospitals, managed care organizations, physician practices, accounting firms, and insurance companies. At the chapter, regional, and national levels, HFMA helps healthcare finance

TABLE 5–3   Professional Associations Geared Toward Health Leaders and Managers *(Continued)*

Health Professional Association (Web Address/URL)	Mission
	professionals meet the challenges of the modern healthcare environment in the following ways: • Providing education, analysis, and guidance • Building and supporting coalitions with other healthcare associations to ensure accurate representation of the healthcare finance profession • Educating a broad spectrum of key industry decision makers on the intricacies and realities of maintaining fiscally healthy healthcare organizations • Working with a broad cross section of stakeholders to improve the healthcare industry by identifying and bridging gaps in knowledge, best practices, and standards **Vision:** "To be the indispensable resource for healthcare finance." **Purpose Statement:** To define, realize, and advance the financial management of health care by helping members and others improve the business performance of organizations operating in or serving the healthcare field.[17]
Healthcare Information and Management Systems Society (HIMSS) http://www.himss.org/ASP/aboutHimssHome.asp	HIMSS is the healthcare industry's membership organization exclusively focused on providing global leadership for the optimal use of healthcare information technology (IT) and management systems for the betterment of health care. Founded in 1961, and with offices in Chicago; Washington, D.C.; Brussels; Singapore; and other locations across the globe, HIMSS represents more than 20,000 individual members and more than 350 corporate members who collectively represent organizations employing millions of people. HIMSS frames and leads healthcare public policy and industry practices through its advocacy, educational, and professional development initiatives designed to promote information and management systems' contributions to ensuring quality patient care. **Vision:** Advancing the best use of information and management systems for the betterment of health care. **Mission:** To lead change in the healthcare information and management systems field through knowledge sharing, advocacy, collaboration, innovation, and community affiliations.[18]
National Center for Healthcare Leadership (NCHL) http://www.nchl.org/ns/about/aboutnchl.asp	NCHL is a not-for-profit organization that works to assure that high-quality, relevant, and accountable leadership is available to meet the challenges of delivering quality patient healthcare in the twenty-first century. Its goal is to improve health system performance and the health status of the entire country through effective healthcare management leadership.[19]
Association of University Programs in Health Administration (AUPHA) http://www.aupha.org/i4a/pages/index.cfm?pageid=3275 Commission on Accreditation of Healthcare Management Education (CAHME) http://www.cahme.org/	AUPHA is a global network of colleges, universities, faculty, individuals, and organizations dedicated to the improvement of healthcare delivery through excellence in health administration education. Its membership includes the premier baccalaureate and master's degree programs in health administration education in the United States and Canada. The association's faculty and individual members represent more than 230 colleges, universities, and healthcare organizations. When asked what they value most highly about AUPHA membership, these members cite the opportunity to meet and network with colleagues who share similar

(continues)

TABLE 5–3   **Professional Associations Geared Toward Health Leaders and Managers** *(Continued)*

Health Professional Association (Web Address/URL)	Mission
	interests, learning about the issues facing the field, and witnessing the latest products and services for the healthcare industry.[20]
	Vision: Improve health by promoting excellence and innovation in healthcare management education.
	Mission: AUPHA fosters excellence and innovation in healthcare management education, research, and practice by providing opportunities for member programs to learn from one another, by influencing practice, and by promoting the value of healthcare management education.[21]
	Program Certification and Accreditation: Programs seeking full membership in AUPHA must have achieved proven excellence as indicated by undergraduate certification or graduate accreditation. Certification and accreditation are processes of external peer review through which programs are examined to determine quality of the curriculum, infrastructure, and outcomes. Certification of undergraduate programs is available through AUPHA. Accreditation of graduate programs is carried out by the CAHME.[22]

LEADERSHIP KNOWLEDGE, COMPREHENSION, SKILLS, AND ABILITIES

Knowledge focuses on recalling information with familiarity gained through education, experience, or association, whereas *comprehension* is the understanding of the meaning of the information such as of a science, art, or technique so as to interpret and translate that information into action. A *skill* is the effective and timely utilization of knowledge that is comprehended; it is the learned power of doing something competently through a developed aptitude. *Ability* is the physical, cognitive, or legal power to competently perform through natural aptitude or learned or acquired proficiency and competence. In essence, knowledge, comprehension, skills, and abilities are sequential, and the notions of "competence" and "proficiency" are critical to these definitions. Leaders grow in knowledge, comprehension, skills, and abilities through education, study, experience, mentoring, and observation. Most, if not all, of these capabilities are learned.

Leaders may find the taxonomies developed by Benjamin Bloom useful as they reflect on their own capabilities and as they evaluate and develop subordinates whom they lead. Bloom's theory is based on three types of learning or three learning domains (categories):

■ Cognitive: mental skills (knowledge)
■ Affective: growth in feelings or emotional areas (attitude)
■ Psychomotor: manual or physical skills (skills)

Trainers often refer to these three domains as KSAs (knowledge, skills, and attitudes [abilities]). Thus this taxonomy of learning behaviors can be thought of as "the goals of the training process." That is, "after the training session, the learner should have acquired new skills, knowledge, and/or attitudes [and abilities]."[25] "Bloom's Taxonomy is a way to classify instructional activities or questions as they progress in difficulty. The lower levels require less in the way of thinking skills. As one moves down the hierarchy, the activities require higher-level thinking skills."[26]

Table 5–4 describes the cognitive domain within Bloom's Taxonomy.[27] The cognitive domain involves knowledge and the development of intellectual skills. This includes the recall or recognition of specific facts, procedural patterns, and concepts that develop intellectual abilities and skills. There are six major categories in Table 5–4, which move from the simplest behavior to the most complex. The categories can be thought of as degrees of difficulties. That is, the first one must be mastered before the next one can be tackled.

TABLE 5–4   Bloom's Taxonomy of the Cognitive Domain (Original Version)

Category and Example	Key Words and Actions
Knowledge: Recall of data or information. *Example: Defines leadership; identifies items from a list.*	Defines, describes, identifies, knows, labels, lists, matches, names, outlines, recalls, recognizes, reproduces, selects, states.
Comprehension: Understands the meaning, translation, interpolation, and interpretation of instructions and problems; states problem in own words. *Example: Explains the steps and sequence of willful choice decision making; translates information and equations into a spreadsheet.*	Comprehends, converts, defends, distinguishes, estimates, explains, extends, generalizes, gives examples, infers, interprets, paraphrases, predicts, rewrites, summarizes, translates.
Application: Uses a concept in a new situation or unprompted use of an abstraction; applies what was learned in the classroom to novel situations in the workplace. *Example: Uses quantitative methods to determine employee performance outliers; uses a policy to determine an employee's merit raise increase or bonus.*	Applies, changes, computes, constructs, demonstrates, discovers, manipulates, modifies, operates, predicts, prepares, produces, relates, shows, solves, uses.
Analysis: Separates material or concepts into component parts so that their organizational structure may be understood; distinguishes between facts and inferences. *Example: Determines sequential work process steps and transition points of a larger work system; gathers information and assessments to identify training needs in a department or unit.*	Analyzes, breaks down, compares, contrasts, diagrams, deconstructs, differentiates, discriminates, distinguishes, identifies, illustrates, infers, outlines, relates, selects, separates.
Synthesis: Builds a structure or pattern from diverse elements; puts parts together to form a whole while emphasizing a new meaning or structure. *Example: Composes an organizational policy, operations, or process manual; organizes, plans, and leads a process improvement project.*	Categorizes, combines, compiles, composes, creates, devises, designs, explains, generates, modifies, organizes, plans, rearranges, reconstructs, relates, reorganizes, revises, rewrites, summarizes, tells, writes.
Evaluation: Makes judgments about the value of ideas or materials. *Example: Selects the most effective, efficient, and efficacious solution to a health delivery problem; explains and justifies a project or annual budget.*	Appraises, compares, concludes, contrasts, criticizes, critiques, defends, describes, discriminates, evaluates, explains, interprets, justifies, relates, summarizes, supports.

Source: Bloom B. S. (1956). *Taxonomy of educational objectives. Handbook I: The cognitive domain*. New York: David McKay. Retrieved May 12, 2009, from http://www.nwlink.com/~Donclark/hrd/bloom.html#cognitive.

A revision of the cognitive domain in 2001 updated the terminology and uses active verbs.

1. **Remembering:** Retrieving, recognizing, and recalling relevant knowledge from long-term memory.
2. **Understanding:** Constructing meaning from oral, written, and graphic messages through interpreting, exemplifying, classifying, summarizing, inferring, comparing, and explaining.
3. **Applying:** Carrying out or using a procedure through executing or implementing.
4. **Analyzing:** Breaking material into constituent parts, determining how the parts relate to one another and to an overall structure or purpose through differentiating, organizing, and attributing.
5. **Evaluating:** Making judgments based on criteria and standards through checking and critiquing.
6. **Creating:** Putting elements together to form a coherent or functional whole; reorganizing elements into a new pattern or structure through generating, planning, or producing.[28]

Next, we turn to the affective domain within Bloom's Taxonomy. This domain includes the manner in which we deal with things emotionally, such as feelings, values, appreciation, enthusiasms, motivations, and attitudes. The five major categories are listed in **Table 5–5** from the simplest behavior to the most complex.

The psychomotor domain includes physical movement, coordination, and use of the motor-skill areas. Development of these skills requires practice, and achievement in this domain is measured in terms of speed, precision, distance, procedures, or techniques in execution. **Table 5–6** lists the seven major categories in the psychomotor domain in order from the simplest behavior to the most complex.

TABLE 5–5   Bloom's Taxonomy of the Affective Domain (Original Version)

Category and Example	Key Words and Actions
Receiving Phenomena: Awareness, willingness to hear, selective attention. *Example: Listens to others with respect; listens for and remembers name of newly introduced person.*	Asks, chooses, describes, follows, gives, holds, identifies, locates, names, points to, selects, sits, erects, replies, uses.
Responding to Phenomena: Active participation in activities; learns from stimulus; attends and reacts to particular phenomenon; shows compliance in responding, willingness in responding or satisfaction in responding (motivation). *Example: Participates in discussions; gives presentations; questions new ideas, concepts, and models to understand them; knows rules and follows them.*	Answers, assists, aids, complies, conforms, discusses, greets, helps, labels, performs, practices, presents, reads, recites, reports, selects, tells, writes.
Valuing: The worth or value a person attaches to a particular object, phenomenon, or behavior; ranges from simple acceptance (compliance) to commitment; based on the internalization of a set of specified values; clues are often expressed in overt behavior and are often identifiable. *Example: Demonstrates belief in the democratic process; is sensitive to individual and cultural differences; speaks up appropriately on matters one feels strongly about.*	Completes, demonstrates, differentiates, explains, follows, forms, initiates, invites, joins, justifies, proposes, reads, reports, selects, shares, studies, works.

TABLE 5–5   Bloom's Taxonomy of the Affective Domain (Original Version) *(Continued)*

Category and Example	Key Words and Actions
Organization: Organizes values into priorities by contrasting different values; resolves conflicts between those values and creates new (or modified) value system; emphasis is on comparing, relating, and synthesizing values. *Example: Recognizes the need to balance freedom with responsible behavior; accepts responsibility for own behavior; explains role of systematic planning to solve problems; accepts professional ethical standards; balances abilities, interests, and beliefs as well as organization, family, and self.*	Adheres, alters, arranges, combines, compares, completes, defends, explains, formulates, generalizes, identifies, integrates, modifies, orders, organizes, prepares, relates, synthesizes.
Internalizing Values: Has a value system that controls one's behavior; behavior is pervasive, consistent, predictable, and characteristically that of a learner. *Example: Shows self-reliance when working alone; cooperates in group activities (teamwork); uses an objective approach to problem solving. Displays professional commitment to an ethical framework and moral practice at all times; revises judgments and behaviors in light of new evidence; values people for what they are and how they behave, not on appearance.*	Acts, discriminates, displays, influences, listens, modifies, performs, practices, proposes, qualifies, questions, revises, serves, solves, verifies.

Source: Krathwohl, D. R., Bloom, B. S., & Masia, B. B. (1973). *Taxonomy of educational objectives, the classification of educational goals. Handbook II: Affective domain.* New York: David McKay. Retrieved May 12, 2009, from http://www.nwlink.com/~Donclark/hrd/bloom.html#cognitive.

TABLE 5–6   Bloom's Taxonomy of the Psychomotor Domain (Original Version)

Category and Example	Key Words and Actions
Perception: The ability to use sensory cues to guide motor activity; ability ranges from sensory stimulation to translation. *Example: Detects nonverbal communication cues; estimates where a ball will land after it is thrown; adjusts height of forklift forks in relation to pallet.*	Chooses, describes, detects, differentiates, distinguishes, identifies, isolates, relates, selects.
Set: Readiness to act; includes mental, physical, and emotional sets; these three sets are dispositions that predetermine a person's response to different situations. *Example: Knows and acts upon a sequence of steps in a care delivery process; recognizes one's abilities and limitations; shows desire to learn a new process (motivation).*	Begins, displays, explains, moves, proceeds, reacts, shows, states, volunteers.

(continues)

TABLE 5–6 Bloom's Taxonomy of the Psychomotor Domain (Original Version) *(Continued)*

Category and Example	Key Words and Actions
Guided Response: The early stages of learning a complex skill, which include imitation and trial and error; adequacy of performance is achieved by practice. *Example: Solves a financial or mathematical equation as demonstrated; follows instructions to conduct an activity.*	Copies, traces, follows, reacts, reproduces, responds.
Mechanism: The intermediate stage of learning a complex skill; learned responses have become habitual and the movements can be performed with some confidence and proficiency. *Example: Uses a personal computer and software program; drives a car.*	Assembles, calibrates, constructs, dismantles, displays, fastens, fixes, grinds, heats, manipulates, measures, mends, mixes, organizes, sketches.
Complex Overt Response: The skillful performance of motor acts that involve complex movement patterns. Proficiency is indicated by a quick, accurate, and highly coordinated performance, requiring a minimum amount of energy; performs without hesitation, an automatic response. *Note:* Same as Mechanism but performed more quickly, better, and more accurately. *Example: Operates a computer and software program quickly and accurately; displays confidence while addressing a group.*	Assembles, calibrates, constructs, dismantles, displays, fastens, fixes, grinds, heats, manipulates, measures, mends, mixes, organizes, sketches.
Adaptation: Skills are well developed and the person can modify movement patterns to fit special situations and requirements. *Example: Responds effectively and efficiently to unexpected situations and experiences; modifies instruction to meet the needs of the learners; uses a machine or medical instrument in a new way (not as intended) successfully.*	Adapts, alters, changes, rearranges, reorganizes, revises, varies.
Origination: Creates new movement patterns to fit a particular situation or specific problem. Learning outcomes emphasize creativity based on highly developed skills. *Example: Constructs a new theory or model; develops a new and comprehensive training program.*	Arranges, builds, combines, composes, constructs, creates, designs, initiates, makes, originates.

Source: Simpson, E. J. (1972). *The classification of educational objectives in the psychomotor domain*. Washington, DC: Gryphon House. Retrieved May 12, 2009, from http://www.nwlink.com/~Donclark/hrd/bloom.html#cognitive.

Understanding and utilizing these taxonomies will assist health leaders in evaluating their own progress in learning about leadership and applying leadership capabilities; moreover, it will assist leaders in structuring the development of their subordinate team members. Motivating and inspiring to focus the collective energy of a diverse workforce toward the mission and vision of the health organization is paramount to leadership success. The next section provides an overview of motivation and inspiration theories, models, and applications.

MOTIVATION AND INSPIRATION

In the health leader's array of knowledge, skills, and abilities, motivation and inspiration rank high on the list. Carnevale states that "creating a climate that enhances motivation, with the commensurate increase in productivity, is a requirement."[29] *Motivation* is all about getting a person to start and persist on a task or project. *Inspiration* is the emotive feeling of value a person experiences while performing a worthy task or project.

Motivation and inspiration in the present day are rooted in the concepts of influence, and to some degree, power. Leaders use motivation and inspiration to influence subordinate actions. Traditionally, leadership thinking rested in the concepts of power and influence. However, the modern-day art of leadership requires a more subtle approach to the misconception of aggressive power and "arm-twisting" influence. The well-educated and complex health workforce will resist the use of errant influence and positional power.

Perhaps not surprisingly, many leaders, academics, and scholars disagree about the best use of power and influence. "There is more conceptual confusion about influence processes than about any other facet of leadership."[30] First this section presents a brief discussion of where influence "exists" for a person; it is followed by a discussion on group affiliation, and then influence as a concept is explored.

Subordinates in health organizations look to leaders, and especially senior executives, as champions and sources of inspiration. Inspirational motivation in health organizations can be achieved when the leader passionately believes in the vision and is able to motivate others through this passion. The leadership team plays an important role in ensuring the success of the organization. This team determines the direction of the organization, while also ensuring that the details behind each event are managed well. Leaders have the responsibility of being concerned about the task of the organization and the support of the organization's stakeholders. Successful health organizations have leaders who not only provide the overall vision for the organization, but also step in and play a pivotal role by motivating and recognizing the efforts of subordinates that contribute to success.[31]

Ethics and morality play a key role in motivating others as well; collectively, they represent a crucial characteristic for a leader to possess. The success of the organization may rise and fall on the perception of the community regarding the morals of the organization. Subordinates and the community expect leaders to use their best judgment and to do what is right. Although leadership distinctions may depend on the execution of skills and abilities, such as charisma, the distinction of authentic leadership rests heavily on perceptions of morality.[32] To gain widespread support, the organization must demonstrate the sincerity of its mission and stay true to the values it supports as an organization.

Locus of Control

To understand where or how people are motivated and inspired, it is important to recognize each person's perspective on influence. Rotter used a personality scale that measured locus of control orientation as a means of assessing influence.[33] People with a strong internal locus of control (a belief that they control their own destiny and success) orientation believe that events in their lives are determined more by their own actions than by chance or uncontrollable forces (leaders and managers tend to be "internals"). In contrast, people with a strong external control orientation believe that events are determined mostly by chance or fate and that they can do little to improve their lives. Research by Miller and Toulouse associated effective (leadership) management with (leaders) managers with an internal locus of control orientation.[34, 35] According to this research, some people are influenced inside themselves (internalizers) and some are influenced outside of themselves (externalizers). In reality, both an internalizer and an externalizer are present inside each person. As a health leader, it is important to understand those people you lead—specifically, to understand which subordinates are more internally oriented and which are more externally oriented.

Group Affiliation

Schutz's theory of affiliation suggests that individuals form groups in response to three kinds of needs:

- Inclusion need: need to be included
- Control need: need for status and power
- Affection need: need to give and receive warmth and closeness

These needs are cyclical; groups pass through observable phases of inclusion, control, and affection.[36] When a leader balances a subordinate's need for inclusion with his or her needs for control and affection within a group environment, the seeds of a powerful organizational or group culture are planted. In a study published in the research literature in 2007, charismatic leadership attributes used by leaders positively contributed to social identification processes and to social identity applied to the workplace.[37] This suggests that leaders can positively influence group affiliation.

Ideally, the leader's subordinate group will be formed into a cohesive team. The health leader's understanding and active use of the insight provided by Schutz's theory could prove very valuable in developing a high-performing, effective, and efficacious team.

Influence

In the simplest terms, leader influence on one or more subordinates may have one of three possible outcomes:

- *Commitment*: The person internally agrees with a decision or request from the leader and makes a great effort to carry out the request or implement the decision effectively.

- *Compliance*: The person is willing to do what the leader asks but is apathetic rather than enthusiastic about it and will make only a minimal effort. The leader has influenced the person's behavior but not the person's attitudes.

- *Resistance*: The person is opposed to the proposal or request, rather than merely indifferent about it, and actively tries to avoid carrying it out.[38]

Clearly, commitment is what every leader desires from each team member or members. The reason motivation is linked with inspiration is that leaders should communicate how the task or project or action is integrated with a subordinate's job activities and provide individualized consideration and concern for that subordinate.

Motivation Based in Social Exchange Theory: Exchange and Expectancy Theories

Social exchange theory requires that leaders must give something in exchange (e.g., higher salary, bonus, increased status) for improved or additional performance by subordinates. Under this theory, relationships can be described in terms of their rewards, costs, profits, and losses. As long as rewards exceed costs (group membership is profitable), group membership is attractive. In social exchange theory, cohesiveness of group members becomes a salient issue.

Exchange theory, as developed by Graen, emphasizes the interaction of the leader with the subordinate or supervised group. The leader exchanges resources, such as increased job or task choices and latitude, influence on decision making, and open communication, for members' commitment to higher involvement in organizational functioning.[39] Under this theory, the leader categorizes followers into two groups: (1) the cadre or in-group and (2) the hired hands or out-group. With the in-group, the leader allows greater subordinate choices and decision making that contribute to higher performance, lower propensity to quit, greater supervisory relationships, and greater job satisfaction. The out-group receives less latitude and, therefore, has poorer performance outcomes. Social exchange theory and the application of Graen's exchange theory are both salient factors in leadership. With a basic understanding of exchange theory, Vroom's expectancy theory of motivation can be studied (refer to Chapter 3 as well).

According to Vroom's expectancy theory,[40] motivation depends on a person's belief that effort will lead to performance, and that performance will lead to rewards that are valued. If any of these three variables (expectancy, instrumentality, and valence) decrease in value, then motivation decreases. Likewise, as the variables increase in value, motivation increases. *Expectancy* is the subordinate's belief that effort will result in quality performance; it focuses on how the employee perceives the relationship between his or her effort and performance.

Instrumentality is the belief in the reward for quality performance; it refers to the perceived relationship between performance and outcome. *Valence* is the level of self-satisfaction in the reward and in the quality performance. In other words, how valuable is the outcome? Does the person think if he or she tries hard, the individual can achieve the outcome, and does the person think he or she can really achieve the outcome?

Social exchange theories and models are closely integrated with goal setting, the subject of the next subsection.

Goal Setting Theory: A Motivational Theory

As described in Chapter 3, goal setting theory,[41–43] which was originally developed by Edwin Locke, is an effective motivational and inspirational leadership approach. Goals are the aim of an action or behavior. They can be set for any verifiable or measurable outcome. "Goals provide order and structure, measure progress, give a sense of achievement, and provide closure."[44] Locke's basic assumption is that goals are immediate regulators of human action. An individual synthesizes direction, effort, and persistence to accomplish goals (**Figure 5–1**).

To maximize the effectiveness of goal setting, specific and challenging goals should be established to focus action and effort over time so as to accomplish tasks. From 1968 to 1980, 90 percent of all studies conducted in this area showed that specific, well-defined, and challenging goals led to greater improvements in performance as compared to vague and easy goals.[45] Individuals must commit to set goals to produce results; the more difficult (challenging yet reasonable) the goal, the better the individual will perform.

Individuals need leadership support (feedback, reward mechanisms, and required resources [time, training, and material goods]) to maximize performance when applying goal setting. "Goal setting and regular communication increase the challenge of the job, make it clear to workers precisely what they are expected to do, and deliver a sense of pride and achievement."[46] Locke suggests seven steps to follow to apply and optimize goal setting:

1. Specify objectives or tasks to be done.
2. Specify how performance will be measured.

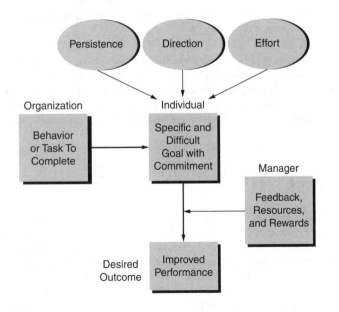

FIGURE 5–1   Locke's Goal Setting Theory Constructs and Application

3. Specify the standard to be reached.

4. Specify the time frame involved.

5. Prioritize goals.

6. Rate goals as to difficulty and importance.

7. Determine the coordination requirements.[47]

Leaders must ensure that the goals they set do not conflict with one another or with organizational goals. For groups, every group member should have verifiable specific goals, as well as an overall group goal to counter social loafing. Smaller groups (three to eight people) are more effective than larger ones in goal setting.[48] The use of management by objectives (MBO) is an approach to utilize goal setting[49] by leaders, whereby mutually acceptable goals can be developed with subordinates.[50] Locke's model coupled with SMART goals is an excellent model; SMART is an acronym for specific, measurable, attainable, relevant and time-bound.[51]

Leaders should be cognizant of risks of goal setting, which include excessive risk taking, and excessive competitiveness. Indeed, goal failure can reduce subordinate confidence and create unwanted stress. However, the benefits of goal setting outweigh the negative potential aspects of applying the theory. "Goal-setting theories provide specific explanations for why people are motivated. Difficult, specific, and mutually developed goals will assist individuals in being motivated. Although goal setting is extremely useful, many individuals are motivated more by climate [current atmosphere or 'feeling' of the workplace; an easily changed phenomenon], culture, and affiliation."[52]

Goal setting integrates well with other motivational theories. Although goal setting is a principal component of many motivational and performance theories, research in this genre has largely focused on locus of control influences and expectancy theory relationships. For the health leader, the merging or synthesis of related theories provides a powerful repertoire for utilization in a multitude of situations. Following are some examples of results from the evaluation of merged theories:

■ Considering the theory of locus of control, internalizers tend to have better performance than externalizers with regard to goal setting and applying goal setting.[53]

■ In the merger of expectancy theory and goal setting theory, goal setting is negatively related to valence (setting low-level goals does not satisfy individuals as well as setting high-level goals) and instrumentality is positively related to goal setting (difficult goals give the individual a greater sense of achievement, self-efficacy, and skill improvement than easy goals).[54]

Clearly, motivation and influence are critical to leadership success. The understanding, application, and enhanced skill and ability a leader gains by using applied theories such as goal setting are invaluable. Of course, as in motivation and influence competence, network building, interpersonal relationship building, and communication competencies are also vital to leadership. Basics concepts of leadership network building, interpersonal relationship building, personal development, and communication are discussed next.

FORMING RELATIONSHIPS, NETWORKS, AND ALLIANCES

Leaders are rarely successful in any organization without the assistance of positive relationships and networks. Knowledge and education can only help an individual achieve certain levels of success. The ability to build relationships and networks is critically important at early stages of leadership development. However, as the junior leader emerges from initial leader development jobs into more responsible and complex positions in dynamic organizations, his or her success is no longer a function of skills and tools as much as the ability to influence the behaviors of those outside the organization; outside stakeholders form the basis for networks and alliances in the organizational environment.[55, 56] In support of this notion, Mintzberg found that leaders spend 44 percent of their time dealing with outside agents and stakeholders, and the rest of their time talking to internal (or other) elements associated with organizational survival.[57, 58]

For health organizations, policies are official expressions and, at least, implied guidelines of expected behavior, decision making, and thinking within the organization. Because policies help organizations attain objectives, they must be consistent with the health organization's mission. However, when determining policies, health organizations must take into account the needs of the stakeholders who make up outside networks and alliances. These external stakeholders include the community, patients, providers, and insurers.

Stakeholders are constituents with a vested interest in the affairs and actions of health organizations. They include individuals, groups, and organizations affected by the health organization's decisions and actions. A well-thought-out and implemented philosophy about stakeholders is a prerequisite to a health organization's strategic planning effort, resource allocation and utilization, customer service strategies, and ability to cope with the external environment in general. Stakeholders can be classified into three groups:

- *Internal stakeholders* "operate entirely within the bounds of the organization and typically include management and professional and nonprofessional staff."[59]

- *Interface stakeholders* "function both internally and externally to the organization" and include medical staff, the governing body, and stockholders in the case of for-profit health organizations.

- *External stakeholders*, such as suppliers, patients, and third-party payers, including government entities and officials, interact with the organization, provide resources, or use services of the organization. The health organization needs this stakeholder group to survive. Other external stakeholders include competitors, special-interest groups, local communities, labor organizations, and regulatory and accrediting agencies.

Health organizations must assess stakeholders to determine which ones are most important, which ones pose potential threats, and which ones have the potential to cooperate with the health organization. Such an assessment suggests appropriate health organization behavior toward stakeholders, ranging from ignoring to negotiating to co-opting and cooperating. Asking a stakeholder group that the health organization has previously ignored to assist the organization with significant influence or resources would be futile. The assessment of stakeholders should also capture conflicting priorities, needs, demands, incentives, and political and financial pressures as related to the association with the health organization.

Balancing the demands of multiple stakeholders with different interests is a major challenge. Levey and Hill suggest that the need for health organization (leaders) managers to balance demands can pose "moral dilemmas arising from responsibilities to patients, governing boards, (professional) staff, and community."[60] Balancing these demands maintains ethical values and social responsibility and prevents inappropriate demands made by single-interest stakeholders from predominating.

The stakeholder philosophy should be consistent with continuous quality improvement. "For example, patients as consumers were passive stakeholders until this decade."[61] Patients are major stakeholders, as are third-party payers; both aggressively seek to influence the health organization. External stakeholders are a fact of life; responding to their legitimate interests while minimizing the effects of inappropriate demands is necessary.

Health organizations are dynamic, heterogeneous entities composed of numerous sub-organizations and interdependent processes. These linkages, when changed, affect other internal departments as well as the external environment. Various types of health organizations are found in both the private (owned by private individuals or groups) and public (owned by government) sectors. Health organizations may be institutions, the most prominent of which are hospitals and nursing facilities, or they may be programs and agencies such as public health departments and visiting nurse associations. All interact with, influence, and depend on their internal environments to provide the range of health services that, in turn, interact with, influence, and depend on the external environment that the organization serves.

In earlier eras, traditional approaches to leadership development were based on the notion that an individual's formal education prior to employment would provide enough learning to span an entire career. Today, however, restructuring efforts, coupled with continuous environmental and technological change, have contributed to rapid job obsolescence at all organizational levels; as a result, leaders need to rely more on outside relationships to ensure organizational success.[62] This emerging focus on managing alliances and networks mandates that leadership development efforts concentrate as much on networking across the entire organization with stakeholders as on the technical requirements of leadership.

Networks can be seen as living systems that adapt and change over time. As more individuals and groups join the network, they become dependent on one another for "group" survival and future growth.[63] If one area of a network is threatened, other partners in the alliance may be less likely to abandon "one of their own" and move off to recruit new replacements if there is a friendship in place. While relationship and network building may be difficult for many early careerists to understand and embrace, the practical reality of working and operating in the health environment requires a formal and informal network to achieve results. This need usually becomes apparent during the first few months of a new position. The application of the knowledge, skills, and abilities presented in this text will assist you in dealing with these kinds of real-world situations as they arise in the workplace.

Health organizations establish supply chains; such a chain is both a network and an alliance between two or more organizations. In today's collaborative, customer-driven, networked economy, forming and sustaining strategic business relationships with customers, suppliers, and partners has become a mission-critical imperative. If done well, the creation of collaborative relationships will lead to greater success and profitability for the organizations involved. As with all other aspects of business, specific steps are followed in forming these relationships—namely, planning, preparing, interaction, and analysis and refinement. These relationships are complex and require investigation and consideration of what each party wants out of the relationship.[64]

Formal and Informal Networks

The support of formal and informal networks—that is, groups of individuals connected in some way—is important for the leader to perform his or her duties. Formal professional networks include peers and superiors at the health organization as well as professional links to members of associations to which the leader belongs. Informal networks tend to be associated with friendship and longevity. Internal networks in the health organization assist leadership to accomplish goals and objectives as well as to move the organizational culture toward the desired state. External networks within the health professions and in the community are also important for career progression and health organization integration and acceptance in the communities served. The basis of building networks, whether internal or network, is interpersonal relationships.

Formal networks in the workplace tend to mirror an organizational wire diagram or organizational structure diagram. These relationships are generally supervisory in nature and carry with them an annual performance appraisal of some sort.

Health leaders in the higher positions can be great leaders—or, unfortunately, not-so-great leaders. If you encounter great leaders, learn from them. With not-so-great leaders, look to them to learn what *not* to do. Some leaders in the upper echelons of the hierarchy may not lead through charisma, motivation, and values-driven philosophies, but rather use coercion and legitimacy of position to manipulate their subordinates. Leaders of this sort do not care about or know the feelings of those under them. They focus only on organizational outcomes and lead through a bottom-line mentality. It may be difficult to work for such leaders; however, for those in job-lock situations with few options for employment elsewhere, the legitimate and coercive boss can dominate a formal network of subordinates for years, with his or her power going unchecked.[65, 66] What is important, when working under a not-so-good leader, is to be a great leader to those who follow you and are subordinate to you. You can be a great leader at whatever level you hold a position.

Informal networks are relationships with others within or outside the health organization that exist through mutual understanding. They are based on the strengths and values of each member of the informal group and the shared aspiration of members' success. Such may be the case with the local community hospital or health organization and the local entity itself. For example, the president of a local health organization cooperative or association benefits from the wide participation of local affiliated hospitals. The larger the network, the more legitimacy and creditability the cooperative or association may have among its peers in the community when it comes time to lobby local government for changes in policy or recognition of its members. In turn, the chief executive officers (CEOs) of the local hospitals and healthcare networks benefit from the opportunity to ally with a large assortment of peers and stakeholders in the local community and establish alliances to achieve various economies of scales on issues, resulting in better outcomes for both parties.[67, 68]

From an individual perspective, the same lesson may be applied to the personal level within an organization. The locally elected union representative may have formal reporting relationships within the vertically integrated facility itself; however, if the internal union leader and the legitimately appointed CEO do not have a positive relationship, contract negotiations and employee complaints may result in less than cordial and collegial discussions. In the worst-case scenario, risk management issues may evolve into lawsuits and litigation rather than leading to open discussion, problem solving, arbitration, and mediation.[69, 70]

From a more pragmatic perspective, the essential tasks of many leaders in nonprofit health organizations may include fundraising and lobbying state and local officials for funding. While a CEO may be able to justify needs and budget expenses to outside agents and stakeholders, many CEOs of these types of organizations find that it is their ability to influence and leverage personal relationships that results in the advantageous distribution of funds and the personal contributions of charitable donors.[71] Given this factor, organizational survival may depend as much on the CEO's informal professional network as on the development of strategic plans and leadership of internal subordinates.

Interpersonal Relationships[72]

Building relationships while in a leadership role is not always easy. Nevertheless, you can build relationships in a professional manner while maintaining your position of power and authority. If honesty, inclusion, and sincerity (the building blocks of trust) are the basis of your quality communication, and if that communication is culturally competent, then you can maintain your role while building relationships. You can gauge the nature of each relationship based on disclosure levels; leaders must consciously draw the line when determining their personal level of disclosure. Disclosing too much or too soon or too often can reduce your position power and authority; being personally "disclosure conservative" is a good initial approach when building new relationships.

For health leaders (or any other leaders, for that matter), interpersonal relationships are required, are beneficial, and enhance leadership capability and success. Certain elements or factors facilitate improved, positive, and mutually beneficial relationships. In 1989, Yukl proposed a taxonomy of managerial behaviors in which one of the four major domains of managerial life was "building relationships"; in this construct, managing conflict, team building, networking, supporting, developing, and mentoring were the actual behaviors and activities leaders were recommended to engage in to strengthen relationships.[73] A health organization leader should establish, enhance, and grow relationships with a myriad of organizational stakeholders both internal and external to the organization. There is no better method to build relationships than going to visit people in their own environment or location; this kind of "management by walking around" is a powerful approach.

The next subsection provides an overview of four key factors that will enhance relationships. Each factor described has monumental importance, though many factors play a role in forging and maintaining solid relationships.

Factors to Strengthen Relationships

A *relationship* encompasses the feelings, roles, norms, status, and trust that both affect and reflect the quality of communication between members of a group.[74] Relational communication theorists assert that every message has both a *content* and *relationship* dimension:

- Content contains specific information conveyed to someone.
- Relationship messages provide hints about whether the sender/receiver likes or dislikes the other person.

Communicating with someone in a manner that provides both content and positive relationship information is important. Language, tone, and nonverbal communication all work together to provide communicative meaning that is interpreted by another person. Consider the following points about nonverbal communication:[75, 76]

- Nonverbal communication is more prevalent than verbal communication and consists of the following elements:
  - Eye contact
  - Facial expressions
  - Body posture
  - Movement

- People believe nonverbal communication more than verbal communication.
  - Sixty-five percent of meaning is derived from nonverbal communication.
- People communicate emotions primarily through nonverbal communication.
  - Ninety-five percent of emotions are communicated nonverbally.

Frequency of communication that is timely, useful, accurate, and in reasonable quantity is needed to reinforce and validate the relationship. Thus one important factor in developing quality interpersonal relationships is *quality communication of sufficient and desired frequency.*

A second factor is *disclosure*, which was mentioned briefly earlier in this chapter. Disclosure relates to the type of information you and the other person in the relationship share with each other; disclosure is one factor that can help you "measure" or evaluate the depth and breadth of a relationship. The "deeper" the information disclosed, the closer the bond of the relationship. Also, the broader the topics of information and experience sharing (e.g., family, work, fishing together, or playing golf) between people, the closer the bond of the relationship. Disclosure or self-disclosure is strongly and positively correlated with trust; that is, more trust means more disclosure. Again, trust starts with quality communication.

Self-disclosure can be categorized and measured. In Powell's model,[77] level 5 illustrates a weak relationship bond, whereas level 1 shows a strong relationship bond:

- Level 5: cliché communication
- Level 4: facts and biographical information
- Level 3: personal attitudes and ideas
- Level 2: personal feelings
- Level 1: peak communication (rare; usually with family or close friends)

Self-disclosure can be summarized as having the following characteristics:[78]

- A function of ongoing relationships
- Reciprocal
- Timed to what is happening in the relationship (contextual/situational/relational)
- Should be relevant to what is happening among people present
- Usually moves in small increments

A third factor in building strong interpersonal relationships is *trust* (mentioned briefly in relation to self-disclosure). Trust is built and earned over time through honest interaction (communication and experiences). It is an essential component of a quality, positive relationship. Honesty, inclusion and sincerity are directly linked to building trust. *Honesty* means being truthful and open concerning important pieces of information that you share with another person. *Inclusion* entails including the other person in the relationship in activities and experiences that are important to the other person, to you, and to both of you. Inclusion is also about making sure the other person is part of the "group" in the organization. *Sincerity* is meaning what you say, meaning what you do, and not keeping record or account of the relationship (not keeping score). Over time, if honesty, inclusion, and sincerity are the basis of your interactions with others, positive and quality relationships will begin to grow.

A fourth factor in forging successful relationships is *cultural competence.* This factor is based not only on ethnical or national dimensions but also on socioeconomic factors. For instance, consider the cultural differences in surgeons as opposed to nurses as opposed to facility technicians or linen staff or consultants. Every stakeholder group, and every individual, has a varying culture of uniqueness. Understanding those cultural issues—"walking a mile in someone else's shoes"—is a factor important to building solid interpersonal relationships. Understanding and modifying your approach to relationship building and enhancement based on cultural differences will serve you well in leadership positions.

COMMUNICATION AND CULTURE

Health leaders need to have exceptional communication skills. They must learn the techniques for clarifying what someone else is saying and for being clear in their own communication. Mintzberg's study on managerial work revealed that managers' activity was characterized by "brevity, variety, and fragmentation"; managers were continually seeking information preferring oral communications to written reports.[79, 80] This finding applies to leaders as well. The preference for oral communication may be difficult for health leaders to enact, but nonetheless important. As an example of personal preference for oral communication, it has been noted that within the first seven months of the Barack Obama administration this President had more White House Press conferences than George W. Bush did in his eight years in the same position.[81] Although verbal communication may be time consuming, given employees', and the public's, need for such communication, it is a very valuable tool that is essential to achieve success.

Simply put, communication is the process of *acting on information*.[82] Communication contributes tremendously to the culture and climate of the health organization. A response—feedback—is an essential aspect of the communication process. Obstacles to communication, called noise, either in the channel or in the mind of the receiver, may contribute to an inaccurate understanding of the intended message. Communication is the main catalyst behind the motivation efforts and strategies utilized by leaders.[83] "Various management [leadership] practices, including goal setting, reinforcement, feedback, and evaluation, require communication."[84] There are three goals of communication:

- Understanding
- Achieving the intended effect
- Being ethical (moral)

Communication is a process of active transaction (transactive), which means messages are sent and received simultaneously. Everything you do or do not do, say or do not say, communicates something. You cannot *not* communicate. Communication media, which encompass what and how to communicate, is discussed next.

Media Richness Theory

Media richness theory,[85–87] which was originally developed by Daft and Lengel and then later updated with the inclusion of computer-mediated communication[88] by D'Ambra and Rice, explains and predicts why certain types of technologies, called media channels or media, are effective (or not effective) in communication efforts. This theory is important to health leaders, in that selecting the appropriate communication media channel, such as a face-to-face meeting, a telephone call, or an email, can predict the likelihood of successful communication to others, such as superiors, subordinates, and peers. Today, it is all too easy to send off an email. In many situations, however, email, as a media channel, is not a good choice to have your communication understood as you meant and, in that, receivers of your message may not take the proper action you expect.

In media richness theory, various media are placed on a "richness" continuum based on the following factors (**Figure 5–2**):

- Potential for instant feedback
- Verbal and nonverbal cues that can be processed by senders and receivers
- Use of natural language versus stilted or formal language
- Level of focus on individual versus a group or mass of people

This theory indicates that ambiguous or potentially ambiguous messages should be sent with richer media to reduce the level of potential (or actual) misunderstanding. *Ambiguity*—also called *equivocality*—is based on the ability of the receiver, in this context, to ask questions. In other words, does the receiver know which questions to ask and how to get started?

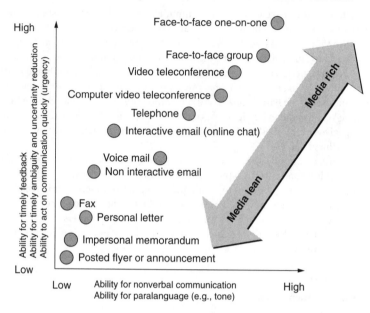

FIGURE 5–2   Media Richness Theory Media Channel Continuum

Different from ambiguity is uncertainty, although these two constructs complement each other. *Uncertainty* is "having the question answered" and having the appropriate information to proceed with an action, task, or project. "Uncertainty is a measure of the organization's ignorance of a value for a variable in the [information] space; equivocality is a measure of the organization's ignorance of whether a variable exists in the [information] space."[89] More information reduces uncertainty.[90] In the workplace, the more similar the work performed by subordinates (or the workforce in general) is, the more ambiguity exists, whereas the more dependent each segment of the work process or work flow is on other segments, the more uncertainty exists (**Figure 5–3**).

It is vital for leaders to reduce ambiguity and uncertainty to the greatest extent possible. The richer the media utilized, the greater the chance of leader communication success, the greater the chance of reducing ambiguity, and the greater the chance of reducing uncertainty. Unfortunately, richer media, such as face-to-face communication, cost more in terms of resources (e.g., time, travel, meeting space) than less rich media.

Health leaders will be more effective if they master the basics of the media richness theory. Following are some important points to reflect on for leadership success:

■ Select media channels to reduce ambiguity.

■ Select media channels to reduce uncertainty.

■ The more complex the issues, the more group members like face-to-face meetings.

■ Computer-mediated communication (CMC) deals more with tasks but less with group relationships.

■ CMC may increase polarization.

■ CMC works best with linear, structured tasks.

■ CMC increases individual "information processing" requirements.

■ People with technological skills gain more power in CMC group communication.

■ More cliques and coalitions form with CMC than with face-to-face communication.

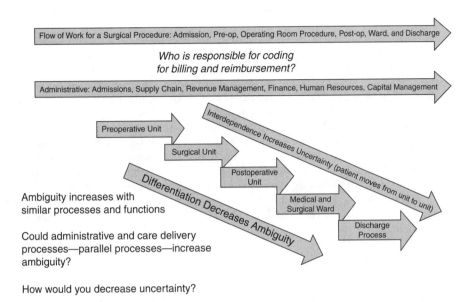

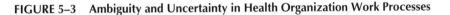

FIGURE 5–3   Ambiguity and Uncertainty in Health Organization Work Processes

Symbolic Convergence Theory

Bormann developed symbolic convergence theory,[91] which explains how certain types of communication function to shape a group's identity and culture, which in turn influence other dynamics such as norms, roles, and decision making. As part of this process, a group develops "fantasy" themes and stories. The key points are that groups develop a unique "group identity" (culture, personality) built on shared symbolic representations related to the group and that these cultures evolve through the adoption of fantasy themes or group stories. Stories provide insight into a group's culture, values, and identity.[92]

Communication Environments

Health organizations function best in communication environments that are open and honest, are free of fear and unnecessary anxiety, and support diverse teams of professionals. Gibb suggests that organizational communication environments promote either a defensive or a supportive communication climate. According to Beebe and Masterson, the following behaviors used by leaders, as well as by others (because subordinates tend to follow the leader's example), contribute to defensive or supportive communicative environments:

- Evaluative versus descriptive communication. Evaluation is "you" language; description is "I" language. Descriptive language leads to more trust and greater group cohesiveness.
- Problem orientation. Such an orientation is more effective in reducing defensiveness than attempting to control communication.
- Strategic versus spontaneous communication. Strategic communication (controlling) suggests manipulation creating distrust whereas spontaneous communication is inclusive.

- Superiority versus equality in communication. Supportive climates occur when participative and equity-based communication is used.

- Certainty versus provisionalism. Flexible, open, and genuine thinking fosters a more supportive climate than "knowing it all."[93]

The health organization's leader and leadership team—from the smallest unit leader all the way to the top of the hierarchy of the organization—set the example and develop the communication environment. The communication environment is a major foundational element of organizational culture. Which type of communication environment do you want to foster as a leader? Is one environment better at enabling more quality and productivity in the health organization than another environment?

Another communication environmental model suggests that a culture may be either disconfirming or confirming based on communicative responses. In essence, a confirming communicative response causes people to value themselves more. A disconfirming communicative response causes people to value themselves less. Health leaders should work to be much more confirming than disconfirming, an effort that takes practice and work. Think about which responses are confirming and which responses are disconfirming.

Listening is yet another valuable leadership skill. Listening contributes to a supporting and confirming communication environment to build a culture of achievement. It encompasses the following aspects of communication:

- Hearing: receiving the message as sent
- Analyzing: discerning the speaker's purpose
- Empathizing: seeing and understanding the speaker's viewpoint

"People seen as good leaders are also seen as good listeners."[94] A simple, yet effective listening model to practice and master has been summarized as follows: "1) stop, 2) look, 3) listen, 4) ask questions, 5) paraphrase content, and 6) paraphrase feelings."[95]

Sometimes, despite the best efforts at communication, conflict may arise. A leader's wise use of conflict management knowledge, skills, and abilities is essential for effectiveness, efficiency, and efficacy in a health organization, as discussed next.

Conflict Management[96]

Conflict is both inevitable and necessary for a vibrant organization. Health leaders will surely meet with situations of conflict and, therefore, must master conflict management styles and techniques. Five frameworks form the basis of modern conflict management theory and application: psychodynamic theory, field theory, experimental gaming theory, human relations theory, and intergroup conflict theory.

Conflict that is channeled and managed effectively is a rational route to change, improvement, thought creation, and organizational longevity, if not outright survival. The existence of conflict means there are opportunities to find improved alternative solutions to the current state of affairs. Of course, conflict can negatively affect the organization; even so, pessimism should not be the overriding default attitude assumed by leadership, management, or human existence for that matter. Leaders and managers can manage conflict and train others to apply skills and tools of conflict to achieve successful and improved outcomes in their professional lives. Leaders communicate meaning in everything they do. If messages are incongruent, goal conflicts and inconsistencies soon become part of the organizational culture.[97–99]

Hand-in-hand with conflict management are interpersonal relationships. Learning, as an organization, to constructively manage and succeed in conflict situations is a foundational construct of leadership and management.

Conflict occurs wherever interdependent people or groups (i.e., people or groups who depend on one another in some fashion for some need) have different goals[100] or aspirations of achievement amid an environment of scarce resources. Simply put, conflict arises when people, individually or in groups, must work together with other individuals or groups who have different goals, needs, or desires in an environment where a full complement of resources is not available to satisfy those goals, needs, or desires. We all live, work, and socialize with other people and share the limited resources available (rarely, if ever, are resources not limited), so conflict will happen and does happen to varying degrees of intensity. At one end of the spectrum, conflict can be a situation identified by two parties, such that those parties identify the problem and work together to solve it (problem-solving style). At the other end of the spectrum is violence (competing style) that inflicts bodily harm, such as in a war, which is the failure of conflict management.

Conflict is both an individual and group phenomenon. Western society tends to teach children to "smooth over" conflict. For example, you may remember a parent saying, "Play nice" or "You have to learn to share." Fairness, morals, social norms, and mores, along with the application of any of the multiple distributive justice methods, contribute to conflict situations when one party believes that a less than equitable distribution of resources has occurred.

Quality conflict management should produce the following outcomes:

- A wise agreement if an agreement is possible
- An efficient solution
  - An innovative solution potentially
  - Movement toward positive change in the organization
- A better relationship between the conflicting parties (or at least not damage the relationship)

Given these expectations, how can the health leader manage conflict? Basically, different situations require different styles; training organizational stakeholders on the effective use of conflict styles is also imperative. Conflict occurs due to differing preferences and nuances, over resources, differing values, difficult relationships, and differing perceptions. Primary tension (initial conflict over an issue or difference) is followed by secondary tension (conflict over the process for actually dealing with the issue of difference), and both require leadership intervention, conflict management, and conflict styles training of the conflicting parties (the preference is to train all subordinates and staff). "Groupthink," a negative group decision, occurs when there is no conflict (**Figure 5–4**).

Conflict Styles

Six basic conflict management styles have been identified.[101–106] Although each person has a dominant or primary style and a secondary style that are relatively stable (like personality style), all six styles can be learned,

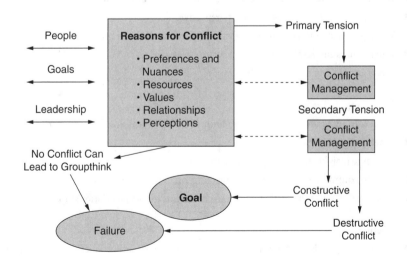

FIGURE 5–4   Conflict Illustrated

applied, and mastered. Conflict styles are a learning skill set. The more you learn and practice, the more flexible you will be in conflict situations. Later in this chapter, a decision tree is shown that can help you select which conflict style to use based on the situation (by answering several yes/no questions). It is imperative to understand and be able to apply different conflict styles because situations will differ daily.

The six styles presented here represent an amalgam of multiple scholars' work created for purposes of expanding your knowledge:

1. Accommodating
2. Avoiding
3. Collaborating
4. Competing
5. Compromising
6. Problem solving

The best style to use in any case depends on the situation. It is important to note that during conflict situations, one party may select (knowing or unknowingly) one style and the other party may select a different style. Only in problem solving do both parties knowingly choose that style and work together. The following summaries identify the situational context associated with each conflict management style.

Accommodating

- When you find you are wrong; to allow a better position to be heard, to learn, and to show your reasonableness
- When issues are more important to others than to you; to satisfy others and maintain cooperation
- To build social capital for later issues
- To minimize your losses when you are outmatched and losing the conflict
- When harmony and stability are especially important
- To allow subordinates to develop by learning from their mistakes

Avoiding

- When an issue is trivial or more important issues are pressing
- When you perceive no chance of satisfying your needs
- When the potential disruption outweighs the benefits of resolution
- To let people cool down and regain perspective
- When gathering information supersedes immediate decision making
- When others can resolve the conflict more effectively
- When issues seem a result of other issues

Collaborating

- To find an integrative solution when both sets of concerns are too important to be compromised
- When your objective is to learn
- To merge insights from people with different perspectives
- To gain commitment by incorporating concerns into a consensus
- To work through feelings that have harmed an interpersonal relationship

Competing

- When quick, decisive action is vital (e.g., emergency situations such as a disaster or terrorism incident or accident)
- On important issues where unpopular actions need implementing (e.g., cost cutting, enforcing unpopular rules, discipline)

- On issues vital to company welfare and survival when you know you are right
- Against people who take advantage of noncompetitive behavior

Compromising

- When goals are important, but not worth the effort or potential disruption of competing
- When opponents with equal power are committed to mutually exclusive goals
- To achieve temporary settlements to complex issues
- To arrive at expedient solutions under time pressure
- As a backup when collaboration or competition is unsuccessful

Problem Solving

- May not always work (it takes two to make this style work)
- Requires the identification of a broader range of strategies
- Points for problem solving:
  - Both parties have a vested interest in the outcome (the resolution)
  - Both parties believe a better solution can be achieved through problem-based collaboration
  - Both parties recognize that the problem is caused by the relationship, not the people involved
  - The focus is on solving the problem, not on accommodating differing views
  - Both parties are flexible
  - Both parties understand that all solutions have positive and negative aspects
  - Both parties understand each other's issues
  - The problem is looked at objectively, not personally
  - Both parties are knowledgeable about conflict management
  - Allowing everyone to "save face" is important
  - Successful outcomes are celebrated openly

The various conflict management styles should be used contingently based on the situation that presents itself in conflict environments. The dynamic nature of healthcare organizations requires leaders to become competent in using each conflict style. Again, training organizational stakeholders is also critically important. To show the contingent nature of conflict styles, a merging with a well-known leadership model is highlighted in **Figure 5–5**. From a leadership contingency perspective, it might be helpful to review the results of the Ohio State

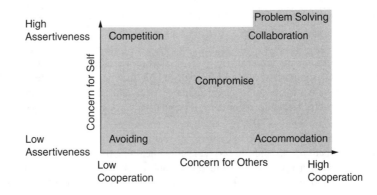

FIGURE 5–5   Conflict Styles Regarding Concern for Self and Others
Source: This figure is an aggregation of multiple scholars' work[96–101] and a modification of the leadership studies at Ohio State and Michigan University accredited to Stogdill and Likert. For the leadership component, Concern for Task was replaced by Concern for Others.

and Michigan Leadership studies, where conflict management styles can be arrayed as shown in the figure, similar to leadership styles.

Essential steps for leaders in conflict management follow. When you are in the early stages of conflict, you should take these steps:

- Stay calm and rational.
- Use facts (do your homework).
- Understand the resource implications and limitations surrounding the conflict.
- Listen to how you feel and know what you want or need.
- Try to imagine what the other(s) feel, want, and need.
- Use a process to select a strategy such as the decision tree method (discussed later).
- Rehearse your strategy.
- Be prepared to modify your approach if necessary.

When you are in the midst of conflict, keep these tenets in mind:

- Separate the people from the problem or conflict as much as possible.
- Focus on interests, not positions.
- Avoid always having a "bottom line."
- Think about the worst and best solutions and know what you can "live with."
- Generate several possibilities before deciding what to do.
- Insist that the result (resolution) be based on some objective standard.

Negotiation is similar to conflict resolution. In fact, Fisher, Ury, and Patton's 1991 work, *Getting to Yes: Negotiating Agreement Without Giving In, Second Edition*, contains some especially salient points for conflict management. These recommendations reinforce guidelines presented earlier in this chapter and lean toward the problem-solving style of conflict:[107]

- Do not bargain over positions.
- Separate the people from the problem.
- Focus on interests, not positions.
- Invent options for mutual gain.
- Insist on using objective criteria to resolve the issue.
- Use your "best alternative to a negotiated agreement." (What is the worst-case scenario if nothing is resolved?)
- Get the other party to negotiate.

Next, we turn our attention to the process of selecting a conflict style based on the situation. With six styles to select from, it is important to study all of them and become familiar with the styles so that the selection method—a decision tree—becomes understandable. Remember that five styles are under your "control," while the sixth style, problem solving, requires that both parties consciously agree to select that style.

Conflict Style Selection

Selecting a conflict style depends on several factors, including the interpersonal relationship with others (that is, those in the conflict against you), resources available (such as time), resources not available, and importance of the issues at hand. In the decision tree model, these factors take the form of high/yes or low/no answers to the following questions:

1. Is (are) the issue (issues) important to you?
2. Is (are) the issue (issues) important to the other party?

3. Is the relationship with the other party important to you?

4. How much time is available and how much pressure/stress is there to come to resolution? (With this question, an answer of "high" means high pressure.)

5. How much do you trust the other party?

To obtain an overview of the decision tree process, examine **Figure 5–6**, noting the questions at the top of the graphic and the associated high/yes and low/no answers to each of these questions. Follow the path until you come to a conflict management style that is recommended given the conflict situation.

An example illustrating two points—use of the decision tree and cautionary notes associated with each style—is provided below. In this scenario, you are in a conflict situation with another employee at the hospital. You have prepared yourself by reviewing all the points made previously in this chapter. Now you answer the questions based on the decision tree model (follow along on the decision tree in Figure 5–6):

1. Is the issue important to you? *You determine the answer is "low."*

2. Is the issue important to the other party? *You determine the answer is "high." (Why else would this person make such a big deal out of it?)*

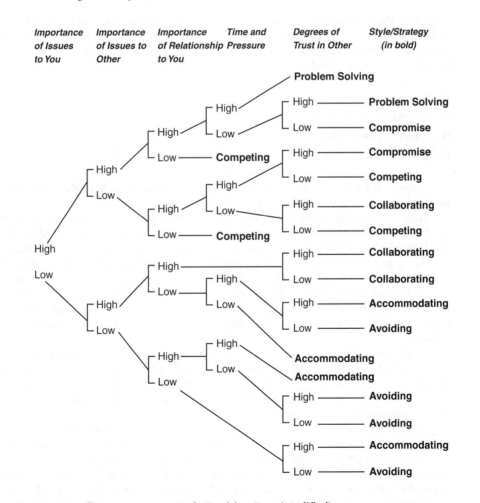

FIGURE 5–6   Conflict Management Style Decision Tree (Modified)
Source: Modified from Folger, J. P, Poole, M. S., & Stutman, R. K. (1997). *Working through conflict: Strategies for relationships, groups, and organizations* (3rd ed.). New York: Addison-Wesley Educational Publishers, p. 201.

3. Is the relationship with the other party important to you? *You determine the answer is "low." (Caution: How does this equate to using the avoiding style? Eventually, the avoidance style will cause the relationship with the other person or party to deteriorate.)*

4. How much time is available and how much pressure/stress is there to come to resolution? *You determine there is "high pressure" to come to resolution.*

5. How much do you trust the other party? *You determine you do not really trust the other person, so the answer is "low."*

6. Outcome: The style recommended is the avoiding style.

Conflict management is a critical and necessary skill that includes both technical (styles and decision tree) and relationship (communication and trust building) components. Conflict is a state of nature; hence the application of conflict styles requires good judgment on the leader's part.

Overview of Culture

Culture is a learned system of knowledge, behavior, attitudes, beliefs, values, and norms that are shared by a group of people.[108, 109] Culture is a difference that makes a difference.[110] Cultural differences have been classified (initially from the work of Hofstede) into the following categories (four categories are presented here, though several more are possible):

■ Language
■ Context (high versus low)
■ Contact (high versus low)
■ Time (monochronic versus polychronic)

Language is the structure, rules, and annunciation of symbols. Spanish, English, Mandarin Chinese, German, and Flemish are examples of language.

High-context cultures place more emphasis on nonverbal communication; physical context is important in interpreting the message and the stress is on the receiver of a message to understand the intended meaning (**Figure 5–7**). Low-context cultures place more emphasis on verbal expression; the sender is responsible for relaying meaning to the receiver verbally. Sometimes, people from a high-context culture will find those from a low-context culture less credible or trustworthy. Someone from a low-context culture may be more likely to make explicit requests for information ("Talk to me," "Do you know what I mean?"). In contrast, a person from a high-context culture expects communication to be more indirect and relies on more implicit cues.[111] People from high-context cultures may consider a low-context person overbearing, dominant, and talkative.

Contact preferences among cultures differ as well. People from some cultures are more comfortable being touched or being in close proximity to others (high contact), whereas some people want more personal space, typically have less eye contact, and are uncomfortable with being touched by others (low contact). Contact, as a variable, is similar to the notion of personal and social space. Some people want larger areas of "space," while others are comfortable with less "space."

Monochronic and polychronic cultures differ with perceptions and use of time. Monochronic cultures are precise; time is to be used and manipulated. Polychronic cultures are not as precise on time; time is what it is, events flow in their intended pattern as they happen. It is not unusual to have a monochronic culture person arrive at a scheduled meeting 5 minutes early, only to be irritated and upset by the time a polychronic culture person arrives 30 minutes past the scheduled time. Although organizational rules such as adherence to schedules (organizational coupling) are important, some understanding of time perception differences can reduce potential "anger" when people from differing cultural perspectives understand the perceptions of one another. Thus

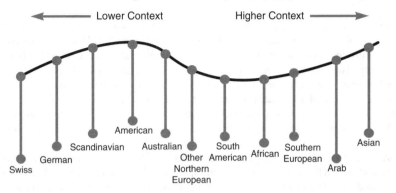

FIGURE 5–7   High- Versus Low-Context Cultures Continuum
Source: Beebe, S. A., & Masterson, J. T. (1997). *Communicating in small groups: Principles and practices* (5th ed.). New York: Addison-Wesley Educational Publishers, pp. 152–158.

strategies to bridge cultural differences, specifically for communicative purposes, are important, as discussed next.

Bridging Cultural Differences in Communication

Individuals hold cultural assumptions when engaged in work within the health organization; this is particularly apparent when involved in group problem solving and decision making. "All communication, problem-solving, decision making, etc. . . . is filtered through the cultural perspective group members hold."[112] Beebe and Masterson recommend the following strategies to bridge cultural differences:

■ *Develop mindfulness.* Be consciously aware of cultural differences; your assumptions and other people's assumptions may be (and probably are) different.

■ *Be flexible.* You may have to adapt and change according to the perceptions and assumptions others hold.

■ *Tolerate uncertainty and ambiguity.* Be patient and tolerant.

■ *Resist stereotyping others and making negative judgments about others.* Do not be ethnocentric; ethnocentrism leads to defensive (not open or confirmatory or supportive) communication environments.

■ *Ask questions.* Develop common ground rules and ask for additional meaning (paraphrase and paraphrase feelings).

■ *Be other oriented.* Be empathetic and sensitive to others where the key is to bridge cultural differences.[113]

Just as there are global cultural differences, so there may be unit or discipline or location differences within the same industry and organization. The next section discusses this phenomenon.

Coordinated Management of Meaning

At the organizational or unit level, individuals and groups embody their own cultural identity; this is certainly true in health organizations. Coordinated management of meaning (CMM) is an interactional theory that focuses on how individuals organize, manage, and coordinate their meanings and actions with one another. This theory was developed by Pearce in 1976 and updated by Pearce and Cronen in 1980. "The theory proposes that the interpretation of a conversation or message will be shaped by the context or nature of the relationship between the interactants as well as the self-concept and culture of each individual."[114] Consider the cultural differences of operating room nurses and technicians and surgeons relative to physical therapists and therapy aides relative to pharmacists and pharmacy technicians while you review the constructs of this theory.

> *Cultural patterns* refer to a socially shaped framework for viewing the world and one's roles and actions within it. The second level, *life scripts*, specifically encompasses the individual's self-concept and expectations for what should happen to him or her. *Contracts* define and specify expectations of the particular relationship based on the kinds of episodes that occur within the relationship. *Episodes* define the kind of activity that occurs between individuals based on the kinds of and sequencing of messages being exchanged. *Speech acts* identify the intent of the speaker and *content* is the decoding of the substance of the message. *Raw sensory data* concern the audio and visual signals that reach the brain.[115]

This logical relationship between levels produces constitutive rules for determining meaning. Constitutive rules stipulate how meanings at one level determine meanings at another level. Regulative rules specify what is appropriate given the nature of the relationship, the episode, and what the other person has said. Thus the CCM theory may be connected to Rokeach's values–beliefs–attitudes model in the following way: (1) values link to cultural patterns and life scripts; (2) beliefs link to life scripts and contracts; and (3) attitudes link to contracts, episodes, and speech acts.

The CMM theory brings into focus practical elements of Shutz's theory of affiliation, communication environments and culture, media richness theory, and interpersonal relationships. It also has strong links to Bolman and Deal's reframing organizational leadership model (presented later in this text). Health leaders who understand motivation and influence and apply culturally sensitive communication approaches can effectively use motivation based theories and models, such as goal setting, to focus a multidisciplinary team of health professionals on the mission and vision of the organization in an effective, efficient, and efficacious manner. **Figures 5–8** and **5–9** graphically illustrate the CMM model and the hierarchy of how meaning impacts people from low (raw data) to high (cultural patterns within the model's continuum).

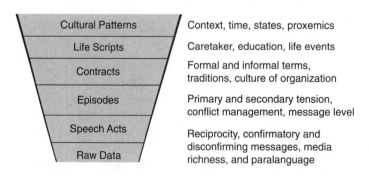

FIGURE 5–8   Coordinated Management of Meaning: Hierarchy
Source: Folger, J. P, Poole, M. S., & Stutman, R. K. (1997). *Working through conflict: Strategies for relationships, groups, and organizations* (3rd ed.). New York: Addison-Wesley Educational Publishers, p. 58.

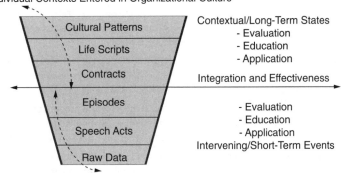

FIGURE 5–9   Coordinated Management of Meaning: Impact
Source: Beebe, S. A., & Masterson, J. T. (1997). *Communicating in small groups: Principles and practices* (5th ed.). New York: Addison-Wesley Educational Publishers.

SUMMARY

A leader has personal responsibility to maintain—if not advance—relevancy in his or her environment. To ensure that he or she does so, leadership competencies and the ability–job fit between a leader and his or her organizational environment are key considerations. Health leaders work in a highly complex environment with a very educated and interdisciplinary workforce. Leadership success is often based on the leader's capabilities related to motivation, influence, interpersonal relationships, communication, situational assessment, and inspiring teams.

Networks and alliances are key ways to expand the leader's sphere of influence. Health leaders must take into account the various factors that play roles in interpersonal relationship building, communication as an environment for leadership effectiveness, communication culture, and conflict management.

For the beginning careerist, using the applications, ideas, and principles presented in this chapter both for your leadership model and for practice will serve you well. Additionally, seeking out a mentor who clearly has earned the respect of others by establishing many quality relationships will benefit you for many years; learn from your mentor in the areas of motivation and inspiration, forming networks and alliances, developing interpersonal relationships, and managing conflict.

DISCUSSION QUESTIONS

1. How would you describe the complexity of the health industry in terms of workforce, environment, and societal expectations? How would a health leader's mastery of competencies, including situational assessment, interpersonal relationship building, influence processes, motivation, and communication capabilities, enable the leader to successfully navigate this complexity?

2. Explain how the complexity of the health workforce may lead to communication failure and conflict. Summarize ways to use quality communication and conflict management skills to successfully motivate subordinates, build interdisciplinary teams, and lead a health organization based on commitment rather than compliance or resistance.

3. Can you predict the outcomes of continuous use of the avoiding and competing strategies as compared to the compromising, accommodating, and problem-solving strategies in a health organization? What might be the outcomes of use of face-to-face meetings as compared to use of memoranda communication channel/media for ambiguous and urgent messages?

4. How would you analyze the health leader competencies in terms of the knowledge, skills, and abilities discussed in this chapter, differentiating the competencies presented here with those not discussed? Support your assessment.

5. How would you design, by combining several theories and models, an influence and motivation leadership model for use in health organizations focused on subordinate commitment? Could you modify this model for use with an interdisciplinary health team or group? Explain why this modification was utilized.

6. Evaluate competencies (knowledge, skills, and abilities) found in leadership practice concerning situation assessment, building interpersonal relationships, influence processes, motivation, and communication that are necessary to successfully lead health organizations; support your evaluation. How would you use those capabilities?

EXERCISES

1. Define the complexity of the health industry in terms of workforce and macro-environmental forces; label possible up-to-date and continuous information sources for the health workforce and macro-environmental factors that are affecting the health industry. Use a cost–quality–access model to determine the cumulative impact of several changes on the health industry.

2. In a three-page (or less) paper, distinguish potentially differing motivational factors for each major health workforce group and predict which applications of building interpersonal relationships, influence, and motivation theories or models would work best for each group.

3. In a two- to three-page paper, construct models of communication for a health organization that could be used by a leader for individuals, groups/teams, and the entire organization. As part of your discussion, demonstrate which elements of your models are similar and dissimilar.

4. Select two theories or models of influence and/or motivation. In a two-page paper, identify the constructs and leadership behaviors/actions, and analyze the effectiveness of the theories or models in a health organization setting for achieving commitment, achieving compliance, and achieving resistance. Relate components of quality leader communication to this analysis and illustrate whether they would result in changes to your outcomes.

5. In a two-page paper, explain how goal setting theory, expectancy theory, and locus of control work together; also, relate how a health leader can utilize the synthesis of these theories to have a productive workforce at the individual subordinate and team or group level.

6. In a two- to three-page paper, evaluate and justify your professional association's combined health leader's competencies considering the complexity of the health industry.

REFERENCES

1. Van der Werff, T. J., & CMC. (2009). Strategic planning for fun and profit. Retrieved July 27, 2009, from Global Future http://www.globalfuture.com/planning9.htm.

2. Choo, C. W. (2001, October). Environmental scanning as information seeking and organizational learning. *Information Research*, 7(1).

3. Griffith, J. R. (1999). *The well-managed healthcare organization* (4th ed.). Chicago: Health Administration Press, p. 1.

4. Rakich, J., Longest, B., & Darr, K. (1992). *Managing health services organizations.* Baltimore, MD: Health Professions Press, p. 17.

5. Rand Corporation. Retrieved May 11, 2009, from http://www.rand.org/cgi-bin/health/showab.cgi?key=1998_77&year=1998.

6. Harvard University School of Public Health. Retrieved May 11, 2009, from http://www.hsph.harvard.edu/news/press-releases/2008-releases/life-expectancy-worsening-or-stagnating-for-large-segment-of-the-us-population.html.

7. Centers for Disease Control and Prevention. Retrieved May 11, 2009, from http://www.cdc.gov/mmwr/preview/mmwrhtml/mm5206a2.htm.

8. Kotter, J. P. (1998). Leading change: Why transformation efforts fail. In *Harvard Business Review on change.* Boston: Harvard Business School Press, p. 7.

9. Health Resources and Services Administration, Bureau of Health Professions. Retrieved May 11, 2009, from http://bhpr.hrsa.gov/healthworkforce/reports/.

10. New York Center for Health Workforce Studies. (2006, October). *The United States health workforce profile.* Health Resources and Services Administration grant report. http:chws.albany.edu. Retrieved May 11, 2009, from http://bhpr.hrsa.gov/healthworkforce/reports/.

11. Hatch, M. J. (1993). The dynamics of organizational culture. *Academy of Management Review, 18,* 657–693.

12. Schneider, B. (1990). Organizational Climate and Culture, San Francisco, California: Jossey-Bass.

13. Hatch, note 11, pp. 657–693.

14. Retrieved May 13, 2009, from http://www.ache.org/aboutache.cfm.

15. Retrieved May 13, 2009, from http://www.mgma.com/about/.

16. Retrieved May 13, 2009, from http://www.aone.org/aone/about/home.html.

17. Retrieved May 13, 2009, from http://www.hfma.org/about/.

18. Retrieved May 13, 2009, from http://www.himss.org/ASP/aboutHimssHome.asp.

19. Retrieved May 13, 2009, from http://www.nchl.org/ns/about/aboutnchl.asp.

20. Retrieved May 13, 2009, from http://www.aupha.org/i4a/pages/index.cfm?pageid=3275.

21. Retrieved May 13, 2009, from http://www.aupha.org/i4a/pages/Index.cfm?pageID=3285.

22. Retrieved May 13, 2009, from http://www.aupha.org/i4a/pages/index.cfm?pageid=3518.

23. Retrieved May 13, 2009, from http://www.ceph.org/i4a/pages/index.cfm?pageid=1.

24. Retrieved May 13, 2009, from http://www.aacsb.edu/.

25. Retrieved May 12, 2009, from http://www.nwlink.com/~Donclark/hrd/bloom.html.

26. Retrieved May 12, 2009, from http://cs1.mcm.edu/~awyatt/csc3315/bloom.htm.

27. Retrieved May 12, 2009, from http://www.nwlink.com/~Donclark/hrd/bloom.html#cognitive.

28. Anderson, L. W., & Krathwohl, D. R. (Eds.). (2001). *A taxonomy for learning, teaching and assessing: A revision of Bloom's Taxonomy of educational objectives, complete edition.* New York: Longman, pp. 67–68.

29. Carnevale, A. P. (1991). *America and the new economy.* Washington, DC: Department of Labor.

30. Yukl, G. (1994). *Leadership in organizations* (3rd ed.). Englewood Cliffs, NJ: Prentice Hall, p. 193.

31. Sorcher, M., & Brant, J. (2002, February). Are you picking the right leaders? *Harvard Business Review,* p. 78.

32. Cooper, T. L. (1998). *The responsible administrator: An approach to ethics for the administrative role.* San Francisco: Jossey-Bass.

33. Rotter, J. B. (1966). Generalized expectancies for internal versus external control of reinforcement. *Psychological Monographs, 80,* 609.

34. Miller, D., & Toulouse, J. (1986). Chief executive personality and corporate strategy and structure in small firms. *Management Science, 32,* 1389–1409.

35. Miller, D., Ketsde Vries, M., & Toulouse, J. (1982). Locus of control and its relationship to strategy, environment, and structure. *Academy of Management Journal, 25,* 237–253.

36. Beebe, S. A., & Masterson, J. T. (1997). *Communicating in small groups: Principles and practices* (5th ed.). New York: Addison-Wesley Educational Publishers.

37. Cicero, L., & Pierro, A. (2007). Charismatic leadership and organizational outcomes: The mediating role of employees' work-group identification. *International Journal of Psychology, 42*(5), 297–306.

38. Yukl, note 30.

39. Graen, C. (1976). Role making processes within complex organizations. In M. D. Dunnette (Ed.), *Handbook of industrial and organizational psychology* (pp. 1201–1246). Chicago: Rand McNally.

40. Vroom, V. H. (1964). *Work and motivation.* New York: McGraw-Hill.

41. Locke, E. A. (1968, May). Toward a theory of task motivation and incentives. *Organizational Behavior and Human Performance,* pp. 157–189.

42. Locke, E. A., Shaw, K. N., Saari, L. M., & Latham, G. P. (1981). Goal setting and task performance: 1969–1980. *Psychological Bulletin, 90*(1), 125–152.

43. Locke, E. A., & Latham, G. P. (1984). *Goal setting: A motivational technique that works!* Englewood Cliffs, NJ: Prentice-Hall.

44. Quick, T. L. (1985). *The manager's motivation desk book.* New York: Wiley, p. 124.

45. Locke & Latham, note 43.

46. Rosenbaum, B. L. (1982). *How to motivate today's workers.* New York: Wiley, p. 103.

47. Locke & Latham, note 43.

48. Locke, E. A., & Chesney, A. A. (1991). Relationships among goal difficulty, business strategies, and performance on a complex management simulation task. *Academy of Management Journal, 34*(2), 400–424.

49. Latham, G. P., & Baldes, J. J. (1975). The practical significance of Locke's theory of goal setting. *Journal of Applied Psychology, 60,* 122–138.

50. Baron, R. A. (1983). *Behavior in organizations: Understanding and managing the human side of work.* Boston: Allyn & Bacon.

51. Value Based Management.net. (2007, May 23). Motivation and management: Vroom's expectancy theory. Retrieved July 27, 2009, from http://www.valuebasedmanagement.net/methods_vroom_expectancy_theory.html.

52. Harris, T. E. (1993). *Applied organizational communication: Perspectives, principles and pragmatics.* Hillsdale, NJ: Lawrence Erlbaum Associates, p. 454.

53. Locke et al., note 42.

54. Mento, A. J., Locke, E. A., & Klein, H. J. (1992). Relationship of goal level to valence and instrumentality. *Journal of Applied Psychology, 77*(4), 395–405.

55. Coppola, M. N., Erckenbrack, D., & Ledlow, G. R. (2009). Stakeholder dynamics. In J. A. Johnson (Ed.), *Health organizations: Theory, behavior, and development* (pp. 255 – 278). Sudbury, MA: Jones and Bartlett.

56. Vicere, A. A., & Fulmer, R. M. (1997). *Leadership development by design.* Boston: Harvard Business School Press.

57. Mintzberg, H. (1989). *Mintzberg on management: Inside our strange world of organizations.* New York: Free Press.

58. Mintzberg, H. (1973). *The nature of managerial work.* New York: Harper & Row.

59. Fottler, M. D., Blair, J. D., Whitehead, C. J., Laus, M. D., & Savage, G. T. (1989). Assessing key stakeholders: Who matters to hospitals and why? *Hospital & Health Services Administration, 34,* 527.

60. Levey, S., & Hill, J. (1986). Between survival and social responsibility: In search of an ethical balance. *Journal of Health Administration Education, 4,* 227.

61. Blair, J. D., & Whitehead, C. J. (1988). Too many on the seesaw: Stakeholder diagnosis and management for hospitals. *Hospital & Health Services Administration, 33,* 154.

62. Lawrence, J. (1999). Exceed your goals. *Hospital & Health Networks, 73*(10), 5–10.

63. Davis, S., & Meyer, C. (1999). *Blur: The speed of change in the connected economy.* New York: Warner Books.

64. Shuman, J., & Twombly, J. (2003, April). The link between entrepreneurial thinking and alliance management. Retrieved July 27, 2009, from The Rhythm of Business, http://docs.google.com/gview?a=v&q=cache:C8yD4L_x-oQJ:www.rhythmofbusiness.com/documents/news/ASAP_Alliances.pdf+forming+relationships,+networks,+alliances&hl=en&gl=us.

65. Harmaakorpi, V., & Niukkanen, H. (2007). Leadership in different kinds of regional development networks. *Baltic Journal of Management, 2*(1), 80–96.

66. Graen, G. B., & Graen, J. A. (2006). *Sharing network leadership.* Charlotte, North Carolina: IAP Press.

67. Levinson, H. (2003). Management by whose objectives? *Harvard Business Review, 81*(1), 107–116. Retrieved May 20, 2008, from http://ezproxy.library.capella.edu/login?url=http://search.ebscohost.com/login.aspx?direct=true&db=bth&AN=8796896&site=ehost-live.

68. Harmaakorpi & Niukkanen, note 65.

69. Lippitt, M. (2007). Fix the disconnect between strategy and execution. Retrieved April 13, 2008, from http://proquest.umi.com.library.capella.edu/pqdweb?did=1327907261&sid=3&Fmt=3&clientId=62763&RQT=309&VName=PQD.

70. Harmaakorpi & Niukkanen, note 65.

71. Grace, K. S. (2006). *Over goal! What you must know to excel at fundraising today.* Medfield, MA: Emerson & Church.

72. Ledlow, G. R. (2009). Conflict and interpersonal relations. In J. A. Johnson (Ed.), *Health organizations: Theory, behavior, and development* (pp. 158–163). Sudbury, MA: Jones and Bartlett.

73. Yukl, note 30.

74. Beebe & Masterson, note 36, p. 71.

75. O'Hair, D., Friedrich, G. W., Wiemann, J. M., & Wiemann, M. O. (1997). *Competent communication* (2nd ed.). New York: St. Martin's Press.

76. Beebe & Masterson, note 36.

77. Beebe & Masterson, note 36.

78. Beebe & Masterson, note 36.

79. Mintzberg, note 57.

80. Mintzberg, note 58.

81. *CBS Evening News.* (2009). Obama going prime time to help ailing health initiative. Retrieved July 25, 2009, from http://www.cbsnews.com/blogs/2009/07/22/politics/politicalhotsheet/entry5179382.shtml.

82. Beebe & Masterson, note 36, p. 3.

83. Cusella, L. P. (1987). Feedback, motivation, and performance. In F. M. Jablin, L. L. Putnam, K. H. Roberts, L. W. Porter (Eds.), *Handbook of organizational communication* (pp. 624–679). Newbury Park, CA: Sage.

84. Harris, note 52, p. 454.
85. Daft, R. L., Lengel, R. H., & Trevino, L. K. (1987). Message equivocality, media selection, and manager performance: Implications for information systems. *MIS Quarterly, 11*(3), 355–366.
86. Daft, R. L., & Lengel, R. H. (1986). Organizational information requirements, media richness, and structural design. *Management Science, 22*(5), 554–571.
87. Daft, R. L., & Wiginton, J. (1979). Language and organization. *Academy of Management Review, 4*(2), 179–191.
88. D'Ambra, J., & Rice, R. E. (1994). Multimethod approaches for the study of computer-mediated communication, equivocality, and media selection. *IEEE Transactions on Professional Communication, 37*(4), 231–339.
89. Daft & Lengel, note 86, p. 557.
90. Daft et al., note 85.
91. Beebe & Masterson, note 36.
92. Beebe & Masterson, note 36.
93. Beebe & Masterson, note 36.
94. Beebe & Masterson, note 36, p. 116.
95. Beebe & Masterson, note 36, pp. 116–117.
96. Ledlow, note 72.
97. Ledlow, G. R., Bradshaw, D. M., & Shockley, C. (2000). Primary care access improvement: An empowerment–interaction model. *Military Medicine, 165*(2), 390–395.
98. Ledlow, G., Cwiek, M., & Johnson, J. (2002). Dynamic culture leadership: Effective leader as both scientist and artist. In N. Delener & C. Chao (Eds.), *Global Business and Technology Association International Conference: Beyond boundaries: Challenges of leadership, innovation, integration and technology* (pp. 694–740). New York: Global Business and Technology Association.
99. Schein, E. H. (1999). *The corporate culture survival guide: Sense and nonsense about culture change.* San Francisco, CA: Jossey-Bass.
100. Folger, J. P, Poole, M. S., & Stutman, R. K. (1997). *Working through conflict: Strategies for relationships, groups, and organizations* (3rd ed.). New York: Longman.
101. Burton, J. (1990). *Conflict: Resolution and prevention.* New York: St. Martin's Press.
102. Cahn, D. (Ed.). (1990). *Intimates in conflict: A communication perspective.* Hillsdale, NJ: Lawrence Erlbaum Associates.
103. Canary, D. J., Cupach, W. R., & Messman, S. J. (1995). *Relationship conflict.* New York: Sage.
104. Cupach, W. R., & Canary, D. J. (1997). *Competence in interpersonal conflict.* New York: McGraw-Hill.
105. Folger et al., note 100.
106. Hocker, J. L., & Wilmot, W. W. (1995). *Interpersonal conflict* (4th ed.). Madison, WI: WCB Brown & Benchmark.
107. Fisher, R., Ury, W., & Patton, B. (1991). *Getting to yes: Negotiating agreement without giving in* (2nd ed.). New York: Penguin Books.
108. Schein, note 99.
109. Beebe & Masterson, note 36, p. 153.
110. Beebe & Masterson, note 36, p. 153.
111. Beebe & Masterson, note 36, pp. 155–156.
112. Beebe & Masterson, note 36, p. 199.
113. Beebe & Masterson, note 36.
114. Folger et al., note 100, p. 57.
115. Folger et al., note 100, p. 58.

CHAPTER

6

Leadership Competence II: Application of Skills, Tools, and Abilities

Thinking always ahead, thinking always of trying to do more, brings a state of mind in which nothing seems impossible.

Henry Ford

This chapter presents additional knowledge and empirically based skills and abilities (a leadership toolbox full of "tools") required for a health leader's success in organizational practice. Strategies for leaders in effecting planning, decision making, and training that result in positive outcomes are addressed; these strategies, in turn, result in practical leadership actions and applications based in "active" leadership.

LEARNING OBJECTIVES

1. Describe planning, decision making, and training in health organizations and provide examples of each.

2. Summarize the planning process and the decision-making process within the context of leadership.

3. Apply and relate at least two different decision-making models to a leadership situation.

4. Differentiate the levels or components of the planning process and distinguish each level or component from the others.

5. Plan and design a quality improvement program based on a system of rational decision making for a health organization.

6. Compare and contrast willful choice to garbage can models of decision making, training leaders to training staff, and cultural competence to ethics and morality.

PLANNING

Planning is an essential leadership skill that requires knowledge about planning and the ability to structure and develop a system of planning. Planning is an essential and critical component, such as in palliative care programs, to successful leadership; effective planning and consistent leadership practice are vital to linking the clinical and administrative domains.[1] Health leaders plan at all levels of an organization. Specifically, they plan the operational actions necessary within their area of responsibility to implement the senior leadership team's strategic or operational plans. Health leaders who can understand, apply, and evaluate planning will have advantages over those who haphazardly plan or fail to plan.

For some scholars, such as Yukl, planning is a step in decision making.[2] For others, planning is a cultural imperative and a method for leaders to guide the organization to its most effective, efficient, and efficacious outcomes.[3, 4] Planning occurs formally, informally, strategically (how the organization can best serve its purpose in the external environment), and operationally (how the internal capabilities and resources of an organization can be used effectively, efficiently, and efficaciously to achieve the strategies and goals of the organization as documented in the strategic plan).

A set of basic definitions will assist in understanding the differences in the term "planning":

- *Planning* is a process that uses macro- and micro-environmental factors and internal information to engage stakeholders to create a framework, template, and outline for section, branch, or organizational success. Planning can be strategic, operational, or a combination of both.

- *Strategic planning* is concerned with finding the best future for the organization and determining how the organization will evolve to realize that future. It is a *stream of organizational decisions* focused in a specific direction based on organizational values, strategies, and goals. The focus is on external considerations and how the organization can best serve the external markets' expectations, demands, and needs.

- *Operational planning* is about finding the best methods, processes, and systems to accomplish the mission/ purpose, strategies, goals, and objectives of the organization in the most effective, efficient, and efficacious way possible. The focus in operational planning concerns internal resources, systems, processes, methods, and considerations.

Planning is vital to the survival of the organization. Indeed, creating a plan is an investment in improving the organization. Improvement is realized through internal change and evolution. Developing and focusing the organization to best meet the needs and demands of its customers and others (stakeholders) that affect the organization lies at the heart of planning. Because the environment, technology, information, people, financing, and governmental policies and laws are constantly changing, the organization itself must evolve to survive, succeed, and prosper. Planning is a journey—but this journey must have a destination, and it must be planned. In other words, it is a planned journey forward in time. In that light, planning includes both a process (developing and achieving goals and objectives) and an outcome (the plan itself).

Planning is a process. This process involves moving an organization along a predetermined path based on its values. Similar to the decisions involved in planning a real-world trip (e.g., which road to take, which stops to make, and who will drive), the organizational planning process entails deciding which goals are important to the organization and which objectives must be met to reach those goals.

Planning has an outcome. This outcome paves the way to a better future state based on organizational values and the external environment. Improving effectiveness, efficiency, efficacy, customer satisfaction, employee satisfaction, financial performance, and many other possible improvements are a part of moving the organization to reach a better future state.

The desired future state constitutes the vision of the organization; the vision is what the combined staff of the organization strive to achieve. If you know where you are going, then planning the trip and getting commitment from your staff becomes much easier. Also, organizational resources (including your energy and time) can be devoted to reaching set goals and having a positive outcome (turning the vision of your organization into a reality).

In this light, the process comprises a journey that must be planned knowing that different ways of doing things, different stops, and different issues will be encountered along the way. The vision represents the final destination. The destination must be determined and the journey must be planned. As a health leader, you are critical in determining the vision (outcome/destination) and the process (journey/goals and objectives) that will ensure the organization reaches its intended vision.

For all health organizations, mergers, departmental restructuring, implementation of new technologies, and market changes may indicate a need for the organization to develop a strategic plan to support its overall plan. Strategic planning can be described as an organizational planning process that analyzes the current situation of an organization and forecasts how the organization will change or evolve over a specified period of time. The health leader is an integral part of a successful strategic plan. Strategic planning on the part of an organization and its leaders require both thought and action, however. In health organizations, strategic thought includes the "ideas, reasons, and processes for changing the future state of your organization."[5] Within the component of strategic thought exists the vision, intent, and planning affecting the path that the organization takes in moving toward its future.

If the strategic plan is a road map, then the organizational vision is the final destination, describing "where the organization is going." The vision depicts a perfect situation in which the future destination can be obtained. The health leader must energize his or her followers to "buy into" the vision so that the organization can begin its strategic journey on the correct path. The strategic vision must be tested and retested to ensure that it has won "buy-in" from all stakeholders (both external and internal).

A vision may require many drafts and revisions to ensure that the needs of all stakeholders are met. In the dynamic world of the health industry, leaders need to recognize that the strategic vision should be tangible. To be tangible, the vision should be stated in the form of concrete ideals rather than using generalizations, should identify a direct relationship between the organizational values and culture to the future direction of the organization, and should communicate a unique future to stakeholders.[6]

Once an organizational vision is developed, intent must be established. Intent describes how the organization will be affected if change does not occur. Organizational leaders must outline how these "impacts" or "crises" could potentially influence the viability of the organization. Examples of crises might include market changes, technological advances that cause older technology to become obsolete, personnel shortages, and decreased reimbursement from payers. From the road map perspective, the wrong intent is analogous to driving in the wrong direction without a road map.

Once the vision and intent have been established, the strategic plan needs to be developed; that is, from the road map perspective, the quickest, most efficient route must be drawn to the final destination (i.e., the vision). One can assume that a good plan will lead to an effective outcome—namely, achieving the vision.

Strategic thought is followed by the component of tactical action, which includes commitment, execution, and accountability. In the health industry, tactical action encompasses the feelings, practices, and metrics for changing the future state of the organization.[7] If strategic thought is the plan for the journey to reach the final destination, then tactical action is the journey itself, including the mechanism for getting there. Tactical action requires commitment within the organization, execution of the plan, and accountability for this effort within organizational leadership.

Commitment, like the strategic vision, requires "buy-in" by the organization and its internal and external stakeholders. It involves a relationship between organizational leaders and followers; in contrast, each party has a clear understanding of the strategic vision and his or her role in reaching this vision. Without commitment on all levels, it will be impossible to achieve the strategic vision effectively and efficiently. From a leadership perspective, a leader can foster commitment within his or her team by serving as a model and demonstrating a strong commitment to the plan and vision. A leader cannot expect to achieve buy-in from followers if he or she has not fully committed to the vision.

During the execution phase of the strategic plan, each team member performs his or her assigned duty. Without a strong, unified commitment, execution of the plan will be a dismal failure. It is the leader's responsibility to enhance motivation and maintain commitment within the team, particularly when team members encounter obstacles. The health leader must be supportive of his or her team members, supporting them by providing them with the needed skills, equipment, and materials to effectively carry out their roles in the plan. In many ways, the health leader's effort in this phase echoes the precepts of House's path–goal theory.

Leaders and followers require consistent feedback about performance during execution of the plan. To ensure that they receive this information, measures must be put in place to gauge successes (or lack thereof) during this time. Successes should be acknowledged between leaders and followers. After all, employees want to know that the plan is working correctly. Lack of success should be analyzed and modified to determine inconsistencies within the execution of the plan.

The Leader's Role in Planning

Most people look for leaders who have a vision and someone who can direct them in the path of the mission. There can be many leaders within a single organization, and each leader will have a vision for his or her own tasks or responsibilities. The morale of the organization can sometimes depend on the attitudes espoused by visionaries of the organization. Staff members of an organization look for the visionaries to lead by example. In planning, leadership should come from within the organization; the effort should be exciting, where followers are excited to follow. Health leaders provide the structure, process, macro direction, shared outcome for all stakeholders, motivation, accountability, influence, obstacle removal, resources, and persistence in the overall effort of *directing, staffing, organizing, controlling,* and *rewarding.*

Planning is the fundamental function of leadership from which all other outcomes are derived. The first step in planning is establishing the organizational situational assessment; the vision, mission, strategies, goals, objectives, and action steps are then developed. Without this structure and signposts as first steps, the organization cannot move forward.

The vision provides the motivational guidance for the organization and typically is defined and promoted by senior leadership. It explains how the organization intends to achieve its goals, whereas the mission defines why the organization pursues the goals it does. Both vision and mission are "directional strategies."

The mission statement is the organization's reason for being. It provides guidance in decision making as well, ensuring that the organization stays on the track that its leaders have predetermined. From the mission statement, strategies to achieve the mission and, ultimately, the vision are devised. Goals are broad statements of direction that come from strategies. This multilevel approach focuses and narrows effort for each section within the health organization. Objectives, in pursuit of achieving goals, are very specific.

Goals further refine the strategies focused on the mission. They are expected to be general, observable, challenging, and untimed.[8] Goals are general in nature; in contrast, objectives are highly specific. Notably, different perspectives often switch goals with objectives and objectives with goals. Whatever framework you select for your organization, try to be consistent. It is not important if goals are at a higher level than objectives, or vice versa; what matters is the process of planning—a planning and execution culture should grow and mature in your health organization. Erven promotes objective development within the "SMART" framework; to be SMART, objectives must be "specific, measurable, attainable, rewarding, and timed."

The phase in which action steps or tactics are established and implemented follows all of the preceding activity. Action steps or tactics represent a fifth level of planning; they provide the most specific approach for describing the *who, what, when, where,* and *how* elements of the activities needed to accomplish an objective.

Planning can be described as an ongoing process of thinking and implementing at multiple levels. At each level, health leaders engage in directing, staffing, organizing, and controlling. Along the way, such leaders must remember that "what gets measured gets done"; thus all planning objectives and action steps must be measurable, assigned to an accountable and responsible person, and set within a time period. Periodic progress reviews, either monthly or quarterly, are essential to see the movement toward success.

In addition to this effort of *directing, staffing, organization,* and *controlling, rewarding* is important. These five elements are crucial as leaders embrace the foundations and functions of planning. Health leaders must publicly praise success and reward those who have achieved predetermined action steps, objectives, and goals.

As U.S. General and President Dwight Eisenhower once said, the plan is important but the process of planning is even more important. The team building, achievement, and success orientation that a culture of planning and implementation brings to an organization is invaluable in ensuring its success over both the short and long term.

DECISION MAKING AND DECISION ALIGNMENT[9]

Decision making occurs in all organizations. Health organizations, for example, face many decisions each day. The decision-making process begins with identifying a question or problem—that is, an area needing improvement or an operational issue. Problems, issues, questions, and operational challenges come to leaders and managers from many different people, both within and outside the health organization.

Leaders and managers usually are taught to utilize the rational decision-making model, which focuses on analytical (quantitative) methods; when necessary, they may couple this approach with group methods (qualitative) such as the normative group technique (brainstorming, alternative categorization, prioritizing alternatives, and selecting an alternative based on group consensus) to triangulate the final result (using both quantitative and qualitative methods) and identify an effective decision.

In reality, decision making is not as sterile and ordered as most have been taught. Both willful choice (rational) decision-making models and reality-based ("garbage can") models are used in organizations amid a myriad of tools and techniques. Thus there are three major domains of decision making:

- Willful choice or rational models
- Reality-based or garbage can models
- Combinations of willful choice and reality-based models

Likewise, three types of decision-making methods are used:

- Quantitative methods: tools such as multiple attribute value, probability-based decision trees, analytical mathematical models, linear programming and similar tools
- Qualitative methods: tools such as focus groups, interviews (formal and informal), normative group techniques and similar tools
- Triangulation methods: combinations of quantitative and qualitative methods where, classically, qualitative methods are perceived as "theory building" and quantitative methods are described as "theory testing, validating, or confirming"

A review of bounded rationality, willful choice, and reality-based decision making models is presented next. More time is spent on reality-based models because this decision-making method is the least well known, but may be the most applicable to health organizational leaders and managers.

Bounded Rationality in Decision Making

Decision making must occur within the bounded rationality of the environmental context in which the problem must be solved. In modern times, with the advent and availability of the Internet, the bounded rationality of information available for decision making is immense and global. As stated in Chapter 2, the bounded rationality for any problem spans the parameters in which the rational resources are available to the decision maker to accomplish positive outcomes. Organizational culture influences decision making as well. As noted in a study of military officers published in 2009, officers with an embedded "forcefulness" and "decisiveness" culture in team leadership roles were more spontaneous and less rational in decision making than their equally ranked team members.[10] Clearly, then, bounded rationality is influenced by organizational culture.

Prior to the dawn of the Information Age and the widespread use of the Internet, information was considered to be a scarce resource that was difficult to find—a perception that has changed dramatically, to the point that we live in an age characterized by "information overload." Unfortunately, the vast amounts of information available do not always include all the information necessary or completely accurate information with which to make the best decisions. Additionally, information may not be in a form that is immediately useable by those needing it. As a result, the most that the health leader can hope to achieve is the best decision possible based on the information that is known. With any decision at hand, different levels of ambiguity and uncertainty will surround the issue. Decisions made easily and with little risk tend to have less ambiguity and uncertainty associated with them, while complex, difficult, and more risky decisions tend to have much more ambiguity and uncertainty embedded within them.

Complicating this feature of human decision making is the fact that, although much more information is available today, decision makers may not have access to all the proper information regardless of tools available to them. Further, searching out that information may require far more time than decision makers have to arrive at a decision. Not all information or sources will be identifiable, but time will advance in any case. The decision maker will need to arrive at the best decision that can be made at the time. As a consequence, health leaders must often "satisfice" by seeking "a satisfactory reward rather than seeking the maximum reward."[11]

Willful Choice Decision-Making Models

Today's decision-making models and current understanding imply that decisions are made by rational, intentional, and willful choice. Choice is guided by four basic principles: (1) unambiguous (you know which questions to ask) knowledge of alternatives; (2) probability and knowledge of consequences; (3) a rational and consistent priority system for alternative ordering; and (4) heuristics or decision rules to choose an alternative.[12]

These models assume that alternatives are selected based on greatest utility (via cost–benefit analysis, for example), given the environmental situation (e.g., as assessed via a strength, weaknesses, opportunities, and threats [SWOT] analysis in strategic planning), for the organization in line with its objectives, goals, and mission. The decision-making models used in engineering, operations analysis and research, management science, and decision theory represent variations on the rational and willful choice model.[13]

The six-step model of decision making[14] applies the analytic willful choice model as follows:

1. Identify the problem.
2. Collect data.
3. List all possible solutions.
4. Test possible solutions.
5. Select the best course of action.
6. Implement the solution based on the decision made.

This practical model assumes that time and information are abundant, energy is available, and goal congruence of participants (everyone is focused on the same set of goals) has been achieved.

Criticism of Willful Choice Models

Well-known leadership and management concepts consider preplanning (short- and long-term) as the method to solve ambiguity (not knowing what to do) in business. As task complexity increases and time availability decreases, however, the challenge of planning and problem solving becomes increasingly more difficult.[15] The rapid pace of operations and change in health care today makes traditionally based organizations less adaptive and flexible in complex environments.[16] Information and time are assumed to be abundant and relatively free resources in rational and willful choice models; moreover, organizational participants in the decision-making process are assumed to have similar (if not the same) goals.[17] Perhaps not surprisingly, these assumptions are the basis of criticisms of the willful choice model. Theories of agency (for conflict management) and economics (scarce resources—namely, time and information) have proposed to resolve contradictory issues associated with willful choice as an explanatory model. Both the theories of agency and economics depend on rational participants to validate the models.[18] The reality of the healthcare industry suggests that individual and group preferences change as underlying variables associated with the decision vary, environmental factors evolve, and other organizational decisions are made.[19, 20] In addition, preferences of participants in the decision-making process often vary in illogical and emotionally dependent ways. Although accounted for in the willful choice models, time and information are not considered to be as valuable or scarce in these models as reality actually suggests they are.

Neoclassical economic theory suggests that the greatest good occurs when individuals are free to pursue self-serving interests.[21] This relationship further confounds the willful choice decision-making models' underlying assumptions. It is unreasonable to assume that each participant in a decision-making process will have similar self-serving goals and similar joint organizational goals most of the time. These contradictions add further credence to the view that willful choice models should be used when participants' goals are similar, time and information are available in sufficient quantities, and participants are well trained in the use of the model.

We do not mean to suggest that one should not use willful choice models, but rather that these models should be used in *appropriate* situations. This leaves the leader and manager in a tough situation: Which model should be used when the willful choice model conditions cannot be met? Other options include reality-based models. In the discussion that follows, the garbage can model is highlighted, as an extension of rational decision-making models. It adds to the available methods of decision making for the leader and manager in health organizations.

Reality-Based Decision-Making Models

Overview of the Garbage Can Model

Reality-based models, such as the garbage can model, are intended to extend the understanding of organizational decision making by emphasizing a temporal context (the situation at one point in time) and accepting chaos as reality. Rational (willful choice) decision-making models are a subset of reality-based models. In ambiguous (do not know what to ask or do) situations where time and information are limited or constrained and "perfect information" is impossible to acquire, where organization structure/hierarchy is loosely coupled, and where the organizational persona seems to embody organized anarchy (chaos), analytical decision-making models do not fit reality. The garbage can model, what was originally designed to reflect decision making in universities, has been cited to explain decision-making processes in various organizations and situations. Also, this kind of model has been introduced as a possible method for understanding processes such as how an organization learns.[22] For the past two decades, researchers have observed that willful choice models of decision making underestimate the chaotic nature and complexity regarding actual decision-making situations; a large percentage of decisions are made by default, when decision-making processes are followed without actually solving anything.[23]

Garbage Can Model Concepts

"Organized anarchy," "chaos," and "bedlam" are terms that describe organizational decision making. "Garbage can decisions can occur in any organization but are more likely to be found in 'organized anarchies,' where decisions are made under ambiguity and fluid involvement of participants."[24] Garbage can models represent attempts to find logic and order in the midst of decision-making chaos. In this model, garbage—defined as sets of problems, solutions, energy, and participants—is dumped into a can as it is produced (streams of "garbage" in time); when the can is full, a decision is made and removed from the scenario.[25]

> Numerous empirical observations of organizations have confirmed a relatively confusing picture of decision making. Many things seem to be happening at once, technologies are changing and poorly understood; alliances, preferences, and perceptions are changing; solutions, opportunities, ideas, people, and outcomes are mixed together in ways that make interpretation uncertain and leave connections unclear.[26]

In management arenas (and specifically in acquisition decisions), the decision-making load, speed required in decision making, uncertainty, and equivocality (i.e., ambiguity—not knowing which questions to ask or what to do) are commonly encountered factors that influence the decision-making process.[27] Thus the temporal nature of decision-making processes, if taken as "snapshots" in time, would show sequential arrival of problems, solutions, and information in a complex mix of participants, environmental factors, and consequences of prior decisions as reality in the "organized chaos" of decision making in organizations. Recognizing that time is not static and multidimensionality is ever present, the garbage can model depicts the chaotic nature of decision making through the jumbled mixture of elements in the garbage can.

Concepts are grounded in the ambiguous and uncertain states of nature for the garbage can model. Originally, three states of nature contributed to the model. All three states are immersed in ambiguity and, to a lesser degree, in uncertainty: (1) The greater the ambiguity of technology, (2) the more diverse the preferences of participants (the fewer preferences that are known, the greater the level of uncertainty) and of the organization, and (3) the greater the level of participation (in more specific terms, attention of participants), the more prevalent the garbage can processes in organizational decision making.

Ambiguity is defined as ignorance. Not only does this definition imply lack of knowledge but it also indicates a lack of understanding of which questions to ask, which information is available, and which kind of connectivity exists between problem and solution sets and the consequences of implementing solutions. Ambiguity of participation exists when participants in the decision-making process have competing time demands that battle for attention that would otherwise be necessary to solve a problem (make a decision). Because measurement of participation ambiguity depends on many extraneous variables in a sea of limitless situational factors, it is difficult to quantify. Yet, attention and energy variations among participants are considered a "given" phenomenon in decision-making processes.

Extending the original concepts in the three-factor model, Takahashi proposed three additional state-of-nature ambiguities to the model: (1) fluid participation, (2) divorce of solutions from discussion, and (3) job performance rather than subjective assessments.[28] Regarding individual preference, Pablo and Sitkin suggest that the more risk adverse a decision maker is, the less tolerant of ambiguity he or she is.[29]

Loose coupling in organizations fosters adoption of the garbage can decision-making approach. Loose coupling, in this sense, is defined as a more informal, differentiated focus, such that members of the organization focus less on following the rules, yet structured connectivity of intra-organizational entities is still present. Loose coupling tends to allow a more flexible organization.[30] Organizations that are loosely coupled can more readily adapt to change and shifts in environmental factors.[31–33] The strength of the feedback loops present determines organizational coupling: Stronger feedback loops imply tighter coupling, whereas weaker loops suggest loose coupling.[34] Four criteria[35] are measured to determine the coupling status in organizations:

- *Formal rules*: The more closely the rules are followed, the more tightly coupled the organization. (In entrepreneurial organizations, formal rules are not as important.)

- *Agreement on rules*: The greater the employee congruence, the tighter the coupling. (Entrepreneurial firms agree on social norms rather than formal rules.)

- *Feedback*: The closer the feedback in time, the tighter the coupling.

- *Attention*: Empowered individuals allocate energy and time to prioritized areas in their "area." (Participation, competence, and empowerment foster focused attention to areas of responsibility.)

In the garbage can model, the concept of loose coupling is required to understand decision making. As a thinking exercise, consider where a health leader should establish the level of coupling in a health organization; refer to **Figure 6–1** when contemplating this question.

Temporal order replaces sequential order. Time is spatial in that a multitude of issues, problems, information flows, and sensing mechanisms can bombard decision makers in short or long time blocks. How problems and information to resolve the problems arrive in time has relatively equal priority with the evaluation of

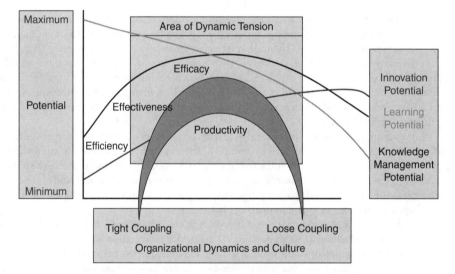

Innovation, learning and knowledge management and organizational coupling
Tension: efficiency, effectiveness, efficacy, productivity.
Where should health organizations focus? Consider mission, vision, strategies, goals, and external (e.g., error-free delivery of care) and internal (capabilities) assessments.

FIGURE 6–1   The Ledlow and Johnson Model (Revised by Ledlow): Coupling and the Tension of Innovation, Learning, and Knowledge Management
Source: Johnson, J., Ledlow, G., & Kerr, B. (2005). Organizational development, training and knowledge management. In B. Fried, J. Johnson, & M. Fottler (Eds.), *Human resources in healthcare: Managing for success* (2nd ed.). Chicago: Health Administration Press.

their importance. Arrival time and sequence in the current context both influence how much attention the decision maker pays to the situation:

> The process is thoroughly and generally sensitive to load. An increase in the number of problems, relative to the energy available to work on them, makes problems less likely to be solved, decision makers more likely to shift from one arena to another more frequently, and choices longer to make and less likely to resolve problems.[36]

Individuals in the decision-making process, directly and indirectly, are interconnected and influence the context of the decision at hand.

Obviously, attention demands influence decision making. Time and energy must be allocated to understand, evaluate, and formulate a problem; then to synthesize relevant information; next to evaluate options; and finally to choose an alternative to counter or terminate the problem. Individuals focus on some things and do not attend to others in the same space of time. Corporate actions, outcomes, and responsiveness are the results of dynamic organizational processes, not heuristics of individual choice.[37] Time and energy combine to form "attention." Attention is a dynamic concept that is highly dependent on load (i.e., the number of decisions that need to be made).

Lending support to the garbage can concept, rational choice in organizational decision making can be skewed by rituals and symbolism. Symbolic rituals associated with decision-making processes, at times, may derail rational attempts to understand the process. Decision making is a process that reassures the organization that values, norms, and logic are upheld; in this light, decision making is a ritual.

Lastly, decision making as a process focuses on showing control and logic in a world of complexity and rapid change. Saying, "We made a decision" and "We own the process" implies control of human existence by logical choice. However the choice ritual makes one feel, decision making is not rational. For this reason, a depiction of organized chaos rationalized by imperfect participants among a myriad of complex and synergized variables is more appropriate, as shown in **Figure 6–2**.

Decision possibilities in the garbage can run the gamut from willful choice models to garbage can–based models. Decisions by "flight," "resolution," and "oversight" are prominent categories in the latter model. *Flight* is defined as a decision maker's intentional movement (attention shift) to another area of concern (problem). *Resolution* comprises a decision that uses classical decision-making processes such as willful choice models.[38] *Oversight* is defined as decision makers activating a process or procedure before a problem becomes apparent,

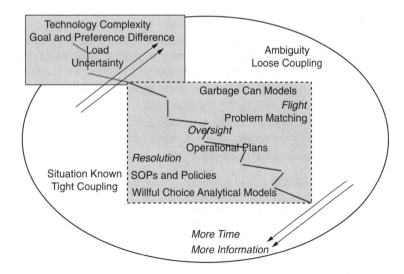

FIGURE 6–2   Conceptual Garbage Can Decision-Making Model

such as development of a standing operating procedure or use of an established and documented process. Much of the research shows that "flight" is a significant result of many decision-making processes; in essence, decisions were "overcome by events" or were not made, but rather allowed to either resolve or escalate themselves. So, what does a leader or manager do to deal with the reality of decision making?

Optimization of Decision Making

If a health organization has decision-making processes that resemble the garbage can environment, understanding the issues and proactively creating an environment that improves decision making can benefit the organization as a whole. Simulation results as part of garbage can studies revealed that decision making by resolution is not the most likely result of decision-making processes unless "flight" results are greatly constrained or decision load is light. Instead, "flight" and "oversight"[39] are more likely to occur—that is, either decisions are not made or predetermined and established processes (such as standing operating procedures) are used to a greater degree than might be noted with willful choice models. Given these findings, why not reengineer organizations to foster decision making based on goals of the organization, where clearly defined yet challenging goals are set and managers direct subordinates to focus, persist, and provide effort in achieving the goals,[40] comprehend technology, and logically apply rational decision-making processes? The answer is simple: Organizations do not exist to make decisions, but rather to serve the external environment. An organization structured to make decisions will not serve its customers well and eventually will be eliminated from the marketplace.

Imperfect decision making can be expected. In light of the ambiguous reality of information, preference, differences, incongruent goals, and sporadically occurring problems coupled with information bombardment of the temporally "exposed" decision maker, the garbage can model represents a reasonable extension of willful choice theories. Humans strive for processes of willful choice, yet, as the garbage can model proposes, fail to achieve rationality in decision making due to time, energy, attention, uncertainty, ambiguous information, and decision-making load issues. Leaders who can grasp the dynamics of the garbage can are better prepared to position their organizations to make good decisions amid organized chaos and competition.

Given this understanding, it seems clear that leaders and managers in health organizations should develop an organizationally sensitive *system of decision making* with the understanding that decision making is not always orderly. To do so, they should focus on the following tasks:

■ Evaluating the situation and decisions that need to be made across the organization (or within your area of responsibility) and categorizing decisions by quantity, urgency, information needed to make the decision, and variance in decision outcomes

■ Developing readily available information concerning core business functions

■ Standardizing, documenting, and training team members on decisions that need to be made routinely, where the same or similar decision outcome is required, and "pushing" those decisions to the lowest levels of the organization as possible but requiring feedback loops

■ Determining decision-making load (quantity in a set time frame) and information available to make decisions for the existing decisions (those not standardized)

■ Determining the importance of a decision to the organization by creating a system of risk determination, prioritization (urgency), and technological requirements for nonstandardized decisions

■ Training team members on the decision-making system and processes

When a decision or decisions need to be made, a health organization leader should take the following steps:

1. Evaluate the priority and risk of the decision to be made, and determine if this is a standardized decision or a decision that needs to be worked through.

2. Evaluate time available, resources available, participant attention, goals, and incentives.

3. Determine which decision making method to use: oversight, based on established documented processes such as standing operating procedures; resolution, using a willful choice model; or by pushing the decision to the appropriate level, individual, or group. It is also important to know when you do not need to make a decision (flight), based on the importance and risk level of the decision at hand.

To develop a reality-based decision making system, the leader and manager must understand that decision making is not a sterile and orderly process in most cases. Importantly, organizational decision making *should be aligned* (decisions should be in accordance) with the *organization's mission and vision* statements and *strategic planning–based goals and objectives.*

Tools of Decision Making

Early careerists need to be aware of the various tools of decision making for future leadership study and practice. Study (e.g., taking a course) and practice of both quantitative and qualitative decision-making tools are highly recommended. This section highlights both methods as well as triangulation, which represents a combination of both quantitative and qualitative methods. It is recommended that each tool mentioned here (and those not mentioned) be searched (perhaps on the Internet), discussed, practiced, and role-played with others in the class, group, or organization. Facilitating the decision-making process in a group or organization is an essential skill of leaders and managers, and a working familiarity with decision-making tools is a prerequisite to such a skill.

Quantitative Methods

Quantitative methods include mathematical and computational analytical models to help leaders understand the decision-making situation (data turned into information, which is then turned into knowledge) and produce mathematical outcomes of solutions. Some models are rather simple; others are highly complex. Quantitative models assist in assigning a "number" to uncertainty. Models include multiple-attribute value and multiple-utility methods, linear programming, probability, and decision trees based on Bayes' Theorem, and can be as complex as discrete and dynamic simulation. In general, simulation uses theoretical distributions and probabilities to "model" the real-world situation on the computer. From this computer model, response variables produce "outcomes" that can be evaluated.

Quantitative models take time and understanding of the important elements (also known as factors or variables) associated with the decision that needs to be made. In most health organizations, quantitative models are gaining momentum, though qualified (highly trained and well-practiced) analysts who understand health processes and can perform a range of quantitative analyses remain difficult to find and hire. Even with quantitative analyses in hand, many times leaders and managers skew decisions toward the qualitative side of decision making.

Six Sigma is a methodology that is growing in prominence in the health industry. Quantitative methods are critical to *Six Sigma,* which is a fact-based, data-driven philosophy of quality improvement that values defect prevention over detection. The Six Sigma technique drives customer satisfaction and bottom-line results by reducing variation and waste. It can be applied anywhere variation and waste exist, and every employee should be involved in its implementation. Six Sigma is used by many business organizations; health organizations are now using this philosophy as well to improve the work processes in their facilities.

Six Sigma is used to evaluate the capability of a process to perform defect free, where a "defect" is defined as anything that results in customer dissatisfaction.[41] The higher the Sigma level, the lower the number of defects. At the Six Sigma level, there are approximately 3.4 errors per 1 million opportunities, a virtually error-free rate.[42] Among early adopters of this approach are some of the most highly regarded health systems in the country—the Cleveland Clinic, the Mayo Clinic, and Johns Hopkins Medical Center, to name a few. These facilities consistently rank among the best hospitals in the world.[43]

Six Sigma is most successful when senior leadership makes a strong commitment to change, and in institutions where patient satisfaction and error-free care are the driving forces. Health organization staff must be trained by professional Six Sigma trainers. The training includes a "lean" thinking that seeks to drive employees toward perfection. It comprises a set of tools of varying degrees of sophistication that can be helpful for a leader to improve the health organization.[44]

A complementary approach to Six Sigma is Lean Sigma. Lean Sigma focuses on fixing the broken systems and processes that hinder medical professionals from doing what they do best, empowering employees to make improvements, reducing time and costs, synchronizing processes, and improving quality and the patient experience.[45] This practice helps to create efficient processes and decrease wasted time in a health facility. Lean Sigma provides the road map for fast and sustainable improvement while creating a work environment that strengthens and sustains the patient experience and increases the effectiveness of the health service and the provider of care.

Qualitative Methods

Qualitative methods include a variety of tools, ranging from personal intuition, discussions with team members, informal interviews, formal interviews, focus groups, nominal group techniques, and even voting. These methods are very useful in the decision-making process, because experience, intuition, and common sense can all be used by individuals as well as by groups.

Study and practice of qualitative methods are essential for leaders to facilitate decision making for themselves, groups, and organizations. The most notable leader decision-making tools of the qualitative nature include intuition, consensus, and coalition-based counsel.

Triangulation

The combination of quantitative and qualitative methods results in triangulation, a more thorough (albeit more time-consuming) method with which to make decisions. For example, a group may use nominal group techniques to develop a small set of possible solutions, then analyze each solution quantitatively. From there the leader can make a decision.

Training the group or organization to use triangulation is a good practice for resolving ("resolution" in reality-based models) decisions. Triangulation can also be used to develop standing operating procedures ("oversight" in reality-based models). Lastly, triangulation can be used to make improvements to processes within the organization. Kaizen theory (discussed later in this chapter) utilizes triangulation in the context of continuous quality improvement.

Decision Making in Quality Improvement

Extending the discussion on decision making, quality improvement integrates well into the overall schema of decision systems. In essence, quality improvement is a distinct system characterized by seven phases: (1) decision making (identification of improvement areas); (2) situational assessment; (3) information gathering; (4) decision making (what to do with assessment and information to improve); (5) planning; (6) implementation; and (7) feedback. Quality improvement, as a system, is an organizational culture "flag" found in many excellent health organizations. The connection in this arena is simple: Where quality improvement systems exist, decision-making systems are embedded throughout the system of continuous quality improvement. Total quality management (TQM), Kaizen theory, and the Shewhart cycle are all quality improvement strategies; they are profiled in the remainder of this section.

Total Quality Management

The TQM principles were initially brought to Japan by Deming after World War II. Consequently, Japanese businesses have been practicing TQM for more than 50 years, with remarkable results: Japan was able to rebuild its war-torn economy and innovate so that it became one of the strongest economies in the world in the latter part of the twentieth century. Despite this proof that TQM can be used over the long term with successful results, many health leaders feel an urgency to adopt new management philosophies every few years.[46, 47]

The key with TQM for any leader is to strive for documented and incremental decreases in variation and redundancy. This is a 14-step process:

1. Constantly strive to improve products and services.
2. Adopt a total quality philosophy.
3. Correct defects as they happen, rather than relying on inspection of end products.
4. Award business on factors other than price.
5. Continually improve the systems of production and service.
6. Institute training.

7. Drive out fear.

8. Break down barriers among staff areas.

9. Eliminate superficial slogans and goals.

10. Eliminate standard quotas.

11. Remove barriers to pride of workmanship.

12. Institute vigorous education and retraining.

13. Require that management take action to achieve the transformation.

14. Engage in proactive management.

The prudent health leader will meet in collaboration with fellow leaders in the organization. Working through a facilitator, write down each of Deming's tenets and outline those current organizational policies, practices, and procedures that have an impact on improving or impeding practices in the organization. When all the information has been collected, the leader will then be ready to establish new guidelines and break down barriers as appropriate.

Kaizen Theory

Kaizen theory is another Japanese-originated philosophy that focuses on continuous improvement throughout a system. Because health leaders are ultimately responsible for all aspects of organizational dynamics within the health enterprise, this approach is noteworthy. Kaizen theory is as much of an organizational culture (how things are done here) as a system that can be taught.

Kaizen originated in Japan in 1950 when business management and government acknowledged that there were problems in the then-current confrontational management system, given the pending labor shortage in Japan. This theory considers the initial quality of a project as well as the incremental improvement of quality when planning for quality improvements. Researchers defined Kaizen theory as a strategy to include concepts, systems, and tools within the bigger picture of leadership. This approach involves people (subordinates) and organizational culture, all driven by the customer. Japanese business leaders then involved the workforce in the solution of the problem. A key idea behind this theory is the need to practice reactive problem solving to promote continuous adherence to quality standards.[48]

Kaizen focuses on continuous improvement (CI) in performance, cost, and quality. In fact, some sources use the terms "Kaizen" and "continuous improvement" interchangeably, reflecting the nature of the theory. El-life described Kaizen, or continuous improvement, as a method that intensively focuses on improving every small detail of a process, recognizing that lots of small improvements, when executed continuously and embedded in the culture of an organization, can yield much more benefit than a few "big" programs.[49] The goal when implementing the concepts of this theory in an organization is to promote a culture of consistent standards and quality by addressing small problems or tasks. In other words, "Kaizen" signifies a series of small improvements that have been made in the status quo as a result of ongoing efforts.[50] Others suggest that CI can be generated and sustained through the promotion of a good improvement model and management support.[51]

A "Kaizen event" is a focused and structured improvement project, using a dedicated cross-functional team to improve a targeted work area, with specific goals and objectives, in an accelerated time frame. It is a complex organizational phenomenon, with the potential for altering both a technical system (i.e., work area performance) and a social system (i.e., participating employees and work area employees).[52] Kaizen events are usually short-term projects, sometimes long only one week.

The introduction of a Kaizen event in the health setting may be problematic, given that leaders could face multiple barriers to the proposed change from the start. For example, some have suggested that demarcations are traditionally more stringent in hospital settings; subordinates in different units in the health organization protect "their" territory. It is, therefore, necessary to have personnel from the different groups involved in patient care represented on a Kaizen team. The structure and composition of this team is crucial to the success of a health organization Kaizen event. Kaizen events typically use a semi-autonomous team (a social system) to apply a specific set of technical problem-solving tools.[53]

In the healthcare arena, a Kaizen team should be composed of people from multiple disciplines to accurately address and manage events. Its members may, for example, consist of a physician, nurse, social worker, and physical therapist, depending on the event being addressed. Working as an interdisciplinary team ensures the sustainability of the improvements. Another positive side effect is that the group members can analyze one

Benchmarks in Qualitative Decision Making for Leaders

1775: Adam Smith, author of *The Wealth of Nations*, observed a pin factory in 1775 and concluded that the process of making a pin could be separated into 14 different steps and processes. After observing the process for a period of time, Smith defined the sentinel events of pin making and assigned these tasks to the personnel who showed expertise in each specific stage. The result: The factory went from producing hundreds of pins a week to thousands! However, Smith found that if certain elements of this fledgling assembly line suffered slowdowns, the entire output could be hindered or halted.

1920: Dr. Walter Shewhart of Bell Telephone developed one of the first true control charts. In a paradigm shift from management philosophies, instead of inspecting outcomes, Shewhart began inspecting the process. He developed some of the first process-control methodologies used in the United States. His primary data methods were statistics (outcomes), sampling (convenience), and control charts that could be supplied to management to measure events as they happened.

1950: Kaizen theory resulted in the increase in productivity in Japan after World War II. Before World War II, Japanese products were seen as low quality and cheap; after the war, when Japanese factories and management philosophies were reestablished, Kaizen principles helped the country establish dominance in the global marketplace. Eventually, the word "Japanese" became synonymous with the word "quality" in regard to factory-made items.

1950–2010: W. Edwards Deming applied Shewhart's principles of quality control in his role as a consultant to several organizations while visiting Japan after World War II. From 1950 onward, he often visited Japan as lecturer and consultant (the Japanese honored him by naming the highest Japanese quality award after him). In spite of this popularity in Japan, Deming's principles were not adopted in the United States until the latter part of the 1980s. Today, the demonstration of TQM, Kaizen theory, and Shewhart principles are staples of many accreditation site visits for health leaders.

another's work processes to see how many steps each process actually includes and how much time is spent doing them. Kaizen covers many techniques and processes of CI; one that may be used in the health setting is the Shewhart cycle.[54]

Shewhart Cycle

The Shewhart cycle is also referred to as the Deming model and the plan–do–check–act (PDCA) cycle. This continuous quality improvement model consists of a logical sequence of these four repetitive steps for CI and learning.[55] The Shewhart cycle is a continuous feedback loop that seeks to identify and change process elements so as to reduce variation. The objective of this process is to plan to do something, do it, check for met requirements, and correct the process to achieve acceptable output performance. Performance improvement teams (PIT) are often developed in health organizations to address specific issues and work on problem solving by implementing the Shewhart cycle.

A PIT, which is a multidisciplinary group, may apply a model such as the Shewhart cycle to concentrate on quality improvement issues. Evidence-based data are used to analyze information within a PIT. Evidence-based practice in clinical performance, as well as administrative components, may help to reduce unnecessary tasks and procedures. The PIT can use the Shewhart cycle to tackle issues that affect the quality of care.

TRAINING

Training is a responsibility of leadership. Usually housed in the human resources department, it is the main vehicle for human resource development (HRD). Training functions as a key role of HRD by working to improve the organization's effectiveness, efficiency, and efficacy by providing employees with the learning needed to improve their current or future job performance based on the mission, vision, strategies, and goals of the organization.[56]

Training comprises a planned set of activities that proceeds through health organizational needs assessment, gap analysis (Do current employees lack certain capabilities?), training module development, trainer identification, logistics of training, the training itself, and training evaluation and refinement. Training in organizations should focus on the organizationally required knowledge, skills, and abilities (KSAs). Training of staff and subordinates is, of course, essential for the long-term success of the health organization. Usually employees who work at the highest levels (leadership) and the lowest levels (e.g., receptionists) receive the least amount of ongoing training in a health organization; this is a problem that needs to be rectified (considering that the lowest levels in a health organization usually welcome and often talk with patients). Leader training is often subsumed in the HRD training structure, when, in fact, it needs to be an ongoing effort that is just as prevalent as staff training.

Why should it be that some people develop into "take charge" types who organize everything around them, while others remain more laissez-faire in their approach to life? Maltby asks the basic question, noting that the "question continues to dominate the study of leadership today. Volumes of research have been written." Many definitions of leadership exist, and Maltby offers one taken from the writing of Jay Conger: This definition holds that leaders establish direction, gain commitment, and motivate members of the group.[57]

Developing some clarity about the "Born or made?" debate is essential to any discussion of leadership training. The current consensus is that the answer to this question is "both": Leaders are born *and* made. Most authors agree that although the elements of leadership certainly can be taught to others, such training is far more effective among those persons with a predisposition to leadership. To be successful, training must be designed to (1) develop and refine certain of the teachable skills; (2) improve conceptual abilities; (3) tap individuals' personal needs, interests, and self-esteem; and (4) help leaders see and move beyond their interpersonal blocks.[58] Two of the more important health organization training efforts, for leaders and all subordinates, are cultural and moral competencies.

Cultural and Moral Competencies

Health leaders must work together as partners to increase general awareness and improve culturally diverse organizations. The U.S. Department of Health and Human Services defines *cultural competence* as behaviors, attitudes, and policies that come together on a continuum to work in an adverse cultural setting. The Robins Group defines it as a way of being that enables people and organizations to engage effectively in a variety of cross-cultural environments. Because every organization is different, what constitutes appropriate cultural competence in one organization may be seen as being wholly inadequate in another organization. Thus cultural competence is "an approach that starts with the core values and cultural expectations of the specific organization."[59] It can also be defined as an understanding of the importance of social and cultural influences on patients' health beliefs and behaviors and a consideration of how these factors interact at multiple levels of the health delivery system (e.g., at the level of structural processes of care or clinical decision making). Clearly, it is important to devise interventions that take these issues into account to assure quality healthcare delivery to diverse patient populations.[60, 61]

Cultural competence provides the knowledge, skills, and abilities that allow health leaders to increase their understanding and appreciation of cultural differences among groups of people. It focuses on behaviors, attitudes, and policies. This foundation facilitates exploration of different cultures, learning about cultural heritages, and appreciation of the effects of diversity on health care and the health industry. Culture and language have powerful effects in terms of how patients access and respond to all health services received from a health provider; leaders need to be aware of these issues.[62, 63]

The Joint Commission suggests that all health leaders should be culturally competent. The U.S. government has presented a series of recommendations for national standards and outcomes-focused research to assure cultural competence in health care.[64, 65] When cultural competency is lacking, patients and subordinates may mistrust both the leader and the health organization. For leaders, cultural competency is a learning process that will allow them to grow and expand their knowledge, sensitivity, and respect for those in the organization and for those whom the health organization serves. Cultural competency is expressed in the healthcare approaches used with patients of diverse ethnicities, races, national origins, and languages. Leaders need to be culturally competent to succeed.[66, 67]

In a global community, the value of cultural competence is clear, particularly as ethnic, racial, and national diversity increases over time. These points of diversity further contribute to the mélange that is the organizational culture. Power can be used to block something from happening, or it can be used to ensure that something does happen. Power is essential if the organization hopes to ever accomplish something: Someone or some group must have the power to make things work. "Power is the basis of the ability to get things done in organizations, and is therefore an essential element of organization and leadership."[68] Cultural competence, in turn, is a capability that adds to a leader's power.

All of these factors combine to form and influence leadership. Planning, decision making, and training can and do take place within organizations that serve and employ a variety of culture types, but only cultural and moral competency can produce an organizational culture that encourages and allows employees to fully respond to leadership.

Ethics and Morality

Ethics can be defined as a theory of moral values.[69] There is a perception that all organizations are expected to work to the highest standards of integrity and ethics. Ethical standards and values are not created by law or regulations, but rather by the board and trustees of an organization; they are then implemented by the leadership. *Ethics* is a framework for decision making and action, whereas *morality* is the level to which the ethical framework is applied. In many university programs, ethics is embedded in a health law or legal course. Ethics and morality are health leader responsibilities—a statement that holds true at all levels of the health organization. In simple terms, ethics relates to doing what is right; it is about using good and fair judgment; it is about responsible fiduciary use and distribution of resources. Ethical and moral behavior, personally and organizationally, is the leader's responsibility.

Health leaders must be ethical and moral agents of the organization. The success of the organization may rise and fall on the perception of the community regarding the morals of the organization. Staff members and the community expect the leaders to use their best judgment; leaders are held accountable for doing what is right. If a slip in morality occurs, unfavorable publicity might obscure all of the health organization's other positive efforts and smear the good name of the organizational "brand." Unfavorable publicity can have a dramatic effect on an initiative already in progress.[70] Although other leadership distinctions may depend on the execution of a skill set (such as planning) or a trait (such as charisma), the distinction of authentic leadership rests heavily on perceptions of morality. To gain support from both internal and external stakeholders, the health organization must display the sincerity of its mission and act consistently with its espoused values.

In nonprofit health organizations, losses due to fraudulent activities are particularly troublesome because they directly reduce the amount of resources available to address tax-exempt purposes.[71] Negative publicity for a health organization may also reduce contributions and lead to loss of grants. Some organizations have publicly indicated their commitment to ethics, whereas others have done little to prevent ethical dilemmas from arising. It is important to read your health organization's ethical statements to see where it stands on these issues.

Over the years, various reports have appeared in the literature on the need for healthcare organizations to develop and implement organizational ethics programs. Health organizations should institute visible and effective leadership training programs in these areas. These programs should promote and inspire the ethical behavior of employees and executives alike. In 2009, Fine suggested that a moral discourse in the health leadership context is important; adding purpose and context to leadership model constructs should be based in ethical considerations and possibly adopt a feminist ethic of care perspective.[72]

In recent decades, several ethical scandals have adversely affected the health industry. Health leaders should be aware of these episodes and take steps to prevent them in their own organizations. Some of the more widely publicized scandals involved embezzlement by the president of the United Way of America,[73] improper use of funds by the head of the National Association for the Advancement of Colored People (NAACP),[74] and investment fraud by the head of the Foundation for New Era Philanthropy.[75] These examples show that ineffective leadership can have a huge impact on health organizations and the industry as a whole. The success of health organizations is sometimes rated by the quality of their charitable and beneficent activities; when these activities are associated with immoral behavior, the negative effects can be devastating.

The leaders of the health organization must demonstrate that they can operate in a consistently ethical and moral manner. Consistent, ongoing, and frequent training in cultural and moral competencies is imperative; this training should begin with new employee orientation and continue throughout the tenure of that employee regardless of position or status.

SUMMARY

This chapter identified additional knowledge and empirically based skills and abilities (a leadership toolbox full of "tools") required for a health leader's success in organizational practice. Strategies for leaders in effecting planning, decision making, and training that result in positive outcomes will ideally result in practical leadership actions and applications based in "active" leadership.

Planning, decision making, and training are integrated processes that are embedded in health organizations. Leaders can consciously make these processes better, more efficient, effective, and efficacious while reducing organizational stress. Understanding the nature of planning and decision making and becoming competent as a decision maker, facilitator, analyst, or decision-making assistant (a person who helps the primary decision makers) are critical for success as a leader and a manager; they are also necessary for success as a team member who is not filling a leadership or management role. Developing a system of planning, decision making, and training, within the organizational context, and becoming a competent user of these systems are vital to achieving and maintaining excellence in health organizations.

DISCUSSION QUESTIONS

1. Discuss the importance of and use of planning, decision making, and training in health organizations and provide examples of each. How can planning, decision making, and training aid in developing organizational culture in health organizations?

2. Explain the planning process within the context of leadership. Explain the decision-making processes used by health organizations. Predict how successful leaders can be when they master these tools of leadership: What might happen if they do *not* master these tools?

3. Use examples to apply and relate at least two different decision-making models to a leadership situation in a health organization. How are the models different? When should each model be used in health organizations?

4. Illustrate the levels or components of the planning process and distinguish each level or component from the others. How does this structure help in planning and in progress review?

5. Relate how a quality improvement program is based on a system of willful choice decision making in a health organization. Can a reality-based decision-making model work in quality improvement? Why or why not?

6. Compare and contrast willful choice to garbage can models of decision making, training leaders to training staff, and cultural competence to ethics and morality. Justify your positions.

EXERCISES

1. Define the overall concepts of planning, decision making, and training; give examples of each as part of your definitions.

2. Generalize how a successful health leader prepares for (a) planning in a health organization; (b) developing a decision-making system in a health organization; and (c) ensuring that all employees are culturally competent in a health organization. Complete this exercise in two pages or less.

3. Prepare a list of internal and external stakeholders for a health organization in preparation of strategic planning; categorize each group.

4. In a two-page paper, compare and contrast in the willful choice and garbage can models of decision making within a health organization context.

5. Organize a planning effort in preparation for a Kaizen theory or Shewhart cycle quality improvement project within a unit (keep it small) of a health organization. Describe this plan in three pages or less.

6. In a two- to three-page paper, appraise the concept of "coupling" within the context of decision making and ethics/morality in a health organization.

REFERENCES

1. Granda-Cameron, C., Lynch, M. P., Mintzer, D., Counts, D., Pinto, S., & Crowley, M. (2007). Bringing an inpatient palliative care program to a teaching hospital: Lessons in leadership. *Oncology Nursing Forum, 34*(4), 772–776.
2. Yukl, G. (1994). *Leadership in organizations* (3rd ed.). Englewood Cliffs, NJ: Prentice Hall.
3. Ledlow, G., & Cwiek, M. (2005). The process of leading: Assessment and comparison of leadership team style, operating climate and expectation of the external environment. In *Global Business and Technology Association Proceedings,* Lisbon, Portugal, July 1995.
4. Ledlow, G., Cwiek, M., & Johnson, J. (2002). Dynamic culture leadership: Effective leader as both scientist and artist. In N. Delener & C. Chao (Eds.), *Global Business and Technology Association International Conference; Beyond boundaries: Challenges of leadership, innovation, integration and technology* (pp. 649–740). New York: Global Business and Technology Association.
5. Eicher, J. P. (2006). making strategy happen. *Performance Improvement, 45*(10), 3148.
6. Eicher, note 5.
7. Eicher, note 5.
8. Higgins, J. (1994). *The management challenge* (2nd ed.). New York: Macmillan.
9. Ledlow, G., & Stephens, J. (2008). Decision making and communication. In J. A. Johnson (Ed.), *Organizational theory, behavior and development* (pp. 213–232). Sudbury, MA: Jones and Bartlett.
10. Thunholm, P. (2009). Military leaders and followers: Do they have different decision styles? *Scandinavian Journal of Psychology, 50*(4), 317–324.
11. Simon, H. A. (1986). Decision making and problem solving. In *Research briefings 1986: Report of the Research Briefing Panel on Decision Making and Problem Solving.* Washington, DC: National Academy Press. Retrieved July 8, 2009, from http://www.dieoff.org/page163.htm.
12. March, J. G., & Weisinger-Baylon, R. (1986). *Ambiguity and command: Organizational perspectives on military decision making.* Marshfield, MA: Pitman.
13. March & Weisinger-Baylon, note 12.
14. Argenti, P. A. (Ed.). (1994). *The portable MBA desk reference: An essential business companion.* New York: John Wiley & Sons.
15. Jelinek, M., & Litterer, J. A. (1995). Toward entrepreneurial organizations: Meeting ambiguity with engagement. *Entrepreneurship: Theory and Practice, 19*(3), 137–169.
16. Jelinek & Litterer, note 15.
17. March & Weisinger-Baylon, note 12.
18. Swanson, D. L. (1996). Neoclassical economic theory, executive control, and organizational outcomes. *Human Relations, 49*(6), 735–757.
19 March & Weisinger-Baylon, note 12.
20. Swanson, D. L. (1995). Addressing a theoretical problem by reorienting the corporate social performance model. *Academy of Management Review, 20*(1), 43–65.
21. Swanson, note 18.
22. Tsang, E. W. K. (1997). Organizational learning and the learning organization: A dichotomy between descriptive and prescriptive research. *Human Relations, 50*(1), 73–90.
23. March & Weisinger-Baylon, Roger. (1986). Ambiguity and Command: Organizational Perspectives on Military Decision Making, Pitman Publishing: Marshfield, Massachusetts.
24. March, James G. & Weisinger-Baylon, note 12, p. 36.
25. Takahashi, N. (1997). A single garbage can model and the degree of anarchy in Japanese firms. *Human Relations, 50*(1), 91–109.

26. March & Weisinger-Baylon, note 12, p. 16.

27. Pablo, A. L., & Sitkin, S. B. (1996). Acquisition decision-making processes: The central role of risk. *Journal of Management, 22*(5), 723–747.

28. Takahashi, note 25.

29. Pablo & Sitkin, note 27.

30. Bennis, W., Parikh, J., & Lessem, R. (1996). *Beyond leadership: Balancing economics, ethics, and ecology* (rev. ed.). Cambridge, MA: Blackwell.

31. Pablo & Sitkin, note 27.

32. Jelinek & Litterer, note 15.

33. March & Weisinger-Baylon, note 12.

34. Van de Ven, A. H., & Poole, M. S. (1995). Explaining development and change in organizations. *Academy of Management Review, 20*(3), 510–541.

35. Jelinek & Litterer, note 15.

36. March & Weisinger-Baylon, note 12, p. 18.

37. Swanson, note 20.

38. Takahashi, note 25.

39. Takahashi, note 25.

40. Locke, E. A., & Latham, G. P. (1984). *Goal setting: A motivational technique that works!* Englewood Cliffs, NJ: Prentice Hall.

41. Black, K. & Revere, L.. (2006). Six Sigma arises from the ashes of TQM with a twist. *International Journal of Health Care Quality Assurance, 19*(3), 259–266. Retrieved May 2, 2009, from ABI/INFORM Global database. Document ID: 1073443771.

42. Morgan, S. & Cooper, C. (2004). Shoulder work intensity with Six Sigma. *Nursing Management, 35*(3), 29–32. Retrieved May 2, 2009, from ABI/INFORM Global database. Document ID: 583229661.

43. Hirst, R., & Weimer, D. (2008). Management systems keep hospitals from meeting goals. *Managed Healthcare Executive, 18*(5), 26–27. Retrieved April 30, 2009, from ABI/INFORM Global database. Document ID: 1500296291.

44. Baker, P. (2005, March). Get the right blend. *Works Management, 58*(3), 26–28. Retrieved April 30, 2009, from ABI/INFORM Global database. Document ID: 816940421.

45. Hirst & Weimer, note 43.

46   Burns, J., & Sipkoff, M. (1998). *1999 hospital strategies in managed care.* New York: Faulkner and Gray.

47. Coppola, M. N. (1998). The hidden value of managing worker's compensation costs in the hospital setting (pp. 227–255). In Burns, J. & Sipkoff, M. (eds). *1999 Hospital Strategies in Managed Care.* New York: Faulkner and Gray Publishers.

48. Singh, J., & Singh, H. (2009). Kaizen philosophy: A review of literature. *ICFAI Journal of Operations Management, 8*(2), 51–72.

49. Ellife, S. A. (2004, May 3). Cutting out the fat. *Journal of Commerce,* p. 22. Retrieved May 29, 2009, from ABI/INFORM Global database. Document ID: 626516031.

50. Singh & Singh, note 48.

51. Chen, C. I., & Wu, C. W. (2004). A new focus on overcoming the improvement failure. *Technovation, 24,* 585–591.

52. Farris, J. A., Van Aken, E. M., Doolen, T. L. & Worley, J. (2008). Learning from less successful Kaizen events: A case study. *Engineering Management Journal, 20*(3), 10–20. Retrieved May 27, 2009, from ABI/INFORM Global database. Document ID: 1582589011.

53. Wennecke, G. (2008, August). Kaizen–LEAN in a week: How to Implement improvements in healthcare settings within a week. *Medical Laboratory Observer, 40*(8), 28, 30-1. Retrieved May 27, 2009, from ProQuest Medical Library database. Document ID: 1555010561.

54. Wennecke, note 53.

55   Singh & Singh, note 48.

56. Blanchard, P. N., & Thacker, J. W. (1999). *Effective training systems, strategies, and practices.* Upper Saddle River, NJ: Prentice Hall.

57. Maltby, D. E. (2009). Are leaders born, or made? The state of leadership theory and training today. Biola University. Retrieved July 8, 2009, from http://www.biola.edu/academics/professional-studies/leadership/resources/leadership/bornormade/.

58. Maltby, note 57.

59. Cultural Competence. (2009). The Robins Group organization development. Retrieved July 8, 2009, from http://kikanzanurirobins.com/cultural_competence_15684.htm.

60. Berry-Cabán, C. S., & Crespo, H. (2008). Cultural competency as a skill for health care providers. *Hispanic Health Care International, 6*(3), 115–121.

61. Jirwe, M., Gerrish, K., & Emani, A. (2006). The theoretical framework of cultural competence. *Journal of Multicultural Nursing & Health, 12,* 3.

62. Berry-Cabán & Crespo, note 60.

63. Jirwe et al., note 61.

64. Rudd, K. M., & Stack, N. M. (2006). Cultural competency for new practitioners. *American Journal of Health-System Pharmacy,* May 2006; 63: 912–913.

65. Berry-Cabán & Crespo, note 60.

66. Markova, T., & Broome, B. (2007). Effective communication and delivery of culturally competent health care. *Urologic Nursing, 27,* 3.

67. Wolf, K. E., & Calmes, D. (2004). Cultural competence in the emergency department. *Top Emergency Medical, 26*(1), 9–13.

68. Van Maanen, J. (2003, October 3). Summary of the three lenses. Retrieved July 8, 2009, from http://www.core.org.cn/NR/rdonlyres/Sloan-School-of-Management/15-322Fall2003/0C7013D1-D849-43FA-995C-42C096FD1B82/0/ses4_three_lenses.pdf.

69. Midkiff, K. A. (2004). Catch the warning signs of fraud in NPOs. *Journal of Accountancy, 197*(1), 28.

70. Hankin, J. A., Seidner, A., & Zietlow, J. (1998). *Financial management for nonprofit organizations.* New York: John Wiley & Sons.

71. Midkiff, note 69.

72. Fine, M. G. (2009). Women leaders' discursive constructions of leadership. *Women's Studies in Communication, 32*(2), 180–202.

73. Murawski, J. (1995, July 13). Former United Way chief gets 7 years in jail: Sentence praised by charities. *Chronicle of Philanthropy,* pp. 37–38.

74. Greene, E. (1995, May 4). The NAACP: What went wrong? *Chronicle of Philanthropy,* pp. 27–29.

75. Stecklow, S. (1997, September 23). New Era's Bennett gets 12 years in prison for defrauding charities. *Wall Street Journal,* p. 15.

Leadership Assessment and Research: Individual, Team, and Organization

Great ability develops and reveals itself increasingly with every new assignment.
Baltasar Gracian, *The Oracle*

This chapter looks at techniques and applications of leadership, ranging from leading small groups of individuals to leading interdisciplinary teams in small- and large-scale organizations. These elements represent ordinal stages for developing competent leadership capabilities; which in turn are built on the "crawl, walk, and run" methodology of health leader development. Mature leaders recognize that different skills are required to lead small groups of individuals than are needed to lead large and complex organizations. Individuals and teams may respond better to verbal communication and direct interaction, whereas leaders of large and complex organizations must develop alternative approaches to communication, such as well-written and -developed policy and mission statements, or nurturing and developing human resources proxies to carry the leader's vision down the hierarchy of the health organization. This chapter examines additional best practices in communication, leadership archetypes, and some delegation, participatory, and collaborative practices in a group or team context.

LEARNING OBJECTIVES

1. Describe the cycle of leadership and identify knowledge, skills, and abilities at each stage of the cycle that contribute to understanding health leadership development.

2. Explain Tuckman's model of the group dynamic process, and summarize its importance to health leaders in group or team supervision.

3. Construct a five-year leadership development plan based on an ultimate health leadership position goal.

4. Compare and contrast a great group or team with one in a groupthink situation and one that is ineffective; distinguish how a health leader performs in each of these group or team situations.

5. Devise a health leader's checklist for leading and managing a group or team focused on superior performance and outcomes.

6. Evaluate health leader development; explain and relate leader development opportunities and events to the cycle of leadership and the knowledge, skills, and abilities necessary to master in each stage of the cycle.

CYCLES OF LEADERSHIP DEVELOPMENT

This chapter offers a methodology for leader development and training based on the crawl–walk–run (CWR) approach. When using this philosophy, leader development starts with a backward planning approach. For example, an early careerist looking to enter into the dynamic world of health may see himself or herself rising to the position of president or chief executive officer (CEO) of a large and integrated healthcare delivery system that spans several geographic miles, employs hundreds (perhaps thousands) of personnel, controls policy for hundreds of millions of dollars' worth of equipment and facilities, and is responsible for the competent and safe care of hundreds of thousands of ambulatory and inpatient visits each year. While this coveted position may be a goal for many entry-level careerists, one has to ask; *How did that person get there?*[1]

The CEO of such an organization did not get to this position overnight. He or she engaged in years (perhaps decades) of incremental training and education that prepared the individual to assume such a complicated position of responsibility. These antecedent, or earlier, leader positions probably involved entry-level positions in the health industry as the administrator for a group practice or administrative department in a hospital or a clinical leader in a clinical service. The person may then have become an assistant or associate administrator in the same facility, or a larger one, where junior executives implemented policy and programs under the supervision of the chief operations officer (COO). The individual may have sought out a CEO position at a small organization with limited inpatient services, with specific rural and/or community missions. This job may have offered opportunity for movement and advancement into subsequently larger and more complex organizations spanning greater responsibility across human resources, financial, revenue, logistical/supply chain, strategic, and other resources. Thus a CEO at a small organization may have moved to a larger organization over time. At each stage in this process, the individual gained competencies in areas relating to human resources, financial, revenue, logistical/supply chain, and strategic areas, to name only a few. These development positions made it possible for the individual to be successful in the complex job that he or she now holds as the president/CEO of a large and complex system.

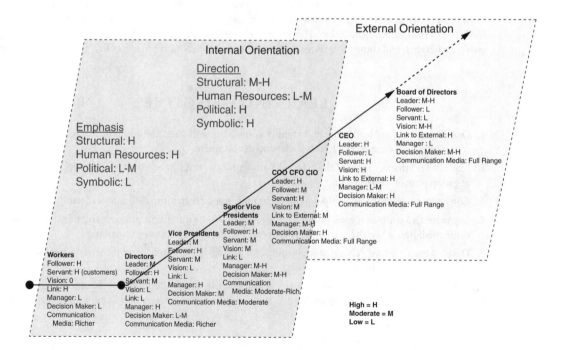

FIGURE 7–1   A Hypothetical Leadership–Management–Follower Progression in a Health System
Bolman and Deal's constructs for reframing leadership and management in organizations are used as components of the model.

In looking at this hypothetical life-cycle model, it became apparent that in each phase in the developmental process, the junior executive gained experience in managing ever larger budgets and leading ever greater numbers of people. The junior executive also transitioned from the responsibility for maintaining only personal equipment and property, or equipment of a colloquial nature, to being responsible for hundreds of individual pieces of property with a value exceeding hundreds of thousands, or even millions, of dollars. Additionally, most all entry-level positions offer at least a limited opportunity for strategic planning. In contrast, the senior healthcare executive makes his or her reputation on the ability to strategically plan for future events while balancing the simultaneous needs of dozens of tightly woven and interconnected echelons of competing priorities.

So again, we ask, *How does a person get to this level of leadership complexity?* In response, we offer the crawl–walk–run (CWR) methodology of leadership development. In **Figure 7–1**, progressive leadership levels are presented in a hypothetical health organization (e.g., under "Workers", "Vision" is assigned a value of 0 because most times the lowest levels of the organization do not develop vision—but should they be involved?). In the figure, Bolman and Deal's leadership orientation constructs, which include structural, human resources, political, and symbolic components, are shown as leader propensities of the positional level; in reality, these constructs are situational and may be used at any level.

THE CRAWL–WALK–RUN METAPHOR

The CWR metaphor for leader development and training is based on how infants learn to progress from the crawling stage to the running stage in their motor ability. This theory is equally applied to their cognitive progress. The CWR premise is both a philosophical perspective and a practical approach to development in any venue. We do not learn to become experts in anything without gaining knowledge, skills, and abilities (KSAs) in a progressive manner.

An old adage says, "You can't run before you can walk." This statement makes obvious theoretical—if not ecological—sense. In education, in the practice called task analysis, each step in performing a task is analyzed to ensure that essential information or skills are not omitted in learning the whole task or process. Everything new that we learn is based on past knowledge and experience along with newly introduced knowledge, skills, and abilities. The process of advancement in health leadership is no different.

THE CRAWL: STRATEGIES FOR MANAGING INDIVIDUALS

The crawl stage begins with self-awareness. In human development, an infant slowly becomes aware of himself or herself and the surroundings. The infant also begins to understand that he or she can interact with the complex world around him or her. After several attempts and experiments, the infant becomes aware of simple cause-and-effect outcomes. The infant then wants to "go places." In getting to where the infant wants to go, he or she crawls.

The readings and personal self-assessments identified in earlier chapters will assist readers in their own understanding of their own self-awareness. After completing this kind of preparation, early careerists will have a road map to success that allows them to initiate their own journey toward leadership competence. The same premise holds true in learning and developing leadership skills. Entry-level management positions are characterized by contact with the unknown and unfamiliar. For example, early careerists are often unsure how to write effective memos and perform management analysis without being given all the variables and constraints to "crunch the numbers." They will likely be unsure of themselves in speaking up at meetings and interacting professionally with senior leaders and clients. They may be uncomfortable when chairing their first meeting, preparing an agenda in advance, scheduling a time, and so forth. There will be some anxiety at initiating ideas, and in the worst-case scenario, taking responsibility for the actions of those below them in the supervisory chain.

There is a specific reason why resumes of health executives boast similar phrases outlining how many persons the executive supervised, the amount of plant and facilities he or she was responsible for, and the size of the budgets managed. Prior to managing hundreds of persons, the early careerist must learn to manage himself or herself and gain experience supervising and keeping track of others in an entry-level and supervisory role.

Explicit Lessons

From a mentoring standpoint, in the crawl stage, early careerists must be given very explicit lessons and directions to learn very basic knowledge, such as what a leader is, what leadership characteristics are, and what leaders do. For example, in the crawl stage in leadership development, the individual does the tasks very slowly and very methodically. This analogy refers to the movement from the conscious incompetent to the conscious competent stage of learning. After experimentation, with greater experience, and recognizing the ability to fail without consequences, the young executive gains confidence in standing up before groups, framing an opinion on basic courses of action, and being responsibility for equipment.[2]

Role Modeling

In the crawl stage, there is need for specific role modeling and/or instruction. Instructions must be explained in detail and their value communicated in the overall plan. After instruction or experience in observing actions, the young executive learns from role models and obtains the knowledge needed to duplicate steps in the process as he or she has been taught. During the crawl stage, the instructions should be relatively simple, so that the early careerist does not need a great deal of supervision to correctly perform the tasks as assigned.[3] Monitoring is still necessary; however, because not all early careerists learn things at the same rate of speed, the progression can be variable depending on who is being taught the basic skill set.

Why Actions Are Done

In the crawl stage, the early careerist must know why actions are being initiated, so that these decisions in dynamic organizations make sense. For example, an early careerist who is harshly judged because an email to a senior supervisor included spelling errors may not know that a marketing brochure mailed to thousands of stakeholders months earlier contained numerous spelling errors. The early careerist may not know that the chief executive placed special emphasis on spelling and grammar on all written documents developed within and outside the organization after the embarrassing event. As a result, what might have seemed to be an innocent email written hastily by an early careerist attempting to solve a complex task that was previously assigned may result in a perception of unprofessionalism individually, and reflect poorly on his or her department as a whole. The early careerist must make it a point to read existing documents, ask questions, and consult with peers and mentors (sometimes peer mentors) who have been in the organization for a longer period of time. These "peer mentors" are probably aware of the unique professional landmines and informal barriers that exist in the organization. Subsequently, the mentor—either a peer or otherwise—can assist the early careerist in navigating the political waters.

Education

The crawl stage involves continuing education to augment previously learned classroom or didactic education.[4] In the crawl stage, the early careerist must grasp the many themes found in an "Introduction to Leadership" class or seminar. These include the topics mentioned earlier, but also encompass the student's definition of "leadership" and the difference between leadership and management. The crawl stage also includes becoming aware of the organizational field of health, the specifics of the health organization, and a burgeoning understanding of how one's own "mental hard-wiring" supports (or fails to support) events and opportunities in the environment. The crawl stage might not be defined so much by doing, as by learning.

The personality tests outlined earlier in this text provide an opportunity for the early careerist—the future health leader—to develop an awareness of his or her strengths and weaknesses within the complex organizational environment. This will help the individual become aware of personal "blind spots" that might keep the early careerist from being successful. For example, a health organization that has a highly kinesthetic preference for learning (learning by doing things) may pose challenges to an early careerist who is fundamentally hard-wired to learn through reading. In the absence of this critical element of self-development, the early careerist will have to enable himself or herself to learn differently, or seek out employment with organizations that are not as action based. Such may be the case in health consulting and sales, where verbal communication and on-the-job training are considered more critical than formal or didactic education.

Developmental Tasks

During the crawl stage of development, the prospective leader may not have the knowledge, skills, or abilities to lead a formal group in completing a complex task or process. Leadership is a very complex profession and requires extensive KSA development before the individual is prepared to lead a formal group in confusing and chaotic situations. It is possible during this stage for the mentor to assign developmental tasks to the early careerist to build these KSAs, such as writing white papers or participating in interdisciplinary process action teams. The crawl stage is also about followership and development of the understanding that to become a leader, one must be a good follower. Some characterize this as understanding the concept of loyalty and servant-leadership development.

The crawl stage is a stage characterized by self-awareness as well as basic knowledge about leadership itself. It is a time to practice what has been learned and to demonstrate one's competencies through written and oral assignments. These beginning developmental lessons provide the foundation for later completion of more intricate and complex tasks in leadership functions.

Self-Improvement

It has been argued that leaders are born, not made. Current understanding suggests leaders can be made or developed; of course, a combination of nature and nurture is at work. However, the patterns of behavior established through early leader development programs cannot be emphasized too strongly as influencing later outcomes. Organizations and industry leaders spend millions of dollars annually to support leadership development and mentoring programs geared toward successfully transitioning early careerists from the crawl stage to the walk stage of development. Moreover, certain activities in which the early careerist engages can specifically assist him or her in advancing up the leader ladder.

First, the crawling leader should be a volunteer. Volunteering to sit on committees, conduct extracurricular management analysis, and assist others who are involved in interdisciplinary team projects, and making it known to the organization that the individual is not limited by his or her own job description, sets a tone of success for the early leader.

Second, the early leader should join and support professional organizations. Joining professional organizations exposes the early careerist to broader pools of health professionals—albeit not in the same organization as the early careerist—who may offer career and mentoring advice. Professional organizations can also provide opportunities for professional advancement and acknowledgment, as well as continuing health, leadership, and management education.

Lastly, the early careerist should be a reader at the crawl stage. In the dynamic world of health, it can become immediately evident if one's relevancy is dated. For example, if an early careerist continues to refer to The Joint Commission as JCAHO, or cites the most recent version of the STARK laws as having been last updated at version II, this may signal to senior executives that the early careerist lacks creditability and relevancy. There are few items that can immediately affect (negatively, in particular) a recent graduate's creditability. Never rely on just one source of information for timely knowledge of health events and industry updates until you are confident and trust the source implicitly. Self-development and personal responsibility cannot be underscored enough in this regard. Early careerists should read fervently and stay attuned to the industry.

Benchmarking

From a mentorship perspective, senior leaders are seeking to develop potential leadership talent in others. Several identifying characteristics are referred to as indicators that an individual will make a good leader. First, managers will look at job performance of individuals and compare their performance with their peers. A good leader will go above and beyond the established requirements to accomplish the goal or complete the project.

They will also do the job well, communicate well, treat people with respect, and be loyal to their supervisor and organization.

Potential leaders have strong interpersonal skills and have the ability to interact with individuals on a variety of levels. Empathy is considered to be an important leadership attribute by many people. Potential leaders develop trustful, reliable, and consistent relationships. They assist others to succeed. Potential leaders know the mission, vision, strategies, goals, and objectives of the health organization and can translate the larger plan into a series of smaller, more specific plans that can be used within their area of responsibility.

Potential leaders also demonstrate clear and concise written and verbal communication skills within the workplace. Strongly developed communication skills may indicate an individual's ability to address conflict. Individuals who are self-driven may be seen as having a strong work ethic and, therefore, may be identified as having leadership potential. Self-driven individuals may also have a tendency to be motivated when presented with a desirable task, demonstrating initiative and drive until the project reaches its completion.

Finally, individuals who have an ability to create an organizational vision and motivate others to "buy into" the vision have potential as future leaders. The ability to translate the health organization's "large" vision into a vision for the specific area of responsibility is a highly valued skill. The application of motivating action to accomplish the work needed to achieve the vision is even more important. Individuals who demonstrate such abilities have a complex understanding of the organizational vision and can be considered forward thinkers.

Once individuals with leadership potential are identified, the next step is to begin the process of developing these skills in the individual to prepare him or her for leadership opportunities of greater scope and scale. According to managers, strategies to promote early leadership development within individuals include exposure, increased responsibilities, special assignments, job rotation, and coaching. Individuals should have exposure to a number of factors, including interactions with senior executives, uncomfortable situations, customers, external resources, internal resources, different levels of organization, and different degrees of risk. Exposure allows the early leader opportunities for trial-and-error learning and making mistakes in a nonthreatening environment. Assigning increased responsibilities to early leaders will allow for this kind of learning and leadership development. Other benefits of these interactions include opportunities to enhance tolerance to stressful situations, communication within the team and organization, and improvements in the leader's influence on his or her team.

Early leaders should also be given the opportunity to complete special assignments that will allow them to develop "transferrable skills." Development of these skills will allow individuals to gain a better understanding and knowledge of the various roles within the organization. Rotating jobs will give the early leader the opportunity to learn about the skills and requirements needed to perform unfamiliar duties within the organization. A leader with a well-rounded knowledge of organizational culture will be able to meet the needs of the employees, their departments, and the organization as a whole.

Finally, early leaders need multiple opportunities to receive coaching and feedback regarding their performance. Opportunities for modeling and mentoring will allow the early leader a safety net as he or she begins to analyze his or her leadership performance.

Sometimes, early leaders may run into situations in which "derailment" may occur. Early leaders who begin to withdraw from communication or engagement; exhibit adverse effects from personal stressors, such as excessive familial or community obligations; fail to follow through on assignments and projects; and demonstrate immaturity and lack of self-control, may be unprepared to handle the early leadership role. If intercepted early, derailment of the early leader can be avoided. Bolt and Hagemann offer strategies to prevent derailment of the early leader, including increasing communication and feedback, developing an action plan, providing more opportunities for coaching, and providing new opportunities or challenges.[5]

Measuring the Success of the Crawl Stage

The discussion of the crawl stage methodology presented here concludes by focusing on the measurement of crawl success by outside agents and stakeholders. This analysis is done through both empirical and evaluative thinking in regard to profession-driven standards and competencies. As a result, it is during the crawl stage that the early careerist begins to fully appreciate the profession that he or she is entering.

Empirical thinking is a skill-based approach that involves the memorization of lists, facts, and other entry-level competencies. Through this type of thinking, the early careerist demonstrates to superiors that he or she understands the technical nature of the organization. Possessing empirical thinking demonstrates to superiors and outside agents that the early careerist has spent time understanding the inputs, processes, and outputs of the organization. Additionally, it demonstrates a basic understanding of the organizational architecture. Empirical thinking may be analogous to the metaphor of an individual "learning the ropes." This phrase was developed by sailors in the British Navy centuries ago. The first task of any new sailor was to "learn the ropes" of the ship—that is, how the ropes were rigged to the masts, tethered to the sails, and connected to the moorings. Every sailor who boarded a ship for the first time "learned the ropes" so that he could contribute to the work of the ship. This same analogy can be applied to the business world.[6] Every profession has certain skills, traits, and entry-level competencies that must be "memorized" or performed to be acknowledged by senior leaders as meeting certain basic performance standards. Passage through this phase entails the movement from the unconscious incompetent or conscious incompetent to the conscious competent or unconscious competent stages of knowing. Execution of profession-driven empirical thinking demonstrates this competency.

The second standard that demonstrates a transition from the crawl stage to the walk stage of development is the execution of evaluative thinking. Evaluative thinking involves the ability to prioritize tasks within the health organization, to assign weighted values to projects based on organizational impact, and to screen the importance of new information filtering into the organization. Evaluative thinking allows the early careerist to make competent decisions on how to manage his or her day, perform tasks as assigned, and prioritize those tasks. A simple analogy may be a decision to spend time cleaning out one's email account versus planning for the weekly staff meeting where you are expected to provide input on a topic. Evaluative thinking allows early careerists to be competent not only in performing tasks, but also performing them in the proper order that allows for maximum output.

Both evaluative and empirical thinking are based on organizational goals and organizational objectives and will differ from organization to organization. For example, the prowess gained in becoming a group practice manager of a multiple-physician cardiac practice will be different than the mastery demonstrated by a CEO in managing a larger healthcare system.

The Crawl Time Line

Assigning an organizational time line to the crawl stage is difficult because the time required to master the "crawl" will be unique from individual to individual. Some "crawl" time may be spent in a degree program; in residencies, internships, or other practicum situations; and in the first professional positions in the health industry. Factors affecting advancement from the crawl stage to the walk stage include the size and complexity of the organization, the interdisciplinary nature of the job(s) to which the individual is assigned, the opportunity for outside professional development, and the desire and motivation of the employee to advance up the corporate ladder. These factors are variable and difficult to predict between organizations and individuals; however, the authors of this book, based on their more than 50 years of health and leadership experience, believe that it may take 5 to 10 years for a recently graduated student to advance prodigiously and effectively through the stages and tasks of the "crawl." This does not mean an early career health leader cannot perform entry-level tasks effectively; rather, it means that to advance to higher, more responsible positions within the industry, crawl-stage development is required.

THE WALK: STRATEGIES FOR MANAGING GROUPS AND TEAMS

In the walk stage, individuals learn more difficult and more complex information about leadership. The prospective leader is still in a safe environment and will most likely make mistakes, just as toddlers often fall down when they progress from crawling to walking. Training is more complex during the walk stage. Perhaps the leadership trainee begins learning about how to make changes in the organization, how to lead a project team, or how to deploy more comprehensive and complex communication skills. For example, the early careerist might learn how to lead successful and effective meetings. This skill incorporates excellent communication skills but also requires learning about facilitation of meetings. This is a skill every leader must have. For example, a meeting attendee who "takes over" or is talkative at inappropriate times should be seated at the corner of the meeting table or where the individual does not have easy face-to-face contact with other meeting attendees; this could reduce their inappropriate behaviors. This "knowledge" comes by learning from a mentor, in coursework, or from role modeling. Further capability elicited from this knowledge is then garnered from doing the task or using the knowledge appropriately.

In the walk stage, there is an increased emphasis on communicating evaluative and empirical information to groups or teams. As part of this phase, health leaders begin to understand the complexities and challenges of managing teams. A *team* is defined as an interdisciplinary group of individuals who are brought together to accomplish specific tasks or projects. The interdisciplinary nature of the team allows its members to accomplish what larger and unspecialized groups cannot perform as well. For example, a baseball team, where each player has demonstrated competency as a pitcher, catcher, infielder, or outfielder, is classified as a team.

A *group* is defined as two or more individuals who come from random disciplines with no apparent collective skills necessary to accomplish complex and specific tasks. A large group of competent baseball pitchers with 95-mph fastballs, for example, may lack the skills of an outfielder who can catch a fly-hit ball and immediately throw the ball from left field to home plate. A team is more specialized, whereas a group tends to be more random and may lack specific skill sets for tasks with great complexity.

In the walk stage, leaders begin to understand the complexities and challenges of managing teams. In the business world, a team is defined as an interdisciplinary group of individuals who are brought together to accomplish specific missions. The Roman army discovered it was difficult for one person to manage more than 12 persons simultaneously. This rule of thumb, or heuristic, has remained a metric for small-group leadership for more than two millennia. Developing leaders would be wise to not attempt to personally manage too many persons simultaneously.

The walk stage becomes far more abstract, which inherently makes it more difficult and more comprehensive. The developing leader will need to access more resources during this stage of development. It is during the walk stage that developing leaders might be required to actually lead a group outside the training situation. Learning in the crawl stage about leading a group or team (from in-training leadership exercises in coursework, perhaps) can serve the leader well when leading a real group in a real situation. Role-playing is one of the activities an instructor could adopt to support this learning, for example. For instance, one company's motto in this regard is "Role before you roll," which means that company employees engage in role-playing before attempting to bring a new product to market.[7, 8]

Interdisciplinary leadership can be understood in terms of shared leadership. Shared leadership requires that all team members "carry responsibility for team process and outcomes, thereby accepting formal and informal leadership roles that shift according to the situation."[9] The leader managing the interdisciplinary team may step in and out as the primary leader, with other individuals taking over at times as primary leader—a "taking your turn" approach. A series of individuals may temporarily fill the role of primary leader when the situation requires the most appropriate individual to be involved. Interdisciplinary leadership requires that individuals demonstrate competence and understanding of other disciplines to serve within the leader role in such a situation.

McCallin calls for a paradigm shift in which interdisciplinary leadership continues to be a form of "shared leadership" with a defined "practice leader." Under this approach, the practice leader accepts the role of managing the team, including the processes of development and coaching. The practice leader is also responsible for "coaching" other team members in the "art of shared leadership," which would include providing learning opportunities to find solutions to problems and achieve desirable outcomes.[10] The concept of coaching is discussed later in this text.

Team Building

In the crawl stage, a person manages him or herself primarily. By comparison, in the walk stage, the individual begins to lead larger numbers of people and manage greater quantities of resources. No leader can be successful without the ability to manage resources and lead small groups. As a result, one of the most critical tasks for young executives to master is the process of leading and building consensus in teams so as to produce positive outcomes for the health organization. While the theoretical process of leading and building teams is often covered in organizational behavior texts, Ledlow and Coppola suggest that no health leader can be truly effective without first having dedicated himself or herself to study of the theory, processes, and dynamics of team evolution. This knowledge may then be put in practice through experience.

Surprisingly, many health leaders are unfamiliar with the process of team building. This may be due to the fact that they moved into organizations with relatively large and stable groups of employees who are comfortable in their positions. It may also be because the leader has become a prominent figure in his or her field of study through excellence in the execution of skills, as might be the case with a surgeon, for example. This level of leader acknowledgment is different for a middle-level health leader and especially for a CEO of a large healthcare system who maintains responsibility for many elements of the enterprise. Without the experience of leading increasingly larger groups, the leader may not be fully aware of the life cycle and evolution associated with standing, ad hoc, and process action teams.

Given the importance of understanding this facet of team life, an overview of team building strategies is provided here. The following analysis is based on the work by Coppola as published in *Healthcare Executive.*[11]

Tuckman's Model of the Group Dynamic Process

It is during the walk stage training that students will most likely learn about the stages of group development. The first lesson is that groups of individuals do not become a cohesive productive group overnight or without training or without time. A descriptive process provides insight or knowledge into this phenomenon. In 1965, Bruce Tuckman described a process of team development that developing leaders in the walk stage would be wise to understand.[12] This process includes five stages: forming, storming, norming, performing, and adjourning. As an addition to the Tuckman model, an initial stage is important in team development; that sixth step is called the "informing stage."[13] Understanding the steps in the team-building process will assist leaders in maximizing team output. Conversely, failing to understand life-cycle issues in team development may result in team failure or decreased team productivity.

Leaders at the walk stage gain their first understanding of this process by managing interdisciplinary teams. During this phase, they come to recognize the importance of building and maintaining teams that produce positive outcomes within their organizations if they are to advance to higher levels of responsibility. However, the dynamics of organizing, maintaining, and guiding teams may be difficult and complex to manage. Teams go through stages of development and an organizational life cycle that may mirror the growth and development of the organization itself. Failing to understand organizational life-cycle issues commonly encountered in team development may result in the leader's inability to manage more complex and interdisciplinary groups in later stages of personal growth and development.

Informing Stage

Prior to the development of any new team, or additions to an existing structured team that rotate members in and out, there is an official notification of membership. This notification may be either verbal or in writing. In some cases, the individuals may be knowledgeable of the mission of the team and be familiar with other team members. During the informing stage, the prospective team member will form generalizations and opinions about the mission of the group. If not provided with enough structure, the individual may make judgments that prove counterproductive when the team initially meets and begins to work. Furthermore, if the candidate is knowledgeable of other team members, he or she may also form opinions and biases (good or bad) about other individuals in the group.

Informing Stage Strategy. Many leaders overlook this important stage of team development and pay little attention to its significance. Numerous threats to team productivity can be overcome in this initial stage through the formal presentation of vision and mission statements as well as clearly defined goals and objectives of the group bounded in a specific time frame of performance and objective measurement. The face-to-face verbal communication of these strategic points by the leader to the group is critical (as suggested by media richness theory); it is a must, not just something to be "if the leader has time and opportunity."

Additional strategic considerations include the time frame for notifying individuals of their team membership and the latent period between notification and the first required meeting. Shorter periods of latency may affect an individual's motivation to be on the team if other important projects are competing for time and attention, not unlike constructs associated with the garbage can model of decision making. Longer periods of latency (90 days or more) may result in an individual moving out of the department or organization where the team assignment was made. A reasonable time for notification to team action is 15 to 30 days.

Other considerations should include a known desire of the individual to be on the team, the special skill set the member brings to the team, and outcomes obtained with similar projects. Finally, an implied task of leaders prior to appointing individuals to a group is a working knowledge of personality dynamics between members. Previous working relationships, both positive and negative, should be included as part of the decision-making process before informing anyone of team assignment.

Forming Stage

The forming stage might also be called the "discovery stage." Typical professionals and working adults may be overtly cordial during this stage and attempt to overcompensate by remaining passive and agreeable. Other commonly encountered dynamics include the initial group membership being dominated through individual conservativism and by those members with a high internal locus of control. If members have worked well together in the past, there will be an initial latent discovery period of testing between members, where mutual support and a reconfirmation of cooperation are established. For members who lack familiarity with one another, there is a desire to be overtly convivial and supportive. New ideas may be offered implicitly or posited as participatory questions, such as "What do you all think would happen if we did 'X?'" If no one has been formally appointed as the mentor or leader of the group, the team may wait for an informal leader to emerge who possesses expert knowledge of small-group leadership or information power necessary to accomplish the team mission.

At this stage, many members of the group may share the perception that there is only one best way to handle the problem or mission. In reality, more than half of the group members may have already made up their minds about what to do, but are reluctant in this genial stage to be perceived as overbearing and lacking participatory collegiality. Conflict is important at this stage to limit "groupthink." Groupthink is a phenomenon, first formally identified by Janus, in which a group may make a decision that is harmful, unwanted, or benign. Conflict that is constructive is important in group processes. Conflict management skills should be part of organizational members' training and specifically group or team training. Emphasis should be dedicated to the problem-solving style of conflict management.

Forming Stage Strategy. It is beneficial in the forming stage to have previously outlined team member roles. This groundwork will catalyze and expedite the protracted collegial followership that professionals often bring into the complexity of team and group dynamics. Establishing clear goals and objectives is important as well, as it aids in the variance and unbounded rationality of excessive "outside the box" decisions. Finally, establishing a time line for the team is important. Many teams will expand their stages of incremental development to fill the time allotted to complete the task. Providing a time to complete initial tasks and objectives may expedite the forming stage. During this stage, the leader has to balance group development (storming and forming) with urgency; this can be a difficult balancing act if significant time constraints are present.

Storming Stage

A team will arrive at the storming stage when a tipping point is achieved and the members of the team no longer feel an obligated sense of prioritizing collegiality over task accomplishment. In the storming stage, members may compete for leadership of the group, try to gain control over the group's creative development, and exhibit frustration with imperfect information or animosity toward others for failing to support their own ideas. In the storming stage, the proverbial "gloves are off" philosophy takes hold, and members become more interested in their personal agendas and goals than in the team objectives.

In the storming stage, disrupters are typically present. Disrupters are people who have not been appointed as formal group mentors or who have not been recognized by the group as informal leaders. As a result, they may seek to exert control and dominance by exercising disruptive behavior. Outside of the leader role, the disrupter is the most common and most easily recognized role in any team dynamic situation.

Storming Stage Strategy.   In this stage of group dynamics, many outside leaders and agents will want to intervene and provide management influence. While seemingly productive, this path might be the worst one for a leader to follow. President Abraham Lincoln is credited with forming a "team of rivals" wherein competing personalities and strong partisan opinions were found to be necessary to achieve positive outcomes and maximize productivity. Intervening too quickly and discouraging professional discourse may result in a perception of group powerlessness and a perception that the team is merely a "rubber stamp" for the leader's vision. Frustration, professional discourse, and passionate competition between team members can be healthy and necessary to achieve higher goals. From a creative standpoint, when partisan personalities will not let go of their personal ideas and agendas, the only option is to develop a new collective idea that is truly accomplished through the input of all team members. Professional discourse is healthy and necessary; leaders should be wary of micromanaging the storming stage too quickly.

Norming Stage

In the norming stage, individuals begin to relinquish their personal agendas. At this point, team roles have been clearly identified within the group and can be recognized by outside agents and stakeholders. Informal and formal leaders begin working together to accomplish tasks and achieve desired outcomes. Other participants in the group may assume one or more roles as followers, innovators, experts, or researchers, among other actor positions. In this stage, lingering disrupters may assume supportive roles or enter into passive positions by accepting delegation. Some individuals may exchange roles over the course of the team's tenure.

Norming Stage Strategy.   Leaders may be initially bewildered by the task organization of the group and the agenda that the group is moving toward. Leaders should be cognizant that the reason the group was formed was to complete a task or mission that could not be accomplished individually or through institutionalized practices and policies. They need to know that team members have gone through the informing, forming, storming, and norming phases and now possess a unique point of view on the problem under study. Leaders need to trust in the process and allow the team to accomplish its task(s). If one or more group members are not "norming" to the group, then the group leader or manager may need to remove them from the group or replace those members. However, replacing members at this stage will set back the group dynamic process and bring the group back to the earlier stages of team development. In essence, if the group leader assesses the situation and determines that certain group members will deter the group from performing the desired work, it is better to go with a smaller team or take more time to replace group members: This choice is the group leader's decision. The team or group is ready to accomplish what it has been formed to do.

Performing Stage

In the performing stage, the team has developed new ideas and carefully thought out objectives that would not have been possible to accomplish by any one individual in the group working along. The adage, "None of us is as smart as all of us," is salient in this context. There is an increased recognition of superordinate goals and a realization that the organization's needs are superior to individualism. A sense of pride in team identity is recognized and a clear sense of "we-ness" over "I-ness" becomes visible. The "we-ness" culture of the group is developed and enhanced when a confirming communication climate is established by the group's leader or manager. This consideration is especially important in health organizations, and even more so with interdisciplinary teams.

In the performing stage, new responsibilities and new requests for information can be processed quickly. The team may be eager to demonstrate its ability to multitask and continue to be challenged. Products, ideas, and tasks are brought to fruition in this stage: There is visible output; there are tangible results.

Performing Stage Strategy.   As the group's leader, first and foremost, you should say, "Thank you!" to team members. Recognize individuals in the group for their contributions. Make a point to understand the role each member played in the development of the new idea or product so that these talents and abilities can be used appropriately next time.

In addition, take a step back and be supportive of the group's work. A potential threat to morale, future team building and group productivity arises when a leader attempts to place his or her superfluous thumbprint on the product for the sole purpose of possession. Leaders need to know when to lead, but they also need to know when to support and trust in the collective wisdom of the team.

Adjourning Stage

In the adjourning stage, both internal and external stakeholders recognize the completion of the group's work. The reason for the team's formation has been accomplished and there is a recognition of new (or updated) programs, polices, or procedures in place. Members are ready to move onto their next positions of responsibility and assume new challenges.

Adjourning Stage Strategy. In this stage, document the process and save the output of member work. Incredibly, the good work of ad hoc (temporary teams or groups focused on a specific project), seasonal teams (e.g., Joint Commission preparation teams) and standing teams (organizational Six Sigma teams) is often lost in the process of personnel turnover and the dynamic turbidity of the environment. More often than not, legacy files and best practices are discarded or reinvented with each new cycle of team formation. Given these possibilities, means of archiving best practices and lessons learned should be established. Now is the perfect time to build knowledge management and organizational learning systems. A team or group section, departmental, or even organizational (depending on the scope and scale of the work) presentation or briefing may be a good start to manage knowledge, diffuse knowledge to others, and provide a platform for organizational learning.

Good to Great Groups and Teams

Once a health leader has mastered the "crawl" stage and understands the process of team life-cycle development and associated challenges in the walk stage, the leader can focus his or her attention on making *good* teams *great*. In health organizations, good group and team accomplishments are important. However, the dynamic and varied world of health also calls for great groups and teams combined with great effort to achieve results that enhance everyone's life. The need for great groups is urgent, so as to solve the most pressing strategic and operational problems in the health industry and within health organizations. The organizations of the future will increasingly depend on the creativity of their members to survive.[14]

Health leaders must understand the type of people who make for great groups. People in great groups have the following characteristics:[15]

■ Intrinsically motivated, buoyed by the joy and challenge of problem solving

■ Focused obsessively on fascinating projects

■ Oblivious to "ordinary," bureaucratic, and trivial matters

> These people love the discovery process and they have dazzling skills (such as [clinical], mathematical, statistical, [financial], or computer). They have the unique ability to identify problems and find creative, boundary busting solutions rather than simplistic ones . . . they have hungry, urgent, quick minds; many have expansive interests with encyclopedic knowledge. They have the ability to see what others don't see (they can almost "see the future") in part because they have command of more data (and the ability to use it) in the first place.[16]

The key for health leaders to understand is to gather, unite, and make an effective group of people, who individually are great, into a synergistic team capable of superior problem solving, persistent energy, and tremendous innovative capacity. Health organizations increasingly will require such teams if they are to compete in a competitive environment amid significant health challenges where information is readily available and just-in-time learning is commonplace:

> Great Groups tend to be less bureaucratic than ordinary ones. Terribly talented people often have little tolerance for less talented middle managers. Great Groups tend to be structured, not according to title, but according to role. The person [who] is best able to do some essential task does it.[17]

Every great group has a strong and visionary leader who has a talent to select or hire people better than the leader; successful health leaders look for people of excellence who have the ability to work well with others. Health leaders, considering goal setting theory, set challenging goals for the group or team: "Look how morale soars when intelligent people are asked to do a demanding but worthy task and given the freedom and tools to do it."[18] Successful health leaders have a vision and a plan to realize it while being expert motivators. They make their group or team feel and know why their work is important; this kind of sharing improves problem solving and increases the pace of work.

Bennis and Biederman suggest the following factors be considered as part of the team building process:[19]

Killers of Groups

- Constraints and trivial structure/tasks
- Error-free environments
- Closed systems
- Military model of leadership (authoritative/strongly directive)

Enhancers

- Freedom and autonomy (failure is a learning event; errors are a natural part of learning)
- Risk taking
- Enabling and encouraging environment (confirming communication environment)
- "If you can dream it, you can do it" mentality

Take-Home Lessons

- *Greatness starts with superb people.* Recruit the best people possible. Recruit problem solvers who happen to be computer programmers, physicists, nurses, physicians, and so on.
- *Great groups and great leaders create one another.* Collaboration is critical; the standard command-and-control models of leadership/management do not work. Leaders of great groups must act decisively but never arbitrarily.
- *Every great group has a strong leader.* A leader is an organizer of genius—a maestro who is a pragmatic dreamer and who has an original, yet attainable vision. A good leader eliminates distractions and trivial matters (consider the path–goal model).
- *The leaders of great groups love talent and know where to find it.* They revel in the talent of others.
- *Great groups are full of talented people who can work together.* Sharing information and advancing the work are the *only* real social obligations.
- *Great groups think they are on a tremendously important mission.* These groups are filled with believers; doubters are dismissed. Their clear, collective purpose makes everything they do seem meaningful and valuable.
- *Great groups see themselves as winning underdogs.*
- *Great groups are optimistic, not realistic.*
- *In great groups, the right person has the right job.*
- *The leaders of great groups give them what they need and free them from the rest.*
- *Great groups share information effectively.* The leader ensures that a communication network exists and that everyone has full access to it.
- *Great groups ship.* (They produce.)
- *Great work is its own reward.* (In Herzberg's two-factor theory, group members are intrinsically motivated by a transformational leader).

Bennis and Biederman used qualitative (as opposed to quantitative) research methods to come to these conclusions. Their work was mostly done through histories, literature review, interviews, and possibly some observation (qualitative methods). Which model do they propose for leading great groups? Which conditions foster the creation of a great group? Which parts or the whole of the model will work (can be applied) in health situations?

Group Size and Composition

Another important factor in group and team dynamics is group size and composition. Shull, Delbecq, and Cummings (1970) determined that group size influences decision processes in several ways; for example, communication becomes difficult as the number of members increase and less time is available for each member to speak.[20] When the size of a group increases beyond eight members, the potential contribution from adding another member should be carefully weighed against the added difficulty of running an effective meeting and the project as a whole.

Janus's notion of "groupthink" (mentioned earlier in this chapter) is noteworthy when considering group issues. "Highly cohesive groups sometime foster a phenomenon called 'group think' (Janus, 1972); group think involves certain kinds of illusions and stereotypes that interfere with effective decision making."[21] Ensuring constructive conflict in the group or establishing and maintaining a "devil's advocate" role or contrarian role in the group can reduce the potential of groupthink.

Overview of Other Essential Skills in the Walk Stage

While learning how to manage and interact with teams is an essential skill that must be mastered by the developing leader, it is not the only skill set required. The developing leader must also gain experience with larger budgets, multidisciplinary task organization, and strategic planning. Several methodologies are available to help the developing leader to gain experience in these areas if there is not a direct opportunity in the workplace to do so.

Becoming involved in the local community can assist the developing leader in developing skill sets that are not immediately available in the workplace. Many local governments and communities have colloquial health boards and advisory committees that routinely seek volunteers. These organizations can assist the developing leader in obtaining experience in strategic planning and managing resources. Many of these boards have strategic plans that look forward into the future for three to five years and can be excellent places for a young health leader to practice skills related to strategic planning and forecasting, analysis, budgeting, and building interpersonal relationships and networks.

As with the crawl strategies, the developing leader in the walk stage can seek relevant opportunities in professional organizations. The opportunity to run for office or lead large committees may be available in the professional organization that will assist the developing health leader in working with teams across large distances (using teleconferencing technology) and provide him or her with an excellent opportunity to exercise leadership skills along an informal chain of influence.

Leading an event and becoming a host of a multidisciplinary health event are also good ways to expand the expression and development of the nascent leader. Hosting a local event and managing a committee of experts who provide continuing health education to a group of senior executives, for example, provides an opportunity for the developing leader to get noticed, to network within the community, and become recognized as someone who can manage people in informal networks.

Mastery of Walk Tasks

In the walk stage, there is an implied understanding that material learned at the crawl stage has been mastered. For example, the chief executive no longer gives detailed and explicit directions and instructions on how to complete tasks to the subordinate health leader; the subordinate health leader knows what to do to accomplish the assigned task. The young executive, at this stage, should have mastered basic skills in regard to participating fully on interdisciplinary teams; completing projects in a timely manner; producing thoughtful and correctly executed whitepapers, business case analysis, or other analyses; and taking on greater responsibility in terms of leading people and managing more materials, financial resources, and other logistical components of the health organization.

The young executive at this stage should begin to serve as a peer role model in the health organization rather than directly seeking mentorship himself or herself. While the CEO always has the responsibility to role-model and mentor junior members of the organization,[22] young executives may begin to discover the benefits of being role models themselves during the walk stage.[23] At this point, the young executive has learned the complexities of the organization and is ready to assume some mentoring duties.[24] Thus the walk stage is characterized by the "powering down" or "pushing down" of the mission, vision, values, strategies, goals, and objectives of the CEO to the subordinate health leader, accompanied by the subordinate health leader's ability to translate higher-order organizational directive and competitive strategies into operational and tactical execution at the departmental, unit, and section levels. The subordinate health leader, by now, should be demonstrating leadership qualities and organizational values to more junior employees in the organization.

The young executive also relaxes from reacting to the environment. In the walk stage, he or she has mastered the basics of the organizational environment and becomes active in controlling events in a strategic and forecasted nature.[25–27] The leader in the walk stage also knows the difference between basic and complex competencies in the organization. A simple example can be found in the naive nature of how an organizations measures productivity or executes a budget. A health leader at the entry level, and definitely at the middle level, after working in an health organization for a period of time, should be responsible for explaining productivity measurement to more junior employees and administrative personnel, rather than seeking counsel from a more senior health leader concerning these issues.[28, 29]

Measuring the Success of the Walk Stage

The young executive in the walk stage has sought out professional education and self-improvement in two forms: didactic (continuing health education) and practical (on-the-job training). When these forms of development are combined, they provide for the ability to exercise competency in both empirical and evaluative thinking. These competencies were exercised in the crawl stage; however, when these two competencies are mastered and the skills of each executed in a combined and simultaneous fashion, one sees the emergence of critical thinking and the ability to apply that thinking to create positive outcomes in the health organization. Critical thinking is apparent when the young executive has demonstrated the capacity to merge both empirical thinking and evaluative thinking into seamless actions and decision making that result in favorable outcomes.[30, 31]

Critical thinking is a skill that involves not only knowledge of content, but also concept formation and analysis. Furthermore, critical thinking encompasses the ability to reason and draw conclusions based on imperfect data, and the ability to recognize and avoid contradiction with imperfect information. Critical thinking is important in moral and ethical analysis where gray areas exist and conflict and partisanship over processes and policy are evident. In extreme cases, the ability to think critically allows an individual to see both sides of controversial topics such as euthanasia and right-to-life issues. In its simplest form, it allows an individual to balance enduring beliefs with behaviors. For example, it may be unwise to tell a subordinate employee that he has gained weight, even though it may be true. Excessive and unnecessary honesty—that is, honest discussions over issues that are not organizationally related or that may be personally hurtful to people's self-esteem—can be undesirable in leaders, and the adroit health leader knows how to balance the importance and consequence of individual action and deeds.[32] This facility directly relates to emotional intelligence.

There is a certain expectation that young executives will be able to anticipate organizational needs, take initiative in solving problems before they become too onerous, and find solutions to issues before they become apparent to others. This ability to anticipate is typically the product of multimodal training experiences that include volunteerism, personal self-improvement, affiliation with professional organizations, maintaining relevancy in the literature, and becoming a mentor to junior employees.[33]

The burgeoning mastery of critical thinking skills may be ineffable and difficult to notice in the workplace; however, the long-term effects of applied critical thinking on an individual's success in the organization are readily identified. The young executive who has mastered these skills is more likely to be promoted and advance within the organization than those individuals who are still educating themselves on empirical and evaluative competencies. Finally, when the young leader is seen advancing in the workplace through demonstrative stakeholder approval of senior leaders, the young leader has successfully graduated from the walk stage.

A conceptual model of critical thinking is depicted graphically in **Figure 7–2**. In this conceptual model, the ability to think critically is a function of combining empirical and evaluative thinking. These two constructs are, in turn, derived from the organizational mission, vision, strategies, goals, objectives, and competencies that represent the skill sets of the organization. In essence, they encompass the knowledge of the health organization, which (ideally) is archived and housed in the health organizational knowledge management system. As the model suggests, obtaining effectiveness in mastering organizational directive and competitive strategies, goals,

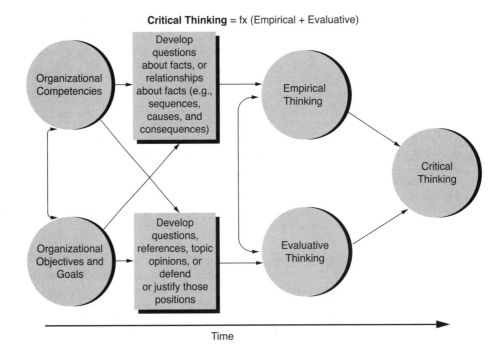

FIGURE 7–2   Conceptual Model of Critical Thinking

Source: Coppola, M. N. (2004, March 8). *Measuring critical thinking through analysis of moment structure (AMOS): A latent variable approach to evaluating effective outcomes.* Whitepaper, Baylor University, Waco, TX.

objectives, and competencies results in a young leader successfully "learning the ropes" of the organization. Over a period of time, with appropriate experiences and opportunities, the young leader hones his or her empirical and evaluative thinking abilities. A tipping point finally occurs when these items are mastered and become an internalized part of the young executive's activities of daily action and decision making. This is an example of unconscious competence: The health leader performs "leadership" as a natural part of who he or she is in the health organization.

The Walk Time Line

Similar to the analysis provided in conjunction with the crawl time line, accessing the necessary time to achieve critical thinking skills is difficult to judge. The walk time line will certainly involve graduate education, or similar continuing health education, resulting in the mastering of competencies associated with industry norms.[34] Mastery of competencies in the health environment might also be achieved through extensive and progressive on-the-job training. As with the crawl stage, advancement from the walk to the run stage will be based on unique factors in the environment that may include access to graduate and continuing health education, opportunities in the workplace to exercise skills, and the individual's motivation to challenge himself or herself by taking on new responsibilities in the health organization. These factors are also mutable and will vary from organization to organization and from individual to individual. As a guideline, it may take 7 to 15 years to master these advanced competencies.

THE RUN: STRATEGIES FOR LEADING ORGANIZATIONS

When aspiring health organizational leaders have progressed successfully through the crawl and walk stages, it is time for them to run. In the run stage, the health leader has been screened and evaluated by outside stakeholders and deemed prepared to lead hundreds of people, manage millions of dollars, and direct strategic plans and policies that may affect the lives of tens of thousands of others; this stakeholder assessment is usually accomplished in the hiring of a senior health leader through screening and interview processes. Candidates who successfully survive these processes are placed in leadership positions, becoming accountable and responsible for the diverse myriad of responsibilities and challenges inherent in every health leadership position. They have the knowledge, they have gained the skills, they have practiced, and now it is time for them to become the leader. This is the most difficult part of the leadership development cycle, because the person who fills this position has a major responsibility—namely, he or she must get things done.[35] At this stage, the leader is ready to be effective as the head of departments or even as the head of the institution or organization. Leaders in this stage have the knowledge, skills, and experience required to lead gender-diverse, ethnically rich populations and motivate highly educated professionals who have received many different kinds of training; they also have the capabilities needed to integrate their health organizations with the communities they serve and to improve the health status of those populations through the organization's products and services.

In the run stage, the execution of complex skill sets allows the leader to lead and operate in the large-scale health organization. These complex skill sets include professional characteristics and qualities, the ability to manage change, the ability to manage crises, and the willingness to accept risk.[36] A final complex competency is the ability to think conceptually.

Professional characteristics of the leader in the run stage include demonstration of ethical behavior and actions, the moral courage to do the right thing, a strong preference for "we-ness" over "I-ness," organizational beneficence, and altruism. The senior leader of the health organization exercises the external presence necessary for the organization to be reflective of the leader's own personal characteristics. It is the leader whose honesty, values, and charisma become the mortar holding together the bricks from which the organization's personality is built.

Moreover, the senior-level executive must be able to manage change. Organizational change may stem from a variety of factors, including technological developments, organizational changes, needs of the employees, economic change, and social movements. The *green movement* is an example of environmental change, wherein conscientious consumers have begun making decisions about which goods and services to buy based on the organization's posture and efforts-related conservation. The health leader who does not look for opportunities in this movement to promote the organization's initiatives and values may face a loss of business as these consumers look for more eco-friendly organizations from which to purchase health products or services.

In managing change, the senior executive must be sensitive to fluctuations in the environment, being able to assess change, plan for change, and facilitate change. In this regard, it is important to remember that "to lead" is "to move the organization forward," and organizations move forward through change. Change becomes a catalyst for organizational improvement, and the senior leader is aware of this opportunity for improvement based on external or internal environmental pressures. Areas of change might include new staff, new services, new technology, redesigned tasks or jobs, and organizational culture change, for example.

In managing change, the executive leader has the most important role when addressing crises to ensure that issues are addressed and handled effectively. It is no small epiphany to say that many leaders earn their reputations on the ability to manage crisis. Hook explains that the principles for managing crisis situations may be classified into three groups: getting organized and oriented, developing a course of action, and implementing the plan.[37]

Another senior-level competency is the ability to accept personal risk and to engage in prudent organizational vulnerability. If the leader cannot do so, then leading an organization will not be possible. Risk taking often is the seminal and actionable element that distinguishes the fully mature and competent leader from those less skilled persons still experimenting with factors in the run stage. An example of a leader engaging in personal leadership risk might be Barack Obama's bid for the U.S. Presidency in 2006. The first-term Senator from Illinois may have hindered his ability to become reelected to the Senate if running for President weakened his ability to legislate for the people of Chicago, or if he professionally embarrassed himself on the national stage. Of course, this run-from-behind personal risk was successful for Obama, and serves as an excellent example of risk taking in leadership.

Conceptual Thinking

The ability to think conceptually might be considered the ultimate goal of a leader. In its simplest form, conceptual thinking is "outside the box" thinking. It is the ability to see what everyone else has not seen, and to think and act in ways that others cannot think and are incapable of enacting. Alternatively, conceptual thinking might be considered as the lack or absence of perceptual blindness. Perceptual blindness is a process of self-selected institutionalism where all future or current problems are addressed based on past practices and procedures. It also incorporates the concept of exercising personal bias and ignoring obvious factors in the environment that are contributing to the existing situation. In this regard, the *theory of the hammer* applies: When an individual has a hammer as a tool, then all the problems look like nails.

Conceptual thinking allows a leader to think strategically. Through strategic thinking, a leader is able to view tomorrow's world without the limits imposed by today's resources and other constraints. Strategic thinking involves anticipation of future events before they happen, and the controlling of events on the horizon. The ability to think strategically, combined with the openness of the leader to explore different methods of practice and policy, allows the leader, and his or her organization, to adopt new technologies early and penetrate new markets ahead of competitors. In short, conceptual thinking provides an organizational advantage for both the leader and the organization within the health industry.

Measuring the Success of the Run Stage

Because the run stage is a continuous process of planning conceptually and thinking strategically, the measurement of the run stage can be framed in terms of the overall success of the organization as defined by market share or other organizational performance metrics. The latter metrics might include the return on investment on new projects and ventures, the rate of penetration into new markets, the development of new product lines, an increase in patient enrollment, satisfaction scores, and other similar measures.

In addition, the successful senior leader will attain a high level of approbation from the external stakeholders in the operational community. These stakeholders may be members of the governing board, outside advocacy groups, or unions. In its simplest form, success at the run stage is based on stakeholder satisfaction, organizational prosperity, and the creation of an organizational culture that is poised to thrive in a dynamic environment.

The Run Time Line

The time line for achieving success in the run stage may cover 10 to 20 years, or even take a lifetime to achieve. For some individuals, success in this stage may never be fully realized. It is reasonable to suggest that some leaders may never be regarded as ready to lead large-scale health organizations, owing to a variety of mutable and immutable factors. Nevertheless, entry into this echelon of excellence should be a benchmark for all early careerists to achieve.

EFFECTIVENESS AND LEADERSHIP DEVELOPMENT

The overall effectiveness of any leader development or organizational life cycle can be measured and gauged only through stakeholder dynamics and health organizational performance. Effectiveness is defined as the ability to achieve approbation from outside stakeholders. In this respect, effectiveness is a qualitative term whose measurement is based on the individual preferences of those measuring the leader themselves. A review of the performance of the President of the United States provides a clear example of this dynamic in action. In approval polls, the President's overall satisfaction rate is based on an amalgam of priorities that are individually calculated by stakeholders and that result in a simple yes/no satisfaction rating. As suggested by the cliché, "Beauty is in the eye of the beholder," leader effectiveness is similarly based on the opinions and subjective judgments of stakeholders.

Stakeholders are constituents with a vested interest in the affairs and actions of the health leader and the health leader's organization. They include those individuals, groups, or organizations that are affected by the leader and that may seek to influence the leader. Stakeholders can be classified into three groups:

■ *Internal stakeholders,* who operate entirely within the bounds of the organization and typically include management and professional and nonprofessional staff.

- *Interface stakeholders,* who function both internally and externally to the organization and include medical staff, the governing body, and stockholders in the case of for-profit healthcare organizations.

- *External stakeholders,* who are generally those acting as suppliers, customers, patients, community members, and third-party payers, including government agencies, and those who provide resources. Other external stakeholders include competitors, special-interest groups, local communities, labor organizations, and regulatory and accrediting agencies.

The leader in any health organization needs these stakeholders to survive. However, the leader must also analyze all stakeholders in the environment to determine which are relevant, which groups could be potential threats, and which have the potential to cooperate. Balancing the demands of multiple stakeholders with different interests poses a major challenge for any leader. Achieving stakeholder approbation on a continual basis is a signature of the leader who has mastered empirical, evaluative, critical, and conceptual thinking skills.

When health leaders are fully competent at leading health organizations, large groups, large projects, and the like, the next salient issue becomes effectiveness. Simply put, how effective is the leader in the health organization? Leading people and managing resources to accomplish the health organization's mission, strategies, goals, and objectives are major components. Creating a robust culture that is able to withstand and thrive in dynamic environments, developing future leaders, and moving the health organization in the appropriate direction to achieve its vision are other elements. **Figure 7–3**, which depicts major constructs of health leadership effectiveness, is provided for thought, reflection, and discussion; use it as a starting point for your own career planning.

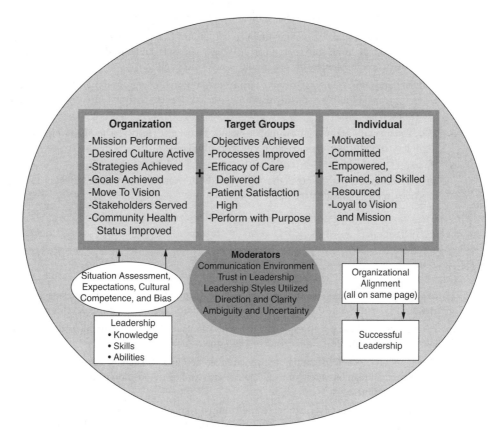

FIGURE 7–3   Macro Constructs of Health Leadership Effectiveness

SUMMARY

This chapter looked at techniques and applications of leadership in leading groups, ranging from small groups of individuals to interdisciplinary teams in small- and large-scale organizations. These elements are ordinal stages for developing competent leadership capabilities, which are in turn built on the crawl–walk–run methodology of health leader development. Mature leaders recognize that different skills are required to lead small groups of individuals than are needed to guide large and complex organizations. Individuals and teams may respond better to verbal communication and direct interaction, whereas leaders of large and complex organizations must develop alternative approaches to communication, such as well-written and -developed policy and mission statements, or nurturing and developing human resources proxies to spread the leader's vision down the hierarchy of the health organization. This chapter examined additional best practices in communication, leadership archetypes, and some delegation, participatory, and collaborative practices used in a group or team context.

DISCUSSION QUESTIONS

1. How would you describe the cycle of leadership? Identify the knowledge, skills, and abilities at each stage of the cycle that contribute to understanding health leadership development. How do you "learn the ropes" in a health organization?

2. Explain Tuckman's model of the group dynamic process and summarize its importance for health leaders in group or team supervision. What is the most important stage and why?

3. Which elements would you include when constructing a five-year leadership development plan based on an ultimate health leadership position goal? What is your goal and how do you get there? Which empirical and evaluative competencies do you need to reach your goal?

4. Compare and contrast a great group or team, a team mired in a groupthink situation, and an ineffective group or team. Could you distinguish how a health leader performs in each of these group or team situations?

5. Which elements or components would be included in a health leader's checklist for leading and managing a group or team focused on superior performance and outcomes?

6. How would you evaluate health leader development as a concept? How would you relate leader development opportunities and events to the cycle of leadership and the knowledge, skills, and abilities necessary to achieve mastery in each stage of the cycle?

EXERCISES

1. In a one-page paper, describe the cycle of leadership and identify essential knowledge, skills, and abilities at each stage of the cycle that contribute to understanding health leadership development.

2. In a half- to one-page paper, explain Tuckman's model of the group dynamic process and summarize its importance to health leaders in group or team supervision.

3. Construct a five-year leadership development plan for yourself. Then, in a one- to two-page paper, outline a development plan based on your ultimate health leadership position goal. How long will it take you to reach your ultimate goal?

4. In a one- to two-page paper, compare and contrast a great group or team, a team mired in a groupthink situation, and an ineffective group or team. Also describe how a health leader performs in each of these group or team situations.

5. Devise a health leader's checklist for leading and managing a group or team focused on superior performance and outcomes; the checklist should be one half to one page in length.

6. In a two- to three-page paper, evaluate health leader development, and relate leader development opportunities and events to the cycle of leadership and the knowledge, skills, and abilities to achieve mastery at each stage of the cycle.

REFERENCES

1. Bolt, J. F., & Hagemann, B. (2009). Harvesting tomorrow's leaders. *T+D Magazine, 63*(7), 52–57.

2. Kinney, M. (2008, July 17). What the Army taught me about teaching. Retrieved July 17, 2009, from Inside Higher Education, http://www.insidehighered.com/views/2008/07/17/Kinney.

3. Global Security. (2005, April 27). Training. Retrieved July 17, 2009, from http://www.globalsecurity.org/military/library/policy/army/fm/7-21-13/chap5.htm.

4. Griffin, C. A., & Lockwood, C. A. (2009, May). Building active learning applications and opportunities into a distance-learning leadership course. Retrieved July 24, 2009, from Northern Arizona University, W.A. Franke College of Business, http://74.125.47.132/search?q=cache:UMTnjj7PPSIJ:www.cba.nau.edu/Faculty/Intellectual/workingpapers/pdf/Lockwood_ActiveLearning.pdf+crawl-walk-run+theory+leadership&cd=5&hl=en&ct=clnk&gl=us&client=firefox-a.

5. Bolt & Hagemann, note 1.

6. Abramson, M. A. (2005). *Learning the ropes: Insights for political appointees.* New York: Rowman and Littlefield.

7. Lynn, D. (2004, May 20). Crawl, walk, run. Retrieved July 17, 2009, from http://startingit.blogspot.com/2004/05/crawl-walk-run.html.

8. Smith, M. K. (2005). Bruce W. Tuckman. Retrieved July 17, 2009, from infed http://www.infed.org/thinkers/tuckman.htm.

9. McCallin, A. (2003). Interdisciplinary team leadership: A revisionist approach for an old problem? *Journal of Nursing Management, 11,* 364–370.

10. McCallin, note 9.

11. Coppola, M. N. (2008, May/June). Managing teams in organizations. *Healthcare Executive* http://www.iqpc.com/News.aspx?id=117213089&m=sixsigma.

12. Smith, note 8.

13. Coppola, note 11.

14. Bennis, W., & Biederman, P. W. (1997). *Organizing genius: The secret of creative collaboration.* New York: Addison-Wesley, p. 8.

15. Bennis & Biederman, note 14.

16. Bennis & Biederman, note 14, p. 17.

17. Bennis & Biederman, note 14, p. 104.

18. Bennis & Biederman, note 14, p. 9.

19. Bennis & Biederman, note 14.

20. Yukl, G. (1994) *Leadership in organizations* (3rd ed.). Englewood Cliffs, NJ: Prentice Hall.

21. Yukl, note 20, p. 410.

22. Mackenzie, K. (2008). The CEO as mentor. *Healthcare Leaders.* Retrieved October 16, 2008, from http://www.healthleadersmedia.com/content/214974/topic/WS_HLM2_MAG/The-CEO-a.

23. Hollister, R. (2001). The benefits of being a mentor. *Healthcare Executive, 16*(2), 49–50.

24. Seijts, G. H., & Latham, G. P. (2001). The effect of learning, outcome and proximal goals on a moderately complex task. *Journal of Organizational Behavior, 22,* 291–302.

25. Terpstra, D. E., & Rozell, E. J. (1994). The relationship of goal setting to organizational profitability. *Group and Organization Management,* 19, 285–294.

26. Thrall, T. H., & Hoppszallern, S. (2001). Leadership survey. Hospitals & Health Networks. *75*(2), 33–39.

27. Seijts & Latham, note 24.

28. Huselid, M. A., Becker, B. E., & Beaty, W. (2005). *The workforce scorecard: Managing human capitol to executive strategy.* Boston: Harvard Business Press.

29. Supon, V. (1998). Penetrating the barriers to teaching higher thinking. *Clearing House, 71*(5), 294–296.

30. Coppola, M. N. (2004, March 9). *Measuring critical thinking through analysis of moment structure (AMOS): A latent variable approach to evaluating effective outcomes.* Whitepaper, Baylor University, Waco, TX.

31. Brookfield, S. D. (1991). Discussion. In M. W. Galbraith (Ed.), *Adult learning methods* (pp. 187–204). Malabar, FL: Krieger.

32. Coppola, note 30.

33. Coppola, note 30.

34. Global Security. (2005, April 27). Training. Retrieved July 17, 2009, from http://www.globalsecurity.org/military/library/policy/army/fm/7-21-13/chap5.htm.

35. Global Security, note 34.

36. Hook, J. R. (2008). Developing senior leaders: A theoretical framework and suggestions for applications. *International Journal of Organization Theory and Behavior, 11*(3), 411–436.

37. Hook, note 36.

Leadership Models in Practice

There are risks and costs to a program of action. But they are far less than the long-range risks and costs of comfortable inaction.

—John F. Kennedy, May 12, 1961

This chapter presents practical models for both students of leadership and mature practitioners of the art and science of leadership to apply to their personal leadership practice. Two evolving models and one established model of leadership are described here; they should assist leaders in honing their personal leadership practice. These models are the *omnibus leadership model,* the *dynamic culture leadership model,* and the *reframing organizations leadership and management model.* These models are prescriptive in that they provide a strategy for success and guidelines for practical implementation. Other differing, yet contemporary, leadership models are also presented from Lynn, Yukl, Hargrove, and Glidewell. An analysis and comparison of four of the models presented in this chapter is included as an example of model comparison and evaluation. Health leaders should consider the constructs of these models and think about how they might apply them in complex health organizational environments. The chapter concludes with a list of recommended leadership measurement tools with which to conduct leader evaluations.

LEARNING OBJECTIVES

1. Outline the constructs and processes of at least two contemporary leadership models presented in this chapter, and identify the prescriptive mechanisms of those models.

2. Distinguish at least two of the contemporary leadership models in this chapter from one other leadership theory or model from the situational leadership thought phase (presented in Chapter 4).

3. Apply at least one contemporary leadership model from this chapter to a real or hypothesized health leadership situation or case, and explain the rationale for your decisions, actions, and behaviors.

4. Analyze and illustrate the contemporary leadership models' constructs that enable a health leader to develop, modify, or revise the organizational culture in a health enterprise.

5. Create a leadership model—either simple or complex—for your own use in health organizations, and relate your model to constructs found in models from this chapter and other constructs from theories and models in previous chapters of this text.

6. Compare and contrast two or more contemporary leadership models.

THE OMNIBUS LEADERSHIP MODEL[1]

In 1905, the world-famous Carnegie Museum of Natural History placed the bones of a prized Apatosaurus on review. The bones remained on display until 1992, when the fossil was reexamined by a different team of paleontologists. These late-century paleontologists noticed that the dinosaur had been assembled incorrectly, and that the wrong head had been placed on the dinosaur almost 90 years earlier.[2] Over the course of the twentieth century, hundreds (perhaps thousands) of scholars and academics had viewed the bones and admired the symmetry and perfection of the fossil—never noticing the 90-year-old error the original paleontologists had made.

Given the profound nature of this mistake, is it possible that the study of leadership is likewise suffering from an ancient error in construction? Has it become a calculus formula that has become memorized, but never derived? It has been suggested that there are as many methods to define leadership as there are ways to measure it. From a research perspective, this flexibility is often very beneficial, as the purpose of research is to look at things in increasing levels of complexity, and with the ultimate goal of discerning intricate parts of the puzzle. But is it possible that, in the literature of leadership theory, the level of complexities has become so intricate that the larger picture is no longer visible? A review of leadership theory suggests the possibility that the answer to this question is "yes."

Furthermore, is it possible that the study of leadership has suffered from *theory creep*? The original conception of "creep" is attributed to former U.S. Secretary of Defense Casper Weinberger, who suggested that "creep" is the absence of a uniform vision, and who noted that this condition results in constant change.[3] The end product of creep results in people solving problems that have no relationship to the original project or process at all. In other words, *the wrong fight is fought.*

The study of leadership theory may have also suffered from theoretical creep. A review of leadership theories in the twentieth century suggests leadership studies have shifted from the broad and wide-ranging trait and "great man" theories to discriminate research efforts that reflect more of an application of unit models of decision making or satisfaction, rather than theory. Supporting this premise, some authors have suggested the problem with organizational theories is that the wrong unit of analysis is applied to inappropriate situations. Furthermore, many authors suggest previous studies may not be looking at leadership issues, but rather evaluating supervisory and interpersonal characteristics.[4–9]

Early Precedents for Misapplied Theories

Early anthropological and scientific literature is regularly flawed and full of assumptions and opinions often presumed to be fact until new insights came to light. A whimsical example is the "flat earth theory," which was largely abandoned after the invention of the telescope and the circumnavigation of the globe by early mariners. Other scientific research is less amusing and could produce harmful consequences.

For example, in the early 1900s through the 1930s, the practice of eugenics was accepted in the United States. An estimated 60,000 people were sterilized when researchers of the era suggested persons with disabilities were a menace to society and could not contribute to humanity.[10, 11] Thirty-five states enforced eugenics-related laws, and the practice was endorsed by the U.S. Supreme Court in the 1927 *Buck v. Bell* decision, in which Justice Oliver Wendell Holmes declared that "three generations of imbeciles are enough."[12] Later, in the early 1940s, faulty research by the U.S. Army Air Corps supported previous research and literature that suggested African Americans were incapable of flying modern aircraft due to intelligence gaps as compared to their white counterparts.[13]

Situations in which new scientific theories replace older ones are constantly documented in the literature. Paleontologist Jack Horner of the Museum of the Rockies posits that Tyrannosaurus Rex ("tyrant lizard king") could not have been a predator. Horner traced back the literature behind the naming of T-Rex by its original discoverer, Henry Osborne, in 1905. Osborne speculated that T-Rex's big teeth and head must have been used in a predatory capacity. This assumption became a widely accepted, often cited, and frequently quoted part of paleontology literature for almost a century. Almost 100 years after the discovery, however, new scientific analysis of the skull and teeth suggested that T-Rex was actually a scavenger.[14]

The organizational literature is likewise peppered with misnomers and reevaluated ideas. Weber's "Protestant work ethic" (PWE) posited that "work gives meaning to life."[15] This theory gained some popular support in early organizational literature, but examination of the literature by later scholars failed to find support for the

PWE theory in contemporary literature. As early as 1990, Peter Drucker suggested that society is in need of many new models in leadership and management. "[The] old theories are feeling the weight of increasing complexities,"[16] he said.

In respect to this effort, earlier attempts to develop a uniform framework for effective leadership analysis have translated into significant academic challenges for researchers in this field. Although the term "leadership" is relatively new to the English language, the idea of leadership has existed for thousands of years. Researchers well recognize that certain individuals stand out from others in a group setting and ultimately direct the group to achieve a specific goal. These individuals have, for centuries, been recognized as leaders. Some such leaders may be associated with business or the military, whereas others become prominent politicians or social activists. Whatever the environmental setting may be, one fact is clear: There is little consensus on exactly what leadership is and which processes create an effective leader.[17]

As noted in earlier chapters of this book, leadership is one of the most widely debated and broadly defined micro-organization theories within the realm of organizational behavior. As a result, the discussion of leadership and leaders has transcended traditional boundaries and is often incorrectly extended to describe behavior and phenomena associated with managers, supervisors, coaches, educators, celebrities, political representatives, inspirational personnel, sports figures, and subject-matter experts. Despite the well-respected body of literature that distinctly separates leadership from other identifiers, the "leadership" label continues to be used to describe a plethora of activity in society.[18] As discussed in the introductory chapter where we framed leadership as a distinct discipline, the overuse and misuse of the term "leader" makes it difficult to study the concept of leadership and differentiate the concept of "leaders" from managers, supervisors, and popular personality figures.

Because of this misapplication, the terms "leader" and "leadership" have dominated fashionable connotations associated with non-equivalent positions, resulting in a popularly accepted—though largely incorrect—hierarchy. According to this "pecking order," being a leader is better than being just a manager, supervisor, or subject-matter expert. Being designated as a leader rather than a manager (or something else) results in an artificial perception of status, which translates into a "feel good" perception for the individual. Perhaps this notion is in part associated with competition for the best employees and other cultural changes that have occurred within society in the last century. A review of "want ads" in *The Washington Post* for senior-level healthcare personnel will turn up few vacancies for "business managers"—but will likely indicate that several positions for "industry leaders" are available.

As a result of these applications, leadership-, management-, and supervisory-related terms have essentially become synonymous within the literature and society. Consequently, leadership constructs are no longer perceived as distinct and mutually exclusive. A review of the literature suggests there is no single construct unique to leadership theory. Researchers working with the leadership theory field are often forced to borrow from the abundance of micro-organizational theories in the discipline to explain phenomena associated with leadership theory.

In response to these propositions, a new model of leadership, originally developed by Coppola at the Army Medical Department Center and School, Academy of Health Sciences, Fort Sam Houston, Texas, is offered here for purposes of discussion, thought, and reflection.[19] This model takes into account constructs and concepts that many traditional models of leadership do not include. These items include *higher order, environment,* and *individual culture* composite elements.

Reviewing Leadership as a New Problem

The study of traditional leadership theory does not always study leadership itself, but rather the outcomes of leaders and the antecedent factors that constitute management practices. Several weaknesses are associated with the traditional leadership models (many of which have previously been discussed in this text) that have been previously published. However, all models have potential for improvement. To begin with, few of the models attempt to define leadership theory before building models that explain the phenomena associated with it. For example, Yukl has suggested that there are at least seven (and perhaps many more) different definitions of leadership that can be found within the literature.[20–22] On which of the various definitions of leadership are the models based when they are tested? Without a uniform definition of leadership, and without agreement on measures and variables, outcomes are most certainly interpreted broadly.

The Euclidean management philosophies of the 1970s and 1980s, in which many of these leadership models have their roots, have since been replaced with more interactive, matrix-like, collaborative, and participatory-based models. These models were introduced to accommodate the paradigm shift in employee expectations, generational changes, and societal expectations (such as more women in the workforce) that has occurred in the last two to four decades. As a result, the application and study of leadership models have not kept pace with this paradigm shift in its totality.

Yukl's research exposes a wide variety of ideas on what constitutes leadership. The existing literature on leadership theory also promotes this definitional gap. Researchers have proposed a variety of theories: trait-based theories, transformational theories, contingency theories, and normative theories. The strength of these theoretical approaches lies in the fact that scholars generally accept them as reliable frameworks for evaluating distinct aspects of leadership. In reality, significant weaknesses exist because no one model can successfully explain all past behavior or predict all future behavior in an omnibus fashion. This differs from the study of constructs and measures in other academic fields. For example, scholars in the health field have regarded Donabedian's model of healthcare quality as a panacea for establishing a basis for any discussion of the subject in any health organization. Similarly, Mintzberg's typology for organizational analysis is a staple for deconstructing organizational hierarchal elements into manageable groups for efficiency and performance analysis.[23, 24]

Brief Overview of Theory

As discussed in Chapter 3, in the mid-1980s, Samuel Bacharach, building on the earlier works of Popper, Kerlinger, and Duban, developed criteria for evaluating theory that has become the benchmark for modern theoretical assessment in organizational literature.[25–28] According to Bacharach, a theory is a statement of relationships among concepts within a set of boundary assumptions and constructs. In this system of constructs and variables, the constructs are related to one another by propositions and the variables are related to one another by hypotheses. As a result, theory is a linguistic device used to organize a complex empirical world.

Similarly, Kerlinger noted that the essence of hypothesis testing is to test the relationship expressed by the variables in the hypotheses, rather than to test the individual variables themselves. Unfortunately, a majority of the leadership literature is centered on testing unit variables such as task accomplishment and satisfaction rather than more broadly defined leadership constructs. Moreover, as discussed previously, the overwhelming majority of leadership studies focus primarily on the outcomes of management and not leadership. These traditions suggest that modern-day thinkers must redirect their efforts and concentrate on defining and testing leadership as a construct.

The New Model

Albert Einstein once said, "Nearly every great advance in science arises from a crisis in the old theory, through an endeavor to find a way out of the difficulties created; we must examine old ideas, old theories, although they belong to the past, for this is the only way to understand the importance of the new ones and the extent of their validity."[29] As suggested, Ledlow and Coppola defined leadership as the ability to assess, develop, maintain, and change organizational culture and strategic systems to optimally meet the needs and expectations of the external environment by moral means. With this definition in mind, some alternatives and suggestions for studying leadership from a theoretical perspective are offered here.

In response to the problems inherent in traditional leadership theory outlined, we posit a series of propositions using the framework developed by Coppola, Kerlinger, Whetten, and Wittgenstein,[30–33] which stipulates that propositions, or statements of opinion based on related facts, are true when describing relationships. The proposed "omnibus leadership model" borrows from previous literature in the field and provides a different aperture for evaluating leaders and leadership theory based on the following propositions:

> *Proposition 1: Leadership theory has become analogous to a calculus formula that is memorized, but not derived.*

In the past, leadership theory and models have followed a pattern similar to that of earlier defunct theories such as the "flat earth" theory and the theory of eugenics—namely, scholars and students memorized the theories and models and passed them on to future generations without ever studying the phenomena firsthand. Likewise, few students have ever done the mathematical calculations to derive the degrees associated with a circle and triangle; rather, they accept the notion that a circle is 360 degrees and the angles within a triangle add up to 180 degrees. We do not dispute these mathematical facts, but do take pause at the widespread acceptance without validation of some of the early leadership literature.

> *Proposition 2: Early models of leadership theory applied a managerial framework to the study of leadership that failed to correctly differentiate other disciplines from leadership.*

Many of the early models of leadership looked at managerial outcomes and not the factors (i.e., constructs) influencing those outcomes for leadership.

> *Proposition 3: It is necessary to reevaluate leadership models to discern whether incorrect unit of analyses or misapplied variables have been extended to the explanation of phenomena associated with leadership theory.*

While we do not suggest that all leader models are inherently incorrect or flawed, we do suggest that—similar to other theoretical disciplines that have acknowledged evolution in their discipline—the study of leadership is more a study of the validation of outcomes attributed to the leader or leadership team than forecasted issues coupled with actions or style selection. This requires prospective and retrospective assessment.

> *Proposition 4: The tautology of the terms "leadership" and "leader" have allowed for the unarrested use and application of the theory in literature.*

The lack of a clear definition of leadership, combined with the lack of a clear understanding of what constitutes the construct of leadership, results in outcomes that do not maximize validity, reliability, and the ability to generalize across situations.

> *Proposition 5: Leadership theory lacks universally defined constructs and variables.*

Dissimilar to the study of quality in health care, where Donabedian's framework has become a benchmark with which to frame results, or the study of evolution, where Darwin's *Theory of Evolution* dominates the landscape, scholars in the management sciences lack a clear signpost for acuity in the leadership field for study. This lack of grounding decreases consistency. In essence, leadership remains in a perpetual "theory building" cycle.

> *Proposition 6: Leadership theory lacks a defined conceptual model.*

No one conceptual model stands out as a panacea for leadership study. This is dissimilar to the proposition offered by the U.S. Constitution, which clearly states that U.S. citizens have the "right to bear arms."

> *Proposition 7: Traditional leadership theories do not differentiate between leadership and dictatorship.*

Leaders who are self-serving, and who also have an agenda for harm and misery, are often labeled as "leaders" because society is unable to place them into any other designation when considering traditional leadership models. Adolf Hitler and Osama bin Laden are only two examples; they are labeled "leaders" by default. Interestingly, the preponderance of the literature associated with Benito Mussolini describes the Italian ruler as "the Italian dictator" and not as a leader—which is unique in the literature of historical despots.

Why a New Model?

When applying traditional leadership models, Adolf Hitler might be described as an effective leader, or at least as someone who demonstrated leadership skills by successfully rebuilding Germany after World War I. A retrospective application of path–goal leadership theory might also justify this position. Without question, Hitler initially inspired hundreds of thousands of followers to join his fascist movement in both Europe and the United States in the late 1930s. A retrospective application of transformational leadership theory might help explain Hitler's success in this regard. Nevertheless, to refer to Hitler as a leader is insulting to the profession of leadership. Hitler is not thought of as a highly regarded leader in the study of leadership theory today; he is considered, at best, to have been a despot and a dictator. Certainly, a model must be created that allows for the differentiation of leadership and dictatorship.

To test this proposition, 170 commissioned U.S. military officers were asked to participate in a leadership test at Fort Sam Houston, Texas, over the period 2004–2006. The test was designed to test an individual's perception of the definition of "leadership" based on a narrative. This narrative was read aloud to a class of graduate students (who were also Army, Navy, Air Force, or Coast Guard officers) in advance, so the entire class heard the narrative at the same time. After the narrative was read, the officers were asked to turn over a piece of paper that had been placed on their desk, and circle the answer choice they thought was most representative of the narrative.

Each class was divided in half so that the narrative was the same. One side of the class had a picture of Adolf Hitler on top of the page; the other side had a picture of Martin Luther King, Jr., on the top of the page. The test was designed to see if the picture of a well-known and accepted leadership figure such as Martin Luther King, Jr., would cause the test takers to support the leadership narrative, whereas the picture of Adolf Hitler would bias the results. The entire one-page test is presented here (including the two pictures used—**Figure 8–1** and **Figure 8–2**), and the test results appear in **Table 8–1**.

Methodology

One side of the room received the following narrative, with a picture of Adolf Hitler appearing on the top of the page. The other side of the room received the same narrative, with a picture of Martin Luther King, Jr., appearing at the top of the page. Neither side of the class knew that the other side was looking at a different picture.

FIGURE 8–1   Martin Luther King, Jr.   **FIGURE 8–2   Adolf Hitler**

It had been several years since the world war. With the war now over, people began looking for a national figure to solve social problems and injustices. Clearly, the country was divided and in need of change. Although many people of the nation were united and content with the status quo, he considered his people and nation to be downtrodden. He dreamed of a better place for his people and thought that his country could be greater than what it was. Slowly, over the years, millions listened and followed him. He inspired people like few before him had ever done. He was also successful in inspiring and motivating people, and accomplishing change. This change and his ability to motivate people were immense and dramatic, and can still be felt to this day. Modern scholars still study his methods and wonder how he did it. Years after his death, people still read his books and are moved by the memory of his dream.

Select **one answer** that best describes this narrative.

This is an example of

  A. A national public figure.
  B. A man with a vision.
  C. Leadership.
  D. Effective strategic management.
  E. None of the above.

TABLE 8–1   Results of Leadership Quiz Based on Character Perception

n = 170 military officers over the period 2004–2006

Question Response	Hitler (*n* = 85)	King (*n* = 85)
A national public figure	34	9
A man with a vision	16	14
Leadership	9	62
Effective strategic management	14	0
None of the above	12	0

The results reveal that military officers were uncomfortable with the option of labeling Adolf Hitler as a leader. Only 9 of 85 students (10.5 percent) felt comfortable with the leader answer when they thought Adolf Hitler's image was associated with the narrative and options. This was not true of the other half of the class, who selected "leader" 73 percent of the time (*n* = 62/85 students) when they assumed that Martin Luther King, Jr.'s picture was associated with the narrative and choices.

Clearly, this exploratory test on image perceptions of leadership with trained military officers in graduate school suggests a problem with perceptions associated with the leadership designation of historical figures. To overcome this dilemma, future leadership models must be capable of screening out despots and dictators from traditional leadership frameworks. The omnibus leadership model provides for this adjustment through its *higher order, environment,* and *individual culture* composite elements, thereby correcting the problem.

Constructs of the Omnibus Leadership Model

Traditional models of leadership focus on outcomes and trace those outcomes back to specific leadership traits, characteristics, or behaviors, with little emphasis placed on the values associated with intrinsic goal-directed behavior. The "nature versus nurture" debate has long existed within the study of leadership. Are leaders born, or can they be made? The environment certainly plays a role in fostering goal-directed behavior, as do family values, available resources, and education (including both didactic and spiritual education). Nevertheless, these constructs are often viewed as confounding variables rather than as leadership progenitors in traditional leadership models. This is a weakness within traditional leadership study.

Furthermore, traditional leader theories fail to fully integrate the various aspects of confounding variables into one multifaceted model that allows for a wider range and utility of leadership study. Specifically, constructs such as cultural distinctiveness, higher power influences, and environmental pressures are often disregarded as antecedent constructs for forecasting leader outcomes or explaining past leader behavior. At the same time, these constructs are excellent theoretical examples for forecasting leader outcomes under appropriate conditions.

For example, in the current environment, which involves a war in the Middle East, some leaders feel that they are driven to goal-directed behavior through a *higher power* mandate. Separate from the realm that is considered religion or spirituality in its common understanding, a "higher power" is often classified as a greater belief in a mantra, or distinctive icon, that guides and directs leader behavior and followership in a predictable manner. Rarely, however, does a discussion of how a higher power affects the values and goal-directed behavior of leaders take place. In fact, many leadership scholars completely ignore altogether the construct of a higher power influence when examining leadership. Some suggest it is politically incorrect to consider this factor, while others posit that it is too difficult to measure and evaluate it. Regardless, the study of a higher power influence on leadership is a burgeoning field of interest in the scholarly community.[34–36]

As previously discussed, the preponderance of traditional leadership models focus on outcomes, using indicators of satisfaction and productivity as indices of success. In doing so, many established models fail to take into account various aspects of the environment and individual culture. Clearly, culture and the environment have profound effects on the study of leadership theory. As a result, an integrated theoretical model developed by Coppola[37] suggests a solution to this problem. The omnibus leadership model (OLM) borrows from previous literature in the field and provides a different aperture for evaluating leaders and leadership theory. This model offers three spatial dimensional constructs—higher order, individual culture, and environment—as signposts for other variables or constructs. Furthermore, from these spatial dimensions, three other constructs—beneficence, character traits, and resources—may be derived.

Higher Order Construct

Within the health and general management environment, the topic of spirituality in leadership is often considered taboo and, indeed, a career-ending conversation for executives and practitioners. Even so, it is well known that spiritual principles are the basis for many values and enduring beliefs that guide the ethical framework and moral development of health leadership practices in our society. Therefore, spirituality (i.e., higher order) as a construct of discussion and examination in health leadership practice should not be overlooked in future research examining leadership theory.

In 2008, a survey of religion performed by Baylor University[38] found that more than 85 percent of the U.S. population consider themselves to be "religious." Furthermore, leadership research conducted by other authors suggests that the distinct absence of the study of spirituality and/or a higher power in leadership study has been a distinct flaw in the traditional study of a leader's ability to influence others and to inspire followership. End-of-life decisions and early pregnancy termination are only two of the issues faced by health executives today that have relevance to this construct; these issues have strong spiritual roots that influence and inform decision making. Obviously, the study of a higher power is necessary in health leadership. More importantly, it opens the conversation of spirituality in leadership and brings it to the table for a professional and intellectual discussion.

Higher-order principles guide the construct of beneficence, or the practice of "doing good" against the construct of malevolence, or the practice of "doing bad." These principles are themselves derived from family values, spiritual teachings, education, "herd mentalities" in the community, and individual interpretation of the aforementioned spatial dimensions—whether they be consistent or inconsistent with practices or norms of behavior. Certainly, higher-order principles guide the development of many leaders, and this construct should not be overlooked in future leadership studies.

Individual Culture Construct

From the individual cultural spatial dimension, the construct of character traits may be derived. Trait theory itself dominated the bulk of traditional leadership methodology over the previous century, and little additional discussion seemed to have been warranted. Nevertheless, it is now clear that cultural distinctiveness acts as an immutable object in the study of leadership theory. Some Asian and Middle Eastern societies clearly favor gender in the practice of leadership hierarchy, whereas other societies are more gender neutral. Age is likewise a factor in many Asian societies and is often used as a proxy suggesting that experience equates with competence. As a result, it would be inappropriate to apply a transformational leadership model to the evaluation of some societies due to the hierarchal gender- and age-based traits associated with those cultures. For example, in traditional Chinese and North Korean cultures, inquisitiveness and outspokenness may be perceived in a negative light, as opposed the Western perception that these behaviors demonstrate a search for understanding and an extroverted approach.

An individual's birthplace culture, or the culture in which he or she lives, will imprint an endurable mark of distinctiveness on the individual that will follow him or her over the course of the person's lifetime. While not entirely immutable, the culture in which an individual is raised or lives will dominate and forecast choices in leader decisions for as long as the person is in charge of people, policy, or other decision-making elements.

Environment Construct

The environment in which many leaders operate is critically important to a leader's success, as Fiedler suggested in his model decades ago. The extent to which the literature has addressed the relationship between individuals and the environment is minimal. In fact, the preponderance of leadership theory ignores the environment altogether. Short of trait theory, very few studies attempt to tie traditional leadership theory to the environment in a manner that predicts and forecasts possible outcomes. In reality, by identifying the environment in which a leader will function, individuals can take advantage of factors in the environment to fit the current situation and maximize outcomes. This approach supports the multidimensional and complex idea that leadership processes include an ecologically valid two-way component between the leader and the environment[39] and that followers are embedded in the environmental context.

Leaders cannot execute their vision, inspire followership, and employ legitimate and charismatic attributes unless appropriate resources are available in the environment to assist in the communication of the leader's message. If the environment lacks appropriate resources to assist in the transfer and the communication of the leader's intent, the leader may not have a significant enough followership to lead anything. For this reason, the environmental construct is a necessary precursor to resource availability. Furthermore, leader recognition is not possible without appropriate resources to deliver the leader's message.

Resources[40] have attracted a reasonable amount of attention in traditional leadership study; however, resources are generally viewed in older theories as variables unto themselves and not as constructs for measurement. In the OLM, resources may be accessed through both human followership and logistical means. For example, in the modern study of leadership, vehicles for message delivery have exponentially been available to small groups of individuals who may have been hermetically sealed from the preponderance of the world culture in the past. The advent of the Internet has allowed small fringe groups of previously marginalized peoples to gain standing and respect in the greater world community. Through a provocative Web site whose message inspires followership, a lone marginalized individual may find standing and prominence on the world stage. Clearly, environmental resources have gained prominence as vehicles for leadership followership.

The Omnibus Leadership Model: A Summary

The OLM meets the needs of future leadership researchers by including the spatial dimensions of higher order, individual culture, and environment. **Table 8–2** provides a template for this model. **Figure 8–3** illustrates the conceptual model of the omnibus leadership theory. The benefit of this theory derives from its ability to capture constructs that assist in explaining why certain leaders are driven to leadership decisions. For example, many leader decisions are based on values learned from childhood relating to cultural and spiritual teachings that can be acted upon in favorable environments. In understanding and applying this model, the foundations on which some leaders base their decisions becomes clear, as does why some leaders have widespread followership. In fact, followership based on cultural and higher-order issues cannot be overlooked in this modern era of the "War on Terror" and an increasingly globalized society.

The OLM provides a framework for screening and evaluating real leaders from the despots and the infamous. For example, using this model as a guide, Hitler is clearly screened out of the leadership category due to his evil malevolence. His actions and outcomes resulted in sociopathic murder and do not qualify him as a

TABLE 8–2 Omnibus Leadership Model

Spatial Dimension	Construct	Description	Variables
Higher order	Beneficence or malevolence	Altruism or sadism	Actions • Self-serving versus other-serving • Teamwork: glory "me" versus glory "we"
Individual (culture)	Character	Extraversion or introversion Type A or B personality archetypes	Traits, abilities, and skills
Environment	Resources Stability Turbidity Dynamic	Human followership and logistical availability	Outcomes • Action versus reaction • Flight versus fight

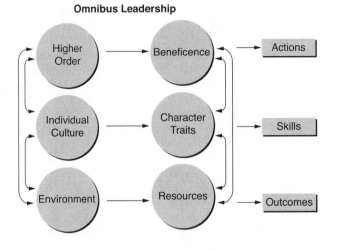

FIGURE 8–3   Conceptual Model of Omnibus Leadership

leader of any sort in modern times. Likewise, their support of suicide bombers causes some modern-day figures to be similarly ruled out of leadership consideration because these acts are obviously nonbeneficent.[41–43]

All leaders are guided by some higher-order principles that may present themselves as unconscious drivers for maintaining enduring beliefs and adopting certain values. Rokeach, in the values–beliefs–attitudes model, suggested that values form the bedrock of who we are as people and, consequently, as leaders. However, without an understanding of the higher-order principles and values that guide a leader, it is not possible to fully understand retrospective actions, or forecast future behavior in a consistent manner.

Measuring the Model

Methods for measuring the OLM in the near term may rely on observational and non-experimental studies. Donabedian proposed a similar observational methodology with the now renowned structure–process–outcome quality model in 1966. Donabedian's original article contained few insights into means of empirical measurement other than to qualify review actions as having merit based on *normative and accepted practices* in the field. Donabedian suggested that subject-matter experts and panels are required to evaluate his new model.[44] Similar methodologies are necessary for the evaluation of the OLM. For example, it was not until the passing of the HMO Act of 1973 that scholars turned to Donabedian's theoretical model to help guide health organizations toward developing quality models. If not for the passage of this act, and the requirement for health organizations to make an argument for quality in their organizations, Donabedian's model may have languished in obscurity for years or decades—or perhaps it would have not been used at all.

A similar argument can be made for John Nash's self-named "Nash equilibrium (NE)" theory, which was first developed in 1950. The NE Theory, and later the Nash bargaining solution (NBS), became the basis for game theory. Nash's concepts were largely regarded as theoretical and intangible when first produced. In subsequent years, however, they were used as the basis for U.S. economic policy making and resulted in the awarding of the Nobel Prize to Nash in 1994 (**Figure 8–4**). Many readers may recall seeing Nash's life portrayed in the movie *A Beautiful Mind.*[45]

Traditional leadership models have typically employed true experimental and non-experimental methods within their leadership frameworks. This approach would continue to be applicable with the OLM. Subjects and data may continue to be collected and analyzed using traditional practices and procedures. However, the OLM will help guide the researcher toward qualifying specific constructs of leadership for discerning certain phenomena.

FIGURE 8–4 John Nash Receives the Nobel Prize

In closing, perhaps the Latin phrase *res ipsa loquitur* ("the thing speaks for itself") may suggest additional structure for the OLM. Leadership is action oriented: "One knows it when one sees it." As a result, leadership theory may continue to confound research efforts. Perhaps leadership scholars must be satisfied with the appreciation of leadership as an art more than a science after all—at least until better theory testing methods are viable.

THE DYNAMIC CULTURE LEADERSHIP MODEL[46]

Superb leadership is required at all levels of the health organization due to the increasingly dynamic nature of the health environment. This reality was the catalyst for the development of the dynamic culture leadership (DCL) model. Leadership in this model is recognized at three levels as the critical ingredient in the recipe for overall success: at the personal level, at the team level, and at the organizational level. The challenge is to focus the knowledge, skills, and abilities of organizational leaders appropriately and to empower the total organization to complete its mission, reach its vision, and compete successfully in an environment that constantly changes. This model is built on various theories and models from the leadership literature and related research. An overview of the DCL model is provided here; this model is intended to fit within the situational and transformational leadership paradigm with an emphasis on organizational culture development.

The DCL model[47] provides both a descriptive and a high-level prescriptive process model of leadership. This model emphasizes a sense of balance that needs to be maintained to achieve a sustainable and continuing level of *optimized* leadership based on the changing macro and micro factors in the external environment.

"Optimized leadership," like the concept "high quality," is not necessarily a norm to be achieved at all times. Rather, it is a worthy goal, an ideal state. No individual (and certainly no organization) can in all situations and at all times enjoy a steady state of higher-level leadership. Nevertheless, many individuals and organizations continuously optimize their ability to function at high leadership levels by consciously (and even unconsciously) cultivating the various elements of the model.

The basic assumptions of the DCL model are as follows:

■ Due to the very dynamic nature of the environment (in this case, the health industry), it is critical for the leadership and management team to bring multiple knowledge, skills, abilities, perspectives, and backgrounds (DCL leadership alignment assessment) to the organization to enable it to successfully and proactively navigate the external environment and focus the internal people and resources on the mission, vision, strategies, goals, and objectives of the organization.

■ Leadership is defined as the ability to assess, develop, maintain, and change the organizational culture to optimally meet the needs and expectations of the external environment through focusing the collective energy of the organization on the mission, vision, strategies, goals, and objectives of the organization.

■ The leadership and management team should consciously determine the culture of the organization and guide and direct culture through communication improvement, organization-wide strategic planning, decision-making alignment, employee assessment and empowerment, and knowledge management and organizational learning (process constructs).

■ Based on the predetermined organizational culture, mission, vision, and strategies, consistency of leadership and management are paramount.

■ Situational and environmental assessment and scanning are key to adjusting organizational culture, mission, vision, and strategies.

■ Transformational leadership and management (including transactional leadership approaches), where both the science and art leadership and management are in concert with the external environment expectations, provide the best approach to lead people and manage resources in a dynamic world.

Optimized leadership is certainly attainable for any person and any organization, but it usually requires concentrated effort to overcome past habits, ideas, and tendencies. Ultimately, *individual* leaders make up the leadership team. The team, therefore, must be diverse in style and competencies while being anchored to a set of values and operating principles of the organization. The assessment instrument for individuals and teams for this model is based on a leadership–management continuum and an art–science continuum.

The characteristics of "leadership" as compared to "management," and "science" as compared to "art," are described in **Table 8–3** and **Table 8–4**. It is important to note that organizations need leaders, managers, scientists, and artists working together to achieve success over the long term. **Figure 8–5** illustrates the macro descriptive model, while **Figure 8–6** shows the prescription (or processes) associated with the model.

The differences in *leadership* versus *management* are shown in Table 8–3; the differences in *science* versus *art* are shown in Table 8–4. It is important to keep in mind that organizations need leadership as well as management mentality/capabilities, as well as science and art mentality/capabilities, if they are to survive and thrive in their external environment.

The DCL model entails a leadership process, as shown in Figure 8–6, that emphasizes leadership team assessment, communication improvement, strategic planning, decision-making alignment, employee enhancement, and learning organization improvement. Leaders who regularly follow the sequence shown in Figure 8–6 have the best potential to deal with change in their environment, while building a culture that will be effective even during times of change. Members of the leadership team must be ever thoughtful in maintaining their consistency relative to the organizational mission, vision, strategies, goals, and values, but also in terms of the model's constructs and process constructs. Examples of inconsistency might include instituting a defensive and disconfirming communication environment within a customer or patient service and care excellence (differentiation) strategy; using a subordinate decision-making tactic (i.e., pushing down decisions to the lowest level appropriate) without involving subordinates in strategic and operational planning; or maintaining a leadership team that is heavily skewed toward "leadership" and "art" while the external environment demands "management" and "science." Examples of consistency would be creating a culture based in a supportive and confirm-

TABLE 8–3   Explanation of the Leadership–Management Continuum in the Dynamic Culture Leadership Model

Leadership	Management
Longer Time Horizon	Shorter Time Horizon
Vision then Mission Oriented	Mission Oriented
Organizational Validity (Are we doing the right things?) – Environmental Scanning and Intuition	Organizational Reliability (Are we doing things correctly and consistently?) Compliance to Rules and Policies and Rule Development
Does the Organization Have the Correct Components (People, Resources, Expertise) to Meet Future as Well as Current Needs?	How Can Current Components Work Best Now?
Developing and Refining Organizational Culture to Meet External Environment Needs	Maintaining Organizational Climate to Ensure Performance
Timing and Tempo of Initiatives and Projects	Scheduling of Initiatives and Projects

Source: Ledlow, G., & Cwiek, M. (2005, July). The process of leading: Assessment and comparison of leadership team style, operating climate and expectation of the external environment. *Proceedings of Global Business and Technology Association,* Lisbon, Portugal.

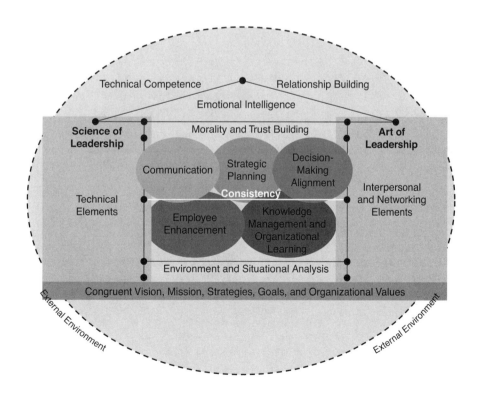

FIGURE 8–5   The Dynamic Culture Leadership Model
Source: Ledlow, G., & Cwiek, M. (2005, July). The process of leading: Assessment and comparison of leadership team style, operating climate, and expectation of the external environment. *Proceedings of Global Business and Technology Association,* Lisbon, Portugal.

TABLE 8–4   Explanation of the Science–Art Continuum in the Dynamic Culture Leadership Model

Science	Art
Technical skills orientation (e.g., forecasting, budgeting)	Relationship orientation (e.g., networking, interpersonal relationships)
Decisions based more on analysis	Decisions based more on perceptions of people
Developing systems (important to organizations)	Developing relationships and networks (important to organizations)
Expert systems	Experts as people
Cost control and evaluation of value are important	Image and customer relationships are important

Source: Ledlow, G., & Cwiek, M. (2005, July). The process of leading: Assessment and comparison of leadership team style, operating climate, and expectation of the external environment. *Proceedings of Global Business and Technology Association,* Lisbon, Portugal.

ing communication environment; using a subordinate-involved planning process with decision making made at the lowest appropriate level; and initiating a customer service and patient care excellence strategy if the external environment expects such a strategy (today, excellent service and care are expected). The overriding theme is that leadership envisions, develops, and maintains an organizational culture that works amid a dynamic environment. A summary of model constructs and process constructs follows.

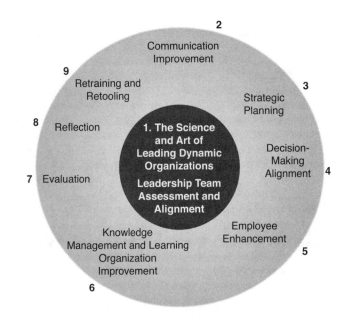

FIGURE 8–6   The Leadership Process (DCL) Model
Source: Ledlow, G., & Cwiek, M. (2005, July). The process of leading: Assessment and comparison of leadership team style, operating climate, and expectation of the external environment. *Proceedings of Global Business and Technology Association,* Lisbon, Portugal.

Briefly, the DCL model incorporates both constructs and "process" constructs as part of the DCL system. In essence, model constructs are primarily the descriptive model. Model constructs include the following:

- *Science of leadership* includes all technical elements involved in leading and managing an organization, such as quantitative and qualitative analysis, decision-making assessments, finance and budgeting, job analysis and design, planning structures and processes, computer skills, and the like. Each process construct of the model has both science and art aspects; an integration of the two must be consistently used to ensure successful leadership of an organization.

- *Art of leadership* includes the elements involved in interpersonal relationships, network building and maintenance, intuition, coalition development, and the like.

- *Technical competence, relationship building, emotional intelligence, morality and trust building,* and *environmental and situational analyses* are required at sufficient levels (and should be at high levels) across the leadership and management team to successfully lead people and manage the resources of the health organization.

- *Congruent vision, mission, strategies, goals,* and *organizational values* are essential so that a culture of *consistency* is developed throughout the organization. The leadership and management team must consciously assess the external environment (macro and micro factors) and predetermine these directional, competitive, adaptive, and cultural development strategies for the organization.

- The *external environment* comprises all organizational stakeholders (anyone or any group that influences, serves, gets service, or is connected to the organization), the macro environmental factors, the micro environmental factors, and the synthesized set of expectations of the health organization.

Prescriptive elements of the model include assessing and aligning a robust leadership and management team that can utilize the knowledge, skills, abilities, and perspectives of all quadrants of the assessment instrument "diamond," being consistent in developing and maintaining an appropriate culture and the sequential and building utilization of the model's process constructs. Process constructs include the following elements:

- *Communication improvement* is the leadership and management team engagement in predetermined modeling, training, rewarding, and assimilating of the communication environment into the organization in the means that best contributes to an effective organizational culture. In health organizations, a confirming and supportive communication environment that is cognizant of media richness of communication channels and competent in conflict management should be the most effective, efficient, and efficacious.

- *Strategic planning* (includes operational planning) is the structured, inclusive process of planning to determine a mission, vision, strategies, goals, objectives, and action steps that are consistent with organizational values and that meet the external environment's expectations of the organization. Subordinate, internal, and external stakeholders should be included, as appropriate to level and responsibilities, in the planning process. Continuous and "living" planning is a cultural imperative in dynamic environments.

- *Decision-making alignment* involves aligning decisions with the strategic and operational plan while understanding reality-based decision making (i.e., pushing down decisions appropriately and using policies and standing operating procedures for routine and consistent decisions).

- *Employee enhancement* is the assessment of employee knowledge, skills, abilities, experience, and trustworthiness and the practice of increasing or reducing responsibilities (such as making decisions) appropriate to the unit, group, and individual in line with the organizational culture as part of development and the strategic and operational plans.

- *Knowledge management and organizational learning* involves capturing what the organization knows and what it has learned so that improvements to effectiveness, efficiency, and efficacy can be achieved. Leadership, willingness, planning, and training are facilitators of organizational learning.[48]

- *Evaluating, reflecting, and retooling* is the leadership and management team's honest assessment of the DCL model cycle and ways to improve the cycle in the next repetition.

Using this process consistently will not only improve the organization's ability to use these processes and produce an organizational culture that reflects the leadership's vision, but will enable the organization to maneuver in dynamic/changing situations.

Leadership team assessment and alignment are important. **Figure 8–7** illustrates the leadership team assessment (Step 1 in Figure 8–6) for 10 members of a hospital leadership team as it compares to the current operational environment and the expectations of the external environment. As shown in Figure 8–7, there is a tension between what the leadership team tends to be (more *leadership* oriented with a reasonable *science* and *art* balance) and the more *management* and *science* emphasis in leadership demanded by the external environment; the operating environment can be found between that tension. The external environment requirements, as perceived by the leadership team, are skewed toward *management* and *science* (the "analytical manager" quadrant). The perception of leadership would lead one to believe that the external environment requires greater cost control, accountability, and adherence to policies and rules, although relationships are still important, as is some leadership focus.

Assessing an organization's leadership team is essential. Aligning the team to bring diversity of style, skills, experience, and abilities is essential for organizations if they are to maintain a robust and resilient, and even opportunistic, personality. In this model and assessment, both cultural diversity and individual diversity are valued because they enable the organization to better respond to dynamic organizational and external environments. In contrast, diversity of focus and diversity of organizational goals are not advantageous; a diverse leadership team brings robustness to solving organizational problems as long as the focus on the vision, mission, and goals are similar across the leadership team. An assessment that looks at leadership as a team, across organizational levels, operating environments, and external environment needs, is far better than simply relying on only individual leader assessments.[49]

Figure 8–7 shows the results of a leadership team style assessment, including operating style and external environment expectations. Note that a considerable disconnect exists between the leadership style and the external environment requirements. The organizational operating style is *balanced,* whereas the leadership style composite is *analytical leader* (skewed toward science and leadership) and the external environment is *analytical manager* (skewed toward science and management). This is hypothesized to represent a leadership coping strategy. Aligning additional leadership team members to bring in more management- and science-oriented

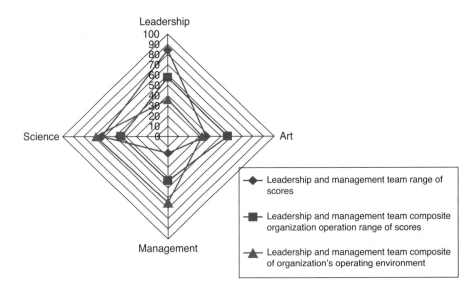

FIGURE 8–7 Comparison of Leadership Team Style, Operating Style, and External Environment Requirements for a Leadership Team

Source: Ledlow, G., & Cwiek, M. (2005, July). The process of leading: Assessment and comparison of leadership team style, operating climate, and expectation of the external environment. *Proceedings of Global Business and Technology Association,* Lisbon, Portugal.

Dynamic Culture Leadership Assessment

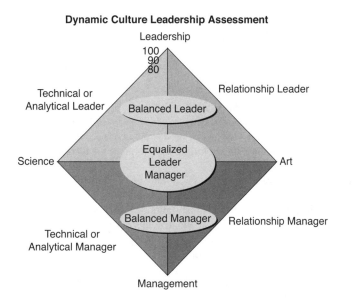

FIGURE 8–8   Categorization Scheme for DCL Model

members may be an appropriate strategy in this case. Alternatives to adding team members would be to "buy" or have consultation with persons who might add management and science abilities to the organization. Such a strategy can cause a problem over the long term, however, in that institutional knowledge could be more easily lost with this approach. When leadership style by organizational level is compared, there is much more propensity for leadership than management, as one looks down the organizational hierarchy, than an organization may be able to tolerate over the long term. In essence, it is important to understand and know the leadership team's style and "personality" as it compares to operating style (how business gets done), as well as the expectations of the external environment.

Leaders are gifted in different ways, with different personalities and varying skill sets. All leaders can grow and become more balanced and achieve greater effectiveness. Notably, some common factors found in those who succeed in becoming dynamic culture leaders, including the desire to learn more about themselves, the motivation to learn and practice new skill sets, and the need to grow and to become more tomorrow than what the person is today. This is not the easiest path to travel, but it is the path that optimizes the likelihood of leadership effectiveness and success.

The DCL model categorizes leaders and managers, scientists and artists, based on the diamond configuration of the assessment tool. Overlaying this categorization scheme on top of the assessment are the following classifications: relationship leader, relationship manager, technical or analytic leader, technical or analytic manager, balanced leader, equalized leader-manager, and balanced manager (**Figure 8–8**). In which category would you put yourself? This same schema can be used in assessing the operating style of the organization (such as relationship-led operation or relationship-managed operation) and the external environment expectations (such as technical or analytically led environment or technical or analytically managed environment).

Organizations are more dynamic today than ever before. With the advent of the Information Age, the fluidity of professional and family life, and the competitive nature of the global marketplace, more of an entrepreneurial environment can be found in many of today's organizations:

Entrepreneurial organizations reflect a different set of underlying assumptions principally because they shift the focus away from producing specific, predetermined behavior by means of direction and formal controls. Instead, they encourage coordination through the shared understanding that will enable individuals to choose effective actions themselves. Organization structure and control systems can no longer be depicted as tools that mechanically determine members' behaviors. We, too, must shift our thinking about organizations away from the organization as an entity, to members' choice and understanding.[50]

Leaders in this environment cannot rest on the laurels of "cookie-cutter" methods, but must instead learn and become effective in developing teams of professionals within dynamic cultures. To see the reality of the dynamic nature of organizations today, one need simply consider the changes wrought by increased human diversity, information overload, the evolution of technology, the increasing sophistication of the consumer, and the introduction of e-commerce.

Leaders need to have a firm grasp of how they can develop an organizational culture that creates a thriving environment for their organization. In 1999, Edgar Schein defined "culture" as the basic assumptions and beliefs shared by members of a group or organization.[51] "A major function of culture is to help us understand the environment and determine how to respond to it, thereby reducing anxiety, uncertainty, and confusion."[52] The key question then becomes, How do leaders shape culture? Schein suggests that leaders have the greatest potential for embedding and reinforcing aspects of culture with the following five primary mechanisms:[53]

- Attention: Leaders communicate their priorities, values, and concerns by their choice of things to ask about, measure, comment on, praise, and criticize.
- Reaction to crisis: This reaction increases the potential for learning about values and assumptions.
- Role modeling.
- Allocation of resources.
- Criteria for selection and dismissal: Leaders can influence culture by recruiting people who have particular values, skills, and traits, and then by promoting (or firing) them.

Schein also described five secondary mechanisms:[54]

- Design of organizational structure: A centralized structure indicates that only the leader can determine what is important; a decentralized structure reinforces individual initiative and sharing.
- Design of systems and procedures: Where emphasis is placed shows concern and ambiguity reduction issues.
- Design of facilities.
- Stories, legends, and myths.
- Formal statements.

It is imperative that health organization leaders understand the various factors that influence culture. Culture is more stable and more difficult to change than "climate," because climate usually does not remain stable over time. Whether employees are "happy" today (a climate indicator) is only of temporal importance. By comparison, culture indicators (e.g., processes, incentive systems, communication environment, understanding of goals and how they fit into the work to achieve success) are much more meaningful and important.

The DCL model is a set of constructs for which its goal is to unify the various leadership theories that previously have received attention. Further, the DCL model can be studied immediately and put to work by leaders and organizational scholars intent on developing highly effective leadership. In their book *The Success Paradigm*,[55] Mike Friesen and James Johnson discuss the importance of leadership in the integration of quality and strategy to achieve organizational success. In this book, the leadership *process* is described as critical for success. The DCL model is presented as an application of theory to advance existing contingency leadership theories, coupled with a strategic process. It is, therefore, presented as a prescriptive model.

Today's complex, ever-changing organizations are experiencing a shortage in leadership effectiveness, not because of a lack of talent or goodwill, but because of the demanding balancing act required for success. This balance of *scientist* attributes and *artist* attributes defined in the DCL model provides the pathway for success. According to experts, *leadership* is the pivotal issue in organizational success. The DCL model is intended to become central to the understanding of leadership in organizations and the people who lead them.

The DCL model, in its current state of development, is being tested in both theoretical and practical ways. It currently provides a conceptual framework for the better understanding of complex organizations and serves as a model for advancing leader effectiveness. Further, tools for leadership assessment and direct application are being refined to advance the practical utility of this model in all organizational settings. In summary, the DCL model includes the following recommendations:

- An assessment of the organization's leadership team and ultimately the development of a team should focus on building a team that is diverse in terms of the leadership, management, art, and science attributes, while simultaneously being rooted in the fundamental values, beliefs, and mission of the organization.

- An organization's leadership should focus on communication improvement, strategic planning, decision-making alignment, employee enhancement, and learning organization improvement, in a regular, cyclical sequence.

- Leaders should become competent in the use of the process constructs (e.g., communication improvement, strategic planning) included in this model, so that predetermined and consistent alternative strategies and applications can be selected based on the situation (refer to Chapters 5, 6, 7, 9, 13, and 15 for information and applications).

- The sequence should be repeated based on the tempo of change in the environment: Rapid change creates a need to work through the sequence at a faster pace. It is estimated that in health care today, this sequence should be planned for every three to four years.

The DCL model, as a leadership team alignment, macro, and culture creation model, integrates well with the "reframing leadership and management in organizations" model, an episodic leader style selection and emphasis platform developed by Bolman and Deal. Both models possess descriptive and prescriptive elements that can be learned and embedded into the organization culture of health organizations.

BOLMAN AND DEAL'S REFRAMING LEADERSHIP AND MANAGEMENT IN ORGANIZATIONS MODEL[56]

Bolman and Deal suggest that leaders must be situational/contingency oriented. Critical variables assist the leader in choosing the emphasis and style they need to use to be successful. Four constructs are considered important in this model: structural, human resources, political, and symbolic. Each of these constructs is important in its own right, but some are more important than others at critical times. Recent research literature from late 2008 used Bolman and Deal's model to suggest several applications for this model in an academic health-care organization.[57]

With Bolman and Deal's model, a leader must pay attention to the four organizational constructs, each of which has assumptions, attributes, and imperatives for the leader to consider. This section summarizes each of these dimensions. As we progress through this model, pay close attention to the application of the model.

The *structural* construct (called a "frame") deals with how organizations "structure" work processes, how they establish formal relationships, and how groups facilitate coupling (coupling is the level of adherence to organizational policies, rules, procedures, and social expectations). The structural frame assumptions are outlined here:

- Organizations exist to accomplish established goals.
- Organizational design/structural form can be designed to "fit" the situation.
- Organizations work best when governed by rationality and norms.
- Specialization permits more productivity and individual expertise.
- Coordination and control are essential to effectiveness.
- Problems originate from inappropriate structures and inadequate systems that can be resolved through restructuring and developing new systems (modern reengineering).

The *human resources* construct or frame embraces McGregor's Theory Y model. This dimension is critical to focus and synergize human energy in an organization. Human resources frame assumptions are as follows:

■ "Organizations exist to serve human needs (rather than the reverse).

■ Organizations and people need each other.

■ When the fit between the individual and the organization is poor, one or both will suffer: individuals will be exploited, or will seek to exploit the organization, or both.

■ A good fit between individual and organization benefits both: human beings find meaningful and satisfying work, and organizations get the human talent and energy that they need."[58] "Moreover, the idea that people have needs is a central element in commonsense psychology."[59]

This model's essential theme regarding human resources management is best summed up in the following quotations:

> The theories of Maslow, McGregor, and Argyris suggested that conflict between individual and organization would get worse as organizations became larger (with greater impersonality, longer chains of command, and more complex rules and control systems) and as society became better educated and more affluent (producing more people whose higher-level needs are salient).[60]
>
> One solution to that problem [treating employees as children] is *participation*—giving workers more opportunity to influence decisions.[61]

The *political* construct or frame deals with resource allocation within an organization. The interesting aspect of this construct is that people create interesting webs of relationships to gain and reallocate resources. Political frame assumptions are based on power, conflict, and coalitions:

■ "The propositions of the political frame do not attribute politics to individual selfishness, myopia, or incompetence. They assert that interdependence, difference, scarcity, and power relations will inevitably produce political forces, regardless of the players. It is naive and romantic to hope that politics can be eliminated in organizations. [Leaders and managers] can, however, learn to understand and manage political processes."[62]

■ This frame suggests that organizational goals are set through negotiations among members of coalitions. A typical organization has a confusing set of multiple goals, many of which are in conflict with one another.

■ "The political perspective suggests that the goals, structure, and policies of an organization emerge from an ongoing process of bargaining and negotiation among the major interest groups. . . . the political view suggests that the exercise of power is a natural part of an ongoing contest."[63]

The *symbolic* construct or frame deals with meaning. This dimension gets at the heart of what organizational members feel about issues and events. Specifically, the meaning of the event is more important than the event. A symbol is something that stands for or means something else.

> The symbolic frame seeks to interpret and illuminate the basic issues of meaning and faith that make symbols so powerful in every aspect of the human experience, including life in organizations. This frame presents a world that departs significantly from traditional canons of organizational theories: rationality, certainty, and linearity. It is based on the following unconventional assumptions:
>
> ■ What is important is not the event but what it means;
>
> ■ Events and meaning are loosely coupled;
>
> ■ Most significant events and processes in organizations are ambiguous and uncertain;
>
> ■ The greater the ambiguity and uncertainty, the harder rationality and logical approaches to analysis, problem solving and decision making are to use;

- Faced with ambiguity and uncertainty, humans create symbols to decrease confusion, increase predictability, and provide direction; and

- Many organizational events and processes are important for what they express than for what they produce: secular myths, rituals, ceremonies, and sagas that help people find meaning and order in experiences.

Symbolic phenomena are particularly visible in organizations with unclear goals and uncertain technologies; in such organizations, most things are ambiguous. Who has power? What is success? Why was a decision made? What are the goals? The answers are often veiled in a fog of uncertainty.[64]

Utilization of the symbolic frame focuses on three types of concepts:

- Concepts of meaning:
  - Dilemmas and paradoxes are everywhere.
  - Organizations are full of questions that have no answers.
  - Organizations are full of problems that cannot be solved.
  - Organizations have many events that cannot be understood fully.
- Concepts of beliefs
- Concepts of faith

The leader uses the following tools within the symbolic frame:

- Myths—to reconcile differences and resolve dilemmas:
  - Fairy tales
  - Stories
- Metaphors—to make confusion comprehensible.
- Scenarios and symbolic activities—to provide direction amidst uncertainty, to provide forums for socialization, to reduce anxiety and ambiguity, and to convey messages to external constituencies:
  - Rituals
  - Ceremonies
- Heroes, heroines, shamans, priests, and storytellers—to provide guides to and interpretations of what life in organizations really mean.

Historically, all human cultures have used ritual and ceremony to create order, clarity, and predictability, particularly in dealing with issues or problems that are too complex, mysterious, or random to be controlled in any other way. We all create rituals to reduce uncertainty and anxiety.[65]

Important to the understanding of organizations and leading organizations, then, is culture. The four frames, when integrated, form a unique culture for each organization.

How do leaders effectively utilize Bolman and Deal's model? First we need to understand which actions leaders use in each frame. Let's look at each frame in an overview.

Structural Leadership

- Leaders do their homework.
- Leaders develop a new model of the relationship of structure, strategy, and environment for their organization.
- Leaders focus on implementation.
- Leaders continually experiment, evaluate, and adapt.

Though structural leadership has received less attention than it deserves, it can be a very powerful approach. Structural leaders lead through analysis and design rather than charisma and inspiration. Their success depends on developing the right blueprint for the relationship between their organization's structure and strategy, as well as on finding ways to get that blueprint accepted.[66]

Human Resources Leadership

- Leaders believe in people and communicate that belief.
- Leaders are visible and accessible.
- Leaders empower: they increase participation, provide support, share information, and move decision making as far down the organization as possible.

> Human resource leadership has generated an enormous amount of attention. Until very recently, in fact, human resource concepts dominated the literature on managerial leadership. The human resource literature has focused particularly on interpersonal relationships between superiors and subordinates and on the value of openness, sensitivity, and participation. When they are successful, human resource leaders become catalysts and servant-leaders.[67]

Political Leadership

- Leaders clarify what they want and what they can get.
- Leaders assess the distribution of power and interests.
- Leaders build linkages to other stakeholders.
- Leaders persuade first, negotiate second, and use coercion only as a last resort.

> Effective political leaders are advocates who are clear about their agenda and sensitive to political reality and who build the alliances that they need to move their organization forward.[68]

Symbolic Leadership

- Leaders interpret experience (transactional [exchange theory] versus transforming [inspire to reach higher needs and purposes]).
- Leaders are transforming leaders who are visionaries.
- Leaders use symbols to capture attention.
- Leaders frame experience (i.e., reduce the ambiguity and uncertainty through symbolism).
- Leaders discover and communicate a vision.
- Leaders tell stories.

> Symbolic leaders are artists, poets, or prophets who use symbols and stories to communicate a vision that builds faith and loyalty among an organization's employees and other stakeholders.[69]

"Wise leaders understand their own strengths, work to expand them, and build teams that together can provide leadership in all four modes—structural, political, human resource, and symbolic."[70] In essence, a situational leader is what is advocated. "Leadership is always an interactive process between the leader and the led. Organizations need leaders who can provide a persuasive and durable sense of purpose and direction, rooted deeply in human values and the human spirit."[71]

The prescriptive aspect of the Bolman and Deal model is summarized in **Table 8–5** and **Table 8–6**. Upon reviewing the tables, you may notice that this model has significant connections to other theories, such as media richness theory.

Bolman and Deal propose that *pluralism* slows research by impeding communication, in that different disciplines and theories use different languages. Because they used interdisciplinary research on leadership to create their model, Bolman and Deal had to develop their own "language" and a common understanding for people to utilize the model. By doing so, these scholars reduced the "Tower of Babel" problem. When you apply, analyze, synthesize, and evaluate leadership theories and models in your own unique circumstances, it will be important to understand and create a common language (and be consistent).

Now we turn to three models that use different constructs but are inherently situational or contingency leadership models. After the summary of each model, an analysis of these models and the Bolman and Deal model is presented as an example.

TABLE 8–5   Bolman and Deal: Choosing a Frame

Frame	Conditions for Salience
Structural	Clear goals and information; well-understood cause–effect relationships; strong technologies and information systems; low conflict; low ambiguity; low uncertainty; stable legitimate authority
Human resources	High or increasing employee leverage; low or declining employee morale and motivation; relatively abundant or increasing resources; low or moderate conflict and uncertainty; low or moderate diversity
Political	Scarce or declining resources; goal and value conflicts; high or increasing diversity; diffuse or unstable distribution of power
Symbolic	Unclear and ambiguous goals and information; poorly understood cause–effect relationships; weak technologies and information systems; culturally diverse

Source: Bolman, L.G., & Deal, T. E. (1991). *Reframing organizations: Artistry, choice, and leadership*. San Francisco: Jossey-Bass, p. 315.

TABLE 8–6   Bolman and Deal: Assessing Frame Selection

Question	Structural Frame	Human Resources Frame	Political Frame	Symbolic Frame
How important are commitment and motivation?	Unimportant	Important	?	Important
How important is the technical quality of the decision?	Important	?	Unimportant	Unimportant
How much ambiguity and uncertainty are present?	Low to moderate	Moderate	Moderate to high	High
How scarce are resources?	Moderately scarce	Moderately abundant to abundant	Scarce or increasingly scarce	Scarce to abundant
How much conflict and diversity are present?	Low to moderate	Moderate	Moderate to high	Moderate to high
Are we working in a top-down or bottom-up manner?	Top down	Top down	Bottom up	Top down or bottom up

Source: Bolman, L.G., & Deal, T. E. (1991). *Reframing organizations: Artistry, choice, and leadership*. San Francisco: Jossey-Bass, p. 326.

LYNN'S LEADERSHIP ART AND SCIENCE IN PUBLIC LEADERSHIP AND MANAGEMENT MODEL[72]

Lynn suggests that most situational leadership models are correct but are difficult to prove. As the number of practitioner-based models of situational leadership increases, Lynn strongly recommends that empirical research and evidence of effectiveness be employed to complement any practitioner model. An interdisciplinary balance of "art" and "science" is the best method for situational model development. "The use of conceptual frameworks delineating agency problems to study the incentive effects of goals is surely a better basis for advising practitioners than ideologically justified advocacy of performance measurement."[73] Agency theory and game theory provide a scientific "platform" from which to research, prove, and apply situational leadership theory. According to Lynn, having a way to think and conceptualize is more important to effective situational leadership than employing half-baked practitioner, "art-based" approaches.

Lynn's situational leadership perspective supports a long-term, individualized approach. Under this model, both practitioner-based and empirically supported concepts are integrated into a conceptual decision-making or thinking approach for leadership. The leader is more important than the organization in this decision-support-based framework. Skills paramount for leaders include evaluation, critical thinking, and synthesis of interdisciplinary ideas so as to develop an individual situational model of leadership.

In 1987, Lynn found that high-level public-sector officials (members of the Reagan administration) tried to change their organizations with varying success. Accordingly, Lynn noted that success depended on four factors:[74]

- Personality
- Skills and experience
- A design for change
- Favorability of the situation

YUKL'S MULTIPLE LINKAGE MODEL[75]

Based on a comprehensive leadership approach, the multiple linkage model was first introduced in 1971, with refinements to the model continuing to appear through the 1990s. This model, which was built on previous leadership models, embraces the contingency approach. The key issue is the interacting effects of leader behavior and situational variables on organizational performance.

Yukl advocates a more complex and comprehensive model than was offered by earlier contingency theories. His model proposes that leaders, in the short term, evaluate and improve intervening variable situations for effectiveness. In the long term, leaders change the situation to better match their organizational strengths and achieve the mission. A transformational leader uses an entrepreneurial style and an articulate and clear vision to shift the situation toward a more favorable environment. Long-term situational variables include the following:

- A formal reward system (subordinate effort)
- Intrinsically motivating properties of the work itself (subordinate effort)
- Technology (performance)
- Geographical distribution (performance)
- Policies and procedures (performance)
- Informal practices that have evolved over time (performance)

Yukl's model suggests that leaders are in control (effective leaders, that is) of the situation more so than—or at least as much as—the organization's status quo or political environment. In this model, empirical evidence is more important than practitioner-based situational leadership schemes. The ability to evaluate short-term intervening variables, establish a long-term vision, and be the primary catalyst (director) driving long-term situational change—these characteristics are the essence of the effective situational leader. According to Yukl, evaluation, learning, interpersonal, and entrepreneurial skills (from empirical evidence) are the leader's most important skills.

HARGROVE AND GLIDEWELL'S IMPOSSIBLE LEADERSHIP MODEL[76]

Hargrove and Glidewell's model is based on "impossible jobs in leadership," such as the positions filled by elected officials, appointed officials, and persons working in the public goods and services arena. In this model, coping—rather than leading—takes center stage. "The commissioner must always be prepared, however, for a shift in focal concerns and be ready to respond by shifting resources to possible (sometimes impossible) professional mitigation of the problems stressed by the new concerns."[77] The prudent public administrator (commissioner) learns to evaluate coalitions—political, governmental, and public—and incorporate coalition concerns into an overall vision for the organization.

An entrepreneurial leader—one who is flexible, is dynamic, and stands with expert power is able to direct the organization through political storms, and manages and maintains emotional and structural equilibrium, through choosing and using situational *coping strategies.* Hargrove and Glidewell suggest that an accommodation strategy works better than a consensus creation strategy in this kind of scenario. Public "impossible jobs" have much ambiguity and uncertainty built into the situation: "'the moves' of commissioners must conform to rules that are constantly changing; in fact, the 'players' often disagree about what the rules are."[78] To deal with this level of uncertainty, the leader must develop a firm sense of intuition.

The more able a leader is at developing contingency plans, and the better he or she masters the ability to effectively and quickly implement contingency plans, the more effective the leader is perceived to be. The leader is tied to the situation he or she inherits in the public sector, especially in "impossible-type jobs"; evaluating coalition power, establishing expert power, choosing and using coping strategies, developing a relatively short-term vision based on accommodation, and celebrating marginal intermittent victories are the essence of such a person's situational leadership model. Hargrove and Glidewell's approach suggests that the organization is the catalyst, rather than the leader, with regard to situational variables and that the "art" of the leader as practitioner is more important than the empirical evidence of effective public leadership. An effective leader who tries to control situational variables may well be a leader who can change expectations of both the political machine and the public.

ANALYSIS AND COMPARISON OF FOUR MODELS

This analysis and comparison section is intended to help readers think critically about leadership models. Can you add insights to this analysis and comparison? The four leadership models analyzed and compared are Bolman and Deal's reframing organizational leadership model, Lynn's art and science of public management model, Yukl's multiple linkage model, and Hargrove and Glidewell's impossible leadership model. The four model citations follow:

- Bolman, L. G., & Deal, T. E. (1991). *Reframing organizations: Artistry, choice, and leadership.* San Francisco: Jossey-Bass.

- Hargrove, E. C., & Glidewell, J. C. (1990). *Impossible jobs in public management.* Lawrence, KS: University Press of Kansas.

- Lynn, L. E. Jr. (1994). Public management research: The triumph of art over science. Symposium on Public Management Scholarship. *Journal of Policy Analysis and Management, 13*(2), 231–287.

- Yukl, G. (1994). *Leadership in organizations* (3rd ed.). Englewood Cliffs, NJ: Prentice Hall.

Five critical concepts can be used to evaluate the perspectives of the four models: (1) the time horizon; (2) the foundation base of the model; (3) the focal point (leader or organization centered); (4) the system employed or suggested for the leader to use; and (5) the important skills that an effective leader must possess to use the respective model. **Table 8–7** presents the analysis and comparison of the models.

TABLE 8–7   Analysis and Comparison of Four Leadership Models

Situational Leadership Model	Time Horizon	Foundation	Focal Point	System Employed	Important Leader Skills
Yukl	Short and long term	Empirical evidence	Leader	Leader behavior in the short term, leader vision in the long term	Evaluation, learning, behavior effectiveness, and vision development
Bolman and Deal	More short than long term	More practitioner than empirical based	Organization	Decision-support system	Evaluation, decision making, application of "inert" knowledge
Hargrove and Glidewell	Short term	Practitioner based	Organization	Coping strategies	Evaluation, accommodation, coping scheme development
Lynn	More long than short term	More empirical than practitioner based	Leader	Individualized conceptual thinking and decision-support models	Evaluation, critical thinking, synthesis of interdisciplinary work

Regarding the time horizon, each model takes a slightly different approach. Yukl suggests that leaders use both a short-term strategy (affect intervening variables) and a long-term strategy (develop a vision and change situational variables). Bolman and Deal take a more immediate perspective overall. Because the reframing model is organization centered, short-term horizons and decision making are more important for the individual leader in this model. Hargrove and Glidewell suggest that, due to the ambiguous and dynamic nature of public jobs, a short-term horizon is most effective for leadership flexibility. Lynn, basing the model on integrating practitioner and empirical approaches, recommends that leaders develop individual synthesized situational models; thus development is a long-term endeavor but individual approaches can be used in both the short- and long-term time horizons.

The four models also use differing perspectives of foundational grounding. Yukl recommends that an empirically grounded model (movement toward a solid theory) is the best approach. Lynn suggests that more empirically supported approaches are needed in the leadership literature. Bolman and Deal offer both empirical support and practitioner-based foundations for their model. Due to the lack of empirical evidence and the best practices (qualitative) nature of their work, Hargrove and Glidewell's model is grounded in practitioner-based evidence.

The focal point of each model can be derived from the disciplinary perspective of the model developer(s) and from the system employed or offered for the leader to utilize. Yukl comes from the behaviorist perspective, which suggests that leaders can individually provide the momentum and the environment for successful leadership. Yukl proposes that by employing behaviors that positively influence intervening variables in the short term and by articulating a clear vision to change situational variables into a more favorable position, leaders provide the focal emphasis of organizational life. Bolman and Deal, and Hargrove and Glidewell, coming from education and public administration disciplines, respectively, and collectively from organizational theory backgrounds, recommend "an organization influences leader" type of model. Evaluation of the situation, developing frames of analysis, and choosing an appropriate frame based on organizational reality are the essence of Bolman and Deal's model, whereas Hargrove and Glidewell suggest that the organizational realities determine the leader's choice of direction and coping strategies. Lynn focuses on the leader to develop a mixed (synthesized) model, individualized to the leader, based on empirical evidence and relying on practitioner-based concepts, to construct a successful situational leadership approach.

All four models suggest that a leader's skill in evaluating the situation (situational analysis) is of paramount concern. Yukl, however, includes the importance of leader behavior development (short-term requirements)

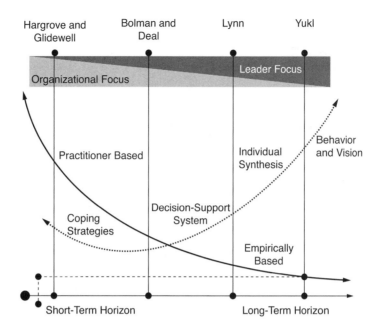

FIGURE 8–9   Four-Model Analysis and Comparison: Evaluation Continua

and vision development. Although all of the models incorporate an implied leader decision-making requirement, the Bolman and Deal model uses decision making in differing situations as a step in the leader's sequence of "frame" analysis. Hargrove and Glidewell mandate negotiation skill—specifically, accommodation—and the development of coping strategies as skills required for the successful leader. Lynn, requiring the leader to dive deeply into Bloom's Educational Learning Taxonomy, requires the leader to synthesize leadership literature and material to develop an individualized situational model.

The four models come from different perspectives; the critical issues, as examined here, can be arranged in a series of continua. **Figure 8–9** offers an integrated look at the four models. Each of these situational leadership approaches is embedded in the developer(s)'s disciplinary perspective. Quite reasonably, each model requires the successful leader to master situation evaluation and learning skills. From there, each model depends on different critical concepts to provide the situational leader with a basis for action and decision making.

LEADERSHIP MEASUREMENT TOOLS

Much of the leadership research has been descriptive and qualitative; by comparison, fewer quantitative data are available. As a result, qualitative research has centered on a "theory building" methodology that uses such methods as biographies, observation activities, informal interviews, and the like. In contrast, quantitative research is a "theory testing" methodology that tries to prove causality—that is, one thing causes another thing to happen. This approach is normally associated with statistical applications such as the general linear model (*t*-tests, analysis of variance [ANOVA], analysis of covariance [ANCOVA], regression) or relationships (such as correlations). The theories highlighted in this text are but a small sample of the myriad leadership models that have been researched throughout the history of leadership. Truly, most leadership research has been conducted using surveys, observation, and factor analysis of experts. Rarely have leadership models that link leader styles, situational variables, and outcomes (performance) been evaluated. However, the models summarized in this text form the basis of much cutting-edge leadership thinking today and are most salient for health organization leadership.

A review of the literature suggests that a plethora of descriptive tools are available to measure or evaluate a leader's style or success. Many of these tests use self-report scales. As a result, they introduce and maintain method bias. Despite this potential weakness, it is possible to control for bias by taking the test multiple times over a period of time. In this manner, a true response score might be found. **Table 8–8** profiles these various test tools (instruments), all of which have been used in the literature with varying degrees of utility. While Table 8–8

TABLE 8–8   Leadership Tests and Measurement Instruments

Test	Measures
Multifactor Leadership Questionnaire (MLQ)	MLQ is designed to measure various characteristics associated with transformational leadership. Three subscales pertaining to transformational leadership are included—charisma, individualized consideration, and intellectual stimulation.
Leadership Competency Inventory (LCI)	Developed for individual use, the LCI measures and identifies four competencies essential to effective leadership: information seeking, conceptual thinking, strategic orientation, and customer service orientation.
Leadership Skills Inventory (LSI)	Developed for individual use, the LSI evaluates and measures competency in terms of planning and organizational skills; oral and written communication skills; decision-making skills; financial management skills; problem-solving skills; ethics and tolerance; personal/professional balance skills; and total inventory score.
Leadership Practices Inventory (LPI), Individual Contributor	Developed for individual use, the LPI assesses five leadership practices: challenging the process, inspiring a shared vision, enabling others to act, modeling the way, and encouraging the heart.
Leadership Practices Inventory	The third edition of this instrument package approaches leadership as a measurable, learnable, and teachable set of behaviors. This 360-degree leadership assessment tool helps individuals and organizations measure their leadership competencies, while guiding them through the process of applying leadership to real-life organizational challenges.
Leader Behavior Questionnaire	Developed for individual use, this instrument helps leaders to determine which changes or further skill development are required for them to make full use of their capabilities for visionary leadership: The questionnaire is made up of 50 items measuring 10 key leadership scales: focus, respect for self and others, communication, bottom-line orientation, trust, length of vision span, risk, organizational leadership, empowerment, and cultural leadership.
Leader Behavior Analysis II, Revised	Developed for individual use, this self-scored questionnaire measures team leadership style flexibility, primary and secondary styles, effectiveness in matching leadership behaviors to the group situation, and tendencies to misuse or overuse various styles.
Leadership Team Alignment Assessment, Dynamic Culture Leadership	The DCL instrument was developed to assess individual and group leadership versus management and science versus art "personalities" in comparison to organizational operating culture and external environment expectations. This assessment incorporates the DCL process: (1) communication improvement; (2) strategic and operational planning; (3) decision-making alignment; (4) employee enhancement; (5) knowledge management; and (6) repeat. A key premise is that a leadership team that is diverse (in leadership personalities), yet focused on organization goals, is better situated for internal and external changes and, therefore, for dynamic culture leadership.
Bolman and Deal's Reframing Organizations Leadership Assessment	This tool was developed for assessment of leadership ability in structural, human resources, political, and symbolic constructs called frames; it determines the leader's dominant, secondary, tertiary and least apt frames.

is certainly not an all-inclusive list of leadership tools on the market, the goal here is to present a balanced approach to the tools on the market that are otherwise readily available and cost-efficient. The DCL assessment instrument is available in the textbook supplement on the publisher's Web page.

SUMMARY

This chapter presented practical models for both students of leadership and mature practitioners of the art and science of leadership. Two evolving models and one established model of leadership were described at length: the omnibus leadership model, the dynamic culture leadership model, and the reframing organizations leadership model created by Bolman and Deal. These models can assist young leaders in honing their personal leadership practice; they are intended to invoke thought, reflection, and discussion. They are also prescriptive in that they provide a strategy for success and a model for practical implementation. Other differing, yet contemporary, situational leadership models were also presented from Lynn (leadership art and science in public leadership and management model), Yukl (multiple linkage model), and Hargrove and Glidewell (impossible leadership model). A variety of leadership measurement tools are also available with which to conduct personal and organizational evaluations.

DISCUSSION QUESTIONS

1. Discuss the constructs and processes of at least two contemporary leadership models presented in this chapter and name the prescriptive mechanisms of those models.

2. Interpret the differences of at least two of the contemporary leadership models in this chapter from one other leadership theory or model from the situational leadership thought phase (from Chapter 4). Why did you select those models?

3. Explain how you would apply at least one contemporary leadership model from this chapter to a real or hypothesized health leadership situation or case; explain the rationale for your decisions, actions, and behaviors.

4. Identify and discuss the contemporary leadership models' constructs that enable a health leader to develop, modify, or revise organizational culture in a health enterprise.

5. How would you create a leadership model—either simple or complex—for your own use in health organizations? Relate your model to constructs found in models from this chapter and other constructs from theories and models in previous chapters of this text.

6. Select two models from this chapter. Compare and contrast those contemporary leadership models. Is one better for leadership use in health organizations?

EXERCISES

1. In a two-page paper, outline the constructs and processes of at least two contemporary leadership models presented in this chapter and state the prescriptive mechanisms of those models.

2. In a three-page paper, identify the differences between at least two of the contemporary leadership models in this chapter from one other leadership theory or model from the situational leadership thought phase (from Chapter 4).

3. Apply at least one contemporary leadership model from this chapter to a real or hypothesized health leadership situation or case; explain the rationale for your decisions, actions, and behaviors in three pages or less. Complete at least one leadership assessment from this chapter and report the results in one page or less.

4. In a two-page paper, analyze and illustrate the contemporary leadership models' constructs that enable a health leader to develop, modify, or revise organizational culture in a health enterprise.

5. Create a leadership model—either simple or complex—for your own use in health organizations and relate your model to constructs found in models from this chapter and other constructs from theories and models in previous chapters of this text in a paper that is 10 pages or less.

6. In a three-page paper, compare and contrast two or more contemporary leadership models. An example can be found within this chapter, but do not use those specific models in your own work.

REFERENCES

1. Ledlow, G., Coppola, N., & Cwiek, M. (2008). Leadership and Transformation. In J. A. Johnson (Ed.), *Organizational theory, behavior and development* (pp. 193–212). Sudbury, MA: Jones and Bartlett.

2. American Museum of Natural History. (n.d). Apatosaurus. Retrieved March 2007 from http://www.amnh.org/exhibitions/expeditions/treasure_fossil/Fossils/Specimens/apatosaurus.html.

3. Crocker, C. (1995). The lessons of Somalia. *Foreign Affairs, 74,* 2–8.

4. Mowday, R. T., & Sutton, R. I. (1993). Organizational behavior: Linking individuals and groups to organizational contexts. *Annual Review of Psychology, 44,* 195–229.

5. Antoinette, S. P., & Bedeian, A. (1994). Leader–follower exchange quality: The role of personnel and interpersonal attributes. *Academy of Management Journal, 37,* 990–1001.

6. Norris, W. R., & Vecchio, R. P. (1992). Situation leadership theory: A replication. *Group and Organizational Management, 17,* 331–343.

7. Weick, K. E. (1995). What theory is not, theorizing is. *Administrative Science Quarterly, 40,* 385–390.

8. Roberts, K. H., & Glick, W. (1981). The job characteristics approach to task design: A critical review of the literature. *Journal of Applied Psychology, 66,* 193–217.

9. Lowe, K. B., & Gardner, W. L. (2001). Ten years of *The Leadership Quarterly*: Contributions and challenges for the future. *Leadership Quarterly, 11,* 459–514.

10. Price, C. (2008, March/April). Eugenics revisited. *Clearly Caring Magazine, 28*(2): 42–43.

11. Worthington, G. E. (1925). Compulsory sterilization laws. *Journal of Social Hygiene, 11,* 257–271.

12. Parfrey, A. (1990). Eugenics: The orphaned science. In A. Parfrey (Ed.), *Apocalypse culture* (pp. 217–228). Los Angeles, CA: Feral House.

13. Dryden, C. (1997). *A-train: Memoirs of a Tuskegee Airman.* Tuscaloosa, AL, University of Alabama Press.

14. McDonald, K. A. (1994, November 16). The iconoclastic fossil hunter. *Chronicle of Higher Education,* pp. A9–A17.

15. Weber, M. (1904–1905/1930). *The Protestant ethic and the spirit of capitalism.* New York: Scribner's.

16. Coppola, M. N. (2004). A propositional perspective of leadership: Is the wrong head on the model? *Journal of International Research in Business Disciplines, Business Research Yearbook, International Academy of Business Disciplines, 11,* 620–625.

17. Coppola, M. N., & Lafrance, K. (2005). *The omnibus model.* Unpublished whitepaper, U.S. Army Medical Department Center and School, Academy of Health Sciences, San Antonio, TX.

18. Coppola, note 16.

19. Coppola, M. N. (2004). *The omnibus model.* Whitepaper, U.S. Army Medical Department Center and School, Academy of Health Sciences, San Antonio, TX.

20. Yukl, G. (1998). *Leadership in organizations* (4th ed.). Englewood Cliffs, NJ: Prentice Hall.

21. Yukl, note 20.

22. Yukl, G., & Van Fleet, D. D. (1992). Theory and research on leadership in organizations. In M. D. Dunnette & L. M. Hough (Eds.), *Handbook of industrial and organizational psychology* (Vol. 3, no. 1, pp. 147–197). Palo Alto, CA: Consulting Psychologists Press.

23. Donabedian, A. (1966). Evaluating the quality of medical care. *Millbank Memorial Federation of Quality, 44,* 166–203.

24. Mintzberg, H. (1979). *The structure of organizations.* Upper Saddle River, NJ: Prentice Hall.

25. Bacharach, S. B. (1989). Organizational theories: Some criteria for evaluation. *Academy of Management Review, 14,* 490–495.

26. Kerlinger, F. (1973). *Foundations of behavioral research.* New York: Rinehart and Winston.

27. Popper, K. (1959). *The logic of scientific discovery.* New York: Harper & Row.

28. Dubin, R. (1978). *Theory building* (rev. ed.). New York: Free Press.

29. Einstein, A., & Leopold, I. (1938). *The evolution of physics.* New York: Harper & Row.

30. Coppola, note 16.
31. Whetten, D. A. (1989). What constitutes a theoretical contribution? *Academy of Management Journal, 14,* 490–495.
32. Kerlinger, note 26.
33. Wittgenstein, L. (1972). On certainty (G. E. M. Anscombe, Ed.). New York: Harper Torch Books.
34. Jordan, S. (2006). *The effects of religious preference and the frequency of spirituality on the retention and attrition rates among soldiers.* Dissertation, School of Human Services, Healthcare Administration Program, Capella University, Minnesota.
35. Fry, L. W. (2003). Toward a theory of spiritual leadership. *Leadership Quarterly, 14,* 693–727.
36. Russell, R. F., & Stone, A. G. (2002). A review of servant leadership attributes: Developing a practical model. *Leadership and Organizational Development Journal, 23*(3), 145–157.
37. Coppola, note 16.
38. Baylor University, Institute for Studies of Religion. (2008). Baylor religion survey.
39. Coppola & Lafrance, note 17.
40. Goodman, R. M. (1998). Identifying and defining the dimensions of community capacity to provide a basis for measurement. *Health Education and Behavior, 25*(3), 258–278.
41. Wintrobe, R. (2003). *Can suicide bombers be rational?* Whitepaper, Department of Economics, University of Western Ontario.
42. Xenophon. (1948). Hiero, or Tyrannicus. Reprinted in L. Strauss, *On tyranny* (pp. 2–11). New York: Political Science Classics.
43. Raskovich, A. (1996). Ye shall have no other gods before me: A legal–economic analysis of the rise of Yahweh. *Journal of Institutional and Theoretical Economics, 152,* 449–471.
44. Donabedian, note 23.
45. Nasar, S. (2001). *A beautiful mind: The life of mathematical genius and Nobel laureate John Nash.* New York: Touchstone.
46. Ledlow et al., note 1.
47. Ledlow, G., Cwiek, M., & Johnson, J. (2002). Dynamic culture leadership: Effective leader as both scientist and artist. Global Business and Technology Association (GBATA) International Conference; Beyond Boundaries: Challenges of Leadership, Innovation, Integration and Technology; N. Delener & C-n. Chao (Eds.), pp. 694–740. First reported in the GBATA publication and provided again herein with permission by New Visions Network, LLC.
48. Busch, M., & Hostetter, C. (2009). Examining organizational learning for application in human service organizations. *Administration in Social Work, 33*(3), 297–318.
49. Conger, J., & Toegel, G. (2002). A story of missed opportunities: Qualitative methods for leadership research and practice. In K. W. Parry & J. R. Meindl (Eds.), *Grounding leadership theory and research: Issues, perspectives, and methods* (pp. 175–197). Greenwich, CT: Information Age Publishing.
50. Jelinek, M., & Litterer, J. A. (1995). Page 168 in Toward entrepreneurial organizations: Meeting ambiguity with engagement. *Entrepreneurship: Theory and Practice, 19* (3), 137–169.
51. Schein, E. H. (1999). *The corporate culture survival guide: Sense and nonsense about culture change.* San Francisco, California: Jossey-Bass.
52. Yukl, G. (1994). *Leadership in organizations* (3rd ed.). Englewood Cliffs, NJ: Prentice Hall, p. 355.
53. Schein, note 51.
54. Schein, note 51.
55. Friesen, M., & Johnson, J. (1995). *The success paradigm.* London: Quorum Books.
56. Bolman, L. G., & Deal, T. E. (1991). *Reframing organizations: Artistry, choice, and leadership.* San Francisco, CA: Jossey-Bass.
57. Sasnett, B., & Clay, M. (2008, December). Leadership styles in interdisciplinary health science education. *Journal of Interprofessional Care, 22*(6), 630–638.
58. Bolman & Deal, note 56, p. 121.
59. Bolman & Deal, note 56, pp. 121–122.
60. Bolman & Deal, note 56, pp. 152–153.
61. Bolman & Deal, note 56, p. 154.
62. Bolman & Deal, note 56, pp. 189–190.
63. Bolman & Deal, note 56, pp. 203–204.
64. Bolman & Deal, note 56, pp. 244–245.
65. Bolman & Deal, note 56, p. 261.
66. Bolman & Deal, note 56, p. 434.
67. Bolman & Deal, note 56, p. 435.
68. Bolman & Deal, note 56, p. 445.
69. Bolman & Deal, note 56, p. 445.
70. Bolman & Deal, note 56, p. 445.
71. Bolman & Deal, note 56, pp. 448–449.

72. Lynn, L. E. Jr. (1994). Public management research: The triumph of art over science. *Symposium on Public Management Scholarship, Journal of Policy Analysis and Management, 13*(2), 231–287.

73. Lynn, note 72, p. 249.

74. Lynn, L. E. Jr. (1987). *Managing public policy.* Boston: Little, Brown.

75. Yukl, note 52.

76. Hargrove, E. C., & Glidewell, J. C. (1990). *Impossible jobs in public management.* Lawrence, KS: University Press of Kansas.

77. Hargrove & Glidewell, note 76, p. 34.

78. Hargrove & Glidewell, note 76, p. 39.

Leadership in Health Organizations

Leadership and the Complex Health Organization

Strategically Managing the Organizational Environment
Before It Manages You

We need leadership on the fundamentals of eating right, exercising, and not smoking.
I am interested in getting people to use the healthcare system at the right time, getting
them to see the doctor early enough, before a small health problem turns serious.
—Donna Shalala, *President of the University of Miami*[1]

This chapter discusses the leader's role in strategically leading the organization. Basic principles of creating and implementing a mission, vision, value, strategies, goals, objective statements, and action steps are presented to add to the planning overview provided in Chapter 6. A matrix tool that assists in understanding relationships within the environment that affect organizational culture and change management is also described. In addition, the leader's self-awareness and understanding of cultural factors are emphasized in terms of their effects on organizational change. The chapter ends with an emphasis on strategic leadership options for managing organizational culture change.

LEARNING OBJECTIVES

1. Identify the strategic direction elements of the strategic plan, identify the other elements of the strategic and operational plan, describe each of these elements in summary, and outline which internal and external environmental factors influence the strategic plan.

2. Distinguish the levels of organizational culture and summarize the actions and behaviors a health leader would perform to proactively and positively change organizational culture.

3. Predict how strategic planning might positively influence organizational culture and the internal environment; describe how strategy selection (e.g., competitive, adaptive) reinforces those changes to organizational culture and the internal environment.

4. Analyze how external and internal environmental factors influence the strategic plan and the organizational culture of a health organization.

5. Design a methodology to perform internal environmental scanning, monitoring, and assessment and external environmental scanning, forecasting, and monitoring for a hospital or group practice, public health organization, long-term care organization, stand-alone allied health practice, or retail pharmacy.

6. Interpret the current external environmental factors in the health industry; turn the interpretation into a critical list for action for a health organization; and appraise each element on the critical list for action as to where it should be addressed by the health organization (e.g., strategic plan, directional strategies, external or internal environment, organizational culture), noting that critical list items may affect more than one area of the health organization.

MISSION, VISION, VALUES, STRATEGIES, GOALS, OBJECTIVES, AND ACTION STEPS

Leaders in health organizations utilize a strategic system of leadership and management. Much of the literature uses the phrase "strategic management system" to describe this system. In reality, a more appropriate name for it is "strategic system of leadership and management," because people are led and resources are managed: Human resources are "managed" from a context of a strategic human resources system considering job analysis, job design, and the like, but the people need to be led. From this context, much of the content in the previous chapters that presented leadership competencies can be considered to represent some aspect of the strategic system of leadership and management. For example, the dynamic culture leadership (DCL) model ascribes to a strategic system of leadership and management with a heavy emphasis on organizational culture. Embedding a strategic and operational planning structure and process, with feedback loops, into the organizational culture is paramount for organizations if they hope to survive in dynamic conditions. Regardless of organizational type or industry or size, strategic systems are required. Indeed, as complexity increases, these systems become even more critical as long as the leadership holds to a consistent application of the system and organizational values.

Health organizations are complex and are of varying sizes. Sizes range from small solo physician practices to a town pharmacy to an integrated group practice to a rehabilitation company to a stand-alone hospital to a large integrated health system. Regardless of the size of the health organization, the speed of change, the complexity of the health industry, and the expectations of perfection by society, all health organizations require leaders' wise use of mission, vision, values, strategies, goals, objectives, and action steps to steer their course. Health leaders use these elements to guide the organization; develop and maintain an effective, efficient, and efficacious organizational culture; and focus the collective energy of the health organization where people are led and resources are managed. The health leadership team most likely will utilize a strategic and operational planning process to formally develop an organization's mission, vision, strategies, goals, objectives, and action steps. As part of this effort, each element of strategic and operational planning will be discussed in rational groupings.

Mission, vision, and values are guideposts[2] that leaders use to focus the health organization's collective energy and resources. "Mission, vision, values, and strategic goals are appropriately called directional strategies because they guide strategists when they make key organizational decisions."[3] A health organization's mission is tied to its purpose. Purpose is what the organization does every day to meet the needs and demands of the external environment (patients, customers, and stakeholders) and to deliver its outputs to a community in some competitive way (effective, efficient, efficacious, and available). Stakeholders include those individuals, groups, community members (individual and collective), and companies that interact with the organization, such as patients, customers, staff members, suppliers, and the community. Stakeholders can directly and indirectly influence the success of the organization.

An extension of purpose is the health organization's mission. Mission is why the organization exists, which business it is in, who it serves, and where it provides its products or services. Swayne, Duncan, and Ginter defined characteristics of mission statements as follows:

1. "Mission statements are broadly defined statements of purpose;

2. Mission statements are enduring;

3. Mission statements should underscore the uniqueness of the organization; and

4. Mission statements should identify the scope of operations in terms of service and market."[4]

Vision is an aspiration of what the organization intends to become—that is, the shared image of the future organization that places the organization in a better position to do its mission and fulfill its purpose. In essence, vision is the dream of what the organization can become. Values are the beliefs and attitudes that an organization holds that guide day-to-day decision making, behavior, and actions. Health leaders "acquire vision from an appreciation of the history of the organization, a perception of the opportunities present in the environment, and an understanding of the strategic capacity of the organization to take advantage of these opportunities. These factors work together to form an organization's hope for the future."[5]

The purpose of a vision statement is to provide a group, organization, or community with a shared image of its direction over the long term. It catalyzes a group's efforts and focuses decisions. Vision statements should:

1. Describe an organization's big picture and project its future;
2. Be grounded in sound knowledge of the business;
3. Be concrete and as specific as practical;
4. Contrast the present and the future;
5. Stretch the imaginations and creative energies of people in the organization;
6. Have a sense of significance; and they should matter.[6, 7]

Leaders must be ever cognizant of the need to be consistent in the development of a mission statement and a vision statement and the need to embrace the values that the health organization holds as important. Yukl suggests using the mission and vision development process as a means for leaders to transform organizations by developing a strategic vision in consultation with the senior leadership team, articulating a clear and appealing vision, developing (senior leadership ownership required) a strategy or strategies to attain the vision, and focusing on the core mission(s) of the organization.[8] Schein argues that mission, vision, and strategies are essential for external adaptation—that is, for conforming with the expectations of the external environment—for organizations.[9] Senior leadership must be committed to and involved in the process of mission and vision statement development, but also involve their subordinates and staff in the process as well.[10]

Morris and Senge call strategists (in this case, health organization strategists) "pathfinders" in that they provide a vision, determine the approaches the organization will take to realize the vision, and provide a clear methodology to implement the plan and succeed.[11, 12] Where there is no vision, the people perish.[13] Health leaders are clearly in the "pathfinder" role for their organizations. "Strategic processes encompass a wide range of topics including analysis, planning, decision making and many aspects of an organization's culture, vision and value system."[14]

Strategies, goals, and objectives are the sequential building blocks of planning to successfully achieve the mission, but also for striving to achieve the vision of the health organization. "Strategic goals are those overarching end results that the organization pursues to accomplish its mission and achieve its vision."[15] Strategies follow "a decision logic of development."[16] Directional strategies lead to adaptive strategies, market entry strategies, and competitive strategies; each of these strategies should also have its own implementation strategy.[17] **Table 9–1** summarizes the types, scope, and role of strategy.

Goals translate the broad strategies of the vision into specific statements for organizational action by focusing the organizational resources so as to achieve the strategy and build the vision. Goals are broader statements—sometimes aspirations—that are hierarchically above objectives. Objectives align organizational resources to meet the stated goals. Objectives should be measurable, assigned to a responsible person (agent or owner), have timelines for completion, and be frequently reviewed by the health organization leadership for progress and resource sufficiency. Action steps (or action plans) are created to produce a step-by-step or task-level implementation sequence for each objective. Each task in the action steps (or plan) has a responsible person (or owner) and a time range for accomplishment, and some tasks may have a measurable variable as well. Action step owners "report" to the objective owner, who "reports" to the goal owner, who ultimately reports to the leadership team; the senior leadership team directs the organization at the strategy level.

Mission, vision, values, strategies, goals, objectives, and action steps are essential components of the strategic system of leadership and management. Health leaders utilize the strategic system's tools, such as planning

TABLE 9–1   Strategy Taxonomy, Scope, and Roles

Strategy	Scope and Role
Directional strategies	The broadest strategies set the fundamental direction of the organization by establishing a mission for the organization (Who are we?) and providing a vision for the future (What should we be?). In addition, directional strategies specify the organization's values and the broad goals it wants to accomplish.
Adaptive strategies	Adaptive strategies are more specific than directional strategies and provide the primary methods for achieving the vision of the organization—that is, for adapting to the environment. They determine the scope of the organization and specify how the organization will expand its scope (grow), contract its scope (shrink), or maintain its scope (remain as is).
Market entry strategies	Market entry strategies carry out the expansion of the scope and the maintenance of scope strategies through purchase, cooperation, or internal development. They provide methods for access or entry to the market. Market entry strategies are not used for contraction (reducing or shrinking) of scope strategies.
Competitive strategies	Competitive strategies include two types of strategies: one that determines an organization's strategic posture and one that positions the organization vis-à-vis other organizations within the market. These strategies are market oriented and best articulate the competitive advantage within the market.
Implementation strategies	Implementation strategies are the most specific strategies and are directed toward value-added service delivery and the value-added support areas such as culture, structure, and strategic resources. In addition, individual organizational units develop action plans that carry out the value-added service delivery and value-added support strategies.

Source: Swayne, L. E., Duncan, W. J., & Ginter, P. M. (2006). *Strategic management of health care organizations* (5th ed.). Malden, MA: Blackwell, p. 229, Exhibit 6-3.

(strategic and operational), to transform, guide, and develop organizational culture, thereby focusing the collective energy and resources of the health organization to effectively, efficiently, and efficaciously serve its purpose. "Strategy-making processes are organizational-level phenomena involving key decisions made on behalf of the entire organization."[18] Vital to strategic thinking, planning, and implementation, understanding the internal environment of the health organization is of paramount concern for the health leader; in fact, Roney suggests that internal assessment is a basic component of any comprehensive plan.[19]

UNDERSTANDING THE INTERNAL ENVIRONMENT

Internal scanning, monitoring, and assessment of the health organization are vital leadership activities. It is well known that effective leaders are effective internal organization scanners, monitors, and assessors. Research on internal organizational scanning, monitoring, and assessment consistently point to active and ongoing leadership emphasis in this arena. In 1986, Komaki reported that leaders and managers who did more monitoring were more effective; in 1990, Yukl found that school principals who monitored internal activity well had higher scholastic achievement in their schools; and in 1987, Jenster noted that successful firms that monitored the progress of their strategic plans performed much better than their competitors.[20]

The most important elements of understanding the internal health organization's environment should focus on systems such as the human resources management system, supply chain system, technological system, information system, and culture and subcultures. The salient theme is one of integrated synergy among all the health organization's systems. Specific areas of scanning, monitoring, and assessing for the health leader include the following issues:

- Competitive advantage and the unique or distinctive competencies the organization possesses (e.g., centers of excellence)
- Strengths and weaknesses of the organization
- Functional strategies for implementation of strategies that are supported by goals, objectives, and action steps
- Operational effectiveness, efficiency, and efficacy
- Organizational culture (Is the culture aligned with the organization's direction?)

Health leaders must create a well-thought-out approach to internal scanning, monitoring, and assessing of the organization against the current strategic and operational plans (which focus effort toward the organization's vision and mission) and the fit with the external environment. How the health leader conducts these processes depends on the viewpoint (or paradigm or context). Leaders develop assumptions and constraints that are internally oriented to achieve understanding of the internal environment. Assumptions in this context are internal (rooted in organizational circumstances) and characterized by a situation or state that exists now or will exist in the future and guides thinking. Constraints include any current conditions that may prevent strategies or goals from being pursued in striving to meet the organizational vision. Constraints are rooted in existing rules, traditions, habits, policies, social norms, or laws that set parameters on what an organization or individual can do.

The remainder of this section discusses topics involved in understanding the internal organizational environment; organizational culture is discussed later in this chapter.

Institutional Factors

Institutional organizations and environments highlight the importance of social, political, and psychological aspects of organizational dynamics. There is really no mystery why so many health organizations are so similar when looking at basic processes and policies. According to Powell and DiMaggio, the creation of a field of organizations triggers a paradox—namely, that rational actors make the organizations similar as they simultaneously try to change the organizations.[21, 22]

An understanding of what constitutes a field is useful in understanding the constructs of institutional theory. Organizations are considered to be in a field if they are institutionally defined and dependent on structural equivalence—that is, if there is a need for an organization to meet certain established competencies that prevent competing organizations from becoming too dissimilar. This situation is an example of the "walks like a duck, looks like a duck, and quacks like a duck" phenomenon: Then it must be a duck. It is important for health leaders to appreciate the fact that a successful CEO in one health organization will likely be successful in another health organization due to the basic organizational similarities found across the field. Much of this success derives from leaders' mastery of "run" stage competencies and thorough understanding of the context of health. The process of defining institutional organizations and environments can be judged based on four dynamics:[23–25]

- An increase in the interaction among organizations in a particular group
- Emergence of interorganizational structures, domination, and patterns of coalition
- An increase in the information load that an organization must address
- A mutual "awareness" among participants in a set or organizations that they are involved in a common enterprise

Institutional View

The institutional view, in essence, is an assessment of the organization's situation as compared against a health leader's predetermined standard, benchmark, or expectations relative to competitors.[26] In this context, organizational strengths and weaknesses are determined, unique organizational competencies are compiled, and functional-level implementation strategies are assessed.

Part of this effort involves listing the organization's strengths and weaknesses. Strengths are what the organization does well, which elements create a competitive advantage, and what makes the organization uniquely appealing to the external environment. Conversely, weaknesses are those elements that the organization does not do well or lacks, and that makes the organization appear less desirable in the external environment. Health leaders must make difficult decisions to lessen or remove weaknesses in their organization, whereas strengths are highlighted and used as building blocks for future expansion.

Unique health organization competencies are focused to create competitive advantage. Competencies merge with resources and processes (or systems—that is, a group of processes) to create capabilities; the assessment of capabilities determines the level of competitive advantage a specific capability confers upon the health organization. Once strengths and weaknesses are determined, how the health organization compares to its competitors and to relevant standards (such as the professional or national standard of care) enables an honest assessment of the organization's competitive advantage. What the organization does—its purpose—is assessed. The assessment should be performed on the patient or customer flow process of pre-service (what exists and is accomplished before caring for a patient), point of service (the patient care process and experience), and after service (patient interaction and organizational activity after the care process); it should also be performed on the organizational culture, structure, and strategic resources (e.g., technology, supply chain, human resources, information systems). The results may then be compared to competitors' performance, with competitive advantage being defined in terms of those organizational characteristics that are evaluated as valuable, rare, imitable, and sustainable.[27] From this assessment, advantages and disadvantages can be discerned. Of equal importance, implementation strategies must be scanned, monitored, and assessed.

Understanding the implementation of strategies in a health organization can be complex. Nevertheless, with a thorough plan and teamwork, implementation strategies can be assessed effectively. Implementation of any strategy is key to success; a strategy in and of itself does nothing if it is not put into practice. Given that many health organizations have similar competencies and enjoy only subtle competitive advantages relative to their competitors, implementation is a very essential organizational "skill" that health leaders must build into their organizations. In fact, effective implementation may be the best competitive advantage a health organization possesses. Implementation strategies are also called functional strategies and operational strategies: Do not let the terminology confuse you—implementation is concerned with putting a strategy into practice, utilizing the strategy, and gaining from the strategy.

In implementation, vertical and horizontal fit are important aspects of assessment. *Vertical fit* comprises the congruence, interoperability, and seamlessness between *different* organizational levels in putting a strategy into practice. In vertical fit assessment and strategic implementation, the following leadership concerns are vital:

■ Organizational coupling (adherence to rules, policies, procedures, and norms)
■ Interdependence between organizational units (interdependence creates uncertainty)
■ Similarity in work functions between units (similarity in work units creates ambiguity)
■ Quality control and in-progress reviews
■ Communication

An assessment of these concerns to reduce weak points and flaws, the appropriate allocation of resources, leadership communication of expectations, goal setting, frequent communication between team members, and appropriate leadership intervention, guidance, and rewards during the process are essential.

Horizontal fit is the coordination and integration of different actions, tasks, functions, or processes performed at the *same* organizational level. Health leaders should consider this assessment from a coordination (sequencing, serial, or parallel processing) perspective; however, similar concerns exist as in assessment of vertical fit.

Institutional organizations focus on the reproduction of organizational activities and routines in response to external pressures, expectations of professionals in the industry, and collective norms of the institutional environment. In this manner, organizations hold themselves hostage to coercive (outside stakeholders telling them what to do), normative (making efforts to benchmark against like organizations in the same field), and mimetic mechanisms (copying the best practices and procedures of similar organizations despite the fact that the organization may or may not have a structure that supports the practice). These behaviors continue to make the organization more similar to other like organizations without necessarily making it more efficient. Health leaders in highly institutional organizations would be wise to become rapidly familiar with the environmental pressures of coercion, mimicry, and other normative external pressures.

Institutional Environments

Overall, institutional environments are preoccupied with ensuring that the correct and appropriate structures and processes are used to pursue organizational goals and objectives. Institutional constraints consist of elaborate rules and regulations to which organizations must conform if they are to receive support and gain legitimacy. Institutional organizations tend to be tightly coupled across all policies, procedures, and cultural norms. In this environment, the leader may be bound to policies so massive that even the simplest new actions and changes require more effort than they are worth.[28] The only way to uncouple this kind of binding to an institutional environment is to reengineer the organization. Entire departments, many personnel, and a wealth of practices may need to be eliminated and new ones established in their place to alter this tightly coupled situation.

Most often, health organizations are a hybrid of institutional and technical environments. Technical environments exist where there is a need for interdisciplinary teamwork and varied skill sets that enable organizations to manage, control, and coordinate work processes effectively, while buffering them from environmental institutional disturbances. Technical environments are characterized by barriers to entry into the industry due to the vastness of knowledge, skills, and abilities of professionals in that environment as well as the high cost of the technology required to produce the products and services of the industry. The medical care sector, for example, seems to combine relatively strong institutional and technical environmental forces.[29]

Resource Dependency

The resource-dependent organization desires to maintain autonomy and remain relatively independent of its environment. At the same time, organizations also recognize the need to form coalitions to bring together resources to help reduce transaction costs. If the environment is unstable, organizations may be less likely to rely on other organizations for support. The stability of the environment may be evaluated by assessing the number and types of organizations, the munificence of those organizations (maturity and size), and the interconnectedness of those organizations (competition and complexity of relationships).

Resource-dependent organizations also assume that leaders can actively increase an organization's effectiveness and influence the environment. Effectiveness is defined as the ability to create acceptable outcomes and actions as perceived by outside organizations and agents.[30] In the health arena, the supply chain component of the organization, and of the industry for that matter, may fit best within this typological category.

One of the basic propositions governing the resource-dependent organization is that leaders must be aware that the most efficient or effective organizations do not always survive. Rather—and perhaps not surprisingly—the organizations with the most power survive. Power is defined as the ability to secure and maintain the most stable and most respected networks of resource chains. Key steps in maintaining power include preparing contingency plans for potential environmental shifts, building redundant networks, and establishing an efficient value chain. As in the supply chain example, volume of purchases and extensiveness of supplier networks act as the power behind efficient and effective supply chain operations in health.

For example, in a stable and healthy environment, resource chains may be several levels deep and have many redundant alternatives. In this milieu, an organization's power may be affected by the introduction of more influential organizations into the environment or by the scarcity of resources and resource levels in periods of environmental famine. Organizations are vulnerable if vital resources are controlled by other organizations, such as manufacturers and distributors of medical equipment, supplies, and pharmaceuticals. Thus organizations purposefully engage in networks of interorganizational relationships to obtain the needed resources and improve their survival chances. In the end, the organization with the best access to suppliers, customers, regulators, and competitors holds the most power in the market and has the greatest survival potential.[31]

The resource-dependent view is also an inventory of the health organization within the context of how it serves its purpose in the external environment. In this paradigm, the health organization's resources, capabilities, competencies, core competencies, and distinctive competencies are assessed.[32] "Resources are the stocks of human and nonhuman factors that are available for use in producing goods and services. Resources may be tangible, as in the case of land, labor, and capital, or they may be intangible, as in the case of intellectual property [includes business and care processes], reputation, and goodwill."[33] Similar to the institutional view, the organization's list of resources and competencies is assessed to determine their value, rareness, imitability, durability, and ultimate importance to the organization.

Definition of these terms in this context is appropriate. *Value* is the subjective worth of the organization's resources in the practice of "purpose" as it delivers its services and products to the external environment; surrogate measures of value can be market share, lives saved, procedures successfully performed, number and percentage of patients successfully treated, percentage of return patients or customers, and financial statements (considered subjective in this context because a financial statement is temporal). *Rareness* reflects how likely one would be able to find the services, products, and processes in the external environment; rareness would denote that one would not find a similar set of services or products or processes. (Of course, a health organization can be rare but of little or marginal value.) *Imitability* describes the speed with which the health organization's resources, processes, and capabilities can be duplicated or copied by other health organizations. *Durability* indicates the speed with which a health organization's resources, processes, and capabilities become obsolete or not usable; this issue is especially important considering the expected standard of care in the health industry.

Health leaders should continuously build and improve the resource and competencies list in this view as assessed by the directional strategies and strategic goals of the organization. A strengths and weaknesses assessment, as discussed previously within the institutional view, is a valuable tool in this context as well. A five-step approach to strategy analysis in this paradigm follows:

1. Indentify and classify resources.
2. Combine strengths and turn them into capabilities.
3. Appraise the profit (margin, for nonprofit organizations) potential of capabilities.
4. Select the strategy that best serves the organization given the macro and micro external environmental factors.
5. Identify resource gaps and invest in weaknesses.[34]

Resource-Dependent Environments

In a resource-dependent environment, the organization requires resources to gain and maintain power and, therefore, must (sometimes reluctantly) interact with the environment.[35] At the same time, a resource-dependent organization conceptualizes the environment in terms of other organizations with which the focal organization engages in exchange relationships. The closed-panel health maintenance organization (HMO) is an example of this type of environment. In this situation, leaders want total control of empanelled providers, enrolled beneficiaries, referrals, and practice plans; they want to dictate the types of services provided and have governance over all other practices and procedures. Today, closed-panel HMOs—at least under the original model develop by Kaiser Permanente—cannot expect to survive for long periods of time in the free market. Leaders who try to maintain a hermetically sealed organization and operation fail to achieve economies of scale and scope and often lose competitive advantage.[36]

Contingency

Contingent organizations are more flexible and rely less on rigid policies and practices. These organizations utilize more loosely established internal best practices; hence they are described as loosely coupled. Within this type of organization, a leader's success is based on a unique amalgamation of internal and external factors—that is, organizational and environmental factors are contingent on one another. Leaders of contingent organizations base many of their assumptions on the fact that many aspects of organizational survival are dependent on factors beyond the organization's control. For the organization to achieve a "good fit" and survive, internal and external demands on the organization must be balanced effectively given the environment. The leadership approach is always based on the organization's current situation in this model. Leaders of this type of organization know that what makes an organization successful today may not keep it successful tomorrow.[37]

The underlying assumptions of contingent organizations are based on the premise that organizational structures are open and are not organizationally egalitarian: There is no one best way to organize, and any one way of organizing is not equally effective in another organization. In keeping with this last postulate, what might work in one organization with one set of particular environmental conditions and employees may not work in a similar organization with its own set of conditions and employees, regardless of the similarity of the organizations.[38]

The contingent view utilizes a scenario-based methodology. Health leaders use an institutional, resource-dependent, or combined approach to scan, monitor, and assess the internal organizational environment, create various likely scenarios for the organization (possible futures in which the organization would survive and thrive), and assess the internal organization's strengths, weaknesses, competencies, patient or customer processes (pre-service, point of service, and after service), and implementation strategies against those scenarios. Each scenario requires the internal organization to be evaluated in terms of its value, rarity, imitability, sustainability, durability, vertical and horizontal fit of strategy implementation, and impact on and congruence with organizational culture. Assessment as compared to competitors, potential competitors, and macro and micro environmental changes should be conducted routinely. A method for evaluating internal health organizations is provided in Table 9–2; multiple contingent scenarios can be evaluated by scoring each scenario against the others.

Leaders operating an organization that practices a contingent strategy need to be aware that the organization's growth may not always support the contingent strategy. *Size* refers to the scale and scope of an organization, especially the number of individuals to be organized. Contingent organizations suggest that size is positively correlated with increasing levels of bureaucratic scale within organizations. Child provided empirical evidence that size and bureaucratic structure are related to organizational performance: As organizational size increases, a higher degree of routinization is required (i.e., more policies, procedures, and tighter coupling).[39] Furthermore, larger organizations will tend to be more highly diverse in terms of organizational structure, be more vertical (more levels of hierarchy), and have greater horizontal differentiation (more divisions and a greater span of control). As a result, growth of contingent organizations suggests a need for a wide variety of specialized tasks; these include larger administrative components, in terms of both the number of hierarchical levels and the number of internal support personnel required.[40]

Contingent Environments

An important factor for a leader operating an organization in a contingent environment is that as the environment becomes more uncertain, organizations respond by employing strategies that change structural characteristics of the organization.[41] Furthermore, organizations tend to cope with uncertainty from the environment by buffering their technical core and protecting the main revenue generation processes of the organization from outside influences. For example, pharmaceutical companies threatened by the expatriation of patents and the possible introduction of generic drugs that threaten their profits and market share may develop a similar product line in which the same pill needs to be taken only once a week instead of daily. By doing so, the organization protects its technical core under a fallacy of daily dosage quality. Leaders in this type of organization use symbolic and political messages more often in times of uncertainty and ambiguity than structural or human resources–oriented pronouncements.

Matrix Assessment

An assessment tool can be a good starting point to assess the internal environment. Taking internal environmental scanning, assessing, and monitoring into account, the successful health leader will create a system, method, or set of tools with which to understand the internal situation. **Table 9–2** shows an example of this kind of tool.

TABLE 9–2   Internal Health Organization Assessment

Current Institutional Resource	Value (1–10, where 10 is best)	Rarity (1–10, where 10 is best)	Imitability (1–10, where 10 is best)	Sustainability (1–10, where 10 is best)	Durability (1–10, where 10 is best)	Fit (Vertical and/or Horizontal) (1–10, where 10 is best)	Organizational Culture (1–10, where 10 is best)
Strengths (list and score each)							
Weaknesses (list and score each as a 1–10 negative number to show how weak each item is)							
Competencies (list and score each)							
Capabilities (list and score each)							
Implementation strategies (list and score each)							
Patient or customer flow process (list [pre-service, point of service, and after service] and score each)							
Organizational culture							

As in the contingent health organization, scenarios are developed as possible future states for the organization. Using the tool in Table 9–2, each scenario would be scored and ranked. Each scenario should be ranked as to the likelihood of its being fulfilled or realized; then the table rankings and scenarios should be compared.

The next phase envisions how to transform the health organization to serve its purpose, fulfill its mission, and achieve its vision in the external environment. What would be required to change weaknesses into strengths (or at least render the factor neutral) for the health organization? What should be changed to improve or change competencies that can be translated into needed or demanded capabilities? Which revisions or resources would be necessary to improve implementation strategies, and which changes would be needed to develop a more appropriate organizational culture? **Table 9–3** can serve as a catalyst to this thought process.

A thorough and continuous internal health organization scanning, monitoring, and assessment system will serve leaders, managers, and the organization as a whole very well. Understanding "who" and "what" the health organization is as part of its current status or "state of nature" is a critical element to leading people and managing resources. Internal assessment is a tangible method for understanding the integration of all of the various resources and capabilities of a complex health organization. How the health organization fits with and serves its purpose in the community is of utmost importance to the leader and leadership team. Understanding the external environment—the topic of the next section—is the next major challenge.

UNDERSTANDING THE EXTERNAL ENVIRONMENT

Understanding the external environment focuses on scanning, monitoring, forecasting, and assessing the macro and micro forces of the external environment. Scanning involves identifying the subtle to dramatic signals of macro and micro forces as they change. Monitoring focuses on deriving meaning from a pattern of observations from scanning macro and micro forces. Forecasting is the active development of projections and likely scenarios based on the patterns identified through monitoring. Assessing entails prioritizing and quantifying the effects of changes in the macro and micro forces external environment, with scenario forecasts being incorporated into that valuation. "External environmental analysis attempts to identify, aggregate, and interpret environmental issues as well as provide information for the analysis of the internal [organizational] environment."[42]

The critical reason for understanding the external environment is to determine how to best situate the health organization to serve its purpose in the short term, yet still be able to adapt and survive in the long term. As mentioned earlier in this text, Rakich, Longest, and Darr provide categories that give leaders a structure through which to scan (environmental scanning), monitor, forecast, and assess a dynamic health industry:

1. Macro-Environmental Forces
   a. Legal, [regulatory, executive orders, and case law] and ethical forces
   b. Political (including government policy) forces
   c. Cultural and sociological (including values [beliefs and attitudes]) forces
   d. Public expectations (including community, interest groups, and media)
   e. Economic forces
   f. Ecological forces
2. Health Care Environmental Forces [also called Micro-Environmental Forces]
   a. Planning and public policy (regulation, licensure, and accreditation) forces
   b. Competitive forces
   c. Health care financing (third-party payers, both public and private, and financial risk)
   d. Technology (equipment, material, and supply entities) forces
   e. Health research and education
   f. Health status and health promotion (wellness and disease)
   g. [Integration with other health disciplines and organizations] public health (e.g., sanitation, environmental protection) forces.[43]

TABLE 9–3 Improvement of Internal Health Organization

Internal Component (State for each component)	Goal (State in simple terms)	Expectation (State in simple terms what is expected from this effort)	Tangible Resources Required (List land, labor, and capital)	Intangible Resources Required (List processes, intellectual property, reputation, and goodwill)	Expected Cost of Resources (List each resource needed and its approximate cost, and sum the costs)	Time Range to Complete (Provide a starting date and an ending date)	Importance Rank (Rank each item by importance to the organization considering the scenario scores)
Weaknesses							
Competencies and capabilities							
Implementation strategies							
Organizational culture							

The Rand Corporation suggests that immense pressure of cost containment is the leading factor for change in the health industry at this time.[44] Multiple forces, however, cumulatively contribute to change in the health industry. Professional associations and societies, the scholarly literature, and professional journals are all sources in which to look for external environmental information.

An evaluation of threats and opportunities of the external environment is essential for the health organization. Threats and opportunities (externally focused) are married to strengths and weaknesses (internally focused) to complete the SWOT analysis used in many strategic planning models and processes. Threats comprise issues, events, or changes that affect the organization negatively and serve as barriers to mission accomplishment and vision attainment. Opportunities are potentially positive issues, events, or changes that, with planning, resourcing, and implementation, can have positive effects on the health organization.

Another aspect of external analysis, particularly regarding forecasting, is the development of assumptions and constraints. Assumptions are perspectives on a condition or state of nature that are supposed to be true or are taken for granted. Assumptions in this context are external (rooted in macro or micro environmental factors) and suggest a situation or state that exists now or will exist in the future that guides thinking. Constraints are current conditions that may prevent strategies or goals from being pursued in striving to meet the organizational vision. Constraints are rooted in existing rules, traditions, habits, policies, social norms, or laws that set limits on what an organization or individual can do or plan to do. An overview of horizontal, vertical, and dynamic external environmental considerations is provided in the remainder of this section.

Horizontal Factors

One of the most difficult leadership skills for health executives to master is to view the health organization as a horizontal organization. Horizontal organizations have cooperative relationships, affiliations, or ownership rights with multiple outside agents and actors. A health actor is any individual, group, or organization that exerts influence on an entity. An agent is a principal lobbyist or representative of a health actor that is trusted with making decisions or statements on behalf of the actor. When poor relationships are in place, actors and agents working in concert can exert so much pressure on the organization that the organization is placed in a position where it must accede to the will of outside parties rather than acting in its own interest. Given this possibility, it is the goal of every healthcare executive to ensure that harmonious and affable relationships are maintained within the horizontal structure.[45]

From a reductionist point of view, horizontal organizations seek to maintain a level of homeostasis with all elements internal and external to the establishment. In horizontal organizations, it is not possible to operate and survive without forming cooperative relationships with multiple outside actors and agents. As a result, horizontal organizations must maintain a careful balance between mutually exclusive organizational needs and the needs of external stakeholders. Failing to balance these simultaneous priorities may lead to organizational failure or loss of competitiveness (i.e., loss of market share or market penetration).

For example, a health organization that views health only from a business-driven perspective (defined as concentrating on rates of return and profit or margin as the primary goal) may find over time that it has lost competitive advantage relative to other organizations in the same industry and could lose the trust and confidence of customers. Such was the perception of the health industry by the U.S. population in the 1980s and early 1990s. The introduction of managed care principles, such as gatekeeper access, specialty care referral, and preauthorization, caused consumers to perceive that health organizations were large, uncaring companies that were more concerned with keeping people away than providing high-quality care for the ill and injured.

A more recent organizational example can be found among the traditional big-oil companies in 2005, 2006, and 2007. Increases of more than 100 percent in fuel prices in less than one year (and even higher increases in some areas) created distrust for these organizations among consumers. Compounding this perception were reports of record-breaking, billion-dollar profits for the fuel companies as well as exorbitant personal salaries and bonuses for their executives. At the same time, customers were forced to pay record-breaking prices for a gallon of gasoline at the pump. These outcomes caused consumers to perceive oil companies as focused on greed and self-fulfillment, and resulted in the Democratic-led Congress of 2007 revoking certain tax incentives for these organizations.

Despite these negative examples, health organization cannot afford to become *too* altruistic and empathetic. For example, engaging in an abundance of uncompensated and charity care may fail to promote organizational survival, prosperity, and growth. Clearly, balance is necessary in a health organization, participating in a horizontal environment.

Vertical Factors

The horizontal organization stands in stark contrast to the vertical organization. The vertical organization builds a monument unto itself and seeks to minimize its reliance on any and all outside stakeholders and actors. In terms of organizational dynamics, there are actually very few truly vertical organizations. Thus, when we speak of vertical organizations, we refer to those organizations that attempt to control the environment first, rather than living in the environment and becoming a participatory member within the community.

Vertical considerations include health providers, possible competitors, suppliers, patients, customers, and other stakeholders associated with health services and goods that are above or below the organization within the continuum of care. For example, a hospital would have vertical considerations at the primary care level (e.g., physician offices and group practices) and above its level in tertiary care (e.g., a large medical center) or rehabilitative care or hospice care. Developing solid relationships and coordination are the keys to the success in this scenario, which explains why many of these organizations work to become vertically integrated.

Vertical integration in the health industry is the ability, through ownership, affiliation, or alliance, to offer products and services that span the continuum of care. A vertically integrated health system may offer primary care, secondary care, tertiary care, long-term care, and hospice care services under its umbrella; likewise, it may include academic medical centers (e.g., in-house education and practice for physicians and surgeons, nurse education and training, allied health education and training), a group purchasing organization and distribution operation (for controlling the supply chain, as described in "The Non-intermediated or Vertically Integrated Health Supply Chain,"[46]), and a research and development operation. This broad span of operations differs significantly from that of a horizontally integrated health organization. Large horizontally integrated health organizations encompass several like organizations across a large area; for example, a health system may include 25 hospitals located across 5 states. Some large health systems are both vertically and horizontally integrated. The degree of integration in each dimension plays a role in determining whether the organization assumes a horizontal or vertical internal "stance" and influences the organizational culture.

One of the last, great vertical organizations was the Ford Motor Company of the early twentieth century. Henry Ford not only built cars, but also owned dealerships, transportation companies, steel mills, oil refineries, rubber plantations, tire manufacturing warehouses, fuel companies, and leather and tanning industries. Put simply, he attempted to control all aspects of automobile manufacturing. This philosophy eventually failed for Ford; however, many organizations still try to minimize their reliance on outside environmental actors and agents.

Some early health organizations, such as the initial Kaiser closed-panel HMO model of the early 1940s, also attempted to replicate the vertical organization structure. In today's dynamic health environment, few organizations can be mutually exclusive while simultaneously relying on no outside influences.

Dynamic Factors

Dynamic organizations are those that do not qualify as either vertical or horizontal organizations. They also do not fit nicely into a model of being an open or closed organization. Nevertheless, many dynamic organizations may be described as having an open and horizontal architecture as opposed to a closed and vertical persona. Open and closed systems can exist in either horizontal or vertical organizations, depending on the organization's size and complexity.

In an open system, organizations are a smaller part of a larger system. Consequently, the environment has a central role in determining organizational survival. Additionally, in an open system model, the system interacts with and adapts to the environment; thus the situation may be described as dynamic. Inherent to open systems are feedback loops and adaptation to the external environment. Open systems do not negate prediction entirely; rather, through control over and understanding of the influences, outcomes are presumed. In such a case, the leader realizes that the environment is defined as the sum of the political, economic, social, and regulatory forces that exert influence on the organization; the organization itself is viewed as an organic living system within the environment. In this regard, no organization is entirely self-contained. As a result, the organization is dependent to some extent on the environment.

Standing in opposition to the open system is the closed system approach to organizational life-cycle analysis. In this design, the leader must be aware that the organization is guided by internal governance. In other words, the sum total of work of the organization is split within internal staff. Additionally, the leadership is hierarchical, probably more technically competent than conceptually driven, and the work of the organization is carried out impersonally and autocratically. In the closed system, the leader and the organization operate in isolation from environmental influences as much as possible. The effects are entirely predictable, because a finite number of variables affect the outcome. Such systems are not the rule, however, but rather the exception.[47–50]

When unpredictable open and horizontal systems actively interact with one another, it takes an accomplished leader to steady the organization in view of the higher levels of complexity. A complex system exists in the dynamic environment when large numbers of interacting organizations and elements begin to establish patterns and relationships that are new and unique. This dynamic can result in rapid and unpredictable change, following no apparent pattern. Complexity, therefore, is an extension of the general system for which the leader must be prepared.[51]

For leaders in the modern era, effectiveness in dealing with the complex dynamics of the health industry requires a deep understanding of the relationships between evaluative and empirical properties discussed earlier in this text. Management within this kind of dynamic environment is most difficult for early careerists to do before they have mastered the complexities of the "crawl" and "walk" elements of professional growth. For example, relationships may exist between segments within the organization along an informal network that have great consequences for organizational outputs. The more dynamic the task environment, the greater the contingencies presented to the organization.

It can be an intimidating task to forecast the future in a dynamic environment. Different possibilities in the environmental characteristics constantly require the creation of new and different ways of positioning the organization for success. Leaders must produce and determine contingencies that can quickly be put in place for countless future scenarios that may evolve. As Daft has suggested, in such an environment, both the destination and the route may turn out to be unexpected and unintended; strategy emerges spontaneously from the chaos of challenge and contradiction, through a process of real-time learning and politics.[52]

Leaders in the current era are more likely to work in open health systems. Thus the importance of an external presence for the leader cannot be overemphasized. The leader becomes the calming voice on behalf of the organization in an otherwise turbid and uncertain environment to countless stakeholders, many of whom the leader has no direct influence upon, other than through the power of his or her organization.

ORGANIZATIONAL CULTURE

From a broad perspective, health leaders assess the external and internal environments of the organization, determine which organizational culture will best meet the needs of the external environment, and then design, develop, implement, and refine the organizational culture. From this "big picture" view, leadership seems simple—yet accomplishing the task of organizational alignment with the external environment requires a focused, clear, appealing vision that is well communicated, combined with leadership and management team actions that are consistent with that vision. From this standpoint, leaders must be knowledgeable and competent about organizational dynamics, culture, communication, assessment and analysis, and change management. All of these areas are important, yet culture is the fabric that weaves all of these components together.

Health leaders can forge a new, better-fitting organization by devising a new culture that meets the needs of a dynamic environment using the best of science and art. If a supportive and confirming communication organizational environment, a planning and accountability emphasis, a push-down decision-making strategy that focuses on appropriate employee empowerment, and a learning and knowledge management-oriented operation are characteristics of the organizational culture needed to best provide health services and products, then the health leader needs an implementation plan or concept. To begin moving an organizational culture toward change, the health leader should take the following guidelines to heart:

- Model the behavior you expect yourself.
- Communicate expectations and train other leaders, managers, and staff.

- Revise structures and reporting relationships.
- Conduct team-based planning and policy development.
- Use primary and secondary mechanisms[53] (discussed later in this chapter).
- Be consistent and communicate often to the organization.
- Continue to scan, monitor, and assess the internal health organization environment while you scan, monitor, forecast, and assess the external environment.

Defining Organizational Culture

Organizational culture is a complex construct that incorporates many concepts and multitudes of variables. It encompasses a large set of largely ignored or invisible assumptions that deal with how group members interpret both their external relationships (external environment) and their internal relationships with one another. Culture is an outcome of group learning. As people solve problems together successfully, a condition for culture formation exists. Health organizational survival is intimately linked to meeting the needs of the external environment (the community that the organization serves). This goal is accomplished by effectively, efficiently, and efficaciously (high quality) developing organizational integration of resources, capabilities, and systems (developing synergy) to produce services and goods that satisfy marketplace demands and expectations.

Each organization deals with external adaptation and internal integration in its own way. The "way" the health organization adapts and integrates forms its collective organizational culture.

Schein gives an excellent summary of the various issues related to external adaptation and internal integration:

External Adaptation Issues[54]

- Mission and strategy: Obtaining a shared understanding of core mission, primary tasks, and organizational functions (both manifest and latent).
- Goals: Developing consensus on goals, as derived from the core mission.
- Means: Developing consensus on the means to be used to attain the goals, such as the organizational structure, division of labor, reward system, and authority system.
- Measurement: Developing consensus on the criteria to be used in measuring how well the group is doing in fulfilling its goals, such as the information and control systems.
- Correction: Developing consensus on the appropriate remedial or repair strategies to be used if goals are not being met.

Internal Integration Issues[55]

- Common language and conceptual categories: If members cannot communicate with and understand one another, a group is impossible by definition. Consider healthcare jargon as an example.
- Group boundaries and criteria for membership inclusion and exclusion.
- Power and status: Consensus in this area is crucial as to who has power and status.
- Intimacy, friendship, and love: What are the rules of the game for peer relationships?
- Rewards and punishments: What are heroic and sinful behaviors?
- Ideology and "religion": How are unexplainable and inexplicable events given meaning?

As you read about and reflect on organizational culture in the remainder of this chapter, note which similarities the research and information here share with research and models of leadership such as the omnibus leadership model, the dynamic culture leadership model, and the reframing organizational leadership model from authors Coppola, Ledlow, and Bolman and Deal. Can you integrate the concepts?

Edgar Schein, who is recognized as the "father of organizational culture," defines culture as a pattern of basic assumptions that are invented, discovered, or developed by a given group as it learns to cope with its problems of external adaptation and integration; these assumptions have worked well enough to be considered valid and, therefore, are taught to new members as the correct way to perceive, think, and feel in relation to their problems, challenges, and opportunities.[56] Sathe defines culture as the "set of important understandings (often unstated) that members of a community share in common."[57] Louis suggests that organizational culture is "a set of understandings or meanings shared by a group of people; the meanings are largely tacit among the members, are clearly relevant to the particular group, and are distinctive to the group."[58] Consider healthcare marketing and advertising in today's very competitive environment: Thirty years ago, very little "healthcare" was advertised (and thus became part of the culture); today, competition is intense and marketing and advertising are essential for survival. Marketing, customer service, entertainment during the care process, and advertising are now key parts of the culture that help ensure health organizational survival.

At the heart of organizational culture are questions about values, beliefs, and attitudes that become translated into behaviors, norms, and social expectations within the health workplace. Culture consists of ideational elements such as beliefs and values that explain and reinforce the foundation of the organization.[59] Which values, beliefs, and attitudes do you hold? How do they differ from your organizational experiences?

> An attitude is a learned predisposition to respond to a person, object, or idea in a favorable, neutral, or unfavorable way. A belief is the way you structure what is true and false and a value is an enduring conception of good and bad.[60]

Layered like an onion (as depicted graphically in **Figure 9–1**), values power beliefs and beliefs greatly influence attitudes. Behaviors are linked to attitudes. Behaviors are easier to change than attitudes, and attitudes easier to change than beliefs and values.

Where can you see, hear, or touch organizational culture?

> Manifestations of culture include rituals, stories, humor, jargon, physical arrangements, and formal structures and policies, as well as informal norms and practices. Content themes (such as values or basic assumptions) are used to capture and show relationships among interpretations of the meanings of these manifestations. These are the building blocks needed for you to understand the theoretical assumptions underlying a culture study, summarize the content of any cultural portrait, and if you wish, develop your own answers to the questions: What is culture? What is not culture?[61]

Schein provides insight into the tangible and intangible components of organizational culture. According to this theorist, three levels of culture interact to form the fabric of culture. Notably, organizational culture cannot be assessed and "known" in a short time or by walking through the corridors and reading policy documents; rather, it is discerned by observing, interviewing, and interacting with the full spectrum of these three levels:[62]

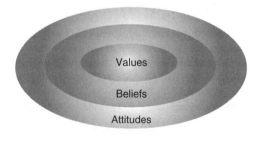

Rokeach's Model

FIGURE 9–1   Values, Beliefs, and Attitudes
Source: Beebe, S. A., & Masterson, J. T. (1997). *Communicating in small groups: Principles and practices* (5th ed.). New York: Addison-Wesley Educational, p. 174.

- *Level 1: Artifacts and Creations.* These elements are the most readily visible components of culture and include the organization's constructed social and physical environment. This level includes technology, art, visible and audible behavior patterns (visible but often not decipherable) such as written and spoken language, overt behaviors, and the ways in which members demonstrate status.

- *Level 2: Values.* Values are testable in the physical environment, but are testable only by social consensus (such as taking care of patients). Central values provide the day-to-day operating principles that the members of the culture use to guide their behavior. As values are taken for granted, they gradually become beliefs and drop out of consciousness, just as habits become unconscious and automatic.

- *Level 3: Basic Underlying Assumptions.* Level 3 elements include the relationship to the environment; the nature of reality, time, and space; the nature of human nature; the nature of human activity; and the nature of human relationships (taken for granted, invisible, preconscious). These implicit assumptions tell group members how to perceive, think about, and feel about things. These assumptions are taken for granted; members would find behavior based on any other premise inconceivable.[63]

Martin also recommends four types of formal practices, of interest to culture researchers, that should be evaluated to begin to understand organizational culture: (1) organizational structure and hierarchy (reporting relationships and locations); (2) tasks and technologies (what employees do to produce goods and services); (3) rules and procedures; and (4) financial controls (authority to commit, audit, and forecast financial resources).[64] Informal practices that should be evaluated (if possible) are not written down, but rather take the form of social rules and norms ("how things really work around here"). Often, these unwritten rules are inconsistent with formal policies and procedures.[65]

Organizational climate is a temporal phenomenon that changes quickly based on the current situation and influences. Climate is a snapshot in time and is dynamic, whereas culture remains stable over a longer time span. In essence, a simple explanation comprises a long series of organizational climate snapshots, strung together over time, that depict a large part of organizational culture; this is especially true in explaining the feeling of the workplace.

Climate can be changed quickly. For example, how would your subordinates and the work climate change if you announced a 5 percent pay reduction to support a budget cut? The next day, you announce that the pay reduction was an error and each employee will actually receive a 5 percent pay increase: Would the climate change? What would happen if you greeted and talked with each employee for a few minutes each morning to check on that person and his or her family and interests, and you followed this routine consistently over several weeks, but then one day you came in with a sad or frowning face, walked into your office, and closed the door, not coming out to greet everyone? How would climate change?

Health leaders can affect climate on a daily basis. With consistent application of behaviors, training, expectations and goals setting, reinforcement, and communication, over time climate influences culture.

Organizational Culture Typologies

Several different typologies of organizational culture exist. A typology is a categorization and description system that attempts to make sense of differing "states of nature" with regard, in this case, to organizational culture. The following subsections describe some of these typologies.

Interpersonal Interaction Model[66]

The interpersonal interaction model categorizes organizational cultures into one of four types:

- *Power culture*: Strong leaders are needed to distribute resources. Leaders are firm, but fair and generous to loyal followers. If the organization is badly led, there is rule by fear, abuse of power for personal gain, and political intrigue.

- *Achievement culture*: Results are rewarded, but not unproductive efforts. Work teams are self-directed. Rules and structure serve the system, but are not an end unto themselves. A possible downside is sustaining energy and enthusiasm over time.

- *Support culture*: Employees are valued both as people and as workers. Employee harmony is important. The weakness is a possible internal commitment without an external task focus.

- *Role culture*: There is a rule of law that outlines clear responsibilities; reward systems are clear, with tight coupling to responsibilities. This type provides stability, justice, and efficiency. Its weakness lies in the impersonal operating procedures and a stifling of creativity and innovation.

Gordon and DiTomaso's Typology

Gordon and DiTomaso's typology of organizational culture is based on the persona of the organization. **Table 9–4** describes this typology.

Daft's Typology

Daft's typology categorizes organizational cultures based on external and internal behaviors and actions. **Table 9–5** describes this typology.

Societal Expression Cultures

There are different types of culture, just as there are different types of personality. Researcher Jeffrey Sonnenfeld identified four types of cultures:[67]

- *Academy culture*: Employees are highly skilled and tend to stay in the organization, while working their way up the ranks. The organization provides a stable environment for employees to develop and exercise their skills. Examples include universities, hospitals, and large corporations.
- *Baseball team culture*: Employees are "free agents" who have highly prized skills. They are in high demand and can rather easily get jobs elsewhere. This type of culture exists in fast-paced, high-risk organizations, such as investment banking and advertising.
- *Club culture*: The most important requirement for employees in this culture is to fit into the group. Usually employees start at the bottom and stay with the organization. The organization promotes from within and highly values seniority. Examples include the military and some law firms.
- *Fortress culture*: Employees do not know if they will be laid off. These organizations often undergo massive reorganization. There are many opportunities for those with timely, specialized skills. Examples include savings and loan companies and large car companies.

TABLE 9–4 Gordon and DiTomaso's Typology

Cultural Practices	Description/Scale
Aggressiveness/action orientation	Emphasis is placed on getting things done, on being a pacesetter rather than a follower.
Innovation	This type indicates the extent to which individual managers are encouraged to take risks and innovate.
Confrontation	This type involves addressing issues openly instead of burying them.
Planning orientation	This element emphasizes managing in a proactive (planning) manner and avoiding surprises.
Results orientation	Emphasis is placed on holding people accountable for and demanding clear end results.
People orientation	A strong emphasis is placed on concern for growth of current employees.
Team orientation	This type refers to the extent that people are encouraged to cooperate and coordinate within and across units.
Communication	This type involves an openness to communicate in other areas of the company that might affect how a job is done.

Source: Gordon, G. G., & DiTomaso, N. (1992). Predicting corporate performance from organizational culture. *Journal of Management Studies, 29*(6), 783–797.

TABLE 9–5 Daft's Organizational Culture Typology

Cultures	Description
Adaptability/entrepreneurial	The organization is characterized by a strategic focus on the external environment through flexibility and change to meet customer needs. The organization actively creates change. Innovation and risk taking are rewarded.
Mission	The organization places major importance on a clear vision of organizational purpose. This type is appropriate for organizations concerned with serving specific customers in the external environment, but without the need for rapid change.
Clan	The organization has a primary focus on the involvement and participation of the organization's members and on rapidly changing expectations from the external environment.
Bureaucratic	The organization has an internal focus and a consistency orientation for a stable environment. There are high levels of consistency, conformity, and collaboration among members.

Source: Daft, R. L. (2000). *Organization theory and design*. Mason, OH: South Western College Publishing.

Defining Leadership from an Organizational Culture Context

Many studies have attempted to elucidate the relationship between the leader and the group and to determine the effect of a leader's personality and style on group formation as highly relevant to the understanding of how cultures form and evolve. Most group and leadership theories develop distinctions parallel to the internal and external task-oriented leadership functions and the internal group-oriented leadership functions. Schein's well-established paradigm of leadership is an excellent example of implied scientific and artistic practice. Schein views the unique and important function of leadership, as contrasted with management or administration, as the conceptualization, creation, and management of *organizational culture*.[68] Culture is a learned and evolved system of knowledge, behavior, attitudes, beliefs, values, and norms that is shared by a group of people.

> Leaders go beyond a narrow focus on power and control in periods of organizational change. They create commitment and energy among stakeholders to make the change work. They create a sense of direction, then nurture and support others who can make the new organization a success.[69]

Health leaders lead people and manage resources within a framework of organizational culture.

Changing and Adapting Organizational Culture

How do health leaders implement their proposals and recommendations? How do they communicate the assumptions underlying these proposed solutions and embed them in the health organization's thought processes? Most often, leaders use an approach that does not consider the contemporary realities of organizational life:

> The problem is simple: we are using a mechanistic model, first applied to managing physical work, and superimposing it onto the new mental model of today's knowledge organization. We keep

breaking change into small pieces and then manage the pieces. But with change, the task is to manage [lead] the dynamic, not the pieces.[70]

When leadership scholars describe the importance of the leader "articulating a vision" for the group, they are referring to this same set of issues—that is, to the development of organizational culture.[71] The next two subsections describe essential concerns for health leaders who want to succeed in developing, changing, and maintaining organizational culture. In the dynamic environment of the health industry, the leader's ability to assess the changing situation (externally and internally) and revise the organization's culture is a vital competence whose successful use requires a set of skills and abilities grounded in these mechanisms. The following subsections provide guidelines with which to measure your leadership effectiveness with regard to organizational culture; these areas—primary embedding mechanisms and secondary articulation and reinforcement mechanisms—are where you, the leader, change, maintain, reengineer, and alter organizational culture.

Primary Embedding Mechanisms [72]

Health leaders have a set of powerful tools, behaviors, and mechanisms at their disposal with which to develop, refine, maintain, or change organizational culture. The importance of these mechanisms cannot be overstated. The primary embedding mechanisms are as follows:

- What leaders pay attention to, measure, and control
- Leader reactions to critical incidents and organizational crises
- Deliberate role modeling, teaching, and coaching by leaders
- Criteria for allocation of rewards and status
- Criteria for recruitment, selection, promotion, retirement, and excommunication

Schein strongly states that leaders communicate both explicitly and implicitly the assumptions they *really* hold. If they are conflicted, their conflicts and inconsistencies are also communicated and become part of the culture. Consistency is the key; health leaders must predetermine where and how to guide the organization and stay on task. The secondary set of mechanisms (profiled next) support the primary set.

Secondary Articulation and Reinforcement Mechanisms [73]

The secondary articulation and reinforcement mechanisms reinforce the primary embedding mechanisms. The following are of the greatest importance:

- The organization's design and structure
- Organizational systems and procedures
- Design of physical space, facades, and buildings
- Stories, legends, myths, and parables about important events and people
- Formal statements of organizational philosophy, creeds, and charters

Schein calls these mechanisms "secondary" because they work only if they are consistent with the primary mechanisms. They are less powerful, more ambiguous, and more difficult to control than the primary mechanisms—yet can be powerful reinforcements of the primary messages if the leader is able to control them. The important point is that all of these mechanisms communicate culture content to newcomers and current staff.

Health leaders do not have a choice about whether to communicate, only about how much to manage what they communicate through words, actions, or neglect: Leaders cannot *not* communicate. Organizations differ in the degree to which the cultural messages are consistent and clear, and this variation in cultural clarity is a reflection of the clarity and consistency of the assumptions of the leaders.[74]

CHALLENGES OF CHANGE

As Morrison points out, there are significant challenges to health reform in the United States. Health leaders should be cognizant of these challenges as they work to positively change the culture of their health organizations, the culture of the health industry, and the expectations of the nation as a whole:[75]

- Recognizing the political, structural, and resource distribution tension between health and health care; understanding that medical care is not the only factor behind health status
- Developing health policies beyond managed competition
- Finding ways to make community-based healthcare systems work
- Clarifying the fuzzy boundaries between for-profit and nonprofit health care
- Dealing with regional diversity in such a large and diverse country

SUMMARY

This chapter discussed the leader's role in strategically leading the health organization. Basic principles of creating and implementing mission, vision, value, strategies, goals, objective statements, and action steps were presented. A matrix tool was described that assists in understanding the various relationships within the environment that affect organizational culture and change management. The leader's self-awareness and understanding of cultural factors are key considerations in the leader's ability to effect change within the organization, which may either narrow or expand the strategic leadership options available for managing organizational culture change.

DISCUSSION QUESTIONS

1. What are the strategic direction elements of the strategic plan? What are the other elements of the strategic and operational plan? What are the various challenges a health leader faces in institutional, resource-dependent, and contingent environments? Which strategies might you suggest the leader could implement to obtain successful outcomes?

2. Discuss the levels of organizational culture. Summarize the actions and behaviors a health leader would perform to proactively and positively change organizational culture.

3. Can you predict how strategic planning might positively influence organizational culture and the internal environment? How does strategy selection (e.g., competitive, adaptive) reinforce those changes to organizational culture and the internal environment?

4. How might external and internal environmental factors influence the strategic plan and the organizational culture of a health organization? In your answer, highlight the basic differences between vertical and horizontal external environments as compared to internal institutional, resource-dependent, and contingent environments. Which strategies might a health leader operating in these environments leverage to ensure success?

5. Discuss a methodology to perform internal environmental scanning, monitoring, and assessment and external environmental scanning, forecasting, and monitoring for a hospital or group practice, public health organization, long-term care organization, stand-alone allied health practice, or retail pharmacy.

6. Explain how you would interpret the current external environmental factors in the health industry; translate your interpretation into a critical list of action items for a health organization. How would you appraise each element on this list in terms of where it should be addressed by the health organization (e.g., strategic plan, directional strategies, external or internal environment, organizational culture), noting that critical list items may affect more than one area of the health organization?

EXERCISES

1. Identify the different challenges a health leader faces in institutional, resource-dependent, and contingent environments. Which strategies should a health leader implement for successful outcomes? Your answer should take the form of a one- to two-page paper.

2. In a one- to two-page paper, summarize the levels of organizational culture and predict the actions and behaviors a health leader would perform to proactively and positively change organizational culture.

3. In a one- to two-page paper, explain how strategic planning can positively influence organizational culture and the internal environment. In your paper, describe how strategy selection (e.g., competitive, adaptive) reinforces those changes to organizational culture and the internal environment.

4. Analyze how external and internal environmental factors influence the strategic plan and the organizational culture of a health organization, highlighting the basic differences between vertical and horizontal external environments as compared to internal institutional, resource-dependent, and contingent environments. Which strategies might a health leader operating in these environments be able to leverage to ensure success? Your answer should take the form of a two- to three-page paper.

5. In a one- to two-page paper, outline a methodology to perform internal environmental scanning, monitoring, and assessment and external environmental scanning, forecasting, and monitoring for a hospital or group practice, public health organization, long-term care organization, stand-alone allied health practice, or retail pharmacy.

6. Evaluate and interpret the current external environmental factors in the health industry; translate your interpretation into a list of critical action items for a health organization. How could you appraise each element on this list in terms of how it should be addressed by the health organization (e.g., strategic plan, directional strategies, external or internal environment, organizational culture), noting that critical list items may affect more than one area of the health organization?

REFERENCES

1. America's best leaders: Q&A with Donna Shalala, President of the University of Miami. (2005, October 22). *US News, Money and Business.* http://www.usnews.com/usnews/news/articles/051022/22shalala.htm.
2. Ledlow, G., Cwiek, M., & Johnson, J. (2002). Dynamic culture leadership: Effective leader as both scientist and artist. In N. Delener & C-n. Chao (Eds)., Proceedings of Global Business and Technology Association International Conference; Beyond Boundaries: Challenges of Leadership, Innovation, Integration and Technology (pp. 694–740).
3. Swayne, L. E., Duncan, W. J., & Ginter, P. M. (2006). *Strategic management of health care organizations* (5th ed.). Malden, MA: Blackwell, p. 187.
4. Swayne et al., note 3, pp. 191–192.
5. Swayne et al., note 3, p. 198.
6. Lerner, H. (2003, November). Vision statements. *Beyond Numbers,* p. 9.
7. Lerner, H. (2003). Vision statements. *Principal's Report, 3*(12), 2. Also appears in Swayne et al., note 3, p. 200.
8. Yukl, G. (1994). *Leadership in organizations* (3rd ed.). Englewood Cliffs, NJ: Prentice Hall.
9. Schein, E. H. (1999). *The corporate culture survival guide: Sense and nonsense about culture change.* San Francisco, CA: Jossey-Bass.
10. Swayne et al., note 3.
11. Morris, G. B. (1988). The executive: A pathfinder. *Organizational Dynamics, 16*(2), 62–77.
12. Senge, P. (1998). The leader's new work. In Hickman, G. (Ed.), *Leading Organizations: Perspectives for a New Era* (pp. 439–457). Thousand Oaks, CA: Sage Publications.
13. Proverbs 29:18.
14. Hart, S. (1992). An integrative framework for strategy-making processes. *Academy of Management Review, 17,* 327–351.
15. Swayne et al., note 3, p. 187.
16. Swayne et al., note 3, p. 227.
17. Swayne et al., note 3, p. 227, Exhibit 6-2.
18. Dess, G. G., & Lumpkin, G. T. (2005). Emerging issues in strategy process research. In M. A. Hitt, R. E. Freeman, & J. S. Harrison (Eds.), *The Blackwell handbook of strategic management* (p. 3). Malden, MA: Blackwell.

19. Roney, C. W. (2004). *Strategic management methodology: Generally accepted principles for practitioners.* Westport, CT: Praeger, p. 44.

20. Yukl, note 8, pp. 103–104.

21. DiMaggio, P, J., & Powell, W. W. (1991). Introduction. In W. W. Powell & P. J. DiMaggio (Eds.), *The new institutionalism in organizational analysis* (pp. 1–38). Chicago: University of Chicago Press

22. Tolbert, P. S., & Zucker, L. G. (1996). The institutionalization of institutional theory. In S. R. Clegg, C. Hardy, & W. R. Nord (Eds.), *The handbook of organization studies* (pp. 175–190). London: Sage.

23. DiMaggio, P. J., & Powell, W. W. (1983). The iron cage revisited: Institutional isomorphism and collective rationality in organizational fields. *American Sociological Review, 48,* 147–160.

24. DiMaggio & Powell, note 21.

25. Meyer, J. W., & Rowan, B. (1977). Institutionalized organizations: Formal structure as myth and ceremony. *American Journal of Sociology, 83*(2), 340–363.

26. Retrieved May 21, 2009, from http://bizcovering.com/business/strategic-analysis-of-internal-environment-of-a-business-organization/.

27. Swayne et al., note 3, p. 159, Exhibit 4-3.

28. DiMaggio & Powell, note 23.

29. Meyer & Rowan, note 25.

30. Pfeffer, J., & Salancik, G. (1978). *The external control of organizations: A resource dependence perspective.* New York: Harper and Row.

31. Coppola, M. N., Hudak, R., & Gidwani, P. (2002, September). A theoretical perspective utilizing resource dependency to predict issues with the repatriation of Medicare eligible military beneficiaries back into TRICARE. *Military Medicine, 167*(9), 726–731.

32. Wheelen, T. L., & Hunger, J. D. (2006). Internal scanning: Organizational analysis. In T. L. Wheelen and J. D. Hunger (Eds.), *Strategic management and business policy* (10th ed., pp. 104–136). Englewood Cliffs, NJ: Prentice Hall.

33. Swayne et al., note 3, p. 162.

34. Wheelen & Hunger, note 32.

35. Pfeffer & Salancik, note 30.

36. Schein, E. H. (1993). Defining organizational culture. In J. M. Shafritz, J. S. Ott, & Y. S. Jang (Eds.), *Classics of organization theory* (6th ed., pp 372–398). London: Thomson.

37. Lawrence, P. R., & Lorsch, J. W. (1967). *Organizations and environment.* Boston: Harvard Business School Press.

38. Itzkowitz, G. (1996). *Contingency theory.* Washington, DC: University Press.

39. Child, J. (1972). Organization structure, environment and performance: The role of strategic choice. *Sociology, 6,* 1–22.

40. Child, note 39.

41. Tosi, H. L., & Slocum, J. W. (1984). Contingency theory: Some suggested directions. *Journal of Management, 10*(1), 9–26.

42. Swayne et al., note 3, p. 57.

43. Rakich, J., Longest, B., & Darr, K. (1992). *Managing health services organizations.* Baltimore, MD: Health Professions Press, p. 17.

44. Rand Corporation. (n.d.). Retrieved May 11, 2009, from http://www.rand.org/cgi-bin/health/showab.cgi?key=1998_77&year=1998.

45. Coppola, M. N., Erckenbrack, D., & Ledlow, G. R. (2008). Stakeholder dynamics. In J. A. Johnson (Ed.), *Health organizations: Theory, behavior, and development* (pp. 255–278). Sudbury, MA: Jones and Bartlett.

46. Ledlow, G., Corry, A., & Cwiek, M. (2007). *Optimize Your Healthcare Supply Chain Performance: A Strategic Approach.* Chicago: Health Administration Press.

47. Weber, M. (1964/1925). *Basic concepts of sociology* (H. P. Secher, Trans). New York: Citadel Press.

48. Weber, M. (1948/1921). Bureaucracy. In H. H. Gerthand & C. W. Mills (Eds.), *From Max Weber* (pp. 196–244). London: Routledge Kegan Paul.

49. Parsons, T. (1960/1957). The distribution of power in American society. In T. Parsons (Ed.), *Structure and process in modern society* (pp. 199–225). New York: The Free Press.

50. Morcol, G. (2005). Phenomenology of complexity theory and cognitive science: Implications for developing an embodied knowledge of public administration and policy. *Administrative Theory & Praxis, 27*(1), 1–23.

51. Miller, K. (1998). Nurses at the edge of chaos: The application of "new science" concepts to organizational systems. *Management Communication Quarterly, 12*(1), 112–127.

52. Daft, R. L. (2003). Organization theory and design (8th ed.). Cincinnati, Ohio: South Western College Publishing, International Thomson Publishing.

53. Schein, note 9.

54. Schein, note 9.

55. Schein, note 9.

56. Schein, note 9.

57. Sathe, V. (1985). *Culture and related corporate realities: Text, cases, and readings on organizational entry, establishment, and change.* Homewood, IL: Irwin, p. 6.

58. Louis, M. (1985). An investigator's guide to workplace culture. In P. Frost, L. Moore, M. Louis, C. Lunberg, & J. Martin (Eds.), *Organizational culture* (p. 74). Beverly Hills, CA: Sage.

59. Martin, J. (2002). *Organizational culture: Mapping the terrain.* Thousand Oaks, CA: Sage, p. 59.

60. Beebe, S. A., & Masterson, J. T. (1997). *Communicating in small groups: Principles and practices* (5th ed.). New York: Addison-Wesley Educational Publishers., pp. 173–174.

61. Martin, note 58, pp. 55–56.

62. Schein, note 9.

63. Schein, note 9.

64. Martin, note 58, p. 86.

65. Martin, note 58, p. 87.

66. Retrieved September 14, 2007, from http://www.entarga.com/stratplan/culture.htm.

67. Retrieved September 14, 2007, from http://www.managementhelp.org/org_thry/culture/culture.htm.

68. Schein, note 9.

69. Kent, T., Johnson, J. A., & Graber, D. A. (1996). Leadership in the formation of new health care environments. *Health Care Supervisor, 15*(2), 28–29.

70. Duck, J. D. (1998). Managing change: The art of balancing. In *Harvard Business Review on change* (p. 56). Boston: Harvard Business School Press.

71. Bennis, W., Parikh, J., & Lessem, R. (1996). *Beyond leadership: Balancing economics, ethics, and ecology* (rev. ed.). Cambridge, MA: Blackwell.

72. Schein, note 9.

73. Schein, note 9.

74. Schein, note 9.

75. Morrison, I. (2000). Health care in the new millennium. San Francisco: Jossey-Bass.

10

Ethics in Health Leadership

Healthcare executives should view ethics as a special charge and responsibility to the patient, client, or others served, the organization and its personnel, themselves and the profession, and, ultimately, but less directly, to society.

American College of Healthcare Executives, 2009

In recent years, the United States has seen the near-collapse of much of its banking system. In hindsight, the chaos was largely attributable to unethical practices and procedures enacted by a few unscrupulous, greedy members of the industry. With the collapse of WorldCom and Enron—both companies that manipulated the stock market and defrauded investors—and the conviction of Bernard Madoff, the mastermind behind a record-setting Ponzi scheme, higher education is realizing the essential need to study ethics and to incorporate those ethical principles and moral practices into the development schema of the next generation of business and health leaders. In support of this view, a review of the top 50 master of business administration (MBA) and master of health administration (MHA) programs in the United States over the last five years, as profiled by *U.S. News and World Report*, suggests that many graduate programs are incorporating ethics-based courses into their curriculums. Clearly, it is critical for nascent health leaders to study health ethics so that they can develop a sound foundation upon which to base decisions, allocate resources, and develop organizational culture.

This chapter presents the ethical responsibilities of health leaders from an organizational perspective. Several ethical theories and frameworks are presented as structures to open up the discussion of ethics. The chapter also discusses professional, educational, and contractual relationships affecting the operation of the health organization.

LEARNING OBJECTIVES

1. Define distributive justice, ethics, morals, and values. Describe how they are used by leaders in decision making.

2. Explain four ethical principles that guide decision making associated with patient care.

3. Apply at least two ethical frameworks or distributive justice theories, with examples of moral practice of a leader, to an ethical issue in a health organization.

4. Analyze arguments and make a recommendation for health leaders to adopt utilitarian or deontological postures in their organization, and differentiate potential decisions leaders would make between the two frameworks to support your analysis and recommendation.

5. Compile a list of options that a leader in a health organization has to develop an integrated system of ethics and moral practice, and summarize the potential impact of each option regarding appropriate ethical adaptation across the organization.

6. Compare and contrast at least three ethical frameworks or distributive justice theories for the topics of patient autonomy, beneficence, nonmaleficence, and justice, and interpret the moral practice associated with those frameworks (at least three) for a right-to-life issue and for the practice of euthanasia.

INTRODUCTION

Defining ethics can be difficult. According to Pozgar, ethics is a moral philosophy between concepts of right and wrong behaviors. Pozgar suggests that ethics "deals with values relating to human conduct with respect to the rightness and wrongness of actions and the goodness and badness of motives and ends."[1] In the context of the health leader, ethics refers to a set of moral guidelines, principles, and suggested standards of conduct for health professionals. All health leaders, regardless of their status as patient care providers, encounter ethical dilemmas or challenges.[2]

The ethical tone and moral expectations in any organization are set by the leader. Unethical leaders set the stage for harmful activities and outcomes that will eventually affect all people and all stakeholders in the organization. It may be said that ethical leaders have a moral responsibility to treat their followers with dignity and respect, and that they must act in ways that promote the welfare of others—most immediately, the welfare of their followers. This consideration is of particular importance for health leaders who rely on actions that involve intrinsic aspects of an individual's values and behaviors to achieve motivational and goal-directed outcomes that support organizational success. Health ethicists have suggested that health organizations have an ethical and moral obligation to provide care that is not only of high quality, but also ethically driven and managed.[3]

Too often, ethics, ethical practice and discussions of ethics are placed in a legal context of liability reduction and "legalism." In fact, the ethical component of many U.S. educational degree programs, both undergraduate and graduate, is embedded in some sort of "legal" or "law" course; the practice of ethics in a profession is likewise relegated to a "Legal Counsel Office." This reality is based on the litigious environment of the health industry; lawsuits and settlements for breaches of ethical expectations and errors in health services delivery run rampant in today's world.

Health leaders model the behavior expected in the organization, including being a moral actor—a visible moral actor—in the health organization. Remember, leaders "do the right thing." Sometimes doing the right thing does not always agree with actions that limit the organization's legal liability, but that has to be the leader's decision. By the end of this chapter, you should be able to answer a key question in this arena: How will you balance "legalism" and "leadership practice" with regard to ethics and moral practice?

WHAT IS ETHICS?

Professional organizations and prospective employers frequently suggest that they are looking for ethical leaders. In response, we might ask ourselves, "What is ethics?" Within the literature, *ethics* is defined as a moral philosophy that focuses on concepts of right and wrong behaviors as linked to resource allocation. It deals with values relating to human conduct with respect to the rightness and wrongness of actions and the "goodness" and "badness" of motives. Ethics in the health field can further be defined as a set of moral principles and rules of conduct for health professionals to follow.[4, 5]

Ethics can, at times, be culturally defined. What may be considered ethically and morally appropriate by one culture may be seen as inappropriate and immoral by another culture. For example, the triage and medical treatment of persons by gender, race, and age may be unethical, if not illegal, in the United States. In the United States, providers may find it extremely *unethical* to make medical decisions based on a patient's age. In fact, Americans may find it extremely distasteful that some countries with socialized medicine and national healthcare systems ration medical care for certain ailments for patients who have passed a certain age.[6] Americans find this form of triage "unethical" or, more simply, "not the right thing to do."

At a general and broad level, however, the United States holds to a system where medical triage is based on a patient's ability to pay. In many ways, persons who have health insurance coverage have access to the entire continuum of care, whereas those without coverage are severely limited in their ability to access the appropriate services within the continuum of care. Many democratic nations find the practice of basing medical care on remuneration "unethical," and not in keeping with the practice of "goodness." This practice, they suggest, violates a sense of beneficence and distributive justice attributed to health services. Clearly, ethics may not only be cultural driven, but also nationally recognized and lawfully upheld based on the beliefs and cultural norms advocated by a national government.[7]

Despite the ineffable and difficult-to-understand nature of ethics, health leaders should study ethics so that they can better understand the human condition and better appreciate the differing points of views presented in the environment. Areas in health where ethics may assist in decision making are highly eclectic. For example, the study of ethics can assist in decision making associated with finance, risk management, resource allocation, customer advocacy, law, and organizational standing policies, to name only a few areas. A health leader in possession of a wider point of view of the dynamic field is better able to handle the complex and challenging issues presented to him or her. This chapter covers some of the areas from which both an early careerist and a seasoned professional may base ethical decision making.

The Difference Between Ethics, Values, and Morals

Ethics is the practice of "goodness and rightness" over "wrongness and badness" within a system of resource allocation and preferences. These principles are based on several factors gleaned from a myriad of experiences, which include, but are not limited to, constructs of values and morals. Societal norms and mores greatly influence ethical frameworks and moral practice; those norms and mores are embedded in the beliefs and values held by the members of that society.

Values are enduring beliefs based on some early form of indoctrination and experience. They are learned from parents, the community, school, peers, professional organizations, and personal self-development, to name only a few areas. Values inform beliefs; beliefs facilitate the development of attitudes; and attitudes contribute to behaviors. Changing attitudes is easier than changing beliefs; in turn, changing beliefs is easier than changing values. A health leader's values provide a basis from which to make decisions and establish preferences. For example, one controversial health debate centered on values focuses on a fetus's *right to life*. Health leaders who have embraced a belief from their own personal experience that life begins at conception may question the "ethics" of abortion. Such an early belief may be based on spiritual experiences or parental teachings. These enduring beliefs are difficult to change and rarely modified within an individual's lifetime. All values are based on some internalized experience or learned behavior. To unlearn and reorient values is difficult; value change is a complex issue for any individual.

Morals are applied practices derived from an ethical framework that is based on values and beliefs. These practices are based on behaviors learned through experience and internalized principles. Different from values, morals comprise the principles on which decision making is based. Morality is the level of compliance to an ethical framework. One way of conceptualizing morality is to think of it as a yardstick that measures each action, decision, or distribution of resources from the standpoint of the accepted ethical framework of a society, organization, community, group, or individual.

Principles are those immutable characteristics of value-based decision making that are broken down into mutually exclusive categories (nominal data) of outcomes or answers such as "yes/no" or "I strongly agree/agree/disagree/strongly disagree" (ordinal data). A principle may be a screening behavior upon which a decision is based. For example, one principle may be the belief, "All those who break the law need to be punished." Once this screening criterion is put into place (yes/no, I agree/disagree), the second step in the process may be acted upon. The progenitor step is to take action and to continue with the consequences of that principle based on an action; in this case, the action is to determine the degree of the punishment. In this second stage, more values-based and evaluative criteria are put into place based on the circumstances and factors associated with the actual breaking of the law. Because values are evaluative and subject to interpretation, a values-driven behavior of providing a "second chance" may result in no punishment for the law breaker or a larger consequence and penalty if forgiveness is not an option in the evaluative process.

FIGURE 10–1   The Grasshopper and the Ants
Source: *The Aesop for Children with Pictures* by Milo
Winter. Copyright © 1919, by Rand McNally & Company.

Following this discussion, we can simply say that morals are the actions and outcomes of the human condition processed over time as evaluated against the ethical framework based on values and resource allocation principles. They arise when values, principles, and preferences (and other factors) are generally internalized through lived experiences. In reality, these lived experiences may take years to compile and practice. Because morals are so difficult to embrace without lived experiences, they are generally taught through storytelling and lessons. Consequently, we learn about the lived experiences of populations in communities, groups in the organizations, and individual experiences in one's own life through the sharing of moral tales. One such example is the moral tale of the *Grasshopper and the Ants* from Aesop's fables.

In Aesop's fable, the ants diligently work through the warm summer days preparing for winter by constructing a summer nest and stockpiling food. During the period of time when the ants are working hard, the grasshopper plays the days away singing (**Figure 10–1**). When winter finally comes, and no food or shelter can be foraged above ground, the grasshopper finds itself starving and cold, while the ants are warm and well fed below ground. It is then that the grasshopper states the lesson of the story: "It is best to prepare for the days of necessity."[8] As an analogy, a health leader might simply suggest that eating right and taking care of your body and mind today ensures a higher quality of life tomorrow.

The "moral" of this story is that it is always best to prepare for one's future in the face of the uncertainty of the environment. However, because this "lived experience" may take an individual's entire lifetime to learn, the experience is shared through the lived experience of others through moral tales. Similar to the propositional statements described in Chapter 3, morals can be statements of opinion presented as if they were true. As a result, they become the "moral compass" by which some leaders conduct their lives in both the personal and professional spheres.

Setting an Ethical Standard in the Health Organization

Health leaders face ethical dilemmas in their daily work of delivering health services and products within the health organization. This stands in contrast to the experiences of their "strictly business"-oriented peers in a nonhealth, for-profit environment. In respect to patient care options, the ethical considerations of the health leader may often be tied to those of the physician, but not always. The physician's ethical duty derives from the Hippocratic Oath and (for many) Section 5 of the Code of Ethics of the American Medical Association, which states that in an emergency physicians should do their best to render service to the patient, despite prejudice of any kind. By comparison, the health leader of an organization may have less of an ethical and legal duty to provide care that exceeds the standing policies and procedures established by the governing board. Health leaders may often find themselves torn between owing allegiance to the financial stability of the organization and the charitable nature of the health profession. As a result, the health organization's policies, screening criteria, and guidelines for services (such as preadmission procedures in a hospital) may often come into conflict with the health of the patient and the patient's compensatory reimbursement potential.

Many hospitals attempt to overcome this dilemma by achieving a balance between the business aspect of operating a health facility and the social aspect of caring for the indigent through the establishment of ethics committees within their managed care organization.[9–11]

Another critical element is the incorporation of stakeholders' ethical expectations for the health organization. Stakeholder expectations are expressed and integrated into the organization in the following ways: through the board of directors or board of trustees membership, which represents the communities served; advocacy on behalf of stakeholder expectations carried out by senior leadership of the health entity; and within internal committee structures of the organization, such as with the ethics committee. Establishing an ethics committee, in particular, is a necessary element in health organization operations and strategy.

The ethics committee has three main purposes: education, consultation, and policy review. Challenges faced by the members of this committee include conflicting internal organizational principles, values contradiction, leadership team decision making, and community and industry ethical attitudinal changes. Other challenges include targeted education, proactive initiatives, and accreditation. Finally, it should be noted that the ethics committee seeks to assess implications for stakeholders during its review of policies. Stakeholders may include the institution and its culture, patients, individuals who receive training in the institution, volunteers, and other health providers in the region.[12, 13]

To aid in the establishment of an ethical organization, the health organization should have an individual appointed on staff as the resident ethicist to assist in decision and policy making. The establishment of an ethics committee that meets on a regular and reoccurring basis can likewise keep the leadership informed of relevant and legitimate ethical issues confronting the health organization.

The health leader may partner with outside stakeholders and agencies to ensure it is meeting certain ethical norms and standards within the environmental setting.[14] Moreover, the organization can seek guidance from ethical policy statements and positions published by such organizations as the American College of Healthcare Executives (ACHE), the American Hospital Association (AHA), the Medical Group Management Association (MGMA), the Association of University Programs in Health Administration (AUPHA), The Joint Commission, and other colloquial and state organizations. Health leaders who are leading a well-rounded organization made up of participatory stakeholders and consumers will ensure that the organization's posture on policies and principles regarding ethics is maintained consistently.[15]

A health leader must remember that it will never be enough to have an organization that *claims* that it is an ethical entity; rather, it must *behave, advocate, and have systems that foster moral action,* such as having recognized committees or boards that separately address clinical and/or research ethics. One such committee is the institutional review board (IRB), the entity that reviews and approves research within a health organization; its role is especially important in the review and strict adherence to human subject laws, policies, and procedures. These ethically associated committees or bodies must have the power and the ability to act and foster change.[16] Unfortunately, according to national polls, 50 percent of health ethics committee chairs feel inadequately prepared to address issues in the health environment.[17] To overcome this problem, a wise health leadership team will invest in professional education and training of the organization's chief ethicist, as well as the members of the committees that make up any advisory panels within the faculty. This investment may offer dividends in future complex leadership dilemmas.

Example: When Actions and Ethics Collide

During the financial collapse of many U.S.-based organizations in the fall of 2008, Congress reacted by providing more than $700 billion to organizations that had run themselves into the ground through bad business practices and risky financial behaviors. It was later learned that the CEOs of many of these financially insoluble organizations would receive annual bonus checks of as much as $620,000.[18] The public was outraged that the leaders of these mammoth financial institutions could be rewarded for incompetency that ruined the financial health of their own organizations and sent hundreds of employees to the unemployment line.

Many industry leaders replied by stating the bonuses that were received were contractually legal. Taxpayers countered by suggesting that although the bonuses may have been legally provided, it was unethical to receive such bonuses when so many people were out of work, and when so many outside stakeholders, including taxpayers, had assumed financial responsibility for the corporate mess.

In an effort to establish a new leadership and ethical tone during the financial collapse of 2008–2009, and in response to taxpayer outrage, one financial organization, American International Group (AIG), made an attempt to change the message. AIG's CEO, Edward M. Liddy, stated that, "I have asked the employees of AIG Financial Products to step up and do the right thing. Specifically, I have asked those who received retention payments of $100,000 or more to return at least half of those payments."[19] In response to his request, 15 of AIG's 20 executives receiving the highest bonuses later agreed to return the money. This good-faith, ethical gesture helped AIG to reclaim some of the public's trust in the banking industry.

Common Ethical Dilemmas in Health Organizations

Ethical dilemmas in health organizations generally arise out of professional or values-based conflicts of interest. According to the American College of Healthcare Executives, a conflict of interest occurs when a person has conflicting duties or responsibilities and meeting one of them makes it impossible to meet the other. The classic example occurs when a decision maker for one organization is also a decision maker or influencer for another organization with which business is transacted. Often, the potential conflict of interest becomes an actual conflict of interest because the decision maker cannot meet the duty of fidelity (loyalty) to both organizations when a decision which impacts both is needed.[20]

Relationship Morality

Ethical dilemmas in the health organization are inevitable. In the field of health leadership, such dilemmas occur at three levels: micro, macro, and meso.

The micro level involves individual issues, such as relationships between individuals and leaders. An example of a micro-level ethical dilemma in the health setting is the reduced decision-making power accorded to some health professionals, such as a physician being forced to order "a cheaper test with less diagnostic power." The micro level of management usually is dyadic, occurring on a person-to-person basis. It is exemplified by health professionals who work directly with patients and face a number of ethical dilemmas in a provider-agent role.

Health leaders should remember to "praise in public and correct in private." All positive actions, behaviors, or performance and, especially, all negative actions, behaviors, or performance (extra emphasis on ethical breaches) should be documented regarding subordinates, staff, and peers. If you observe an ethical breach by a superior leader, privately discuss the issue with the individual and ask the person to correct the situation and report the issue to his or her superior leader. If the individual refuses or does not comply, it is your duty to discuss the ethical breach with that person's superior leader. This is tremendously difficult to do—but it is the right thing to do. Always confront the leader who has committed an ethical breach immediately and, at first, privately; always document the scenario in a confidential memorandum that you keep in a secured location unless you need to provide evidence to senior leadership at a later time. You cannot let ethical breaches go without confronting the person who committed the ethical error; you cannot let the ethical breach go uncorrected and unreported. If you do, you are modeling a negative behavior—namely, corruption and ethical cover-up. Although the choice is sometimes difficult, it is up to you to decide to be moral (or not). This decision-making process includes not only your actions and behaviors, but also, as a leader, the actions and behaviors you observe in others.

The macro level of ethical dilemmas involves societal or community issues that reflect governmental actions or social policies. These dilemmas are typically culturally based. For example, closing down a hospital's emergency department when it may be the only source of entry into the health system for the uninsured may be a prudent business decision, but the lack of consideration shown for the impoverished by this decision may violate the value of the health organization's responsibility to provide care.

The meso level involves organizational or professional issues. A restrictive agreement between health organizations and managed care organizations, such as the use and contractual arrangement for durable medical equipment, is an example of a meso-level ethical dilemma.[21]

Business and Financial Ethics

Business and financial ethics has been acutely observed since the Enron and other scandals began to erupt in the past decade. The Sarbanes-Oxley Act, which requires the senior leader to validate and confirm financial statements and performance, is a governmental reaction to the public outrage over unethical business and financial behavior by organizations. Health leaders need to deal fairly and honestly in business and financial matters. In the health business, telling the truth is paramount. Of course, telling every financial or business secret and breaking confidentiality are neither reasonable nor moral. If you cannot tell the truth, it is better to say nothing. The golden rule applies to business and financial operations of the health enterprise: "Do unto others as you would have them do unto you." Avoid and acknowledge conflicts of interest; remove yourself from situations where conflicts of interest might compromise your ability to make decisions fairly. Follow the law, regulatory requirements, accreditation recommendations, and good business practices. Never leverage "good" for "bad" intentions.

Build systems that are efficient, effective, and efficacious while treating people with respect, dignity, and honesty. Apply those same principles to the moral application of day-to-day business activities. This is never more important than when you are in discussions with bond raters; those organizations decide your organization's bond rating (e.g., AAA, B, C), which has a direct correspondence with the interest rates charged on your organization's loans. Tell the truth, and act according to that truth. A good bond rating, for example, does not get better if trust is broken; a poor bond rating does not get better with broken trust. These ratings do improve, however, if trust is the basis of discussions and interactions.

In addition, health organizations must have regular external audits, conducted by a firm with a solid reputation, of their financial records, flow of funds, and policy compliance. Especially important is the audit of financial information and systems of claims and reimbursement to taxpayer-funded programs such as Medicare and Medicaid. If errors or systemic problems are found, either by the external audit firm or by internal staff, immediate communication with the appropriate fiscal intermediaries and government agencies must occur. As an ethical health organization, application of this process is also appropriate with any commercial payer or for any contract with an outside entity.

Contracts and Negotiations

Ethical standards regarding negotiations and contracts are of particular interest and importance. Whenever a health organization is engaged in a negotiation or contract process, the organization is most likely working with some external entity. A successful negotiation usually concludes with a contract; this contract may be written or verbal and should specify terms, conditions of performance, payment, liability conditions, and outcomes if either party breaches the contract (i.e., does not perform its agreed-upon actions to the level of quality stated). Representing the health organization honestly by stating the needs and conditions of a particular negotiation or contract event, the elements of performance, the payment, and the commitment to comply with the ultimate terms are paramount in this type of negotiation.

A successfully completed negotiation and signed or verbally agreed-to contract must be complied with; when compliance may be at risk, communication with the other party or parties must occur in a timely fashion. Negotiations and contracts should include involvement of the health organization's legal counsel to ensure compliance with all applicable laws and regulations, and to ensure a reasonable amount of liability protection. All negotiations and contract processes should consist of well-thought-out elements that adhere to the values and ethical expectations of the organization.

Health leaders must not engage in negotiations or contracts that are inherently illegal—for example, making inappropriate payments. This is the professional ethical expectation for all negotiations and contracts.

Right-to-Life Issues

It is not possible for a health leader, especially a CEO, of a large and munificent health organization to avoid policy discussions on right-to-life issues. The term "right to life" has transcended boundaries in the recent era and is no longer associated with only abortion-related issues. Health leaders will find themselves faced with a variety of right-to-life issues that include abortion, the death penalty, and euthanasia.

Despite the increased number of situations associated with the generalization of right-to-life issues, health leaders in government, secular, nonsecular, for-profit, and nonprofit health organizations alike will be faced with decisions brought to their attention regarding abortion issues from the medical staff, stakeholders, and patients. In response, they may have to issue a policy statement on abortion procedures in the facility or provide institutional guidance on the practice. In doing so, health leaders must balance their personal views and organizational goals simultaneously and perhaps select one value and principle over the other if the personal and professional dilemmas related to abortion procedures cannot be reconciled.

For health leaders who have very specific and partisan views regarding abortion, the selection of a health organization as an employer may need to be carefully evaluated. For example, if you believe that abortion is wrong and immoral, seeking a position in a health organization that refuses to abort a fetus should be your focus. Many religious-based health organizations, such as Catholic-, Lutheran-, Baptist-, and Methodist-based or value-founding organizations, will not perform procedures that go against their values regarding right to life.

The famous *Roe v. Wade* debate is an example worth noting regarding the contradiction of values within a society. These contradictions in values, especially as health is concerned, in a society are at the heart of ethical challenges faced by health leaders. As health leaders progress up the ladder of responsibility and accountability, the ethical issues encountered become both more frequent and more challenging.

Roe v. Wade.   The following excerpt was adapted from Harris's *Contemporary Issues in Healthcare Law and Ethics:*[22]

> In 1973, the U.S. Supreme Court delivered a decision in the case of *Roe v. Wade* based on a woman fictitiously named Jane Roe who sought an abortion in the state of Texas but did not "fit within the sole exception" as a medical necessity to save the life of the mother. The ruling gave women the right to abort a fetus for any reason up until the fetus became viable. The term *viable* was defined as a fetus brought to 28 weeks gestational age, or a fetus that could live on its own outside the womb with reasonable medical aid. Women were still given the option to pursue an abortion after 29 weeks if there was/is substantial cause to protect the life of the mother.
>
> The Court further ruled that the Texas abortion statute violated the constitutional right of personal privacy and it "emphasized the physician's right to practice medicine without interference by the state." The ruling additionally gave states opportunities for placing more regulations and statutes to protect maternal health and potential life.
>
> In 1992, the U.S. Supreme Court ruled on the case of *Planned Parenthood of Southeastern Pennsylvania v. Casey,* in which the court upheld the ruling of *Roe v. Wade* [stating that] a woman had the right to terminate a pregnancy prior to the point of viability, but the court rejected the trimester framework as previously ruled in *Roe v. Wade.* However, the court left open the interpretation of "point of viability" to future medical developments.
>
> In 2000, the Supreme Court ruled that a statute banning partial-birth abortions in Nebraska was unconstitutional as it contained an exception to "preserve the life of the mother," but not an exception to "preserve the health of the mother." In 2002, President George W. Bush signed into law the *Born-Alive Infants Protection Act,* which treats every infant who is born alive, including those as a result of abortion, as a "person." The debate continues.

Euthanasia.   Euthanasia can be defined as the active termination of an otherwise viable human life in a painless manner. It can also be defined as a passive methodology in which life-sustaining treatment is withheld or withdrawn. Euthanasia issues are generally grouped with right-to-life issue in health facilities, and provide similar dilemmas for leaders to ponder.

Euthanasia is becoming an acceptable alternative to heroic medical care as some patients are securing *advanced directives* that state life support should not be provided to them under certain medical conditions. Research also suggests that hospice and palliative care may actually increase incidence of euthanasia requests, as individuals who seek out these services are more accepting of their condition and may be more likely to "plan" for their deaths. Additionally, the concept of the "slippery slope" may be justified in the argument against legislation of voluntary euthanasia for elderly individuals who are pressured to "opt for death when they perceive themselves to be a burden for loved ones."[23]

UNDERSTANDING THE PATIENT'S SPIRITUALITY BASE IN DECISION MAKING

Within the health and general leadership environment, the topic of spirituality in leadership is often considered taboo and may even be a career-ending conversation for executives and practitioners. This stance is beginning to soften in society; spirituality in leadership is beginning to be discussed more openly in more organizations. At the same time, it is well known that spiritual principles are the basis for many values and enduring beliefs that guide the moral and ethical development of health leadership practices in our society.[24, 25] Therefore, spirituality as a construct of discussion and examination in health leadership practice should not be overlooked in future research examining leadership theory.

For example, a survey of religion by Baylor University in 2008 found that more than 85 percent of the U.S. population considers themselves to be "religious." A similar study of Canadians found that 72 percent claimed to have spiritual needs, while 70 percent believed in miraculous healing. These factors have tremendous implications for health professionals in terms of meeting the physical, emotional, and personal needs of their patients and their patients' families. As Pesut has suggested, "professionals are now expected to play a role that was once borne by the institutional church, which may include helping individuals to reconcile spiritual beliefs with their health care decisions."[26]

Within the study of leadership theory, it has been suggested that the distinct absence of the study of spirituality in ethics and leadership results in a gap in the process that seeks to understand the decisions ultimately reached by patients in regard to end-of-life decisions. End-of-life decisions such as pregnancy termination and euthanasia are, of course, only two of the key issues faced by health executives today; notably, these issues inherently touch on strong spiritual roots and affect decision making. As a result, the concept of spirituality in leadership should not be overlooked when discussing ethical decisions in the modern health environment.[27–29]

To adjust to the spiritual needs of patients entering the health system, leaders should strive to be aware of the diverse beliefs within their organizations and foster a high degree of sensitivity and respect for those beliefs. Specific beliefs and practices to consider include, but are not be limited to, the following:

- Healing rituals
- Dying, death, and care of dead bodies
- Harvesting and transplanting organs
- End-of-life and right-to-life decisions
- Use of reproductive technologies

In an article published in 2009 titled "Incorporating Patients' Spirituality into Care Using Gadow's Ethical Framework,"[30] Pesut suggests that there is a growing need to address spirituality in client care. In addition, Pesut notes that several health professional organizations are now addressing spirituality as an ethical obligation to care. She further states that in many situations, spiritual values and beliefs provide a source of encouragement as patients endure experiences of suffering.

One challenge of addressing spirituality in health is the use of "language and narratives" that may be foreign to health professionals outside of a specific faith. Language and terminology that are consistent and easily understood by one faith-based group of individuals may be misunderstood or misconstrued by an individual unfamiliar with that faith-based group's tradition. As an elementary example, if we describe our friend "John" as a "big man," are we operationalizing "big" as someone who is tall, fat, muscular, or popular? In summary, while understanding faith-based beliefs is important for health professionals so that they will be sensitive to and respectful of those beliefs, the leader should be careful when asked to provide faith-based advice.

ETHICAL CODES ADOPTED BY THE HEALTH INDUSTRY

This section discusses some of the philosophical viewpoints associated with ethical decision making. Understanding these values-driven apertures may assist you in your own decision-making process in future ethical events where your individual judgment will have to be exercised. It is always prudent to remember that not all individuals exercise ethical decision making in the same way or consistently over time. Health leaders are reminded to refer back to the personality tests done earlier in this text, which emphasized that not everyone thinks alike. In understanding *both* his or her own personality dynamic and the various apertures from which health professionals make decisions, the health leader will have an advantage in elucidating the dynamics of the patients and human resources in the organization.

The philosophies or ethical frameworks discussed here are distributive justice, utilitarianism, egalitarianism, libertarianism, deontology, and pluralism.

Distributive Justice

At the foundation of ethics is distributive justice. This set of theories or ideologies attempts to instill a set of values, ideals of fairness based on those values, and beliefs in the allocation of resources (e.g., food, water, housing, wealth/money, opportunities, materials) throughout a society. At its roots, ethics is a framework that is based on a distributive justice theory or combination of those theories; ethics is an extension of resource allocation and the methods of that allocation, while morality or morals are the level of congruence to that ethical framework. "Principles of distributive justice are normative principles designed to guide the allocation of the benefits and burdens of economic activity."[31]

Taken individually, distributive justice theories are neither right nor wrong in and of themselves. Instead, situations, contingencies, and values must be considered in the selection (creating an ethical framework) and application (level of morality) of the distribution of resources. Would the distribution of resources be the same in a mass-casualty situation in an emergency room, such as an influx of patients from a bus accident, as when conducting cholesterol checks at a health fair in the community? Of course not. The tough part of selecting an ethical framework based on values and beliefs and the application of that framework (morality) comes down to one simple truth: Resources are scarce in society, in health organizations, in departments, in units, in families, and for individuals.

Resource scarcity—the reality responsible for creation of disciplines such as economics, political science, and distributive justice/ethics—is the catalyst that requires a method for resource distribution. If all resources were abundant, how many conflicts, political maneuvers, or crimes would society have to deal with or resolve? Selection of a distributive justice theory is based on values and beliefs of a society, organization, group, or individual; developing an ethical framework from that theory; and applying that framework are responsible for some of the cultural conflicts, group tensions, and individual conflicts in the world, society, organization, or group. If two groups are strongly attached to their different ethical frameworks, resource distribution that fosters "fairness" for both groups can be difficult; that is one reason why negotiation is a valued skill. Lastly, avarice or greed may play into the scenario; scarcity can motivate greed and motivate competition. (In ancient Greece, avarice or greed was considered one of the seven deadly sins.)

In health, social justice and market justice discussions are integrated as part of the selection of resource distribution mechanisms. Social justice advocates that:

> [I]n a just society, minimal levels of basic needs like income, housing, education, and health should be provided to all citizens as fundamental rights. These basic needs are usually provided through various forms of social insurance; while market justice supports that the inexorable logic of supply and demand operating within the economic marketplace are key to determining the optimal outcomes of health care resources (with minimal or no intervention by government).[32]

These issues muddy the waters surrounding distribution of resources, especially in the health industry. Some of the well-known distributive justice theories are presented here in summary. What theories work best in health organizations? Does one theory fit all health situations?

Utilitarianism

Utilitarianism is a theory that takes as its primary aim the attainment of maximum possible happiness of a society as a whole. This goal is to be achieved in such a way that one first checks what makes every particular individual in a society happy, then sums up all these various wants and preferences, and finally finds out how to satisfy the greatest number of them. A policy which makes happy the greatest number of persons, or the one which frustrates satisfaction of desires of the least number of them, is the only one which is right to choose. Utilitarianism shows interest in distribution of goods only if this has some impact on maximization of overall happiness.[33]

Utilitarianism seeks to maximize utility (usefulness) from the distribution of resources in a society. This theory would balance social and market justice.

Egalitarianism

Egalitarianism is a set of closely related theories that without exemption advocate the thesis that all members of a society should have exactly equal amount of resources. Simpler theories of this kind are satisfied with the claim that everyone should be given, at all costs, completely equal quantity of certain crucial material goods, like money. More careful and sophisticated egalitarian thinkers are aware that such a distribution would have too many shortcomings: those with greater needs for which they are not themselves responsible (like the handicapped people), would get less satisfaction than others because they would have to spend a great share of their resources just to catch up to others (if ever) in normal functioning; lazy and idle people would be rewarded and the talented and industrious would be discouraged.[34]

John Rawls, in *A Theory of Justice* (1971),[35] posited a supplementary position to egalitarianism known as the "difference principle." In essence, egalitarianism negatively affects those who are less fortunate, such as the disabled and mentally challenged; based on this reality, more resources should be allocated to those who are less capable of performing productive work. This theory is more aligned with social justice.

Libertarianism

Libertarianism suggests that the market or market forces should determine the distribution of resources in a society. The Nobel Prize–winning economist Milton Friedman, who died in 2006 at the age of 94, is the best-known advocate on behalf of modern market forces as the key factors in an economy; he joined a long line of economists associated with this model, including the major historical figures Adam Smith and John Keynes. According to this perspective, market justice is the force that controls distribution. No pattern or criteria are important in the distribution of resources in a market-based approach; instead, those persons who work diligently and intelligently should receive the fruits of their labor. Market justice is strongly associated with libertarianism.

Deontology

Deontology is the opposite of utilitarianism. It is an ethical framework and philosophy of resource allocation that suggests actions should be judged right or wrong based on their own values and principle-driven characteristics. Within this theory, there is no planning for the consequences of an action. As a result, the preponderance of the masses is not a major consideration, and the needs of the one can outweigh the needs of the many. In many ways, deontology is a case-by-case or individual-based framework for resource allocation considering the factors associated with that individual. Social and market justice are both considered valid considerations in this framework.

Pluralism

Pluralists hold that goods which are normally distributed in any society are too different to be distributed according to only one criterion. To almost every one of these various kinds of goods we should apply a criterion that is characteristic for it. Thus we have diverse spheres of justice in which there are different criteria that tell us which distributions are morally right. If the result is to be just, a criterion which holds in one sphere should not be applied in another one. For instance, rewards and punishments should be distributed according to performance, jobs according to ability, political positions according to wishes of citizens as expressed at the elections, medical care according to needs, income according to success on the market, and the like.[36]

Both social and market justice are applicable in a pluralistic view.

Societal Application of Distributive Justice Theories

How does a society justly distribute resources? Resources include goods, materials, technologies, and funding/money—but also time and effort. As a health leader, the cost, quality, and access paradigm should be considered along with distributive justice considerations. Because health organizations are a scarce resource in a community, how resources are allocated and to whom are particularly salient issues and can be thorny points for health leaders. Does everyone get all the health services they need? How do you know? Does everyone get all of the services they want? How do you know? Has your organization done needs assessments and other analyses to determine these needs and wants?

An example of the application of distributive justice theories can be found straight out the window of the health organization's facility. Look at the parking lot. Parking in many places is a scarce resource. How are parking spaces allocated by your health organization, by your university or college, your clinic, your agency, or your association? In most health organizations, spots close to entries of the facility are reserved for disabled patrons, customers, patients and family members, and expecting or recent mothers (deontology); these are prime parking spaces that remain empty on many occasions. Other spaces may be reserved for surgeons, physicians, nurses, pharmacists, administrators, emergency room staff, and possibly others (utilitarianism) so that those professionals can get to work and start performing their various missions in the facility so as to do the greatest good, using scarce skills, for the greatest number of patients. Other spaces may be reserved by payment of a lease for the parking space (or valet parking) for those persons who do not want to hunt for a parking space (libertarianism); spaces more advantageous or closer to the facility usually cost more in terms of the monthly lease payment. The rest of the spaces are open on a "first come, first served" basis, so that everyone has an equal chance at the space (egalitarianism). In the totality of the parking lot situation, pluralism is used to allocate this scarce resource. Thus distributive justice theories are the foundation of the ethical framework used to allocate parking spaces in a manner in which society can justify within the norms and mores of that society.

Selected Application of Philosophies

Distributive justice theories can serve as ethical frameworks that may assist a health leader in framing his or her decision-making policies, systems, and processes. Two of these theories are presented in this section as contrasting frameworks for discussion: utilitarianism and deontology. Not all health organizations use only utilitarianism or deontological frameworks; for example, a health department's immunization program most likely uses an egalitarian framework. Issues surrounding patient rights of autonomy, beneficence, nonmalificence, and justice are addressed here as well. The selected ethical codes or frameworks should be integrated with the cost, quality, and access paradigm after considering any changes to the health system or resource allocation of health resources. While these topics could take several chapters of discussion, we address them here for consistency and familiarization within the leadership framework.

Health Leader Framework: Utilitarianism

Utilitarianism is the view that an action is deemed morally acceptable because it produces the greatest balance of good over evil, taking into account all individuals affected. This theory posits that the needs of the many outweigh the needs of the few. It also suggests that the end results and outcomes outweigh the process and the procedure used to reach those results and outcomes. The ultimate goal with utilitarianism is "mass happiness," or the bringing of the greatest good to the preponderance of the people. Due to the end-results focus of this methodology for decision making, the outcomes are often viewed as justifiable measures despite the consequences of the process. Under this perspective, the outcomes dictate the rules, and decisions are based on the predetermined desires of leaders.[37, 38]

Medicare and Medicaid may be thought of as a utilitarian decision when the benefits were first introduced in 1963. The decision to redistribute the income of working persons in the United States by taking a certain percentage of every employee's wages so that other certain individuals who were older than the age of 65 or who were indigent could receive subsidized care was initially (by many) seen as a socialist movement in America. The policy itself, almost by definition, provides for the greater good at the expense of others.[39] These programs are different, however. Medicare is an entitlement program; most people have to pay into the program over time to become eligible for the program. In contrast, Medicaid is a welfare program, for which eligibility is based on various criteria and for which a citizen does not have to pay into to become eligible. From a macro view, however, both programs could be seen as utilitarian in nature.

As the CEO of a health organization, you may someday be involved in a "bond initiative" where you lobby the county or local jurisdiction to increase local taxes in support of a new health venture in your local community. Your argument for this bond initiative may be based on a utilitarian effort.[40]

Health Leader Framework: Deontology

Deontology is the opposite of utilitarianism. This ethical framework and philosophy suggests actions should be judged right or wrong based on their own values and principle-driven characteristics. Within this theory, there is no planning for the consequences of an action. As a result, the preponderance of the masses is not a major consideration in this theory, and the needs of the one can outweigh the needs of the many.

This system of thought also focuses on personal responsibility and "what one ought to do." According to this principle, the moral decision will be reached when one follows the "rules" or "duty" without deviation.[41] Immanuel Kant introduced a deontological theory that assesses conditions from the vantage of inputs rather than outcomes. Kant's categorical imperative judges morality by examining the nature of actions and the will of agents rather than the goals achieved. Although Kant's theories are useful in making the moral judgments involved in the decision-making process, deontology holds that consequences are less important than intent.[42]

Providers of care are often the greatest users of deontology principles. In perfect and unconstrained conditions, providers of care would love to practice a more exact science of medicine in which expensive laboratory tests and consults could confirm or disconfirm the judgment and instincts of a more imperfect physical exam. This may have been the practice of medicine in the era before managed care, when preapproved specialty consults were unnecessary for access and fee-for-service, indemnity, and open systems were the norm. Modern patient care providers are bound by capitation, gatekeeper access restrictions, and per-member, per-month withholds on premiums. As a result, modern physicians are less likely to practice a form of deontology than their predecessors from the pre-managed care era.

Autonomy, Beneficence, Nonmaleficence, and Justice

Similar to the ethical principles of utilitarianism and deontology that guide, forecast, and help frame the discussions and actions of senior leaders in a health organization regarding policy implementation and organizational resource allocation, the patient frameworks of autonomy, beneficence, nonmalifience, and justice help guide a health leader's agenda in respect to patient care decisions. Ethical issues surrounding patient care generally revolve around four commonly accepted and established healthcare practices:

- *Autonomy*: The patient's right to self-governance and medical decision making.
- *Beneficence*: The requirement of the health organization to do "good."
- *Nonmaleficence*: The requirement for the health organization to do no harm.
- *Justice*: The obligation to give each patient fair resource allocation (services and products associated with the care process).

In health organizations, the tenets of patient autonomy and justice often come in conflict with the obligations of beneficence and nonmaleficence. This potential for conflict explains why the provider of care—in most cases, the physician—is the agent for the patient who structures and delivers the correct regimen of diagnostic procedures and treatments. This point is especially salient if the patient is deliberately seeking uncompensated care or some other secondary benefit.

THE DIFFERENCE BETWEEN MEDICAL ETHICS, CLINICAL ETHICS, AND BIOETHICS

Clinical ethics refers to the ethics of the clinical practice of medicine and to ethical problems that arise in the care of patients. It includes traditional professional medical ethics, which places the patient at the center of consideration. Traditional medical ethics have proved deficient in the face of technological advances of recent years; this reality has given rise to bioethics. Bioethics' first concern was with "the intersection of ethics and the life sciences," which was later expanded to include human values.[43] Thus today's health organizations have to balance and develop systems to adhere to medical and clinical ethical standards as well as emerging bioethical standards.

Goals of Organizational Ethics

Today, health costs are on the rise, patients are demanding more from their health professionals, and government and third-party payers have tightened controls on reimbursement for services, hospital length of stay, and allocation of resources. In this environment, it is becoming increasingly more difficult for the health professional to practice morally while meeting all other health, professional standard of care, and organizational demands. Tension between demands for health services and demands for profits/margins are imposing enormous pressures on health professionals to achieve cost reductions, increased revenues, and enhanced quality of care.[44]

Some individuals can manage to "do the right thing" in practically any situation and consistently place the needs of others above their own. Unfortunately, the individuals who achieve this feat seemingly so naturally can be difficult to locate and identify. In health organizations in general, but particularly in nursing, there is a need for the ability to learn to use increasingly complex technologies, develop a solid background in biological sciences, and yet operate with compassion and caring every day for every patient (many times with high patient loads). Few individuals innately have the ability to learn nursing's technical complexities and already have full command of ethical values to the point that they can act from a targeted decision-making perspective rather than from instinct.

Individuals' ethical values generally are built over a lifetime. Study of the old philosophers can give a voice and a rationale to active decision making that the individual can then describe and defend. For immediate guidance, values statements and codes of ethics can be used to guide decision making.[45]

Health Leaders Are Part Ethicist

Attention to various branches of philosophical and professional ethics assists in building and maintaining an ethical climate within the organization. Because they are knowledgeable about ethical frameworks, experienced leaders can act more mindfully of the consequences of their actions and decisions, and they are able to explain their positions to patients and external stakeholders more easily. Health leaders must incorporate an ethical framework and expectation of moral actions and behaviors from all organizational stakeholders; this is most true for internal stakeholders and acutely important for direct subordinates. Leaders should ponder and answer the questions listed under the "A Health Leader's Challenge: Where to Start?" section later in this chapter, but should also ensure that ethic frameworks, moral practice, and regulatory compliance are inherently embedded in the health organization. To make sure that these concerns are addressed effectively, the organization can take the following steps:

- Establish and charter ethics committees with authority
- Require staff attendance, participation, and evaluation of educational programs
- Create a system of policy development and review
- Seek consultation by utilizing consultants with similar values and moral practices
- Integrate professional, clinical, and business ethical performance through leader role modeling and subordinate reinforcement (rewards and punishments)

- Foster a positive ethical climate within an open and supportive communication environment (e.g., it is acceptable to tell leadership about a mistake or error)
- Review relationships with external stakeholders, partners, and entities with which the health organization has contract relationships to evaluate ethical framework and moral practice congruence with the health organization

A HEALTH LEADER'S CHALLENGE: WHERE TO START?

All of the dilemmas mentioned in this chapter have an ability to influence an organization's financial stability, community legitimacy, and stakeholder dynamics. Leaders in health organizations should be prepared for relationship conflicts at several levels within the health organization and strategically plan for negative consequences before they occur.[46] The following list of questions is intended to provide a model for health leaders with regard to creating a system of ethics and morality in their organizations.

1. Which values does the organization hold?
2. On which distributive justice theoretical framework should ethical decisions be based?
   - Does that framework apply to all situations? If not, when does the framework not apply and which framework takes its place?
   - How do values of the health organization get put into practice?
3. How does the health organization establish an ethical framework and moral application of principles (e.g., through planning, group discussions, professional associations, laws and regulations, community expectations, community needs)?
4. Does the health organization have an ethical statement or creed that is highly visible and accessible by all stakeholders?
5. To embed the ethical foundation and moral actions, which systems need to be in place, such as committees, policies, procedures, enforcement of those policies and procedures (e.g., should coupling be tight or loose regarding ethical frameworks and moral behavior and actions?), and leadership role modeling considering customers' and patients' expectations, business conduct and operations, negotiations, contract agreements and compliance, legal/regulation compliance, error remediation (e.g., how are errors resolved?), and health service and product delivery?
6. How can leadership decisions remain consistent with the ethical framework over time? How do you know when you are consistent?
7. How can the organizational culture incorporate the ethical framework and moral application of principles that the health organization holds important?
8. How does the health organization integrate its ethical framework and moral applications into its strategic planning, decision making, and daily operations?
9. How does the health organization communicate its ethical framework and moral application to the communities it serves and to its external stakeholders?
10. How does the health organization ensure internal staff and subordinate adaptation to the ethical framework and moral application of that framework both to long-term (e.g., training, annual updates, rewards and punishments) employees and to new employees (e.g., orientation, training)?
11. Who keeps the health leadership team accountable to the ethical framework and moral application of established principles?
12. Is the ethical framework and moral application of those principles reasonable, relevant, and realistic? How are boundaries established?
13. Who (e.g., individuals, groups, legal counsel) has the authority to initiate an ethical incident report, an ethical discussion, an ethical incident investigation, or an ethically attributed reward or punishment? Is the health organization legally or liability oriented to ethical considerations, leadership oriented, or both? (What may be legally "moral" so as to limit liability may not be leadership "moral" in terms of doing what is right.)

SUMMARY

This chapter presented the ethical responsibilities of health leaders from an organizational perspective. Distributive justice theories, which describe the ideology of resource distribution in a society, were presented as a framework to open up a discussion of ethics. Organizational ethics consists of a process to address ethical issues associated with the business, financial, and management areas of health organizations. Professional, educational, and contractual relationships all have ethical components that can affect the operation of the health organization.

DISCUSSION QUESTIONS

1. How do you (personally) balance legalism and leadership practice with regard to ethics?

2. Define distributive justice, ethics, morals, values, and conflict of interest. How are they used by health leaders in decision making?

3. Explain four ethical principles that guide decision making associated with patient care. How can leaders use these principles in decision making within a health organization?

4. How could you apply at least two ethical frameworks or distributive justice theories, with examples of moral practice of a leader, to an ethical issue in a health organization? What would be the results?

5. Should health leaders adopt utilitarian and/or deontological postures in their organization? How would you differentiate the potential decisions that leaders would make under these two frameworks?

6. Which options does a leader in a health organization have for developing an integrated system of ethics and moral practice? What would be the potential impact of each option regarding appropriate ethical adaptation across the organization?

7. How would the utilization of at least three different ethical frameworks or distributive justice theories affect patient autonomy, beneficence, nonmaleficence, and justice? How would the application of moral practice associated with those frameworks (at least three) be different for a right-to-life issue and for the practice of euthanasia?

EXERCISES

1. In a one-page paper, define distributive justice, ethics, morals, and values, and describe how they are used by leaders in decision making.

2. In a one-page paper, explain four ethical principles that guide decision making associated with patient care.

3. In a two-page paper, apply at least two ethical frameworks or distributive justice theories, with examples of moral practice of a leader, to an ethical issue in a health organization.

4. In a two- to three-page paper, analyze arguments and make a recommendation for health leaders to adopt utilitarian and/or deontological postures in their organization; differentiate potential decisions leaders would make in the two frameworks to support your analysis and recommendation.

5. Compile a list of options a leader in a health organization has to develop an integrated system of ethics and moral practice. In a one- to two-page paper, summarize the potential impact of each option regarding appropriate ethical adaptation across the organization.

6. Read "The Case Study of the Transferred Employee" and answer the following questions in a two- to three-page paper.

    a. What do you do?

    b. Do you change the documents?

    c. Do you go back and confront your supervisor?

    d. What is your decision, and why did you make it?

    e. What is your next course of action?

    f. Which other factors do you consider and which other actions do you take?

    g. Which ethical framework or distributive justice theory best supports your decisions regarding the case, and why?

The Case Study of the Transferred Employee

You are an administrator of a department in a health organization that has recently been reorganized. Personnel from other units have been permanently transferred into your department so that your department can take on additional tasks in support of the mission of the health organization.

After two months have passed, one of your new employees comes to you asking for you to complete his annual job performance appraisal. You are surprised because all annual performance appraisals were supposed to be completed by the supervisors of the departments losing the personnel before they were transferred into your department. Because you do not feel you know the new employee well enough to do an annual performance appraisal, you call the former supervisor and ask that she complete the performance evaluation herself on the employee. The losing supervisor refuses, saying that the issue is now your problem. The losing supervisor further states that no one from the human resources department told her that she was supposed to do a performance appraisal on the employee before the employee left her division. The losing supervisor also confides that writing a performance appraisal 90 days after it is due will trigger a "red flag" with human resources, which may reflect negatively on the losing supervisor's management and the supervisory effectiveness of her department.

Frustrated with the situation, you approach your supervisor and ask for his guidance. He suggests that you change the date on the employee's internal transfer documents, making it seem as if the employee arrived in your department yesterday. Your supervisor also says that he will talk to the other department leader and make sure she did an evaluation for 12 months on the employee, and not just for 9 months. He also suggests that you could provide some input on the evaluation because the employee did work for you for the last 60 days. Your supervisor says, "This happens all the time." He continues by stating, "It is easily corrected by creating a new set of documents." He assures you that there is nothing illegal about this practice, and that this methodology is used frequently to correct otherwise careless administrative actions in the facility.

Your supervisor then tells you to go back to your office, retrieve the transfer documents already in place, and replace them with new ones containing the dates you and he just talked about. As you walk back to your office, you begin to feel uncomfortable with the prospect of taking an administratively correct set of documents, destroying them, and then replacing them with some newly created documents that do not represent the actual dates of the transfer. You believe that this practice provides further support for an otherwise ineffective human resources system. However, as a new department head, you are uncomfortable losing favor with the boss who controls your future in the organization.

To protect yourself, you call the organization's legal counsel to get some advice on an informal basis. Legal counsel tells you that your supervisor is, indeed, correct; it is not illegal to change the documents if changing them results in a correction to a previously made administrative error. You counter by telling legal counsel that this may not have been a human resources or administrative error as much as it is an attempt to avoid a negative human resources action. Legal counsel suggests you go back and discuss the issues with your supervisor if you are uncomfortable doing anything regarding this matter. This suggestion makes you even more uncomfortable, because your boss is not an individual who enjoys repeating himself or being challenged or questioned by his employees. Such events are perceived by your boss as the actions of disloyal employees. You are certain that going back to your supervisor will result in an uncomfortable event for you.

REFERENCES

1. Pozgar, G. D. (2004). *Legal aspects of health care administration* (9th ed.). Sudbury, MA: Jones and Bartlett, p. 2.
2. Pozgar, note 1.
3. Joseph, A. M. (2007). The impact of nursing on patient and organizational outcomes. *Nursing Economics, 25,* 30–34.
4. Pozgar, note 1.
5. Hewitt-Taylor, J. (2003). Issues involved in promoting patient autonomy in health care. *British Journal of Nursing, 12*(22), 1323–1330. Retrieved February 17, 2005, from Academic Search Premier database.
6. Johnson, J. A. (2009). *Comparative health systems.* Sudbury, MA: Jones and Bartlett.
7. Coppola, M. N, Croft, T., & Leo, L. (1997, September/October). Understanding the uninsured dilemma: A necessity for managed care survival. *Medical Group Management Journal, 44*(5), 72–82, 100.
8. Gibbs, L. (translation) (2002). Aesop's fable of the grasshopper and the ants. *Aesop's fables.* Oxford: Oxford University Press (World's Classics).
9. Coppola et al., note 7.
10. Southwick, A. (1988). *The law of hospital and health care administration.* Chicago, IL: Health Administration Press.
11. Beauchamp, T. L., & Childress, J. F. (2008). *Principles of biomedical ethics.* Princeton, NJ: Oxford University Press.
12. McDonald, F., Simpson, C., & O'Brien, F. (2008). Including organizational ethics in policy review processes in health-care institutions: A view from Canada. *HEC Forum, 20*(2), 137–153.
13. Emmanuel, L. (2000). Ethics and the structures of healthcare. *Cambridge Quarterly of Healthcare Ethics, 9,* 151–168.
14. Povar, G. J., Blumen, H., Daniel, J., Daub, S., Evans, L., Holm, R. P., et al. (2004). Ethics in practice: Managed care and the changing health care environment. *Annals of Internal Medicine, 141*(2), 131–137. Retrieved February 15, 2005, from Academic Search Premier database.
15. Reiser, S. J. (1994). The ethical life of health care organizations. *Hastings Centre Report, 24*(6), 28.
16. McGee, G., Spanogle, J. P., Caplan, A. L., & Asch, D. A. (2001). A national study of ethics committees. *American Journal of Bioethics, 1*(4), 60–64. Retrieved February 27, 2005, from Academic Search Premier database.
17. McGee et al., note 16.
18. Muir, D. (2008, October 30). Congress speaks out about CEO bonuses. *ABC News Online.* Retrieved August 11, 2009, from http://abcnews.go.com/Business/story?id=6150746&page=1.
19. Stout, D. (2009, March 18). A.I.G. chief asks bonus recipients to give back half. *The New York Times.* Retrieved on August 11, 2009, from http://www.nytimes.com/2009/03/19/business/19web-aig.html.
20. American College of HealthCare Executives. (2005). *Board of Governor's Certification Exam Study Guide.* Chicago, IL: Health Administration Press.
21. Peer, K. S., & Rakich, J. S. (1999). Ethical decision making in healthcare management. *Hospital Topics, 77*(4), 7–13. Retrieved February 15, 2005, from Academic Search Premier database.
22. Harris, D. M. (2003). *Contemporary issues in healthcare law and ethics.* Chicago, IL: Health Administration Press.
23. Leathard, A., & Goodinson-McLaren, S. (2007). *Ethics: Contemporary challenges in health care social care.* Bristol, UK: Policy Press.
24. Coppola, M. N., & Ledlow, J. R. (2009). *A scholarly discussion of spirituality in healthcare leadership: Why not?* American College of Healthcare Executive (ACHE) abstract (unpublished). West Texas Region.
25. Pesut, B. (2009). Incorporating patients' spirituality into care using Gadow's ethical framework. *Nursing Ethics, 16*(4), 418–428.
26. Pesut, B. (2009). Incorporating patients' spirituality into care using Gadow's ethical framework. *Nursing Ethics, 16*(4): 19.
27. Baylor University, Institute for Studies of Religion. (2008). Baylor religion survey.
28. Coppola & Ledlow, note 24.
29. Giesler, N. L. (1981). *Options in contemporary Christian ethics.* Grand Rapids, MI: Baker Book House.
30. Pesut, B. (2009). Incorporating patients' spirituality into care using Gadow's ethical framework. *Nursing Ethics, 16*(4): 418–428.
31. Retrieved August 13, 2009, from http://plato.stanford.edu/entries/justice-distributive/.
32. Retrieved August 13, 2009, from http://medicalethics.suite101.com/article.cfm/social_justice_v__market_incentive.
33. Retrieved August 13, 2009, from http://www.distributive-justice.com/theory/p-utilitarism-en.htm.
34. Retrieved August 13, 2009, from http://www.distributive-justice.com/theory/p-strict-egalit-en.htm.
35. Rawls, J. (1971). A theory of justice. Boston: The Belknap Press of Harvard University Press.
36. Retrieved August 13, 2009, from http://www.distributive-justice.com/theory/p-pluralism-en.htm.
37. Kovner, A. (1995). *Jonas's health care delivery in the United States* (5th ed.). New York: Springer.
38. Giesler, note 28.
39. Crisp, J., Potter, P. A., Taylor, C., & Griffin Perry, A. (2008). *Potter and Perry's fundamentals of nursing* (7th ed.). St. Louis: Mosby.

40. Ven, V., Poole, H. W., & Scott. M. (1995). Explaining development and change in organizations. *Management Review, 20*(3), 510–540.
41. Kovner, A., & Jonas, S. (1999). *Jonas and Kovner's health care delivery in the United States* (6th ed.). New York: Springer.
42. Kay, C. D. (1997, January 20). Notes on deontology. Retrieved July 31, 2009, from http://webs.wofford.edu/kaycd/ethics/deon.htm.
43. Spencer, E. M., Mills, A. E., Rorty, M. V., & Werhane, P. H. (2000). *Organization ethics in health care.* New York: Oxford University Press.
44. Proenca, E. J. (2004, January). Ethics orientation as a mediator of organizational integrity in health services organizations. *Health Care Management Review, 29*(1), 40–51. Retrieved February 15, 2005, from ProQuest multiple databases.
45. Spencer et al., note 40.
46. Curtin, L., & Flaherty, M. J. (1982). *Nursing ethics: Theories and pragmatics.* Bowie, MD: Robert J. Brady.

11

Measuring the Outcomes of Leadership Initiatives

While the sage advice "you can't manage what you can't measure" is still very much true, in an e-business environment it is also true that "you can't measure what you can't monitor."

—Peter Drucker[1]

This chapter discusses how leaders can measure and assess the impact and progress of their leadership efforts within the health organization. We have all heard the phrase, "If you can't measure it, you can't manage it." Measurement and assessment of health leadership is one of the more underrepresented aspects within the health industry. This chapter defines common issues related to this consideration for health leaders and recommends ways in which to measure outcomes. A distinction is made between measuring leader efficiency, effectiveness, performance, organizational efficacy, and the leader's goal, with these elements being combined to create a composite quality leadership outcome assessment.

LEARNING OBJECTIVES

1. Describe how health leaders measure and capture information (i.e., use metrics) related to efficiency, effectiveness, performance, efficacy, and quality in health organizations.

2. Explain the importance of measurement and developing criteria for efficiency, effectiveness, performance, efficacy, and quality in health organizations.

3. Demonstrate applicable models and tools that represent the constructs of efficiency, effectiveness, performance, and quality in health organizations.

4. Compare and contrast two or more models of health leader assessment and evaluation and analyze the process of capturing metrics for this assessment and evaluation within a health organization.

5. Compile and categorize health leader measures/metrics for assessment and evaluation of effectiveness, efficiency, performance, efficacy, and quality; compile and categorize measures/metrics for assessment and evaluation of the health organization; finally, relate the two lists.

6. Appraise, evaluate, and justify the use of performance and quality measures/metrics for a specific type of health organization (e.g., hospital, group practice, rehabilitation center).

INTRODUCTION

This is a very important chapter for health leaders to embrace and understand within the context of leadership practice. In this chapter, we discuss the very important duties a leader has in regard to managing his or her facility from perspectives of efficiency, effectiveness, efficacy, performance and productivity, benchmarking, optimization, and quality. How do you know you are leading the health organization well? This chapter will assist you in answering that critically important question.

The trend in the U.S. health industry is for leaders to become more efficient, effective, and efficacious in leading people and managing resources, while simultaneously achieving high performance and quality outcomes within their organization. To keep up with this trend, measurement and assessment has become a necessary competency for leaders. However, before any leader can become skilled in this area, he or she must understand the difference between the *constructs* of efficiency, effectiveness, efficacy, performance, and quality, and identify how the operationalization of salient variables for these constructs can assist in leading highly successful organizations.[2]

As discussed earlier in this text, terms such as "efficiency" and "effectiveness" are called constructs. Constructs are those things that lack identification through one of the five senses. As a result, to maximize opportunities for achieving highly effective, efficient, efficacious, performing, and quality organizations, it is incumbent on the health leader to recognize the differences between these constructs (as they are generally understood in the health arena) and be able to use common indicators (e.g., variables) that are also understood by internal and external stakeholders. Failing to use appropriate terminology (e.g., constructs and variables) that is universally understood and applied consistently within and outside the organization may result in conflicting messages. For this reason, it is incumbent upon the leader to "stay on message," adhere to industry standards in terms of the definition and use of commonly accepted and widely employed health terminology, and measure these variables consistently.

EARLY EFFORTS OF THE U.S. HEALTH SYSTEM IN MEASUREMENT

Measuring organizational and leader performance has always been uniquely important within the health industry. In the early part of the twentieth century, a convergent evolution was occurring within the U.S. healthcare industry that sought to benchmark and measure the performance of organization and leadership efforts. During this time, medical societies, private health organizations, and many health leaders collectively adopted as a goal the improvement of the quality and delivery of health services and products. In fact, Abraham Flexner wrote one of the earliest works on hospital performance, called *Medical Education in the United States and Canada*.[3] This early work on standards and measures led to improvement in the scientific method, and also to improved curriculum and standards in medical education. Nevertheless, despite these policy changes and the widespread acceptance of Flexner's work, leaders of early U.S. hospitals and health systems remained largely reluctant to change traditional practices and procedures.

Despite Flexner's recommended innovations, a review of the early archives of leadership and management of hospitals from the early 1900s suggests that studies of hospital performance were viewed as bothersome. Although he wrote one of the earliest published works on hospital efforts to improve hospital efficiency, Dr. Ernest Codman of Massachusetts General Hospital noted that "*the carrying out of comparative studies is troublesome, difficult, and time-consuming and may point to the desirability of making changes in procedure in organizations which are bothersome, to say the least.*"[4]

Nonetheless, capitalizing on the growing trend in U.S. medicine in the early twentieth century to deliver higher quality and more productive care, the American College of Surgeons instituted an efficiency program of its own during that time. In 1918, this organization launched a program geared toward standardizing hospital procedures and organization. More than any other single factor, the masterful implementation of these standards has been responsible for the most constructive changes in the efficiency of hospital operations in the United States; the legacy of this effort continues to influence leaders in health organizations today. Since 1918, standards, processes, and procedures for health leaders have grown from the simplistic and finite to the dramatically complex and seemingly infinite.

CONSTRUCTS, VARIABLES, AND TOOLS TO MEASURE HEALTH LEADERS AND THEIR ORGANIZATIONS

How can you evaluate a health leader's performance and the performance of the health organization? Numerous tools and methods, comprising various constructs and variables, are available to assist with assessment and evaluation of leadership and the organization as a whole. This chapter summarizes several of these organizational and individual methods, although many more approaches to evaluation exist.

It is extremely difficult to separate leadership performance and evaluation from organizational performance and evaluation because leadership, in its broadest definition, exists to enable and facilitate a health organization in performing well and fulfilling its purpose effectively, efficiently, and efficaciously. Health leaders should develop an assessment and evaluation system for the health organization, for the leadership and management group within the organization, for groups categorized appropriately in the organization, and at the individual level. This system of assessment and evaluation is closely related to internal and external organizational processes of assessment, monitoring, forecasting, and evaluation, although the focus in this context is on improving group and individual leadership competencies, outcomes, and processes. As in program evaluation, when assessing leadership, as part of a strategic system that goes down to the individual health leader, eight constructs are salient. According to Veney and Kaluzny, evaluation must contain methods and measures of relevance, adequacy, progress, effectiveness, impact, efficiency, and sustainability[5]; efficacy is the eighth consideration.

Why is health leadership assessment and evaluation important? A key justification is that success in improving organizational performance and outcomes rests primarily in the competent leadership of the health organization. Also, promoting competent leaders to higher levels of responsibility in the health organization is of utmost concern. Consider the following points made by the National Center for Healthcare Leadership (NCHL):

- The attrition rate for senior-level health executives could reach 40 percent in the next decade.[6]
- The cost of turnover for a middle- to senior-level leader in the health industry is approximately $250,000.[7]
- Sixty-six percent of health organizations fail to provide formal leadership training to prepare the next generation of leaders.[8]

Health leaders who show competence at lower levels of the health organization should, over time, be given greater level of responsibility, accountability, and authority. As a person gains experience and masters leadership at lower and middle organizational levels, opportunities for senior-level leadership should be visible on the horizon. To reach senior leadership and perform well at entry and middle leadership levels, the health leader's ability to honestly and objectively assess and evaluate his or her own performance is critical. From a theoretical perspective, emotional maturity or emotional intelligence is a prerequisite for honest self-evaluation.

Emotional Intelligence [9] and Self-Efficacy

Knowing oneself, therefore, becomes absolutely essential. Emotional intelligence constructs support the self-monitoring and adaptation of the dynamic culture leader fairly well. "It [emotional intelligence] doesn't measure how well you did in school or what your GMAT scores were, but rather, how well you handle yourself and your relationships."[10] It used to be said that "It doesn't matter what you know, but who you know." Today, a new rule applies: "It matters what you know, and who you know, and perhaps most importantly, what you know about yourself!"

The four basic constructs of the emotional intelligence model are (1) self-awareness; (2) self-management; (3) social awareness; and (4) social skills.[11] These constructs are slanted toward the art of leadership. Even so, they can and should merge to form a secondary level of "intelligence" that monitors the technical and relationship orientations of the leader on an ongoing basis. Thinking about when to emphasize science or art, as in the dynamic culture leadership model—or, even better, how to merge the two—should become an intuitive exercise within the subconscious processes of the health leader. Conscious engagement and mastery lead to subconscious implementation. This is the internal gyroscope that many successful health leaders learn to depend upon:

> Those who use the emotional intelligence framework to guide their thoughts and actions may find it easier to create trust in relationships, harness energy under pressure, and sharpen their ability to make sound decisions—in other words, they increase their potential for success in the workplace.[12]

The health leader connects the four emotional intelligence constructs together with this "internal gyroscope" to analyze both himself or herself and the organization, and to merge the appropriate levels of leadership science and art in creating an organizational culture that can withstand the ever-changing environmental challenges. The more emotionally intelligent and mature the health leader is, the better he or she will be able to assess and evaluate his or her own, the leadership group's, and the organization's performance honestly and objectively. The health leader's level of self-efficacy, coupled with emotional intelligence, is worthy of discussion as well.

A high level of self-efficacy is important for the health leader. Self-efficacy is an individual's capability to produce a desired effect:

> Perceived self-efficacy is defined as people's beliefs about their capabilities to produce designated levels of performance that exercise influence over events that affect their lives. Self-efficacy beliefs determine how people feel, think, motivate themselves and behave.[13]

Rotter's internalizer/externalizer-based theory, which focuses on the locus of control, intuitively supports leadership capabilities and high levels of self-efficacy. Internalizers, it would seem, would have higher levels of self-efficacy. Health leaders need to be self-efficacious in their capability to lead people and manage resources, but must also instill a sense and organizational culture of efficacy for excellence in patient care. Only in this way can subordinates be directed to accomplish the mission, goals, and objectives of the organization, and to improve health status of the community as a whole.

Developing a system to assess and evaluate your leadership capabilities at the individual through the organizational levels is vital to your growth and development as a health leader; seeking to improve and lead better on a continuous basis should be a long-term career goal. To assist in developing your assessment and evaluation system, this section first outlines the strategic system of leadership and management—specifically fulfillment of the strategic plan—within the context of evaluation.

Strategic Plan

At a basic level, strategic planning addresses the following question: Has or is the organization fulfilling and achieving its mission and vision? Using directional strategies such as mission and vision, evaluation of leadership, the strategic system of leadership and management, and the organization can be undertaken. This evaluation is rather subjective in a broad sense, but can be very specific at the objective level, where measures should be employed. A more objective view—that is, a more measurement-based approach in evaluating strategic plan and strategies—is to assess the progress made toward accomplishing action step tasks, objectives, and goals that are linked to specific strategies. Objectives are evaluated by variables of interest that are inherently integrated into the objective itself. Are action step tasks associated with each objective being accomplished? Is the variable of interest for the objective moving toward (or has it reached) the desired level? This combination of subjective and objective assessment should be conducted several times throughout any given year (such as on a quarterly basis).

From a strategic system of leadership and management, leadership and the organization as a whole can be evaluated by the leadership team, the board of directors (or trustees), shareholders (if the organization is a publically traded company), the corporate organization, or the community at large (stakeholders). In this assessment, strategies and goals contain constructs important to the organization, and objectives contain measurable variables.

Market Share/Growth

Another high-level construct that assesses a health organization's performance is market share rate and the trend of that rate. In other words, how much of the geographical-bound percentage of qualified and available customers or patients come to the organization for care? Market share is a percentage, such as 50 percent or 70 percent. The more market share an organization possesses, the more power it wields in the community. Patient or customer satisfaction rates are associated to a certain extent with market share and with the level of repeat or return business (i.e., when a patient returns to the organization for additional or different health care in the future).

The direction of the organization's market share is important. If you evaluate the market share held by a health organization during only a single time period, you really cannot assess much. If you assess the trend in the organization's market share over multiple years, however, then you have a much better basis for making judgments about organizational performance. Growth, decline, and maintenance of market share and the organization's performance are subjective and relative. Health organizations that strategically want or need to grow should realize that market share growth occurs over time; they also should recognize that leaders in the organization should be held accountable for a predetermined evolution of market share growth. Conversely, if a growth strategy results in a decline in the organization's market share, the leadership team, strategies, and goals should be reevaluated within the context of the external environment. If the environment is extremely competitive, with new competitors entering the marketplace, that factor should weigh into the evaluation. This high-level method of evaluation must consider the environment and the unique circumstances of the health organization.

Benchmarking

Benchmarking is a critical tool for leaders to understand and embrace as a method for tracking programs and performance in the health organization. Benchmarking is a continuous process of measuring performance and services against best-in-class cases or organizations; it is an ongoing process of gathering information from peers and competitors in the industry and applying that information to internal performance assessment. It is *not* a linear or one-time process for hospital or group practice administrators. Health leaders must continually measure their organization's performance against its peers in the industry to establish benchmarks for meeting the current and future needs of patients, stakeholders, the community, and beneficiaries (if in insurance).

Similar to internal assessment, benchmarking is an eight-step process:

1. Determine which independent and dependent variables to benchmark.
2. Plan the process.
3. Collect internal data.
4. Collect external data.
5. Analyze differences.
6. Transform the data into information and then into knowledge (information that is actionable).
7. Plan the action.
8. Reassess the situation (periodic reassessment).

Determining what to benchmark and analyzing differences between outcomes to determine if there are relevant and incremental differences in processes may be the two most important steps in determining a benchmarking scheme for the health leader. The key point to recognize in the process of benchmarking is that benchmarking is not a linear process, despite the sequential and procedural list of steps associated with implementing the program. Often, when evaluating benchmarking schemes, it will be necessary to reevaluate the plan or revisit the interpretation of the data collected. By continually refining the process and encouraging group participation and interaction, health leaders can hone in on a relevant benchmarking decision.[14]

Performance Variables in Benchmarking

Benchmarking performance variables (also called indicators) measure the organization's performance against other organizations like it or groups of organizations like it based on size, geographic location, or other criteria.

Benchmarking data can be purchased and acquired through professional associations and societies, firms specializing in benchmarking and health data/information, some consulting firms, and state associations (e.g., state hospital associations). These data and information may include a variety of constructs and associated variables—for example, financial performance; patient care mortality and morbidity by service line (e.g., cardiac care, cancer care, pediatrics), diagnosis-related groups (DRG), or *International Classification of Disease,* ninth or tenth revision (ICD-9 or ICD-10) category; and measures of efficiency, effectiveness, and efficacy ranging from patient satisfaction rates to staff satisfaction, pay scales, turnover rates, and market share. Benchmarking data are invaluable in comparing the effectiveness, efficiency, and efficacy of leadership performance and organizational performance against those of similar organizations. Many health organizations use "dashboards" to conduct ongoing assessments of their organization's performance, from the construct level down to the variable level.

Organizational Satisfaction, Absenteeism, and Turnover

Internal organization performance and outcomes can provide a method to assess and evaluate health leadership. Although many internal performance and outcome measures exist, the three major constructs for performance and outcome evaluation are organization employee/staff satisfaction, employee absenteeism, and turnover. Organization employee/staff and physician satisfaction is the employee's or staff's perception of the level of approval they have for the direction and approaches utilized by the health organization, the fulfillment they experience in performing their responsibilities, the contentment they have with the work environment, and the agreement (trust) they have with equitable treatment. Satisfaction from this perspective is significantly correlated with leadership and leader performance. This satisfaction should be assessed over time (i.e., as a trend) to determine leadership effectiveness in terms of this construct because satisfaction is relatively temporal and dynamic (similar to organizational climate, as discussed in Chapter 9). Higher levels of satisfaction are preferable, but some dynamic tension is desirable and expected (perfect satisfaction is rare and may not be conducive to productivity).

Absenteeism—that is, missing scheduled work due to illness or social loafing—is usually a result of less-than-satisfied employees or staff members. Poor work conditions, lack of clarity in responsibilities, mistreatment, inequitable application of rewards and punishment, less than competitive pay and benefits packages, decision and policy inconsistency, and lack of perceived appreciation from the employee's perspective are root causes of the symptom of absenteeism. Acute absenteeism is a real problem for health organizations given their patient care processes and standards. Moderate to high levels of absenteeism usually are attributed to poor or inattentive leadership and management.

Excessive turnover is a result of similar prolonged problems. Turnover is the cumulative resignation (quitting their jobs) of employees, staff, and physicians over time. High turnover rates correspond directly to inconsistent leadership and management practices and have root causes similar to those associated with high absenteeism. High turnover rates are the ultimate action of employees, staff, or physicians in expressing their dissatisfaction with the health organization. A low to moderate level of turnover is expected in a dynamic and transient world, but high turnover is a leadership problem; this problem is most usually reflective of poor or inconsistent leadership and management.

National-Level Systems

Groups or organizations utilize systems of performance and quality evaluation. Many health systems, integrated health systems (systems with insurance plans), and health insurance plans, for example, use the National Committee for Quality Assurance's (NCQA's) Healthcare Effectiveness Data and Information Set (HEDIS)[15] report card and Quality Compass system:

> HEDIS is a tool used by more than 90 percent of America's health plans to measure performance on important dimensions of care and service. Altogether, HEDIS consists of 71 measures [variables] across 8 domains [constructs] of care. Because so many plans collect HEDIS data, and be-

cause the measures are so specifically defined, HEDIS makes it possible to compare the performance of health plans on an "apples-to-apples" basis. Health plans also use HEDIS results themselves to see where they need to focus their improvement efforts.[16]

Constructs and variables, along with an integrated "State of Healthcare Quality" report are essential reading for health leaders (the endnote contains the URL for the citation).[17]

At the highest level, a national strategic plan for health prevention and promotion is embodied in the *Healthy People 2020* initiative; Healthy People 2000 and 2010 were earlier versions of the current plan:

> Healthy People 2010 provides a framework for prevention for the Nation. It is a statement of national health objectives designed to identify the most significant preventable threats to health and to establish national goals to reduce these threats.[18]

This plan incorporates several health constructs (called leading indicators) and variables to measure progress toward the desired goal (such as reducing deaths from colorectal cancer).[19]

Health leaders must determine which constructs and variables they want to improve at the organization; how they will perform group benchmarking against peers; which group performance and quality they will seek, such as inclusion in health plan HEDIS indicators; and at the national level, how those indicators relate and integrate with their particular health organization's mission and vision. A physician group practice in a rural area would not include constructs and variables outside its scope of practice as part of their self-assessment, but would strive to improve the variables relevant to their practice, such as immunization rates, cancer screening for their patients, and improvements to administration of their practice.

Next, individual leadership assessment and evaluation tools are described. This discussion is followed by examples of health leader development process and competency models and, lastly, organization performance measures.

TOOLS TO MEASURE LEADERSHIP OUTCOMES AND COMPETENCIES

Health leaders are assessed and evaluated in many ways. These methods encompass organizational performance and outcomes to individual performance, outcomes, and mastery of competencies. In this section, individual leadership outcomes and competencies are described as sources of individual leadership improvement that lead, in turn, to improved organizational performance and outcomes.

Competencies for Assessment and Evaluation

A recent collaboration of five professional associations has created five domains that include a total of 300 competencies for the health leader and manager. Recall the extract of competencies, focusing on leadership and management from Domain 2, Leadership, described in Chapter 5. The summarized file for all domains can be found on the supporting Web site for this text.

Objectives

Health leaders can be assessed and evaluated by objectives. Using goal setting theory applications, the health leader and her or his supervisor (another leader or board member) should establish specific, yet challenging goals for a specified time period (e.g., quarter, year, two years). These goals, for which the health leader is held accountable, can target the individual, group, section/divisional, or organizational levels. They may also contain group goals, wherein a group (leaders, or leaders and subordinates) as a whole is responsible for achieving the objective. Even though health leaders may have multiple goals across the spectrum just described, these goals should be consistent and aligned with organizational mission, vision, strategies, and goals.

The health leader's goals should have a good vertical and horizontal fit with other goals established by the organization, meaning that they should not conflict or contradict with others' goals. Measureable variables, such as organizational satisfaction rates, absenteeism, turnover rates, productivity rates, and market share, should be associated with each goal. Some goals may have several variables linked to the goal. Rather than having 20 goals, 5 to 10 well-devised, important goals that are challenging and for which adequate resources are available are preferable.

Surveys

Health leaders can be assessed and evaluated by a survey of their subordinates; the survey may be distributed to the leader's peers as well. Such a survey should elicit the respondent's assessment of the leader's attention and accomplishment of organizational objectives and goals, work environment variables (those similar to satisfaction and/or organizational climate), communication ability, and the appropriate competencies described previously. Survey results should be validated and standardized to other leaders' results; national or regional leadership assessment and evaluation surveys are used by many health organizations for this purpose. Simply developing a survey without experience, internal assessment, and validation of the instrument is not advised. Surveys should be used only in conjunction with other leader performance and outcome information.

360-Degree Evaluation

A 360-degree evaluation is a survey that is given to all those in the organization who work with and work for the leader under assessment. Superiors, subordinates, and peers assess the health leader in this approach. As stated previously, survey results should be validated and standardized to other leaders' results; national or regional leadership assessment and evaluation surveys are used by many health organizations for this purpose. Simply developing a survey without experience, internal assessment, and validation of the instrument is not advised. Like surveys, 360-degree evaluation should be used only in conjunction with other leader performance and outcome information.

MODELS FOR LEADERSHIP ASSESSMENT AND EVALUATION

This section presents three models for review and reflection—namely, models provided by the National Center for Healthcare Leadership (NCHL), General Electric (GE) Healthcare Performance Solutions, and the National Public Health Leadership Institute (NPHLI). When studying these models (which are depicted in **Figure 11–1**, **Figure 11–2**, and **Figure 11–3**), consider the leadership theories, models, knowledge, skills and abilities, and subsequent competencies a health leader should possess, understand, discern, apply, and master. Then review the leadership competencies provided by the five professional associations listed in this chapter. Do you see an integration of multiple constructs? Which variables would you measure to assess and evaluate your own leadership capabilities? Do you see constructs in these models that are similar to those discussed in previous chapters of this text? Do you see constructs or elements that are familiar to you? Can you list leader constructs and variables to assess performance? What would you measure?

In Figures 11–1, 11–2, and 11–3, would you add other constructs (such as a strategic supply-chain system) for leader evaluation? Can you prioritize the constructs by importance? Which variables would you measure, and how would you measure them for constructs that are important?

Health leaders do their jobs, seek continuous improvement of their leadership capabilities, and use moral approaches to ensure that their health organizations survive and thrive, while providing excellent patient care services or products. It takes all leaders throughout the organization to focus the collective energy of the health organization to serve its community and fulfill its purpose. Health leaders develop the organizational culture, select the strategies, and lead people and manage resources to consistently improve health services, care practices, and the health status of their communities. The capability to perform these essential leadership tasks is

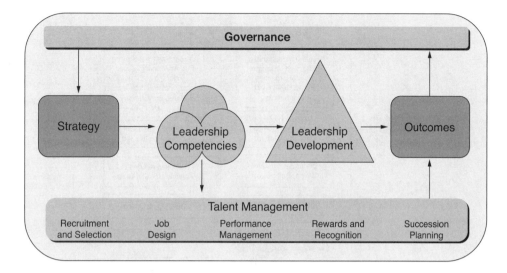

FIGURE 11–1   National Center for Healthcare Leadership and GE Institute for Transformational Leadership Development Construct Model
Source: National Center for Healthcare Leadership (NCHL) & General Electric Institute for Transformational Leadership. (n.d.). Preparing leaders to achieve organizational excellence, p. 5. Retrieved June 1, 2009, from http://www.nchl.org/ns/calendar/NCHL_Overview_1.08.pdf.

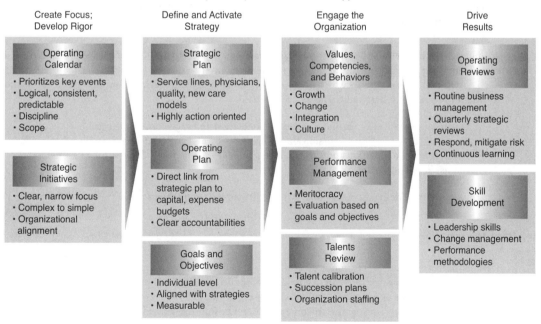

FIGURE 11–2   GE Institute for Transformational Leadership Development Variable and Process Model
Source: National Center for Healthcare Leadership (NCHL) & General Electric Institute for Transformational Leadership. (n.d.). Preparing leaders to achieve organizational excellence, p. 8. Retrieved June 1, 2009, from http://www.nchl.org/ns/calendar/NCHL_Overview_1.08.pdf.

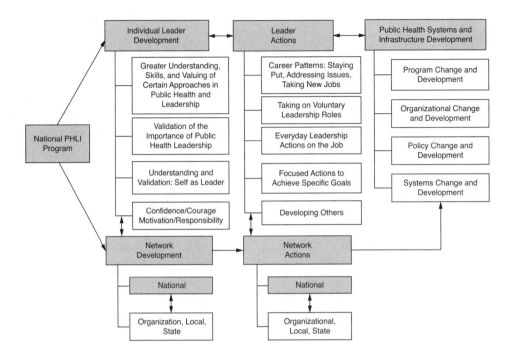

FIGURE 11–3   National Public Health Leadership Institute Model of Leadership Evaluation
Source: Umble, K., Diehl, S., Gunn, A., & Haws, S. (2008). Developing leaders, building networks: An evaluation of the National Public Health Leadership Institute 1991–2006. National Public Health Leadership Institute, Gillings School of Global Public Health, University of North Carolina, p. 28. Retrieved June 1, 2009, from http://www.phli.org/evalreports/index.htm.

grounded in the health leader's ability to assess, evaluate, and develop leadership knowledge, skills, abilities, and subsequent competencies, and ultimately to translate them into practice.

Next, this chapter continues with a discussion of efficiency, effectiveness, performance, efficacy, and quality. Many times, effectiveness and efficiency are confused:

> Organizational effectiveness has an external orientation and suggests that the organization is well positioned to accomplish its mission and realize its vision and goals. Efficiency, on the other hand, has an internal orientation and suggests that economies can be realized in the use of capital, personnel, or physical plant.[20]

Effectiveness is "doing the right thing," while efficiency is "doing things right."[21, 22]

Health Efficiency

Defining health efficiency is very important. Efficiency is defined as a Pareto optimal allocation of resources. An allocation is "Pareto optimal" or "Pareto efficient" if production and distribution cannot be reorganized to increase the utility of one or more units without decreasing the utility of other units. This concept is also referred to as technical efficiency, because the outcome will always be improved based on economic performance measures without reference to subjective weights or comparisons. Efficiency is further measured in terms of the productivity of selected outputs and inputs. This measure can be stated in the form of a ratio:

$$\text{Efficiency} = \text{Outputs/Inputs (subject to constraints)}$$

In layperson's terms, one can think of efficiency as analogous to a triathlon, where an individual is expected to swim, cycle, and run for great distances. Now think of the sequence of events. Between the arduous swimming and running events is the cycling event. Studies have been done to validate that the fastest scores in triathlons are achieved when the three events are structured with a swim, a cycle, and then a run; reversing the order results in slower times in the triathlon event. The most "efficient" way to do the three events—that is, the one that results in the least amount of time for the overall triathlon—is to conduct them in the following order: swimming, cycling, and running.

In a similar fashion, task organization and careful planning can make a health leader more "efficient" in his or her job. Efficiency in this case results in the ability to accomplish the same tasks within shorter periods of time or to accomplish more tasks in a given workday. Obviously, efficiency is extremely important to a health leader from an individual perspective; it is also important from an organizational perspective, given that hundreds or thousands of simultaneous activities may be occurring during the course of a normal day of operations.

Some examples will illustrate how efficiency plays out in the health arena. Is it possible to increase patient visits to a clinic by 25 percent without adding providers to the clinic to examine those patients? From an efficiency standpoint, think of acute care and the physician office visit sequence of events. Usually the patient makes an appointment, arrives at the clinic or practice, and sees the physician. The physician then orders some diagnostic tests to be performed on the patient (e.g., a blood test, culture, or urinalysis). Next, the physician makes a preliminary diagnosis (many times without the diagnostic test results), writes a prescription or treatment regimen for the patient, and follows up with the patient after the diagnostic test results are provided to the physician. If the diagnostic test result is different than the physician expected, then the patient may have to return for additional examinations or may need different treatments. Given this traditional sequence of events, how inefficient is the process? If you create a system for prescreening and assessment (i.e., an algorithm or protocol), have the patient receive the diagnostic test based on that prescreening process, and make the diagnostic test results available before the physician examines the patient, the efficiency for both patient and physician are enhanced. By changing this traditional process, efficiency is enhanced by as much as 25 percent for the physician; as a consequence, the physician can see more patients and have more confidence in the diagnosis and treatment regimen.

> Efficiency refers to whether program results [organizational results] could be obtained less expensively. Questions of efficiency concern the relationship between the results obtained from a specific program and the resources expended to maintain the program.[23]

Efficiency has an internal orientation and focuses on those resources, including time, required to achieve a desired outcome or result. Efficient operation, as in the context of organizational performance, can be understood as "(1) effective operation as measured by a comparison of production with cost (as in energy, time, and money); and (2) the ratio of the useful energy delivered by a dynamic system to the energy supplied to it."[24]

> To economists, efficiency is a relationship between ends and means. When we call a situation inefficient, we are claiming that we could achieve the desired ends with less means, or that the means employed could produce more of the ends desired. "Less" and "more" in this context necessarily refer to less and more value. Thus, economic efficiency is measured not by the relationship between the physical quantities of ends and means, but by the relationship between the value of the ends and the value of the means.[25]

Selecting and operationalizing the appropriate inputs and outputs to measure (variables) are critical steps in producing the best efficiency analysis for health leaders. Failure to use the best available measures may lead to inadequate representation of efficiency for the organization. It should also be noted that within the health industry, the word "productivity" is sometimes used interchangeably with "efficiency." It is not uncommon to see these terms used haphazardly in organizational parlance. Finally, it is important to recognize that several different kinds of efficiency measures may exist in a health organization. The tables in the next section present snapshots of the different types and definitions of efficiency.

Defining and Measuring Efficiency

The important thing to know about efficiency that makes it different from all other terms is that efficiency is a quantitative term expressed as a ratio. More so than with any other term used in health, the definition of efficiency must include a numerator and a denominator expressed as a ratio. For example, from a reductionist point of view, if your car is supposed to get 100 miles/gallon of gas, but after you drive it for a week, you average only

---

TABLE 11–1 Efficiency Calculation

Efficiency is a quantitative term. It is derived through a process of dividing outputs by inputs: $E = O/I$.

Inputs can be defined based on *design capacity*.

Design capacity is determined through predetermined structures and process. For example, a clinic might be designed to see 220 patients per day based on available full-time employees (FTEs) and treatment rooms.

Outputs are defined based on outcomes.

Outcomes are captured from actual data generated by the organization. For example, outputs are the actual numbers of patients seen per day. In this case, suppose 180 patients were seen by the facility:

Efficiency calculation: $E = O/I$; $E = 180/220 = 82\%$

The health leader can see that his or her new clinic is operating at only 82 percent efficiency. Two possible areas to investigate are immediately evident:

1. The facility is not meeting its operational capacity.
2. The facility's design capacity was originally miscalculated or forecasted erroneously.

---

95 miles/gallon, your car's efficiency can be measured as a function of outputs divided by inputs: 95/100 = 95 percent efficiency. **Table 11–1** summarizes the calculation of an efficiency ratio.

A variety of health efficiency measures are available to leaders that are universally understood and applied in health organizations. Basic ratio analysis (i.e., efficiency) is the cornerstone of U.S. health system metrics. An example is the percentage of occupied bed-days, where the result is the ratio of patient-occupied beds and total beds. Other ratios can be used as well, such as infection rates per total patients seen, and morbidity and mortality rates for overall patient encounters. Most health service research over the last 50 years has emphasized ratio analysis to discern the contributions of single input or output variables. Once meaningful and prudent ratios are calculated, they can be compared against those from previous years and from other organizations for benchmarking purposes. Ratios can provide useful information on how an item of interest has performed in the past and may perform in the future. They can provide quick and easily understandable information to health leaders and should be one of the first calculations performed in any new organization.[26] In the examples in **Table 11–2**, note that all of the measures can be subjected to ratio analysis once the correct variables are selected for manipulation.

Examples of Best Practices in Industry[27]

In the 1990s the healthcare supply chain found at Sisters of Mercy Health System was much like those found at many organizations. The fragmented and duplicative systems across Mercy were dependent on six different in-

---

TABLE 11–2 Types of Efficiency Measures in Health from a Leader Perspective

- **Cost efficiency** focuses on the optimal distribution of funds to meet daily activities in the health setting.
- **Productivity,** or process efficiency, measures the work expended to produce healthcare products.
- **Economic efficiency** measures the resources consumed per unit of service output.
- **Response efficiency** refers to how quickly a system reacts to a request for service.
- **Technical efficiency** focuses on optimizing inputs to create outputs in such a way that no other reorganization could use resources more fully.
- **Operational efficiency** is defined as achieving the full potential for all resources available. It differs from technical efficiency in that there is emphasis on avoiding waste.

---

formation technology (IT) materials management software solutions, were unable to negotiate the maximization of supplier discounts, and were heavily relying on outside vendors to help facilitate the management of the health system's supply chains.

The decentralized work found in the mimicking of similar processes at each health system wasn't managed for process efficiency or cost savings at the enterprise level. This realization created a new organization at the system level, with the intent to create an integrated supply chain that better utilized available technologies for inventory management and implements supply chain best practices from in and out of industry. With the creation of a new centralized supply chain, departmental data could then be shared across the system and Mercy's reliance on outside vendor information was dramatically lessoned.

The creation of resource optimization and innovation (ROI) helped consolidate the supply chain throughout Mercy at the corporate level, align major processes utilizing a shared materials management software solution, create an internal group purchasing organization, and allow for the enterprise-wide management of supply chain distribution and repackaging processes within Mercy. The creation of an internally owned and managed repackaging and distribution facility, the Consolidated Services Center (CSC), permitted improved supply chain responsiveness by better catering to customer hospitals, improving fill rates over the 85 to 90 percent that other

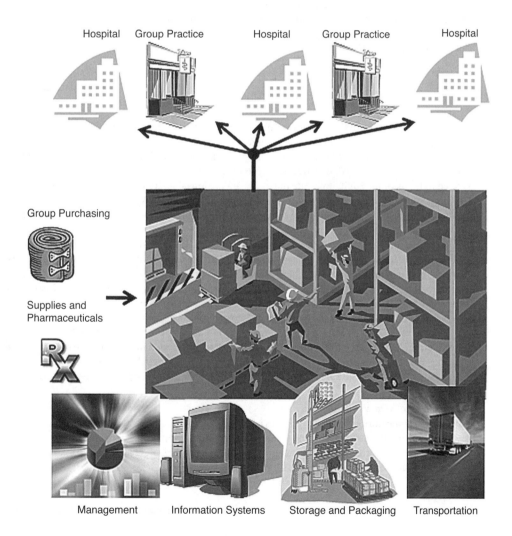

FIGURE 11–4   What Is a Consolidated Services Center?

Source: Corry, A., Ledlow, G., & Shockley, S. (2005). Designing the standard for a healthy supply chain. In *Achieving supply chain excellence through technology* (ASCET) (Vol. 7, pp. 199–202). San Francisco, CA: Montgomery Research.

distributors achieved, streamlining the receiving process, and reducing complexity by 70 percent through combined deliveries of [medical/surgical supplies] and pharmaceuticals; created standard inventory management metrics such as fill rate percentage to measure departmental and centralized performance; permitted more timely deliveries to facilities (with an internal truck fleet), improving cost savings by eliminating third-party markup fees (approximately $3 million annually) and by purchasing directly from manufacturers; and permitted bulk purchasing and contracting for economies of scope and scale. With these efficiency improvements and taking advantage of economies of scope and scale, the Sisters of Mercy supply chain now returns $6 for every $1 invested in this core business function.

Optimization

"Optimization" is sometimes used as a synonym for efficiency. In reality, this term refers to an isolated case of efficiency where the ratio of outputs to inputs is 1 (or 100 percent). Most times, optimization is something to be strived for, rather than actually achieved.

Optimization is defined as achieving perfect efficiency goals. It results from maximizing the outputs for the design capacity for the unit under study. When something is optimized, it is operating at 100 percent efficiency; thus there can be no greater output based on designed inputs than that which has resulted from the process of generating those results. Process optimization should identify and consistently maintain the best combination of manufacturing conditions, operating procedures, and technologies to consistently achieve the highest level of long-term outputs.[28]

Health Effectiveness

Effectiveness differs from the concept of efficiency insofar that it may be a qualitative variable and not always a quantitative variable.[29] The concept of effectiveness is also very subjective and may be based on emotion- and value-driven behaviors. For example, the concept of efficiency will always have a ratio associated with it so that the metric can be calculated. Effectiveness, in contrast, may not always be a quantitative term. It may simply be stated in terms of the ability to create outcomes and actions that are perceived as acceptable by outside stakeholders. Such outside perceptions may be subjective and may not always be generalizable outside the context under assessment. Care must be taken to generalize effectiveness to the entire population because effectiveness is strongly rooted in the perceptions of the individual.[30]

Think of the current presidential administration trying to craft a new policy. Although the new policy may not have been implemented yet, or have any metrics associated with it such as costs and numbers of persons served, there is always a perception of approval or disapproval of the concept based on individual values, enduring beliefs, and other personal factors. Effectiveness is (or can be) a highly opinionated assessment, not supported by any creditable argument for satisfaction or dissatisfaction other than the opinion of the person (or group of individuals) making the evaluation of the item under discussion.

As far as health items are related, the cliché that "Beauty is in the eye of the beholder" is a reasonable metaphor for forecasting effective outcomes. Positive and empirical outcomes may be one way to judge a health leader.[31] However, if the population at large does not place the same value on the outcomes as the health leader does, then the leader may be judged to be *ineffective* despite the otherwise positive metrics he or she is producing.

Defining and Measuring Effectiveness

Defining and measuring health effectiveness is difficult due to the ineffable nature of the values of the persons who are making the decisions on the behavior under study. In this regard, the effectiveness of a health leader may be based on a variety of factors, including both empirical variables (such as outcomes measures) and latent variables (such as employee satisfaction). As a result, effectiveness becomes the sum of both quantitative and qualitative factors that are individually interpreted by stakeholders.[32]

Effectiveness = Degree of (Qualitative + Quantitative factors) (interpreted by stakeholders)

For example, a physician who is producing high volumes of output for the organization—that is, seeing a large number of patients per day—could make a cogent argument that he or she is contributing greatly to the organization in terms of revenue generation. However, if the physician has a poor bedside manner that ultimately results in some patients complaining about the physician–patient encounter, then the outcomes of number of patients seen per day must be evaluated in the context of patient satisfaction measures. Over time, a profile for each patient care visit per provider can be collected and matched against satisfaction rates for that provider. In this scenario, effectiveness becomes a factor of both average number of patient visits and average number of complaints per patient. Thus the senior health leader has both metrics and a method with which to evaluate the overall effectiveness of the physician.[33]

The situation becomes more problematic when tangible outcome measures for effectiveness (e.g., patient satisfaction scores or number of complaints) are not available. Consider, for example, the collegiality or manners associated with an employee in an organization. Perhaps the employee is highly regarded by his or her patients, and also produces good outcomes for the organization in the form of high numbers of visits, high patient satisfaction ratings, and low secondary incidence rates. Now suppose this same employee does not get along well with his or her fellow employees, is disruptive or institutionalized in regard to organization change, and is viewed as a general malcontent by his or her superiors. Despite the good outcomes this employee generates for the organization, when asked by the senior leadership if the employee is "effective," the answer may be "no" based on the intangibles surrounding the employee.

As these examples demonstrate, the concept of effectiveness can be highly subjective. For this reason, the young health leader should be cognizant of his or her persona and impressions made when interacting with internal and external stakeholders.[34]

Other ways to measure health effectiveness may be more tangible. For example, health organization effectiveness should be defined and measured in terms of the unique situation of the organization and the community or stakeholders whom it serves. A survey consisting of a series of questions may be the best method for assessing effectiveness; although these answers might seem subjective at the surface, objective measures can be incorporated in the instrument to assess the overall effectiveness of the health organization. It may be difficult to answer each question from the standpoint of the entire health organization, so service line or product line assessments should be performed and then evaluated in total to provide a better, more precise picture of health organization effectiveness. Critical questions included on such a survey would include the following:

- Are the health organization's mission and vision statements grounded and informed by a community or stakeholder assessment of needs and future needs (forecasts)? (This assessment question is closely linked to external environment scanning, monitoring, forecasting, and assessment.)
- How has the health organization served its purpose and accomplished its stated mission?
- How well have the services and products of the health organization been perceived, adopted, or utilized by patients, customers, and stakeholders? (Measures such as patient satisfaction rates, mortality and morbidity rates, market share percentages, and return business/customers/patients rates can be used as a proxy evaluation set.)
- Are standards of care or practice being met or exceeded in the health organization?

Examples of Best Practices in Industry

Example 1: The Genesis Project[35]   Sisters of Mercy, a four-state system based in St. Louis, includes 19 hospitals along with outpatient care, physician practices, and a health plan; [it] has 4,122 licensed beds. With over 26,000 [employees], the Mercy system embarked on a $260 million project that will encompass technology upgrades throughout the system in clinical, patient access, revenue, resource planning, and supply chain areas. The supply chain operation began its movement to consolidation several years ago with the implementation of one shared materials management system, McKesson's Pathways Material Management. The Genesis Project enhances an integrated approach to that evolution for further standardization of supply chain practices and the initial standardization of clinical, revenue, and ERP [enterprise resource planning] practices and technologies.

The Genesis Project is an ambitious effort for the system [that was] launched in 2004, addressing the following six daunting challenges facing today's healthcare organizations: concerns about quality and outcomes; higher expectations of patients; shortages of clinical personnel; capacity issues; financial pressures; abilities to have physicians and institutions operate as a team.

> In response to compelling environmental factors and based on a belief that through innovation we
> can positively impact the lives of our customers and communities, the Sisters of Mercy Health Sys-
> tem is committed to improving patient safety, simplifying work processes, and enabling commu-
> nication flow among patients and their families, coworkers, and physicians.[36]

The Genesis Supply Chain Management (SCM) team supported improved patient safety outcomes (such
as utilizing critical inventory levels and ensuring product availability), and service by enhancing the supply
chain/procurement process to provide seamless, accurate, and efficient access to supplies for patients, care-
givers, and coworkers.

> Exercising leadership requires distinguishing between leadership and authority and between tech-
> nical and adaptive/operational work. Clarifying these two distinctions enables us to understand
> why so many people in top authority positions fail to lead: they commit the classic error of treat-
> ing adaptive challenges as if they were technical problems.[37]

The Genesis Project is not simply a technologically based upgrade of information systems, but a thorough
assessment and standardization of business processes and flows to better meet the needs of the communities
served. Among other major changes in processes and responsibility throughout the enterprise health system,
Genesis will bring about a huge shift from "home-grown" health system–defined and –designed processes, to
new standardized, corporate, consolidated processes and management of resources. By standardizing metrics,
naming conventions, functional area processes, documentation practices, role definitions, and charging practices management, true enterprise-level management of system resources, promotion of best practices, and accurate information management [will become possible].

Example 2: The American College of Surgeons' Standards   The early roots of some of the United States' early
quality control organizations demonstrate how values and opinions informed perceived judgments and outcomes associated with effectiveness criteria. In 1917, the American College of Surgeons (ACS) developed a set
of Minimum Standards for Hospitals. The ACS used these standards to conduct on-site hospital inspections. The
following year, after surveying 692 hospitals, only 89 of the hospitals were found to meet the ACS standards. Although these results were intended for public release, the ACS burned this list of deficient hospitals at midnight
in the furnace of the Waldorf Astoria Hotel in New York. This cover-up prevented both the media and the general public from discovering that some of the most prestigious hospitals in the country did not meet the standards as set forth by the ACS.[38]
    Although the burning of the list may be seen as unethical and self-serving, the intent of the leaders (at the
time) was to maintain the perception of high hospital effectiveness in the Unites States. The introduction of this
one metric into an otherwise highly regarded and trusted population of hospitals may have done more harm
than good. As suggested early, effectiveness may be in the eye of the beholder—but it may also be based on an
appropriately selected group of metrics and values.

Health Performance

The health literature to date reveals no single, universally accepted methodology for the measurement of performance in organizations for leaders to guide their strategy and vision.[39] Consequently, health leaders are faced
with another very complicated construct that must be defined and measured based on other variables and metrics in the environment. Here, we offer one solution that incorporates the use of efficiency and effectiveness criteria upon which health leaders can base policy and decision making when dealing with performance
constructs.[40]
    As previously noted, effectiveness is a values-based term that is derived from qualitative and quantitative
measures. Ultimately, it is defined as the achievement of outcomes acceptable to stakeholders. Efficiency, by
comparison, is an empirical concept, defined by the statistical interpretation of outputs achieved by organizing
inputs and outputs. How, then, do we interpret health organization performance?

One way to look at this complicated construct is to define performance based on the constructs of efficiency and effectiveness. The concept of performance in health organizations weds the empirical concept of efficiency with the stakeholder concept of effectiveness, thereby creating a new, measurable latent variable called performance:[41]

$$Performance = (Effectiveness\ criteria + Efficiency\ ratios)$$

Defining and Measuring Performance

For a health leader, the most important definitional issue in measuring organizational performance is capturing the correct measures to make organizational decisions. Various performance measures are available depending on the perspective being used to conceptualize performance. Once captured, these measures may highlight the potentially conflicting features of performance in an organizational system. In selecting organizational performance variables, it is critically important to stay focused on the domain of activity. For example, once a general framework or model has been selected to guide the performance measure to capture, it is necessary to determine which particular functions or activities will be evaluated on a continual basis. Most complex organizations serve a variety of aims and objectives. There is no simple measure of overall effectiveness of a health organization, which explains why several domains of activity (e.g., staffing turnover, organization FTEs, services offered) need to be captured and evaluated. There is always room to continuously improve at least some aspect of organizational performance—something for the leader to consider. A second consideration in the process is the level of analysis. An organization may wish to gather information at the clinic, department, or organizational level; having this echelon of information captured at different chokepoints in the organization provides an opportunity for the leader to effect change and engage in policy making.[42]

Examples of Best Practices in Industry

Because performance measures will differ based on the type of organization (for-profit or nonprofit; hospital, clinic, or retail pharmacy) and the product being produced by the organization, measures of performance will vary greatly between and within similar populations of organizations. High-performing for-profit hospitals will certainly look at revenue generation as a metric of performance, as this aspect is important to members of the hospital board; similarly, the employed persons in the organization may look at high revenue generation as a metric for job security. A nonprofit hospital may place more emphasis on the number of persons served and the degree of services offered to the population simultaneously as indicators of performance. Because the mission of the nonprofit organization is to provide services to the indigent or to increase the services offered to a rural community, this metric may be viewed as a performance measure. Local and regional professional organizations and internal and external stakeholders will all have different views on the achievement of performance criteria for organizations under study; leaders should quickly familiarize themselves with those measures.

Health Efficacy

Efficacy suggests possession of a special quality or virtue that gives effective power.[43] Efficacy is "the power to produce an effect."[44] Efficacy, as related to health and health care, is defined as the resources of the care process (continuum of care related to prevention, promotion, diagnosis, treatment, rehabilitation, and palliative care) that are attributed to realizing a desired or improved outcome for the patient and his or her family within an environment of respect and dignity. This is an individual patient perspective, whereas a community view of efficacy related to health and health care would be defined as the resources of the care process (continuum of care related to prevention, promotion, diagnosis, treatment, rehabilitation, and palliative care) that are attributed to realizing a desired or improved health status for the community that adds value to improve production and quality of life of its members.

Seemingly the opposite of efficacy is malefience, which is the "act of committing harm or evil"[45]; health organizations are duty bound to *not* do harm. "Efficacy and effectiveness relate to one of the most important questions in medicine—does a particular intervention work or not?"[46] Basically, efficacy is the value of health organizations in maintaining, restoring, and improving health and providing appropriate palliative care to those who desire health services. These definitions are different from the self-efficacy discussed earlier in this chapter.

Defining and Measuring Efficacy

Health organizations are expected to provide error-free services and products; in essence, high levels of efficacy are expected by all stakeholders. This charge is rooted deeply in the values of health professionals and in health organizations' cultural paradigms. This expectation requires health leaders and their organizations to consider and apply strategies that bring efficacy concerns and realities to the top of the list of priorities. Health leaders must balance effectiveness and efficiency but cannot compromise on efficacy. This aspect of their operation is vital for the health organization's survival and the perception of the health organization in the community and industry.

Measuring health organization efficacy focuses on outcomes that are clinically and administratively based. Using the professional or national standard of care and standards of practice, what are the health organization's outcomes relative to national, regional, or similar organizations' benchmark statistics? Quality is highly associated with health efficacy.

Examples of Best Practices in Industry[47]

The Sisters of Mercy Health System (Mercy) has launched the "Mercy Meds" medication administration program, which will bring bedside barcoding and other medication safety features to more than 3,000 patient beds in 10 hospitals. In addition to ensuring the safest, most reliable delivery of medication by using advanced barcode technology, the Mercy Meds program enables nurses and hospital pharmacists to spend more time with patients. Because of its multiple safety components and coordinated approach, the Mercy Meds program represents one of the most comprehensive patient safety initiatives to be implemented by a healthcare system.

> The 2006 Institute of Medicine report that cited 1.5 million people are harmed annually by medication errors, takes into account not only the incorrect administration of medication, but also the failure to prescribe or administer medication. Technology can solve a majority of the problems linked to medication errors by reducing variation and ensuring compliance. Some of the main reasons errors occur include nurse and pharmacy staffing shortages, high patient acuity, [poor] handwriting, and medication distribution process problems. Barcodes and radio-frequency identification are the mainstays of medication administration improvements among hospitals.[48]

From the time a doctor prescribes a medication to the time it is dispensed by the pharmacy and administered to the patient, Mercy has documented more than 70 steps in the process. Mercy Meds simplifies the process by eliminating unnecessary steps and implementing technology where possible to help identify potential medication issues.

With Mercy Meds, hospital pharmacists review patients' medication orders and enter prescription information into a computer. When giving medication to a patient, nurses wheel a computer to the patient's bedside that accesses information regarding the patient's medication regimen. Nurses use a handheld scanner to scan their own ID badge, the patient's barcoded ID wrist badge, and the barcode on the medication to verify accuracy. The computerized system also prompts nurses to check for potential medication issues, such as the patient's blood pressure and diet, before giving the medication. By using the barcode technology, the medication administration is automatically and accurately documented in the patient's electronic medication record.

Less than 5 percent of the nation's 5,000 hospitals currently use barcode systems, partly because only 35 percent of pharmaceutical doses come with barcodes. The Mercy Meds program is unique because the Mercy health system has become its own pharmaceutical distributor, allowing it to store, repackage, barcode, and distribute all medications used across Mercy, eliminating potential safety gaps that stem from using pharmaceuticals without barcodes. In addition, the Mercy Meds program includes the use of computer-controlled medication storage cabinets on the nursing unit. The cabinets enable nurses to access medications in an easy and timely manner, and provide another safety check in the medication process.

In February 2004, the U.S. Food and Drug Administration (FDA) issued a final rule that [required] drug manufacturers to barcode prescription drugs by 2006. In addition, consumer advocacy groups such as the National Quality Forum (NQF) and the Leapfrog Group for Patient Safety have endorsed several medication "safe practices" that should be used universally in clinical settings to improve patient safety. The Mercy Meds program greatly surpasses both the FDA rule and the NQF/Leapfrog safe practices in both timing and scope by combining unit-dose, barcoded medications with bedside barcode scanning technology, and increasing nursing and pharmacist participation in medication safety. "Mercy is committed to ensuring an exceptional level of patient safety," said Ron Ashworth, [former] president and chief executive officer of the Sisters of Mercy Health System. "We believe the benefits of Mercy Meds are essential in today's increasingly complex healthcare environment."

A primary goal of the initiative is to increase nurses' time at patients' bedsides, which will result in better hospital experiences and better health outcomes. Mercy Meds also positions hospital pharmacists as integral members of the collaborative patient care team, bringing their unique medication expertise and insight directly to the hospital floor.

"Mercy Meds allows Mercy to capitalize on our technical and clinical expertise, but most importantly, it helps us bring an increased level of comfort and peace of mind to our patients and their loved ones," said Kelly Turner, Manager—Pharmacy Services, Sisters of Mercy Health System.

Health Quality

There may be no construct more important to health leaders than the ability to define, operationalize, and measure quality in the organization.[49] As discussed in earlier chapters of this book, quality is a very complicated construct that has several different meanings considering the myriad of stakeholders. Stakeholders of interest in the defining of quality include patients, providers, employers, and payers. These stakeholders are discussed in more depth elsewhere in this text; for now, it is sufficient to recognize that each of these stakeholders will have different (and competing) concepts of organizational quality. The leader of any health organization will not be successful unless he or she is aware of these stakeholder interests and perceptions of quality and is prepared to meet these demands in the delivery and organization of health services and products.[50]

Similar to the definition of leadership itself, health quality has several definitions with no one universal frame for application among the populations of health organizations in the United States. As a base of reference, the authors of this book suggest quality is absolute and universally recognizable by all stakeholders. According to Coppola, quality is a mark of uncompromising standards and the accomplishment of high achievement. It is also the process of continuous improvement that is systematically evaluated against stakeholder demands and environmental requirements. Quality is the conformity to certain specifications set forth by stakeholders so that the equifinality and totality of the organization outputs satisfy both stated implicit needs and the implied and expected desires of all stakeholders. From a reductionist point of view, quality is the sum of organizational performance metrics plus stakeholder factors and expectations and meeting (or exceeding) the professional standards of care:[51]

Quality = Performance + Stakeholder factors and expectations + Professional standards of care

Defining and Measuring Quality

Several organizations are acutely interested in health quality. The National Quality Forum, for example, focuses on health quality: "The mission of the National Quality Forum is to improve the quality of American healthcare by setting national priorities and goals for performance improvement, endorsing national consensus standards for measuring and publicly reporting on performance, and promoting the attainment of national goals through education and outreach programs."[52] The Agency for Healthcare Research and Quality (AHRQ) is the federal organization charged with monitoring and improving health quality in the United States: "AHRQ is the lead Federal agency charged with improving the quality, safety, efficiency, and effectiveness of health care for all Americans. As one of 12 agencies within the Department of Health and Human Services, AHRQ supports health services research that will improve the quality of health care and promote evidence-based decision making."[53]

Quality is the perceived and actual value that a service or product delivers to the receiver of the service or product:

> There are many issues to consider when selecting a quality measure. The first step in selecting measures is to identify the measurement purpose and intended use of the measure. Quality measurement can be used to drive performance improvement. The quality improvement process is often iterative and therefore measurement may be repeated over time.[54]

Depending on the area assessed for quality, the measure and how to measure will differ from area to area. A good explanation, examples, and lists of measures and comparisons of measures can be found on the AHRQ's Web site.[55]

In 1966, Donabedian proposed an observational methodology for evaluating quality based on the constructs of structure, process, and outcome as necessary precursors to measuring quality. This model of health quality has since become the industry standard. Donabedian's original treatise on measuring and evaluating quality contained few guidelines for empirical measurement; rather, Donabedian recommended classifications of reviewing procedures. Successful review was based on the effective application of merit-based approaches and on normative and accepted practices in the field (stakeholder dynamics). Donabedian stated that experts on the subject matter and also panels should evaluate structure, process, and outcome variables.

Since 1966, the empirical literature has identified methods and methodologies capable of measuring quality, given appropriate data. Building on Donabedian's framework, and earlier methodologies developed by other authors, the framework shown in **Figure 11–5** is proposed.[56, 57]

■ *Structure*: Structure criteria and measures assess the context, or system, in which care or service is provided. These criteria are frequently generated from federal and state regulatory or accreditation organizations and include individual and organizational licensure, compliance to safety codes, The Joint Commission standards, and NCQA standards, to name a few. Structure can also include the resources required to deliver care, the environment in which care is delivered, the facilities, the equipment (e.g., bandages, linen, drugs), and the documentation of procedures, policies, and guidance to staff.

■ *Process*: Process measures assess the way in which care or services are provided. Examples of process measures include numbers of referrals and health screening rates. These measures also encompass the actual procedures and practices implemented by staff in their prescription, delivery and evaluation of care, and the monitoring, evaluation, and actions to adjust the provision of care.

■ *Outcomes*: Outcome measures assess the end result of a care or service process. Traditional outcome measures include mortality, morbidity, and infection rates. They may also include the effects of care received by patients as a result of health service intervention, the benefits to staff as a consequence of providing this care, and the costs to the organization of providing care.

Examples of Best Practices in Industry

Like performance constructs, quality can be a difficult and complex construct for leaders to define, let alone measure. A plethora of metrics, measures, and stakeholder dynamics come into play when attempting to universally define a complex construct such as quality and apply it in a consistent manner to health organizations.

Starting in 1990, *U.S. News and World Report* began to publish an annual survey of "America's Best Hospitals" that has remained a standard for profiling and ranking hospitals in the United States for 20 years. This model uses constructs of structure, process, and outcomes defined by a set of uniform variables that collectively

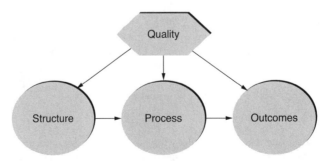

FIGURE 11–5   Quality Perspective from the Donabedian Model

make up a system of Likert-scale survey questions that are sent out to various key and influential stakeholders across the country. The survey also takes into account the reputation of the hospital (effectiveness criteria) as well as the evaluation of certain DRGs groupings (efficiency criteria).[58]

Although the results are not perfect (and are disputed by some), the *U.S. News and World Report*'s attempt to improve upon the earlier American College of Surgeons' survey conducted in 1917 is certainly successful in many ways. The improvement is that structure, process, and outcomes composite scores are reported with—and without—scores for reputation. The score for a facility's reputation (effectiveness criteria) is included as a stand-alone metric; it is also included in calculations of the overall scores for the top hospitals. In this regard, it is possible for hospitals to have highly regarded effective criteria as measured by key and influential stakeholders, as well as in terms of the operationalized metrics of the raw survey scores themselves. While not all leaders approve of survey results serving as indices of their organization's quality performance, leaders need to be aware of their existence, and their impact on the overall perceived quality of the facility, warranted or not.

SUMMARY

This chapter discussed how leaders can measure and assess the impact and progress of their leadership efforts within the health organization. Measurement and assessment of health leadership initiatives is one of the more underrepresented facets of the health industry. This chapter defined common issues encountered by health leaders who undertake such measurements and recommended ways in which to measure outcomes. Distinctions were made between measuring leader efficiency, effectiveness, performance, and organizational efficacy. The health leader's goal is to combine these elements to create a composite quality leadership outcome assessment. **Table 11–3** summarizes these terms as a take-away message for readers.

TABLE 11–3   Summary of Measurement-Related Terms

Term	Definition	Function
Benchmarking	Benchmarking is a continuous process of measuring performance and services against best in class cases or organizations.	Compare item A to best-in-class item B
Efficiency	Efficiency is a quantitative term expressed as a ratio. It is derived through the process of dividing outputs by inputs.	$E = Outputs/Inputs$
Optimization	Optimization is defined as achieving perfect efficiency.	$E = Outputs/Inputs$, such that $E = 100\%$
Effectiveness	Effectiveness is the sum of both quantitative and qualitative factors that are individually interpreted by stakeholders.	Effectiveness = Degree of (Qualitative + Quantitative factors), as interpreted by stakeholders
Performance	Performance in healthcare organizations weds the empirical concept of efficiency and the stakeholder concept of effectiveness, thereby forming a new, measurable latent variable.	Performance = (Effectiveness criteria + Efficiency ratios)
Quality	Quality is absolute and universally recognizable by all stakeholders.	Quality = (Performance + Stakeholder factors)

Source: Coppola, M. N. (2010). *Quantitative analysis coursepack* [in-progress textbook]. Texas Tech University Health Sciences Center, Lubbock, TX.

DISCUSSION QUESTIONS

1. How do health leaders measure and capture information (metrics) of efficiency, effectiveness, performance, efficacy, and quality in health organizations? Where are stakeholders' expectations important to this process?

2. Can you explain the importance of measurement and developing criteria for efficiency, effectiveness, performance, efficacy, and quality in health organizations? Why is this important to health leader evaluation?

3. Which types of applicable models and tools represent constructs of efficiency, effectiveness, performance, and quality in health organizations? Are some better than others?

4. Compare and contrast two or more models of health leader assessment and evaluation, and analyze the process of capturing metrics for this assessment and evaluation within a health organization. Which models seem most appropriate and why?

5. List health leader measures/metrics for assessment and evaluation for effectiveness, efficiency, performance, efficacy, and quality. List measures/metrics for assessment and evaluation of the health organization. How are the two lists similar and different? Do benchmarks fit into this discussion? Why or why not?

6. How would you appraise, evaluate, and justify the use of performance and quality measures/metrics for a specific type of health organization (e.g., hospital, group practice, rehabilitation center)?

EXERCISES

1. In a one- to two-page paper, describe how health leaders measure and capture information (metrics) of efficiency, effectiveness, performance, efficacy, and quality in health organizations.

2. In a one-page paper, explain the importance of measurement and developing criteria for efficiency, effectiveness, performance, efficacy, and quality in health organizations.

3. The CEO of your health organization comes to your office and states that she is not happy with the efficiency of the new ambulatory care clinic; she does not believe that the new clinic is being effective. Come up with three different measures for efficiency and three different measures of effectiveness that you feel are uniform and applicable to ambulatory care clinics.

   a. Using the model building techniques you learned about in Chapter 3, develop a construct representing "patient satisfaction with ambulatory care" that includes two variables and four measures based on the metrics you developed for this exercise.

   b. Based on the metrics you developed for this exercise, develop a dashboard for each metric that will provide the CEO with a snapshot of the performance items you have already suggested are important.

4. In a one- to two-page paper, compare and contrast two or more models of health leader assessment and evaluation, and analyze the process of capturing metrics for this assessment and evaluation within a health organization.

5. Compile and categorize health leader measures/metrics for assessment and evaluation for effectiveness, efficiency, performance, efficacy, and quality; compile and categorize measures/metrics for assessment and evaluation of the health organization. In a two- to three-page paper describe and compare the two categorized lists.

6. Appraise, evaluate, and justify the use of performance and quality measures/metrics for a specific type of health organization (e.g., hospital, group practice, rehabilitation center).

REFERENCES

1. Drucker, P. (1993). *The practice of management* (reissue ed.). New York: Harper Business.
2. Aday, L. A. (1998). Introduction to health service research and policy analysis. In L. A. Aday, C. E. Begley, D. R. Lairson, & Balkrishnan, R. (Eds.), *Evaluating the healthcare system: Effectiveness, efficiency, and equity* (Chapters 2–5, pp. 45–172). Ann Arbor, MI: Health Administration Press.

3. Flexner, A. (1910). *Medical education in the United States and Canada.* Boston: Merrymount Press.

4. Codman, E. A. (1917/1996). A study in hospital efficiency: As demonstrated by the case report of the first five years of a private hospital. Oakbrook Terrace, IL: Joint Commission on Accreditation of Healthcare Organizations.

5. Veney, J. E., & Kaluzny, A. D. (2004). Evaluation and decision making for health services (3rd ed.). Washington, DC: Beard Books.

6. Beeson, J. (2004, November/December). Building bench strength: A tool kit for executive development. *Business Horizons, 47*(6), 3–9. Also in NCHL and GE Institute for Transformational Leadership. (n.d.). Preparing leaders to achieve organizational excellence. Retrieved June 1, 2009, from http://www.nchl.org/ns/calendar/NCHL_Overview_1.08.pdf, p. 2.

7. Industry estimate: 2.5 times annual salary, based on $100,000 annual salary. NCHL and GE Institute for Transformational Leadership. (n.d.). Preparing leaders to achieve organizational excellence. Retrieved June 1, 2009, from http://www.nchl.org/ns/calendar/NCHL_Overview_1.08.pdf, p. 2.

8. WittKieffer. (2004, May). View from the top: CEO perspectives on leadership talent, executive development and succession planning in healthcare organizations. Conducted in conjunction with California State University, Los Angeles, CA. Also in NCHL and GE Institute for Transformational Leadership. (n.d.). Preparing leaders to achieve organizational excellence. Retrieved June 1, 2009, from http://www.nchl.org/ns/calendar/NCHL_Overview_1.08.pdf, p. 2.

9. Ledlow, G., & Cwiek, M. (2005, July). The process of leading: Assessment and comparison of leadership team style, operating climate and expectation of the external environment. Proceedings of Global Business and Technology Association, Lisbon, Portugal.

10. Lanser, E. G. (2000). Why you should care about your emotional intelligence: Strategies for honing important emotional competencies. *Healthcare Executive, 15*(6), 7.

11. Lanser, note 10, p. 7.

12. Lanser, note 10, p. 9.

13. Retrieved June 4, 2009, from http://www.des.emory.edu/mfp/BanEncy.html.

14. Coppola, M. N. (1998). The hidden value of managing worker's compensation costs in the hospital setting. In J. Burns & M. Sipkoff (Eds.), *1999 hospital strategies in managed care* (pp. 227–255). New York: Faulkner and Gray.

15. Retrieved August 21, 2009, from http://www.ncqa.org/tabid/59/Default.aspx.

16. Agency for Healthcare Research and Quality, National Committee for Quality Assurance. (n.d.). Retrieved June 1, 2009, from http://www.ncqa.org/tabid/187/Default.aspx.

17. Agency for Healthcare Research and Quality, National Committee for Quality Assurance. (n.d.). Retrieved June 1, 2009, from http://www.ncqa.org/Default.aspx?tabid=136.

18. Retrieved June 1, 2009, from http://www.healthypeople.gov/About/.

19. Retrieved June 1, 2009, from http://www.healthypeople.gov/LHI/lhiwhat.htm.

20. Swayne, L. E., Duncan, W. J., & Ginter, P. M. (2006). *Strategic management of health care organizations* (5th ed.). Malden, MA: Blackwell, p. 56.

21. Swayne et al., note 20, p. 56.

22. Veney & Kaluzny, note 5.

23. Veney & Kaluzny, note 5, pp. 5–6.

24. Retrieved June 3, 2009, from http://www.merriam-webster.com/dictionary/efficiency.

25. Retrieved June 3, 2009, from http://www.econlib.org/library/Enc/Efficiency.html.

26. Coppola, M. N. (2003). *Correlates of military medical treatment facility (MTF) performance: Measuring technical efficiency with the structural adaptation to regain fit (SARFIT) model and data envelopment analysis (DEA).* Doctoral thesis, Medical College of Virginia Campus, Virginia Commonwealth University, Richmond, VA.

27. This section is excerpted from the following source: Corry, A., Ledlow, G., & Shockley, S. (2005). Designing the standard for a healthy supply chain. In *Achieving supply chain excellence through technology (ASCET)* (Vol. 6., pp. 199–202). San Francisco, CA: Montgomery Research.

28. Coppola, M. N. (2010). *Quantitative analysis coursepack* [in-progress textbook]. Texas Tech University Health Sciences Center, Lubbock, TX.

29. Coppola, note 28.

30. Coppola, note 28.

31. Starfield, B. (1992). *Primary care: Concept, evaluation, and policy.* New York: Oxford University Press.

32. Coppola, note 28.

33. Coppola, note 28.

34. Coppola, note 28.

35. The first example was taken from Corry et al., note 27.

36. Sisters of Mercy Health System. (2004, April). The Genesis Project: Background paper.

37. Conger, J., Speitzer, G., & Lawler, E. III. (1999). *The leader's change handbook: An essential guide to setting direction and taking action.* San Francisco, CA: Jossey-Bass, p. 56.

38. Roberts, J. S., Coale, J. G., & Redman, R. R. (1987). A history of the Joint Commission on Accreditation of Hospitals. *Journal of the American Medical Association, 258*(7), 936–940.

39. Coppola, M. N., Ozcan, Y. A., & Bogacki, R. (2003, October). Evaluation of performance of dental providers on posterior restorations using amalgam or composite material: Does experience matter? A data envelopment analysis (DEA) approach. *Journal of Medical Systems, 27*(5), 447–458.

40. Coppola, note 28.

41. Coppola, note 28.

42. Coppola, note 28.

43. Retrieved June 3, 2009, from http://www.merriam-webster.com/dictionary/effectiveness.

44. Retrieved June 4, 2009, from http://www.merriam-webster.com/dictionary/efficacy.

45. Retrieved June 4, 2009, from http://www.merriam-webster.com/dictionary/maleficence.

46. Retrieved June 4, 2009, from http://www.medicinescomplete.com/journals/fact/current/fact0403a02t01.htm.

47. The material in this section was retrieved June 4, 2009, from http://www.mercy.net/quality/technology/news1484.asp.

48. Ganguly, I. (2009, June). Effective medication administration, *Advance for Health Information Executives, 13*(6), 21.

49. Coppola, note 28.

50. Coppola, M. N., Harrison, J., Kerr, B., & Erckenbrack, D. (2007). The military managed care health system. In P. Kongstvedt, *Essentials of managed care* (5th ed., pp. 633–655). Sudbury, MA: Jones and Bartlett.

51. Coppola, note 28.

52. Retrieved June 4, 2009, from http://www.qualityforum.org/about/mission.asp.

53. Retrieved June 4, 2009, from http://www.ahrq.gov/about/ataglance.htm.

54. Retrieved June 4, 2009, from http://www.qualitymeasures.ahrq.gov/resources/measure_selection.aspx.

55. Retrieved June 4, 2009, from http://www.qualitymeasures.ahrq.gov/resources/measure_selection.aspx.

56. Donabedian, A. (1966). Evaluating the quality of medical care. *Milbank Memorial Fund Quarterly, 44,* 166–206.

57. Coppola, M. N. (2008). Anatomy and physiology of theory. In J. A. Johnson, *Health organizations: Theory, behavior, and development* (pp. 9–29). Sudbury, MA: Jones and Bartlett.

58. McFarlane, E., Murphy, J., Olmsted, M. G., Drozd, E. M., & Hill, C. (2008). America's best hospital methodology. Retrieved August 15, 2009, from http://www.usnews.com/usnews/health/best-hospitals/methodology/ABH_Methodology_2008.pdf.

12

Understanding the Executive Roles of Health Leadership

Necessity does the work of courage.

—George Eliot, *Romola*

This chapter examines the complex cycle of relationships within health organizations. The needs and desires of nurses, physicians, administrators, and medical function leaders are presented. This chapter also places special emphasis on the relationships between major stakeholders within health entities. For the purpose of this discussion, we designate major health organization stakeholders as payers, providers, patients, and organizational entities. We additionally elaborate on the complexities of stakeholder relationships as they are concerned with cost, quality, and access issues. Finally, the chapter presents a conceptual model called the "parity of health care" that combines stakeholders and stakeholder issues into one schematic that assists in explaining and forecasting relationships in the dynamic world of the health industry.

LEARNING OBJECTIVES

1. Identify the steps, characteristics, and behaviors a health leader should take to build relationships with internal, "interface," and external stakeholders.

2. Explain the Parity of Health Care model and its usefulness to health leaders.

3. Construct a health organization stakeholder list and predict at least two motivations of each stakeholder considering cost, quality, and access to health services and products.

4. Compare and contrast internal health organization stakeholder motivations and issues.

5. Using previously discussed theories and models, combine two or more theories or models into a practical stakeholder management and relationship development model.

6. Evaluate internal and external health organization stakeholders, and justify their motivations, needs, and aspirations with regard to health services and products.

LEADERSHIP FOR PHYSICIANS, NURSES, ADMINISTRATORS, AND MEDICAL FUNCTION DIRECTORS

Health leadership is, indeed, situational and contextual, influenced by cultural constructs, and moderated by relational factors. The myriad of internal stakeholders and their differences are complex in both breadth and depth. In simple terms, health leaders need to lead people and manage resources so as to direct the collective energy of the organization toward successfully achieving the mission of the organization. This mission is always to serve patients and the community. This idea may be simple to state, but it is difficult to realize in practice. Similar to a conductor leading an orchestra, health leaders must ensure a seamless and harmonious operation such that all participants are collectively moving forward to accomplish the mission of the organization simultaneously. To do so, leaders must understand and motivate the various stakeholders in different ways while staying true to the organization's preferred strategies, goals, and objectives.

Physician Leaders

Health leaders need physicians to diagnose, treat, and refer patients to their organization. Without physicians, health organizations would not receive reimbursements or other revenues for the patient care process. With this point in mind, health leaders need to create a symbiotic, trusting, and integrity-based relationship with physicians. This is especially true of physician leadership. Health leaders should visit and know all physicians who practice and refer patients to their organization; these visits should be regular events that occur at times when physicians are not engaged in patient care. Health leaders should seek input from physician leadership on important decisions within the organization and provide frequent feedback on the decision process as well. The relationship a health executive builds with the physician leadership is critical.

It is always very important to respect a physician's education, background, decision-making priorities, and skills. A health leader should constantly be communicating the organization's vision, strategies, goals, and objectives in a clear and consistent manner while weaving the value of physician involvement and work into the discussion. Health executives should also try to maximize physicians' time to diagnose, treat, prescribe, and refer patients by creating or reengineering processes and systems that focus on their skills.

One of the greatest fears that physicians have with regard to any proposed "national health care" system is that they might lose control of their clinical practice autonomy. Physicians believe that any time spent away from direct patient care on additional bureaucratic requirements lowers patient care quality. Additionally, providers view decreased patient contact as inhibiting access to patients. Organizations can alleviate some of this fear by continuing to solicit physician input in all policy analyses and decision making that affect the care process or the logistics of the care process. For example, provider participation in policy making and strategic planning are essential to program success. To discount physician involvement and influence in health policy will ultimately doom policy implementation. Include physicians in all health and care delivery policy decisions that might affect their day-to-day autonomy or decision making.

Nurse Leaders

Nurse leaders are important to the health organization, in that they provide care for patients on an ongoing basis. In most health organizations, nurses account for the largest personnel expense for the entity as a whole. Nurses are needed to "staff" hospital beds, work in health programs, provide home health services, and perform any number of other jobs in health entities. Nurse leaders, like physician leaders, want to be respected, trusted, and sought out for input into decisions affecting the care process. Nurses want good work environments, with reasonable patient care loads (usually four to six patients per nurse per shift for average-acuity patients); they want to be treated with respect by administrators, physicians, and other medical staff personnel, and to have some level of self-governance (e.g., nurse education, and scheduling).

Building a solid relationship with nurse leaders is like building a relationship with anyone else: Trust, respect, and honesty form the foundation for interaction. As with physicians, health leaders should meet with nurse leaders and ask how to best build great relationships. Most nurses will respect the health leader's courage and intent to build a good relationship within the organization.

Administrative Leaders and Medical Function Leaders/Department Heads

Building professional and effective relationships with administrators and medical function leaders (e.g., pharmacists, and laboratory staff) are important in building a cohesive team of superiors, peers, and subordinates. Relationships with these leaders should be built on trust, respect, and honesty. However, different leaders will have different foci and motivations. For example, the finance leader is concerned with the bottom line and efficient use of resources. The pharmacist may be interested in error-free operations and streamlining supply chain logistical tasks. The laboratory leader may be focused on acquiring new capital equipment to keep up with the technology diffusion in this field. As this discussion suggests, administrators' and medical function leaders' "wish list" is both dynamic and nearly endless. As a result, managing these competing interests and priorities is challenging for any health leader. Even so, regardless of their job and organizational placement within the facility, it is important to listen to, respect, and understand the needs of these stakeholders.

Stakeholder Dynamics

Stakeholder dynamics are critically important for leaders of health organizations. This reality becomes more salient as leaders rise to positions of greater responsibility within the health organization. Key stakeholders in any health entity will include groups, individuals, and associations. Within these three classifications, stakeholders can further be defined as internal, interface, and external stakeholders.

In a health organization, internal stakeholders operate within the organization and consist of management, professional, and nonprofessional staff. Interface stakeholders function both internally and externally to the organization; they include medical staff, the governing body, and, if applicable, stockholders. External stakeholders include patients and their families, suppliers, third-party payers, competitors, special-interest groups, regulatory and accrediting agencies, local communities, and labor organizations.[1, 2] All of these stakeholders exert an influence on every issue and must be recognized and evaluated for their potential to support or threaten the organization and its competitive goals.[3, 4]

Health organizations have a particularly complex set of stakeholders. They include patients and families; payers; buyers (employers); regulatory agencies, such as The Joint Commission; community groups, such as public health departments, local employers, churches and civic organizations; providers, including medical staff members, employees, and volunteers; suppliers and financing agencies; associate organizations such as physician professional organizations; as well as other providers, including competing organizations and agencies whose service lines may be either competing or complementary, such as home care agencies and primary care clinics.[5]

Key stakeholders are those most important to health organizations. These stakeholders directly or indirectly control reimbursement, information, approvals, or other resources valued by the organization, or are in a position to impose costs on the organization.[6]

While the number of stakeholders in health organizations may be high, four main types of stakeholders should be considered in any healthcare decision making: These include patients, payers, employers, and providers. These four stakeholder groups have recently been labeled with a new term in managed care called the *managed care quaternion*.[7] Collectively, the stakeholders in the managed care quaternion affect all aspects of health organizational life, including patient care, payment, reimbursement arrangements, external costs, and other policy affecting organization survivability. Patients, payers, employers, and providers all play a vital role in the operations of any health organization. With any one of the four major stakeholders of the managed care quaternion omitted in the decision-making process for a healthcare entity, failure at some level is highly probable.

The Managed Care Quaternion and the Iron Triangle

The managed care quaternion (MCQ) model was developed in the early part of 2003 by Coppola.[8] It has since gained popular support within governmental organizations, as well as within some state Medicaid agencies, as an aid to health planning and policy making. It has also been used to forecast future healthcare needs. Furthermore, the MCQ concept is slowly working its way into the mainstream of health education. It will be an important model for health leaders to become familiar with as a tool for decision making in the next decade. However, the MCQ model alone is not a model that can be used as a basis for policy or decision making. Instead, it is more beneficial to view this model in concert with the *Iron Triangle* of health care.

The concept of the Iron Triangle was developed by Kissick in the early 1990s during the managed care revolution in the United States.[9] Kissick coined the term "Iron Triangle" to demonstrate the difficulty in selecting priorities for health as they relate to healthcare costs, quality, and access. Kissick suggested that an understanding of these resource elements would assist managed care organizations in establishing their logistical priorities.

For example, Kissick recognized that cost is only one important resource for the healthcare industry. In the Iron Triangle, costs form one angle of the three points, with quality and access being the other two resource priorities. These three factors together are kept in balance by the expectations, cultural goals, and economics of the society that supports the industry. Any angle (or construct) in the triangle can be increased, but only at the expense of the other two. For instance, quality in the U.S. health industry can be improved through large expenditures for additional technology or in training allied health providers; however, the increased expenditures may result in restricted access of this improved health care to only those persons who can pay for the higher quality of care. Put simply, the normal increase in one construct may adversely affect some combination of equifinality of the other two.

The concept of the Iron Triangle has been used by health leaders for more than a decade to guide development of strategic plans, organizational vision, and mission statements. Furthermore, this notion has become a staple and core competency in most health and business programs in the United States. Every young graduate student in this country should be familiar with the Iron Triangle—and be able to relate it to resource priorities in organizational analysis.

Kissick's model is a vital tool to health leaders; however, the model itself fails to take into account outside actors and agents. In this regard, it is incomplete as a means for conducting dynamic organizational analysis. When the Iron Triangle and the MCQ model are combined, they form a dynamic model called the "Parity of Health Care." This model describes, explains, and can forecast competing issues and organizational dynamics in the healthcare arena (**Figure 12–1**). The Parity of Health Care model is explained in more detail later in this chapter; we present it here for visual stimulation. Readers of this chapter should refer back to this model as the various components are described later in this chapter.

Optimally, it will be every health leader's goal to deliver high-quality care, services, or products, while simultaneously increasing access to services or products and lowering costs. Unfortunately, as health leaders try to make improvements in one area, there is often a tradeoff consideration in another area. For instance, increasing access to pharmacy benefits by opening an after-hours pharmacy window may improve access and be

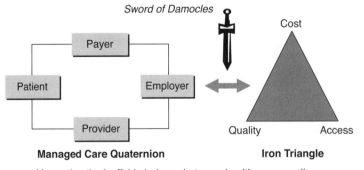

Measuring the ineffable balance between healthcare paradigms

FIGURE 12–1 The Parity of Health Care Model

seen as a quality initiative, but this service may not generate enough new revenue to pay for itself. If the pharmacy window continues to draw scarce resources from other areas in the health facility, its growing drain on the overall fitness of the organization may result in negative influence on other areas—perhaps in professional development and training opportunities, for example. In this case, the decreased opportunities for continuing health and medical education may translate into lower-quality outcomes for customers. The decrease in quality outcomes may be the result of the organization failing to take advantage of industry best practices that peer organizations have implemented due to their emphasis on professional development and training.

This complicated relationship forces health leaders to think conceptually and in nonlinear approaches. As a result, they must perform careful analyses of new policy ideas or agendas to ensure that the organization will maintain an effective balance between health costs, quality, and access. The cost, quality, and access tradeoffs associated with the interrelationships among actors must be considered.

The following sections provide an overview of the key stakeholders of the MCQ model, relating them to various dynamics of the Iron Triangle. The goal here is to illuminate the complicated and delicate nature of health dynamics.

Payers

Payers are a key stakeholder, as they provide reimbursement for services and products provided by health organizations. This group of stakeholders includes patients (who may pay for at least some, if not all, of their expenses on an out-of-pocket basis); governmental insurance programs, including Medicare and Medicaid; and private health insurers. Payer organizations attempt to keep the cost of care as low as possible and, more recently, have begun their own efforts to improve the quality and safety of care.[10]

Payers seek the lowest costs possible for health services and products and are usually willing to sacrifice the time costs of patients to achieve that goal. Accordingly, access is a secondary issue to the cost of care; the quality tradeoff is only marginally discussed after the cost of care. While risk management issues certainly come into play with large-scale health-based plans, the payer will, unfortunately, often go with the lowest physician bidder who can validate equally effective health outcomes in an environment of acceptable access. Such is the paradox and dilemma of being a large-scale health payer.

Leaders of health organizations need to be aware that large insurance companies may be more interested in health costs as opposed to outcomes of health services or products. This tendency is somewhat due to the migration of beneficiaries from plan to plan over short time periods; most health insurance plans are focused on medical expense ratios and maintaining profit margin because long-term prevention and outcomes linked to beneficiaries are rarely beneficial to the health insurance plan in which the beneficiary is enrolled at the time. Furthermore, while interested in health policy as a vehicle to lowering costs, the legislation that surrounds policy making is only a means to an end when it comes to cost controls. However, purchasers of health care may see reasonable price controls as a quality indicator and demand to see comparative data from different organizations. Such has been the case lately with many car insurance companies, which freely offer their prices for automobile insurance to consumers, allowing them to compare these prices against those offered competitors. This transparent and open system of pricing not only translates into an imprimatur of honesty and candidness for the organization, but also can be perceived as an effort to promote a partnership in the insurance industry rather than advocate for a cost-driven industry.

Accordingly, leaders of health organizations in the current decade may be placed in situations where they are forced to provide comparative data. Comparative data in health may include information to assist the purchaser to distinguish between health organizations' quality outcomes and services delivered. The payer, if not an individual patient, may also be concerned about the total cost per employer per year and acuity-adjusted disability periods if economies of scale are achieved to negotiate large-scale discounts of fees for services. As a result, health organizations need a strategy that allows them to know ahead of time how to implement a partnership with outside purchasers that is seen as a cooperative relationship rather than a utilitarian, profit-driven liaison.

Importance of Medicare and Medicaid. Two of the largest payers that early career health leaders and established leaders will most commonly deal with today in the United States are Medicare and Medicaid. Many issues play a role in the development of policy, payment decision making, and resource management for these payer organizations.

Medicare.   Medicare is an entitlement program where beneficiaries are required to "pay into" the system to be entitled to Medicare coverage once eligibility criteria are met. Medicare is administered through a series of intermediaries. Organizations such as Trail Blazers, Blue Cross and Blue Shield, and Aetna act as Medicare agents in determining interpretations of Medicare law and case management of patients. This system allows individual health organizations to work with one primary organization for funding and regulation compliance rather than all organizations going through one central Medicare supplier in Washington. D.C. The downside to having a larger number of agencies administering this program is that each agency has its own interpretation of the Medicare law, and some lack of consistency across the nation is found.

Medicare has gone through many permutations over the past four decades. The Balanced Budget Act of 1997 brought Medicare, the federally funded healthcare payer, to this point in history: Medicare has 43 million beneficiaries and is the United States' largest health insurance program. With estimated costs of $430 billion per year, spending is growing more rapidly than revenue. If current trends continue, the program will be unable to pay for all medical bills by 2018.[11] Leaders need to keep this point in mind in any analysis that incorporates the payer cost mix within the organization.

The Medicare system is under constant construction and renovation, with the most recent efforts being directed at the Medicare disability programs. This portion of Medicare provides health services for Americans who are declared disabled through the Social Security Administration. With the election of President Barack Obama, lawmakers and more than 75 disability advocacy groups have begun lobbying Congress to decrease the wait time for Medicare's disability benefits to take effect.[12]

Medicaid.   Medicare is the federally funded insurance plan for Americans age 65 and older as well as some other groups, such as those individuals with kidney failure. In contrast, Medicaid services are provided through individual states and supplemented with federal dollars through a block grant program. Medicaid is a welfare program that requires beneficiaries to meet state-based criteria for coverage. Leaders of local state-funded hospitals need to be keenly aware of the varying payments and restrictions that are found in their state.

Medicaid funds are geared toward low-income individuals and often pay for basic health service and product needs. The one exception is children younger than age 18, who often receive dental and vision care as well as the standard medical care through Medicaid and/or the State Children's Health Insurance Program (SCHIP). Medicaid programs are often difficult to navigate for both leaders of health organizations, health providers, and patients alike. The bureaucracy limits options for services due to the difficult requirements for becoming part of the system. Many physicians do not accept assignment for services because of low reimbursements and slow payment for services provided. As part of current legislative efforts, policy makers have been focusing on increasing reimbursement rates as a means of encouraging provider participants and building a more extensive provider network for beneficiaries. Also, many states have moved to Medicaid managed care plans in an effort to rein in costs and stabilize quality.

Patients

Ironically, the term "patient" was derived from a Latin verb meaning "to suffer." It is used to describe those persons who are recipients of care. The patient is an individual who will use some part of the health system in a facility for reasons known only to that person and his or her caretakers. Patient needs, interests, and expectations vary depending on the problem and the patient's past experiences. Understanding patients is important to health leaders because they are the individuals who use the facilities and ultimately pay for services and products.[13, 14]

Traditionally, health patients have been more interested in the indicators of satisfaction, access to care, facility accommodations, and service quality than in how an organization is structured to provide that care. This is especially true if the patient has insurance resulting in little to no out-of-pocket cost; moral hazard is a phenomenon that explains the increase in health services and product utilization noted when the patient incurs few financial demands at the time of service or product delivery. Now, however, a new era of health consumerism exists. Patients, who have learned to expect more from the products and services they purchase, are beginning to benchmark their health services against similar services they receive from the best organizations outside the health industry. They are using their experiences and observations to ask pointed questions in this growing era of patient autonomy. For example, if a package shipping company can answer calls in one ring, why can't the insurance claim center meet the same standard? If an investment advisor can offer a convenient after-hours appointment within a week, why can't a physician do so? If a company will accept without question the return of a product that doesn't fit properly, why won't the triage center trust a consumer who shares information about medical symptoms?

The health industry has not kept pace with the expectations of increasingly demanding patients. Complaints about quality and access to care are common. Making convenient appointments with the "right" practitioner remains a challenge for the average patient. Administrative minutiae have become more time consuming than the actual delivery of health services, and stories of medication errors and the lack of patient safety in different settings are increasingly prevalent. In the midst of this turbulence, organizations known for health excellence, such as Harvard Pilgrim Health Care and many Blue Cross and Blue Shield plans, are falling on hard financial times. As a result of these trends, health leaders who do not control costs while simultaneously managing patients' expectations of quality and access will fail to receive the confidence of their patients, and their organizations may find themselves facing the problems of financial instability and lower revenues. To quell this possibility, health leaders must manage patient expectations of access and quality, all the while controlling costs, if they want to compete and survive in this highly competitive dynamic health environment.[15]

Hospitals spend countless hours creating surveys, working on process improvement issues, and studying best practice alternatives. This information gained through these efforts is then used to identify what a patient actually needs to have in order to be processed through the service line comfortably and effectively. A patient's wants and needs are important to identify within the realm of the hospital's community. For instance, a hospital located within an oil-producing area should have the capability of dealing with the problems commonly experienced in this area—this is a *need*. An example of a *want* would be fresh flowers in an inpatient room every day or covered parking for all patient and guest vehicles. These concerns are important to patients, and patients realize that major changes will affect the cost of health services and products. Therefore, a patient's wants and needs must be carefully analyzed and implemented to benefit the needs of the patient, while simultaneously maintaining or exceeding the professional standard of care.

As previously stated, patients have traditionally been more interested in access to care and quality than in how an organization is structured to provide that care. Today, these issues are still important to patients, but now patients are requesting a voice in how their local organizations are run. This voice and input may include demands for services not offered and extended hours for services not currently offered. Patients also want to be treated as individuals; the health industry needs to respect their cultures.[16] Leaders also need to know that many patients are surfing the Internet for published service and product benchmarks. One survey found that Internet users were successful in locating many of the hospital benchmarks they were interested in with regard to certain health issues in less than 6 minutes.[17] Given the ready access patients have to this information, health leaders need to be aware of what is written about their organizations and what is publically available.

Health leaders are always striving to provide the necessities that patients need. One important necessity is the role that hospitals have in treating patients as individuals. Treating patients as individuals, and not just as a medical record numbers, means that facilities must respect all patients' values, privacy, and culture. Culture refers to a cohesive body of learned behaviors, taught from one generation to the next. One's culture constitutes one's rationale and rules for living; it makes experiences meaningful. Cultures are not simply a hodgepodge of disparate habits.[18, 19]

Providing cultural satisfaction is a complex issue because all patients have cultural views that may or may not be congruent with those of the health organization's staff. Ultimately, it is important for the leader to set aside cultural differences and to accommodate and incorporate cultural satisfaction into his or her health organization; after all, to maximize a patient's recovery is to make the patient as comfortable as possible.

Patients' Views on Costs.   Patients today are concerned with their out-of-pocket costs, health insurance premium costs, and pharmaceutical costs: Health expenditures have become a major concern for most Americans. Many view the rising costs of health services and products as a sign of a failing health system. Within the past decade, several debates have dealt with the issues of universal health care, electronic medical records, and insurance reform. As a consequence, the new patient now typically views the health organization not only as a place for medical care, but also as a business that does not care about the financial concerns of the patient stakeholder.

It is incumbent upon every health organization to create a vision that will benefit its community. This vision usually becomes a reality if costs and patients' objectives come together to form a broad picture. Patient objectives are items that patients would like to have accomplished as part of their interaction with the health organization. These objectives can be personal or they can belong to a group of stakeholders. An example of a personal objective would be satisfying the itinerary that a therapist sets at the beginning of treatment. An example of a group objective would be petitioning the hospital to provide for more handicap access routes for easier maneuverability. Objectives can be considered goals; however, these are generally items that need to be accomplished. Goals, by comparison, are items that the organization wants to reach, but for which there are no deleterious effects if they are not attained. Objectives are very important to cost analysis when dealing with patient care.

Patients' Views on Quality.   The Institute of Medicine (IOM) defines quality as follows: "the degree to which health services for individuals and populations increase the likelihood of desired health outcomes and are consistent with current professional standards."[20] Patients are motivated to participate in their care when they receive quality care. The patient is the key to how a health organization scores regarding quality. This is accomplished, first by patients recognizing what quality means to them, then by measuring the health professionals' performance, and finally by assessing the organization's ability to meet patient needs. Patients' views of quality reflect their perceptions of their treatment while in the health organization, hospital, clinic, or doctor's office, the service provided, and the competency of the staff. These views are analyzed by the organization through patient surveys, questionnaires, and discharge interviews. Information is then analyzed, and performance improvements or performance initiatives are implemented within the health system. Health leaders should maximize these opportunities when possible.

Patients' Views on Access.   Several factors affect access to health services and products: cultural and linguistic barriers, inability to get through by telephone, long wait times in the physician's office, inability to secure appointments, physician office hours that are not convenient for patient, lack of transportation, and being uninsured or underinsured. In a study conducted by the National Health Interview Survey (NHIS), a survey of 23,413 participants concluded that even when adults have a regular source for medical care, such as a personal physician, various problems in accessing care from their primary care physician—including long waiting times in the office, limited availability of appointments, lack of transportation, or difficulty reaching the physician by telephone—can increase the use of the emergency department at the hospital, which acts as a surrogate to primary care with the personal physician. This diminishes the benefits of having a regular source of primary care. Solutions that might improve access to medical care, such as implementing open access scheduling, can not only benefit patients, but also can benefit health policy related to cost-effective healthcare delivery systems and relieve overcrowding in emergency department waiting rooms.[21]

Health leaders know that the largest obstacle standing in the way of access to care is actually the inability to pay for health insurance or healthcare services. According to the U.S. Census Bureau, 45.7 million Americans are uninsured.[22] Insurance coverage greatly increases the probability and potential to access health services and products. Lack of health insurance and inability to pay for health services is a huge problem. For many Americans, it has grim consequences, because uninsured persons often put off necessary care until an illness or disease has escalated either to a difficult or impossible situation that is challenging to treat. Because of their lack of access, these patients typically seek treatment through the emergency department of a local hospital or institution as a last resort. As this trend continues (and is affected by the Emergency Medical Treatment and Active Labor Act [EMTALA]) and results in more patients who cannot fully pay for services or cannot pay at all, hospitals will face serious debt that must either be written off or funded by taxpayers. This reality of uncompensated care can have long-term negative effects for the health organization and its leadership.

Providers

Providers, sometimes referred to as practitioners, are key stakeholders in a health organization. Most people think of providers as the physicians and surgeons who treat the patients. In reality, nurses, physical and occupation therapists, technicians, and other clinical staff are also providers. They all play critical roles in the healthcare process.

There are two categories of providers: primary and secondary. Primary providers include hospitals, health departments, long-term care facilities, nursing facilities, HMOs, ambulatory care institutions, and home healthcare institutions.[23] Secondary providers include educational institutes such as medical schools, organizations that pay for care, and pharmaceutical and drug supply companies. Essentially, providers are both the individuals and the organizations involved with providing health services and products.

The primary interest of providers is the best treatment for the patient; primary, secondary, and individual providers share this interest. Hospitals, health departments, and other participants in providing care also want to provide the best care for those in need of health services and products. Medical school interests are to educate students to their fullest potential so they may then care for and treat the sick. Pharmaceutical companies are working around the clock to develop new and improved medicines to improve patients' health and cure illnesses. All providers want to offer the best care possible, but that best care is not always available—thus the problem of access is an important consideration.

Cultural and Ethnic Impacts on Providers.   At one time, treating a population was a fairly straightforward process. The U.S. population seeking care at hospitals was mainly white, and most doctors (and nurses) were white. Ethnic minorities sought treatment along ethnic lines and stayed among themselves. Less than 100 years after segregation in health treatment was the norm, the United States has evolved into a true melting pot in which "minorities" are projected to be the "majority" by 2050. Any person of color can now walk into any doctor's office and any hospital and expect the same treatment as his or her white counterpart.

But is that really true? The problem when it comes to people of color and today's health system is that there continue to be latent bias and disparity when it comes to health providers and their treatment of these patients. There is still a large difference in the treatment of people of color and ethnic minorities that goes beyond language; there is a cultural divide as well.

The Impact of Cost, Quality, and Access on Providers.   Many factors affect providers regarding cost, quality, and access. When looking at the cost issue, providers are forced to balance the costs of care with the costs of maintaining the organization in a financially viable situation; from a systems perspective, if the cost of care exceeds the health organization's ability to survive, where will patients receive care if the health organization closes? There are several reasons for cost increases over time: Improved equipment costs more, improved practitioners with better skills cost more, and increased use of information technology costs more. In fact, information technology has been one of largest factors in contributing to the rising costs of health care.[24]

Access has also been affected by these trends. Owing to the higher costs to provide care, more out-of-pocket costs for patients, and staff shortages, access to health services has declined. Many rural and urban areas lack health providers and are determined by government to qualify as health professions shortage areas (HPSAs) and/or medically underserved areas (MUAs). There is an ongoing shortage of health professionals such as nurses, medical technicians, and physicians working in certain specialties. Many hospitals, health organizations, and even medical schools have closed because of lack of funds or the inability to implement new technologies.[25] Moreover, the cost of malpractice insurance continues to increase, adding yet another cost into the system—and one that providers pass along to the patients, payers, and employers.

With higher costs, it might be assumed that quality and access would also increase. Unfortunately, the relationship between these variables is quite the opposite. As Chaudhry and Harris point out, much of the technological improvements being implemented in health care are not affecting the overall quality of care. At the same time, there are continuous advances being made in the treatment and care of patients. Providers are implementing new surgical procedures and tools, such as minimally invasive procedures; new pharmaceuticals are being introduced daily; and new and improved ways of treating illnesses are constantly being updated. It is apparent that plenty of quality improvements are being made within health organizations, but at what cost?[26]

Employers
Employers, especially large employers, are the largest stakeholder group purchaser or payer of health services and products in today's complex world of health delivery. Employers are more often the conduit to a health plan that ultimately reimburses for the cost of care; this reality is based on health insurance as a benefit to employment and as an enticement to employment for potential employees. Employers tend to pay between 60 percent and 80 percent of insurance premiums, while the employee pays the balance of the premium from their pay or salary. In this regard, the health leader needs to understand that health care is a prospective commodity that is paid for in advance. Reflecting this view, employers may focus on health care as a means of ensuring continued productivity in the workforce (keeping the workforce healthy, treating illness quickly to return workers to work) and emphasize the quality and timeliness of care; employers want to see a return on investment for the health insurance they pay for in prepaid premiums.

An example of employer constituent group efforts to improve and justify health outcomes to employer inputs (efficiency measure based on health outcomes [productivity of workforce] as compared to employer insurance premiums paid) is the LeapFrog Group. The LeapFrog Group serves as a forum for airing employer concerns. It also develops initiatives, such as those aiming at reducing adverse drug events, to improve the value of health services from the perspective of the employer. Similarly, both federal and state governments are large employers that attempt to improve their value proposition with regard to health services.

Employers face many challenges in today's business world. In the current era of complex managed care and potential national health care, organizational entities may find themselves between "a rock and a hard place" due to their inability to manage health costs at one extreme and their choice to give up healthcare benefits altogether at the other extreme.[27] Employers' healthcare costs are large and growing, with little hope of relief in sight. The overwhelming costs associated with employers' health benefits have prompted some employers to drop healthcare benefits for their employees. Many leaders of large organizations find it more cost-effective to hire part-time employees who work fewer than 40 hours per week, thereby making them ineligible for benefits such as health insurance coverage, which is provided only to full-time workers. (A full-time worker, also known as a full-time equivalent [FTE], typically works approximately 2,080 hours per year, whereas a part-time worker works less than full time, usually 16 to 24 hours per week.) Currently, the proportion of the U.S. gross domestic product (GDP, the summed value of all goods and services produced in the United States in a year) attributed to health costs is approximately 16 to 17 percent, which means that 16 to 17 percent of the costs of all products and services made or delivered in the United States are attributable to healthcare costs. Considering that the world is rapidly merging into a global economy, can U.S. employers compete with a product or service made in another country that devotes only 8 or 10 percent of its GDP to health care?

Today, the majority of large health organizations do not support establishment of a national health plan. A recent survey of more than 450 health organizations found that almost 85 percent did not want a national health policy in place of the current system. This strong consensus indicates that there is a need to look at alternative options to assist employers with their health benefits. As Ted Nussbaum states, "Most large companies believe they have a fairly good understanding of how they should manage their health care and how it impacts their workforce."[28]

Employers' Perspective Concerning Cost, Quality, and Access. Employers' perspective on healthcare cost, quality, and access over the last two decades has been overshadowed by increased costs of health in the United States. Employer-sponsored health insurance is the primary source of medical benefits for Americans who do not qualify for Medicare or other government-run programs. Employers provide health insurance benefits primarily to attract and retain employees. Nevertheless, faced with the rising costs of health services and products, many businesses, both small and large, have begun reconsidering their decisions to provide health insurance benefits. Employers have been faced with many uncertainties and modifications because of the increasing costs of providing health benefits to their employees. They have used many new strategies to decrease their costs such as cost shifting or cost sharing methods, consumer-directed health plans, high-deductible plans, and/or prevention or disease management plans.

Cost sharing and cost shifting have become widely accepted methods for attempting to reduce employer health costs. These initiatives ask employees to "share a higher portion of their health costs" by paying larger shares of the premium or assuming higher deductibles and/or copayments. The co-insurance initiative was introduced in the 1970s and 1980s as a method to reduce employer health costs; with this approach, employees are required to "pay a percentage of the actual cost of the healthcare services provided."[29]

Employers have also adopted consumer-directed health plans (CDHPs) to help reduce the rising costs of providing health services and products to their employees. CDHPs place more responsibility on employees and allow employees to "manage their health care spending and to make informed choices about the use of health care."[30] These plans usually come with high deductibles and consumer-controlled savings health savings accounts. Employers offer two primary types of health savings accounts: health savings accounts (HSAs) and health reimbursement accounts (HRAs). HSAs are employee-owned healthcare accounts that can be funded by employers and employees and used for qualified medical expenses. HRAs are employer-established and -funded accounts that "provide non-taxed funds that employees can use for medical expenses."[31] Employers have turned to CDHPs as a means to facilitate cutting healthcare costs by asking employees to consider costs when making decisions about their health. Health leaders must understand and navigate these complex issues while building relationships with employer stakeholders.

Prevention and disease management programs have also been created by employers to assist with reducing the costs of providing health benefits to their employees. With these programs, employers focus on disease prevention and disease management as means to avoid onset or progression of disease, with the ultimate goal being to have better-managed diseases, resulting in less absenteeism and more productive employees. Employers have faced challenges when trying to implement these prevention and disease management programs, however—namely, because of the lack of short-term cost cuts the programs offer and the generally low rates of employee utilization.[32]

Employers continually face challenges related to escalating costs as they seek the best way to provide quality health services and products to their employees. If they hope to flourish over the long term, employers also must attract and keep quality employees, who typically expect health coverage as a benefit to employment. Cost-effective benefit programs are crucial for employers to compete in the job market and obtain and retain beneficial employees. Thus, along with analyzing costs, employers must also keep in mind the quality of health benefits that their health plans provide.

Quality is an attribute that must be at the forefront for employers when making decisions about the type of health benefits to offer employees. Employers need to provide good, quality health services and product coverage to boost their probability of having healthy and productive employees. As discussed previously, many of the current trends in health design are aimed at increasing employees' power in managing their own health, a trend known as consumerism. At the same time, employers seek to provide employees with the education they need to obtain necessary, high-quality, cost-effective care and services and, in turn, become less likely to participate in treatments and services that are "unnecessary and ineffective from either a quality or cost perspective."[33]

Employers have been petitioning to have more price and quality transparency in health so that employees can make more informed decisions. Employees currently have difficulty in identifying high-quality, efficient treatment centers because of the lack of information available about quality and price. Employers have begun promoting the use of the agencies such as the National Data Cooperative and Quest Analytics to provide employees with information concerning quality and price of health services, thereby enabling patients to make informed, responsible decisions. Ideally, the widespread availability of quality and price information will assist the employees with making prudent choices for their health decisions and, in turn, save employers money.[34]

Cost and quality are two very important elements for employers to consider when choosing health benefits, but access is also critical for successful health benefit programs. Employers must provide access to the most up-to-date medicine and medical advances to help their employees manage acute and chronic illnesses; this move is intended to ensure that their workforce is as healthy—and as productive—as possible. One new concern related to recent medical advancements stems from the use of biotechnology medications, which may delay the onset of some conditions and are used to treat many high-cost diseases such as cancer. Employers have struggled with the dilemma of whether they should offer their employees access to these often exorbitantly expensive biotechnology medicines. Pitney Bowes, a large *Fortune* 500 company, found that improving employees' access to biotechnology medicines resulted in fewer acute cases, fewer hospitalizations, and less absenteeism. Therefore, it may be a profitable investment for employers to adjust their health benefits and allow employees access to biotechnology medicines and other medical advancements and technologies.[35]

Regarding access to health services and products, employers continue to search for methods of cost containment. Some have chosen not to provide any health benefits—that is, they provide no access at all. One increasingly popular way to cut back on employers' costs involves restricting or cutting health benefits for retired employees. Galvin and Delbanco report that "offering health coverage to retirees has less payback for employers" and employers can find "short-term and long-term cost savings" by taking away these benefits. Strategists suggest that this type of restriction may be just the first step for employers seeking an exit strategy. According to Galvin and Delbanco, many employers feel incapable of finding the answer to the challenge of decreasing the costs of providing health coverage to employees and believe that they would be better off getting out of the business of providing health benefits to all employees. Clearly, employers are faced with a tough challenge ahead of them in deciding whether to provide access to health services and products through employer-based insurance benefits and, if they choose to do so, in determining the most cost-effective and high-quality benefits that can be offered.[36]

PARITY OF HEALTH CARE

The Parity of Health Care is a unique model that juxtaposes two mutually exclusive models together in an interrelated medium that allows leaders to forecast the impact of new policy decisions on the organization. As previously discussed, the Parity of Health Care model incorporates the managed care quaternion and the Iron Triangle. Refer back to Figure 12–1 as this model is discussed here.

Perhaps the most significant issue the U.S. health system has grappled with since the inception of managed care, and the recent adoption of a Public Option Health Care Plan under the Obama Administration, is the balance between the business and financial priorities of care and stakeholder needs. These relationships can be conceptually viewed in the Parity of Health Care model. For example, the MCQ model helps to explain the complex interactions among employers, patients, providers, and payers in regard to partisan and competing views about health. Moreover, these health stakeholders have dissimilar views and preferences when overlaid with Kissick's Iron Triangle. The triangle comprises logistical factors of cost, quality, and access. Because each MCQ stakeholder may have different views associated with Kissick's cost, quality, and access options, the potential number of outcomes can be difficult to negotiate.

Table 12–1 demonstrates the complexity of this reality and assists in explaining why sustained consensus is difficult in developing health policy. For example, if one stakeholder (say, the payer) prioritizes cost–quality–access concerns as wanting the lowest out-of-pocket costs first, places receiving the highest quality of care possible during that low-cost visit second, and positions immediate access for that care third, it may have trouble finding a provider stakeholder with identical priorities. As Table 12–1 makes clear, stakeholders can be demanding; however, they may rarely have all three priorities sequenced in a manner that will meet a competing stakeholder's similar priorities. As can be seen in Table 12–1, even a slight variation in the prioritization of Iron Triangle options results in a myriad of interrelated and intrarelated competing priorities that can be difficult for even the stakeholders to resolve themselves, let alone in tandem with other stakeholders along the continuum of care.

The challenge for health professionals regarding employers, patients, providers, and payers is to maintain high satisfaction with each stakeholder along the continuum of care as in relation to aspects of cost, quality, and access. For example, a primary care clinic without extended and weekend office hours may be regarded as low quality by the patient and the employer, but high quality by the payers and by the providers who work in the clinic. However, if employers and patients continue to perceive lack of extended and weekend office hours as equivalent to low quality, dissatisfaction with the overall health plan may result. In a worst-case scenario, that factor might result in the termination of the health contract. Thus health professionals are in a constant struggle to maintain high satisfaction with all elements of the MCQ model.

TABLE 12–1 Parity of Health Care Model: Competing Priorities of Stakeholders

Payer	Patient
Cost–quality–access	Access–cost–quality
Access–cost–quality	Quality–access–cost
Quality–access–cost	Quality–cost–access
Quality–cost–access	Access–quality–cost
Access–quality–cost	Cost–access–quality
Cost–access–quality	Cost–quality–access
Employer	**Provider**
Access–quality–cost	Quality–cost–access
Cost–access–quality	Access–quality–cost
Cost–quality–access	Cost–access–quality
Access–cost–quality	Cost–quality–access
Quality–access–cost	Access–cost–quality
Quality–cost–access	Quality–access–cost

Another example of the complexity of relationships can be seen by revisiting the example of construct development in Chapter 3. Consider the phrase "the right to bear arms" as an example of the complexity surrounding the meaning of multiple-construct propositional phrases. For more than 200 years, the greatest scholars and minds in the United States have debated on the true meaning of the founding fathers' objective in granting the "right to bear arms" to the American people. However, as we can see if we further deconstruct the propositional phrase the "right to bear arms," we can easily see that this phrase has three related propositional constructs applied to one unit of analysis. That one unit of analysis is "people," and since people have differing opinions of priorities, meanings, terminology, and application, we can begin to see why the phrase "the right to bear arms" is so complex. By comparison, understanding and applying the Parity of the Health Care model is many more times as complex, due to the addition of four distinct units of analysis competing over three different logistical priorities. The factorial nature of competing priorities within this model results in more than 500 potential combinations of echelon rankings among all stakeholders—now that is complexity! Given this complexity associated with forecasting only one stakeholder's priorities over a sustained period of time, it becomes clear why it is so challenging for health leaders to accurately predict all future needs for all stakeholders.

The Sword of Damocles

In understanding the difficult nature of the relationships between the Iron Triangle and the managed care quaternion, we offer a metaphor from classical literature called the *Sword of Damocles*. In Greek mythology, the Sword of Damocles represents ever-present peril. It is also used as a metaphor to suggest a frailty in existing relationships. For example, in the Parity of Health Care model, the Sword of Damocles represents an inability of any one stakeholder to reach sustained consensus on the priorities assigned to healthcare cost, quality, and access. With health priorities constantly changing due to environmental demands, it is no wonder why agreements on health policy are difficult to reach. However, an understanding of the Parity of Health Care model can be helpful to health leaders for strategically forecasting threats to relationships amid stakeholders, while also balancing priorities among those stakeholders. If anything is apparent, it is that continuous external and internal assessment and evaluation and relationship building among stakeholders are critical to leadership success.

Health planners must be cognizant that solutions developed to solve health problems in the current environment may not be valid solutions to tomorrow's new issues. As environmental demands continue to place pressures on the relationships within the parity of health care, health leaders must renegotiate priorities. Health planners and leaders should be aware of this fact and view change as a new opportunity for success and not simply problems of the dynamic environment. Always consider that the Sword of Damocles represents the frailty of established relationships among stakeholders, and that constant maintenance and attention are required to ensure that these relationships remain healthy.

SUMMARY

Organizations and organizational leaders cannot be successful if they do not understand the wide-ranging impact of stakeholder influence. All too often in health policy making and strategy analysis, organizations become overly concerned with isolating themselves (i.e., the organization) as the principal actor from which all other factors revolve. Such was the case with Enron and WorldCom, which viewed customers, allies, employees, and investors as tertiary catalysts and insignificant stakeholders in the quest for growth and wealth. Health organizations are no different, regardless of whether they have for-profit or not-for-profit status. Stakeholder dynamics are critically important in organizational survival and success. To be successful in the competitive economy of the twenty-first century, health leaders must be cognizant of stakeholder dynamics and appreciate how the principal actors and components of each interrelate and influence one another. Health leader success will be in large part determined by developing and maintaining relationships with stakeholders and by aligning the health organization based on external and internal assessment and evaluation.

DISCUSSION QUESTIONS

1. What are the steps, characteristics, and behaviors a health leader should take to build relationships with internal, "interface," and external stakeholders?

2. What is the Parity of Health Care model? Explain its usefulness to health leaders.

3. Select a health organization stakeholder and predict at least two motivations of that stakeholder considering cost, quality, and access to health services and products. Are the stakeholder's issues justified?

4. Which issues arise when you compare and contrast at least two internal health organization stakeholder motivations and issues? How does a health leader empathize with those stakeholders to build a relationship?

5. Using previously discussed theories and models, which two or more theories or models would you use to construct a practical stakeholder management and relationship development model? Which constructs make those theories or models useful in stakeholder management?

6. Which theory or model would you use to evaluate internal and external health organization stakeholders? How do those theories or models justify stakeholder motivations, needs, and aspirations with regard to health services and products?

7. Why was the Parity of Health model developed? What utility, advantages, and strengths does it offer to forecasting stakeholder dynamics in health care?

EXERCISES

1. In a one- to two-page paper, identify the steps, characteristics, and behaviors a health leader should take to build relationships with internal, "interface," and external stakeholders.

2. In a one-page paper, explain the Parity of Health Care model and describe its usefulness to health leaders.

3. Construct a health organization stakeholder list. In a two-page paper, predict at least two motivations of each stakeholder, considering cost, quality, and access to health services and products.

4. In a one- to two-page paper, compare and contrast internal health organization stakeholder motivations and issues.

5. In a three-page paper, using previously discussed theories and models, combine two or more theories or models into a practical stakeholder management and relationship development model.

6. In a two-page paper, evaluate an internal health organization stakeholder and an external health organization stakeholder and justify their motivations, needs, and aspirations with regard to health services and products.

REFERENCES

1. Griffith, J. R., & White, K. R. (2007). *The well-managed healthcare organization* (6th ed.). Chicago: Health Administration Press.

2. Young, A. E., Wasiak, R., Roessler, R. T., McPherson, K. M., Anema, J. R., & van Poppel, M. N. M. (2005). Return-to-work outcomes following work disability: Stakeholder motivation, interests and concerns. *Journal of Occupational Rehabilitation, 15*(4), 543–556.

3. Franche, R. L., Baril, R., Shaw, W., Nicholas, M., & Loisel, P. (2005). Workplace-based return-to-work interventions: Optimizing the role of stakeholders in implementation and research. *Journal of Occupational Rehabilitation, 15*(4), 525–542.

4. Blair, J. D., & Fottler, M. D. (1998). *Strategic leadership for medical groups: Navigating your strategic web.* San Francisco: Jossey-Bass.

5. Griffith & White, note 1.

6. Blair & Fottler, note 4.

7. Coppola, M. N., Erckenbrack, D., & Ledlow, G. R. (2008). Stakeholder dynamics. In J. A. Johnson, *Health organizations: Theory, behavior, and development* (pp. 255–275). Sudbury, MA: Jones and Bartlett.

8. Coppola, M. N., Harrison, J., Kerr, B., & Erckenbrack, D. (2007). The military managed care health system. In P. R. Kongstvedt (Ed.), *Essentials of managed care* (5th ed., pp. 633–655). Sudbury, MA: Jones and Bartlett.

9. Kissick, W. L. (1994). The past is prologue. In *Medicine's dilemmas: Infinite needs versus finite resources.* New Haven, CT: Yale University Press.

10. Griffith & White, note 1.

11. Antos, J. (2007, April 10). Saving Medicare from a fiscal breakdown. *Real Clear Politics.* Retrieved November 15, 2008, from http://www.realclearpolitics.com/articles/2007/04/saving_medicare_from_a_fiscal.html.

12. Antos, note 11.

13. Smeltzer, S. C., & Bare, B. G. (2004). *Medical surgical nursing* (10th ed.). Philadelphia: Lippincott.

14. Coppola et al., note 7.

15. Smeltzer & Bare, note 13.

16. Smeltzer & Bare, note 13.

17. Eysenbach, G., & Kohler, C. (2002). How do consumers search for and appraise health Information on the World Wide Web? Qualitative study using focus groups, Usability tests, and in-depth interviews [Electronic version]. *British Medical Journal, 324,* 573–577.

18. Press, I. (2006). *Patient satisfaction: Understanding and managing the experience of care* (2nd ed.). Chicago: Health Administration Press

19. Press, note 18.

20. Institute of Medicine. (2006, July 20). Crossing the quality chasm: The IOM health care initiative. Retrieved October 15, 2008, from http://www.iom.edu/CMS/8089.aspx.

21. Rust, G., Ye, J., Baltrus, P., Daniels, E., Adesunloye, B., & Fryer, G. E. (2008). Practical barriers to timely primary care access: Impact on adult use of emergency department services. *Archives of Internal Medicine, 168*(15), 1705–1710.

22. Retrieved August 29, 2009, from http://www.census.gov.

23. Bodenheimer, T. (2005). High and rising health care costs. Part 3: The role of health care providers. *Annals of Internal Medicine, 142,* 996–1002.

24. Chaudhry, B., Wang, J., Wu, S., Maglione, M., Mojica, W., Roth, E., et al. (2006). Systematic review: Impact of health information technology on quality, efficiency, and costs of medical care. *Annals of Internal Medicine, 144,* E12–E22.

25. Harris, K. M. (2002). Can high quality overcome consumer resistance to restricted provider access? Evidence from a health plan choice experiment. *Health Services Research, 37*(3), 551–571.

26. Rosenthal, M. B., Fernandopulle, R., Song, H. R., & Landon, B. (2004). Paying for quality: Providers' incentives for quality improvements. *Health Affairs, 23*(2), 127–141.

27. Galvin, R., & Delbanco, S. (2006). Between a rock and a hard place: Understanding the employer mind-set. *Health Affairs, 25*(6), 1548–1555.

28. Bruno, M. (April 23, 2008). Employers almost universally against universal healthcare. *Financial Week.* Retrieved November 2008 from http://financialweek.com/apps/pbcs.dll/article?AID=/20080423/REG/210997508/1008/HUMANRESOURCES.

29. Hodge, B., & Martin, M. (2008). Benefit design critical to protecting out-of-pocket costs for employees. *American Journal of Managed Care, 14*(8), S246–S251.

30. Galvin & Delbanco, note 27.

31. Claxton, G. (2006). Consumer-directed health plans: Health Care Marketplace Project. Kaiser Family Foundation. Retrieved November 26, 2008, from http://www.kaiseredu.org/tutorials/CDHP/Consumer-Directed.ppt#291,1,Consumer-Directed Health Plans.

32. Claxton, note 31.

33. DiCenzo, J., & Fronstin, P. (2008). Lessons from the evolution of 401(k) retirement plans for increased consumerism in health care: An application of behavioral research. *Employee Benefit Research Institute Issue Brief, 320*(1), 3–26.

34. Griffith, J. R., & White, K. R. (2006). *The well-managed healthcare organization* (6th ed., pp 415–465). Chicago, IL: Health Administration Press.

35. Horn, D., Mahoney, J., Wells, K., & Lednar, W. (2008). Leading employers share strategies for managing promising, high-cost biotech medications. *American Journal of Managed Care, 14*(8), S264–268.

36. Galvin Galvin & Delbanco, note 27.

Leading People and Managing Resources into the Future

13

Complexity, Speed, and Change: Leadership Challenges for the Next Decade

Great necessity elevates man; petty necessity casts him down.
—Goethe, *Wisdom and Experience*

This chapter discusses the globalization of leadership, taking into account that many leadership theories and practices presented in this book are based on Western ideologies. The need to leverage technology, lead through followership, and understand the basics of influence and power are addressed in respect to climate, culture change, and environment, along with suggested strategies for utilization by the health leader.

LEARNING OBJECTIVES

1. Describe and outline issues related to globalization, power, followership, and culture change from a health leader's perspective.

2. Give examples of tools that a health leader can use to change and adapt culture in the health organization.

3. Relate global leadership style differences and similarities using appropriate constructs to transformational leadership practices.

4. Analyze a health leader's use of power as it relates to followership, culture change, and knowledge management.

5. Categorize global leadership differences according to a leader's use of power, technology, and knowledge management.

6. Evaluate approaches to knowledge management, organizational learning, and transformational leadership with health organization culture change.

CULTURAL DIFFERENCES IN LEADERSHIP

As globalization increases, health leaders need to be culturally aware, understanding, and capable of leading people from diverse backgrounds. In today's global economy, it is commonplace for subordinates, peers, and superiors to be from different geographic, national, and cultural backgrounds. Likewise, patients, customers, and their families are growing more diverse. This trend requires a culturally competent and adaptive perspective for both the health leader and the health organizational culture the leader maintains. It adds complexity to the health leader's landscape from both internal and external environmental perspectives. In turn, this complexity lends credence to demands for a dynamic culture leadership mentality and process to create a robust organizational culture amid an environment of change—the speed of change is also increasing.

Globalization causes concern when discussing differing perceptions across cultures:

■ Individualist (self oriented) and collectivist (team oriented) cultures will have significantly different perceptions of work and performance.

■ Power distance (higher power means more physical space): High-power cultures tend to be authoritarian, whereas power is more equally distributed in low-power cultures.

■ Uncertainty avoidance (risk taking and plan implementation without all information and organizational coupling) is thick with rules and guidelines.

■ Gender equality: Assertive, material, and competitive cultures tend to be masculine, whereas collaborative, harmonious, and nurturing cultures take on a feminine persona.

■ High-context communication cultures transfer meaning with more emphasis on the situation, whereas low-context communication cultures emphasize the sender's responsibility to transfer communication meaning more than the situation.[1]

Situational leadership applications fit nicely in the paradigm of a culturally competent leader considering the complexity of globalization. Leadership expectations differ depending on the culture, society, nation, or ethnic group to which leaders belong (and reside and practice). It is difficult to find much in the literature on leadership outside the "Western" perspective, for example. The Western perspective in the literature is predominately based on research conducted in the United States, the United Kingdom, Australia, or Europe. "To date [as of 2004] more than 90% of the organizational behavior [including leadership] literature reflects U.S.-based research and theory."[2]

In an attempt to bridge Western and Eastern thought on leadership, the new paradigm of "thinkers" in an interconnected world has evolved. Health leaders who are successful have many of the characteristics encompassed by this new paradigm:

■ Thinking in open systems in contrast with fixed, ideal states

■ Integration of multicultural characteristics into decision making

■ Viewing things globally (acting locally)

■ Global distribution

■ Use of technology to scan the environment

■ A full tool box and knowledge of how to use all of the tools

■ Personal characteristics of resourcefulness, fearlessness, toughness, competence, humor, and playfulness[3]

With this introduction, the most recent worldwide study on leadership, the GLOBE Study, is presented.

GLOBE LEADERSHIP STUDY[4, 5]

The most comprehensive global assessment of leadership styles, propensities, and expectations is an ongoing project called the GLOBE Study; to date, 170 researchers from 62 cultures have worked on this project.[6] Much of the GLOBE Study cultural constructs were derived from the previous work of Hofstede.[7] The following constructs used in the study pertain to cultural variation:

■ Performance orientation (How aggressive is task accomplishment?)

■ Assertiveness (How forceful and firm is the leader?)

- Future orientation (Is tomorrow more important than yesterday or today?)

- Humane orientation (People oriented, compassionate, and empathetic?)

- Institutional collectivism (Is the total organization a "team"?)

- In-group collectivism (Is there a small-group orientation?)

- Gender egalitarianism (Are males and females equal in respect, reward, and punishment?)

- Power distance (How much physical space is normal based on the leader's or person's perceived power?)

- Uncertainty avoidance (How risk adverse is the leader? Does implementation of a plan or task proceed without all information? How intuitive is the leader?)[8]

In the study, each construct embodied a set of variables pertinent to the construct. Findings were based on each construct. Although a summary and highlights are presented in this chapter, it is recommended that health leaders read and study the findings of the entire GLOBE Study[9]; the research can be found at the Web page cited in the references.

The cultural dimension named "performance orientation" emerged from the research as exceptionally important. It "reflects the extent to which a community encourages and rewards innovation, high standards, excellence, and performance improvement"[10] A few of the characteristics of societies that have high and low performance orientation are described in **Table 13–1**.

The cultural dimension named "uncertainty avoidance" also emerged from the research as very important; it is "the extent to which a society, organization, or group relies on social norms, rules, and procedures to alleviate the unpredictability of future events."[11] "An alternative way of thinking about uncertainty avoidance is that it's about the extent to which ambiguous situations are felt as threatening (about the extent to which deliberate measures such as making and enforcing rules and procedures are taken to reduce ambiguity)."[12] Some characteristics of societies that have high and low uncertainty avoidance orientation are provided in **Table 13–2**.

As for leadership styles, 21 constructs, each having a set of variables that were measured, were found valid in interpreting leadership style and performance across all 62 societies, which were clustered in 10 societal groups. Leadership styles were categorized and measured by 6 groupings of the 21 constructs:

- Charismatic/value based

- Team oriented

- Participative

- Autonomous

- Humane

- Self-protective[13]

TABLE 13–1   High and Low Performance Orientation Societal Characteristics

High performance orientation societies have characteristics such as . . .	Low performance orientation societies have characteristics such as . . .
• Value training and development	• Value societal and family relationships
• Value competitiveness and materialism	• Value harmony with the environment
• View formal feedback as necessary for performance improvement	• View formal feedback as judgmental and discomforting
• Value what one does more than who one is	• Value who one is more than what one does
• Expect direct, explicit communication	• Expect indirect, subtle communication

Sources: House, R. J., Hanges, P. J., Javidan, M., Dorfman, P. W., & Gupta, V. (Eds.). (2004). *Culture, leadership and organizations: The GLOBE Study of 62 societies.* Thousand Oaks, CA: Sage, p. 245, Table 12.1; and Grovewell, LLC. Retrieved June 6, 2009, from http://www.grovewell.com/pub-GLOBE-dimensions.html. Reprinted with permission.

TABLE 13–2   High and Low Uncertainty Avoidance Societal Characteristics

High uncertainty avoidance societies have characteristics such as . . .	Low uncertainty avoidance societies have characteristics such as . . .
• Use formality in interactions with others	• Use informality in interactions with others
• Are orderly and keep meticulous records	• Are less orderly and keep fewer records
• Rely on formalized policies and procedures	• Rely on informal norms for most matters
• Take moderate, carefully calculated risks	• Are less calculating when taking risks
• Show strong resistance to change	• Show only moderate resistance to change

Sources: House, R. J., Hanges, P. J., Javidan, M., Dorfman, P. W., & Gupta, V. (Eds.). (2004). *Culture, leadership and organizations: The GLOBE Study of 62 societies*. Thousand Oaks, CA: Sage, p. 618, Table 19.1; and Grovewell, LLC. Retrieved June 6, 2009, from http://www.grovewell.com/pub-GLOBE-dimensions.html. Reprinted with permission.

From the associated constructs or traits (**Table 13–3**), each leadership grouping or style can be "defined" for the purpose of making comparisons between the styles. There is considerable overlap in some of the styles. Can you develop a continuum of preferred/desirable to less preferred/undesirable leadership styles based on the constructs?

> Much of the analysis in the book [and Web page] is focused on explaining how the nine cultural dimensions (e.g., "performance orientation," "assertiveness," and seven others) as *independent* variables relate to the six culturally endorsed leadership theory dimensions (e.g., "charismatic/value based," "team oriented," and four others) as *dependent* variables across the 10 societal clusters.[15]

A summary of each style used in the GLOBE study is provided in **Table 13–4**; the cultural constructs are listed in priority for each style as either positively related (+) or negatively related (–). Can you relate this aspect of the GLOBE Leadership Study to earlier leadership behavior-based studies such as the Michigan or Ohio State

TABLE 13–3   The Six Global Leadership Groupings/Styles and Associated Constructs in the GLOBE Study[14]

Charismatic/Value Based	Team Oriented	Self-Protective
• Charismatic/visionary	• Team collaborative	• Self-centered
• Charismatic/inspirational	• Team integrative	• Status conscious
• Charismatic/self-sacrificing	• Diplomatic	• Conflict inducer
• Has integrity	• Malevolent	• Face saver
• Decisive	• Administratively competent	• Procedural
• Performance oriented		

Participative	Humane Oriented	Autonomous
• Autocratic	• Modest	• Autonomous
• Nonparticipative	• Humane oriented	

Sources: House, R. J., Hanges, P. J., Javidan, M., Dorfman, P. W., & Gupta, V. (Eds.). (2004). *Culture, leadership and organizations: The GLOBE Study of 62 societies*. Thousand Oaks, CA: Sage, p. 676, Table 21.1; and Grovewell, LLC. Retrieved June 6, 2009, from http://www.grovewell.com/pub-GLOBE-dimensions.html. Reprinted with permission.

TABLE 13—4   GLOBE Study Cultural Constructs Associated to Leadership Style

Charismatic/ Value-Based Leadership Style	Team-Oriented Leadership Style	Participative Leadership Style	Humane-Oriented Leadership Style	Autonomous Leadership Style	Self-Protective Leadership Style
Performance orientation (+)	Uncertainty avoidance (+)	Performance orientation (+)	Humane orientation (+)	Performance orientation (+)	Power distance (+)
In-group collectivism (+)	In-group collectivism (+)	Gender egalitarianism (+)	Uncertainty avoidance (+)		Uncertainty avoidance (+)
Gender egalitarianism (+)	Humane orientation (+)	Humane orientation (+)	Assertiveness (+)		
Future orientation (+)	Performance orientation (+)		Performance orientation (+)		
Humane orientation (+)	Future orientation (+)		Future orientation (+)		
Power distance (−)	None	Uncertainty avoidance (−)	None	Humane orientation (−)	Gender egalitarianism (−)
		Power distance (−)		Institutional collectivism (−)	In-group collectivism (−)
		Assertiveness (−)			Performance orientation (−)

Source: House, R. J., Hanges, P. J., Javidan, M., Dorfman, P. W., & Gupta, V. (Eds.). (2004). *Culture, leadership and organizations: The GLOBE Study of 62 societies.* Thousand Oaks, CA: Sage, pp. 46—48. Reprinted with permission.

leadership studies? Which other leadership theories or models can be integrated with the GLOBE Study? How do the constructs or traits that define or describe each leadership style in Table 13–3 connect to the cultural constructs?

This charismatic/value-based style, which is employed by leaders who are inspiring, visionary, self-sacrificing, and performance oriented, was universally considered the most desirable style.[16] The team-oriented leadership style and the participative leadership style were nearly universally desirable as styles, albeit not in all societal clusters.[17] Autonomous and humane-oriented (modest and compassionate) leadership styles were neither desirable nor undesirable in most societal cultures and clusters.[18] The self-protective leadership style (self-centered, status conscious, and conflict inducer) was undesirable.[19] "Attributes that facilitate, such as decisiveness, and inhibit, such as irritability, outstanding leadership"[20] were consistent across the study.

Highlights of the GLOBE study by societal groups show the diversity in leadership style preferences, expectations, and societal norms. Ten societal clusters were identified in the study, but some of these clusters will be combined for purposes of their review in this chapter.

Western Perspective[21]

The Western perspective of leadership styles, for this summary, includes Germanic Europe, Anglo, and Nordic Europe clusters. For these Western clusters, charismatic/value–based leadership was the most preferred and desirable leadership style, followed by the team-oriented leadership style. Very close in preference to the team-oriented style was the participative leadership style. Significantly less preferred and less desirable was the humane-oriented leadership style. The autonomous and self-protective leadership styles were not preferred and not desired for this perspective. Thus, in priority of preference, the Western perspective favored the charismatic/value–based style, team-oriented style, and participative style of leadership. The humane-oriented style was preferred or desired to only a minor degree, while the autonomous and self-protected styles were not preferred or desired.

Translating the Western perspective into modern leadership theories and models, transformational leadership, the omnibus leadership model, and the dynamic culture leadership model are readily integrated into this perspective. In balancing leadership emphasis between performance (mission accomplishment) and concern for people, having a team orientation, looking toward the future (vision achievement), and understanding a dynamic environment, there is considerable congruence between these models and the Western perspective of leadership style preference. Are there other leadership theories, models, principles, or competencies that integrate well with, or support, this perspective?

Asian Perspective[22]

The Asian perspective of leadership styles includes the Confucian Asia (China, close neighbors of China, Japan, and close neighbors of Japan) and Southern Asia (from Afghanistan to Vietnam, including the southern belt of Asian countries) clusters. For these Asian clusters, charismatic/value–based leadership was the most preferred and desirable leadership style, followed by the team-oriented leadership style. Next in preference to the team-oriented style was the humane-oriented leadership style. Significantly less preferred and less desirable was the participative leadership style. The autonomous and self-protective leadership styles were not preferred and not desired for this perspective, yet were more readily tolerated than in the Western perspective. Thus, in priority of preference, the Asian perspective favored the charismatic/value–based style, team-oriented style, and humane-oriented style of leadership. The participative style was preferred or desired to only a moderate degree. The autonomous and self-protected styles were not preferred or desired, but are more readily tolerated by the Asian perspective than by the Western perspective.

Modern leadership theories and models salient for the Asian perspective could include transformational leadership, the "reframing organizational leadership" model, the omnibus leadership model, the dynamic culture leadership model, and an older theory, Theory Y (from behavioral leadership models). Can you match and integrate these contemporary leadership theories and models to the Asian perspective based on the GLOBE Study findings?

Middle Eastern Perspective[23]

For the Middle Eastern perspective of preferred leadership styles, the cluster includes the land mass from southern Turkey to Iran to northwest Africa to the Mediterranean Sea. In this societal cluster, team-oriented leadership, and then charismatic/value–based leadership, were the most preferred styles. Participative and humane-oriented leadership styles were moderately preferred, while self-protective and autonomous leadership styles were least preferred. Tolerance for the self-protective leadership style mimicked the Asian perspective, while autonomous leadership was the least desired leadership style.

Modern leadership theories and models that integrate well with the Middle Eastern perspective would include the dynamic culture leadership model, transformational leadership, and the omnibus leadership model. Can you match and integrate these contemporary leadership theories and models to the Middle Eastern perspective based on the GLOBE Study findings?

Latin Perspective[24]

In terms of the Latin perspective of preferred leadership styles, the cluster includes Latin America and Latin Europe (southern Europe bordering the Mediterranean Sea). In this group, charismatic/value–based leadership was the most preferred and desirable leadership style, followed by the team-oriented leadership style. Next in preference to the team oriented style was the participative leadership style. Significantly less preferred and less desirable was the human-oriented leadership style. The autonomous and self-protective leadership styles were not preferred and not desired for this perspective. The Latin and Western perspectives are very similar based on the results of this study.

Which leadership theories and models can you relate to the Latin leadership perspective? Can you list the characteristics of the theories and models in terms of the preferred leadership styles of the Latin societal cluster?

African Perspective[25]

The African perspective covers sub-Saharan Africa. It is similar to the Western and Latin perspectives, although the humane-oriented leadership style was more preferred in African cultures than in Western or Latin cultures. Charismatic/value–based leadership was the most preferred and desirable leadership style, followed by the team-oriented leadership style. Next in preference to the team-oriented style was the participative leadership style. Slightly less preferred and less desirable was the human-oriented leadership style. The autonomous and self-protective leadership styles were not preferred and not desired for this perspective.

Eastern European Perspective[26]

The Eastern European perspective includes eastern Germany (former East Germany) to Russia and south to the Balkans (in essence, countries in the former Eastern European Bloc or Communist Bloc). This perspective is similar to the Middle Eastern perspective, where team-oriented leadership, and then charismatic/value–based leadership, were the most preferred styles. Participative and humane-oriented leadership styles were moderately preferred, while the self-protective leadership style was least preferred. Tolerance for the autonomous leadership style was the greatest in the Eastern European perspective as compared to all other societal groups; this style was not preferred but would be considered a more neutral style.

GLOBE Summary

The major theme that health leaders need to understand, apply, and synthesize from the international research on leadership is that charisma, values, team orientation, and performance matter. Health leaders should focus on accomplishing the mission, striving for the vision of the organization, leading people and managing resources, and mastering and applying sound practices of leadership (leadership competencies); these demands are vitally important for leaders across the globe.

This section reviews the constructs or traits that are highly prized and accepted across the world. Culturally sensitive health leaders should strive to have the following characteristics:

- Charismatic and visionary
- Charismatic and inspirational
- Charismatic and self-sacrificing
- Consistently able to lead with integrity
- Decisive
- Performance oriented
- Team collaborative
- Team integrative
- Diplomatic
- Benevolent
- Administratively competent

As a health leader, it is inevitable that you will lead and work with persons from different countries, from different societies, and from different backgrounds. To demonstrate cultural competence, respect and understanding of different ways of doing things, different expectations, and different perspectives is essential. The leadership challenge is to integrate these differences into the group and organization while focusing on the mission (performance orientation), striving for the vision (future orientation), communicating well (visionary and integrating people into the mission and vision), leading people well and genuinely (charisma and humane-orientation), managing resources effectively (administrative competence), building teams (team orientation), and being diplomatic, yet decisive.

The health leader needs to accomplish these tasks—a big set of tasks—within a solid moral framework built on truth, honesty, and integrity. Without morality, integrity, and honesty, regardless of cultural perspective, the leader's work is meaningless. In simple terms, the health leader must develop and maintain an organizational culture that fulfills the mission and vision while incorporating the vast diversity and complexity that the world holds within a sound ethical framework. The health leader must accomplish this feat in an environment of dynamic change while meeting and exceeding the professional standards of care and health administration.

LEVERAGING TECHNOLOGY

Leveraging technology in a health organization, like the practice of leadership itself, creates competitive advantage—that is, more effectiveness, efficiency, and efficacy—in the practice of medicine, in the clinical environment of care, in patient outcomes, and in the administration of the enterprise. In the health context, technology is anything that is utilized in the practice of medicine, in patient care processes, and in the leading of people and management of resources. Examples of technology, in an attempt to cover the enormity of the term, include chairs, computers, harmonic scalpels, MRIs, patient beds, knowledge of and the process of budgeting, computer software, a forklift, an intercom system, pagers, cell phones, knowledge of and the process of diagnosing disease, and utilization of media richness theory for improved communication. Technology is encompassed in the following definitions: the practical application of knowledge, especially in a particular area; a manner of accomplishing a task, especially using technical processes, methods, or knowledge; and a capability given by the practical application of knowledge.[27]

Technology, especially networked computer technology, can be leveraged by the health leader and the leadership team to facilitate communication so as to better lead people; to scan and monitor the efficiency, effectiveness, and efficacy of the organization; and to manage resources. True individual health leader technology leverage comes when the leader can allocate more time to interpersonal relationship building, both internal and external to the organization; "leadership by purposefully walking" around and talking to subordinates, peers, and superiors; and establishing a balance in the leader's religious, professional, social, and personal life.

Technology is constantly evolving, increasing the complexity and speed of change. "The nature of the work or technology is changing and subordinates need to learn new skills and procedures."[28] Yukl and Fiedler consider technology to be an important situational variable in their respective leadership models, the multiple linkage model[29] and the contingency leadership model.[30] Likewise, technology is a critical situational variable—one that affects ambiguity—in the garbage can model of decision making.[31] Schein identifies technology as an element in the category of artifact and creation of culture (a Level 1 element).[32]

Health leaders should be cognizant of putting sound clinical and business practices into place, focusing on both the human and technological elements, to leverage technology most effectively.

> Exercising leadership requires distinguishing between leadership and authority and between technical and adaptive/operational work. Clarifying these two distinctions enables us to understand why so many people in top authority positions fail to lead: they commit the classic error of treating adaptive challenges as if they were technical problems.[33]

Simply put, fixing a problem by changing or increasing the technology most likely will not work, but rather will further confound the problem. Human adaption to quality clinical and business processes, linked to organizational culture, needs to be effective, efficient, and efficacious such that technology can be leveraged to complement and merge as seamlessly as possible to the people the health leader leads.

> Health organization structure and control systems can no longer be depicted as tools that mechanically determine subordinates' and team members' behaviors. Health leaders must shift their thinking about organizations away from the organization as an entity, to subordinates' choice and understanding.[34]

How subordinates and team members fit into the processes and work with the technology needs to be communicated, documented, trained for, and continuously improved. Health leaders in this environment cannot assume that "cookie-cutter" methods will suffice, but instead must learn and become effective in developing teams of professionals within dynamic cultures. To appreciate the dynamic nature of organizations today, one need simply consider the realities of human diversity, information overload, the evolution of technology, the sophistication of the consumer, and e-commerce; many of these changes are rooted in technological advances.

Creating a health organization culture in which subordinates, team members, and leaders alike keep current with technological advances and best practices in clinical and administrative arenas is paramount. In their assessment of great groups or teams, Bennis and Biederman suggest that teams whose members want to excel desire new technology. Technology is embraced—the newer and the better—because creating the future is exciting.[35] Health leaders can leverage this excitement and enthusiasm by creating a conducive culture aligned with the organization's mission and vision, communicating how people fit in with the technology employed, fostering a continuous learning emphasis, and developing systems of learning and knowledge management.

LEADERS AS FOLLOWERS

Every health leader was, most likely, a follower at some point. In fact, a health leader is likely to be simultaneously both a leader and a follower. Knowing what role you are in within a given situation and context is clearly important. The most successful health leaders were, and are, great followers. As a health leader, which traits, attitudes, and characteristics do you like to see in a follower? Good followers have a great attitude; commit to their responsibilities; complete their assigned (and at times unassigned) tasks; communicate to superiors, peers, and subordinates well and often; are loyal; and focus on the mission and vision of the organization within the appropriate strategies, goals, objectives, and action steps in their purview. Great followers are honest, are moral, and put the organization's success ahead of their own interests. In many ways, great followers have attributes of great leaders.

Being a "transformational follower" means you are positively contagious to others as a role model. Transformational followers have a service "charisma," focus on the leader or leadership's organizational agenda and work to achieve it, communicate and follow up with all connected to their responsibilities and work, are loyal to leadership and the organization, stay appropriately coupled to the organizational norms and expectations, and deliver quality performance within a moral foundation.

The best method to understand how a health leader can be a great follower is to ask your superior, your leader, what his or her expectations for you are regarding followership. Leadership requires followership; followership requires leadership. Many of the same attributes of leadership pertain to followership, except that the leader sets the agenda and tempo for the follower's work and work environment. Being a great health follower goes hand in hand with being a great health leader.

POWER, INFLUENCE, AND THE BASIS OF POWER

Power is a leader's or agent's capacity to influence another person's, group's, or organization's values, beliefs, attitudes, and behaviors. Using power to influence a change of behaviors is less difficult than changing attitudes; attitudes are less difficult to change than either beliefs or values. Power and influence can be characterized in several ways; the two methods presented here are the most universal.

Power can be discussed in terms of Kelman's social influence theory[36, 37] and the process of social influence. Power and influence, serving as a catalyst, prompt three responses to varying degrees; that is, the subordinate or target of a leader's power- and influence-based request or requirement many demonstrate instrumental compliance, internalization, and/or identification.

- Instrumental compliance is defined as a subordinate's or target person's fulfillment of the leader's requested action for the purpose of obtaining a tangible reward or avoiding a punishment controlled by the agent. This is an example of transactional leadership in action from a foundation of the social exchange theory.

- Internalization is defined as a subordinate or target person's commitment to support and implement requests (and actions required to fulfill the request) made by the leader because they are perceived to be intrinsically desirable and correct in relation to the target's values, beliefs, attitudes, and self-image. In this response, the request or proposal becomes integrated with the target person's underlying values and beliefs. It is an example of transformational leadership in action.

- Identification is defined as s subordinate's or target person's imitation of the leader's behavior and/or adoption of the same attitudes to please the leader. This is an example of social learning theory in action, closely linked to role modeling.

Another method to consider in terms of the use of power and influence on subordinates, peers, stakeholders, and possibly superiors results in three possibilities: commitment, compliance, or resistance.

- Commitment occurs when the person, group members, or organizational members who are the focus of power and influence from the leader internally agree with a decision or request from the leader; they then implement an approach to fulfill the request or implement the decision effectively, efficiently, and efficaciously. Commitment implies attitude change in the subordinates.

- Compliance occurs when the person, group members, or organizational members are willing to do what the leader desires but in a mechanical or apathetic manner, applying only moderate to minimal effort. Compliance implies that the subordinate's behavior, but not his or her attitude, has changed due to the leader's influence.

- Resistance happens when organizational members are opposed to the leader's request and actively avoid carrying it out, perhaps even taking steps to block actions to fulfill the leader's request.

Of course, there are varying degrees of commitment, compliance, and resistance. Health leaders should assess the organizational culture and the individual team member's personal impact and perception, such as with the coordinated management of meaning model discussed in Chapter 5, when using power and influence, and should plan accordingly. Obviously, health leaders want commitment and at least compliance, while eliminating resistance.

The most recognized basis of power and influence comes from French and Raven's Power Taxonomy. **Table 13–5** is presented in tandem with Kelman's model for purposes of synthesis and comparison.

Agenda power—the authority and control of agenda items—is similar to information power but can be recognized as a source of power as well: Consider the secretary's or assistant's control of meeting agenda items on behalf of the leader (superior). Moreover, health leaders have power from legitimate or formal power, also called position power: "Position power includes potential influence derived from legitimate authority, control over resources and rewards, control over punishments, control over information, and control over the organization of the work and the physical work environment."[38]

Power is maintained, if not increased, by wise use of power. The use of power is particularly important in organizational culture; who controls resources, who receives those resources, and how resources are used contribute to the cultural disposition of the organization. Bolman and Deal, in their reframing organizational leadership model (specifically, under the "political" construct), overtly suggest that leaders must use power and resource distribution wisely. Again, consistent and predetermined leadership actions, when using power and distributing resources, are paramount to ensure leader success.

Power and influence, and the basis of power, change in all organizations. "Power is not static; it changes over time due to changing conditions and the actions of individuals and coalitions."[39] Subcultures in health organizations have also been shown to create and build resistance to power, influence, and change.[40] Controlling your emotions is "power's crucial foundation"[41] across all professional situations. Health leaders who control their emotional "self," are cognizant of their sources and level of power, and who are sensitive to subcultures in the organization and to sources and level of power in others, will best navigate amid coalitions and groups in moving the health organization forward in a positive direction.

TABLE 13–5   French and Raven's Power Taxonomy and Kelman's Power and Influence Outcomes

French and Raven's Power Taxonomy	Description	Kelman's Influence Processes
Reward	Person complies to obtain rewards controlled by the agent	Instrumental compliance
Coercive	Person complies to avoid punishment by the agent	Instrumental compliance
Legitimate (also called formal)	Person complies because the agent has the right to make the request; person is under the chain of authority	Instrumental compliance, internalization, and identification
Expert	Person complies because the agent has special knowledge	Internalization
Referent	Person complies because he or she admires or identifies with the agent and wants the agent's approval	Identification
Information*	Control of information by agent is source of power	

*Added by Yukl.

Sources: French, J. R. P., & Raven, B. H. (1959). The bases of social power. In D. Cartwright (Ed.), *Studies of social power* (pp. 150–167). Ann Arbor, MI: Institute for Social Research; Kelman, H. C. (1958). Compliance, identification and internalization: Three processes of attitude change. *Journal of Conflict Resolution, 2,* 51–56; Kelman, H. C. (1974). Further thoughts on the process of compliance, identification, and internalization. In J. T. Tedeschi (Ed.), *Perspectives on social power* (pp. 125–171). Chicago: Aldine; Yukl, G. (1994). *Leadership in organizations* (3rd ed.). Englewood Cliffs, NJ: Prentice Hall, p. 202.

Empowerment and Power

Empowerment is, in essence, the delegation of power, influence, and authority to another person—usually to a subordinate from a superior. Empowerment does not mean delegation of responsibility, although some responsibility rests in the subordinate that has delegated authority.

> All the [leadership] models suggest that these leaders use empowerment rather than control strategies in order to achieve transformational influence over their followers. They in essence advocate the transformational influence of leaders where the main goal is to change followers' core attitudes, beliefs, and values rather than to induce only compliance behavior in them. Again they all agree that these forms of leadership lead to attitudinal changes among followers characterized by identification with the leader and internalization of values embedded in the leader's vision and ideology.[42]

Empowerment involves the matching of an employee's knowledge, skills, and abilities to *appropriate* tasks, levels of authority, and levels of power and influence. Once the assignment is made, the health leader forgoes command over that task or authority until it is completed; again, this statement does not mean that responsibility is delegated. Oversight, mentoring, and guidance are advised in accordance to the capabilities of the subordinate employee. Empowering subordinates and team members conveys trust and individualized consideration, which fosters ownership. This practice encourages employees to achieve their maximum potential throughout their careers, allowing an organization to develop leadership from within.

Empowerment is about providing motivation, developing subordinates, and appropriately aligning the decision-making processes in the health organization. Health leaders and leadership teams that understand what motivates subordinates and team members will know how to keep them satisfied, productive, and fulfilled in the workplace.

In 1959, psychologist Fredric Herzberg described a two-factor theory of motivation that aligns well with empowerment. Herzberg's theory distinguished between intrinsic (from the work itself) and extrinsic (outside of the actual work) motivators. Essentially, intrinsic factors are needed to motivate an employee to higher performance, and extrinsic motivators are needed to ensure an employee is not dissatisfied. Intrinsic and extrinsic motivational constructs are called "satisfiers" and "dis-satisfiers," respectively. In summary, the two-factor theory of motivation consists of intrinsic motivators—challenging work, recognition, responsibility, effectiveness, personal growth, and achievement—and extrinsic motivators—salary, work conditions, company policies, job security, status, and administration. Health leaders who appropriately (considering individualized consideration of the subordinates they lead) enhance and increase intrinsic factors and maintain or enhance extrinsic factors, according to the industry market norms, will most likely have motivated subordinates. Empowerment is a large key to this positive situation.

ENDURING ORGANIZATIONAL VALUES AND BELIEFS

Every health organization has a foundation of values and beliefs that its holds dear and that form the essence of the organizational culture. The values and beliefs of health organizations focus on the relationship with patient care amid the pressures of the external environment, business expectations, and survival/longevity of the organization. These values and beliefs cause health leaders to decide on a strategy that may be less efficient but is more efficacious for the patients and communities they serve. Both values and beliefs are closely linked to societal norms and mores, although increased globalization can loosen these attachments and open up new possibilities to the society. Values tend to remain very stable over time and help organizations make sense of where they are and how they serve their purpose in the community. Beliefs are stable as well, and should focus on excellent patient care, effective and efficient operations, and teamwork in the health organization. How health leaders influence values and beliefs that foster attitudes and behaviors is the focus of this section.

Values, Beliefs, Attitudes, and Behaviors

Transformational health leaders have an advantage in solidifying or changing values, beliefs, attitudes, and behaviors in the organization. "Charismatic leaders have insight into the needs, hopes, and values of followers and are able to motivate commitment to proposals and strategies for change"[43] Values and beliefs are expressed in strategic plans, organizational charters, and statements. Attitudes are the perceptions and opinions of members of the health organization that describe how they perceive the world around them. Behaviors are observed in actions. Health leaders should frequently express expectations about values, beliefs, attitudes, and behaviors to subordinates and other organizational stakeholders. Knowing your team members and subordinates also assists in knowing which values, beliefs, attitudes, and behaviors are consistent or inconsistent with the organization's expressed values, mission, and vision.

Health leadership styles can influence followers' values, beliefs, attitudes, and behaviors. Transactional leadership focuses on behaviors: Changing, motivating, and directing the behaviors and actions of subordinates based on social exchange is the essence of transaction-based leadership. It is possible that transactional leadership can alter attitudes; once the social exchange catalyst is removed or changed, however, it is highly likely that attitudes will return, at least somewhat, to their original state. Transformational leadership focuses on attitudes that lead to desired behaviors by changing the individual subordinate's or subordinate group's understanding, feeling, and connectedness with the health organization's mission, vision, or task at hand. Indirectly, transformational leadership can influence subordinates' beliefs over time and again, over time, shape the health organization's culture. Transformational leadership can also influence subordinate values, although such changes tend to occur only over a longer time horizon and are linked to the intensity and capabilities of the leader and the level of leader loyalty from subordinates.

Change means adjusting, revising, and redirecting effort and actions (behaviors), including how subordinates envision and feel about their place in the organization (attitudes), to a new course. This type of change is more typical of organizational change. Less frequently, change may modify the beliefs and values of subordinates in the health organization.

For the health leader, it is important to reflect on the interconnected nature of values, beliefs, attitudes, and behaviors of individuals in the organization with organizational culture and the collective values, beliefs, attitudes, and behaviors with organizational culture; these constructs may either reinforce or conflict with one another in a dynamic way. Temporal (one point in time) assessment of these constructs can be accomplished much like organizational climate can be assessed. Over time (many temporal points in time in a sequence), values, beliefs, attitudes, and behaviors influence the organizational culture. Health leaders with consistent focus and direction can change, modify, and redirect individual and collective values, beliefs, attitudes, and behaviors as part of the macro-organizational culture development process. Edgar Schein's primary embedding and secondary reinforcement mechanisms are an excellent approach to accomplish this aspect of organizational culture development for health leaders. Transformational leadership principles in practice are likewise both important and productive.

Leadership and Change

Health leaders who understand and are competent in applying transformational leadership principles (charisma is a component of transformational leadership) are best poised to create positive change in the health organization. Those who master transformational leadership principles and applications are best suited for initiating positive change.

To accomplish this goal, the transformational leader must be a competent communicator. Transformational leadership in action is best seen when several elements synergize to change the culture and improve the organization. "Transformational leadership refers to the process of building commitment to the organization's [mission, vision, strategies, goals and] objectives and empowering followers to accomplish these objectives"[44]

An early conception of transformational leadership was developed by Burns in 1978 from descriptive research on political leaders; "leaders and followers raise one another to higher levels of morality and motivation."[45] Expectation and goal setting, empowerment, and increased use of appropriate media channels for communication can combine to focus a team, thereby enabling its members to accomplish significant tasks in system improvement.[46]

Transformational leadership is different from simple charismatic leadership in several respects (an idea attributed to Bernard Bass). Although charisma is a necessary component for transformational leadership, by itself it is not sufficient to account for transformation:

> Transformational leaders influence followers by arousing strong emotions and identification with the leader, but they may also transform followers by serving as a coach, teacher, and mentor. Transformational leaders seek to empower and elevate followers, whereas in charismatic leadership the opposite sometimes occurs. That is, many charismatic leaders seek to keep followers weak and dependent and to instill personal loyalty rather than commitment to ideals.[47]

Schein's primary embedding mechanisms and secondary reinforcement mechanisms to develop and maintain culture (discussed in Chapter 9 of this text) are salient within the context of change; transformational health leaders who use these mechanisms with a conscious and predetermined vision for a health organizational culture are best equipped to effect positive change. When this synthesized strategy is used consistently and morally, change can be accomplished more quickly, deliver greater benefits, and enhance the health leader's status within the organization.

Strategies in Creating a Culture of Change

Health leaders can use transformational leadership strategies,[48] primary embedding and secondary reinforcement mechanisms,[49] and the dynamic culture leadership (DCL) model[50] processes to develop and synthesize a model to serve as a strategy for creating a culture of change in the health organization. A review of transformational leadership is presented here, followed by a discussion of the various culture change mechanisms and the DCL process.

Bernard Bass, building on work by Burns, developed the theory of transformational leadership.[51] This model measures the leader's influence on followers. A health transformation leader would create trust, admiration, loyalty, and respect in the followers through the leader's actions, behaviors, and persona.[52] Followers are motivated by the leader to do more than expected, as the leader makes followers more aware of the importance of task outcomes, induces them to transcend their own self-interest for the sake of the team, and activates their higher-order needs.[53] To do so, the leader uses the following transformational behaviors and actions:

- **Charisma:** leader influences followers by arousing strong emotions and identification with the leader
- **Intellectual Stimulation:** leaders increase follower awareness of problems and influence followers' view of problems from a new perspective
- **Individualized Consideration:** providing support, encouragement, and developmental experiences for followers
- **Inspirational Motivation:** extent that the leader communicates an appealing vision using symbols to focus subordinate effort and model (role modeling; Bandera's social learning theory) appropriate behavior[54]

As described in Chapter 9, primary embedding mechanisms[55] are a set of powerful tools, behaviors, and mechanisms that a health leader can use to develop, refine, maintain, or change organizational culture:

- What leaders pay attention to, measure, and control
- Leader reactions to critical incidents and organizational crises
- Deliberate role modeling, teaching, and coaching by leaders
- Criteria for allocation of rewards and status
- Criteria for recruitment, selection, promotion, retirement, and excommunication

Schein strongly states that leaders communicate both explicitly and implicitly the assumptions they really hold. If they are conflicted, their conflicts and inconsistencies are also communicated and become part of the culture. Consistency is the key: Health leaders must predetermine where and how to guide the organization and stay on task.

Another set of mechanisms support the primary set and are called secondary reinforcement mechanisms.[56] The secondary articulation and reinforcement mechanisms reinforce the primary embedding mechanisms. The following are of greatest importance to the health leader:

- The organization's design and structure
- Organizational systems and procedures
- Design of physical space, facades, and buildings
- Stories, legends, myths, and parables about important events and people
- Formal statements of organizational philosophy, creeds, and charters

Schein calls these "secondary" because they work only if they are consistent with the primary mechanisms. The secondary mechanisms are less powerful than primary mechanisms, more ambiguous, and more difficult to control, yet can be powerful reinforcements of the primary messages if the leader is able to control them.

The important point is that all of these mechanisms communicate culture content to newcomers and current staff. Together, they represent a rich set of tools, behaviors, decisions, and mechanisms a health leader can use to develop and maintain organizational culture. Health leaders must be consistent and conscious of how and when they utilize these mechanisms.

The DCL model[57] process suggests prescriptive elements that include assessing and aligning a robust leadership and management team to ensure that all of these individuals can utilize a broad range of knowledge, skills, abilities, and perspectives while being consistent in developing and maintaining an appropriate organizational culture. The leader's use of the sequential and building elements of the model's process constructs facilitates the development of the predetermined organizational culture desired. Process constructs include the following elements:

- *Communication improvement* is the leadership's and management team's predetermined modeling, training, rewarding, and assimilation of the communication environment into the organization in the manner that best contributes to an effective organizational culture. In health organizations, a confirming and supportive communication environment that is cognizant of media richness of communication channels and competent in conflict management should be the most effective, efficient, and efficacious.

- *Strategic planning* (which includes operational planning) is the structured inclusive process of planning to determine mission, vision, strategies, goals, objectives, and action steps that are consistent with organizational values and that meet the external environment's expectations of the organization. Subordinate, internal, and external stakeholders should be included, as appropriate to their level and responsibilities, in the planning process. Continuous, "living" planning is a cultural imperative in dynamic environments.

- *Decision-making alignment* involves aligning decisions with the strategic and operational plan while understanding reality-based decision making (pushing down decisions appropriately and using policies and standing operating procedures for routine and consistent decisions).

- *Employee enhancement* is the assessment of employee knowledge, skills, abilities, experience, and trustworthiness and the practice of increasing or reducing responsibilities (such as making decisions) appropriately to the unit, group, and individual, in line with the organizational culture in development and the strategic and operational plans.

- *Knowledge management and organizational learning* involves capturing what the organization knows and what it has learned, so that improvements to effectiveness, efficiency, and efficacy can be achieved.

- *Evaluating, reflecting, and retooling* is the leadership and management team's honest assessment of the DCL model cycle and understanding of how to perform the cycle better in the next repetition.

Using this process consistently will not only improve the organization's ability to use these processes and lead to the development of an organizational culture that reflects the leadership's vision, but also enable the organization to maneuver effectively in dynamic situations. Process repetition and consistency are foundational to success in this model.

From these three integrated aspects of leadership, a strategy for creating positive change in the organization can be realized. By scanning, monitoring, forecasting (for the external environment), and assessing the health organization (internal) and its setting, context, and location in the environment (external), the health leader and/or leadership team needs to develop a predetermined direction, a preliminary vision, and a picture of the best organizational culture that can achieve that direction and vision while attending to the health organization's current mission. This process and the decisions it produces should be documented and planned over time. Health leader actions must then be planned to achieve the better future envisioned for the health organization. Health leaders must plan, practice, and hold themselves and other leaders accountable for consistency to realize the desired outcomes of the plan.

To turn the desired future into reality, change will most likely be required in the health organization and among its stakeholders. Active situational leadership—that is, selecting the appropriate mix of transformational and transactional leadership, frequent quality communication to subordinates and stakeholders, appropriately inclusive planning, decision-making alignment, empowerment, and organizational learning and knowledge management—should merge with an appealing vision of the future of the health organization so that the organization can achieve success. Can you integrate the concepts, actions, behaviors, and aspects from this section to develop an initial model of leading change? Are some elements particularly important in this respect? **Table 13–6** summarizes one model for leader-facilitated positive health organization change.

Change, Conflict, and Transition Planning

At the macro level of analysis, transformational leadership involves shaping, expressing, and mediating conflict among groups of people in addition to motivating individuals.[58] Anytime there is change, there is conflict. Managing this conflict is necessary for two reasons: (1) Conflict is inevitable and (2) it can create positive results. By being consistent in their delivery of the message of change and the organizational vision, health leaders can continuously reinforce the change while calming nervous tension or anxiety in the organization. Each step of the transition through change should be planned, with subordinates and team members being included, as appropriate, in developing aspects of the change and transition plan. Including internal and external stakeholders in organizational changes that will affect them is a great method for moving through the transitions and changes with less turbulence. Nevertheless, smooth change is rare—so expect some turbulence and resistance. Frequent supportive, descriptive, yet firm communication is a great tool for health leaders; media-rich channels of communication (e.g., face-to-face with individuals and groups) are recommended for communicating change.

Another change in health organizations that is inevitable involves leadership position changes. If transitional planning and succession planning has occurred, this transition tends to go more smoothly. Succession planning—the deliberate development and placement of internal leadership and management over time—should be a part of every health organization's culture.

Maintaining a Culture of Adaptive Change

Once a culture of change is established in a health organization, it is important to nourish and maintain that culture:

> The organizational culture is a learned pattern of behavior, shared from one generation to the next. It includes the values and an assumption shared by members about what is right, what is good and what is important. Since demands on most organizations are unlikely to be steady and stable, only cultures that can adapt and change will be associated with superior performance over long periods of time.[59]

TABLE 13–6   Leadership-Facilitated Organizational Change: Application of Theories and Models

Predetermined Organizational Culture to Develop	Individual Leader Actions and Behaviors	Leadership Team Actions and Behaviors	Organizational Actions and Behaviors by Leaders and Subordinates	Organizational Outcomes
Vision predetermined and culture changes predetermined by leadership team	Transformational leadership characteristics: • Charisma • Intellectual stimulation • Individualized consideration • Inspirational motivation • Performance orientation • Decisiveness • Team integration and collaboration • Being diplomatic • Being benevolent • Being administratively competent • Transactional leadership (reward for performance) where appropriate	Primary embedding mechanisms: • What leaders pay attention to, measure, and control • Leader reactions to critical incidents and organizational crises • Deliberate role modeling, teaching, and coaching by leaders • Criteria for allocation of rewards and status • Criteria for recruitment, selection, promotion, retirement, and excommunication Secondary reinforcement and articulation mechanisms: • Design and creation of the organization's design and structure • Design and creation of the organizational systems and procedures • Design of physical space, facades, and buildings • Creating and telling of stories, legends, myths, and parables about important events and people • Developing and publishing formal statements of organizational philosophy, creeds, and charters	Dynamic culture leadership process: • Leadership alignment • Communication improvement • Strategic and operational planning • Decision-making alignment • Employee enhancement • Knowledge management and organizational learning • Evaluation, reflecting and retooling, and repeating the process	Predetermined vision and organizational culture incrementally transformed and realized

Health leaders can and should develop a predetermined organizational culture focused on transformation, continuous improvement, and the ability to thrive in a dynamic environment. A transformational culture for health organizations facilitates adaption and change over time.

Transactional cultures exhibit the following attributes:

■ Concentrate on explicit and implicit contractual relationships.

■ Job assignments include statements about rules, benefits, and disciplinary codes.

■ Jargon/values/assumptions usually set or imply a price or reward for doing anything.

■ Rewards are contingent on performance.

■ Management by exception is commonly practiced.

■ Employees work individually.

■ Employees do not identify with the organization, its vision, or mission.

■ Leaders are negotiators and resource allocators.

■ Innovation and risk taking are discouraged.

Transformational cultures exhibit the following attributes:

■ Express a sincere sense of purpose and feeling of family.

■ Commitments are long-term.

■ Mutual interests are shared along with a sense of shared fates and interdependence.

■ Leaders serve as role models, mentors, and coaches.

■ Leaders work to socialize new members into the organization.

■ Shared norms are adaptive.

■ Organizational purposes, visions, and missions are emphasized; not threats.

■ Norms change with changes in the organization's environment.[60]

In thinking about the concepts covered in this chapter, can you incorporate leadership competencies regarding diversity, power, and changing and transforming organizations into an initial application model? After engaging in reflection, can you construct a leadership model that you can use in leading people and managing resources in a health organization? To assist in this effort of developing a leadership model to positively change a health organization, reflect on the following suggestions:

■ Model the behavior you expect yourself.

■ Communicate expectations and train other leaders and managers and staff.

■ Revise structures and reporting relationships.

■ Conduct team-based planning and policy development.

■ Use primary embedding and secondary reinforcement mechanisms.

■ Utilize the DCL model sequential processes.

■ Be consistent and communicate often to the organization.

■ Continue to scan, monitor, and assess the internal health organization environment while you scan, monitor, forecast, and assess the external environment to guide the health organization appropriately.

Which elements are clearest to you? Can you list the leadership elements that are important to realize change in a health organization?

KNOWLEDGE MANAGEMENT AND A LEARNING ORGANIZATION[61]

Learning organizations are living, open, robust systems.[62] Knowledge management in and of itself is an innovative strategy of change, adaption, and evolution. This process involves accumulating and creating knowledge and facilitating the sharing of knowledge throughout the organization. "The ability for a healthcare organization to develop systems to manage knowledge directly impacts the level of institutional knowledge and organizational learning."[63] Knowledge management empowers the organization to fulfill its mission and vision. The ability to reach the vision of the organization, in turn, provides a greater ability to compete in a dynamic environment. If knowledge is created, captured, and managed appropriately in a consistent manner over time, a culture of learning is created. To manage knowledge effectively within the organization, it is first important to create a working definition of knowledge and to define what knowledge is not.

Clear distinctions can be made between data, information, and knowledge. Data comprise a set of objective facts about certain objects, events, people, or observations. Data become information when these facts are used to inform or convey a *relevant* message to the receiver. Information is capable of yielding knowledge, but is not synonymous with knowledge. Information becomes knowledge when decision makers determine how to take advantage of the information to further health organizational goals or as part of the decision-making process. Knowledge is "actionable" information. It conveys understanding as it applies to a particular problem.

In creating a practical working definition of knowledge, the organization should understand and emphasize these differences. A working definition of knowledge offered by Davenport and Prusak states that knowledge is a dynamic mix of contextually based experiences, values, contextual information, and insights that provide a framework for evaluating and incorporating new experiences and information.[64] In creating a system of knowledge management for the health organization, there are three processes of importance: knowledge accumulation, knowledge creation, and knowledge sharing.

Accumulating Knowledge

To learn, a health organization must have data, information, and knowledge to draw from. Essential data and information that is critical to the mission and core systems and processes of the health organization must be identified. Because knowledge management is an organizational phenomenon, the health organization should first identify and clarify the organization's mission, vision, and core values. Identifying these organizational concepts provides an understanding of the current state of the organization, which will influence how priorities and boundaries for capturing and creating knowledge are set. The next step in accumulating knowledge is to discover existing knowledge and put it into a health organizational context. This step involves gathering and organizing knowledge to make it useful to others. If the intent of knowledge is to inform and influence decision making, then its focus must be on the future. Allowing for discussion and frequent debate is a vehicle to accumulate existing knowledge.

Creating Knowledge

Knowledge generation and usage is a never-ending work in progress. The health organization must continually acquire and create new knowledge. Experiments are crucial to the creation of new knowledge because they provide data and information; employees learn by taking chances and, sometimes, by making mistakes. Unintended mistakes should be viewed as opportunities to learn and improve patient care and business processes; they should be acceptable in the organization. At the same time, patient care should always strive to be error free (although mistakes do occur at times). People learn from mistakes and then push the answers out to others.

According to Nonaka, two types of knowledge—tacit and explicit—are important to the knowledge creation process.[65] Explicit knowledge is knowledge that is transferrable by the use of language. It is something that we can say or tell someone. Tacit knowledge is much more difficult to convey, because it is the result of subjective and experiential learning and, therefore, may not always be documented. Tacit knowledge is the means by which explicit knowledge is captured, assimilated, created, and disseminated.

Sharing Knowledge

Capturing and storing knowledge are the cornerstones of knowledge management. Although knowledge is stored many ways in a health organization, the most popular approach combines a database form with the use of a technology-related platform. Once knowledge is stored properly, it can be disseminated throughout the organization and applied to specific situations and the decision-making process.

Knowledge databases should be broad in scope to provide for greater ease of usability. Leaders must be obsessive about noting and correcting errors in their stock of knowledge. What do they know or think they know? How does what they know or do not know affect specific decisions? Which errors reside in their knowledge and what are the consequences of those errors? Once errors are identified, a plan to rectify those errors must be developed.

For knowledge to be usable, the target audience of the knowledge database must be clear. Organizations today can deliver knowledge via a variety of technology platforms. Technology is a means to access information and knowledge but is no substitute for interaction. Put simply, communication and the learning process are inherently types of personal dialogue.[66]

Knowledge Management and Organizational Learning Summary

Based on the concepts of knowledge accumulation, knowledge creation, and knowledge sharing, a five-step approach to knowledge management is proposed:[67]

1. Identify what is critical to the organization.

2. Discover existing knowledge and put it into an organizational context.

3. Acquire or create new knowledge.

4. Establish knowledge databases.

5. Distribute knowledge to the appropriate audience.

Building a culture of learning within the health organization to foster the development and sharing of knowledge is an essential element in establishing and maintaining an effective, efficient, and efficacious knowledge management system. As the acceptance of evidenced-based medicine and administrative practice grows, establishing and maintaining a knowledge management system within a culture of organizational learning will be critical to ensure the success of both the health organization and its leadership team.

SUMMARY

This chapter discussed the globalization of leadership, taking into account that many of the leadership theories and practices presented in this book are based on Western ideologies. The need to leverage technology, lead through followership, and understand the basics of influence and power are important with respect to climate, culture change, and environment. Knowledge management and organizational learning are also keys to keeping the health organization attuned to its dynamic environment and flexible enough to embrace change when necessary. As part of this effort, the health leader may use a variety of integrative models as the basis for fostering change—including change in the culture—within the organization.

DISCUSSION QUESTIONS

1. Describe and outline issues related to globalization, power, followership, and culture change from a health leader's perspective.

2. Which tools can a health leader use to change and adapt culture in the health organization? Are some tools better than others? Why?

3. What are the major global leadership style differences and similarities (based on appropriate constructs)? Do leaders from certain cultures seem to be able to use transformational leadership practices more effectively than leaders from other cultures? Why or why not?

4. How can a health leader use power? Which kind of power works best in the setting of followership, culture change, technology, and knowledge management?

5. Can you categorize global leadership differences according to a leader's use of power, technology, and knowledge management? Which leaders from various cultures would use each type of power most successfully? Which leaders from various cultures would lead culture change efforts best? Why?

6. What are the best approaches to knowledge management, organizational learning, and transformational leadership within health organizations? How can a health leader facilitate culture change using transformational leadership practices, tools, and processes?

EXERCISES

1. In a one- to two-page paper, describe and outline issues related to globalization, power, followership, and culture change from a health leader's perspective.

2. In a one- to two-page paper, give examples of tools a health leader can use to change and adapt culture in the health organization.

3. In a two- to three-page paper, relate global leadership style differences and similarities using appropriate constructs for transformational leadership practices.

4. In a two-page paper, analyze a health leader's use of power as it relates to followership, culture change, and knowledge management.

5. In a two- to three-page paper, categorize global leadership differences according to a leader's use of power, technology, and knowledge management.

6. In a four-page paper, evaluate approaches to knowledge management, organizational learning, and transformational leadership in relation to health organization culture change.

REFERENCES

1. Harris, T. E., & Nelson, M. D. (2008). *Applied organizational communication: Theory and practice in a global environment* (3rd ed.). New York: Lawrence Erlbaum Associates, summary of Chapter 2.
2. House, R. (2004). Preface. In House, R. J., Hanges, P. J., Javidan, M., Dorfman, P. W., & Gupta, V. (Eds.), *Culture, leadership and organizations: The GLOBE Study of 62 societies* (p. xxv). Thousand Oaks, CA: Sage.
3. Bennis, W., Parikh, J., & Lessem, R. (1994). *Beyond leadership: Balancing economics, ethics and ecology* (2nd ed.). Oxford, UK: Blackwell, p. 23.
4. House, R. J., Hanges, P. J., Javidan, M., Dorfman, P. W., & Gupta, V. (Eds.). (2004). *Culture, leadership and organizations: The GLOBE Study of 62 societies.* Thousand Oaks, CA: Sage.
5. Grovewell, LLC. Retrieved June 6, 2009, from http://www.grovewell.com/pub-GLOBE-dimensions.html.
6. Triandis, H. C. (2004). Foreword. In House, R. J., Hanges, P. J., Javidan, M., Dorfman, P. W., & Gupta, V. (Eds.), *Culture, leadership and organizations: The GLOBE Study of 62 societies* (p. xv). Thousand Oaks, CA: Sage.

7. Hofstede, G. (1980). *Culture's consequences: International differences in work-related values.* London: Sage.

8. Triandis, note 6.

9. Grovewell, note 5

10. House et al., note 4, pp. 20, 239; Grovewell, note 5.

11. House et al., note 4, p. 30; Grovewell, note 5.

12. House et al., note 4; Grovewell, note 5.

13. Triandis, note 6.

14. House et al., note 4, p. 676, Table 21.1; Grovewell, note 5.

15. Grovewell, note 5.

16. Triandis, note 6, p. xvii.

17. Triandis, note 6, p. xvii.

18. Triandis, note 6, p. xviii.

19. Triandis, note 6, p. xviii.

20. Triandis, note 6, p. xvii.

21. House, R. (2004). Introduction. In House, R. J., Hanges, P. J., Javidan, M., Dorfman, P. W., & Gupta, V. (Eds.), *Culture, leadership and organizations: The GLOBE Study of 62 societies* (pp. 42–45). Thousand Oaks, CA: Sage

22. House, note 21.

23. House, note 21.

24. House, note 21.

25. House, note 21.

26. House, note 21.

27. Retrieved June 8, 2009, from http://www.merriam-webster.com/dictionary/technology.

28. Yukl, G. (1994). *Leadership in organizations* (3rd ed.). Englewood Cliffs, NJ: Prentice Hall, p. 91.

29. Yukl, note 28.

30. Ledlow, G., & Coppola, N. (2008). Leadership Theory and Influence. In J. A. Johnson (Ed.), *Organizational theory, behavior and development* (pp. 167–192). Sudbury, MA: Jones and Bartlett.

31. March, J. G., & Weisinger-Baylon, R. (1986). *Ambiguity and command: Organizational perspectives on military decision making.* Marshfield, MA: Pitman.

32. Schein, E. H. (1999). *The corporate culture survival guide: Sense and nonsense about culture change.* San Francisco, CA: Jossey-Bass.

33. Conger, J., Speitzer, G., & Lawler, E. III . (1999). *The leader's change handbook: An essential guide to setting direction and taking action.* San Francisco, CA: Jossey-Bass, p. 56.

34. Jelinek, M., & Litterer, J. A. (1995). Page 168 in Toward entrepreneurial organizations: Meeting ambiguity with engagement. *Entrepreneurship: Theory and Practice, 19*(3), 137–169.

35. Bennis, W., & Biederman, P. W. (1997). *Organizing genius: The secret of creative collaboration.* California: Perseus Publishing.

36. Kelman, H.C. (1958). Compliance, identification and internalization: Three processes of attitude change. *Journal of Conflict Resolution, 2,* 51–56.

37. Kelman, H. C. (1974). Further thoughts on the process of compliance, identification, and internalization. In J. T. Tedeschi (Ed.), *Perspectives on social power* (pp. 125–171). Chicago, IL: Aldine.

38. Yukl, note 28, p. 197.

39. Yukl, note 28, p. 209.

40. Jermier, J. M., Slocum, J. W. Jr., Fry, L. W., & Gaines, J. (1991). Organizational subcultures in a soft bureaucracy: Resistance behind the myth and façade of an official culture. *Organization Science, 2*(2), 170–194.

41. Greene, R. (1998). *The 48 laws of power.* New York: Penguin Books, p. xix.

42. Conger, J. A. (1999). Charismatic and transformational leadership in organizations: An insider's perspective on these developing streams of research. *Leadership Quarterly, 10*(2), 157.

43. Yukl, note 28, p. 207.

44. Yukl, note 28, p. 350.

45. Yukl, note 28, p. 350.

46. Ledlow, G. R., Bradshaw, D. M., & Shockley, C. (2000). Primary care access improvement: An empowerment–interaction model. *Military Medicine, 165*(2), 390–395.

47. Yukl, note 28, p. 353.

48. Yukl, note 28.

49. Schein, note 32.

50. Ledlow, G., Cwiek, M., & Johnson, J. (2002). Dynamic culture leadership: Effective leader as both scientist and artist. In N. Delener & C-n. Chao (Eds.), *Global Business and Technology Association (GBATA) International Conference: Beyond boundaries: Challenges of leadership, innovation, integration and technology* (pp. 694–740).

51. Bass, B. (1998). *Transformational leadership: Industrial, military, and educational impact.* Mahwah, NJ: Lawrence Erlbaum Associates.

52. Yukl, note 28.
53. Yukl, note 28.
54. Yukl, note 28, pp. 352–353.
55. Schein, note 32.
56. Schein, note 32.
57. Ledlow et al. note 50.
58. Yukl, note 28, p. 351.
59. Bass, note 51, p. 62.
60. Bass, note 51, pp. 64–65.
61. Much of this section was completed in collaboration with Kelley Chester, doctoral candidate, Georgia Southern University, 2007–2009.
62. Bennis et al., note 3.
63. Johnson, J., Ledlow, G., & Kerr, B. (2005). Organizational development, training and knowledge management. In B. Fried, J. Johnson, & M. Fottler (Eds.), *Managing human resources in healthcare organizations* (2nd ed., pp. 202–222). Chicago, IL: Health Administration Press.
64. Davenport, T. H., & Prusak, L. (2000). *Working knowledge: How organizations manage what they know.* Boston: Harvard Business School Press.
65. Nonaka, I. (1994, February). A dynamic theory of organizational knowledge creation. *Organization Science, 5*(1).
66. Fahey, L., & Prusak, L. (1998, Spring). The eleven deadliest sins of knowledge management. *California Management Review, 40*(3).
67. This model is from the unpublished work of Kelley Chester, doctoral candidate, Georgia Southern University, 2007–2009.

14

Leadership: A Critical Factor for the Future Success of the Industry

The first step to leadership is servanthood.

—John Maxwell

This chapter emphasizes that the practice of leadership, like the practice of medicine, is a constant effort of development. What kind of leader do you want to become and be? Leaders have an obligation to stay current and relevant in the field of leadership practice. This chapter presents issues and strategies to help leaders maintain their relevancy and creditability in the organization. Discussed in this chapter are opportunities and advantages in completing continuing education as well as in participating in community and professional organizations. In addition, the humble leader can admit to *not knowing* everything that occurs in a health organization; this chapter emphasizes that it is okay to say, "I don't know," when leading complex health entities.

LEARNING OBJECTIVES

1. Describe the leader you want to become and be in a health organization.

2. Explain the attributes of a successful health leader.

3. Relate leadership and leadership-oriented theories and models to attributes, behaviors, and actions of successful health leaders.

4. Identify and assess the key principles of inner leadership, leading people, managing resources, leader credibility and relevance, and community outreach for a health leader.

5. Combine three or more leadership-oriented theories and models to principles of inner leadership.

6. Appraise and defend a "perfect" health leader/mentor by explaining the knowledge, skills, abilities, and competencies of the "perfect" mentor.

WHAT KIND OF LEADER DO YOU WANT TO BE?

This is a serious question: What kind of leader are you? For many people who are just starting their careers, this question may be rephrased: What kind of leader do you want to become? Armed with what was learned from the behavior phase and the situational phase of leadership thought, can you learn, practice, and develop leadership knowledge, skills, abilities, and competencies starting today and continue that development through-out your lifetime? Remember the definition of leadership presented earlier in this book: *Leadership* is the *dynamic* and *active* creation and maintenance of an organizational *culture* and *strategic systems* that focus the collective energy of both *leading people and managing resources* toward *meeting the needs of the external environment,* while utilizing the most efficient, effective, and efficacious methods possible by moral means. To become the kind of leader you want to be, you will need to be *active* in your approach to the art and science of leadership. The process of "practicing the art of leadership" is discussed in more detail in this chapter. However, one characteristic you will have to embrace is the process of internalizing leadership as a continuous process if you want to be a leader who always gets better, always stays credible, and always wants to be the best.

The desire to be a great leader comes from within. For example, Fairholm summarizes several principles of "inner leadership." Inner leadership is based on many of the principles of empowerment. Empowerment engages the inner leader in the kinds of actions necessary to internalize leadership as a constant process. By doing this, the leader becomes capable of assuming the following responsibilities:

- Goal setting
- Delegating to followers
- Encouraging participation
- Encouraging self-reliance
- Challenging followers
- Focusing on workers
- Specifying followers' roles[1]

When looking at this series of inner leadership principles, how many theories and models come to mind that have already been studied that can be applied to them? How many could be put into practice? Which theories and models would work well together, and which ones might contradict one another? For purposes of synergy of theories and models, reflect on **Table 14–1**, which shows a few of the linkages. Many more connections are also possible: Can more linkages to theories and models be listed?

Earlier in this text, there was an opportunity to do a personal self-assessment of leadership "hard-wiring." This self-assessment should have led to a greater understanding of a leader's strengths and weaknesses. Furthermore, a leader's predisposition toward a certain mental hard-wiring might lend itself to a natural tendency to emulate some of the many leadership styles discussed in this text. Looking at Table 14–1, which theories and leadership methods best fit with your experiences and natural talents? While this process may seem somewhat mechanical and prescriptive, without an understanding of his or her own style and natural tendencies, a leader cannot emphasize strengths and work on weaknesses. Lastly, while this approach might seem mechanical and deliberate in one's role as an early leader, with practice and over time, a leader should be able to seamlessly incorporate personal style and abilities into a blended practice of leadership.

You should be able to list other connections and links to theories and models presented previously in this book and from knowledge gained from other courses. Again, it is important to create a vision for yourself of what kind of leader you want to be. Because it is important to communicate a clear and appealing vision to your subordinates, you need to develop a personal leadership vision. You will need to sell that vision of your leadership to potential employers in job interviews and by your performance in the job:

> Today, senior leaders of major organizations consistently rank leadership development as their number one concern. Leaders and the art they perfect is not bestowed on those, it is developed over time and with great effort; good leaders are not born but are produced over time and with great effort.[2]

It's Okay to Say, "I Don't Know"

Leaders of health organizations are probably at a greater disadvantage than leaders of any other large organizations. Their unique challenges stem from the complexity of health organizations and the lack of understanding of "what goes on" in the health facility. To outsiders and less informed individuals, a physician is a physician, a nurse is a nurse, and any one administrator is equally as competent as the next. The complexities, competencies, skills, and specializations between administrators, physicians, nurses, and other allied health personnel and employees are lost on the layperson.

Leaders of health organizations not only have to be aware of the same accounting, marketing, logistical, human resources, and compliance regulations as their manufacturing and service industry peers, but also the challenges of managing Food and Drug Administration (FDA)–designated controlled substances, licensing and certification issues, innovation and technology, and the rapidly changing multispecialty best practices in areas of medicine or patient care. Moreover, this feat must be achieved in an environment of near-perfection when it comes to patient care.

In addition, the leader in a health organization may have absolutely no experience or professional education related to many of the daily activities that go on in the health facility. For example, in popular fast-food franchises, the list of menu items is finite and can be generalized. With few colloquial exceptions, the same items on the menu of one fast-food restaurant will be identical to the menu items at the same franchise restaurant across town. Managers of these local restaurants are required to be keenly aware of the ordering, processing, and

TABLE 14–1   Inner Leadership Principles Linked to Theories and Models

Inner Leadership Principle	Link to Other Leadership or Related Theory or Model (1)	Link to Other Leadership or Related Theory or Model (2)	Link to Other Leadership or Related Theory or Model (3)
Goal setting	Goal setting theory (Locke and Latham)	Expectancy theory (Vroom) and path–goal model (House)	Dynamic culture leadership; planning and specifically objectives (Ledlow)
Delegating to followers	Garbage can model of decision making (March and Weisinger-Baylon)	Motivation by empowerment (several models: Bolman and Deal's reframing organizations and Ledlow's dynamic culture leadership)	Kaizen, total quality management, continuous quality management, process improvement
Encouraging participation	Situational leadership model (Hersey and Blanchard)	Kelman's model (instrumental) and the model of influence considering commitment, compliance, and resistance	Reframing leadership and management in organizations (Bolman and Deal)
Encouraging self-reliance	Transformational leadership model (Burns and Bass) and locus of control (Rotter)	Dynamic culture leadership (specifically, knowledge management and organizational learning)	Organizational culture primary and secondary mechanisms (Schein)
Challenging followers	Competency-based leadership (Bennis)	Transformational leadership (Burns and Bass)	Communication environment, conflict management and media richness theory (Daft and Lengel)
Focusing on workers	Transformational leadership (Burns and Bass)	Cultural competence	Coordinated management of meaning (Pearce and Cronen)
Specifying followers' roles	Shutz's theory of affiliation	Communication clarity	Tuckman's model of group dynamics

delivery of all food items on the menu, as well as the intimate details of how everyone in that franchise does his or her job. This is never the case with the health leader, who will rely on the competence, honesty, and reporting of those who work for him or her in the organizational hierarchy over and above firsthand knowledge.[3–5]

For example, in many manufacturing organizations, the leader must know the skills and duties of those persons who work underneath him or her in the organizational hierarchy. This is a difficult task for the leader of a health organization. A leader in a multispecialty, primary, secondary, and tertiary health organization will never be as competent at doing the individual tasks of any two individuals across specialties within the organization. In almost all cases with leaders who rise to positions of greater responsibility in health organizations, there will be dozens, even hundreds, of people in the organization who know more about their own jobs than the leader does. More so in health organizations than any other manufacturing- or service-driven organization, the leader must be comfortable with the prospect of "not knowing" the inner complexities of the organizing that or she is running. At the same time, the health leader must be able to develop and employ systems and processes that create an efficient, effective, and efficacious healthcare environment. The leader *must* be comfortable with a personal and professional posture of admitting to himself or herself that he or she does not know everything that goes on in the organization. Leaders who try to know everything, manage everything, and control everything are destined for personal frustration, professional disappointment, and, ultimately, leader failure.

MAINTAINING RELEVANCY AND CREDITABILITY

In becoming comfortable stating, "I don't know," within a health organization, the next logical question a leader has to ask himself or herself is this: How do I maintain relevancy and credibility with my peers and colleagues? These critical self-assessment issues must be constantly addressed and evaluated by the leader, at least on an annual basis. Additionally, both relevancy and creditability are mutually exclusive issues the leader must pursue from individual strategies.[6, 7]

Credibility

For example, credibility is a complex construct that can be measured through experience, outcomes and employee trust. A leader with little previous experience in the day-to-day operations of the health organization may not be perceived as credible. However, the defining of experience becomes even more complex when discussing the specific nature of the experience of the individual. For example, nurses may not be perceived as having creditable experience in leading health organizations if their 20-year familiarity with leading people in health organizations has been restricted to leading only other nurses. Similarly, professional administrative leaders without clinical degrees may look at a physician leader with skepticism if the physician has risen to a position of authority based on his or her medical and clinical prowess rather than by taking on administrative and management developmental activities. The circle may continue if physicians view the administrator with only a master's degree as an individual without experience to know enough about hands-on patient care to manage physicians.

As this discussion suggests, credibility is highly wedded to trust. While professional rivalries and professional competition are part and parcel of leading complex health organization, the leader should never lose focus on maintaining and instilling positive relationships with peers and staff.[8] Without gaining the trust of those in the organization, the leader will not be effective in his or her job. Consequently, trust is also highly wedded to outcomes all along the continuum and process of daily operations.[9, 10] Likewise, building a trusting relationship with peers and colleagues is a key element in achieving credibility and positive outcomes.

Outcomes

Outcomes in regard to credibility are not restricted to financial, logistical, and morbidity/mortality metrics. Perhaps most importantly, they are related to outcomes with human resources. Organizational satisfaction, leader and employee development opportunities, and formation and maintenance of positive relationships with stakeholders are some of the most critical factors for a leader to consider. How a leader treats employees in regard to acknowledging input, respecting candor, protecting employee autonomy, and maintaining a positive leader climate are some of the most important factors that any leader can focus on in his or her organization.[11] The loss of trust of even a single person, considering that person's influence in the organization, can begin a professional downturn for the leader. In fact, President Lyndon Johnson once said he had lost the trust of America because he lost the trust of one man: Walter Cronkite, the famous anchorman of CBS News. Cronkite said in 1968 during the evening newscast that he thought the Vietnam War could not be won. President Johnson was later quoted as saying, "If I've lost Cronkite, I've lost Middle America."

Relevancy

Relevancy is an easier behavior trait for a leader to maintain. Relevancy is defined as a leader's ability to maintain a position of continued and sustained contribution to the organization's success. All other factors are antecedent to this ability.[12] Relevancy may be one of the most important hierarchal dispositions of the leader in any health organization. If the organization is growing its market share, increasing its local or national prominence, and improving in terms of other quality factors measured on a regular basis, these changes can be indicators of the relevance of the leader of the organization. However, as discussed earlier in terms of leadership styles and strategies, an organization that achieves high outcomes while discounting employee satisfaction is a weak model of leader effectiveness.[13, 14] As a result, both creditability and relevancy are partnered elements of success. The path to achieving high outcomes in both of these areas is multifaceted and revolves around four key areas: joining professional organizations, service, continuing education, and personal professional development.

Professional Organizations

As discussed previously in this text, membership in professional organizations is critical to establish a leader's credibility and relevancy. For the sake of fairness, we will not identify any one organization in this chapter as the panacea for professional success. Rather, the selection of a professional organization in which to seek membership is a personal issue, and this decision should be tied to a leader's current work environment. For example, a leader who was previously vested in a professional organization specializing in hospice care may no longer find the organization "relevant" if he or she decides to seek a leadership position within a multispecialty group practice. The goals of the two health organizations are not parallel. Outside stakeholders will clearly see that the leader has failed to maintain relevancy by not vesting himself or herself in a more creditable professional entity.

The greatest benefit offered by any professional organization is the opportunity to network and collaborate with peers from similar organizations. Despite the competitive nature of the business of health care, professional organizations seek to share best practices between and within similar organizations along the continuum of care. Professional organizations are also multidirectional warehouses where topical information from the environment is captured and then disseminated to leaders and organizational entities. For instance, professional organizations were seen as the leading entities for the dissemination of HIPAA information when these regulations and compliance standards were introduced in the latter part of the 1990s and early 2000s, over and above the information provided by governmental agencies.[15]

Professional organizations also provide opportunities for mentoring and networking. Young leaders who become fully vested in professional organizations that are willing to share information and best practices will find the favor returned in later years when new policies, practices, or procedures need to be developed quickly with minimal resources. Many health leaders will freely share and contribute knowledge to peers within professional organizations out of professional courtesy and respect for the common organization they share. Failing to join, contribute to, and maintain a presence in a professional organization of choice will surely decrease opportunities for both organizational and personal growth.

Service

Professional service can be defined in a variety of ways. It is suggested that health professionals consider service from a volunteer perspective that involves contributing to their own organizational entity, their community, and their personal professional organization of choice.

Leading by example and volunteering are critical parts of any leader's success. For instance, through his volunteer work as a reading tutor, which continued nearly up until the time of his death, Senator Edward Kennedy spent many hours around Washington, D.C., working with elementary school-aged children.[16] His leading by example resulted in the development of a district-wide volunteer initiative that resulted in hundreds of school-aged children in the nation's capitol having an adult mentor to read to them. Similarly, the health leader should be aware that if he or she wants the organization's employees to demonstrate organizational citizenship behavior (OCB)—that is, doing extra work for the organization that benefits the organization, albeit without compensation—the leader must model this behavior himself or herself and lead by example.

Many organizations thrive on the OCB initiatives of their employees. Simple activities such as sponsoring the department's annual Christmas party or starting a before-work exercise program demonstrate an individual's potential to the organization beyond those things documented in annual performance reports. Likewise, service to the community by volunteering to sit on after-hours community boards or participating in charitable outreach programs not only establishes an individual as a leader outside the organization, but also provides positive marketing for the organization itself. Service to professional organizations can also be rewarding in many ways that benefit both the individual and the organizational entity if the professional is able to rise, or become elected, to a national position of prominence. As a result, the service to the organization, service to the community, and service to the profession will collectively result in increased opportunities for both personal growth and organizational success.

Continuing Education

A few years ago, the authors of this book participated in a seminar where the speaker was discussing strategies to pass a Joint Commission accreditation site visit. The speaker was very well known to the group and had achieved a level of national prominence and respect by his peers. However, this particular speaker had not worked in the practical world of health care for several years. After a very brief period of time, it became clear to a few members of the audience that the speaker was addressing old standards and procedures that were no longer applicable to more recent initiatives in accreditation site visits. Many in the audience were not aware of the subtle outdated information that was presented; however, a few people did get up and walk out of the room. It was clear that the speaker had not maintained creditability and relevancy in regard to his personal continuing education since he had left his CEO position in a major facility.

Continuing education (CE) will be different for practicing patient providers and administrators. The elements of CE are generally described as twofold: (1) continuing health education (CHE), or nonclinical education, and (2) continuing medical education (CME), or clinical education. Other variations exist; however, these two are the prevalent forms in the health field of CE.

For clinical professionals, the need for CME is immediately evident. New pharmaceuticals, procedures, and materials are constantly being introduced and changing in ways that may affect patient care. Medical professionals who do not keep abreast of these changes place both themselves and the organization in professional peril.

For nonclinical professionals, the need for CHE may be less mandated by state and national licensing agencies. Nevertheless, failure to seek out CHE is progressive, noticeable, and professionally and organizationally damaging for a professional. A leader who is unaware of how national policy affects billing, organizational strategy, and compliance issues can place the organization at risk or, as in the seminar speaker example, expose the organization to a loss of reputation.

CE opportunities are generally widely available to a leader in the modern era. Webcasts, podcasts, computer-based training, online seminars, and teleconferences have made CE readily available to those serving in both rural and urban communities. A leader who seeks to maintain both personal and organizational relevancy and legitimacy will seek out those CE opportunities best suited to the organizational needs on a continual basis.

Mentoring and Professional Development

No individual is ever too old or experienced for mentoring and additional professional development. Self-proclaiming that a level of personal success has been reached such that there is no one individual left to role-model best practices or act as a benchmark for achievement can be both a narcissistic act and a fatally flawed methodology for achieving personal and organizational success. It is incumbent upon the leader to become a mentor to the next generation of health leaders.[17] Oftentimes a 30-year-old employee with five to seven years experience under his or her belt may be a more effective role model to a new employee than a more seasoned and (possibly) intimidating senior leader who is much older.

Seek out a mentor, ask questions, and follow examples of those leaders you find successful. You have a world of possible informal mentors to observe, including both those who perform well and those who do not; seek out those who perform at a high level and are moral leaders. If a mentor cannot be found in your current organization, seek a mentor (through a professional organization or association) from another organization; this is not a rare situation.

Professional development is a necessary component of staying relevant within the industry. Leaders all along the health continuum should seek opportunities to attend seminars and presentations on a continual basis. Additionally, staying current with the public and professional literature is important. Associations, topical publications, and top-tier news organizations provide a myriad of material to enhance a leader's knowledge base. A leader should allow for at least 30 to 60 minutes of professional reading each day to maintain a sense of relevancy with events in his or her environment. Quality books on leadership, management, systems, leading people, managing resources, and the like should be read as well.

Which book did you read last month and what are you reading this month? Try to finish a quality leadership and/or management book at least once a month.

DEVELOPMENT OF SYSTEMS TO LEAD PEOPLE AND MANAGE RESOURCES

As a health leader, you are responsible for leading people and managing resources (Has that been said often enough?). To accomplish these essential and broad tasks, leaders must develop, refine, evaluate, and implement systems that facilitate leading people and managing resources. Nearly all of the theories and models in this book—and many of the applications of these theories and models—have provided a foundation for developing these systems. We encourage health leaders to put the dynamic culture leadership (DCL) model into practice as a basis to a system to lead people and manage resources. Yes, we are biased toward our model, but it is a solid starting point (other methods exist and can be used equally effectively, of course). Personally, you as a health leader must "plug into" the systems you create. As a continuously developing situational and moral leader, your style, behaviors, and actions must be consistent with the organizational culture, values, strategies, and goals.

There are many systems in place in most health organizations, such as the human resources system, revenue management system, financial system, patient care system, and supply chain system. Considering these systems from a leadership perspective, are the systems and their associated processes aligned and consistent with the organizational culture required to succeed in the external environment? How do you keep these systems aligned and consistent? How would you use the DCL model to improve and integrate, with consistency, these systems? Remember—health leaders lead people and manage resources.

Take Care of People

The most important resources in any organization are the human resources. Individuals in any health organization will always be the most significant component of organizational success. Leaders will be wise to keep this fact close and personal. Without skilled, dedicated, and competent individuals to do the work of the organization in an ongoing manner, the organization is sure to fail. Always remember that the employees whom the leader directs will reflect the values and goals of the organization as well as communicate those goals and values to the customers whom the organization serves. Taking care of people is not only based on monetary and work environment factors, but also on moral grounds.[18]

Leaders should also recognize the importance of taking advantage of the diversity in the workforce. It is a well-known fact that workforce diversity lends itself to achieving a higher degree of technical quality and organizational efficiency. Diversity increases the personnel resource pool available to the leader, which in turn tends to eliminate groupthink and increase differentiation. An increase in differentiation allows the organization to pursue new and innovative concepts that will increase its ability to survive—and thrive—over the long term.[19]

Take Care of Resources

Resources are the materials and technologies that the leader needs to perform the business of the organization. Resources, in turn, are used as the inputs for the organization to process its outputs. This is true regardless of whether the organization has a service or manufacturing orientation. It is incumbent upon the leader to provide appropriate resources to the employees of the organization so that they can carry out the business of the entity. The leader must also stay abreast of emerging technologies that can aid employees in becoming more productive in the performance of their jobs. As a fiduciary agent of the health organization, the leader who can manage and take care of resources is better able to lead people. Managing resources tends to be easier than leading people; however, leaders must be competent at both aspects of leadership.

As a leader, you should develop and maintain a list of all resources under your management. This list should identify where the resource is housed, who uses it, how and when it is maintained (in-house, under warranty, or by contract), and, if appropriate, its calibration or performance quality assurance record. All resources (the tangible ones) should be on a maintenance schedule and checked according to the standards of practice for that resource; this is especially critical for resources that are used on, near, in, or with patients, providers, and staff. Also, all resources should be inventoried routinely (at least once a year) by you or your trusted representative; you should see and compare serial numbers for resources in use as compared to your list of resources. This inventory can be done with a quick check of 8 to 9 percent of resources on a monthly basis. During this inventory, verify if routine maintenance has been accomplished on the resource, if necessary supplies are available for use with the resource, and if the resource is in good working order.

As for intangible resources (such as dollars in a budget), leaders should keep track of committed and obligated funds. Leaders should meet routinely with the controller and/or financial officer of the health organization. It is suggested that young leaders meet with the financial officer once a month for the first six months of employment and then quarterly (at a minimum) thereafter to ensure fiscal responsibilities are being met and managed properly.

Pay Attention to Details

There is a careful balance in leadership between micromanagement and being detail oriented. In assessing the effectiveness of the work of the leader, the leader's communication of vision, mission, values, and goal statements should be explicit. Implicit communication will be effective only if there are ingrained values and norms in the organization that clearly support ambiguity in direction and goal orientation. For example, a leader looking to relax dress standards for "casual Fridays" away from a coat and tie to something like khakis and three-button shirts would be incorrect in assuming that all employees consider casual dress to include polo shirts and items featured in *GQ* magazine. As the leader, ensure that you communicate your expectations explicitly. Additionally, attend to the details of the organization without micromanaging the process of work. Finally, if you are not predisposed to paying attention to details, you can develop that skill and learn by consistency and perseverance. Set a goal to be detail oriented (see the discussion of goal setting theory in Chapter 5).

Attend to the Communities Served by the Organization

Health leaders are expected to be knowledgeable about the community in which they operate. Even more importantly, health leaders are expected to become involved in the communities that their organizations serve.

The reality of the modern business of health is that large organizations and individual populations of providers will tend to do business with the leaders of the organizations with which they have a personal relationship.[20, 21] While the Stark laws[22] prevent physicians from referring patients to only those facilities in which they have a financial interest, organizations, populations of physicians, and other entities will be more likely to do business with organizations with which they have an existing personal relationship. Without violating parameters of ethics, the reality of the environment is that trust remains a major factor in doing business in the health field.

Leaders can establish and maintain trust with organizations, populations of providers, and outside stakeholders by becoming involved and integrated in the community rather than isolating their personal and professional practices. To truly "live" in the community, the health leader will be expected to become a part of the process and participate in activities (or minimally support activities) along both horizontal and vertical community bridges. An effective leader will see being involved and becoming part of the community as a natural direction of organizational outreach. Those leaders who find this interaction to be too much of a chore might be advised to reread the job-fit characteristics outlined earlier in this text to see if the dynamic role of health leadership is truly their professional calling.[23, 24]

Share Your Knowledge

Health leaders are some of the most open, knowledge-sharing, and innovative industry leaders operating in the global community. The health community contains hundreds of health-related journals, industry trade publications, magazines, newspapers, and Web sites where best practices and innovative techniques are freely shared. Authors of these articles vigorously promote their ideas and personal success stories as benchmarks for success for peer organizations and affiliated professionals to adopt so that (often competing) organizations can improve their effectiveness. This behavior stands in stark contrast to that observed in nonhealth professions, such as the fast food and soft drink industries, where simple cola formulas and food recipes are regarded as top-secret property.

As a health leader, you have an obligation to contribute to the body of knowledge of the profession.[25] Leaders should personally author, or provide support and opportunity for those in the organization to author, descriptions of best practices and methods that increase outcomes along the continuum of care. Publishing, speaking at local and national conferences, and sharing information and knowledge will increase not only the leader's personal credibility and relevancy in the community, but also act as a proxy for increasing the recognition of the organization.

Partner with Community Leaders

The "Henry Ford," resource-dependent model of vertical integration, which attempts to control every aspect of production and throughput in an organization, has long since been cast aside. It is no longer possible to control every employee involved in sales and revenue generation connected to organizational survivability in the health industry. Joint ventures are becoming more common in the healthcare field as organizational entities try to achieve economies of scope and scale. Physician practice plans, sharing of administrative third-party entities, and contracting with part-time employees are models of success for future health organizations. As a result of these ventures, leaders will have to partner with other health leaders who are effective in their own specialty niche, such as technology or billing. In many cases, a leader may belong to an invisible network of suppliers, administrative personnel, record keepers, and human resources. Problems with simple one-item elements, such as a decrease in the availability of blood products from a single-source supplier, can threaten an organization's creditability and survivability in this environment if backup plans and collegial networks of support are not in place to assist the organization when it faces lean, changing, and turbid environments. Today's savvy health leader will be aware that the leader of a perceived rival organization today may be the organization's rescuer tomorrow in resource-restricted environments if positive relationships have been maintained.

INTEGRITY

Earlier in this book, we discussed the differences between, and application of, values, ethics, and morals. We have also addressed consistency in leadership outcomes associated with trust, honesty, and ethics. In this chapter alone, we have presented issues revolving around relevancy and creditability. The end result of consistency in practice and awareness by stakeholders of this genuine predisposition to care is a construct recognized by outside agents as integrity.[26, 27]

Integrity may be defined as the consistency of actions over time.[28] Lack of integrity is impossible to disguise for long periods. True integrity may be demonstrated through a leader's ability to lead by example, becoming a "Do as I do" leader, and taking responsibility for actions. If an early careerist can embrace these life rules as a compass for daily activities, he or she certainly has a high chance of achieving enviable professional development and success.

RELATIONSHIP BUILDING AND COMMUNICATION

Building relationships and communication have been emphasized in earlier chapters of this book. The ability to build and maintain relationships is critical for successful health leaders. Highly competent communication skills are also a health leader imperative for success. This section reiterates the foundations of relationships and communication. Read it while you keep all health organization stakeholders in mind, such as physicians, nurses, allied health staff, administrators, other leaders, community members, and patients. Can you visualize what you would do to build relationships and communicate with key stakeholder groups?

Factors to Strengthen Relationships

Relationships refer to the feelings, roles, norms, status, and trust that both affect and reflect the quality of communication between members of a group.[29] Relational communication theorists assert that every message has both a *content* and *relationship* dimension, where

- Content contains specific information conveyed to someone and
- Relationship messages that cue or provide hints about whether the sender/receiver likes or dislikes the other person.

Communicating with someone in a manner that provides both content and positive relationship information is important. Language, tone, and nonverbal communication work together to provide communicative meaning that is interpreted by another person. In particular, care must be taken with nonverbal communication:[30, 31]

- Nonverbal communication is more prevalent than verbal communication.
  - Eye contact
  - Facial expressions
  - Body posture
  - Movement
- People believe nonverbal communication more than verbal communication: Sixty-five percent of meaning is derived from nonverbal communication.
- People communicate emotions primarily through nonverbal communication: Ninety-three percent of emotions are communicated nonverbally.

Frequency of communication that is timely, useful, accurate, and in reasonable quantity must be considered to reinforce and validate the relationship. One important factor in this regard is *quality communication of sufficient and desired frequency,* which enhances the likelihood of developing quality interpersonal relationships.

Another key factor is *disclosure*. Disclosure relates to the type of information you and the other person in the relationship share with each other; disclosure is one factor that can help you "measure" or evaluate the depth and breadth of a relationship. The "deeper" the information disclosed, the closer the bond of the relationship. Broader topics of information and experience sharing (e.g., family activities, work, fishing together, or playing golf) suggest a closer bond within the relationship as well.

Self-disclosure can be categorized and measured. In the model below, level 5 illustrates a weak relationship bond whereas level 1 shows a strong relationship bond. Disclosure or self-disclosure is strongly and positively correlated with trust (i.e., connected such that more trust means more disclosure)—and trust starts with quality communication. Shown are Powell's self-disclosure levels:[32]

- Level 5: cliché communication
- Level 4: facts and biographical information
- Level 3: personal attitudes and ideas
- Level 2: personal feelings
- Level 1: peak communication (rare; usually with family or close friends)

In summary, self-disclosure can be described as follows:[33]

- A function of ongoing relationships
- Reciprocal
- Timed to what is happening in the relationship (contextual/situational/relational)
- Relevant to what is happening among people present
- Usually moves by small increments

A third factor in establishing effective relationships is *trust*. Trust is built and earned over time through honest interaction (communication and experiences). Honesty, inclusion, and sincerity are directly linked to building trust. Trust is an essential component of a quality, positive relationship. Honesty is being truthful and open concerning important pieces of information that you share with another person. Inclusion focuses on including the other person in the relationship in activities and experiences that are important to both of you. Inclusion is also about making sure the other person is part of the "group" in the organization. Sincerity is meaning what you say, meaning what you do, and not keeping a record or account of the relationship (not keeping score). Over time, if honesty, inclusion, and sincerity are the basis of your interaction with others, positive and quality relationships will begin to grow.

The fourth factor in relationship building is *cultural competence*. This factor is based on not only ethnical or national dimensions, but socioeconomic factors as well. For instance, consider the cultural differences in surgeons versus nurses versus facility technicians or linen staff or consultants. Every stakeholder group, and every individual, has a unique culture. Understanding those cultural issues, or "walking a mile in someone else's shoes," is a factor important to building solid interpersonal relationships. Understanding and modifying your approach to relationship building and enhancement based on cultural differences will serve you well in leadership positions.

Communication and Culture

Health leaders need to have exceptional communication skills. They must learn the techniques for clarifying what someone else is saying and for being clear in their own communication. Mintzberg's study on managerial work revealed that managers' activity was characterized by "brevity, variety, and fragmentation"; managers were continually seeking information and preferred oral communications to written reports.[34, 35] This finding applies to leaders as well. The preference for oral communication may be difficult for health leaders to enact, but is nonetheless important. As an example of personal preference for oral communication, it has been noted that within the first seven months of the Obama administration this U.S. President had more White House press conferences than his predecessor did in his eight years in the same position.[36] Verbal communication may be time consuming. Even so, given employees' and the public's need for such communication, it can be a very valuable tool for success.

Simply put, communication is the process of *acting on information.*[37] Communication contributes tremendously to the culture and climate of the health organization. A response—that is, feedback—is an essential aspect of this communication process. Obstacles to communication (noise), either in the channel or in the mind of the receiver, may contribute to an inaccurate understanding of the intended message. Communication is the main catalyst behind motivation efforts and strategies utilized by leaders.[38] "Various management [leadership] practices, including goal setting, reinforcement, feedback, and evaluation, require communication."[39] There are three goals of communication:

■ Understanding
■ Achieving the intended effect
■ Being ethical (moral)

Communication is a process of active transaction (transactive), which means messages are sent and received simultaneously. Everything you do or do not do, say or do not say, communicates something. You cannot *not* communicate.

HAVE FUN

Leaders of health organizations can endure only if they are having fun. Managing complex problems on a continuous problem-solving cycle[40] can lead to burnout and leader turnover. Those leaders who endure in the profession truly see the art and science of leading complex health organizations as a pseudo-hobby and as an extension of their own personality. If this is you, you have the potential to have a long and productive career in the health field.

SUMMARY

The practice of leadership, like the practice of medicine, is a constant effort of development. Each potential leader should pose the question, "What kind of leader do I want to become and be?" Leaders have an obligation to stay current and relevant in the field of leadership practice. Opportunities and obligations that have been successful in leveraging leadership resources for decades were discussed in this chapter, along with the affable quality of a leader to say, "I don't know," and learn from those around him or her.

DISCUSSION QUESTIONS

1. Describe the leader you want to become and be in a health organization. What is unique about your description?
2. What are the attributes of a successful health leader in the industry today?
3. What are three leadership and leadership-oriented theories and models, and how are they related to the attributes, behaviors, and actions of successful health leaders?
4. What are the key principles of inner leadership, leading people, managing resources, leader credibility and relevance, and community outreach for a health leader?
5. Combine three or more leadership-oriented theories and/or models with principles of inner leadership. Which theories or models did you select and why?
6. Appraise and defend a "perfect" health leader/mentor by explaining the knowledge, skills, abilities, and competencies of the "perfect" mentor. Is this similar to the type of leader you want to be and why?

EXERCISES

1. In a one-page paper, describe the leader you want to become and be in a health organization.

2. In a one- to two-page paper, explain the attributes of a successful health leader in the industry today.

3. In a one- to two-page paper, relate leadership and leadership-oriented theories and models to attributes, behaviors, and actions of successful health leaders.

4. In a two- to three-page paper, identify and assess the key principles of inner leadership, leading people, managing resources, leader credibility and relevance, and community outreach for a health leader.

5. In a two-page paper, combine three or more leadership-oriented theories or models with principles of inner leadership.

6. In a three-page paper, appraise and defend a "perfect" health leader/mentor by explaining the knowledge, skills, abilities, and competencies of the "perfect" mentor.

REFERENCES

1. Fairholm, G. (2003). *The techniques of inner leadership: Making inner leadership work.* Westport, CT: Praeger.
2. Murphy, E. C., & Murphy, M. A. (2002). *Leading on the edge of chaos: The 10 critical elements for success in volatile times* (p. 54). Paramus, NJ: Prentice-Hall.
3. Walsh, A., & Borkowski, S. (1995, Summer). Differences in factors affecting health care administration development. *Hospital & Health Services Administration. 40,* 263–277.
4. Ulrich, D., Zenger, J., & Smallwood, N. (1999). *Results-based leadership.* Boston: Harvard Business School Press.
5. Welch, R. L. (2000). Training a new generation of leaders. *Journal of Leadership Studies. 7*(1), 70–81.
6. Metzger, M. J., Flanagin, A. J., Eyal, K., Lemus, D. R., & McCann, R. (2003). Credibility in the 21st century: Integrating perspectives on source, message, and media credibility in the contemporary media environment. In P. Kalbfleisch (Ed.), *Communication yearbook* (Vol. 27, pp. 293–335). Mahwah, NJ: Lawrence Erlbaum Associates.
7. Sperber, D., & Wilson, D. (1986/1995) *Relevance: Communication and cognition* (2nd ed.). Oxford, UK: Blackwell.
8. Volk, M., & Lucas, M. (1991). Relationship of management style and anticipated turnover. *Dimensions of Critical Care Nursing, 10*(1), 35–40.
9. Dunham, N. C., Kindig, D. A , & Schulz, R. (1994, Fall). The value of the physician executive role to organizational effectiveness and performance. *Health Care Management Review, 19,* 56–63.
10. Morrison, R., Jones, L., & Fuller, B. (1997). The relation between leadership style and empowerment on job satisfaction of nurses. *Journal of Nursing Administration, 27*(5), 27–34.
11. Kouzes, J., & Posner, B. (1995). *The leadership challenge: How to keep getting extraordinary things done in organizations.* San Francisco, CA: Jossey-Bass.
12. Burns, J. (1978). *Leadership.* New York: Harper and Row.
13. Grinspun, D. (2000). Taking care of the bottom line: Shifting paradigms in hospital management. In D. L. Gustafson (Ed.), *Care and consequences* (pp. 22–24). Halifax, NS: Fernwood.
14. Upenieks, V. (2003). What constitutes effective leadership? *Journal of Nursing Administration, 33*(9), 456–467.
15. Coppola, M. N, Burke, D., Dianna, M., & Rangappa, S. (2002). Physician practice awareness and preparedness for HIPAA: A national survey. *Group Practice Journal, 51*(5), 13–19.
16. Local volunteer group remembers Sen. Kennedy's work. Retrieved September 14, 2009, from http://www.wjla.com/news/stories/0809/653842.html.
17. Prather, J. (2009). Soldiering on: Baylor Army grad mentors the next generation. *Baylor Line Magazine.* Retrieved September 12, 2009, from http://www.bayloralumniassociation.com/baylor_line/past_issues/win09_soldiering_on.asp.
18. Cole, M. (1999). Become the leader followers want to follow. *Supervision, 60*(12), 9–11.
19. Gillert, A., & Chuzischvili, G. (2004). Dealing with diversity: A matter of beliefs. *Industrial and Commercial Training, 36*(40), 166–170.
20. Six, F. (2004). Trust and trouble: Building interpersonal trust within organizations. Retrieved November 4, 2004, from http://hdl.handle.net/1765/1271.
21. Hamel, G., & Prahalad, C. K. (1994). *Competing for the future.* Boston: Harvard Business School Press.
22. Social Security Act Amendments of 1994 (P.L. 103-432).
23. Laschinger, H., Finegan, J., Shamian, J., & Casier, S. (2000). Organizational trust and empowerment in restructured health care settings: Effects on staff nurse commitment. *Journal of Nursing Administration, 30*(9), 413–425.

24. Wheatley, M. (2002). *Turning to one another: Simple conversations to restore hope to the future.* San Francisco, CA: Berrett-Koehler.

25. Hansen, M., Nohria, N., & Tierney, T. (1999). What's your strategy for managing knowledge? *Harvard Business Review, 77*(2), 106–116.

26. Carter, S. L. (1996). *Integrity* (pp. 7, 10). New York: Basic Books/HarperCollins. On page 242 Carter credits influence to some extent by the fine discussion of integrity in Martin Benjamin's book *Splitting the Difference: Compromise and Integrity in Ethics and Politics* (Lawrence, KS: Lawrence University Press of Kansas, 1990).

27. Lewicki, R., & Bunker, B. (1996). Developing and maintaining trust in work relationships. In R. N. Kramer & T. R. Tyler (Eds.), *Trust in organizations: Frontiers in theory and research* (pp. 114–139). Thousand Oaks, CA: Sage.

28. Storr L. (2004). Leading with integrity: A qualitative research study. *Journal of Health Organization & Management, 18*, 415–434.

29. Beebe, S. A., & Masterson, J. T. (1997). Communicating in small groups: Principles and practices (5th ed., p. 71). New York: Addison-Wesley Educational Publishers.

30. O'Hair, D., Friedrich, G. W., Wiemann, J. M., & Wiemann, M. O. (1997). *Competent communication* (2nd ed.). New York: St. Martin's Press.

31. Beebe & Masterson, note 29.

32. Beebe & Masterson, note 29.

33. Beebe & Masterson, note 29.

34. Mintzberg, H. (1989). *Mintzberg on management: Inside our strange world of organizations.* New York: Free Press.

35. Mintzberg, H. (1973). *The nature of managerial work.* New York: Harper & Row.

36. Obama going prime time to help ailing health initiative. (2009). *CBS Evening News.* Retrieved July 25, 2009, from http://www.cbsnews.com/blogs/2009/07/22/politics/politicalhotsheet/entry5179382.shtml.

37. Beebe & Masterson, note 29, p. 3.

38. Cusella, L. P. (1987). Feedback, motivation, and performance. In F. M. Jablin, L. L. Putnam, K. H. Roberts, & L. W. Porter (Eds.), *Handbook of organizational communication* (pp. 624–679). Newbury Park, CA: Sage.

39. Harris, T. E. (1993). *Applied organizational communication: Perspectives, principles and pragmatics* (p. 454). Hillsdale, NJ: Lawrence Erlbaum Associates.

40. Coppola, M. N. (1997, July/August). The four horsemen of the problem solving apocalypse. *Army Medical Department Journal, PB 8-97-7/8*, 20–27.

15

Leading Nonperforming Employees: Leadership Responsibility

Accountable work has consequences: rewards for work well done and sanctions for work that is not well done.

—Brian Dive, *The Accountable Leader*

This chapter discusses the role leaders have in health organizations when confronted with nonperforming employees. Positive aspects and opportunities for reiterating and defining standards of performance are addressed and articulated. Readers are encouraged to always see nonperforming employees in a positive light and to look for opportunities to coach, nurture, educate, and mentor these employees. Nonperforming employees can be viewed as opportunities to create and inspire personal loyalty and to create organizational loyalty, too. When all else fails, last-resort options and consequences of risk management and termination may be necessary.

LEARNING OBJECTIVES

1. Describe the importance of dealing with nonperforming employees in the workplace.
2. Distinguish between the different types of nonperforming employees in the organization.
3. Relate progressive strategies for moving nonperforming employees toward a more productive posture within the organization and predict outcomes of each strategy.
4. Diagram and differentiate the steps—that is, the progressive actions from initial recognition of the problem to termination—a leader should take when confronting nonperforming employees.
5. Categorize and summarize methods for implementing continuing education in the organization.
6. Evaluate the risk management issues associated with dismissing employees and/or asking them to engage in performance improvement plans.

INTRODUCTION

In earlier chapters in this text, we noted that people are the most important "resources" in the health organization. Human resources must be managed to meet the needs of the organization; however, as has been reiterated many times in this text, people are led. Human resource systems provide the framework to manage the professionals who represent the "people" in the health organization. Without dedicated and high-performing employees, no organization can be a success. A health organization will only be as good as the people who work in it—including the leader. Working alongside dedicated, autonomous, and hard-working employees can be a sincere pleasure for any leader. Unfortunately, the opposite may be true when leading nonperforming employees. In addition to all the other responsibilities of leadership the person in charge has to perform, there may be no task more difficult than working with nonperforming employees.[1] As a test of this proposition, we challenge you to ask any leader with whom you are familiar what his or her top three leadership challenges were in the current or a past leadership job. Typically, most leader replies will revolve around communication challenges, the health industry environment, and the difficulties of leading nonperforming employees.

At a recent keynote address to a university in Washington, D.C., former Secretary of State and Army General Colin Powell suggested that it is a leader's responsibility to lead not only the performing employees in an organization, but also the nonperforming employees. He stated that the entire organization will be watching the leader and how he or she leads these individuals.[2]

For the purpose of this chapter, we classify nonperforming employees into two categories: the unproductive employee and the employee who seeks to avoid work. Both types can pose a variety of complex challenges to the leader. Unfortunately, dealing with nonperforming employees cannot be delegated by the leader to a subordinate; this is true in most cases. It will always remain the personal responsibility of the leader to remedy the issues surrounding those who are not contributing to the workplace and to the health organization's mission. These situations are reminiscent of McGregor's Theory X and Theory Y employees; nonperforming employees would fall in the Theory X category.

Unproductive Employees

The unproductive employee may be an employee who lacks appropriate motivation or education needed to maintain productivity in the workplace. Such employees may be willing to perform the work of the organization; however, they may not have enough foundational or continuing education to actually "do" the work the job requires. Employees who were hired years ago with special skills and talents may find themselves working in organizations where those skills, tools, and abilities are no longer relevant. For example, an employee who is negligent in maintaining currency with innovation in medical informatics may gradually begin to become less productive in the workplace if this lack of currency results in an inability to do daily work. This specific aspect of nonperformance—an employee's lack of knowledge, skills, and abilities—will be addressed later in this chapter.

On the other end of the spectrum of unproductive employees are those who may no longer be inspired by the organization's leadership, policies, or mission to perform diligently on the job. Reflect on Herzberg's two-factor theory of intrinsic and extrinsic factors: Intrinsically, the employee may not be committed to the mission of the health organization; extrinsically, the employee may not be satisfied with new norms, policies, or pay or reward systems. For instance, an employee who is accustomed to receiving praise, additional responsibility, and being thought of as the "go-to" person in the organization under the supervision of one leader, may become less productive in the organization if supervised by a different leader whose style differs from that of his or her predecessor. Other factors may also affect the reality of employees becoming unproductive in the workplace. It will be incumbent upon the leader to discover the cause of these outcomes before trying to effect change. Using Herzberg's two-factor theory to identify potential intrinsic and extrinsic causes of an employee's lack of motivation to perform is a solid method of determining causes or catalysts that have led to nonperformance.

Regardless of the cause of the subpar performance, the leader needs to be aware that employees who are unable to perform the work of the organization on a continual basis affect other employees in the business.[3] For instance, other employees in the work unit may be forced to pick up the slack for the unproductive employee. This practice results in one or more employees having to do more tasks just to maintain the organization's effectiveness. Shouldering this extra burden for long periods of time will result in high employee dissatisfaction with the leader's effectiveness at remediating unproductive employees as well as a lack of desire to continue the work of the organization. Fortunately, strategies for improving the behavior and outcomes of unproductive employees are generally simple and easy to implement in the organization; ultimately, if the employee continues to be unproductive, dismissal may be the solution if the health leader has the will to move to that stage of progressive action.

Work Avoidance Employees

The second type of nonperforming employee is more troublesome. These employees are work avoiders (also known as malingerers). Malingerers attempt to avoid the work of the organization altogether, either for some personal reason or for secondary gain. Malingerers are employees who, *for whatever reason,* are no longer willing to perform the work of the organization on a daily basis. They feel entitled to continue to draw a paycheck from the health organization without delivering the requisite work productivity. This feeling of entitlement may have nothing to do with the employees' current work (or output) contributions to the workplace. As a result, employees who have adopted a work avoidance or malingering attitude toward the daily activities of work in the organization will affect the bottom line of the organization. Nonperforming employees such as these are similar to what Locke, as part of his goal setting theory, deems "social loafers." This situation should never be tolerated because it can create a new organizational culture characterized by entitlement and low productivity. This negative organizational culture may also lead to patient care errors, financial errors, and fraud.

Evidence of the leader becoming weak in handling malingerers will ultimately create a distrustful environment for all employees in the organization. The employees will eventually come to see the leader as ineffective, easily manipulated, and frail. Some employees may abandon their personal goal of achieving excellence in the workplace, allowing mediocrity and apathy to run rampant in the organization. Unfortunately, strategies for managing malingerers are more complex and time consuming than those used for managing unproductive employees, and can be both physical and emotionally draining. However, it is a leader's responsibility to lead not only the high performers in the organization, but also the low performers.

A Responsibility

A leader who allows nonperforming employees to continue along this path in the organization is not doing his or her job as a leader—it is as simple as that. Concomitant with successfully building teams and creating a positive work environment, the leader must take center stage in improving the work of nonperforming employees or dismissing these employees from the health organization. Both of these options are the most difficult job of leadership, regardless of the industry in which the leader works.

Verbally reprimanding or dismissing a nonperforming employee can invite in a host of unpleasant consequences. At a minimum, it can create discomfort in the workplace if informal relationships are tightly interconnected in professional organizational reporting chains. In more complex situations, the nonperforming employee may retaliate and file a complaint with any number of organizations, either internal or external to the organization. In this case, the leader places both the organization and himself or herself in a position of professional peril if appropriate documentation does not support verbal or other actions that confirms the lack of productivity of the employee and the steps initiated to remedy the lack of performance. Furthermore (and often even more troublesome), the result of any complaint filed against the leader by an employee may be viewed (incorrectly) by outside stakeholders as circumstantial evidence of a leader's inability to lead people in the organization. As a result, some leaders may become "gun-shy" about the potential for such employee retaliation. The outcome may be an inappropriate decision by the leader to do nothing or to take easy action over more difficult action and avoid the employee rather than confront the poor behavior.

In the worst-case scenario, steps taken to deal with nonperforming employees may lead to litigation. The unfortunate reality of defending against frivolous and nuisance employee complaints is that it often results in the organization expending significant financial and leadership resources in responding to these allegations. Thus, concurrently with taking legitimate action against nonperforming employees, the leader must ensure that his or her actions are supported by local laws, senior leadership, and internal policy. The leader must also ensure that the process is thoroughly documented.[4]

Leader Assessment of Nonperforming Personnel

As with all human endeavors, problems may arise that hinder, block, or eliminate the health organization's efforts to fulfill its mission and reach its vision state. People, employees, subordinates, peers, and, sometimes, superiors may be the catalysts or root of the problem. Even when the organization has a thoroughly vetted hiring system including a multilevel and multiple-approach interviewing process, some employees may not perform to the level required to meet the standards of the health organization. Sometimes organizational change creates a situation where employees can no longer perform to the level expected. When employees are not performing up to expectations, it is a health leader's duty and responsibility to intervene to remedy the situation.

Leader intervention in this situation takes courage, integrity, communication, and documentation; alignment with organizational values, direction, mission, vision, strategies, and goals; and compassion for the nonperforming employee. The leader at the closest level to the nonperforming employee should be the one to start the process of intervention, although more senior leaders may play a role if the situation dictates their involvement. Health leaders who do not intervene with nonperformers are simply reinforcing and modeling behaviors that are at odds with the leadership's predetermined organizational mission, vision, strategies, goals, objectives, and, ultimately, the culture needed for the organization to thrive in the health industry. As with all aspects of leadership, consistency is critical in intervening with nonperformers.

Given the two main categories of nonperforming employees, several approaches may be taken to evaluate nonperforming employees. Three approaches of evaluation are discussed in this section. First is evaluation of the lack of employee commitment or compliance or employee resistance to organizational norms, standards, policies, and procedures; this is an example of loose coupling by the employee when the organization requires a tighter level of coupling. In this modality, employee motivation is critical. Second is evaluation of the lack of knowledge, skills, or abilities or lack of competency of skills and abilities that create a nonperformance situation on the part of the employee; this can also incorporate the lack of the required licensures, certifications, or education/training. Third, evaluation may address whether the employee is inconsistent or unreliable in commitment or compliance with the health organization's norms, standards, policies, and procedures or inconsistent in job or task performance; that is, the employee may not fit into the culture of the organization. These situations are examples that directly link back to the model of commitment, compliance, or resistance. An individual's personality plays a major role in a leader's understanding of that employee.

Personality, as a construct, can assist in understanding the individual employee. "People like to believe that their behavior is sensible and rational, as opposed to foolish and irrational."[5] Personality is a complex and constantly evolving and adapting system of mental structures, mental processes (such as needs, wants, memories, and self-image), and the way in which individuals see themselves in relation to their environment.[6, 7] An employee's personality changes over time to adapt to the situation as well as his or her activity level, development, education and training, occupation, marital status, health, and socioeconomic status.[8] Employees' self-image—in essence, the values and beliefs they see in themselves and how they portray that image in the environment where they live and work—does remain relatively stable, however. For example, "the achievement-oriented person will continue to seek success, the conscientious person will continue to be reliable and the aggressive person will continue to be combative over time and across situations."[9]

Health leaders are increasingly interested in selecting, hiring, promoting, and sustaining employees who are able to adapt to changing situations; stay loyal to the organizational mission, vision, strategies, goals, and objectives; and perform their duties well. Likewise, employees who are not able to adapt to change, have questionable loyalty, and demonstrate marginal performance are not selected, not hired, and not promoted, and may face removal or punishment. Health leaders must foster hiring, rewarding, promoting, and resourcing of subordinates and other employees who can adapt to change, are organizationally loyal, and perform their duties well. When leaders do less than reward and credit subordinates with organizationally complementary and supportive personalities, then they are essentially reinforcing personalities and behaviors that go against the organizational direction, the organizational culture, and the leadership as a whole.

Reward those subordinates who exhibit the personalities and behaviors you want, and redirect those who do not meet your expectations. This simple fact is directly tied to the process of developing organizational culture through Schein's primary embedding mechanisms, as discussed in Chapter 9.

The next section presents several methods to intervene with the nonperforming employee in hopes of enhancing his or her performance and value to the organization.

Reiteration, Adaptation, and Commitment of Organizational Norms and Standards

The health marketplace is a highly competitive environment. Employees who have successfully made it through a set of screening criteria based on their education and experience as depicted on a resume, and later evaluative criteria based on personal interviews, have demonstrated that they are skilled and competent when applying for a job. No employer hires any employee with the preordained knowledge that the employee will be terminated within months or a few years after initial employment. The slow creep away from a position of performance may be gradual. The actual slip into nonperformance may even go unnoticed until negative outcomes emerge. In such cases, initial strategies for the leader are clear and simple.

Health leaders, when confronted with nonperforming subordinates, should reiterate organizational expectations, norms, and performance standards. Frequent communication of expectations should be verbalized, modeled, and documented to all subordinates and employees across the organization. Nevertheless, nonperforming employees may need explicit counseling of each expectation, norm, and performance standard. As in transformational leadership, individualized consideration and intellectual stimulation are key considerations when dealing with nonperformers; the leader must express how that nonperforming individual fits into the scheme of the organization and meshes with the organization's mission, vision, strategies, and goals.

Many times in health organizations, change results in the need to become more organizationally efficient and cost-conscious. In these situations, the leadership may change the requirements of compliance with policies and procedures. The requirement to be consistent and compliant with organizational policies, standards, and norms can be explained in terms of a construct called organizational coupling; both loose and tight coupling are possible, along with many degrees in between. When tighter organizational coupling becomes the new norm, some employees may find it difficult to adapt to the new culture. The strength of communication feedback loops determines organizational coupling; stronger feedback loops imply tighter coupling, whereas weaker loops suggest loose coupling.[10] Jelinek and Litterer suggest four criteria for determining the coupling status in organizations:

1. Formal rules: The more closely the rules are followed, the tighter the coupling.
2. Agreement on rules: The greater the employee congruence with the rules, the tighter the coupling.
3. Feedback: The closer the feedback in time, the tighter the coupling.
4. Attention: Empowered individuals allocate energy and time to prioritized areas in their "area" (participation, competence, and empowerment foster focused attention to areas of responsibility).[11]

To meet organizational norms, especially in compliance with policies, the health leader should facilitate frequent norm- and standards-oriented communication with the nonperforming employee to reinforce the new norm. Rewarding the performance of those employees in compliance with the norms and punishing those employees not in compliance are both part of a leader's duty in reinforcing and solidifying the organizational norm.

The leader should be aware that the creep into nonperformance may not be intentional or readily evident to the employee under discussion. An employee who has always managed medical records the same way for years may be unaware of new compliance regulations governing the disposition of these records. In a similar fashion, an employee who has worked for several years in an environment where subtle errors in internal memos or spreadsheets were tolerated may find himself or herself at odds with a new leader who has higher standards for this same information. The health leader should take opportunities whenever possible to reiterate workplace standards that reflect the positive aspects of committing to organizational standards rather than the negative aspects. For example, an employee who turns in a flawless report without spelling or mathematical errors should be publically praised so that the other employees are aware of benchmarks.[12] Examples of standards should be readily available to all employees; this is an example of how an organizational cultural artifact may be used as a model. This practice also helps to reemphasize the leader's performance standards and expectations of other employees without singling out noncompliant employees in the organization.

The passive role-modeling approach may not work for some employees who are too tightly wedded to their workplace habits. In such situations, it will be incumbent upon the leader to call the employee in for a positive, reassuring, and coaching/mentoring discussion where workplace standards are clearly presented simultaneously with the employee's efforts in meeting those standards. The employee's efforts should be praised, and the employee should be made to feel reassured and valued. This approach is critical in the process of reiterating standards. A leader who comes across too strongly, in an admonishing or overly critical manner, may not only lose the loyalty of that employee for the remainder of the time that they continue to work together, but may also create a perceived environment of intolerance in which the employee is not comfortable taking risks or engaging in organizational citizenship behavior. A careful balance must be maintained. An experienced leader will become comfortable and proactive in this strategy. The ideal outcome is the employee understanding the leader's vision and embracing it as his or her own.

The choice of whether to document these types of informal or verbal coaching sessions will be an individual decision made by the leader. The preponderance of employees will reflect on the conversation positively and improve their efforts toward meeting the organization's standards. This verbal, unrecorded, and unwritten exchange may be the only action necessary. However, should subsequent conversations need to take place over similar actions within a brief period of time, the leader may adopt a strategy of following up the conversation with a friendly and nonthreatening (no attribution) note or email that documents the conversation and the items discussed. This step will become important only if the leader believes that the employee will not take positive and individual steps to improve performance. It also begins the process of documentation to protect the organization at a later time should levels of nonperformance escalate.

STRATEGIES FOR COACHING, MENTORING, PEER MENTORING, AND EDUCATING NONPERFORMERS

Coaching, mentoring, peer mentoring, and educating nonperforming employees are other methods of changing the employee into a performer. These techniques have varying levels of time commitment and formality and are associated with potentially different outcomes. For example, coaching, as a central function, facilitates change and development.[13] Coaching, in the context of the nonperforming employee, is instructing, guiding, correcting, and challenging the employee to perform to expectations.

Coaching

Leader coaching is a continual process that goes beyond task accomplishment. It is a constant process of trying to improve task accomplishment through encouraging and valuing the employee. Coaching involves evaluating an employee's current efforts, motivating him or her to achieve greater outcomes on subsequent projects, and instilling a sense of pride and commitment to the organization. Leaders should constantly seek coaching opportunities in daily activities of work. These techniques can range from a simple visit to an employee's work station to discuss organizational progress, to more complex engagements where a leader shares his or her experience doing similar projects through demonstration. Leaders should be careful not to remove themselves from the direct coaching of employees in the organization; leaders must be "available" and "aware" of the activities they are responsible for and the people engaged under them in this work. Coaching, like leading itself, cannot be delegated.

It is difficult[14]—and perhaps impossible—to coach someone via email or memo (although weaker leaders may try to do so). Coaching is often a face-to-face reality of doing business in the modern health organization. However, these coaching techniques can also take place with groups of individuals in larger sessions addressing common points of productivity for all employees. Coaching is based in transformational leadership constructs such as individualized consideration, intellectual stimulation, and performance expectations for the employee. Personal, face-to-face, frequent, and planned actions are necessary to be a coach. Coaching in a professional sense is usually specific to a set of activities or work processes or tool utilization within a specific time period.

Mentoring

Leader mentoring has a similar, but slightly different role than coaching. Mentoring tends to be of broader scope (career oriented rather than specific to activities or projects or tool utilization) and requires a longer time commitment as compared to coaching, although the leader actions and behaviors used in coaching are often similar to those used in mentoring. Mentoring is discussed in detail in Chapter 16. The discussion here only briefly touches on mentoring in the context of leading nonperforming employees.

Mentoring nonperforming employees can be frustrating at first. The nonperforming employee may see mentoring as targeted behavior and feel that he or she is being singled out unfairly. The nonperforming employee may not look favorably on the leader's increased attention. Nevertheless, mentoring nonperforming employees should be considered one of the many leadership options available for improving performance.

Although professional mentoring usually requires a longer commitment of several months to a year or more, it can result in a professionally intimate relationship.[15] Mentoring is the practice of coaching coupled with instruction on the subtle elements of the profession while securing increasingly more challenging opportunities for the mentee by the mentor. Health leaders are, inherently, coaches and mentors. Both roles, subtly different, are performed to improve the future career of the employee and, therefore, the outlook for the organization as a whole. Both roles are also future oriented.

Similar to leader role modeling that is imbued with transformational leadership characteristics, coaching and mentoring complement the leadership persona. Hudson suggests that coaches and mentors follow these guidelines:

- Model mastery in professional areas that others want to obtain
- Guide others to high performance in emerging scenarios
- Advocate, criticize, and extend corporate [organizational] culture [to include culture change] and wisdom
- Endorse and sponsor others without using [or needing to] power or having control over them
- Facilitate professional development and organizational system development[16]

Deeprose recommends team coaching and mentoring in which the coach facilitates communication, conducts long-range planning, supports career development of team members, mediates or resolves conflicts, and measures performance.[17] Education and training are highlighted next.

Peer Mentoring

Peer mentoring differs from mentoring in several important ways. Peer mentoring occurs when information between two peers is freely shared without leader supervision or intervention. Peer mentoring can result in several positive benefits to the organization and those who participate in it. These benefits include opportunities for leader development at lower levels of the organization, opportunities for employees to improve the collegiality of their relationships with one another, and increased overall organization efficiency.[18] In the context of managing nonperforming employees, peer mentoring provides for a semi-formal process of aligning a well-performing employee or subordinate with a nonperforming or marginal-performing employee or subordinate. Much of the same coaching and mentoring concepts apply, but role-modeling and knowledge, skills, and abilities transfer in the process of the work environment are especially pronounced in this context. Many employees label peer mentoring as "on-the-job-training." While it *is* training on the job, it also entails purposefully matching an excellent performer with a lower-performing employee.

Peer mentoring is an effective way to facilitate the creation and sharing of knowledge, through its intentional linking of high performers and low performers.[19] Peer mentoring is also an old and time-honored tradition in organizations. Successful organizations have found ways to promote and leverage this behavior for centuries. One such example can be found in the *Wilson & Company Employee Handbook* from 1919. The employee handbook states (sic):

> Older employees can do a single service by giving new employees the benefit of their experience. Appoint yourself a Committee of One to take the new employee in your Department in tow. Point out the things he or she should know. You may be sure that your efforts will be appreciated. Remember too, the power and the responsibility of Example.

While this example specifically addresses new employees, the same philosophy can be applied to a nonperforming employee in any organization in the modern era.

It would be wonderful if all employees in the health organization were so conscientious and forward think-ing about the leadership of new or nonperforming employees. Organizations that have employees within their walls who see peer mentoring as an obligation of employment to the entity are truly rare and unique. In cases where this philosophy does exist, there may be little evidence of nonperforming employees in the organization at all. If this is not your organization (and likely so), it may be incumbent on you as a leader to ask high-performing employees to "adopt" nonperformers as a method of improving overall organizational performance. This method serves three main purposes: (1) it frees the leader's time to focus attention on other priorities of interest in the organization; (2) it provides an opportunity for leadership development of junior employees; and (3) it improves organizational effectiveness. A good leader leverages the resources available to him or her in the organization. If you are able to leverage your own employees in the task of improving nonperforming employee performance, do it!

Education and Training

Education and training are formalized, objective-based periods of instruction that explicitly sets learning ob-jectives and details expected mastery of knowledge, skills, abilities and behaviors. Education is a formal process, such as the path followed while earning a degree. In contrast, training is usually a workplace-oriented activity. Both education and training can enhance the knowledge, skills, and abilities of a nonperforming employee; ed-ucation and training can also positively influence behaviors, attitudes, and, to some degree, values and beliefs. The longer the learning time, the more potential impact the effort will have for the employee.

No industry in the United States is under more scrutiny in terms of the need for continuing education (CE) than the health professions. Unfortunately, the same high degree of CE that is offered to medical and allied health professionals may not be freely available to administrative, management, and general workers of the health organization. While it may be cost-prohibitive to send all employees to one- and two-day conferences on an annual basis, the organization should provide educational and training opportunities for all employees on a frequent and cyclical basis. Education and training must complement, enhance, or enable the organizational cul-ture envisioned by the leadership of the health organization.

The leader must be cognizant that CE is vital to the survival of the health organization. Education of all employees begins with their basic orientation in the health organization after being hired and ideally should continue throughout their tenure in the organization. A health organization cannot be recognized as "high performing" unless it continuously ensures that its employees are exposed to opportunities that enable them to update their skills with modern medical procedures and equipment, administrative techniques, and tech-nologies. For the health leader, creating such opportunities can be challenging, but significant effort must be made to ensure that health practitioners and administrative personnel maintain appropriate and up-to-date levels of professional competence. This competence directly contributes to the development of high-performing employees. Depending on the health professional specialty, CE may be required to maintain licensure, credentials, or status in professional associations as well as privileges to practice in the health organization.

Workshops

Workshops are closely associated with training and can assist nonperformers in correcting behaviors and ac-tions—that is, moving them toward those desired by the leadership. Both workshops and training need to be well planned, delivered, and logistically supported to achieve the expected outcomes of the activities. Gordon, Morgan, and Ponticell, as well as Blanchard and Thacker, advise leaders who are providing retraining, work-shops, or other education to subordinates, and especially to nonperformers, to consider nine principles before and during any such initiative:

1. Identify the types of individual learning strengths and problems, and tailor the training around them.
2. Align learning objectives to organizational goals.
3. Clearly define program goals and objectives at the start.
4. Actively engage the trainee, thus maximizing attention, expectations, and memory.

5. Use a systematic, logically connected sequencing of learning activities so that trainees have mastered lower levels of learning before moving onto higher levels.

6. Use a variety of training methods (such as auditory, visual-verbal, visual-nonverbal, and kinesthetic methods).

7. Use realistic, job-relevant training materials.

8. Allow trainees to work together and share experiences.

9. Provide constant feedback and reinforcement while encouraging self-assessment.[20, 21]

Learning

Even with nonperforming employees, effective health leaders must find the proper balance of education and training to assist them in developing the skills they need to perform their primary job, make sound decisions, and uncover underlying connections to deal with more general issues in the workplace. They are encouraged to work closely with professional educators and trainers so that education programs will be aligned with expected outcomes and provide realistic experiences that will produce the competencies essential to effective performance. As in most institutions, the fundamental forms of employee education in health settings materialize through the use of passive, active, and experiential learning techniques.

In *passive learning* (the most basic form), the employee simply sits quietly while receiving the information. Lectures are the classic illustration of this style of learning. If not necessarily the most enjoyable technique, reading manuals is another traditional form of passive education. More sophisticated techniques include demonstrations, videotapes, and self-taught or self-paced course materials. In addition, some large health organizations are putting training materials on their intranets that may include sophisticated graphics and video.[22] This type of learning uses visual-verbal (text), visual-nonverbal (graphics, pictures, and videos), and auditory learning modalities.

Active learning techniques include anything that the employee does in a classroom setting other than merely passively listening to a lecture. They encompass everything from listening, where the students/employees absorb what they hear; to short writing exercises, in which students/employees react to lecture material; to complex group exercises, in which students/employees apply course material to real-life situations and new problems.[23] This form of learning uses a combination of visual-verbal (text), visual-nonverbal (graphics, pictures, and videos), auditory (listening), and kinesthetic (doing) learning modalities.

Somewhere in between the activity levels of the passive and active learning alternatives is *experiential learning*, which involves learning through the work process. Basic on-the-job training of a new employee is the most common example. Another is rotation, in which an employee is temporarily placed in a different job setting so that he or she can acquire new knowledge and practice new techniques used by that unit.[24] The primary learning modality in experiential learning is kinesthetic.

Performance Appraisals

The performance appraisal is the assessment of the individual employee. In this activity, the health leader truly and honestly assesses an employee's performance across the spectrum of expectations. This process is a component of the health organization's performance management system. Performance appraisals are conducted periodically, such as annually, semi-annually, or quarterly. With nonperforming employees, more frequent appraisals, such as on a quarterly or monthly basis, may be prudent until the salient issues of nonperformance are resolved. Performance appraisals are the end of a performance assessment cycle. Setting expectations, such as by using the goal setting model from Locke and Latham's goal setting theory, and measuring performance are critical components of this process. The assessment cycle should follow a logical sequence of "setting performance goals and development plans with the employee, monitoring the employee's progress toward achieving objectives and goals, providing continual coaching, training and education as appropriate, conducting periodic performance reviews using measurable goals and development plans as guides, and establishing the next cycle's plan and goals."[25]

Health leaders should set aside significant time—perhaps an hour to 90 minutes—to conduct a face-to-face performance review with each employee; again, this step is especially critical with nonperforming employees.

Using a media-rich communication channel, such as face-to-face meetings, will foster feedback and a sense of urgency, and it better enables the leader to express expectations to the employee. Fried recommends that performance reviews should be reserved for the following situations:

- Giving employees the opportunity to discuss performance and performance standards
- Addressing employee strengths and weaknesses
- Identifying and recommending strategies for improving employee performance
- Discussing personnel decisions, such as compensation, promotion, and termination
- Defining a variety of regulatory requirements that deal with employee performance, and discussing compliance [and commitment] methods[26]

Successful health leaders use performance management systems to assess organizational, group, section, or team performance while evaluating individuals within those structures. Taking time to develop, revise, and utilize this system not only sets expectations and standards, but it also transfers culture and cultural meaning to others, and it sets measurable goals and objectives for everyone to commit to moving the organization forward to reach its vision.

Performance appraisals should reflect the actual work of the employee in the health organization. They should be based on performance metrics, output, and organizational potential. Unfortunately, many performance appraisals overrate employees' performance. In many cases, appraisals are used as tools to maintain harmony or professional collegiality in the workplace—this is not the purpose of the evaluation. Moreover, failing to maintain accurate and thoughtful reporting on the evaluation can reflect poorly on the leader's ability to manage the workforce.[27]

Lenient evaluations can become even more problematic when the upwardly mobile leader advances within the organization, or seeks a position outside the organization, and leaves a satisfactory performance history on nonperforming employees that makes it difficult for the next leader to take any form of corrective action. This self-serving bias negatively affects the performance of the organization and everyone in it.[28] Put simply, performance appraisals should never be used to maintain relationships, build professional bridges, or avoid the difficult task of confronting an employee's weak performance.

Modeling

There is a time-honored quote related to leadership that cannot be attributed to any one source. It is often repeated and highly cited in leadership, management, and organizational behavior literature as a panacea for success:

Do as I do

No individual in the organization is watched more closely than the leader, and no one's actions are analyzed more intensely than those of the leader. From the time the health leader arrives at the organization to the time he or she departs, subordinate employees will form judgments and opinions in regard to the leader's actions, words, and deeds. In particular, the chronically nonperforming employee may seek to leverage his or her own erratic behavior by pointing out the leader's shortcomings. A leader who has become too comfortable and relaxed in his or her job may informally signal to employees that this behavior may be emulated in the workplace. Any performance improvement in any employee must start with the leader role-modeling the behavior expected in the health organization.

For example, health leaders should always model the behavior they expect of subordinates, peers, and superiors (yes, even superiors—they are watching you as well). Modeling is contagious, and it becomes even more so when you are in a leadership position. Everyone watches leaders, and their actions set the tone by modeling appropriate and desired behaviors. According to social learning theory[29] (which is mostly attributed to Albert Bandura), the desired result or outcome of modeling is the mimicking of observed behavior by others. Leaders model behaviors and actions all the time, even when they do not realize it. Conscious modeling sets the expectation for behaviors and actions for all employees in the organization. For nonperforming employees, modeling can greatly assist in their learning. The more employees around the nonperformer who model the desired behavior, the more peer pressure builds to create adaption in the nonperformer.

RECOGNIZING THAT EMPLOYEE FAILURE CAN BE A FAILURE OF LEADERSHIP

Nonperforming subordinates are not solely to blame for their predicament; their nonperformance is also a failure of leadership. A health leader's ability to intervene positively and change a nonperformer into a performer is at the heart of this reality. The health leader should do all that is possible, such as creating an intervention plan for the nonperforming subordinate (based on the suggestions in this chapter), to turn around an employee so that he or she becomes a valuable part of the organization. Most people want to do a good job, be valuable, and contribute to the health organization's mission; this is a Theory Y perspective. Health leaders should do all they can to positively intervene when nonperformance is *first recognized*.

Be Sensitive to Personal Issues as the Causes of Nonperformance

Abraham Lincoln once said, "Most folks are about as happy as they make their minds up to be." If his statement is accurate, then a successful health leader would benefit greatly from learning to recognize and understand the problems that arise when leading employees, because there will be instances when employee problems that are carried from home into the workplace significantly affect an employee's ability to perform his or her job.

The majority of employees with personal problems will share those problems outright with their leader if he or she takes the time to listen. At other times, the leader needs to pay closer attention to an employee's mood or performance to identify personal problems that are cause for concern. Poor performance is typically a good early indication of trouble. If employees are going through a really tough time, their issue will almost always affect their performance. The most common signs that may indicate an employee needs help include (but are not limited to) coming in late frequently, avoidance of other employees, repeated absences, complaints about finances, argumentativeness, lack of concentration, and missed deadlines.

Initially, the health leader may chose to ignore the problem or wait until it goes away. Although this technique sometimes works, a successful leader must not let problems drag on longer than necessary. On the contrary, a health leader should not choose to ignore poor performance or behavior just because he or she is aware of an employee who is experiencing a problem. The leader has a right to expect adequate performance from all his or her employees. Continue to coach, counsel, and discipline as needed.

If reasonable accommodations can be made to reduce the stress or personal issues faced by the employee, then try to implement the accommodations. Many personal problems tend to be short lived; if the personal problem is long term or significant, referring the employee to counseling is a prudent step for the health leader. If the health leader senses that the personal issue of the employee could escalate, refer the employee to counseling and inform the human resources department of the health organization based on established procedures.

Be sensitive, yet firm about your expectations; be reasonable, but set boundaries. Comply with the health organization's policies (if you do not know them, ask the human resources department) with regard to employee personal issues that have affected or could affect either the employee's performance or the health organization's reputation.

Transformation, Transactional, and Situational Leadership Opportunities

As a health leader, you should recognize that many aspects of leadership discussed in this chapter mirror aspects of the transformational, transactional, and other situational leadership models. Using transformational characteristics (emphasized in coaching and mentoring, for example), transactional characteristics (for example, setting goals and outlining rewards and punishments, such as termination), and recognizing other situational leadership characteristics (such as the in-group and out-group concepts detailed in Fiedler's contingency theory) can greatly assist the health leader in intervention with the nonperforming subordinate or employee. The reader is advised to review transformational, transactional, and other situational leadership models presented earlier in this text.

OPTIONS FOR DISCIPLINE

Many disciplinary options may be used with nonperforming employees. From reducing authority, responsibility, and salary or pay, to demotion, to termination, the health leader has many ways to leverage transactional leadership in hopes of improving an employee's performance. The idea that "the punishment should fit the crime" is important, however: Small defects in employee performance should not engender large punishment actions by the leader. Likewise, gross violations of performance and behaviors should be subjected to more severe punishment and leadership actions. Remember—others are watching how leaders deal with nonperformers or violators of policies and procedures; fair and equitable treatment is always correct. Initially giving the employee the "benefit of the doubt" is a good rule as well.

The more severe the punishment for nonperformance, the more responsibility the health leader has to measure performance accurately, document expectations thoroughly, and engage in counseling of the nonperformer. In health organizations, considering the complexity of the organization, everyone should know and understand those behaviors and actions that are heavily frowned upon by leadership. At the same time, they should know that second chances are given. Some leader mercy will assist in creating a less stressful workplace. The leader should always keep a record of all nonperformance, indicating times, dates, activities, and locations where nonperformance is noticed.

Verbal and Written Warnings

Once nonperformance is noticed, the health leader should start with verbal warnings and discussion with the nonperforming employee. Written warnings and documentation should follow if the nonperformance is not corrected. Health leaders should also report their actions regarding written warnings and documentation to their superiors, so that the chain of leadership stays informed about the problem and can reinforce the direct leader's efforts.

Progressive Corrective Action

Progressive corrective action is usually effective in remedying employee performance problems. All too often, a health leader tolerates an employee's unacceptable performance for as long as possible without taking disciplinary action. When the employee's conduct finally becomes intolerable, the health leader then tends to overreact and recommend action of which its severity exceeds the severity of the actual infraction. By using a sequential progressive process, it is hoped that many employee problems can be corrected at an early stage, thereby benefiting both the health organization and the employee.

To achieve the most effective use of progressive corrective action for nonperforming employees, health leaders should become familiar with their health organization's human resources policies and departmental regulations. This ensures that infractions can be quickly and accurately identified and dealt with appropriately. Similarly, it is extremely important that good judgment be used in determining the degree of corrective action that is warranted in each employee's case. It is always a great idea to consult with the director of human resources prior to taking any action toward an employee. Also, in all instances where corrective action is required, it is the responsibility of the immediate health leader to initiate the action. In other words, sometimes you need to be the "bad guy" in the eye of the nonperforming employee before you enlist any assistance from senior leaders.

The high-performing employees will see you as a "leader" for their unit if your actions are warranted and appropriate given the violations committed by the nonperforming employee.

Progressive corrective action will generally result in one of four measures: (1) documented verbal warning, (2) documented written warning with improvement plan of action, (3) suspension, or (4) dismissal, depending on the severity of the employee's performance issues and the number of times the individual has been counseled. You should ask for, read, and retain a copy of your health organization's progressive corrective action policy from the human resources department. If the policy or an aspect of the policy is not clear or does not seem to be appropriate for the situation, meet with the human resources leader and health organization legal counsel for guidance *prior to* initiating the process identified in the policy with the nonperforming employee.

Verbal Warning

The health leader uses a verbal warning to single out the employee's exact performance or behavior problem. It is important to always provide the employee with an opportunity to explain his or her perspective of the situation. Follow up with a request for a specific positive and measurable change, and confirm with the employee his or her understanding of what is expected. Always advise the employee that the verbal warning will be documented and that a copy of the documentation of the discussion will be provided for the employee (as well as placed in his or her personnel file). Likewise, it is highly suggested that an acknowledgment of receipt of the warning be signed and dated by the employee prior to conclusion of the meeting.

Written Warning

The health leader begins the written warning process much like the verbal warning process. However, after requesting a specific change and achieving confirmation from the employee that he or she understands what has occurred, the leader proceeds to explain to the employee the importance of positive performance standards by the organization's employees. This discussion tends to go much more smoothly when the health leader expresses a desire and willingness to help the employee remain employed. This message is further reinforced with the creation of a written performance improvement plan. Even so, the health leader should advise the employee of the written warning, and explain that a copy of the documentation of the discussion will be provided for the employee (and placed in his or her personnel file). Correspondingly, it is always helpful to have the employee demonstrate an understanding of the desired behavior by signing and dating an organizational form of acknowledgment stating that disciplinary action could occur should there be a recurrence of the behavior.

Suspension

With suspension, the health leader initiates a similar counseling session as in the verbal and written warning phases. However, after providing the employee with an opportunity to explain the situation and advising him or her that the previous discussions/actions have been ineffective in modifying his or her behavior and performance, the health leader suspends the individual without pay for a specific number of days based on organizational policy. As with verbal and written corrective actions, the health leader has the employee sign and date an acknowledgment form for the corrective action, and the employee is informed that a copy of the acknowledgment will be placed in his or her personnel file.

Dismissal

Dismissal is the health leader's option of last resort. An employee who does not correct problems identified during the earlier phases of the progressive corrective action process is indicating an inability or unwillingness to change his or her behavior. That is, the employee clearly does not wish to work to reach satisfactory performance standards. It is during this time that the health leader must do what is best for both the organization and the employee. Indeed, discharge may well be the best solution for both parties.[30]

Before a dismissal action is undertaken, the health leader should have exhausted efforts to rehabilitate the nonperforming employee, and the health organization's human resources department, senior leaders, and legal counsel should have been aware of the situation for some time. Of course, according to health organization policy, some actions and behaviors of employees warrant immediate dismissal from the organization. In these situations, the health leader should immediately contact the senior leader (the health leader's superior), the human resources department, and legal counsel and follow their guidance as to the procedure to dismiss an employee based on a specific action, behavior, or event.

Employee Improvement Programs

Employee improvement programs are systematic methods to enhance performance of not just nonperformers, but also marginal performers. Leader identification and employee matriculation into such a program starts with a *person analysis* based on a series (a trend) of performance appraisals, documented counseling sessions, and verbal performance discussions:

> The person analysis identifies individuals who are not meeting the desired performance requirements or goals. The expected performance compared to the actual performance provides a performance discrepancy form which the training intervention can be designed. Data sources for the person analysis include supervisor ratings, performance appraisals, observation, interviews, questionnaires, tests, attitude surveys, checklists, rating scales, in basket exercises and simulations, and self ratings, and assessment centers.[31]

In essence, an employee improvement program is a professional "boot camp" focused on performance building, behavior change (such as termination of alcohol or drug abuse), and cultural adaptation. These programs can be semi-formal to formal in nature, may be held on-site at the workplace or off-site, and can be of either short-term or long-term duration.

Performance Improvement Plans

The performance improvement plan is designed to facilitate constructive discussion between a health leader and an underperforming employee. This discussion focuses on clarifying the work performance to be improved. Performance improvement plans are implemented at the discretion of the health leader when it becomes necessary to help an employee improve his or her performance. The plan should always be developed with input from the affected employee as a means to gain the employee's commitment to achieve the desired level of performance.

If a formal performance improvement plan is developed and documented, the employee should receive a copy of it; another copy should be placed in the employee's personnel file. In the event that the documented issues lead to more severe disciplinary actions, such as suspension or dismissal, the plan is signed by the employee and the leader or manager. Be aware that many employees will refuse to sign this type of document, especially when they dispute the evaluation. In this case, the health leader should document the employee's refusal to sign the plan. The employee's refusal to sign does not change the requirement for the employee to follow the improvement plan.[32]

Responsibilities to Document Nonperformance

Health leaders are duty-bound to document employees' failure or refusal to perform to standards or comply with organizational policies, standards, or norms. What the leader does with this documentation depends on the length of nonperformance of the employee, the severity of the nonperformance, and the motivation of the employee to correct, adapt, or adjust the undesirable behaviors and actions to meet expectations. Due process is the sequence of leader actions of identifying the problem, documenting the problem, counseling the nonperformer, remediating the situation, and providing enough time for the nonperforming employee to correct the behaviors and actions so that they align with organizational expectations. Due process is required for public-sector employees[33] by law, but is a good system for all other employees (called "at-will" employees, because they can be dismissed without cause) to deal with nonperformance.

When all fails to correct performance, termination is the usual remedy. Termination should be a near-to-last or last resort, undertaken only after exhausting the due process policy and all other options for intervention with the nonperforming employee. Termination is expensive because the hiring process to replace the nonperformer can be costly in dollars, time, and (potentially) legal liability. Of course, paying for nonperformance over time can also be expensive. Rubin and Fried cite four basic reasons for termination or dismissal for cause of a nonperforming employee:

- Misconduct, including fraud, embezzlement, and commission of a criminal act
- Violation of corporate policy or practice
- Material failure to perform employment obligations
- For professionals, loss of license[34]

Termination or dismissal of an employee is a serious matter. Health leaders should put the following recommendations into action concerning employee termination or dismissal:

1. Analyze the risk before terminating the employee, including all documentation pertaining to the employee.
2. Avoid procrastination.
3. Strategically select the date to terminate the employee by avoiding Fridays or significant personal dates of the employee.
4. Consult human resources personnel (and legal counsel, if necessary).
5. Act.[35]

It is the responsibility of the health leader, the human resources department, and the organization as a whole to assess risk and legal liability concerning any action—but most especially a negative action such as dismissal—that affects a subordinate or employee.

Risk Management and Legal Liability Associated with Creating Employee Improvement Programs and Termination

Risk and legal liability issues arise when steps such as creating employee improvement programs and terminating employees are undertaken. Anyone, for nearly any reason, can file a civil lawsuit against a health organization. For example, a suit may be filed if an employee who is targeted for intervention (e.g., with an employee improvement program) or an employee who has been terminated believes that he or she was treated unfairly, inconsistently (based on precedents set by the organization's dealings with other employees), or abruptly. The best countermeasures for these risks are health leader documentation, documented (with the employee's signature) counseling with the nonperforming employee, informing senior leaders in the organization about the situation of nonperformance, and early and ongoing counsel from the health organization's legal counsel or legal team.

Today's society is very litigious, so following published organizational policies and procedures regarding nonperformance, documentation, fair warning, and remedial intervention for the employee, along with continuous advice from in-house or retained legal experts, are key responsibilities of the successful and prudent health leader. Health leaders must train and guide subordinate leaders and managers in this process as well. In essence, health leaders need to build a documented and supportable case to negatively change the subordinate's status in the organization; this pertains to demotion, loss of bonus(es), termination or dismissal, or any other action that affects the employee negatively.

SUMMARY

This chapter discussed the role leaders have in health organizations when confronted with nonperforming employees. Positive aspects and opportunities for reiterating and defining standards of performance were addressed and articulated. Health leaders are encouraged to always see nonperforming employees in a positive light and to look for opportunities to coach, nurture, educate, and mentor these individuals. They should also see nonperforming employees as opportunities to create and inspire personal loyalty and to create organizational loyalty. When all else fails, last-resort options may become necessary, in which case the consequences of risk management and termination must be assessed carefully.

DISCUSSION QUESTIONS

1. Using your gender as a starting point, outline how you would admonish and reprimand a same-sex employee. Would this process be different than the one used with an opposite-sex employee? Why or why not?

2. Dealing with nonperforming employees is as unique as an individual's leadership style. How would you begin to inform an employee about his or her nonperforming behavior? Why would you start this way? How does the initiation of your leader actions work with your preferred leadership style (consider the results of your self-assessments from Chapter 2). How are your perceptions different from those of other members of the class? Do your initial findings support the theory that internal hard-wiring affects your leadership decision making in regard to nonperforming employees? Can you distinguish differences between different leadership styles?

3. How many verbal and undocumented warnings should an employee get before the formal process of written documentation starts? At what point do you think you would "give up" on coaching and mentoring an employee and move toward dismissal? How would you apply progressive action steps to nonperformance?

4. How would documentation of your attempts to make a nonperforming employee aware of his or her nonperformance assist you in risk management situations later on if the employee filed a complaint? How do your leader actions set a new standard or reinforce an existing standard for the organization, division, branch, or section? Analyze and infer how leader actions can set new standards or reinforce existing standards.

5. Discuss the differences and similarities between coaching, mentoring, and conducting a performance improvement plan. Do the techniques support one another, or are they mutually exclusive? Why? Devise a general plan for a "generic" nonperforming employee.

6. Discuss special circumstances in which the admonishment and reprimanding of an employee can be delegated to someone other than the employee's immediate supervisor. Justify when delegation in these cases is appropriate.

EXERCISES

1. In a one-page paper, describe the importance of dealing with nonperforming employees in the workplace.

2. In a one-page paper, distinguish between the different types of nonperforming employees in the organization.

3. In a two-page paper, describe progressive strategies for moving nonperforming employees toward a more productive posture within the organization and predict outcomes of each strategy.

4. In a two-page paper, diagram and differentiate the steps in the progressive action sequence, from initial warnings to termination, that a leader should take when confronting nonperforming employees.

5. In a one-page paper, categorize and summarize methods for implementing continuing education in the health organization.

6. In a two- to three-page paper, evaluate the risk management issues associated with dismissing an employee or asking an employee to comply with a performance improvement plan.

REFERENCES

1. Dive, B. (2007). *The accountable leader.* London: Kogan Page.
2. Powell, C. (2009, October 24). Keynote address at Capella University Colloquium, Arlington, VA.
3. Srisupatpongsa, K., & Jones, G. (2001). *Action to be taken with a non-performing employee decision model implementation.* Whitepaper developed by Saint-Gobain Crystals and Detectors, Houston, TX. Retrieved September 22, 2009, from http://mdm.gwu.edu/forman/GSmodels/Employee%20Action.pdf.
4. Eyres, P. (2005). Avoid successful lawsuits by non-performing employees. *Connections.* Retrieved September 22, 2009, from http://www.connectionsmagazine.com/articles/5/092.html.
5. James, L. R., & Mazerolle, M. D. (2002). *Personality in work organizations* (p. 9). Thousand Oaks, CA: Sage.
6. Allport, G. W. (1937). *Personality: A psychological interpretation.* New York: Holt.
7. Millon, T. (1990). The disorders of personality. In L. A. Pervin (Ed.), *Handbook of personality: Theory and research* (pp. 339–370). New York: Guilford.
8. James & Mazerolle, note 5.
9. James & Mazerolle, note 5, p. 1.
10. Van de Ven, A. H., & Poole, M. S. (1995). Explaining development and change in organizations. *Academy of Management Review, 20*(3), 510–541.
11. Jelinek, M., & Litterer, J. A. (1995). Toward entrepreneurial organizations: Meeting ambiguity with engagement, *Entrepreneurship: Theory and Practice, 19*(3), 137–169.
12. Branham, L. (2005). *The 7 hidden reasons employees leave: How to recognize the subtle signs and act before it's too late.* New York: AMACOM.
13. Hudson, F. M. (1999). *The handbook of coaching: A comprehensive resource guide for managers, executives, consultants, and human resource professionals* (p. 3). New York: Jossey-Bass.
14. Cahill, M., & Payne, G. (2006). Online mentoring: ANNA connections. *Nephrology Nursing Journal, 33*(6), 695–697.
15. Hudson, note 13, p. 6.
16. Hudson, note 13, p. 6.
17. Deeprose, D. (1995). *The team coach: Vital new skills for supervisors and managers in a team environment.* New York: AMACOM.
18. Bryant, S. E., & Terborg, J. R. (2008). Impact of peer mentor training on creating and sharing organizational knowledge. *Journal of Managerial Issues, 20*(1), 11–31.
19. Bryant & Terborg, note 18.
20. Gordon, E., Morgan, E., & Ponticell, J. (1995, September). The individualized training alternative. *Training and Development,* 52–60.
21. Blanchard, P. N., & Thacker, J. W. (1999). *Effective training systems, strategies, and practices.* Upper Saddle River, NJ: Prentice Hall.
22. Austin, C., & Boxerman, S. (2002). *Information systems for healthcare management.* Ann Arbor, MI: AUPHA Press/Health Administration Press.
23. Paulson, D. R., & Faust, J. L. (2009). Active learning for the college classroom. Retrieved September 24, 2009, from http://www.calstatela.edu/dept/chem/chem2/Active/#authors.
24. Shi, L. (2007). *Managing human resources in health care organizations.* Sudbury, MA: Jones and Bartlett.
25. Fried, B. J. (2008). Performance management. In B. J. Fried. & M. D. Fottler (Eds.), *Human resources in healthcare: Managing for success* (p. 261). Chicago, IL: Health Administration Press.
26. Fried, note 25, p. 262.
27. Holmes, B. (2003, June). The lenient evaluator is hurting your organization. *HR Magazine,* 11–14.
28. Greenberg, J. (1991, March). Motivation to inflate performance ratings: Perceptual bias or response bias? *Journal of Motivation and Emotion, 15*(1).
29. Retrieved June 19, 2009, from http://teachnet.edb.utexas.edu/~lynda_abbott/Social.html.
30. *Dismissing an employee.* (2007). Boston: Harvard Business School Publishing.
31. Johnson, J., Ledlow, G., & Kerr, B. (2005). Organizational development, training and knowledge management. In B. Fried, J. Johnson, & M. Fottler (Eds.), *Human resources in healthcare: Managing for success* (2nd ed., p. 213). Chicago, IL: Health Administration Press.
32. Flynn, W. J., Mathis, R. L., & Jackson, J. H. (2007). Healthcare human resource management (2nd ed.). Mason, Ohio: Thomson South-Western Publishing.
33. Rubin, B. L., & Fried, B. J. (2008). The legal environment of human resources. In B. J. Fried & M. D. Fottler (Eds.), *Human resources in healthcare: Managing for success* (p. 135). Chicago, IL: Health Administration Press.
34. Rubin & Fried, note 33, p. 134.
35. Rubin & Fried, note 33, pp. 133–134.

C H A P T E R

16

Responsibilities of Mentorship and Succession Planning

Health organizations that embrace a mentoring culture hope to cultivate leaders that remain in the organization to build trust and loyalty.

—Finley, Ivanitskaya, and Kennedy[1]

In this chapter, mentoring is discussed from a historical perspective. Mentoring has been part and parcel of leadership activities for many millennia. From its historical beginnings, mentoring has evolved to the point that it can influence modern-day organizational success, survivability, and prosperity. Mentoring can increase employee satisfaction and stabilize the organization during times of turbulent change. Lastly, mentoring can influence transitions in an organization when senior leaders depart an organization and others move into new positions.

The concept of mentoring was first discussed about 800 B.C. as illustrated in Greek mythology: *The Odyssey,* written by Homer, tells the story of a king named Odysseus who went to fight in the Trojan War, leaving his son Telemachus with a trusted friend named *Mentor.* This chapter discusses the importance and responsibilities that leaders have in mentoring. Strategies are posited for mentoring across constructs of culture and gender. Correlations with mentoring and organizational success are documented and addressed. Ways to implement a mentoring program within the organization that supports succession planning are covered as well. The chapter ends by presenting a template to develop a leadership system for use in leadership practice.

LEARNING OBJECTIVES

1. Describe the importance of mentorship and succession planning to the long-term success of the health organization.
2. Distinguish between the concepts of mentee and protégé.
3. Discuss some of the barriers in establishing a mentoring program in health organizations regarding gender, ethnicity, age, and race, and apply methods to reduce those barriers.
4. Explain the steps involved in establishing a mentoring program in an organization.
5. Differentiate and list similarities between leading, mentoring, and succession planning in health organizations.
6. Combine theories and models, develop an implementation plan, and evaluate a personal leadership system for practical application in a health organization.

HISTORY OF MENTORING

The term "mentor" is derived from the character named *Mentor,* who was a faithful friend of the Greek hero Odysseus in Homer's epic story, *The Odyssey.* When Odysseus went off to war, he left Mentor behind to serve as a tutor to his son, Telemachus. Mentor served ably in this role, earning a reputation as being wise, sober, and loyal. It is from the relationship between these two characters that the classic understanding of the term "mentorship" has evolved. However, it was not until 1883 that the word "mentor" appeared in a dictionary. When the word first entered into the American parlance and lexicon, it was defined as (sic) "a wise and faithful counselor or monitor."[2, 3] Certainly, roles and opinions of the mentor and the process of mentoring have changed over the years.

Mentoring as a distinct theory did not emerge in the modern era until 1978, when Levinson and his colleagues first looked at the benefits and measures associated with the mentor's and mentee's relationship to the organization.[4] In the 1980s, books and journals solidified the understanding of mentoring as a separate behavioral process, distinct from leadership and coaching.[5, 6] Several authors have found successful mentoring in the workplace to be a specific cause of success in organizations. As a result of these perceptions, mentoring eventually worked its way into organizational activities that supported both entity survival and organizational performance.[7, 8]

In contemporary terms, mentoring can be either a formal or an informal relationship between two people: a mentor and a mentee. A mentor is a person of greater knowledge or wisdom who shares his or her experiences to help develop the abilities of a person junior to the mentor; the junior leader is called a mentee. However, mentoring, like the study of leadership, is a complex study. Similar to leadership, the term "mentoring" (as found in the literature) is associated with a wide range of definitions. Words such as "guidance counselor," "expert," "leader," "advisor," and "coach" are often used in these definitions.

As originally defined, mentoring was a process where a wise and trusted advisor helped a less experienced person or professional.[9, 10] Over time, this definition has evolved, with some theorists suggesting that mentoring must also be a voluntary relationship of equality, openness, and trust between the counselor and the counselee.[11] Other scholars have suggested a mentor is defined as an individual influential in the work environment who has advanced experience and knowledge and who is committed to providing upward mobility and support to a certain person's career.[12] Finally, some have suggested that mentoring is analogous to a parent–child relationship, where the best interests of the mentee are placed over and above the mentor.[13] Regardless of the definition selected, in health leadership development, mentoring is generally the process of developing a relationship that can be either informal or formal, that involves two or more people, and that has the goal of securing some personal or professional outcome agreeable to the parties in the activity.

Why Mentor?

Health organizations that embrace a mentoring culture hope to cultivate leaders who remain in the organization, thereby building trust and loyalty.[14] Mentoring has shown to provide for greater stability of employees in an organization as well as to improve both the individual and organizational loyalty of employees. Ideally, these two benefits will ultimately result in improved organizational performance and survivability.

Health leaders should look at mentoring as a fundamental responsibility. Not only do the mentor and the mentee benefit from this exchange of ideas and information, but the organization benefits greatly as well. Consider this ancient Chinese proverb:

> If you want one year of prosperity, grow grain;
> If you want ten years of prosperity, grow trees;
> If you want one hundred years of prosperity, grow people.

The majority of health leaders would agree that leadership qualities are transferred by means of example (modeling). As such, it is important to know and understand that subordinates are always watching and learning from leaders' direct and indirect actions. For this reason, leaders need to accept the task of intentionally training those junior to them in all facets of their profession.

Additionally, it is important that subordinates learn the art and science of decision making. In this context, the goal is not necessarily for the mentee to make the decision, but rather that he or she understand the process through which the decision was made by the leader. A great by-product of such learning will be better teamwork and cohesion within the organization. For instance, once subordinates understand the central theme of a problem, they will be compelled to support decisions made by senior management, and when feasible they will be able to explain the decisions to other employees. Whether people agree or not, once they understand the issues surrounding a problem, they are less likely to gossip or cause dissension within the organization. Accurate information and communication always improve morale and team cohesion. This principle directly connects to the motivation and influence processes, especially in terms of the commitment, compliance, or resistance of subordinates regarding a leader-made decision.

THE DIFFERENCES AMONG LEADING, COACHING, AND MENTORING

Due to the very difficult nature of defining terms (i.e., constructs) in organizational behavior and leadership, it is not surprising that the terms "leading" and "mentoring" are often thought of as being synonymous. In reality, this is not the case. Leading is a macro organizational concept that involves the goal-directed behavior of followers toward organizationally selected mission, vision, values, and goals. Many employees in the organization may not see their boss's boss on a monthly or quarterly basis (or even over the scope of a year). For this reason, it is the leader's responsibility to carefully direct and lead those under him or her in a manner that results in consistent goal-directed behavior. This must be accomplished across the organization regardless of size or geographic displacement of employees.

Mentoring is quite different from this leadership activity. Mentoring is an individual process of taking a mentee "under the mentor's wing" and personally helping the individual to succeed in a professional career. The action is analogous to a mother or father bird shielding a young hatchling from all the threats of the environment (**Figure 16–1**). The process requires a combination of intense face-to-face coaching, leading, educating, and parenting to ensure that the mentee is successful at his or her job. Personal time resources and costs are invested in this activity.

FIGURE 16–1   Bird Under Wing

Many people in the field of health consider their personal adoption by high-level leaders in the organization as mentees to be a great compliment. Many mentors also fiercely protect their mentees (like a parent would) against internal politics and organizational threats (such as downsizing).

Coaching differs from both mentoring and leading. Coaching is more specific—that is, it is geared toward teaching specific skills or activities to the coached individual or trainee. It involves a transfer of skills, and a one-on-one development of the trainee's own knowledge and thought processes. It also emphasizes the development of team skills and creates a supportive environment that encourages and motivates the coached individual. The end state is that the personal qualities of the coached individual are developed in a positive way. Coaching occurs on a personal level but can also be done in groups over short periods of time.

Defining Protégé and Mentee Relationships

Mentoring can be defined according to organizational factors and specific job functions. Career functions help the protégé to develop career skills, by assigning challenging assignments to the individual, and psychosocial functions, by encouraging the protégé to pursue his or her dreams.[15] When a mentee takes on specific roles and responsibilities that are specifically directed toward preparing the mentee to ultimately replace the mentor in a certain position, the relationship between mentee and mentor is better defined as one of a mentor and protégé.

Protégé is derived from a French verb that means "to guide and support someone younger." In the business world, the protégé is guided and advised by the mentor, who has worn the same shoes and traveled the same path. Unlike in the relationship between mentor and mentee, where success in the profession is the ultimate goal of the mentee, the protégé is carefully guided in a controlled succession of education and progressive job opportunities that may ultimately lead to the protégé replacing the mentor in the job that the mentor currently occupies. This type of behavior is most often seen in family-dominated businesses where financial control and ownership of the organization will pass from parent to child. It is also seen in the British monarchy, where certain members of Parliament (in the House of Lords) inherit their positions based on birthright.[16]

Table 16–1 summarizes the key definitions related to mentoring, distinguishing it from similar, yet different leadership, coaching, and protégé relationships.

TABLE 16–1 **Mentoring-Related Terms Defined**

Term	Defined
Leadership	Concerned with overall organizational success of vision, mission, and goals of the organization. The leader directs dozens of personnel, who in turn supervise and mange hundreds or thousands of other employees.
Mentoring	Concerned with the overall success of the individual within the profession. This process is personal and intimate, and requires face-to-face interaction.
Mentor	A person of greater knowledge or wisdom who shares experience to help develop the abilities of a junior person.
Mentee	A person who seeks guidance or wisdom from a mentor.
Protégé	Concerned with personal succession. This process is wedded to a long-term commitment to leader development, resulting in the transfer of organizational responsibilities and organizational controls from mentor to protégé.
Coaching	Concerned with the overall success of groups of individuals in the organization. This process is personal, but not intimate, and it may not require direct contact and interaction.

Mentoring Across Cultural and Gender Barriers

Mentors and mentees must be matched according to their personality types and attitudes, rather than based on any cultural or demographic similarity.[17] By following this concept, the organization ensures that the resulting interpersonal relationship will strengthen the employee's creative thinking skills, while fostering a culture of respect and sharing in the workplace. The encouragement and promotion of fundamental values provide for rewards and the employee's integrative learning.[18] However, white male leaders should be aware of the potential for disproportionate mentoring opportunities: Non-Caucasians and females should receive mentoring opportunities in the workplace as well. Human nature tends to focus our efforts toward those who are like us; consider this book's earlier discussion of the trait, behavioral, and situational leadership phases. Both potential mentors and potential mentees should remain open to mentoring based on behavior, performance, and aptitude.

In support of this point, Finley, Ivanitskaya, and Kennedy found in their 2007 mentoring study of health leaders that 95 percent of the respondents to their survey were Caucasian, and 84 percent were men.[19] Two explanations for these findings are possible. First, the preponderance of health mentors who actively engaged in this role may have been Caucasian and male. Second, for some strange reason, minorities and females did not feel it was important to engage in a study of mentoring due to possible preconceived notions of the futility of the study in changing existing organizational practices.

Regardless of the exact reason for its existence, this trend is disturbing. It may not be satisfactory for a Caucasian male in the organization to only adopt same-gender and same-race mentees. The leader should be cognizant of the disproportionate opportunities for mentoring open to non-male, non-Caucasian employees, and should actively be on the lookout to establish mentoring opportunities among minorities and women in the workplace. It is not uncommon for some women and minorities in organizations to feel that they do not possess the necessary competencies for success if a culture of gender and racial diversity is not embraced.[20–22]

Earlier in this chapter, it was noted that the word "mentor" came from Greek mythology and the book, *The Odyssey*. However, what we failed to mention was that Athena (a goddess in myth) presented herself as a much older man to the child Telemachus, so that he would more readily accept the old man named Mentor as a wise sage. This example illustrates that for millennia the process of mentoring was male specific. Why would a Greek goddess deem it necessary to present herself to a mortal child in male form to gain his confidence and trust? This trend may continue to this day as well. A review of the literature suggests that the preponderance of the literature associated with the study of mentorship is male and nonminority-centric.[23, 24]

Hezlett and Gibson found that the major factor contributing to decreased levels of employee dissatisfaction, burnout, workplace disharmony, stress, and early retirement was mentoring.[25] They suggest that these factors are within the control of the organization to effect change. Also, because the consequences of these factors are known to disrupt organizational performance, the question might be, Why not implement a mentoring program (as opposed to not starting one)? Leaders in large organizations should always promote, within their organizational culture, opportunities for employees to seek out mentors. Mentoring also supports—if not enables—an organizational learning culture and possibly a knowledge management culture. The establishment of formal mentoring programs will assist in this process.[26]

It will always be the responsibility of the top leader in the organization to establish mentoring programs and to ensure their ongoing success. Nevertheless, all leaders at all levels of the organization can do their part in mentoring by leading by example and ensuring that personnel in their chain of supervision are mentored even if the corporate culture of the organization is not formally supportive of this process.[27]

Mentoring as a Means to Foster Organizational Success

Mature and experienced organizations will see mentoring as another method to help the entity achieve its mission, objectives, and goals. Additionally, mentoring programs can fit seamlessly into an organization's daily practice of doing business. As such, these programs do not interfere with the daily business of the entity, but complement and enhance the working activity.[28, 29]

According to the CEO of the American College of Healthcare Executives (ACHE), health leaders must "confront daily challenges by developing strong healthcare executives for tomorrow."[30] Furthermore, as noted earlier in this text, no health organization can be successful if it lacks strong and competent leaders. Mentoring helps foster the development of these leaders.

One of the primary objectives of mentoring is to ensure that organizational skills, organizational knowledge, and organizational best practices are transferred from the mentor to the mentee. As a result of this knowledge transfer, the organization benefits through the development of more highly trained and competent employees who are loyal, more efficient, and more competent in their jobs.[31]

Most mentors report longer job tenure related to having a formal mentor. Mentoring is a tool that both leaders and health organizations can use to help foster organizational success. It is considered a path for forging long-term personal and professional relationships, for acknowledging and fulfilling the basic spiritual and psychological human needs in support of today's and tomorrow's loyal employees. The process of mentoring can be used to instruct organizational culture, pass on technical expertise, develop creative problem solving, foster critical thinking, and build interpersonal skills.

Finley, Ivanitskaya, and Kennedy suggest that mentoring has myriad benefits for health executives. In their research, these authors discovered that mentoring was associated with both primary and secondary gains for the entire organization. Elements of satisfaction, performance, and productivity were all improved when the organization supported mentoring. However, the greatest benefit to the overall process was a culture shift, such that mentoring was seen as a responsibility of all employees in the organization and not just a duty of the CEO.[32]

A 2005 survey by Block and colleagues found that a major element in the turnover of nurses in health organizations was the nurses not having or receiving any mentorship in the organization. Considering the shortage of nurses in the nursing profession and the highly competitive nature of the health industry, it is much easier for nurses to find outside or alternative employment in the health industry than many of their similar, allied health peers. The job dissatisfaction experienced by nurses may be reduced by a leader-supported and organizationally based mentoring program.[33] Organizations that see the benefit in this approach and implement such a program most likely will decrease their turnover rates, increase employee and patient satisfaction, and maintain a competitive advantage in the workplace.

STARTING A MENTORING PROGRAM

Leaders in any health organization should establish, or provide an opportunity for the creation of, a formal mentoring program. Mentoring in health organizations, like a cargo net, may go up and down or from side to side. For example, it goes up when a new employee mentors an experienced worker on technology matters; it goes from side to side when employees relate common learning, knowledge, experiences, and skill sets with their coworkers within the organization.

Formal organizational mentoring programs must incorporate six critical elements to respond to the mentees' basic needs:[34, 35]

1. A mentoring program must have "clear strategic goals that are established and understood by all organizational members."

2. The program must have a "method to carefully select mentors."

3. It should "provide for confidentiality between the mentor and mentee."

4. Participants must be "trained with the skills needed to be successful mentors or mentees."

5. The mentor and mentee must "understand the importance of being politically savvy."

6. There must be "someone responsible for monitoring and assessing the status of the organization's planned mentoring efforts."

Mentoring helps prepare young health professionals to assume increased responsibilities in the health organization by encouraging job competency, professional development, higher education, and serving the needs of the organization. It can cover a wide range of areas, such as guiding a young administrator through the steps of professional development and career management; clarifying an individual's understanding of health operations in various health and care settings; becoming affiliated with professional organizations; and engaging in continuing educational and training programs. In the same way, mentoring sets a leadership example for new members of the medical community. It also includes sharing knowledge of the health organization itself, including an understanding of the organization's mission, vision, and strategic imperatives. Sharing knowledge regarding techniques, procedures, and skills is an important part of the process, but taking a personal interest in the individual's development is what separates mentoring from supervising—and is exactly what today's young health professional needs.

Mentoring and Technological Change

Although the Internet offers a vast and often bewildering array of information resources, there is still no substitute for human relationships. Tele-mentoring is emerging as a way to pair teachers and learners with subject-matter experts who can provide advice, guidance, and feedback on learning projects. Technology is also assisting mentoring in organizations as corporations with offices around the country and around the world connect mentors and protégés via electronic mail or videoconferencing.[36] In addition, tele-mentoring is proving essential in distance learning. The isolation that often contributes to distance learners dropping out can be overcome by pairing learners with faculty tele-mentors. Empire State College, for example, has successfully used this strategy to improve retention and completion for distance learners and adult students in individualized degree programs.[37] At Iona College, faculty mentors use telephone, written, and e-mail interaction to guide video-based learning for adult students.[38]

The combination of digital technologies and organizational change is making individuals more responsible for their own learning and career development. Freelancing, consulting, and "portfolio work" make it more difficult for people to connect with traditional sources of mentors in organizations.[39] At the same time, telecommuting increases the worker's physical distance from the workplace and decreases the ability to acquire the tacit or craft knowledge that comes from interaction with experienced workers. For these reasons, mentoring becomes even more important for individuals who are attempting to develop an array of flexible skills and for organizations that are seeking to maintain institutional knowledge.[40]

Mentoring and Organizational Change

Organizational trends such as downsizing, restructuring, teamwork orientation, increased diversity, and individual responsibility for career development are contributing to the resurgent interest in mentoring. Downsizing has heightened the need to preserve institutional memory and to share the information and experiences that remain in the company.[41] Mentors represent continuity; as mentors, older, experienced workers can continue contributing to their organizations and professions. The Mentoring Institute maintains that, in the past, mentoring typically "just happened" as experienced people recognized and developed new talent or as beginners sought the counsel of knowledgeable elders. Now, the institute describes a "new mentoring paradigm": Today's protégés are better educated but still need a mentor's practical know-how and wisdom (craft knowledge) that can be acquired only experientially. Therefore, many organizations are instituting formal mentoring programs as a cost-effective way to upgrade skills, enhance recruitment and retention, and increase job satisfaction.[42, 43]

Many mentoring programs have been geared specifically toward women and minorities as a way of helping them break into the "good old boy network" and through the "glass ceiling." However, the value of opening these opportunities to all is being recognized. Gunn suggests that a more democratic approach to mentoring is emerging, with such programs being thrown open to more employees at more levels.[44] For example, a high-level new employee hired because of specific expertise may still need the coaching in organizational culture that mentors can provide—a form of partnership that entails a two-way transfer of skills and experience. This more inclusive mentoring strategy is seen as an alternative to the career ladders and security that organizations are no longer providing. Another democratic approach is a trend toward group mentoring, in which the mentor is a learning leader of a team or "learning group" within a learning organization.[45] Members of a diverse learning group can learn from one another (peer mentoring) as well as from the learning leader.

Loeb goes further by suggesting that one-on-one mentoring is becoming less viable as competition increases and people change jobs more frequently, becoming less identified with one organization. He recommends that individuals manage their own career development with the help of a "board of advisors," where multiple mentors within and outside of their organizations provide a wide range of expertise and advice about both specific organizational politics and culture as well as broader trends in a profession or field.[46]

RESPONSIBILITIES OF THE MENTOR AND THE MENTEE

The Mentor

An effective mentor must, at a minimum, have a heightened awareness of or sensitivity to the needs of others, and be willing to pause and listen (empathy). Formal mentoring requires dedication and commitment both to the individual and to the organization. On some occasions, a member's need for mentoring may go beyond the capabilities, time, or resources of the assigned mentor. In such cases, referral to a more appropriate resource is necessary. It is the mentor's responsibility to recognize these limitations and offer alternatives. The mentor is encouraged to set the stage by establishing a mentoring agreement with the individual to be mentored. Such an agreement defines the objectives to be achieved and timelines for accomplishment. This kind of "contract" will help ensure an effective mentoring relationship from the start.[47]

The Mentee

The effective mentee must be a receptive and willing participant. There must be noticeable enthusiasm on the part of the mentee to take responsibility for his or her own growth and development. Similarly, the mentee must be eager to learn and grow through new challenges and opportunities. An important aspect of the relationship for the mentee will be receptiveness to feedback and sharing personal information with the mentor. In the same manner, a mentee has to discover the mentor that is right for him or her. Also, the mentee must understand that mentorship is not necessarily a lifelong proposition. The relationship may last for only several months to several years, or it might last for the duration of either the mentor's or the mentee's career. The nature of the relationship will depend on the dynamics of the relationship, the mentee's needs, and the willingness of the mentor to continue to work with the mentee.

The Mentee–Mentor Relationship Mix

The mentee and the mentor fulfill a mutually symbiotic relationship while benefiting the organization. In addition to the obvious benefits already discussed in regard to organizational performance and knowledge transfer, the role of a mentor can be psychologically and personally gratifying. The mentor feels that he or she has ensured the success of the organization where the mentor has worked for years as well as that he or she has completely fulfilled the responsibilities of a leader by ensuring that the next generation is prepared to meet future challenges. The rewards for the mentee are more readily evident through increased abilities and opportunities.

Kelly discusses four primary elements necessary to make a mentor and mentee relationship work:[48]

- Socialization: the process of integrating the mentee into the organization's culture
- Technological assistance: the process of acquainting the mentee with the informatics of the profession
- Career advancement: personal and specific goal directed actions that support the mentees growth in the organization
- Emotional support: as a parent supports a child, so does the mentor take care of the mentee

There are also some downsides to mentorship. For example, there may be a perception on the part of the mentee's peers or subordinates that the mentee is receiving preferential treatment. There can be additional challenges in this regard with cross-gender mentoring relationships. Also, mentor–mentee relationships evolve over time and can terminate with negative feelings or unfulfilled expectations on the part of one or both parties.

Mentoring Story

Dr. Coppola was the youngest officer in the history of the Army Medical Service Corps to receive the Army's Mentoring Award. Previous recipients had all been general officers or colonels. In fact, Dr. Coppola had received a similar award, called the Peer Award, from the Medical College of Virginia Campus, Virginia Commonwealth University's graduate program, while he was there as a doctoral student.[49] When asked why he thought he had been selected for both awards, Coppola replied, "I was always more interested in the success of those around me than in my own success or accomplishments." He went on to say, "I suppose I had my own method of evaluating my own performance, and that metric was the fact that the people around me, and those who worked for me, were advancing and excelling. My own success was always secondary."

When encouraged to expand on the specific tasks he engaged in with his subordinates and peers to receive such high approbation, Coppola replied, "It's really just a matter of freely giving your time. I never said 'no' to anyone who ever came to me for help or advice. I also made it a point to get out of my office and visit with my subordinates and peers other than during the normal professional activities of work. Moreover, I never waited for my employees to come to me. I'd often offer career and professional advice without being asked. Mentorship is really not a once-a-year activity during a performance evaluation. When you actively take a 24/7 interest in an employee's professional career, its appreciated by your employees and becomes valued."

Soldiering On: Baylor Army Grad Mentors the Next Generation

FIGURE 16–2   Dr. Nicholas Coppola, Mentor

When Dr. Nicholas Coppola retired from the U.S. Army in June 2008, he was leaving a job he loved. A 1997 graduate of Baylor's Army graduate program in health administration in San Antonio, Coppola went on to earn a PhD from the Medical College of Virginia in 2003 before returning to proudly direct Baylor's San Antonio graduate program for five years.

But Coppola didn't just hang up his uniform and walk away forgotten. Shortly after retiring, he learned that he had been chosen to receive both the 2008 Army Medical Service Corps (MSC) Mentor of the Year Award and the 2008 Educator of the Year Award.

While both honors are meaningful, he says he was especially humbled at receiving the Mentorship Award. Coppola was selected by junior officers all over the military system as the senior officer who demonstrated "exceptional, measurable, and visible mentorship recognizable to all members of the MSC regardless of rank or duty description" and "displayed altruistic and selfless service to MSC officers worldwide."

He says, "I got notice of the award about a week or so after I officially retired. After twenty-six years, I was going through some very typical self-analysis. Did I do everything I could do to assure that the next generation is prepared? I guess it's sort of like fathers sending children off to college—did I do enough?"

He has now moved to Lubbock with his wife, Susannah, and three children, where he is program director and an associate professor with the Master of Science in Clinical Practice Management program of the Texas Tech University Health Science Center.

But thanks to dedicated mentors like Coppola, other graduates from Baylor's MHA program will be equally well equipped. "As I looked at my goals and visions and objectives," he says, "I was always focused on preparing the next generation of soldiers to assume leadership in military health care."

Source: Pratner, J. (2009). Soldier on: Baylor Army grad mentors the next generation. *Baylor Line, 71*(1).

But Coppola was never one to shy away from one-time mentoring events, either. If a soldier with whom he had little contact needed or requested some mentorship, Coppola would make sure he was available to share time with that individual.

"I was always cognizant that I might not ever see that individual again," Coppola said, "However, if I could make a favorable impression on young healthcare executives that resulted in a positive outcome in their careers down the road, that was my only personal motivation."

When prompted to sum up his mentoring philosophy, Coppola replied, "I made sure I was not a 9 A.M. to 5 P.M. mentor. I always took an active interest in the person's family, career, and personal interests. Activities like these are not something that leaders generally get evaluated for—*nor should they seek recognition for*—but are simply the right things to do. Lastly, I suppose I always saw my soldiers and students as extensions of my own family. And when your subordinates know you mean this—and do this—everything else falls into place by itself."

SUCCESSION PLANNING

As emphasized throughout this chapter, mentoring the next generation of healthcare leaders is a critical component of organizational success. With an aging workforce, it is more and more incumbent on organizations to include leadership succession planning early in the life-cycle model rather than later.[50]

In addition to losing skilled and highly qualified employees, the organization faces the reality of the loss of talent and institutional memory, which are even more difficult to replace. Positive relationships with outside stakeholders, collegiality with local organizations within the competitive environment, and the ability to be productive and efficient are incalculable intangibles that represent huge losses to any organization as the workforce ages.[51] An appropriate succession plan can help alleviate this dilemma.

The primary purpose of succession planning is to ensure that there is appropriate training and development of junior employees, thereby preparing them to assume more responsible positions of leadership. Succession planning, like leadership development and mentoring, is a continuous process that must start years in advance of retirements or leader transitions in the organization. According to Thurgood, "Leaders in a variety of organizations must understand the role and importance of effective leadership, leadership development and succession planning in achieving organizational success. Unfortunately, leadership and leadership development do not confine themselves to a single 'checklist,' comprehensive model, or flow chart."[52]

The health industry is no more stable or resistant to the impact of the economy and stakeholder dynamics than any other organizational entity.[53] Furthermore, the unfortunate reality of some recent trends—namely, the discovery of unethical practices of business leaders—suggests a strong need for health organizations to engage in appropriate succession planning.[54] As Swayne, Duncan, and Ginter have suggested, the health industry must be ready at all echelons within the organizational architecture to advance and replace leaders on a moment's notice. These leaders should possess the talent, skills, and organizational knowledge to maintain the performance of the organization during times of stress.[55] Establishing a mentoring program (in addition to other sound principles of continuing education and leader development) in an organization will ensure that several levels of the organization (leader redundancy) are established and will remain stable should the primary leader or mentor suddenly depart. Cultivating a mentoring program is one methodology that ensures succession plan success.

LEADERSHIP DECISIONS FOR YOUR LEADERSHIP SYSTEM

How much of the material and content in this textbook is relevant, memorable, and useful? Ideally, your answer to this question will be "Much," "A lot," or "Most." In reality, all of the material and context is important; application of some of the material and context is absolutely necessary, whereas application of other material and context is situational. What is important is how you critically think about, assess, plan, determine, implement, monitor, improve, and maintain how you lead, how the organization where you lead performs, and how well you meet the needs and expectations of the communities and external environment you serve.

First, as a leader in your organization (or future organization), what vision do you have for the area (or section or department or division) you lead based on the organization's strategic plan (mission, vision, strategies, goals, objectives, and values)? Write that vision down, along with the key values your leadership system holds onto. Be aware, however, that your leadership system vision and values must "fit" the organization you serve. From your vision and values, which kind of organizational culture (for your area of responsibility) are you developing? Write that statement down. Lastly, list key organizational links such as strategies, goals, and objectives that fall within your leadership area of responsibility (directly and indirectly). These items, vision, values, culture, and linkages form the foundation from which you can "launch" your leadership system, regardless of the size of your leadership area of responsibility (large or small).

This section concentrates on envisioning your leadership "system": Select those theories and models that are the most applicable, determine how you would apply those theories and models, consider whether a synthesis of theories and models would be most appropriate, and contemplate how you would evaluate your overall approach. This important exercise is very personal; these decisions have to fit you. However, this is a wonderful tool to bring and discuss with your mentor or supervisor. To facilitate this work, a template such as the one shown below could be utilized for your leadership "system" (in reality, this template could be many pages long; an example is shown in **Table 16–2**). You should review your notes and highlights from Chapters 2, 4, 6, 8, 10, and 11 from this textbook to prepare for this exercise. Once you finish filling out the template, how consistent are the different parts of your leadership "system"? Consistency should be evaluated and measured by scoring each construct or item to your leadership system vision.

Vision of your leadership system:

_____
_____
_____
_____
_____

Values of your leadership system:

_____   _____
_____   _____
_____   _____
_____   _____
_____   _____

Organizational culture (Write a statement based on your vision and values that explains your envisioned culture.):

_____
_____
_____
_____
_____
_____

Organizational strategies, goals, etc. . . (Which organizational links influence your leadership at your level and in your area of responsibility?):

_____
_____
_____
_____
_____
_____

TABLE 16–2 Leadership System Template Example

Construct	Applicable Theories And Models (Must Fit You)	How To Apply (Single Theory or Model or a Synthesis of Theories and Models)	Evaluation (What Is Successful Utilization?)	Time Period
Leadership style	Dynamic culture leadership (DCL); transformational leadership; transactional leadership; reframing organizational leadership and management.	Use DCL as a sequential system to lead and manage; transformational leadership coupled with transactional leadership as a personal leadership style; and reframing organizational leadership as situational to emphasize appropriate frames in action and communication.	Plan and complete the sequence of DCL; keep a daily reflective journal of your leadership style to evaluate transformational and transactional leadership and in communication; determine the appropriate framework to emphasize in a log.	Within 18 months. Start the journal immediately and continue it for one year; periodically (weekly) assess the journal. Start the log immediately and assess it weekly along with the journal.
Organizational culture leadership	Edgar Schein's primary embedding mechanisms and secondary reinforcement mechanisms; coordinated management of meaning; Shutz's theory of affiliation; goal setting theory.	Integrate the primary and secondary mechanisms with your leadership style and measures of subordinate performance based on goal setting for each subordinate that focuses on team building and performance.	Determine measurement of key variables; monitor and report them for the team. Assign and monitor subordinate goals and progress toward those goals, placing equal weight on team performance goals. Maintain a behaviors and actions log that reflects the desired culture and identifies any behavior that does not match the desired culture (praise publically good behavior and counsel in private behavior to improve).	Within 6 months. Integrate primary and secondary mechanisms into daily work and subordinate goals (as appropriate); monitor with performance appraisals every 6 months for 2 years. Keep the actions log and review it (not pointing fingers at anyone with "bad" log entries) with the subordinate group monthly for one year.

Communication environment	Confirming communication environment; media richness theory; conflict management.	How would you utilize a synthesis of these theories and models?	How would you evaluate this?	What time frame seems to be reasonable?
Planning	Which theories and models would you use?	How would you utilize a synthesis of these theories and models?	How would you evaluate this?	What time frame seems to be reasonable?
Decision making	Which theories and models would you use?	How would you utilize a synthesis of these theories and models?	How would you evaluate this?	What time frame seems to be reasonable?
Employee enhancement	Which theories and models would you use?	How would you utilize a synthesis of these theories and models?	How would you evaluate this?	What time frame seems to be reasonable?

To assess your consistency, based on your vision, values, organizational culture, and organizational links statements and lists, score each construct (use the cell/box in Table 16–2 that lists the construct for each) for commitment to that foundation on a 10-point scale; sum the number of consistency points and divide by the number of constructs to get an average. A higher average is better, but the number should definitely be above 8.

As you can see, assessment of your leadership system is a very extensive exercise that requires considerable critical thinking—thinking about implementation and about evaluation. The necessity for leaders at all levels to conduct this exercise is simple: If you do not know where you and your organization are going, if you do not know how to get there, and if you do not know how to evaluate your progress, then how can you expect those whom you lead to know what to do? You as the leader must be clear, concise, and consistent in your expectations, implement a plan to meet your expectations, monitor its progress, and expect those whom you lead to perform.

Although you may not want to develop a personal leadership system plan for each possible construct, consider the following list of constructs as possibilities to include in your leadership system exercise. For each construct, how would you determine measureable variable(s) for it? This exercise is both a great starting point and a routine monitoring plan you can discuss with your mentor or supervisor. A summary (not expansive) construct list based on the dynamic culture leadership (DCL) model follows; note that each item listed could be expanded into more than one item:

■ Leadership style
■ Leadership alignment
■ Leadership development
■ Organizational culture
■ Cultural competence
■ Communication environment
■ Communication improvement
■ Strategic planning
■ Operational planning
■ Decision making
■ Decision-making processes and procedures
■ Employee enhancement
■ Employee performance appraisal
■ Employee training
■ Organizational learning
■ Knowledge management
■ Performance evaluation
■ Resource acquisition and distribution
■ Management of resources
■ Network development
■ Coalition building
■ External assessment
■ Internal assessment
■ Ethical framework
■ Patient/customer satisfaction
■ Quality assurance/performance/improvement

What kind of health leader do you want to be? What kind of organization do you want to lead? Can you envision it? Determining your leadership system and plan and being consistent are critical. If you know where you are going, you are more likely to get there! Leading, especially in health organizations, is a challenging enterprise but a rewarding one; leadership in health organizations is also necessary and needed if we are to make progress as an industry.

$$\text{Leader Success} = \text{Individual (Nature} + \text{Nurture)} \times \text{Situational Adaptation}$$
$$\times \text{Organization Culture Creation} \times \text{Personal} + \text{Subordinate Accountability}$$

Leadership is the *dynamic* and *active* creation and maintenance of an organizational *culture* and *strategic systems* that focus the collective energy of both *leading people and managing resources* toward *meeting the needs of the external environment* utilizing the most efficient, effective, and, most importantly, efficacious methods possible by moral means.

In Chapter 1, the following point was made: The purpose of this text is to provide you with not only a foundation for the study of leadership practice and theory, but also the broader concept of understanding the complexities of leading people and health organizations across multiple and interconnected disciplines. A second goal of this text is to bridge theory and the abstract concepts of leadership with the practical or concrete operational behaviors and action of leaders. This goal integrates with the popular evidence-based leadership discussions of today. These goals were met by utilizing a four-tiered strategy that walked students, early careerists, and practicing health leaders through the foundations of leadership, leadership principles and practices, and the complexity of leadership in health care, and finally into the world of leading people and managing resources into the future. Put simply, this text has sought to build your leadership knowledge, skills, and abilities.

Although the discipline of leadership, with its myriad of related topics, theories, and models, is rather large and extensive in the literature and knowledge base, the authors' perspectives on the most pertinent leadership content, theories, models, principles, and strategies that produce results in the health industry are captured in this text. The authors of this text—Drs. Ledlow and Coppola—have put many of these theories and models into practice quite successfully over the course of their practitioner careers.

The health industry is different from other service and product industries. To appreciate this difference, consider that many times efficacy is more important than efficiency in health care; patient outcomes are more important than profits and margin; the "rational man" theory of economics is set aside when certain injuries or illnesses invade our families, such that chaos or irrational economic decisions prevail; and society holds the health industry to an extremely high standard—it expects perfection. Moreover, health organizations are extremely complex, run continuously, and are highly regulated and closely scrutinized. These realities create a distinctive leadership niche, that of the health leader. This text is specifically for the health leader.

We hope you agree that our intent for this text was to make you a better leader. The textbook was written to facilitate your development as a health leader. Content for many constructs were presented several times, as introduction, as foundational material, and in one or more contexts. This repetition, we hope, created multiple opportunities for you to think about, use, and begin to build your leadership system plan. We look forward to hearing from you and watching your success as a leader in our industry. Remember: People are led and resources are managed!

SUMMARY

The concept of mentoring dates back at least to Homer's *Odyssey*; "mentor" was not formally introduced as a recognized word in American parlance until 1883, however. For several decades, this term may have been lost, or wrongly communicated as a synonym for leadership, coaching, or advising. Finally, in the 1970s and 1980s, the concept of mentoring as a distinct and separate study from leadership and motivation became widely accepted. Since then, the formal institution of mentoring programs has resulted in decreased employee turnover, increased organizational success, and increased employee satisfaction.

Mentoring is different from leadership and coaching. Leadership is a macro concept focused on inspiring followership and completing defined tasks and objectives. Coaching is a more personal relationship that emphasizes the emulation of skills and abilities; however, it may not have any deep personal meaning to either the coach or the coached subject. In contrast, the mentee/protégé relationship is characterized by deep, personalized, and intimate interactions that are motivated by a mentor's personal desire to see the mentee/protégé succeed.

Although the concept of mentoring has been around for almost two generations now, the unfortunate reality is that that mentor–mentee relationships are often male dominated and race specific. More needs to be done to draw females and minorities into the fold of mentoring relationships.

Health leaders should be aware that mentoring begins with setting the right example at all times and in all situations.[56] Setting the right example means taking responsibility for the preparation of future leaders so that the organize can endure tomorrow's challenges. This type of preparation is performed with a professional and caring understanding from the supervisor to the subordinate, from the mentor to the mentee. Leading by example is behavior that both influences and improves functions within the organization, including employees' job performance, career socialization, upward mobility, and the preparation of future leaders.[57]

This chapter presented a method to combine, evaluate, and develop a personal leadership system for practice. Such a system can provide a framework for discussion and improvement plan development with your mentor or supervisor as you become a better, more efficient, more effective, more efficacious, and successful health leader.

DISCUSSION QUESTIONS

1. Describe the importance of mentorship and succession planning to the long-term success of the health organization.
2. Distinguish between the concepts of mentee and protégé.
3. Discuss some of the barriers in establishing a mentoring program in health organizations regarding gender, ethnicity, age, and race, and apply methods to reduce those barriers.
4. Explain the steps involved in establishing a mentoring program in an organization.
5. Differentiate and list similarities among leading, mentoring, and succession planning in health organizations.
6. Combine theories and models, develop an implementation plan, and evaluate a personal leadership system for practical application in a health organization.

EXERCISES

1. In a one-page paper, describe the importance of mentorship and succession planning to the long-term success of the health organization.
2. In a one-page paper, distinguish between the concepts of mentee and protégé.
3. In a two- to three-page paper, discuss some of the barriers in establishing a mentoring program in health organizations regarding gender, ethnicity, age, and race, and apply methods to reduce those barriers.
4. In a one- to two-page paper, analyze the steps in establishing a mentoring program in an organization.
5. In a one-page paper, differentiate and list similarities between leading, mentoring, and succession planning in health organizations.
6. Combine theories and models, develop an implementation plan, and evaluate your personal leadership system for practical application in a health organization by using the leadership system template provided in this chapter.

REFERENCES

1. Finley, F. R., Ivanitskaya, L. V., & Kennedy, M. H. (2007, July/August). Mentoring of junior healthcare administrators by senior executives: A description of mentoring practices in 127 U.S. hospitals. *Journal of Healthcare Management,* *52*(4), 260–270.

2.   Dancer, J. M. (2003). Mentoring in healthcare: Theory in search of practice? *Clinician in Management, 12,* 21–31.

3.   Homer. (1996). *The odyssey* (R. Fagels, Trans.). New York: Viking.

4.   Levinson, D. J., Darrow, C. N., Klein, E. B. Levinson, M. A., & McKee B. (1978). *Seasons of a man's life.* New York: Knopf.

5.   Johnson, W. B., & Ridley, C. R. (2004). *The elements of mentoring.* New York: Palgrave Macmillan.

6.   Finley et al., note 1.

7.   Kram, K. E. (1983). Phases of the mentor relationship. *Academy of Management Journal,* 608–625. and

8.   Kram, K. E. (1985). *Mentoring at work: Developmental relationships in organizational life.* Glenview, IL: Scott, Foresman.

9.   Cahill, M., & Payne, G. (2006). Online mentoring: ANNA connections. *Nephrology Nursing Journal, 33*(6), 695–697.

10. Clutterbuck, D. (1992). *Mentoring.* London: IPM.

11. Hafford-Letchfield, T., & Chick, N., (2006). Talking across purposes: The benefits of an interagency mentoring scheme for managers working in health and social care settings in the UK. *Work Based Learning in Primary Care, 4,* 13–24.

12. Kelly, M. J. (2001). Management mentoring in a social service organization. *Administration in Social Work, 25*(1), 17–33.

13. Pratner, J. (2009). Soldier on: Baylor Army grad mentors the next generation. *Baylor Line, 71*(1).

14. Finley et al., note 1.

15. Johnson & Ridley, note 5.

16. http://www.degree-essays.com/essays/politicsessays/house-of-lords.php

17. Hankin, H. (2004). *The new workforce: Five sweeping trends that will shape your company's future.* New York: AMACOM.

18. Hankin, note 17.

19. Finley et al., note 1.

20. O'Neill1, R. M., & Blake-Beard, S. D. (2002, April). Gender barriers to the female mentor–male protégé relationship. *Journal of Business Ethics, 37*(*1*), 51–63.

21. Linehan, M., & Walsh, JS., (1999). Mentoring relationships and the female managerial career. *Career Development International, 4*(7), 348–352.

22. Martin, P. Y. (2004). Gender as a social institution. *Social Forces, 82,* 342–266.

23. O'Reilly, N. (2008). Women helping women: How mentoring can help your business. *Business Credit,* 56–57.

24. Gibson, S. K. (2004). Mentoring in business and industry: The need for phenomenological perspective. *Mentoring and Tutoring, 12*(2), 250–275.

25. Hezlett, S. A., & Gibson, S. K. (2005). Mentoring and human resource development: Where we are and where we need to go. *Advances in Developing Human Resources, 7*(4), 446–449.

26. Kram, note 8.

27. Allen, T. D., Eby, L. T., Poteet, M. L., Lentz, E., & Lima, L. (2004). Career benefits associated with mentoring for protégés: A meta-analysis. *Journal of Applied Psychology, 89*(1), 127–136.

28. Kelly, note 12.

29. McAlearney, A. S. (2008). Using leadership development programs to improve quality and efficiency in healthcare. *Journal of Healthcare Management, 53*(5), 319–332.

30. Dolan, T. C. (2004). Mentoring at every level. *Healthcare Executive, 19*(5), 6–7.

31. Young, A. M., Cady, S., & Foxon, M. J. (2006). Demystifying gender differences in mentoring: Theoretical perspective and challenges for future research on gender and mentoring. *Human Resource Review, 5*(1), 148–175.

32. Finley et al., note 1.

33. Block, L. M., Clafrey, C., Korow, M. K., & Mccaffrey, R. (2005). The value of mentoring within nursing organization. *Nursing Forum, 40*(4), 134–141.

34. Rigotti, M. (1997). *Mentoring of women in the United States Air Force.* Maxwell AFB, AL: Air University.

35. Oswald, P. (1996, March). *Distance learning in psychology.* Paper presented at the 10th Annual Conference on Undergraduate Teaching of Psychology, Ellenville, NY.

36. Jossi, F. (1997, August). Mentoring in changing times. *Training & Development, 51*(8), 50–54.

37. Alliance. (1995). *Celebrating excellence.* Washington, DC: Alliance, an Association for Alternative Degree Programs; American Council on Education.

38. Oswald, note 35.

39. Dyson, E. (1997, February). Education and jobs in the digital world. *Communications of the ACM, 40*(2), 35–36.

40. Raghuram, S. (1996). Knowledge creation in the telework context. *International Journal of Technology Management, 11*(7), 859–870.

41. Jossi, note 36.

42. Jossi, note 36.

43. Mentoring Institute. (1998). *The new mentoring paradigm.* Sidney, BC: Author. Retrieved September 29, 2009, from http://www.mentoring-resources.com/.

44. Gunn, E. (1995, August). Mentoring: The democratic version. *Training, 32*(8), 64–67.

45. Kaye, B., & Jacobson, B. (1996, August). Reframing mentoring. *Training & Development, 50*(8), 44–47.

46. Loeb, M. (1995, November 27). The new mentoring. *Fortune,* p. 213.

47. Krause, M. K. (2007). ABCs of being a mentor. *Healthcare Executive, 22*(3), 62–66.

48. Kelly, D. L. (2003). *Applying quality management in healthcare: A process for improvement.* Chicago: Aupha Press.

49. Alumni spotlight. Retrieved January 5, 2010, from http://www.had.vcu.edu/alumni/spotlights/Apr05_Coppola.html.

50. Feeg, V. D. (2008). Mentoring for leadership tomorrow: Succession today. *Pediatric Nursing, 34*(4), 277–278.

51. Lahaie, D. (2005). The impact of corporate memory loss: What happens when a senior executive leaves. *International Journal of Health Care Quality Assurance, 18*(4/5), 35–45.

52. Thurgood, K. (2008, December). *Construct for developing an integrated leadership model: Linking the correlates of effective leadership, development and succession planning.* Dissertation project submitted to the faculty of the School of Business, Capella University, Minnesota.

53. Institute for the Future. (2003). *Health and healthcare 2010* (2nd ed.). San Francisco: Jossey-Bass.

54. Ncube, L. B., & Wasburn M. H. (2006). Strategic collaboration for ethical leadership: A mentoring framework for business and organizational decision-making. *Journal of Leadership Organizational Studies, 13*(1), 7–92.

55. Swayne, L. E., Duncan, W. J., & Ginter. P. M. (2006). *Strategic management of healthcare organization* (5th ed.). Malden, MA: Blackwell.

56. Powers, R. (2008). Army commissioned officer career information: Mentoring. Retrieved September 28, 2009, from http://usmilitary.about.com/library/milinfo/arofficerinfo/blmentoring.htm.

57. Stoddard, D. A., & Tamasy, R. J. (2003). *The art of mentoring: Ten proven principles for developing people to their fullest potential.* Colorado Springs, CO: NavPress.

APPENDIX

Leadership in Practice: Cases and Insights

INTRODUCTION

Health leaders utilize their knowledge, skills, and abilities in practical situations. In this important section of the book, four experienced, successful, and dedicated health executive leaders use real scenarios to guide your thinking and reflection about using and mastering leadership capabilities in realistic circumstances. In each of the eight "Leadership in Practice" cases, you should connect the leadership actions to applications of theories and models discussed in the text. Background on the health executive leaders is provided at the beginning of their cases to help you understand the type of character, dedication, and credentials senior health leaders bring to their organizations. Lastly, consider our definition and model of leadership when reading and studying the "Leadership in Practice" cases:

Leadership is the *dynamic* and *active* creation and maintenance of an organizational *culture* and *strategic systems* that focus the collective energy of both *leading people and managing resources* toward *meeting the needs of the external environment* utilizing the most efficient, effective and most importantly, efficacious methods possible by moral means.

Leader Success = Individual (Nature + Nurture) × Situational Adaptation
× Organizational Culture × Personal + Subordinate Accountability

The insights in the "Leadership in Practice" cases are important, and the background and organizational information are similarly important to provide you with an understanding of the context in which these extraordinary professionals work and produce their leadership outcomes. These health leaders are dedicated to mentoring, sharing, and fostering growth and capability in the next generation(s) of health leaders. Each health leader has prepared insights for you in his or her own style, focusing on timely and important topics. Dr. James H. Stephens, Dr. Donald M. Bradshaw, Michael Sack, and Dr. Susan Smith—thank you for your eagerness to develop our future health leaders.

INTRODUCING THE HEALTH LEADER

James H. Stephens, DHA, MHA, FACHE
Distinguished Assistant Professor, Georgia Southern University
Past Health System and Hospital Chief Executive Officer

FIGURE A–1   Dr. James H. Stephens
Courtesy of Suzanne Oliver

Biographical Sketch
Dr. James H. Stephens has taught at three universities for 10 years at the bachelor's, master's, and doctoral levels. He is the founding program director of the master of healthcare administration program in the Jiann-Ping Hsu College of Public Health at Georgia Southern University. The other two universities where Dr. Stephens has taught are Ohio University and University of Indianapolis. Dr. Stephens is on his second career: Previously, he held senior executive positions at large medical centers and health systems for 25 years, including 18 years at the president and CEO level. He is a Fellow in the American College of Healthcare Executives, has been the recipient of many professional and civil awards and honors, and has been on many healthcare and community boards of directors.

TABLE A–1   Dr. James H. Stephen's Credentials

Degree	Institution Where Degree Was Earned	Institution Location	Year Degree Was Conferred
DHA	Central Michigan University	Mt. Pleasant, Michigan	2006
MHA	Indiana University	Indianapolis, Indiana	1974
BS	Indiana University	Bloomington, Indiana	1972

What Is Your Leadership Style?
I used a combination of several leadership styles in my former executive positions. A summary of my leadership style follows.

> *Servant-Leader:* I believe it is important for leaders to think of themselves as serving others to accomplish the health organization's mission and living its values. This style also makes you a better listener, which is a skill many leaders lack. I believe you have to learn how to follow before you ask others to follow you. A

servant-leader's results will be measured beyond the organization, and the story will be told in the changed lives of others.

Transformational Leader: With this style, the leader acts as a mentor to others in the organization so they can be developed into leadership positions. This is done by building trust among followers and demonstrating sincere interest in building relationships, which in turn builds healthy work environments. To be truly effective and successful, an organization will need many leaders at all levels.

Contingency Leadership: This style fits the leader to the particular organization's culture by changing leadership styles, selecting leaders whose styles fit the particular situation, or changing the situation to better fit the leader's style.

Which Skills of Leadership Are Most Important to You?

TABLE A–2   Which Skills of Leadership Are Most Important to Dr. James H. Stephens

Skills	Skills	Skills
Build trust among followers.	Be a good listener.	Be decisive in decision making.
Believe in and be the main promoter of the organization's mission.	Have excellent oral and written communication skills.	Have a significant understanding of corporate finances so as to protect and appropriately utilize the organization's resources.
Have the right vision for the organization.	Be an expert in leading change.	Be competent in the corporate culture of complex organizations and operations.
Execute short- and long-range strategic plans successfully.	Have interpersonal skills to build internal and external relationships.	Be diplomatic and tactful.
Be a facilitator of a healthy and productive organizational climate and culture.	Enhance personal and professional growth of individuals.	Be socially skilled.

What Are Your Three Biggest Leadership Challenges?
1. Building trust among the organization's key stakeholders
2. Implementing major organizational change
3. Maintaining a balance between your professional, family, and personal life

What Are Your 3 Most Important Leadership Improvement Areas?
1. Be a better listener and communicator.
2. Understand that not all individuals wish to be effective leaders.
3. Keep up with the ever-changing state and federal regulatory requirements, policies, and laws.

Leadership in Practice: Stephens Case 1

Replacing the Radiology Contract

Describe the leadership challenge of your case.
1. I was a new CEO for the health system and had not developed any relationship with the medical staff leadership (president, chief of staff, and chiefs of clinical services) or members (more than 500 physicians).

2. The previous health system CEO was aware of the many issues associated with the radiologists but had failed to address the situation.

3. The senior radiologists had been at the medical center for 20 years and had good relations with older physicians.

4. The medical center was the market leader; however, the radiology equipment was old and not state of the art.

5. The senior radiologist members were not trained in new clinical radiology treatments.

6. The radiologists were refusing to come in to the medical center at nights or weekends despite surgeons' and ER physicians' requests.

7. The medical center was in potential danger of losing market share because of a poor performing radiology department.

Discuss how you met and dealt with the leadership challenge, and discuss the outcome or resolution of the challenge.

As a new president and CEO of a 350-bed medical center located in the Midwest, I had many organizational issues facing me upon my arrival. The medical center was a member of a national Catholic Health System, and I was the first lay CEO in the 95-year history of this medical institution. The organization was experiencing a financial downfall, employee morale was low as a result of a layoff of 100 employees, the medical staff was aging, and its main hospital rival was starting to take patient market share away from the medical center. However, the immediate problem was with the radiologist group, which had six members. In my first 50 days on the job, I encountered a "bee line" of physicians complaining about the quality and cooperation of the radiologist group, including the president and several department chiefs of the medical staff.

The radiologist group had been at the medical center for many years and was generating significant income for each of its members. There had been a long history with this group in terms of poor working relationships with the hospital's radiology department employees and with physicians, especially with the emergency room department physicians and surgeons. The previous medical center CEO was quite aware of these issues, but refused to pursue any corrective action. I felt this situation was unacceptable, so a plan to resolve the various problems was developed. I met with the president of the medical staff, the chief of the medical staff, and the hospital management staff of the radiology department to formulate a listing of major concerns to share with the radiologist group and to seek resolution. The problem list included:

■ The emergency room physicians and the surgeons were having a difficult time finding a radiologist at night or on weekends (this was a significant problem because the medical center's emergency room was the trauma center for the region).

■ Most of the radiologists left early in the afternoon, so no one was available to consult with physicians of the medical staff on specific patient medical issues.

■ The radiologists had no interest in acquiring state-of-the-art radiology equipment or in enhancing their medical training for the new technology.

■ There were not enough radiologists to handle the medical center patient volume, and they had no interest in recruiting additional radiologists.

■ The radiologists were not meeting the 24-hour turnaround standard to interpret radiology patient films.

■ The radiologists treated the department employees harshly and with no respect.

■ Two of the radiologists were not board certified and had no interest in becoming certified.

■ The radiologists had communication issues with other departments of the medical center.

After the problem list was finalized, I met with all the radiologists and reviewed the list with them. During this meeting, I stated I would give them one year to resolve all the issues. They were also advised that if the problem list was not resolved by the end of the year, their contract with the medical center would be cancelled. At the end of the one-year period, the radiologist group had not resolved even a single item on the problem list. I then started to recruit a new radiologist group, which took about 5 months. The new group included nine radiologists who all were board certified and anxious for the medical center to finance an $8 million program to replace its old radiology equipment with state-of-the-art radiology equipment.

Once the new radiology group had been signed to a new contract and the capital funds to purchase new equipment was approved out of the budget by the governing board, I asked the members of the old radiology group to meet with me. The president of the medical staff and the chairperson of the board of trustees were informed of the meeting and the actions that I planned to take with this group. I reviewed with the radiologists that none of the items on the problem list had been resolved, which was disappointing not only to me but also to members of our medical staff and the radiology department employees. I handed each radiologist an official letter stating that his or her contract with the medical center would be cancelled within the next 90 days. Needless to say, all were quite surprised: It is highly unusual to fire an entire radiology group in a large medical center.

At the end of the 90-day period they left, albeit not very professionally, and the new group started. The old radiologist group filed a lawsuit that dragged on for 8 years; the medical center's legal fees were $700,000. The medical center did win the legal case, and the new radiologist group enhanced the radiology department revenue by an additional $1 million in the first year (i.e., $1 million more than the old radiologist group had brought in). The new radiologist group took the problem list and began to resolve every one of the items on it. The conclusion to this situation was that the medical staff and the medical center employees were very pleased with the new radiologist group and with the installation of the state-of-the-art radiology equipment. The medical center's image was enhanced both internally and externally, so that it was recognized as the medical institution with the best radiology service in the area. Once this critical issue was resolved, I began developing plans to resolve the other very important issues facing our organization.

To recap this situation, as the new health system CEO, I met with the entire radiologist group to share with them the issues that had been brought to my attention by the medical staff leadership and members, as well as by the radiology department management staff. I wanted to hear their side regarding what had been said about their service and behavior. The radiologists had the attitude that the previous health system CEO did nothing about the issue, and that things would be the same with me. This was a serious miscalculation. Within a month I had a second meeting with them and gave to each radiologist a list of items that they, as a group, would need to rectify in the next 12 months or I would cancel their contracts. They did not believe me, which was their second miscalculation. During the year, I developed a strong relationship with the medical leadership. After one year, none of the items had been corrected by the radiology group, so I held a meeting and gave them letters stating that their contracts would be canceled in 90 days. Before this meeting occurred, I had obtained the support of the medical staff leadership. I had also been recruiting a new radiology group, in anticipation of this outcome.

Leadership Styles Used in This Case

I used all three leadership styles, all of which were incorporated into my leadership philosophy:

1. I used servant leadership in protecting our mission—namely, that we treat all individuals with respect and that we, as a medical center, provide the highest-quality level of health care within our means and resources.

2. I used the transformational leadership style in developing a trustworthy relationship with the medical staff leadership, who supported me when I was making a very difficult decision

3. The contingency leadership style played a role by changing the leadership style so that I was decisive and prepared to face ligation for my actions in dealing with the radiologist group and a possible backlash from the medical staff.

Leadership Skills Used in This Case

1. The leader developed a trust relationship with the medical staff leadership.

2. The leader understood the long-term impact on the medical center related to changes in its market share.

3. The leader demonstrated courage in making a decision that might have strained the relationship with senior members of the medical staff and potentially spurred ligation from the radiologist group against the health system.

4. The leader demonstrated strong communication skills while presenting the medical center's case so as to win the support from the medical staff leadership.

5. The leader was effective in leading change by removing a physician group without a major uprising by the medical staff while replacing the existing radiologist group with a very qualified and cooperative new radiology group.

6. The leader was very professional and diplomatic during the entire process even though the old radiologist group was not professional.

Outcomes

The old radiology group filed a lawsuit about 60 days after their final day at the medical center. They wanted to settle the case many times but I refused. After 8 years and $700,000 in legal fees, the judge in the case dismissed it and it was over. The new radiologist group increased the radiology department revenue $1 million above what the old group had done in their first year and even better in the following years. The medical staff, the radiology employees, and I were all very pleased with our new group.

INTRODUCING THE HEALTH LEADER

Donald M. Bradshaw, MD, MPH, FAAFP, FACHE, FACPE
Senior Partner, Martin, Blanck & Associates

FIGURE A–2   Dr. Donald M. Bradshaw
Courtesy of Jody L. Bradshaw

Interests
Facilitating and providing quality health care; mentoring exceptional leaders and managers; developing innovative and creative answers to challenges, issues, and problems.

Biographical Sketch

Donald M. Bradshaw is a physician with board certification in family medicine and healthcare management. He started his career in clinical medicine and teaching, and then transitioned to administrative medicine, earning a master of public health degree and certification by both the American College of Healthcare Executives and the American College of Physician Executives.

For the past 10 years, Dr. Bradshaw has successfully led Army community hospitals and a teaching medical center. He led a dynamic healthcare system in the Southeastern United States and Puerto Rico consisting of 8 facilities and an operating budget in excess of $1 billion dollars, while serving more than 750,000 eligible beneficiaries. Prior to joining Martin, Blanck & Associates, Dr. Bradshaw was Commanding General (CEO) of the Army's Southeastern Regional Medical Command (SERMC) and Eisenhower Army Medical Center (EAMC). SERMC is the Army's healthcare system for seven states in the U.S. Southeast and Caribbean; it includes more than 10,000 staff members, 5 hospitals, and 4 free-standing clinics. EAMC is a referral and teaching medical center. Dr. Bradshaw retired from the U.S. Army in October 2009.

What Is Your Leadership Style?

My leadership is cooperative and collegial in the development of vision, mission, priorities, and resourcing. I understand that ultimate responsibility rests with me, even as I delegate authority and roles to subordinates. I then allow those subordinates freedom of action within mutually agreed-to boundaries. I ensure accountability and encourage a freedom to innovate. I underwrite well-thought-out risks, and accept that not every idea or plan will be completely successful. However, organizations must learn, grow, and continue to focus on patient/customer satisfaction linked to staff satisfaction and effectiveness. Subordinates are expected to lead and manage their responsibilities as part of the organizational team. Simultaneously, they should be learning and growing to expand their knowledge, skills, attributes, and attitudes. They must also grow their subordinates to ensure future leaders and managers throughout the organization.

What Are Your Three Biggest Leadership Challenges?

1. Effective communication to all levels of organization

2. Developing "middle managers" to lead, manage, understand accountability, and develop others

3. Encouraging innovation and creativity balanced with standardization and consistency throughout the organization

What Are Your Three Most Important Leadership Improvement Areas?

1. Communication, communication, communication

2. Balancing accountability with subordinates' authority and freedom of action

3. Counseling marginal or poor performers

Which Skills of Leadership Are Most Important to You?

TABLE A–3   Which Skills of Leadership Are Most Important to Dr. Donald M. Bradshaw

Skills	Skills	Skills
Vision	Character—especially integrity	Integrity
Effective, multidimensional communication	Team building	Patient/customer focus
Ability to make, communicate, and enforce tough decisions	Subordinate development	

Organizational Background

Martin, Blanck & Associates is a leading healthcare consulting firm that brings a team of partners with unparalleled leadership experience—as health executives, policy makers, physicians, and other providers—who have served throughout the federal government and the private sector. The company helps its private-sector and government clients move forward in a challenging environment, by identifying solutions and helping to implement them.

Martin, Blanck & Associates provides critical assistance to firms interested in pursuing business opportunities in the federal, state, and nonprofit sectors—with particular expertise in federal health systems. It provides healthcare policy and program development, management, informatics and strategic planning advice, training management, and healthcare studies and analytical support to local, national, and international organizations in both the public and private sectors.

This firm provides assistance throughout the acquisition life cycle, including the following services:

■ *Strategic acquisition planning.* Martin, Blanck & Associates assists its clients in identifying product features, target markets, and business development strategy. This includes analyses of the potential customers and the competition. The company helps its clients meet with customers to introduce products or services, and it assists in identifying important milestones to take a business concept to a delivered product or service.

■ *Responding to Requests for Proposal (RFP).* Martin, Blanck & Associates has a proven track record in helping large and small firms compete for business in the federal sector. It can manage the entire response, or just key subcomponents of an RFP release (e.g., written proposals, oral presentations and coaching, critical review/red team participation and consultant support, production, and delivery).

■ *Ongoing customer support.* Martin, Blanck & Associates helps both new market entrants and existing market participants sustain a close relationship with customers and remain aware of new opportunities or competitive threats. It provides ongoing intelligence and monitoring, and offers subcontracted program management services to provide clients with direct support.

Leadership in Practice: Bradshaw Case 1

Implementing an Information System: Electronic Health Record

Describe the leadership challenge of your case.

Our task was to implement an outpatient electronic health record (EHR) within our health system, which consisted of multiple, geographically separated clinics and a community hospital. We were part of a vertically integrated, staff-model, worldwide healthcare system; the EHR was developed by our parent organization, and the training package was centrally contracted. Because we were early in the process of implementing the EHR, important leadership roles were to capture strengths, weaknesses, and lessons learned concerning the EHR system. The greatest challenge was to use the EHR implementation to evaluate the entire care process and not just take our present processes of information flow, patient flow, and staff communication to the electronic record, but improve the efficiency, effectiveness, and efficacy of the care processes utilized.

Discuss how you met and dealt with the leadership challenge, and discuss the outcome or resolution of the challenge.

We addressed this challenge in several areas by utilizing a situational assessment that included an analysis of the following areas:

1. Equipment and infrastructure (e.g., computers, printers, bandwidth, classrooms).

2. Patient flow. After this analysis, we reengineered patient flow while determining the scope of practice and duties of providers and staff; we then modeled changes caused by or necessary to support EHR implementation.

3. Staffing implications for EHR implementation (not only the trainers and IM/IT staff, but additional support staff in clinics, appointment and admissions sections, shifting duties among present staff, dealing with labor unions, and other relevant issues).

4. Implications for reimbursement/compensation caused by decreased patient care during implementation (salary verses workload-driven compensation models).

5. Adequacy of the centrally contracted trainers compared to our organization's needs: If additional local trainers are required, how do we find, hire, and train those local trainers?

In essence, moving to an EHR across the entire system required changing our existing models of delivering care. Leadership issues in change management included the following points:

1. Developing a vision, message, and communication plan for the EHR implementation.

2. Identifying champions (physicians, nurses, support staff) for each area of the system.

3. Identifying early adapters who would stimulate change and "anchors" who were resistant to change.

4. Determining the appropriate implementation model (rapid change for the entire organization over several weeks versus clinic-by-clinic implementation over several months).

5. Determining the appropriate training model (large groups with individual follow-up versus one-on-one, over-the-shoulder, on-the-job training) and structure (in groups by function versus by clinical team) and timelines. Because central contractors were deemed adequate only for the initial training, we needed additional trainers for maintenance training.

Leadership imperatives for the implementation of the EHR included the following needs:

1. Ensuring synchronization of equipment, training, and staffing

2. Ensuring adequate training, both initially and then over the long term (refresher, new employees, and revisions); scheduling; and ability to modify training and scheduling based on individual needs and unexpected events (e.g., staff or trainer illness, system downtime, local surge in illness or demands)

3. Creating incentives for using the EHR system and publish results

4. Developing a system to ensure rapid response to questions, suggestions, and needs

5. Celebrating success

The results of the EHR implementation were successful. Over a nine-month period, an implementation plan was developed, training was completed, and the necessary changes were implemented with a marked improvement in effectiveness and efficiency of care. After implementation, more than 95 percent of patients had records available at clinic visits (baseline was less than 70 percent), documentation vastly improved in legibility, records were linked to electronic prescriptions with improved safety, and health promotion and preventive measures were facilitated through systematic reminders and ease of tracking. Additionally, improved staff satisfaction with their new or changed roles, due to reengineering, was realized.

Over the four months of initial implementation, we did see 15 percent less productivity (e.g., more training time, slower patient flow, longer visits required, patient education) in outpatient clinics. Implementing a single EHR for primary care and specialty clinics was challenging: The EHR was developed for primary care, so specialty care applications for drawing, scanning, and other needs had to be developed. Also, EHR continues to be a challenge owing to issues related to ongoing training, accuracy of coding, and some provider dissatisfaction with movement through the electronic record (multiple screens, slow response, and multiple logins).

Leadership in Practice: Bradshaw Case 2

Ineffective Subordinate Leader

Describe the leadership challenge of your case.

The chief medical officer (CMO; also called the chief of medical staff) at the hospital was a nice guy, well liked by staff, but ineffective. He had limited experience in critical areas such as credentials, risk management, and project management. He could not manage the medical staff effectively.

Discuss how you met and dealt with the leadership challenge, and discuss the outcome or resolution of the challenge.

First, I had to determine how much of a knowledge deficit the chief of the medical staff had, how much was attitude, how much was personality, and if he was willing to learn and grow.

Second, I had to determine critical areas that could not wait on his growth because they might lead to loss of workload (and the corresponding funding), loss of accreditation, or loss of key medical staff members. I then had to determine possible short-term solutions for these critical deficit areas for the CMO.

Third, I had to determine which options were available to lead him:

■ Could I move him or relieve him of his duties?

■ Could I develop him without destroying his capabilities to lead medical staff over the long term?

■ Could I work with him at all? (Was the relationship open to and capable of sustaining counseling, growth, accountability, open communication?) If not, could someone else provide the mentoring?

Fourth, I had to develop a plan to stimulate his growth, including setting appropriate timelines and goals. At this point, I counseled him, identifying what he was accountable for in this process.

To implement the plan for his growth and improvement, the following occurred:

■ The CMO's skills were assessed through a variety of tools (he had already taken several assessments including a 360-degree management-style evaluation tool) and interviews.

■ New chairs of several critical committees were temporarily appointed, with the announcement that the CMO was assuming specific other duties for the six-month period that would prevent him from providing focused leadership during this time frame.

■ A plan for the CMO's development was created, including specific readings, courses, and time spent "shadowing" various experts (e.g., the credentials staff); specific targets for improvement were set.

■ I counseled the CMO initially every week and then every two weeks, identifying specific written and verbal projects for him to complete and provide to me and the medical staff.

The results of the CMO improvement program were generally successful. This executive did complete his time as CMO; we did have a Joint Commission survey and achieved full accreditation with commendation. Other staff members developed their leadership skills as they chaired committees and led specific projects. The CMO was placed back into a full-time clinical role with minimal administrative duties and remained a productive member of the organization. However, his leadership void did result in some distress and power shifts with the COO and senior nurse executive, which required additional time from me to monitor, listen, and occasionally "referee" disagreements. Looking back on this situation, once the CMO's assessments were completed and it was clear his greatest lack was an ability to hold others accountable, I should have moved this individual back to a clinical position without leadership responsibilities earlier.

Leadership in Practice: Bradshaw Case 3

Values and Vision Conflicts

Describe the leadership challenge of your case.

As the CEO of a hospital within a larger system, you are faced with your higher leadership developing a plan to reorganize the reporting and accountability system within the entire organization that includes the hospital you lead. The goals of the reorganization are to streamline reporting, improve clarity of responsibilities, cut down on leaders with multiple supervisors, and hold leadership at all levels accountable for performance. You feel certain that the proposed plan will actually increase the complexity, decrease clarity, fail to decrease multiple chains of supervision, and decrease accountability. You have expressed your beliefs to leadership, but they appear not to listen and proceed with the proposed actions. It appears much of the weight behind their decision is political (limit loss of jobs in any one area, market it as better focus on prevention and community health, and continue to build up headquarters centralization of control).

You are the spokesperson who must tell your hospital staff, your patients, and your community about the reorganization. As senior leader, you are charged with communicating why they should support this reorganization, why they should not be concerned for their jobs, why this change is good and meets the stated goals, and how the reorganization will be implemented at your hospital.

The following are leadership issues at the local level:

1. Do you readdress your concerns with higher leadership?

2. Do you discuss your concerns with other hospital CEOs (your peers) within the organization? If so, for what purpose or what action?

3. Do you support the "party line" when marketing this reorganization internally and externally?

4. Do you resign?

5. Do you start a job search?

Additionally, the following are topics for discussion based on the reorganization plan:

1. Loyalty to larger organization when it conflicts with your perception of loyalty to your own staff and organization.

2. Communication within the larger organization and specifically your communication, impact, and participation in decision making.

3. Your personal integrity and reputation: How do you maintain them in various situations?

4. Your standing within the bigger organization: Should you consider the decision to go ahead with the reorganization to indicate a failure of alignment of your goals, leadership style, and/ purpose with those of your employer, and begin a job search for a company with better alignment?

5. Means to additional information or other (peer) input and advice without appearing disloyal, not a team player, or overly opinionated.

6. Ways to transmit the higher organizational level's messages to your staff, community, and political leaders.

Discuss how you met and dealt with the leadership challenge, and discuss the outcome or resolution of the challenge.
First verify all of your concerns. Do you understand the plan? Then go to your "mentors" or people you trust (preferably outside the organization); discuss your concerns to get a broader understanding and additional opinions about them, and to have others challenge your concerns. If your concerns are validated, readdress them with higher-level leadership in a nonconfrontational manner to better understand their decision-making process, develop better communication, and develop a fuller understanding of the issues.
Then you have one of several choices:

1. Support the plan and implement it to the best of your ability.

2. Find other CEOs (if any) who agree with you and go as a group to higher leadership. Be prepared to present your own plan and alternatives, not just negatives or complaints.

3. Take this rejection of your position as an indicator that this organization may not be a good long-term fit for you and begin a job search. (Continue to do your best so you leave with a positive reputation.)

You should always strive to develop ways to improve your communication with higher levels of leadership and provide your input early in change processes. An absolute imperative is that you *do not* complain to your staff or community leaders about upper management's decisions.

INTRODUCING THE HEALTH LEADER

Michael Sack
President and CEO, Hallmark Health, Melrose, Massachusetts

FIGURE A–3   Michael Sack
Courtesy of Hallmark Health System, Inc.

A short list of leadership characteristics that Michael Sack finds critical and valuable:

- Ethical behavior
- Enthusiasm
- Personal authenticity
- Motivation
- Discipline
- Sincerity
- Goal-oriented perspective

A short list of leadership challenges:

- Delivering a consistent message to all parties that is realistic and motivating
- Creating a culture of belief and achievement
- Selecting and building a competent, successful leadership team
- Engaging clinical practitioners in protocol assessment and constructive changes
- Ensuring operational performance effectiveness
- Developing administrative and medical leadership

Organization Background
Hallmark Health System is the premier, charitable provider of vital health services to communities in the north-ern metropolitan Boston area. This system includes Lawrence Memorial Hospital of Medford; Melrose–

Wakefield Hospital, Melrose; Hallmark Health Cancer Center, Stoneham; CHEM Center for MRI, Stoneham; CHEM Center for Radiation/Oncology, Stoneham; Hallmark Health Medical Center, Reading; Hallmark Health VNA and Hospice, Malden; Lawrence Memorial/Regis College Nursing and Radiography Programs, Medford; and Hallmark Health Medical Associates. Hallmark Health is affiliated with Massachusetts General Hospital for cardiology services and with Tufts Medical Center for neonatology services.

Mission, Vision, and Values
Hallmark Health System's mission is to provide, in a community-based setting, the highest quality health care to Boston's northern suburbs. Its vision is to be the healthcare system of choice in the region, with demonstrated service to and support from area residents and physicians.

Customers
Hallmark Health System has stated that its intention is to help anyone who is looking for high-quality service and care in a local setting. The goal is to give patients access to the same level of services and expertise found in Boston, but in a much easier to navigate community setting.

Services
Hallmark Health System provides care in a wide array of clinical categories, including internal medicine, surgery, maternal/newborn services, psychiatric care, walk-in service, and emergency services. It also offers quality-focused specialty care in the areas of cardiac and endovascular health, bone and joint replacement, bariatric surgery, and cancer care. In addition, the company offers convenient access to the latest imaging and diagnostic services, including MRI, CT scan, digital mammography, ultrasound, interventional radiology, and a full range of laboratory and physical rehabilitation services. Two outpatient medical centers and a home care agency round out the full line of services offered throughout this healthcare system.

Core Values
As a core part of its values, Hallmark Health System is committed to the communities that it serves. To help fulfill this community benefit commitment, the company has established community outreach teams. The teams help Hallmark Health System determine where its support would have the greatest impact on the health and well-being of everyone in the community. Some of these efforts include organizing more than 40 local health programs in over 8 communities, including providing more than $2 million in community service programs that include flu shot clinics, a tri-city WIC (Women, Infants, and Children) program, various health screenings and education programs, and much more. The company has also collaborated with local agencies to foster emergency preparedness programs and disaster readiness. As a system, Hallmark Health provided more than $8 million in uncompensated care in 2009 to people in the communities it serves.

Commitment to Quality
Hallmark Health System's leadership believes that quality care starts internally, by working together to build the teams, policies, and commitment necessary to deliver the level of care its patients deserve. The company then takes these internal guidelines and translates them into new, high-quality care and service for patients as measured by clinical and industry guidelines and standards. Its success to date is reflected in the recent recognition and ratings Hallmark Health System has received and the future recognition and ratings that it promises to continuously strive to obtain.

Leadership in Practice: Sack Case 1

Physician Leadership Development

Describe the leadership challenge of your case.

Running a healthcare delivery organization requires sound, committed physician leadership. Where do you get it?

Hallmark Health System is an integrated healthcare delivery organization serving communities located at the northern edge of Boston. It was formed in 1998 by the merger of four community hospitals with some overlap in service area and in physicians, all of whom are private, independent practitioners. Because they competed with one another, and because they did not support the organizational merger, there was no established physician leadership to help guide the new organization. As a result, there were four of everything following the merger. Each meeting had to have representation from each former organization. Nothing got done in the hospitals with engaged, helpful physician input. Most concerning, decisions were stalemated; when a decision was made, generally dissatisfaction predominated.

For the first few years following the merger, the new entity's significant financial losses diverted board and management attention away from active efforts to develop medical staff unity and promote strategic harmony. In 2003, a change in administrative leadership occurred.

Among my many initial priorities, the development of a bond of trust between physicians and management was my key initiative. To do so, I recognized formal medical staff leaders and sought informal leaders with whom I could form personal and professional relationships. Finding few individuals who met these criteria among the formally oriented, typically formerly competitive individuals, I turned to the task of developing new leadership talent. I recognized the need to bridge, or transition, from the current structure to a new one.

Discuss how you met and dealt with the leadership challenge, and discuss the outcome or resolution of the challenge.

I created leadership positions for the Hallmark Health System; the people who filled those positions were appointed by me and came from outside the medical staff organizational structure. The medical executive committees held jurisdiction over all other leadership roles through medical staff elections. I did not disrupt their authority but made it quite clear that the chiefs of departments would report to these "administrative medical directors."

Goals and objectives were established for the positions. After six months, it became clear the administrative medical directors were helpful in terms of physician interactions and problem solving. Private attending chiefs were happy to have someone else to assist in planning, in handling operational details, and in spending time in meetings.

Simultaneously, I developed a Medical Leadership Academy for individuals desiring or selected to be medical staff leaders. This program consists of quarterly sessions in which outside faculty are present and leading discussions on topics such as organizational finance, meeting management, dealing with disruptive behavior, and collaborative problem solving. There has even been a session on self-awareness and personal style. If an individual becomes an organizational leader, he or she is required to attend at least one leadership training session per year.

As a result of these initiatives undertaken over the past two years, we now have new individuals who appreciate their leadership roles and who are involved more effectively in our organization. Their involvement in and guidance on strategy decisions are helpful, and their influence on their colleagues is tremendous. The cost of the stipends for these positions and the cost of the training academy are amply offset by the more collegial atmosphere, reduction of tension, reduced opposition, and improvement in outcome measures.

Leadership in Practice: Sack Case 2

Cultural Change

Describe the leadership challenge of your case.

Corporate mergers are rarely easy. Creating a sense of unity and mutual respect can be a challenge. First, there needs to be an understandable purpose for the merger. Second, there must be fair and committed leadership. Third, the focus that cements the formerly separate components into a seamless whole must be an attitude of accountability for results.

I have been involved in three such efforts with varying degrees of success. All have withstood challenges and have adapted over time into successful organizations.

Discuss how you met and dealt with the leadership challenge, and discuss the outcome or resolution of the challenge.

My first experience was as a junior executive involved in merging two hospitals in a small town. There were no other hospitals or places for hospital employment. Services were initially divided between the two sites, both of which were old and greatly in need of capital repairs. The compelling purpose for the merger was to avoid closure for either or both organizations. Strong community leaders joined forces and mandated that the two hospitals consolidate their operations and reduce duplication of services. New administrative leadership was brought in and tasked with rationalizing the services, generating a strong balance sheet, and ultimately developing a replacement facility. Duplicate services were consolidated, new programs were established, forums were frequently held in public town hall meetings, educational sessions were provided for physicians, and communication with employees was emphasized. Over a period of six years, services were "right sized," a culture of togetherness prevailed, and the cornerstone for a new replacement facility was laid. Over the past 25 years, the organization has thrived, has expanded twice, and is now a major regional tertiary care center.

My second experience was as a senior executive who was recruited to manage a smaller hospital that was taken over by a larger, nearby competing institution. This situation was a much more difficult challenge. There was no sense of togetherness, nor was such cohesion expected, because this deal was not a merger of equals—the connection was forced. Few operations were formally merged, but departmental managers from the larger organization typically became responsible to manage the corresponding department in the smaller organization. "Take over" and "mandate" were prevailing attitudes. One culture was stripped away and replaced.

Perhaps not surprisingly, tension was high and significant personnel losses occurred. With the loss of identity, there was an erosion of community support for the smaller hospital. After six years of effort, the smaller organization was converted into a behavioral health and CARF (Commission on Accreditation of Rehabilitation Facilities)-accredited rehabilitation facility. The larger organization was expanded to assume all acute care operations.

This organization continues to be successful, but took a dramatically different path in reaching its current state. Cultural acceptance never occurred between the two facilities. A culture did emerge, but only through the adoption of the larger organization's existing culture by new employees, new doctors, and leaders of clinical directions.

My third experience was as the chief executive officer in the merger of three competing organizations in a large suburban service area where there are other competing organizations. The merger was prompted by significant over-bedding in the area. At the point when the merger occurred, four other hospitals had already closed. The belief was that the overlap in service areas by these three organizations would facilitate economies of scale and lead to greater ease of operational integration among them.

So far, the boards and management of these three organizations have become integrated reasonably well. The wild card has been the medical staffs. Resistance among physicians to the prospect of working together has made operational consolidation and the achievement of economics of scale difficult. In fact, one of the three hospitals was eventually closed.

This merger has provided some valuable lessons. Namely, just because a name connects one organization to others, it does not guarantee that patients and doctors will make the same connection and use the affiliated hospitals. In this case, physicians' reluctant attitude made it difficult for integration to occur and the result was a drastic loss of patient volume. Services that were expanded in anticipation of increased activity went underutilized. A change in administrative leadership brought me to the organization. My goal was to develop two separate but related hospitals servicing separate populations through a single medical staff with distinct differences by campus. This plan created confusion among the hospital employees, however.

Six years later, we are focusing on creating a common culture by emphasizing a separation in purposes of various elements of Hallmark Health System. There is a corporate, business organization with a unifying oversight of business functions. There are two clinical care delivery organizations that retain their heritage and community recognition. Although this separation is working, a stagnant patient population base, the aging of facilities, and demand for new technology now require new investment and development of a new purpose. The recognition that business practices play a key role in physician payment reform, operating efficiency, and collaborative practice is gaining acceptance and bringing people together.

At this point, we are reconsidering our organizational culture and developing a new vision that will support future successes for Hallmark Health System. The loss of pride, the confusion over which organization we were, and the uncertainty of our purpose in the immediate aftermath of the merger have been replaced with a much more cohesive, enthusiastic sense of pride. Our emphasis on accountability for results and a strong return to our roots in the communities served have resulted in favorable operating performance. We have also recruited many new physicians, which is helping to minimize the competitive atmosphere. Everyone is more willing to work together for the common purpose of improving the care offered throughout the health system. New leadership—which includes some leaders recruited from the outside and some promoted from within—has helped stabilize the situation and focus on the organization's goals, promote thoughtful dialogue, and facilitate open communication. Persistence, respect, and clear communication of purpose and results are keys to success.

INTRODUCING THE HEALTH LEADER

Susan Reisinger Smith, DHA, MSN, RN
Chief Executive Officer, Regency Hospital of Central Georgia

FIGURE A–4   Dr. Susan Reisinger Smith

Interests
Healthcare administration, health legislation issues, chronic health issues and informatics.

Biographical Sketch
Susan Reisinger Smith has 29 years of combined experience in administrative and managerial positions, including acute care hospital operations, long-term acute care hospital operations, acute rehabilitation, ambulatory care, and industrial health. She has been a hospital CEO for the past 5 years. Because it is important to her to develop the next generation of health professionals, she serves as an adjunct faculty member. Her continued desire is to research the chronic health issues and escalating healthcare costs caused by social, environmental, and stakeholder influences. Dr. Smith is a licensed registered nurse.

Leadership Style
Throughout my career, I have been able to grow and develop from a manager to a leader utilizing the theory of transformational leadership. "Transformational leadership occurs when in their interactions, people raise one another to higher levels of motivation and morality" (Kouzes & Posner, 2007, p. 122). My efforts as a leader have proved effective in changing organizations by utilizing effective communication of shared values and truthfulness. I have been able to enlist others and develop a team by communicating openly successes and failures, rewarding and recognizing others, fostering empowerment, and developing a sense of ownership at all levels. I believe that leadership is not an individual act by the leader, but rather a team effort that seeks to achieve successes and overcome failures. Collaboration and a feeling of personal ownership throughout the organization are critical necessities to accomplish its goals and sustain winning strategies.

I utilize leadership evaluation tools to assist in my professional growth and in transforming organizations. I am constantly evaluating myself and others for improvement by seeking feedback and listening. Lack of communication listening skills can lead to missed opportunities, failures, and mistrust. According to Manion (2005), it is important for leaders to speak from the heart and share their beliefs, regardless of the feeling of vulnerability (p.77). Moreover, leaders should provide feedback and emphasize that every person's contributions are appreciated and valued. An employee who understands the leader's values will be less distrustful of leadership and willing to participate and be accountable in achieving organizational goals.

According to Kouzes and Posner (2007), "You can't do it alone is the mantra of exemplary leaders . . . collaboration can be sustained only when you create a climate of trust and facilitate effective long-term relationships among your constituents" (p. 242). My future success will depend on my ability to engage in continual learning and understanding of the organizational dynamics while understanding influence of the systems, both internally and externally.

What Are Your Three Biggest Leadership Challenges?

1. Keeping people inspired and motivated through the "rough times"

2. Achieving sustainability over the course of healthcare reform, and continuing sustainability after the reform is complete

3. Fostering a sense of ownership throughout the organization on a continuous basis

What Are Your Three Most Important Leadership Improvement Areas?

1. Confidence in my leadership—both within the organization and in the community

2. Communication techniques in achieving goals, and setting achievable goals to foster a sense of success

3. Success at building teams

Which Skills of Leadership Are Most Important to You?

TABLE A–4   Which Skills of Leadership Are Most Important to Dr. Susan Reisinger Smith

Skills	Skills	Skills
Conduct a self-evaluation (know who you are: self-evaluation; understand your own beliefs and values: self-esteem and confidence)	Ability to build a foundation	Ability to create a vision
Ability to take risks	Transparency (excellent communication and listening skills)	Inspire commitment (building commitment in the face of controversy and conflict)
Creative thinking	Always learning: learning never ends (commitment to growth of people: mentoring)	Clear understanding of what it takes to sustain an organization; understanding of the "Iron Triangle"
Systems thinker: capacity to see the big picture	Ability to foster harmony—recognize and reward employees	Ability to empower individuals; trust
Ability to balance your personal life and work	Foster collaboration	Energize, inspire, and motivate staff
Ability to build teams	Ability to create and manage change	Purpose management skills

Organization Background

Regency Hospital Company is in the business of providing long-term acute care through 24 hospital locations in several states. Regency Hospital of Central Georgia is a 34-bed, long-term acute care hospital located in Macon, Georgia, which opened in April 2004. Expansion is expected to create a 60-bed facility in Macon (scheduled to open in December 2010). More information can be found at the following Internet address: http://www.regencyhospital.com/locations/georgia-central-georgia.aspx.

Long-term acute care hospitals are the most appropriate setting for severely ill, medically complex patients, and chronically ill patients needing long-term acute care. Care for the chronically ill patient takes a highly planned and coordinated effort by a nursing, therapy, and rehabilitative team working in conjunction with physicians, as well as a case management team, to ensure the best possible outcomes are achieved for the patient and his or her family within a reasonable period of time.

Leadership in Practice: Smith Case 1

Evidenced-Based Leadership: A Formula for Success?

Describe the leadership challenge of your case.

Will standardizing leadership through evidence-based practices enable organizations to continue to provide excellent service, outcomes, and sustainability?

Discuss how you met and dealt with the leadership challenge, and discuss the outcome or resolution of the challenge.

Many environmental changes are requiring organizations to engage in significant, systematic, and sustained change to improve outcomes and viability. Bill O'Brien, former CEO of Hanover Insurance, has stated, "The ferment in management will continue until we build organizations that are more consistent with man's higher aspirations beyond food, shelter, and belonging" (Senge, 2006, p. 5). Most organizations have a vision, mission, and value statement, yet many organizations fail from lack of commitment and ownership. Improving an organization's performance and effectiveness requires the "vision of one who created it, and the efforts of many that make the vision come to life and survive" (Johnson, 2009, p. 109).

Evidence-based leadership is a concept that provides "best practices" regarding how to achieve successful applied leadership skills. Evidence-based leadership is defined as a philosophy based on using current "best evidence" to make decisions about what the organization needs (Studer, 2008, p. xi). Will standardizing leadership through evidence-based practices enable organizations to continue to provide excellent service, outcomes, and sustainability?

Applied leadership utilizes evidence-based leadership practices to develop and model leadership behaviors for organizational success and sustainability. According to Kouzes and Posner (2007), five practices are commonly used by exemplary leaders: modeling the way, inspiring a shared vision, challenging the process, enabling others to act, and encouraging the heart (p. 14). Modeling the way requires leaders to demonstrate the types of behaviors that they expect of others. Successful leaders understand that their behaviors must represent the whole organization. Leaders must also inspire others to commitment to the organization through motivation, enthusiasm, inspiration, and excellent communication skills. Leaders provide a vision so others can see how things could be. Exemplary leaders will not avoid challenging existing processes and will take risks in their search for opportunities to innovate, grow, and improve the organization. Successful leaders foster collaboration and build support and faith in others through teamwork, trust, and empowerment. They encourage the heart by providing support, recognition, and celebration of successes.

Many organizations have attempted to use evidence obtained through measuring outcomes, testing, and other reporting methodologies to improve their performance by eliminating variances contributing to negative outcomes. "Quick fixes" implemented to improve outcomes based on organizational data have typically led to the creation of rules and interventions, which then inevitably resulted in only short-term improvements, inconsistencies, and even failures. These interventions for achieving success generally do not take advantage of best practices that might foster team collaboration by sharing of skills, and do not communicate opportunities to improve outcomes that would have long-term effects.

According to Senge (2006), "Organizations that truly excel in the future will be the organizations that discover how to tap people's commitment and the capacity to learn at all levels" (p. 4). Improved technologies and an increasingly complex work environment are creating an increased need for organizations to become more "learningful" (p. 4). Successful organizations promote leadership development programs to foster a culture of learning and ownership. They recognize that effective implementation of best leadership practices must reside with the user. Regardless of the level of knowledge base mastery, the challenge for the leader becomes one of applying the knowledge base to the day-to-day operation with colleagues and clients who possess various knowledge bases and whose expectations of leadership development cover a broad continuum (Kunkel, 1980). Kouzes and Posner (2007) found that "leadership is an observable set of skills and abilities rather than an innate set of character traits. . . effective leaders are the leaders who are constantly learning" (p. 341).

Applied leadership development focuses on key components of successful evidence-based practices. These practices include a change in leadership from a top-down perspective to group-centered leadership, from a hierarchal mode of operations to adoption of a stewardship attitude, and a vision that is value based (National Council on Disability, 2001). Leadership development requires self-development, an assessment of one's strengths and weaknesses, and an understanding of one's values, motivations, and passions (National Council on Disability). Unfortunately, many leaders refrain from best practices and standardization of leadership practices. According to Studer (2008), "leaders want standardization for others, but prefer autonomy for themselves . . . it is appropriate for leaders have their own individual style, but standardization is important for certain leadership procedures as a key to eliminate variances and achieve lasting organizational results" (p. 81). Studer defines variance as the difference between what the results can be and what actually occurs (p. 81).

The National Council on Disability (2001) defines a leader as one who fosters change; is value based; recognizes that all people are potential leaders; understands that leadership is a group process; fosters continual learning, creativity, flexibility, and resilience; and has a vision. Leadership is not a solo act, but rather a team effort (Kouzes & Posner, 2007, p. 223). The traditional view of "leading" others requires an evidence-based shift to shared power. Leaders must be skilled in creating a climate of trust and facilitating relationships to foster collaboration (p. 224). Indeed, collaboration among the members of the organization is a critical necessity to accomplish and sustain winning strategies. Given this understanding, leaders must question whether personal autonomy is more important than achieving the organization's desired results (Studer, 2008, p.81).

Leadership requires the understanding of one's values. Values influence behavior on both an organizational level and an individual level. Values form the basis of how we see ourselves as individuals, how we see others, and how we interpret the world. They are used to decide between alternatives; they serve as the cornerstones of who we are and how we do things. Strong values are what is put first, defended most, and least likely to be sacrificed even when the system process requires a change. The exemplary leader must understand how to manage his or her personal values when they conflict with the organizational values.

Evidence-based leadership requires effective communicative skills, including the ability to listen in different cultural settings. Downs and Adrian (2004) state, "For organizations to perform effectively, it is essential for periodic monitoring of the communication process that is necessary for excellent organizational development" (p. 2). Communication techniques influence how effective the process of hiring and training of employees is, how people are motivated, how instructions are received, and how interventions are in difficult situations. "We all come from different backgrounds and bring different experiences to the table . . . dealing with cultural differences or with messages stemming from nonverbal communication . . . barriers to effective communication can be a disruptive force" (Whitehead, 2006, para. 1). Ineffective listening is a barrier to effective organizational communication. A leader who cannot listen will create gaps in interpretation. Communication techniques developed from evidence-based practices offer the value of knowledge gained through failures, successes, and measured outcomes.

Standardizing leadership through evidence-based best practices will enable organizations to continue to provide excellent service, outcomes, and sustainability. Evidence-based leadership establishes an infrastructure that provides individuals, collegial groups, and employees with the time and resources needed to analyze data, scrutinize evidence, identify areas of action and development, and be involved in action research (Caldwell & Lewis, 2005). Leaders who embrace this approach utilize a management style that encourages a constant informed interchange of professional information among colleagues (Caldwell & Lewis, 2005). Evidence-based practices enhance a person's abilities to reuse evidence to work faster, shorten learning cycles, identify new opportunities, increase quality of deliverables, and increase the volume of work on matters of priority (Caldwell & Lewis, 2005). The goal of standardization of leadership through evidence-based practices is to create a self-sustaining culture that has the energy and vision to achieve excellence (Studer, 2008, p. 86).

Exemplary leaders will develop an organizational culture that fosters continual leadership learning and collaborative decision making. Ultimately, the success of the organization depends on the leader's ability to apply evidence-based leadership techniques to foster ideas and motivate creative solutions that will lead to relationships built on trust and commitment. The leader must focus on a strategic plan based on learning, embracing standardized leadership best practices, and utilizing applied leadership techniques for continual success. The leader must not wait until signs of decline or negative outcomes appear to seek out leadership learning. Instead, the leader must model the way proactively, inspire a shared vision, challenge the process, enable others to act, and encourage the heart. How leaders effectively utilize evidence-based leadership standards is connected to how effectively they manage the knowledge and techniques learned. Evidence-based leadership provides leaders with the tools to effectively share the information, effectively communicate with other people, and utilize outcomes to alter and improve the organizational system's ability to sustain environmental influences. This type of leader, through standardized practices, will be able to create a lasting culture of individual accountability and a sense of ownership throughout the organization.

Leadership in Practice: Smith Case 2

Ownership and Accountability Culture

Describe the leadership challenge of your case.
　How does a leader create a climate and sense of "ownership" in the organization?

Discuss how you met and dealt with the leadership challenge, and discuss the outcome or resolution of the challenge.
　Hospitals are service organizations. The success of a hospital depends on customers' perception of the services it delivers. Health organizations are challenged to meet the demand for services universally with no untoward events; perfection in delivery of care is the norm. Over the years, each healthcare organization has likely drilled into employees the institution's standards through staff meetings and memos. These standards include those that the organization's leaders believe are necessary both to achieve success and to meet regulatory requirements. Unfortunately, many organizations are unable to obtain "buy-in" from each and every employee regarding the importance of its standards. What is often missing in such cases is the participation of the employees in developing the organization's underlying principles that would enable it to achieve the kind of quality service that is expected by customers. Instruction is not enough; employees and leaders must be able to see and feel what is necessary to create and sustain a great organization.

　Accountability is critical to the success and sustainability of an organization. People who do not work together, but rather operate in silos, lack cohesiveness, and their activities soon become fragmented. In this milieu, poor communication develops and flourishes, feelings of distrust become evident, and attaining the organization's goals becomes ever more difficult. Optimal service delivery for hospital organizations requires communication between departments, coworkers, and leadership for essential positive outcomes. A sense of "ownership" or a feeling of pride must exist among all members of the organization.

　Establishing "buy-in," or a sense of ownership and accountability throughout the organization, requires both extensive effort by the leader and a concerted effort to ensure transparency. For starters, it means having the employees establish the organization's standards of conduct or behaviors. This step might begin, for example, by creating the organization's principles or "credo." These principles must be established so as to create the foundation for achieving high-quality service and organizational goals. The behaviors must be demonstrated by all, including top-level leaders. Leaders who follow the principles signal that no one is excused from adhering to the principles.

Principles for the credo may include, but are not limited to, the following examples:

- I will wash my hands.
- I will be happy to provide assistance.
- I will reduce risks and promote safety.
- I will communicate effectively.
- I will respect privacy and confidentiality.
- I will never say, "I don't know"; instead, I will say, "Let me find out for you."
- I will never say, "It is not my job."
- I will take the initiative.
- I am committed to my colleagues.
- I will make every effort to reduce anxiety for our customers and my coworkers.

Once the credo is made, it must be made visual and placed where all employees will be reminded of it on a daily basis. Each employee must sign one copy of the credo and keep it for themselves, and sign a second copy to be maintained by the organization. New prospective employees should be shown a copy of the credo during their interview to disclose the organization's principles prior to any job offer. When this extra step is taken during the interview or application process, the organization can be sure that future employment seekers will have an understanding of its minimum expectations. Periodically, the credo will need review by the employees to add new principles, tweak current ones, and provide detailed expectations related to current principles to improve understanding and compliance.

The next step toward achieving a feeling of ownership within the organization focuses on making the organization's goals part of every employee's evaluation process. This step requires the leader to define the goals to be measured to ensure organizational success. Specifically, goals must be measurable and weighted by significance. For example, a hospital must provide excellent patient satisfaction to have a positive reputation in the community and surrounding areas. Patient satisfaction survey questions can identify weak areas that require improvement to increase patient satisfaction. These weak areas might include time to answer a call light, temperature of food, communication with patients about test results, discharge instructions, and attitudes of the providers.

Financial viability is every organization's objective. Financial goals may include measurement of average length of stay, optimal discharge percentage range, readmissions, equipment replacement costs and repairs, and operating expenses per patient-day. High turnover rates among staff members are not only costly for organizations, but can also have an effect on quality, patient outcomes, and an organization's reputation. Including the staff turnover rate as part of the evaluation process encourages staff to recruit and retain existing employees, which will assist in lowering the organization's operating costs and improving its quality of care.

Nosocomial infection rates are a measurement that healthcare institutions track. Not only does the infection rate of an organization have an immediate effect on the patient's outcome, but it also affects the cost of care, the length of stay, and the hospital's reputation. Adding nosocomial infections and other risk issues such as falls and treatment/medication errors to the evaluation process encourages staff to be more aware of their own actions as well as the actions of their coworkers.

Adding the objective evaluation piece to employees' overall evaluations encourages employees to become creative in seeking solutions to improve systems that may be hindering performance and service. Once the goals are established for the evaluations, quarterly postings on "how we are doing" can communicate to staff what is working well, what requires immediate attention, and what can be improved.

The two basic techniques discussed here—employees establishing the organization's principles and incorporating the organization's objective measureable goals into the individual employee evaluations—are both designed to enhance staff engagement and feelings of ownership. Ideally, their implementation will result in enhanced organizational sustainability.

Table A–5 links the lessons learned through the "Leadership in Practice" cases presented in this appendix to salient text chapters.

TABLE A–5   Summary of "Leadership in Practice" Cases and Insights

Case	Title of Case	Textbook Chapter Link (Parts 1 and 2)	Textbook Chapter Link (Parts 3 and 4)
Stephens Case 1	Replacing the Radiology Contract	Chapters 5 and 6	Chapters 10 and 15
Bradshaw Case 1	Implementing an Information System: Electronic Health Record	Chapter 6	Chapter 12
Bradshaw Case 2	Ineffective Subordinate Leader	Chapters 2 and 5	Chapters 15 and 16
Bradshaw Case 3	Values and Vision Conflicts	Chapters 5 and 6	Chapter 10
Sack Case 1	Physician Leadership Development	Chapter 7	Chapter 12
Sack Case 2	Cultural Change	Chapter 4	Chapters 9 and 13
Smith Case 1	Evidenced-Based Leadership: A Formula for Success?	Chapters 4 and 8	Chapters 11 and 14
Smith Case 2	Ownership and Accountability Culture	Chapter 5	Chapters 9 and 14

REFERENCES

Caldwell, B., & Lewis, J. (2005). Evidence-based leadership. *Educational Forum, 69,* 182–191.

Downs, C., & Adrian, A., (2004). *Assessing organizational communication: Strategic communication audits.* New York: Guilford Press

Johnson, J. A., (Ed.). (2009). *Health organizations: Theory, behavior, and development.* Sudbury, MA: Jones and Bartlett.

Kouzes, J., & Posner, B. (2007). *The leadership challenge* (4th ed.). San Francisco, CA: Jossey-Bass.

Kunkel, R. C. (1980). Toward applied leadership development: Gamblings of a rookie dean. *Journal of Teacher Education, 31*(1), 30–34.

Manion, J. (2005). *From management to leadership: Practical strategies for health care leaders* (2nd ed.). San Francisco: Jossey-Bass.

National Council on Disability. (2001, February). *Applied Leadership for effective coalitions.* Washington, DC: Author.

Senge, P. (2006). *The fifth discipline: The art and practice of the learning organization.* New York: Doubleday.

Studer, Q. (2008). *Results that last.* Hoboken, NJ: John Wiley & Sons.

Whitehead, B. (2006, January). Identifying and overcoming barriers to effective communication. *WebConferencingZone.* Retrieved October 26, 2008, from http://www.web-conferencing-zone.com/4106-barriers-to-effective-communication.htm.

Index

In Defense of Human Rights

The argument that religion provides the only compelling foundation for human rights is both challenging and thought-provoking, and answering it is of fundamental importance to the furthering of the human rights agenda.

This book seeks to establish an equally compelling non-religious foundation for the idea of human rights, engaging with the writings of many key thinkers in the field, including Michael J. Perry, Alan Gewirth, Ronald Dworkin, and Richard Rorty. Ari Kohen draws on the Universal Declaration of Human Rights as a political consensus of overlapping ideas from cultures and communities around the world that establishes the dignity of humans, and he argues that this dignity gives rise to collective human rights. In constructing this consensus, we have succeeded in establishing a practical non-religious foundation upon which the idea of human rights can rest.

In Defense of Human Rights will be of interest to students and scholars of political theory, philosophy, religious studies, and human rights.

Ari Kohen has been Assistant Professor of Justice Studies and Political Science at James Madison University, USA; from August 2007, he will be Assistant Professor of Political Science at the University of Nebraska-Lincoln, USA.

Routledge innovations in political theory

In Defense of Human Rights

A non-religious grounding in a pluralistic world

Ari Kohen

Routledge
Taylor & Francis Group

LONDON AND NEW YORK

First published 2007
by Routledge
2 Park Square, Milton Park, Abingdon, Oxon, OX14 4RN

Simultaneously published in the USA and Canada
by Routledge
270 Madison Ave, New York NY 10016

Routledge is an imprint of the Taylor & Francis Group, an informa business

Transferred to Digital Printing 2008

© 2007 Ari Kohen

Typeset in Sabon by Wearset Ltd, Boldon, Tyne and Wear

British Library Cataloguing in Publication Data
A catalogue for this book is available from the British Library

Library of Congress Cataloging in Publication Data
A catalog record for this book has been requested

ISBN10: 0-415-42015-6 (hbk)
ISBN10: 0-415-47969-X (pbk)
ISBN10: 0-203-96376-8 (ebk)

ISBN13: 978-0-415-42015-0 (hbk)
ISBN13: 978-0-415-47969-1 (pbk)
ISBN13: 978-0-203-96376-0 (ebk)

For Saba and Safta, who taught me, through their everyday actions, about the twin virtues of human rights and education and set me on this path before I even learned to walk.

Contents

Acknowledgments

In completing a project as daunting as a first book, it is impossible not to incur some fairly large debts. My hope is to thank everyone who provided support, encouragement, advice, insight, and assistance along the way; if anyone is left out, I hope they prove to be as forgiving as they were helpful.

In my time as a student, I was privileged to study with some of the finest professors of political science, from whom I learned an incalculable amount about the discipline and about the art of teaching: Rom Coles, Peter Feaver, Michael Gillespie, Hein Goemans, Ruth Grant, Mike Munger, Eric Petrie, Michael Schechter, Tom Spragens, and Dick Zinman. In addition to this list, I must single out Peter Euben and Elizabeth Kiss. To say that Elizabeth read every draft of this book would be sufficient to justify special thanks; in fact, though, she read multiple versions of every page. She served as a sounding board and offered constructive criticism of nearly every idea, in addition to coaxing and cajoling me to meet my own deadlines. Peter's humor kept me afloat over and over again, especially through my dark days of wading through the Xs and Ys of analytical philosophy; in addition, his careful reading of early drafts and his dogged insistence that I work harder in places where I did not want to have made this a much better book than it otherwise would have been.

I was very fortunate to spend half-a-year teaching at Wake Forest University while working on this project; I could not have wished for better colleagues than John Dinan, Pete Furia, and Kathy Smith. During that time, I was also able to get to know Michael Perry, whose excellent treatment of the problem of justifying human rights serves as my point of departure for this book; I have benefited a great deal from my numerous conversations with him and the whole of this project has been greatly improved by his comments on drafts. Thank you to Michael and also to Christopher Eberle, to whom he introduced me, for allowing me to read and quote from unpublished manuscripts. I would also like to thank the Irmgard Coninx Foundation, which brought me to Germany on three occasions in 2005 and 2006 to present drafts of several chapters at their "Reframing Human Rights" roundtables; at those meetings, I learned a

great deal in particular from Sabine Berking, Mark Goodale, Stefan Gosepath, Hans Joas, Michael Kilburn, Ingo Richter, and Ralf Müller-Schmid.

I also owe a debt of gratitude to my colleagues at James Madison University, especially the members of the political science research group – Chris Blake, Scott Hammond, Kay Knickrehm, and Valerie Sulfaro – who offered insightful comments on a number of chapters. This project was also helped along by a summer research grant from the JMU College of Arts and Letters in 2005. Finally, the students in my classes at Duke, Wake Forest, and James Madison must also be acknowledged, as they have been willing to discuss difficult topics with me, and their critical thinking about the concept of rights helped me to consider this project in new ways.

Two chapters of this book previously appeared in *Human Rights Review* and *Journal of Human Rights*, in different forms and with slightly different titles. Thank you to the editors of those journals – Gary Herbert and Tom Cushman – for their assistance, comments, and permission to reprint the articles here with changes. Thank you also to the anonymous reviewers at those journals for their helpful comments. My editors at Routledge, Heidi Bagtazo and Harriet Brinton, deserve special thanks for taking on this project and for patiently answering my seemingly endless stream of questions; so too do the anonymous reviewers who read the manuscript, offered constructive criticism, and suggested that it ought to be published.

I benefited immensely from the friendship and the careful readership of an impressive group: Melinda Adams, Allison Anders, Mark Axelrod, Chip Bolyard, Abe Bonowitz, SueZann Bosler, Elizabeth Brown, Andrew Cohen, Phil and Jenny Demske, Gerry DiGiusto, Mike Ensley, Dan Eschtruth, Aba Gayle, Ted Goodman, Marisa Gwaltney, Brian Halderman, Bill Hawk, Kristin Houlé, Seth and Gretchen Jolly, Clare Kramer, Dave and Robin LaRoy, Zachary Liss, Caroline Lubert, Mark Moon, Leila Neeson, Brian Newman, Bill Pelke, Jason Reifler, Marnie Riddle, Mark Sanborn, John Scherpereel, Bill Schulz, Kevin Scott, Tom Scotto, Mike Strausz, Len Van Wyk, George White, and Sebastian Wolfrum. A few from this group – Bill Curtis, Howard Lubert, Dennis Rasmussen, Janie Thames, Michael Tofias, and Margaret Williams – went above and beyond the duty imposed by friendship, carefully reading drafts of each chapter or listening to me talk about the project for hours; more than that, though, the intelligence and excitement that they bring to every conversation make them ideal friends and colleagues.

It remains to me, then, to thank my family. Thank you, first, to Ilana, who has supported me since she first followed me into this world; she has endured all of my efforts to cast her as my sidekick in our neighborhood adventures or my chorus in our basement musicals, and she has become a kind and intelligent woman of whom I am incredibly proud – a leading lady in her own right. My parents, Belle and Jerry Kohen, taught me from

the first that education was of primary importance, and they backed up their words with nine years of driving my sister and I to a school that was nearly an hour from our house and better than those close by. Their love and encouragement have made the distance between our homes seem shorter than it is. Finally, to my grandparents – Frances and Leonard Fink, and Zoli and Sheri Kohen – thank you for being the exemplary people you are. You have always offered me wise counsel and excessive birthday presents, and you have always challenged me with difficult questions and a ubiquitous bunch of grapes after heavy four-course meals. The four of you together provide a spiritual center for a family that has spread out across the country, one which ensures our return, at regular intervals, from any distance. The person I am today owes so much to the lessons about love and support you taught me when I insisted that I was too tired and that you should carry me.

Prologue
Starvin' for Justice

Each summer, a group of activists arrives at the marble steps of the Supreme Court of the United States to protest the death penalty. This assembly, usually numbering no more than twenty but occasionally swelling to as many as fifty, begins its vigil on June 29 and remains until July 2. They carry banners, they distribute leaflets, they urge passersby to sign petitions, they host a rock concert, they sell t-shirts, buttons, and bumper stickers, they carry out a mock execution, they give interviews to reporters, and they drink a lot of water. The bulk of their activities are designed to educate the public about capital punishment, but they drink as much as they do because their four days and nights at the Court are spent without food. For thirteen years, the group – known as the Abolitionist Action Committee – has marked the anniversaries of two landmark Supreme Court cases in this way.[1]

The Fast & Vigil to Abolish the Death Penalty – or Starvin' for Justice, as it is known amongst participants – draws activists from a variety of organizations, including the American Civil Liberties Union, Amnesty International, Citizens United for Alternatives to the Death Penalty, Dorothy Day Catholic Worker House, Murder Victims' Families for Reconciliation, and the National Coalition to Abolish the Death Penalty. Some live in the area, but many travel from as far away as Alaska, California, Texas, Michigan, and Florida; they have also been joined in the past by people from Canada, Italy, and Great Britain. The participants hold their position on the death penalty for a variety of reasons, but all clearly have a deep commitment; some have lost loved ones to violent crime or to execution, some have been exonerated and released from death row, some believe in the right to life as a universal principle of human rights, and some believe that only God may give or take a life.[2] Whatever their reason for spending these four days at the Supreme Court, a strong bond is quickly built amongst long-time and first-time attendees.

Happy to be in one another's company, Fast & Vigil participants must agree to abide by only two simple rules: the first is a pledge of nonviolence and respect, while the second states that "those who choose not to fast are asked not to discuss or consume food at the Fast & Vigil site."[3] A third,

unwritten, rule makes clear that opposition to the death penalty has occasionally made strange bedfellows: participants are discouraged from discussing their views about abortion, especially with passersby. When asked about the group's stance on abortion, participants generally respond by saying that individuals have their own opinions but that the group as a whole does not take a position. Behind all of this is the recognition that such conversations are both off-topic and can quickly cause tempers to flare. As Ronald Dworkin notes, "The war between anti-abortion groups and their opponents is America's new version of the terrible seventeenth-century European civil wars of religion."[4] Importantly, all of the activists at the Supreme Court believe that human life is intrinsically valuable. Some of them, however, believe that abortion and the death penalty are both morally wrong because both take human lives. Others do not believe that an unborn fetus constitutes a human being in the same way that the occupant of a cell on death row does (if at all); therefore, they contend, only the death penalty involves the deliberate killing of a human being. In one sense, the debate that would likely rage if these conversations took place at the Fast & Vigil is a political one, and the merits of both sides have been thoughtfully weighed by the Supreme Court. But it is also a religious debate, concerning as it does the sanctity of life, as well as the rights of the state in opposition to the dictates of God. And for now, the Catholics, Protestants, Lutherans, Unitarian Universalists, Jews, Buddhists, agnostics, and atheists who attend the Fast & Vigil avoid discussions of religion. For four hot and hungry days, no one asks *why* anyone else is opposed to the death penalty; it is enough simply to know that they *are*. Even so, I suspect that many are curious about the motivations of their companions at the Court.

Indeed, when dealing with complex moral issues like the death penalty or abortion, it might be insufficient to make claims about human rights as though they are self-evident. The failure to look closely at the reasons behind the common belief that the right to life is nonderogable has resulted in the occasional uncomfortable moment. Just before breaking the fast in 2003, for example, one of the Catholic Workers spoke passionately about the belief she presumed that everyone shared, singling out the "crime" of abortion as she encouraged those who had fasted against the death penalty to continue to oppose all forms of murder. Many of those who were fasting, however, did not share her conviction that abortion and the death penalty were two sides of the same coin, and were particularly offended because she had not been an active participant throughout the Fast & Vigil. Those who were offended, however, kept their discomfort to themselves and no discussion took place between the Catholic Worker and those she had offended; in the end, it was easier for the former to keep their feelings to themselves than it would have been to delve into a conversation about the reasons for protesting the death penalty and not abortion. A more lighthearted example comes from an

overheard conversation between a protester and a Supreme Court tourist. The former – holding a sign that read, "Stop State Killing!" – was approached by the latter, who patted him on the shoulder and thanked him for speaking out on such an important issue. After the two had exchanged pleasantries for a moment, the tourist pointed toward some protesters with signs that explictly declared opposition to the death penalty and said, "I can't agree with those sons of bitches, though." Perplexed, the protestor replied, "I have to tell you, actually, I'm one of those sons of bitches." The tourist had mistakenly associated state killing with abortion rather than the death penalty and was shocked to learn that everyone around him was protesting the latter, something he believed in strongly. In his mind, it was clear that abortion is murder and therefore constitutes a moral wrong; capital punishment, however, is not murder and he declined an invitation to consider whether there is any kind of contradiction in this sort of thinking.

Interestingly, the offended protesters from the first example and the horrified tourist from the second example have two things in common. They hold opposite positions on abortion and the death penalty, but neither is opposed to killing as such. Also, neither seems to be scratching the surface of their convictions, examining the reasons that underlie their quite different positions on these controversial issues. But, for the purpose of this project, it is the reasons, not the convictions, that are of primary importance. The reasons behind believing that either abortion or the death penalty is a violation are the most crucial components of any claim about the inalienable right to life (of either the unborn fetus or the murderer), as they provide the basis for our understanding of the idea of human rights. Indeed, even if we turn our attention to less controversial claims, like the right not to be tortured, we must confront the question of whether there is any reason to believe that we are the bearers of rights. As Michael Perry notes, "The fundamental challenge to each and every human rights claim – in particular, to each and every claim about what ought not to be done to any human being or what ought to be done for every human being – is a demand for reasons."[5] For some, there is a particularly salient feature or quality inherent in human beings from which our rights spring. For others, the focus on qualities is a wrong turn taken long ago by theologians and philosophers; instead, they argue that one can articulate reasons that do not depend on human nature but on the political decisions of the past fifty years. Human rights, they contend, are grounded in the many international treaties, conventions, and declarations that have been drafted, signed, and ratified since the creation of the United Nations.

To return to our protestors and, in particular, to my earlier comment that many are curious about their companions' motivations, we need only consider the Catholic Worker who assumed that she would not be offending anyone by expressing her opposition to abortion in front of people committed to ending the death penalty. Indeed, she might be surprised to

find that individuals are so dedicated given that they do not believe human beings are the sacred children of God. This Catholic Worker is a real-life example of the academic argument put forward by Perry that "For many religious persons . . . the idea of human rights simply does not make sense, it does not exert a claim, apart from, cut off from, the Gospel vision of the world and of our place in it – or from some equivalent religious vision."[6] With this in mind, we can easily imagine her asking for a list of the reasons that motivate the non-religious human rights activist. For, if convicted murderers are not considered sacred – have no relation to God – why should our society be prohibited from putting them to death? If a captured terrorist has knowledge of an impending attack on innocent civilians, and if that terrorist is not created in the image of God, why must we refrain from utilizing torture to extract precious, life-saving information?[7] In all that follows, I will offer what I believe is a compelling, non-religious answer to questions of this sort. I will do so, in part, as a response to the argument put forward by Perry that, at the very heart of the idea of human rights, lies a fundamentally religious concept, the notion of the sacredness of persons. Along the way, I will examine a variety of contemporary non-religious theories of human rights – those of Alan Gewirth, Ronald Dworkin, and Richard Rorty – and offer critiques of each.

Lest anyone assume that this project is simply one more example of philosophy done for its own sake, let me close this prologue with a quotation that describes what I take to be the very real stakes of the argument that follows. Amy Gutmann poses the question quite nicely when she asks:

> What, pragmatically minded people might ask with some incredulity, is at stake in the equally heated – and quite common – arguments about the metaphysical and moral foundations of human rights? These arguments – for example, about human agency, dignity, and natural law – tend to be quite abstract, and it may therefore be tempting to assume that not much of practical importance is at stake.[8]

While this point is well-taken, she continues with an answer with which I am very much in agreement:

> What is at stake in determining the foundations of human rights is often the very legitimacy of human rights talk in the international arena. If human rights necessarily rest on a moral or metaphysical foundation that is not in any meaningful sense universal or publicly defensible in the international arena, if human rights are based on exclusively Eurocentric ideas, as many critics have (quite persistently) claimed, and these Eurocentric ideas are biased against non-Western countries and cultures, then the political legitimacy of human rights talk, human rights covenants, and human rights enforcement is called into question.[9]

As I will argue throughout this book, the idea of human rights is based on universal ideas about the inviolability of the human person. It is an idea that can be embraced by both Western and non-Western cultures and communities, and its fulfillment is one for which deeply religious and deeply non-religious people alike can work.

Introduction
The first day of class

On the first day of a new semester, I always begin by asking students enrolled in my International Conflict and Violence class to define a list of terms that will play an important role in all of our discussions. And each semester they have the least amount of trouble defining the same term: human rights. Some point out that there exists quite a long list of these rights, that the list was finalized in 1948, and that it came to be known as the Universal Declaration of Human Rights; others include in their definitions the fact that violations of these rights occur with disturbing regularity all over the world. To be fair, there are always a few students who take the easy way out and tell me that human rights are rights that all human beings have. Circular though it sounds, there is technically nothing wrong with this definition; human rights *are* rights that we all hold solely by virtue of our being human. And there is much to be gleaned from a closer look at this simplistic definition. For once they have started defining terms, students typically want to continue, and they add to their initial definition of human rights by looking more closely at the idea of rights. Rights, they note, are guarantees; if I have the right, for example, to speak freely, then no one may prevent me from doing so. If I am so prevented, I need only claim my right – pointing to the language of the American Bill of Rights or the Universal Declaration – and I should quickly find my grievance redressed. At the very least, there is a system in place by which such grievances can be brought forward, complete with courts to adjudicate the issue. This, my students argue, is the power of rights: they imply an obligation on another's part.[1] Further, and with only a minor amount of encouragement, these students will take their idea forward a few additional giant leaps, noting that, because they are rights that are guaranteed to all human beings, human rights cannot be bartered, sold, stolen, or otherwise removed. In other words, the only way one can truly lose one's human rights is to cease to be human, a seemingly impossible scenario.

All of this, my students tell me, is relatively simple. They have, after all, just finished defining much more difficult terms like terrorism and nationalism. It becomes infinitely more challenging when I ask them for the reasoning behind the idea that human beings have all of these rights. From

where, for example, do I derive my right to free speech? And is there something about me that compels governments the world over to refrain from imprisoning me indefinitely in the absence of a proper trial? What reasons can we give to shore up our belief that no one ought to be subjected to torture or other ill-treatment? William F. Schulz makes this point effectively with a similar, poignant question:

> In Shakespeare's *The Merchant of Venice*, Shylock cries out, "I am a Jew. Hath not a Jew eyes? Hath not a Jew hands, organs, dimensions, senses, affections, passions? Fed with the same food, hurt with the same weapons, subject to the same diseases, healed by the same means? If you prick us, do we not bleed? If you tickle us, do we not laugh? If you poison us, do we not die?" What do we say to the killer who responds to Shylock, "Yes, a Jew has eyes but so does a pig"?[2]

It is here that my students run into trouble and really begin to disagree with one another. Some argue that God is the ultimate guarantor of our rights, that we are all the children of God, and that we are entitled to certain standards of treatment because we are all created in God's image. This answer, while perfectly valid, does not appeal to those in the room who do not believe in God but who still believe that they and others have rights. Instead, some argue that their rights are based on human dignity, while others contend that rights are nothing more than incredibly useful social constructs (perhaps the most fashionable term in the academic lexicon today). Though I have only participated in a handful of discussions on this topic, I am fairly confident that most sound like the one I am recounting here and like the one from a Houston classroom that Schulz recounts:

> "Do only Americans have the right to a fair trial or to free speech?"
>
> "No," most of the kids replied. "Everybody does."
>
> "OK, but since our constitution only applies to Americans, on what basis would we argue with somebody who says either 'Your Constitution is just plain wrong' or 'Well, OK, maybe your Constitution is right for you but not for me and my people. We don't believe in all those rights you allow your people to have'?"
>
> At this point the more alert students were starting to turn some of these questions over in their minds.
>
> "I'd say, 'It's because God gave us those rights,'" somebody interjected.
>
> "But what if the person we're talking to doesn't believe in God, or what if he or she is of a different religion than we are and says, 'Well, my God didn't give me those rights'? What do we say then?"
>
> "We could say that human beings just deserve those rights," a smart kid retorted. "Rights are what make us human. Chairs and

tables don't have rights. Rights are just the right thing to do. It's just the moral thing."

"But what if somebody tells us that he or she thinks what makes us human is obeying the wishes of our leaders, even if the leaders deny us our rights. What if somebody tells us he or she thinks it is perfectly moral to torture a person or throw someone in jail without a trial. How do we refute that?"

After we had gone round and round on these questions for a few minutes, a girl in the back tried to settle the matter: "Well, OK," she said. "Maybe we can't argue others into believing our way for sure. But what we *can* do is to say to them, 'Look, this is just the best way to live. Do you really want to live in a world without any rights? We think this way works best, and we think you should try it too.'"[3]

The students in Schulz's classroom seem satisfied at this point, but mine have traditionally not been as easy to please. If three different people can believe three completely different things about the source of our rights, then perhaps they stand on shakier ground than anyone imagined. Interestingly, it is the religious group that is most dissatisfied at the end of the day, though they are not frustrated with their own answer. They want to know where human dignity comes from if not from God and they want to know why anyone ought to respect a social construct the minute it becomes inconvenient to do so or when it is clear that it is not *their* social construct. It is easy enough, they argue, to understand the language of human rights if one believes that human beings are the sacred children of God, but a good deal more must be said if one is not of that belief.

Indeed, Michael Perry makes this argument in a particularly forceful and engaging manner. This book will consider in depth his assertion that:

> There is no intelligible (much less persuasive) secular version of the conviction that every human being is sacred; the only intelligible versions are religious .... The conviction that every human being is sacred is, in my view, inescapably religious – and the idea of human rights is, therefore, ineliminably religious.[4]

Perry's argument presents one of the most thought-provoking aspects of human rights theory and answering his challenge is, on my reading, of fundamental importance to the furthering of the human rights agenda. For if we are able to discern a compelling non-religious foundation for the idea of human rights that can stand alongside the religious one, we will have made it easier for an ever-widening group to reach a consensus on the manner in which they ought to treat one another, even if they are unable to reach any other agreement.[5]

Chapter 1 focuses both on Perry's argument that a religious framework provides the only intelligible grounding for any theory of human

rights and also on a provocative critique of the idea of rights. I begin by presenting Perry's claim that at the center of the idea of human rights lies a fundamentally religious concept, the notion of the sacredness of persons. To do so, I examine Perry's discussion of Christianity, his example of a persuasive religious grounding for human rights. It is also important to consider Perry's definition of a religious worldview – one that is "grounded or embedded in a vision of the finally or ultimately meaningful nature of the world and of our place in it."[6] Further, I consider whether the expansive scope of Perry's definition stretches our understanding of religion beyond its breaking point and, of course, whether conventional religious worldviews fit comfortably within it. In the end, I agree with Perry that a religious worldview – one that contains a vision of equality and of human connectedness – provides a persuasive grounding for the idea of human rights; however, I also argue that organized religion has done a particularly poor job of translating these concepts into action and that, in fact, the history of religion can be seen as antithetical to the concept of human rights. Finally, I examine one of the most profound challenges to the idea of using religion as a justification for human rights, that of Friedrich Nietzsche. If human rights take God as their source, then certainly the death of God spells disaster for the entire concept. Alternatively, if the concept is constructed by human beings, then it is the result of self-interested calculation, a tool of the weak to keep true greatness enslaved to the sort of mediocrity that ensures the survival of the weakest. As Perry correctly argues, one comes away from a reading of Nietzsche with the sense that human rights either cannot or should not be defended.

The remainder of the book proceeds from the spiritual void that Nietzsche's theory opened and grapples with Perry's conclusion – in the face of that vacuum – that accepting Nietzschean conclusions makes the idea of human rights untenable. A number of contemporary theorists have attempted to locate a non-religious defense of human rights that can work around the twin problems of self-interest and the death of God. Chapter 2 looks at the first of these, Alan Gewirth's argument from pure reason. In this chapter, I examine his reasoning for constructing a theory, namely that existing theories are fundamentally flawed and leave the idea of human rights without a logically consistent foundation, before considering in careful detail Gewirth's own claims for the Principle of Generic Consistency (PGC). Having looked at his critique of numerous other theories, as well as at his own argument about human action grounding basic rights to freedom and well-being, I then offer a critique of Gewirth's PGC. Ultimately, the chapter's conclusion is that Gewirth's theory relies too heavily on the notions, first, that we have a meta-desire not to contradict ourselves and, second, that we are unable to find persuasive justifications for our behavior that might allow us to avoid self-contradiction. If one is not troubled by charges of self-contradiction or, as is more often the case, one does

not recognize that one's victim is as much a human being as oneself, Gewirth's theory will not seem particularly persuasive.

Chapter 3 considers a non-religious conception of sacredness based on creative investment, as outlined by Ronald Dworkin. I begin by examining how Dworkin arrives at his conclusion about the value of life without necessarily referring to God, and then use the lens of the contemporary abortion controversy to think through the implications of his argument. After addressing the debate over why Dworkin thinks human life has value – based on human and biological creativity – I consider Perry's objections to this theory of non-religious sacredness, namely that its subjective reasoning cannot bear the weight necessary to ground the idea of human rights. While Perry is correct about the problem this presents for Dworkin, I argue that his overall approach is mistaken, as the concept of sacredness simply cannot be understood in the absence of a religious cosmology. Having said that, I argue that Perry's conclusion about the necessity of religion to human rights does not hold; looking closely at the etymological roots of the terms "sacred" and "dignity," I challenge Perry's conflation of those terms. Instead, I argue that the contemporary language of human rights is based on the concept of human dignity rather than sacredness, and that – contrary to existing theoretical work on this subject – the two words should not be treated as synonyms.

Chapter 4 seeks to answer the lingering question left open at the end of the previous chapter: on what basis might a non-religious person claim that human persons possess inherent dignity? Though our knowledge remains incomplete at present, I want to argue that the information we have begun to compile about the human mind can yield some interesting conclusions about the idea of human dignity. I begin by briefly constructing an argument for a human nature that is rooted in evolutionary biology. Having done so, I then make a case for locating personhood in the human mind; in particular, I consider arguments in favor of and against linking personal identity with either higher- and whole-brain activity. Next, I turn to a discussion of the differences between the fetus, the human animal in a persistent vegetative state, and the human person with a view to sorting through some possible sources of personhood. I conclude by offering a resolution to these controversies – which David DeGrazia calls "the boundaries of our existence"[7] – and, in so doing, demonstrating the priority of dignity to personhood. Ultimately, I argue that an intelligible grounding for human dignity – itself a foundational component of human rights – can be arrived at through an argument about the way our minds function; more specifically, I contend that dignity might be thought of as a feature of higher-brain activity and, in making this case, I provide one possible answer to the question of how a non-religious person might arrive at the concept of human dignity.

Chapter 5 looks closely at Richard Rorty, who "has recommended that we simply stop trying to defend the idea of human rights"[8] and that we,

instead, simply focus on expanding our contemporary human rights culture. Doing as Rorty recommends, Perry and many others argue, could open the door to any number of illiberal (and dangerous) possibilities. That said, it might instead suggest a plausible non-religious grounding for the idea of human rights. It is to a discussion of these two possibilities that I turn in this chapter, beginning with a detailed look at the Rortyan ideal of liberal irony and the question of whether this sort of irony is a desirable, or even psychologically possible, character trait. I then bring the disagreement between Rorty and those theorists he refers to as metaphysicians into sharper focus by examining the figure of the illiberal ironist, who is armed with the same tools as his/her liberal counterpart but reaches the opposite conclusion about whether to prevent human suffering. Finally, the chapter considers the place of sympathy and solidarity in what I take to be Rorty's answer to his detractors. I argue throughout that Rorty has been unsuccessful in abandoning metaphysical claims, as he relies on the foundational idea that sympathy and solidarity are natural and universal characteristics of humanity; indeed, Rorty's thoughts on the self-creating aspect of the brain dovetail nicely with the argument – made in the previous chapter – about the universal complex human mind. In making this case, Rorty has (perhaps unwittingly) succeeded in providing an answer to Michael Perry's assertion that "the idea of human rights is ... ineliminably religious"[9] by suggesting a plausible non-religious foundation. The final chapter builds upon the possibility to which Rorty's theory alludes, while avoiding the problem of attempting to do away with foundations.

Chapter 6 puts forward what I take to be a plausible non-religious foundation for the idea of human rights. In particular, I argue that compelling religious foundations have led non-religious rights theorists to focus on finding features or qualities inherent in human beings from which our rights spring, a mistake that can be seen clearly in the theories of both Gewirth and Dworkin. Following Rorty, I contend that these features or qualities are not found so much as they are created. While I believe that Rorty's argument – that telling sentimental stories is the most practical method for increasing our sense of solidarity with those we once considered "others"[10] – is an interesting response to Perry, I depart from it here because Rorty is unsuccessful in abandoning the idea of universal truths about human nature. Though I agree with Rorty – indeed, I have fleshed out and made explicit his implicit argument in my fourth chapter – I make a more procedural and practical argument here, one that steps back from arguments about a universal human nature. To do so, I look to the Universal Declaration of Human Rights to claim that human rights represent a political consensus of overlapping ideas from cultures and communities around the world. It is not simply that no single tradition was victorious in setting out the foundation of human rights that others could accept, though it is true that none was; instead, the Declaration's

chief virtue is that everyone was able to agree upon and endorse a *common* foundation: the dignity of the human person. The nations of the world may disagree on a great many things – philosophical as well as practical – but they have all agreed on this important point: every human being is entitled to the rights enshrined in the Universal Declaration by virtue of the inherent dignity that is common to us all. Some might argue that our dignity stems from our sacredness, from the *Imago Dei*, while others might prefer my argument for a less other-worldly source. At bottom, though, we have all agreed that human beings possess dignity and that, by virtue of this agreement, they have rights; this idea can be embraced by those who subscribe to what Perry calls a religious cosmology and also by those who do not. In constructing this consensus, then, we have succeeded in establishing a practical non-religious foundation upon which the idea of human rights can rest.

1 Michael Perry and the religious cosmology
Foundations and critiques of human rights

The concept of human rights ultimately rests on the premise that there are some things that ought to be done for human beings and other things that ought not to be done to human beings in light of the fact that they are human. These rights stem from the "recognition of the inherent dignity and of the equal and inalienable rights of all members of the human family."[1] Some would argue that this notion has its roots in the natural law and natural rights tradition that is an important strand of Western political thought,[2] and others would point out that Eastern philosophy neither ignores nor is fundamentally opposed to the concept of rights.[3] Finally, many people would claim that human rights have their origin in the Jewish and Christian traditions, while others would argue that nearly every major religion has its version of the Golden Rule.[4] It may well be from the insistence that we treat others as we wish to be treated ourselves that we can deduce the rights we have today, but there is also a long-standing debate about whether rights can be found in traditional religious texts at all. In examining the Bible, for example, we might conclude instead that people have duties to one another – and to God – but no rights, per se.[5] To put a finer point on it, there are injunctions against killing and stealing in the Old Testament, but these do not necessarily correspond to rights to life and property; likewise, the New Testament encourages people to treat one another as they themselves want to be treated, but does not provide a mechanism for anyone to claim injury in the event that they do not. In other words, these ancient religious texts do not seem to speak in the language of rights to which we have become accustomed. At the same time, strands of every major world religion seem to be quite supportive of the notion of inherent dignity, which underlies our contemporary understanding of human rights.

To say that religious texts are inclusive of human rights is very different from saying, as Michael Perry does, that a religious worldview provides the only intelligible grounding for those rights. Indeed, the most provocative question is not whether the concept exists in each of the world's religions, but whether it can exist independently of religion. As Perry asks:

What are we to make of such talk: talk about "the inherent dignity" of all human beings – about all human beings as members of one "family" – and about the importance, therefore, of all human beings acting toward one another "in a spirit of brotherhood"? It is easy enough to understand such talk as *religious* talk . . . . But is it possible, finally, to understand such talk in a nonreligious ("secular") sense?[6]

A good deal of work must be done to answer this question, and this chapter will begin to do so. The first section presents Perry's claim that at the center of the idea of human rights lies a fundamentally religious concept, the notion of the sacredness of persons. To do so, I examine his example of a persuasive religious grounding for human rights, the Christian conception of human flourishing that stems from a life of loving and serving others. It is also important to consider Perry's definition of a religious worldview – one that is "grounded or embedded in a vision of the finally or ultimately meaningful nature of the world and of our place in it"[7] – and that is the focus of the second section. Importantly, this section also looks closely at the tension that exists between organized religion and human rights, as well as whether the expansive scope of Perry's definition stretches our understanding of religion beyond its breaking point and, of course, whether non-traditional religious worldviews fit comfortably within it. In the end, I argue that a religious worldview – one that contains a vision of equality and of human connectedness – provides a persuasive grounding for the idea of human rights; however, I will also show that organized religion has done a particularly poor job of translating these concepts into action and that, in fact, the history of religion can be seen as antithetical to the concept of human rights. The final section examines one of the most profound challenges to the possibility of a religious justification for the idea of human rights, posed by Friedrich Nietzsche. If human rights take God as their source, then certainly Nietzsche's postulation of the death of God spells disaster for the entire concept. Alternatively, if the concept is socially constructed, then it is the result of self-interested calculation, a tool of the weak to keep true greatness enslaved to the sort of mediocrity that ensures the survival of the weakest. As Perry correctly argues, one comes away from a serious reading of Nietzsche with the sense that rights either cannot or should not be defended.

Human sacredness and human rights

"The fundamental challenge to each and every human rights claim," Perry tells us, "is a demand for reasons."[8] He has authored a book and a number of articles in an attempt to examine whether the extant reasons are compelling ones. On Perry's reading, all hitherto articulated non-religious reasons either fall well short of providing a solid foundation for human rights or are unintelligible. I will look closely at Perry's critiques of

both Ronald Dworkin and Richard Rorty in later chapters; in this chapter, I focus solely on the grounding for human rights that Perry believes can withstand serious scrutiny, the conviction that every human being is sacred. He begins his argument with a quotation from R.H. Tawney that sets our stage. Tawney argues that "*The essence of all morality is this: to believe that every human being is of infinite importance, and therefore that no consideration of expediency can justify the oppression of one by another.*"[9] Clearly, here, we have an articulation of the basic idea of human rights, that the human person is inviolable. Tawney continues, however, by noting that, "*to believe this it is necessary to believe in God.*"[10] Although Tawney's own reasoning for the necessary connection between human rights and religion is not given, Perry clearly articulates what he believes it to be, as he ascribes to Tawney the belief "that the conviction that every human being is sacred is inescapably religious."[11] Leaving aside the slight discrepancy in word choice – Tawney says "is of infinite importance," which Perry's translates to "is sacred" – both articulate the same basic point, namely that the human person is inviolable because of her relationship to God. It is human sacredness, then, that Perry focuses on throughout and his project is to confirm that the sacredness of persons can only be understood as a religious concept. Doing so, he argues, will show precisely why "For many religious persons ... the idea of human rights simply does not make sense, it does not exert a claim, apart from, cut off from, the Gospel vision of the world and of our place in it – or from some equivalent religious vision."[12]

To make his point clearer, Perry offers the example of Christianity to provide some detail on the connection between human sacredness and the inviolability of persons. While Perry focuses on his own religious tradition, he also makes clear that he recognizes there are "ample materials in other religious traditions out of which one can construct, or reconstruct, a relevantly similar version of the conviction [that every human being is sacred]."[13] At the heart of Perry's example is a rather simple, well-known injunction and it provides the ballast for Christians' understanding of human rights: "the instruction given by Jesus at a Passover seder on the eve of his execution: 'I give you a new commandment: love one another; you must love one another just as I have loved you.'"[14] Of course, Jesus was not only speaking of the people at the table; instead, he had in mind a far broader understanding of those who should be loved and of the type of love – love-as-agape – that should be afforded them. This is very much in line with the example that Perry gives in a more recent essay about the religious nature of the notion of human inviolability. He sketches out the belief system of a woman named Sarah whose faith helps her to love as Jesus commanded:

> She loves all human beings. She loves even 'the other'. She loves, that is, not only those for whom she has personal affection, or those with

whom she works or has other dealings, or those among whom she lives; she loves even those who are most remote, who are unfamiliar, strange, alien, those who, because they are so distant or weak or both, will never play any concrete role, for good or ill, in Sarah's life.[15]

It is easy enough to understand how Sarah might love those who are close to her, but one might justifiably wonder, in reading about Sarah, whether her love for those who do not touch her life in any way can properly qualify as love. Further, Perry suggests that:

Sarah loves even those from whom she is most estranged and towards whom she feels most antagonistic: those whose ideologies and projects and acts she judges to be not merely morally objectionable, but morally abominable ... Sarah loves even her enemies; indeed, she loves even those who have violated her.[16]

The depth of religious belief that this would require is, for many, unimaginable. It seems to me, in fact, that Sarah would not merely be a run-of-the-mill believer but a saint, a person of a fundamentally different quality from the people that we meet in our daily lives. But Perry is not alone in making this claim about the staggering requirements of religious love. Raimond Gaita, in a quotation that Perry employs, suggests that "the language of love ... compels us to affirm that even those who suffer affliction so severe that they have irrevocably lost everything that gives sense to our lives, and the most radical evil-doers, are fully our fellow human beings."[17] In looking carefully at Gaita's words, however, we might wonder whether the sort of acknowledgment or affirmation he proposes is not quite a bit different from actually loving those who directly violate us. I might, for example, affirm the humanity of the man who steals from me, but isn't it something else entirely to love him?

But these are not puzzles for those who subscribe to the religious worldview that Perry sketches. For them, it is entirely possible to love those who are near to us, far from us, love us in return, or seek to do us harm. For Christians, love is not necessarily associated with affection; it can be, instead, something spiritual and selfless, as evidenced by Jesus' example. Perry says:

love-as-agape does not require that we feel affection; such love consists, minimally, in wishing that the evildoers—who are understood/ seen to be truly, fully human—somehow achieve their perfection as human beings. In Sarah's case, this means that Sarah wants even the evil-doers somehow to achieve eternal union, in love, with God and with all their sisters/brothers.[18]

It is in this discussion of what constitutes human flourishing that Perry's example of a religious worldview begins to take a more definitive shape.

Underlying Sarah's feelings toward others, Perry tells us, is a particular understanding of the reason for our existence itself:

> For us – or, at least for most of us – it is a fundamental conviction, born not merely of our own experience, but of the experience of the historically extended communities ("traditions") that for many of us have been formative, that an important constituent of one's own well-being – of one's authentic flourishing as a human being – is concern for the well-being of one's sisters and brothers.[19]

On this reading, the Christian seems to care deeply about the welfare of other people – and, indeed, views them as inviolable – for a somewhat self-serving reason. On the one hand, those who subscribe to this worldview work toward their loving attitude for the good of the other, regardless of the position that the other takes toward them. On the other, though, they love the other because they believe "that a life of loving connection to one's sisters and brothers is . . . a flourishing life and that a life of unloving – uncaring – alienation from one's sisters and brothers is . . . a withering life."[20]

Christians who love their sisters and brothers receive great benefit from their loving attitude: "Sarah explains that the extent we become persons who love one another, to that extent we fulfill – we perfect – our created nature and thereby achieve our truest, deepest, most enduring happiness."[21] Perry wants to address this problem; in fact, he argues that Sarah's motives can be impeached only by those who misunderstand rationality and action. On this point, it will be useful to quote him at some length:

> Does Sarah do what she does for the other – for example, does she contribute to Bread for the World as a way of feeding the hungry – for *self-regarding* reasons? Does she do so, say, because it makes her happy to do so? She does not. (This is not to say that feeding the hungry doesn't make Sarah happy. It does. But this is not why she feeds the hungry.) Given the sort of person she is, the reason – the *other-regarding* reason – Sarah feeds the hungry is: "The hungry are my sisters and brothers; I love them." Now, a different question: Why is Sarah committed to being the sort of person she is, and why does she believe that everyone should want to be such a person? *Pace* Augustine, Sarah's answer is self-regarding: "By becoming persons who love one another, we fulfill our created nature and thereby achieve our truest, deepest, most enduring happiness." According to Sarah, it is not individual acts of love that necessarily make one happy; it is, rather, becoming a person who loves the other "just as I have loved you." "[S]elf-fulfillment happens when we are engaged from beyond ourselves. Self-fulfillment ultimately depends on

self-transcendence. This is essentially the claim that is made by religion, that the meaning of our lives is to be found beyond ourselves."[22]

In a series of footnotes to this discussion of self- and other-regarding reasons for action, Perry embraces what he sees as a decidedly Aristotelian viewpoint. For Aristotle,

> Happiness is the single final answer to the question "why do that?", the answer that survives the conflict with every rival interest or desire. In referring to happiness, we refer, not to the satisfaction of impulses, but to the fulfillment of the person."[23]

Whether we accept Perry's analysis depends on the importance we assign to the idea of purity of motives. While it is certainly possible to question the motivations that Christians like Sarah possess, it is equally (if not more) important to note that the result she achieves is one that does a good job of grounding human rights. While Sarah might not have purely other-regarding reasons for loving others, it might be that there is no such thing as a purely other-regarding reason and that, in fact, Sarah comes closest to this ideal. The quotation above, I think, is helpful in highlighting how she comes so close. Clearly, Sarah has a desire to feed the hungry. Following Harry G. Frankfurt, we will call this and her many other reasons for action first-order desires, "desires to do or not to do one thing or another."[24] He goes on to note that "Besides wanting and choosing and being moved *to do* this or that, men may also want to have (or not to have) certain desires and motives."[25] In addition to her first-order desire to feed the hungry, then, Sarah has a second-order desire to be the sort of person who is fulfilled through service to others. While her first-order desire might be purely other-regarding, as Perry claims, Frankfurt would argue that she follows through on it because of her very personal second-order desire. It might be the case that Sarah's reasons for action are purely other-regarding rather than self-regarding, but it seems more likely that one cannot act in a purely other-regarding manner. Much of Perry's discussion of Christian love, in fact, deals with the lover rather than the one being loved, but this does not change the fact that Sarah has a profound respect for the human rights of others and acts upon it. As we have seen, Sarah achieves fulfillment as a human being when she loves her sisters and brothers; conversely, "to fail to love the Other as sister/brother – worse, to hate the Other – is to succumb to the pathology of estrangement; it is, to that extent, to wither as a human being rather than to flourish."[26]

Given our desire to live a flourishing life, filled with happiness, rather than a withering life, we ought to love our brothers and sisters. The end, however, is not simply living a fulfilling life; as Perry notes, there is a more important reason – for Christians like Sarah – to love other human beings: the long shadow of the afterlife. Rather than attempting to figure out who

counts as one's sister or brother so that one may behave toward them as Jesus instructs, Perry points out that failing to love everyone leads to a fundamental estrangement with God. And this rupture has disastrous and irreparable consequences, as noted in the "Last Judgment" passage in the Gospel of Matthew that Perry quotes:

> When the Son of Man comes in his glory, and all the angels with him, he will sit on his throne in heavenly glory. All nations will be gathered before him, and he will separate the people one from another as a shepherd separates the sheep from the goats. He will put the sheep on his right and the goats on his left.
>
> Then the King will say to those on his right, "Come, you who are blessed by my Father; take your inheritance, the kingdom prepared for you since the creation of the world. For I was hungry and you gave me something to eat, I was thirsty and you gave me something to drink, I was a stranger and you invited me in, I needed clothes and you clothed me, I was sick and you looked after me, I was in prison and you came to visit me."
>
> Then the righteous will answer him, "Lord, when did we see you hungry and feed you, or thirsty and give you something to drink? When did we see you a stranger and invite you in, or needing clothes and clothe you? When did we see you sick or in prison and go to visit you?"
>
> The King will reply, "I tell you the truth, whatever you did for one of the least of these brothers of mine, you did for me."
>
> Then he will say to those on his left, "Depart from me, you who are cursed, into the eternal fire prepared for the devil and his angels. For I was hungry and you gave me nothing to eat, I was thirsty and you gave me nothing to drink, I was a stranger and you did not invite me in, I needed clothes and you did not clothe me, I was sick and in prison and you did not look after me."
>
> They also will answer, "Lord, when did we see you hungry or thirsty or a stranger or needing clothes or sick or in prison, and did not help you?"
>
> He will reply, "I tell you the truth, whatever you did not do for one of the least of these, you did not do for me."
>
> Then they will go away to eternal punishment, but the righteous to eternal life.[27]

In stressing the religious response to the "who is my sister/brother" question, however, Perry lends more weight to the claim that religious people are more concerned about themselves than they are about others. In other words, it seems that one ought to act toward other human beings with love and compassion because one's eternal fate hangs in the balance.

Having looked at the idea of love-as-agape in some detail, the relationship between this sort of love and human rights continues to seem a bit tenuous, apart from the connection that Perry wants to make through the idea of sacredness. But Perry attempts to answer critics – such as myself – who see ulterior motives in the idea of Christian love, and who wonder whether love and human rights are at all related. He says:

> The imperative to "love one another as I have loved you" can be understood ... not as a piece of divine legislation, but as a (truly, fully) human response to the question of how to live .... What makes the imperative a *religious* human response and not merely a secular one is that the response is the existential yield of a religious conviction about how the world (including we-in-the-world) hangs together: in particular, the conviction that the Other is, finally, one's own sister/brother – and should receive, therefore, the gift of one's loving concern.[28]

For Perry, then, there is a direct link between a belief in God and the idea of human rights. For Christians, this link can be expressed as follows: I believe in God, who created all human beings in His image and who instructed us to love one another as He loves us. I have concluded, in believing that we are all created in God's image, that we are all sisters/brothers and that we are all sacred. I have further concluded, in believing that we ought to love one another, that a life of human flourishing can only be achieved by treating others as sisters/brothers and as sacred. Either way, my belief system compels me to recognize the human person as inviolable and to respect the human rights of the Other. This connection might not be as explicit in other belief systems as it is in Christianity, but Perry argues that it is assuredly present because the concept of a religious worldview has similar features across the many diverse world religions, despite some differences in expression and application. In his own words:

> Just as there are differences among the precise religious visions adhered to by different sects within Christianity, there are differences among the precise visions adhered to by different world religions.... But such differences as there are ought not to obscure the fact that the experience of all human beings as sacred is widely shared among different sects and religions, albeit expressed – mediated – differently in different traditions.[29]

The idea of a religious worldview

As we have seen, Perry argues that a religious worldview is necessary to achieve the sort of robust understanding of human rights that we hold

today. This is all well and good theoretically, of course, but it begins to break down once we consider the actual interaction between religion and rights.[30] Historically, respect for God's commandments did not seem to line up with a love of the Other or even a basic consideration for the Other's life. In some instances, in fact, God actually destroys human beings Himself or commands human beings to commit murder, as in the famous stories of Noah and Abraham. While God punishes the first recorded instance of murder – Cain's slaying of his brother, Abel – with banishment, it is not terribly long before men have become entirely corrupt and God decides to destroy them all: "And the earth was corrupt before God, and the earth was filled with violence.... And God said unto Noah: 'The end of all flesh is come before Me; for the earth is filled with violence through them; and, behold, I will destroy them with the earth.'"[31] Perhaps just as famous as the story of Noah and the flood is that of God's test to determine whether Abraham was a true believer.[32] In it, He commands Abraham to sacrifice his only son, Isaac, to Him and Abraham prepared to comply without hesitation. Only after the preparations have been completed and Abraham is poised to carry out God's request does an angelic representative intercede:

> And Abraham stretched forth his hand, and took the knife to slay his son. And the angel of the Lord called unto him out of heaven and said: "Abraham, Abraham." And he said: "Here am I." And he said: "Lay not thy hand upon the lad, neither do thou any thing unto him; for now I know that thou art a God-fearing man, seeing thou hast not withheld thy son, thy only son, from Me."[33]

In addition to these two examples, the Old Testament is filled with numerous stories involving slavery, intolerance, murder, and even genocide. Perhaps the most troubling is the proposed annihilation of the kingdom of Amalek, not only because of the genocidal intent of the Israelites but because Saul's failure to completely destroy them results in God's extreme displeasure and Saul's eventual loss of his kingdom. To capture the spirit of this passage, it will be necessary to quote at some length:

> "Thus saith the Lord of hosts: I remember that which Amalek did to Israel, how he set himself against him in the way, when he came up out of Egypt. Now go and smite Amalek, and utterly destroy all that they have, and spare them not; but slay both man and woman, infant and suckling, ox and sheep, camel and ass." And Saul summoned the people, and numbered them in Telaim, two hundred thousand footmen, and ten thousand men of Judah.... And Saul smote the Amalekites, from Havilah as thou goest to Shur, that is in front of Egypt. And he took Agag the king of the Amalekites alive, and utterly destroyed all the people with the edge of the sword. But Saul and the

people spared Agag, and the best of the sheep, and of the oxen, even the young of the second birth, and the lambs, and all that was good and would not utterly destroy them; but everything that was of no account and feeble, that they destroyed utterly. Then came the word of the Lord unto Samuel, saying: "It repenteth Me that I have set up Saul to be king; for he is turned back from following Me, and hath not performed My commandments".... And Samuel came to Saul; and Saul said unto him: "Blessed be thou of the Lord; I have performed the commandment of the Lord." And Samuel said: "What meaneth then this bleating of the sheep in mine ears, and the lowing of the oxen which I hear?" And Saul said: "They have brought them from the Amalekites; for the people spared the best of the sheep and of the oxen, to sacrifice unto the Lord thy God; and the rest we have utterly destroyed."... And Samuel said: "Hath the Lord as great delight in burnt-offerings and sacrifices, As in hearkening to the voice of the Lord? Behold, to obey is better than sacrifice, And to hearken than the fat of rams. For rebellion is as the sin of witchcraft, And stubbornness is as idolatry and teraphim. Because thou hast rejected the word of the Lord, He hath also rejected thee from being king."... Then said Samuel: "Bring ye hither to me Agag the king of the Amalekites." And Agag came unto him in chains. And Agag said: "Surely the bitterness of death is at hand." And Samuel said: As thy sword hath made women childless, So shall thy mother be childless among women. And Samuel hewed Agag in pieces before the Lord in Gilgal.[34]

The destruction of the Amalekites, rabbinic commentary tells us, was the final act of vengeance in a long-standing "feud between the tribes of Israel and this untamable race of savages" that dated back to an attack by Amalek on the weak and defenseless Jews in their exodus from Egypt.[35] While the commentary goes to some length to recognize that "The moral difficulty in connection with this command is very real," the conclusion reached by the rabbis is that "the truest mercy sometimes lies in the dispensation of sternest justice, and Israel here was the instrument of Divine Retribution."[36] Despite the forgiving nature of this rabbinic commentary for what would today be considered an obvious and horrific example of a crime against humanity, it is clear that the connection between a religious cosmology and loving the Other is a tenuous one "in a world – *our* world, the *real* world – that is often fiercely partial/local rather than impartial/universal."[37]

It would be an obvious mistake, however, to conclude from these well-known Old Testament examples that the New Testament ushered in a world filled with a much more pacific and loving humanity. Indeed, the Holy Land of Jesus' day was populated by those who murdered one another over trivialities, were very hasty in their decisions to hurl stones at sinners, routinely refused assistance to the poor and infirm, and

colluded with the Roman authorities in their application of the death penalty.[38] And yet the New Testament on the whole spends markedly less time on the violence and abuse that people faced than the Old Testament – apart, of course, from the terrible violence of Jesus' own death by cruci-fixion – and focuses instead on the example of love, charity, and kindness that Jesus brought to humanity. Much more damaging to Perry's vision of the connection between Christianity and human rights are the centuries of atrocities carried out in the name of God once the persecuted Christians became the rulers following the conversion of the Roman emperor Constantine in 312. The following passage offers an illustration of the extremely violent and almost-immediate in-fighting that began once Christianity became an officially recognized and state-sanctioned religion in Rome:

> The eighty or ninety sects, into which Christianity speedily divided, hated one another with an intensity that extorted the wonder of Julian and the ridicule of the Pagans of Alexandria, and the fierce riots and persecutions that hatred produced appear in every page of ecclesiasti-cal history. There is, indeed, something at once grotesque and ghastly in the spectacle. The Donatists, having separated from the orthodox simply on the question of the validity of the consecration of a certain bishop, declared that all who adopted the orthodox view must be damned, refused to perform their rites in the orthodox churches which they had seized, till they had burnt the altar and scraped the wood, beat multitudes to death with clubs, blinded others by anointing their eyes with lime, filled Africa, during nearly two centuries, with war and desolation, and contributed largely to its final ruin. The childish and almost unintelligible quarrels between the Homoiousians and the Homoousians ... filled the world with riot and hatred. The Catholics tell how an Arian Emperor caused eighty orthodox priests to be drowned on a single occasion; how three thousand persons perished in the riots that convulsed Constantinople when the Arian Bishop Mace-donius superseded the Athanasian Paul; how George of Cappadocia, the Arian Bishop of Alexandria, caused the widows of the Athanasian party to be scourged on the soles of their feet, the holy virgins to be stripped naked, to be flogged with the prickly branches of palm-trees or to be slowly scorched over fires till they abjured their creed. ... In Ephesus, during the contest between St. Cyril and the Nestorians, the cathedral itself was the theater of a fierce and bloody conflict. Con-stantinople, on the occasion of the deposition of St. Chrysostom, was for several days in a condition of absolute anarchy. ... About fifty years later, when the Monophysite controversy was at its height, the palace of the emperor at Constantinople was blockaded, the churches were besieged, and the streets commanded by furious bands of con-tending monks.[39]

And this, of course, is just the beginning. In a little more than a thousand years – from Constantine's conversion to the outbreak of full-scale religious warfare between Catholics and Protestants in Europe – pious Christians would burn, drown, and torture hundreds of thousands – if not millions – of people with beliefs that differed from their own. These beliefs could be ones that were quite different (as exemplified by the persecution of Jews during the Spanish Inquisition), but just as often what constituted heresy was either not terribly far removed from the orthodox understanding of the day or a harmless derivation.[40] And this, of course, leaves out the centuries of destruction visited upon native populations around the world in the name of Christianity, as well as the violence meted out in full measure to the Muslims and Jews during the Crusades. As just one example, consider this eyewitness account of Jerusalem's capture during the First Crusade in 1099:

> Wonderful sights were to be seen. Some of our men (and this was more merciful) cut off the heads of their enemies; others shoot them with arrows, so that they fell from the towers; others tortured them longer by casting them into flames. Piles of heads, hands and feet were to be seen in the streets of the city. It was necessary to pick one's way over the bodies of men and horses. But these were small matters compared to what happened at the Temple of Solomon, a place where religious services are normally chanted ... in the temple and the porch of Solomon, men rode in blood up to their knees and bridle reins. Indeed it was a just and splendid judgement of God that this place should be filled with the blood of unbelievers since it had suffered so long from their blasphemies.[41]

Confronted with this sort of behavior, Perry's vision of a religious grounding for the idea of human rights begins to sound a bit hollow. For, although the New Testament preaches quite the opposite sort of behavior from that which we now associate with many of its most fervent believers, it shares with other human rights violating regimes one destructive feature: what both Aleksandr Solzhenitsyn and Raymond Aron refer to as ideology, a totalizing theoretical justification that grounds believers' actions. This point is made clearly and forcefully by Solzhenitsyn in *The Gulag Archipelago*, his gripping account of Stalin's concentration camps. He argues that:

> To do evil a human being must first of all believe that what he's doing is good, or else that it's a well-considered act in conformity with natural law. Fortunately, it is in the nature of the human being to seek a *justification* for his actions. ... Ideology – that is what gives evil-doing its long-sought justification and gives the evildoer the necessary steadfastness and determination. That is the social theory which helps

to make his acts seem good instead of bad in his own and others' eyes, so that he won't hear reproaches and curses, but will receive praise and honors. That was how the agents of the Inquisition fortified their wills: by invoking Christianity; the conquerors of foreign lands, by extolling the grandeur of their Motherland; the colonizers, by civilization; the Nazis, by race; and the Jacobins (early and late), by equality, brotherhood, and the happiness of future generations.[42]

The trouble, Solzhenitsyn argues, is not necessarily with seeking to justify our actions; instead, it lies in doing so with ideological reasons. In agreement with him on this point is Aron, who notes – as Perry does – that a loss of faith in God leaves human beings in the difficult position of not knowing "whether humanity is progressing towards an atomic holocaust or Utopian peace."[43] Faced with this unsettling question, one might ask, as Abraham Heschel does, "Are we alone in the wilderness of time, alone in the dreadfully marvelous universe, of which we are a part and where we feel forever like strangers? Is there a Presence to live by? A Presence worth living for, worth dying for?"[44] For Aron,

> That is where ideology comes in – the longing for a purpose, for communion with the people, for something controlled by an idea and a will. The feeling of belonging to the elect, the security provided by a closed system in which the whole of history as well as one's own person find their place and their meaning ... all this inspires and sustains the true believer.[45]

In an attempt to confront this criticism head-on, Perry notes that "There has been an obvious tendency on the part even of the world's 'great' religious traditions to tribalism, racism, and sexism – and worse.... A self-critical attitude toward one's own tradition is 'the route to liberation from the negative realities of [the] tradition.'"[46] This seems to me, however, to be far from a sufficient reply and, in fact, I wonder whether any reply to charges as grave as these can ever be sufficient. Indeed, the vigor and creativity with which the human person has been violated in the name of religion casts serious aspersion on the idea that religion and human inviolability are intimately connected.

That said, it is important that we avoid throwing the baby away with the bathwater; despite the abhorrent and criminal behavior of those who claim to live religiously, it can still be the case that a religious cosmology underpins the idea of human rights. Leo Strauss correctly asserts, after all, that the "reductio ad Hitlerum" is fallacious logic, as "A view is not refuted by the fact that it happens to have been shared by Hitler."[47] The same can – and, no doubt, ought to – be said of a "reductio ad religium," as many people who consider themselves to be religious are quite loving, charitable, and kind. What exactly does Perry have in mind, then, when he

says that a belief or conviction is a religious one and that it is embedded in a religious vision? He takes as his starting point the haunting question of the meaning of life – which, he acknowledges, may not be one that everyone attempts to answer – and considers the possible solutions. The question might arise, he says, after "a searing encounter with such a common but elemental event as sickness, old age, or death. Another principal occasion is an encounter, whether personal or vicarious, with evil and the terrible, primal suffering that evil causes."[48] At moments such as these, when our own mortality comes sharply into focus, there is a strong impulse to wonder whether there exists some greater purpose beyond our own small lives, some ultimate plan for humanity. In the face of encounters such as these, Perry tells us, a person is left "with a feeling that she is, or might be, a stranger, an alien, an exile, homeless, anxious, vulnerable, threatened, in a world, a universe, that is, finally and radically, unfamiliar, hostile, perhaps even pointless, absurd."[49] For Perry, there seem to be only two paths open to us when confronted in this manner. The first possibility, for Perry, is to adopt what he calls a religious vision of the universe, "a vision of final and radical reconciliation, a set of beliefs about how one is or can be bound or connected to the world – to the 'other' and to 'nature' – and, above all, to Ultimate Reality in a profoundly intimate way."[50]

Two interrelated questions arise from Perry's definition of a religious vision. The first is one that he seems to invite almost immediately after articulating his position, for he goes on to suggest that an "all-encompassing" worldview, like Marxism, is not a religious one.[51] His reasoning is that Marxism – and presumably other, unnamed worldviews with similar features – "is not grounded or embedded in a vision of the finally or ultimately meaningful nature of the world and of our place in it."[52] It is an interesting question, though, whether Marxism is truly incompatible with the sort of religious worldview that Perry has in mind. Indeed, Marxism seems to share a great deal with organized religion and many have argued that Marxism acquired a religious status of its own. As Raymond Aron argues:

> What the Christian, without being aware of it, is taken in by in the working-class world and in Marxist ideology are the reminders, the echoes, of a religious experience: proletarians and party militants, like the early Christians, live in anticipation of a new world; they have remained pure, open to charity, because they have never exploited their fellow-men; the class which carries within it the youth of humanity rises up against the corrupt past .... The Communists, who claim quite unashamedly to be atheists, are nevertheless imbued with a faith: they do not aim exclusively at a rational exploitation of natural resources and of communal life; they aspire to control all cosmic forces and all societies in order to solve the riddle of history and to turn mankind away from meditation on the Fall on to the path of self-sufficiency.[53]

Marxism, on Aron's reading, is very much a religion unto itself. It has replaced Christianity's righteous believers, whom Marx personally found distasteful, with a different group of oppressed people; in other words, Marxism substitutes the proletariat for the faithful, but offers no substantive distinctions between itself and organized religion. Karen Armstrong makes an argument similar to Aron's: "Even though [Marx] adopted a Messianic view of history that was heavily dependent upon the Judeo-Christian tradition, he dismissed God as irrelevant."[54] She says that "Since there was no meaning, value or purpose outside the historical process, the idea of God could not help humanity."[55] Important to note, clearly, is the emphasis on the historical process in this description, as well as in Aron's, for it is history itself that provides Ultimate Meaning within Marxist dogma. In Marx's own words, "Communism is the riddle of history solved, and it knows itself to be this solution."[56]

If Aron and Armstrong are correct about their reading of Marxism, then our second question comes to the fore, namely whether every worldview we can imagine can be classified as religious under Perry's expansive definition. One might wonder, for example, whether Buddhism, a prominent world religion practiced by more than 350 million people, qualifies under Perry's definition of a religious worldview. Indeed, Buddhism has no conception of God per se (despite the idea of *bhakti* (personal devotion) to the Buddha, which is somewhat reminiscent of Christians' devotion to Jesus and which Armstrong notes was developed despite its being in tension with a number of important teachings).[57] Although Buddhism, then, is quite different from the Christian vision of the universe that Perry sketches, the central teaching "that enlightenment was humanity's proper destiny"[58] clearly points to the idea of an ultimately meaningful universe and our place in it. As Armstrong argues:

> Just as enlightenment and Buddhahood did not involve invasion by a supernatural reality but were an enhancement of powers that were natural to humanity, so too the deified Christ showed us the state that we could acquire by means of God's grace. Christians could venerate Jesus the God-Man in rather the same way as Buddhists had come to revere the image of the enlightened Gautama: he had been the first example of a truly glorified and fulfilled humanity.[59]

Buddhism, then, despite the notable absence of a deity, seems to fit squarely into Perry's definition, as he tells us it should: "Not every religious tradition tells the same story about the way in which the world is ultimately meaningful; often the stories are different, even if sometimes the stories are quite similar."[60] Buddhists are certainly understood to be religious in the conventional sense and Marxism is generally regarded as having fairly strong religious undertones; at this point, then, it seems that Perry's definition of a religious worldview is expansive enough to

accommodate religious worldviews of very different sorts. Organized religions like Judaism, Christianity, and Buddhism clearly hold human life in the highest esteem and provide a foundation for the idea of human rights; Marxism also places a great deal of emphasis on humanity's role in the historical process and it might even be argued that Marx's concept of human emancipation can ground the idea of human rights. Having considered some conventionally and unconventionally religious worldviews and their connection to the idea of human rights, it will be instructive to look briefly at a worldview that is viewed as anathema both to religion and rights – Martin Heidegger's nihilism – and see how it fares under Perry's definition.

If, as noted above, the first possibility when confronted by questions of our own mortality is to adopt a religious vision of the universe that provides us with Ultimate Meaning, the second possibility could not be more dissimilar, for it is to embrace the path taken by Martin Heidegger. Heidegger's thoughts on metaphysics take Perry's conclusion about the search for Ultimate Meaning as their beginning and, like Perry, arrive before long at Nietzsche and nihilism. For Heidegger, men are constantly led to question the purpose of their existence. Insofar as they are thrust into the Nothing by the fact of their mortality, they must ask, "Why am I?" Every person, he argues, is struck by this question at least once in a lifetime, in a moment of either great joy (when everything becomes focused into love of one thing), despair (when everything is meaningless), or boredom (when nothing is of interest).[61] In each of these three cases, things run together and there ceases to exist a hierarchy of concerns regarding beings in the world. Heidegger suggests that hierarchy requires distance between objects and that, in times such as these, people no longer recognize the possibility of a future outside a particular moment and beings cease to have value. It is at these moments, then, that the question of Being arises for a particular individual. Because of the question's relation to the Nothing, human beings stake their entire existence on its asking – and only in doing so can they live authentic lives. It is to Nietzsche and the problem of nihilism that Heidegger turns, and his project is to show not that the end of metaphysics brings about nihilism but that European philosophy has nihilism at its core. He focuses his attention on Nietzsche because Nietzsche is, for Heidegger, the philosopher who takes metaphysics to its logical end: "Nietzsche had to conceive of nihilism that way [as nihilistic, rather than recognizing its hidden essence] because in remaining on the path and within the realm of Western metaphysics, he thought it to its conclusion."[62] Important, here, is Heidegger's assertion that Nietzsche is the last in a long line of metaphysical thinkers that can be traced back to Plato, the first to distinguish between Being and beings. Indeed, in positing his idea of the Good, of the Being of beings, Plato sought to answer the question of Being but in doing so relegated Being itself to the status of other beings.[63]

Central to the advent of nihilism is Nietzsche's well-known and oft-quoted phrase that God is dead. Nietzsche's claim is not that there is no God, but instead that God was once alive – as the Being of all beings – and that we have killed Him.[64] Heidegger's explanation traces this idea back to Cartesian philosophy which, in positing the world as world picture rather than as creation, replaces God with the individual as the Being of beings. In suggesting the idea of the world picture grounded in the experience of the individual, Descartes asserts that nature is the picture of matter in lawful motion and that man – in learning the laws visible in this picture – can master nature. For Nietzsche, the consequence of the death of God is not so much the Cartesian claim that man takes on God-like power, but that the highest values devalue themselves. Put succinctly, the lack of faith in a god necessitates the acceptance of the total absence of foundations for individual values, beliefs, and thoughts.[65] In other words, human beings have a great many choices to make, but absolutely no reason to choose any one thing over another. While Nietzsche saw either mass suicide or self-overcoming as the only possible results of this nihilistic manner of thinking, Heidegger is appreciably more hopeful. He makes the claim that to say something has no value is to say that it is not. In attempting to assert the non-existence of Being by thinking the Nothing, however, an individual always makes an assertion of Being because Being introduces through the "is." He notes that "Even when we say simply that the nothing 'is' nothing, we are apparently predicating an 'is' of it and making it into a being; we attribute what ought to be withheld from it."[66] This is the great use Heidegger sees for nihilism: in attempting to assert that there is no foundation – no Being – human beings are forced by nihilism to raise anew the question of Being.

The things that truly order our lives, according to Heidegger, are mostly invisible to us and only by raising anew the question of Being can we begin to recognize what drives us. For Heidegger, men are in the control of something beyond themselves but have concealed this fact from themselves and are, consequently, unable to see their destiny. This is not to say that an aim for human life is lacking, but that people fail to appreciate that aim. The value of raising anew the question of Being is that it brings man back to a place where Being can assert its control over man in an obvious way and provide him the direction necessary to live an authentic life. It is here, interestingly, that Heidegger and Nietzsche must be separated, as Perry should undoubtedly classify the former but not the latter as a religious thinker. The distinction for Perry – and, therefore, for this project – is clear. For, as Perry says:

> To ask if the conviction that every human being is sacred – the conviction that every human being is "inviolable", has "inherent dignity", is "an end in himself", or the like – is inescapably religious is to ask if the conviction can be embedded in … either an antireligious

cosmology, according to which the world is, at the end of the day, not meaningful but meaningless, or a cosmological agnosticism that neither affirms nor denies the ultimate meaningfulness of the world.[67]

In the end, Heidegger's cosmology is neither an antireligious nor an agnostic one; despite the emphasis it places on nihilism, it actually seems to fit relatively well into Perry's definition of a religious worldview. The problem with Heidegger's religious cosmology is that it leaves open decidedly anti-liberal possibilities, as no value judgment exists regarding Heidegger's great hope, the return to the question of Being. Instead, Heidegger seems content to advise people to wait beside the abyss and follow whatever is disgorged, for good or ill, in an effort to live authentically. The danger is that the product of the abyss is just as likely to be what respectable liberals consider evil as it is what they consider good. In this sense, Heidegger is very much the careful reader of Nietzsche, whose thoughts on the virtues of self-overcoming do not concern themselves with the suffering that might accompany it: "Genuine charity demands sacrifice for the good of the species – it is hard, it is full of self-overcoming, because it needs human sacrifice."[68]

But this is precisely what horrifies Perry, whose quotations make clear his apprehension: "Nietzsche declared: 'Naiveté: as if morality could survive when the *God* who sanctions it is missing! The 'beyond' absolutely necessary if faith in morality is to be maintained.'"[69] In a world without God, the range of possibilities for human interaction is broad enough that it allows for amoral or immoral action. It is in this sort of world that men might sanction violence against targeted groups and systemically violate the rights of others. It is a world in which stories such as this one, taken from the Iraqi repression of its Kurdish minority, are commonplace:

> Some groups of prisoners were lined up, shot from the front and dragged into pre-dug mass graves; others were shoved roughly into trenches and machine-gunned where they stood; others were made to lie down in pairs, sardine-style, next to mounds of fresh corpses, before being killed; others were tied together, made to stand on the lip of the pit, and shot in the back so that they would fall forward into it – a method that was presumably more efficient from the point of view of the killers. Bulldozers then pushed earth or sand loosely over the heaps of corpses.[70]

In such a world, the idea of human rights, according to Perry, is both unintelligible and unpersuasive.

If human beings want a world in which human rights are respected, Perry would argue, they must eschew the path of nihilism that Nietzsche and Heidegger are willing to consider. A religious worldview must provide people with more than just meaning, for Heidegger's seems to promise

that. For Perry, the worldview must be both religious and liberal, no mean feat, as it must provide people with an answer not only to the question of why we ought not to destroy one another, but why we ought to go so far as to love one another:

> The answer … is that the Other (the outsider, the stranger, the alien), too, no less than oneself and the members of one's family or of one's tribe or nation or race or religion, is a "child" of God – God the creator and sustainer of the universe, imag(in)ed, analogically, as a loving "parent" – and therefore a "sister"/"brother"[71]

It is in caring about other people, in treating them as brothers and sisters, that we live a truly meaningful human life. Those who think otherwise are, for Perry, "no less in the grip of a pathology of estrangement than if [they] were to reject that an important constituent of [their] own well-being is concern for the well-being of [a] child, or spouse, or parent."[72]

That said, it is important to note that Perry's Nietzsche is a sort of philosophical bogeyman. Perry has been, in my estimation, uncharitably selective in his reading; indeed, all of the quotations that Perry employs come from Nietzsche's *Will to Power*, an infamous collection of often incomplete notes and ideas published after his death. As Walter Kaufmann notes:

> These notes were not intended for publication in this form, and the arrangement and the numbering are not Nietzsche's. Altogether, this book is not comparable to the works Nietzsche finished and polished, and we do him a disservice if we fudge the distinction between these hasty notes and his often gemlike aphorisms.[73]

There is a great deal more to Nietzsche than the death of God and the destruction of morality, though I will not ultimately argue with Perry's characterization of the basic problem that Nietzsche presents for the idea of human rights. In many ways, however, Nietzsche puts forward a much more nuanced critique of liberal human rights and the culture that spawned them. We turn, then, to a more robust discussion of nihilism and to Nietzsche's postulation of the death of God, which Perry views, it seems, as his antipodes.

Nietzsche and the death of God

For Nietzsche, the problem of modern society lies in the sense of security that liberalism fosters in its citizens. Modern men, he seems to suggest, might be nothing more than happy slaves, convinced by rationalism that they ought to continue their work because progress makes each day better than the last. An answer to this problem, Nietzsche asserts, can be found in an examination of man's use of history to serve the goals of the present.

People have the tendency to overemphasize the importance of the past and become absorbed in a love of history. Nietzsche goes so far as to poke fun at those who can find fault with everything associated with the present.[74] On the other hand, it is just as easy to ignore the past and lose sight of everything by focusing solely on day-to-day living. One overzealous approach is as harmful as the other. He is quick to point out that neither extreme can provide an answer for how men ought to live. Instead, it is a blending of the two that can bring people closest to their target. History, according to Nietzsche, must be considered in light of the present; if it fails to challenge or speak to the experience of modernity, we have used it improperly.[75] In this way, there can be no universal truth about history. Indeed, the strongest people must be able to synthesize history as plants use sunlight. These strong men will mold and shape the past into a form that illuminates the present in a useful manner for them; what cannot be used is simply forgotten. "The stronger the roots of the inmost nature of a man are, the more of the past will he appropriate or master."[76] Those who are not gifted with this ability may be permanently traumatized, paralyzed with fear or anxiety, and unable to move forward after a harmful experience.[77] These people, unable to close a horizon around themselves that leaves the forgotten outside, cannot continue to exist as the strong do. As Nietzsche notes, *only the strong personalities can endure history; the weak are completely extinguished by it.*[78]

The strong man, for Nietzsche, has no repression in his soul and is more a force of nature than a human being. He is filled with the uncorrupted joy of mastership, of being the best. The weak man, however, is forced to follow the orders of the strong and repress his own passions and appetites. This daily repression leads to a powerful resentment that is relieved only through an imagined revenge encapsulated in a doctrine under which the meek supposedly inherit the earth. As Nietzsche argues:

> Dante, I think, committed a crude blunder when, with a terror-inspiring ingenuity, he placed above the gateway of his hell the inscription "I too was created by eternal love" – at any rate, there would be more justification for placing above the gateway to the Christian Paradise and its "eternal bliss" the inscription "I too was created by eternal *hate*" – provided a truth may be placed above the gateway to a lie! For *what* is it that constitutes the bliss of this Paradise?
>
> We might even guess, but it is better to have it expressly described for us by an authority not to be underestimated in such matters, Thomas Aquinas, the great teacher and saint. "*Beati in regno coelesti,*" he says, meek as a lamb, "*videbunt poenas damnatorum, **ut beatitude illis magis complaceat.***"[79]

Although this religious belief justifies their suffering, Nietzsche asserts that the knowledge offered by religion serves only to keep the truth about the

world hidden from weak men. This fraudulence underpins Nietzsche's criticism of both Christianity and morality, as priests and the rulers they buttress seek to further consolidate their power by asserting the concept of an effectual truth which can only be discovered through blind faith. This sort of easy knowledge, Nietzsche argues, is precisely what weak men hope for: "'Enlightenment' enrages: for the slave wants the unconditional; he understands only what is tyrannical."[80] For Nietzsche, two interesting questions arise when religious truth is shown to be a falsehood. First, how will humanity deal with the realization that religion is man-made and outmoded? Subsequently, what will become of humanity once morality – that pillar that religion itself fosters – is also shown to be its own construct?

It is clear to Nietzsche, at the close of the nineteenth century, that man has arrived at a philosophical crossroads. The first path leads to nihilism resulting from the failure of humanity to recover from its loss of belief in religion and rationalism. The second, however, is the path of the Overman and it winds through what Nietzsche calls a revaluation of all values. He argues that:

> Life itself is *essentially* appropriation, injury, overpowering of what is alien and weaker; suppression, hardness, imposition of one's own forms, incorporation and at least, at its mildest, exploitation – but why should one always use those words in which a slanderous intent has been imprinted for ages?[81]

To recognize that the strong individual – not the common man or God – is the creator of morality is the cornerstone of this second path. Learning that values neither arise from a universal truth nor are God-given leads to the understanding that they are created by human desires. "The noble type of man experiences *itself* as determining values; it does not need approval; it judges, 'what is harmful to me is harmful in itself'; it knows itself to be that which first accords honor to things; it is *value-creating*."[82] Nietzsche, then, does not preach the destruction of all morality as Perry fears; he encourages the creation – by strong individuals – of the values that are necessary for their lives. Of course, Nietzsche is no democrat and only a certain sort of person can undertake this sort of constructive work. "In the end," he says, "it must be as it is and always has been: great things for the great, abysses for the profound, nuances and shudders for the refined, and, in brief, all that is rare for the rare."[83] For Nietzsche, equality is a construct to keep the strong enslaved to the weak. In its name, most geniuses have been labeled dangerous or insane, killed or institutionalized. And this is not particularly surprising, as Nietzsche asserts that the production of genius will necessitate suffering and that, most often, the geniuses will not be the sufferers. He asserts that "One must shed the bad taste of wanting to agree with many. 'Good' is no longer good when one's neighbor mouths it. And how should there be a

'common good'! The term contradicts itself: whatever can be common always has little value."[84]

This repudiation of the ideal of a common good is one that would terrify someone like Thomas Hobbes, who argues that men collectively give up their power to a sovereign because they desire self-preservation above all else. According to Nietzsche, this is nonsensical: weak men are certainly willing to give up the meager amount of power they have in nature, but strong men must be subdued in order to accomplish the goal of *Leviathan*. Indeed, if men exist in nature with no other purpose than the satisfaction of their individual appetites, the strong should have little trouble following as many of their divergent drives and passions as possible, all at the expense of the weak. The weak, then, desperately need to create and maintain the commonwealth to ensure their own survival, irrespective of the cost. They do so, first, by building resentment against the strong through the doctrine of eternally-rewarded meekness taught by the purveyors of religion. Then they assert the notion of equality, as Hobbes famously does, claiming that the weakest man – or a group of them – can eventually kill even the strongest.

While this statement of equality is not in dispute, Nietzsche argues that what actually separates the strong from the weak is that the former have no fear of death. They have come to terms with the wisdom of Silenus: "What is best of all is utterly beyond your reach: not to be born, not to *be*, to be *nothing*. But the second best for you is – to die soon."[85] The strong live solitary and instinctual lives, by the rules of nature rather than artificially created maxims, fulfilling passion after passion until they die. "For solitude is a virtue for us, as a sublime bent and urge for cleanliness which guesses how all contact between man and man – 'in society' – involves inevitable uncleanliness. All community makes men – somehow, somewhere, sometime 'common.'"[86] While a fundamental falsehood is required to remove these strong individuals from their natural state, this move is not necessarily bad in itself. It is, for example, easy to imagine a society – like that of the ancient Greeks – that enslaves some people in order to better produce a race of artistic men in touch with the world as it is. The trouble arises when just the opposite occurs, when the mechanism by which the weak are able to continually subdue the strong is the perpetuation of the Socratic principles that so infuriate Nietzsche. By privileging the rational over the instinctual, society begins to reprioritize toward more sterile ends and genius is soon entirely suppressed.

This is the corrupted world in which – centuries earlier – Hobbes provides a quasi-scientific method for tricking and destroying genius in order to better establish a regime that preserves the lives of the thoughtless and artless masses. Hobbes' commonwealth – and the modern liberal society that eventually arose from it – has nothing to offer the strong man. Trapped within its confines, it is only a matter of time before his sense of loss becomes too great to bear. He is that revolutionary, then, that rages at

the sovereign until his detention or execution at the behest of the terrified citizenry. Unlike the opinion presented in *Leviathan*, however, Nietzsche suggests that these revolutionaries are the only men of sufficient strength and vision capable of reorganizing society in such a way that the production of genius becomes its goal. If the revolutionaries succeed in their violent uprising, the lives of weak men might indeed be as "poore, nasty, brutish, and short"[87] as they would be in the state of nature. The difference, for Nietzsche, is that they will have served a higher purpose by living and dying in a society that produces great genius. In other words, a slave in Athens is far better off than any modern man.

Nietzsche, then, is not simply the brash critic of Christianity and morality that Perry cites disapprovingly. He is one who seeks a revaluation of all values, who laments the passing of an age when genius was cultivated and weakness denigrated, and who deeply resents the gentle liberal virtue of tolerance. An aristocrat at heart, Nietzsche decries the fictional notions that all men are created equal and should act toward one another in a spirit of brotherhood. The truth about mankind, he argues, accords with the wisdom of Silenus – and human life, therefore, is valuable only insofar as it prepares the way for the Overman. Warfare, suffering, and death are grist for the Nietzschean mill because these call forth all that is great and powerful about men to the detriment of all that is weak and facile. This is the depth of Nietzsche's critique of liberalism and the idea of human rights, one with which Perry does not even begin to contend because he becomes transfixed by the idea of Nietzsche the Antichrist who scorns the notion of morality. In fact, Nietzsche mainly vilifies the slave morality that begins with resentment and imaginary revenge; in the end, he dreams of a revaluation of all values that will bring forth a new morality, one that is simultaneously inspiring and terrifying to those who take his writing seriously.

Conclusion

It is no accident, Werner Dannhauser tells us, that Nietzsche and Nazism are so commonly and closely linked. He writes that:

> The problem of Nietzsche's connection with fascism is unfortunately not resolved by claiming, as many interpreters of Nietzsche are prone to do, that Nietzsche was no fascist, that he was a violent critic of German nationalism, and that he would have loathed Hitler. These things are undoubtedly true, and uttering them shows the absurdity of a crude identification of Nietzsche's doctrines with Hitler's ravings.... But the fact remains that in various ways Nietzsche influenced fascism. Fascism may have abused the words of Nietzsche, but his words are singularly easy to abuse. Nietzsche was an extremist, and no man was more gifted than he in making an extreme view seem appealing by presenting it with great audacity and eloquence.[88]

And, for Michael Perry, much of the connection between the totalitarian, rights-abusing regimes and the theorists from whom they drew their inspiration can be explained by the absence and abuse of the idea of a religious cosmology in Nietzsche's writing. Such a view, I have argued, is overly simplistic and encourages a critique that fails to deal with the complexity of Nietzsche. That said, I think Dannhauser's argument is a compelling one: Nietzsche was clearly abused by the Nazis, but the language he frequently employs *is* singularly easy to abuse. As he forcefully points out:

> A man who counsels men to live dangerously must expect to have dangerous men like Mussolini heed his counsel; a man who teaches that a good war justifies any cause must expect to have this teaching, which is presented half is jest but only *half* in jest, to be abused. Nietzsche praises cruelty and condemns pity without reflecting sufficiently on whether man must really be advised to be more cruel than he is, or what the effect of such a view will be on cruel men."[89]

Perry's consideration of *Will to Power* as the authentic Nietzsche is undoubtedly unfair, as it fails to present much of what is praiseworthy about him: "Nietzsche was a man with a noble vision of man's future. His own delicacy, integrity, and courage shine through his writing. He was also free of the crude racism which was to be an important element of fascism, and he had only contempt for political anti-Semitism."[90] Of course, I have attempted to show that a more complete consideration of his work does not bring to light a more democratic or pacific Nietzsche. In looking carefully at Nietzsche, then, we should not be surprised that religious thinkers and human rights theorists find much to dislike, and that those who set themselves against both religion and rights find much to praise.

   Though he likely would not have supported the Nazis, Nietzsche's philosophical critique of rights and religion was certainly used to prop up their repressive ideology. To my mind, this makes Perry's project all the more troubling, as he argues that *only* a religious cosmology can ground the idea of human rights. In a pluralistic world – one in which most people do not hold the same religious worldview and many hold worldviews that would not fit within Perry's definition – it seems to me that a wider framework is needed, not a narrower one, to ground the idea of human rights. This is, of course, quite different from showing that Perry is incorrect about religion providing a compelling grounding for human rights, and I do not think he is. As I have shown, the language of rights can certainly find a solid foundation in many of the world's great religious texts, especially – as Perry notes – the Christian Gospels. The language of love and respect for the other, as well as of the equality of persons, provides a strong justification for the belief that people ought to be treated with respect and compassion, and that they ought not to be abused or otherwise

harmed. As this chapter has also demonstrated, however, religious people do not have the best track record when it comes to respecting human rights. Indeed, from the biblical destruction of the Amalekites to the Spanish Inquisition to the Taliban government of Afghanistan, some of the most terrible violations of human rights have occurred in the name of religion. These failings of organized religion should not necessarily be seen as damaging beyond repair Perry's thesis, as these are certainly misuses of a theory in much the same way that Nazism abused Nietzsche's thought. They do, however, constitute a serious hurdle that, I have argued, Perry fails to overcome in his argument in favor of the intimate connection between religion and rights.

Having said all this, the question that remains to be considered in the chapters that follow is one that Perry poses at the outset of *The Idea of Human Rights*: "Must we conclude," he asks:

> that the idea of human rights is ineliminably religious, that a fundamental constituent of the idea, namely, the conviction that every human being is sacred – that every human being is 'inviolable', has 'inherent dignity', is 'an end in himself', or the like – is inescapably religious?"[91]

For Perry, the answer is clear and affirmative, but for a number of other theorists – like Alan Gewirth, Ronald Dworkin, and Richard Rorty – to whom we will turn in the coming chapters, the answer is quite the opposite. Our task, then, is to adjudicate this dispute with a view to determining whether a religious worldview is needed to protect the concept of rights from Nietzsche's atheistic assault or whether a non-religious grounding can also provide us with compelling responses to those who would deny or disregard the idea of human rights.

2   The possibility of non-religious human rights
Alan Gewirth and the Principle of Generic Consistency

There is a well-known and often-quoted passage in Aleksandr Solzhenitsyn's *The Gulag Archipelago* in which the author makes a striking and controversial claim about his experience in the Soviet work camps. He says:

> If only it were all so simple! If only there were evil people somewhere insidiously committing evil deeds, and it were necessary only to separate them from the rest of us and destroy them. But the line dividing good and evil cuts through the heart of every human being. And who is willing to destroy a piece of his own heart? ... Confronted by the pit into which we are about to toss those who have done us harm, we halt, stricken dumb: it is after all only because of the way things worked out that they were the executioners and we weren't.[1]

Primo Levi, a survivor of the Nazi Holocaust, disagrees vehemently with Solzhenitsyn's claim. In *The Drowned and the Saved*, Levi says:

> I do not know, and it does not much interest me to know, whether in my depths there lurks a murderer, but I do know that I was a guiltless victim and I was not a murderer. I know that the murderers existed ... and that to confuse them with their victims is a moral disease or an aesthetic affectation or a sinister sign of complicity; above all, it is a precious service rendered (intentionally or not) to the negators of truth.[2]

This debate between survivors of history's two most brutal regimes has captured the imagination of a wide variety of human rights theorists. The passages, in whole or in part, appear in numerous books and can now be found on a wide variety of Internet websites; something about them strikes a chord with us and encourages us to enter into the debate. As Jonathan Glover points out, "One question about those who ran the Gulag or the Nazi genocide is about the rest of us too. Could *anyone* have done these things?"[3]

The haunting experience of the atrocities of the twentieth century has produced a greater understanding of humanity's dark side, through the works not only of Solzhenitsyn and Levi, but also Arthur Koestler, Milan Kundera, Elie Wiesel, and countless other authors' personal narratives and fictionalized accounts. An encounter with this body of literature – or, more powerfully, with the regimes themselves – directly informs much of contemporary rights theory, as philosophers, legal scholars, and politicians have attempted to come to terms with all that we have learned about ourselves and to keep our dark side in check. Glover is particularly clear on this point; he says, "If persuaded that an otherwise convincing ethical theory could justify the Nazi genocide, I should without hesitation give up the theory. In reconstructing ethics, revulsion against these things which people have done has a central place."[4] The century's most repressive regimes drew inspiration – however misguided – for their doctrines of racial purity and proletarian dictatorship from the foundations provided by the philosophy of Nietzsche and Marx (among others). It is, then, to philosophy that we turn for an answer to the claim that rights necessarily serve the interests of one group at the expense of another (the weak against the strong, for Nietzsche, and vice versa for Marx). As Alan Gewirth notes:

> In a century when the evils that man can do to man have reached unparalleled extremes of barbarism and tragedy, the philosophic concern with rational justification in ethics is more than a quest for certainty. It is also an attempt to make coherent sense of persons' deepest convictions about the principles that should govern the ways they treat one another."[5]

In this chapter, I examine Gewirth's argument for a non-religious foundation for the idea of human rights as a possible response to Michael J. Perry's claim

> that the idea of human rights is indeed ineliminably religious, that a fundamental constituent of the idea, namely, *the conviction that every human being is sacred – that every human being is "inviolable", has "inherent dignity", is "an end in himself", or the like* – is inescapably religious.[6]

In the first section, I look at Gewirth's reasons for constructing a theory, namely that existing theories are fundamentally flawed and leave the idea of human rights without a logically consistent foundation. The second section then considers Gewirth's own claims in detail. For the purposes of this chapter, Gewirth's argument will be thought of as having two major components, though in his own text it is actually broken down into some fifteen parts.[7] We will, of course, look carefully at each of these steps in his

argument, but for the purposes of critique, it will help to think of each step as belonging to one of these two major components. The first of these is Gewirth's notion that:

> every agent logically must hold or accept that he has rights to freedom and well-being as the necessary conditions of his action, as conditions that he must have; for if he denies that he has these rights, then he must accept that other persons may remove or interfere with his freedom and well-being, so that he may not have them; but this would contradict his belief that he must have them.[8]

And the second is that "the agent logically must accept that all other prospective purposive agents have the same rights to freedom and well-being as he claims for himself."[9] These components are used to construct the frame of Gewirth's argument for the Principle of Generic Consistency (PGC), a theory of non-religious universal human rights. Having looked at his critique of numerous other theories, as well as at his own argument, the third section offers a critique of Gewirth's PGC, concluding that the problem for Gewirth's theory is that it relies on the notions, first, that we have a meta-desire not to contradict ourselves and, second, that we are unable to find persuasive justifications for our behavior that might allow us to avoid self-contradiction. If one is not troubled by charges of self-contradiction or, as is more often the case, one does not recognize that one's victim is as much a human being as oneself, Gewirth's theory will not seem particularly persuasive. Ultimately, my critique of Gewirth is centered around the idea of justification. To my mind, a compelling grounding for human rights must do more than achieve logical coherence in order for it to have justificatory weight; I argue for the necessity of *inclusivity*, *persuasiveness*, and *practicality* to any foundational theory of human rights.

Gewirth's case against previous theories

If there could be only one thing said about Alan Gewirth, it should be that he is thorough. Thanks to his meticulous work, we are able to examine – in some detail – a number of non-religious theories that he feels are unable to successfully defend the idea of human rights against its critics. In sorting through these theories, which range from that of Thomas Jefferson to the Universal Declaration of Human Rights and H.L.A. Hart to John Rawls, Gewirth provides a comprehensive critique of those who have attempted his project before him. In order to be considered successful, Gewirth suggests, an argument for human rights must specify what a person has a right to; in addition, it must be universally applicable and must incorporate the principle of equality. He begins with the intuitionist argument made by Thomas Jefferson and again by Robert Nozick: "Jefferson held it to be 'self-evident' that all humans equally have certain rights, and Robert

Nozick has peremptorily asserted that 'individuals have rights.' "[10] For Gewirth, these sorts of claims fail immediately, for prudential as much as for theoretical reasons:

> Such assertion is not, of course, an argument for the existence of human rights; it would not serve at all to convince the many persons throughout history who have had different intuitions on this question. Hence, the answer fails to satisfy *the condition of providing an argument.*[11]

He turns, then, to a number of theorists who – in his view – provide reasoned argumentation for the logic of their positions and tries to demonstrate the ways in which they do not satisfy his three necessary conditions. Based on his critique of Jefferson and Nozick, it seems to me that Gewirth must also be looking for arguments that can "convince the many persons throughout history who have had different intuitions" about whether or not human rights exist, and so I include *persuasiveness* as another necessary condition.

Gewirth next quickly dispenses with what he calls the formal principle, namely that people have a right to be treated equally unless some reason can be determined for treating them unequally. He does so by pointing out, first, that the formal principle fails to specify what ought to count as a good reason for treating people unequally; "and, of course, very many differences, including intelligence, sex, religion, color, economic class, have been held to be thus relevant."[12] Further, he notes that the formal principle can result in both egalitarianism and inegalitarianism, which means that it "fails to satisfy ... *the condition of determinacy*, since it may serve to justify mutually opposed allocations of rights."[13] Gewirth then turns to a consideration of Joel Feinberg's argument that rights arise from interests. The trouble with Feinberg's assertion – apart from what Gewirth calls "the murkiness of the concept of 'interests' "[14] – is that not every interest automatically necessitates a right to fulfill that interest. The criminal certainly has an interest in committing his crime, for example, but he does not thereby derive a right to do so. More than that, Gewirth asserts that animals, as well as humans, have interests and that humans have unequal interests; Feinberg's interest principle offers no justification for the idea that rights belong only to humans or that they belong to all human beings equally.[15] An argument might easily be made that some people deserve more than others or have more of a right to fulfill their interests than do others. Nietzsche, for example, makes precisely this sort of argument.

From Feinberg's argument, Gewirth turns to a similar theory of interests offered by William Frankena, who "held that humans 'are capable of enjoying a good life in a sense in which other animals are not [which] justifies the *prima facie* requirement that they be treated as equals.' "[16] The trouble, here, is that Frankena falls into the trap of the naturalistic fallacy,

arguing that an "ought" can be derived from an "is." Human beings may, in fact, be able to enjoy a good life in the way that Frankena asserts; the recognition of this fact of human existence, however, does not require that humans be treated in a certain way. Next, Gewirth turns to Susan Moller Okin and her strategy of defining "a human right as 'a claim to something (whether a freedom, a good, or a benefit) of crucial importance for human life.'"[17] Gewirth's argument against Okin – and, indeed, against all definitional approaches – is that defining human rights as claims to important goods does not prove that these rights are actually necessary or that they ought to be fulfilled. In addition, it might be that other rights theorists (or anti-rights theorists) simply disagree with the definition that Okin puts forward or with the goods that she considers to be crucial.

The final three theories that Gewirth considers receive much greater detail in their explication and ultimate rejection. The first "is H.L.A. Hart's famous presuppositional argument. He says: 'If there are any moral rights at all, it follows that there is at least one natural right, the equal right of all men to be free.'"[18] The first problem, clearly, involves the way in which Hart sets up his claim. Precisely because his argument begins with a presupposition about the existence of moral rights, someone might just as easily suggest that there are no moral rights at all. Hart has not demonstrated that there are moral rights; he has simply put forward an "if, then" sort of suggestion. A second difficulty with Hart's argument is the same one that snared Feinberg, which is the unquestioned assumption of equality. As Gewirth points out:

> If special moral rights are to be used to show that there is an *equal* right of *all* men to be free, then such universal equality must be found in the special rights themselves. But Hart has not shown that all men equally derive rights from the transactions of promising, consenting, and imposing mutual restrictions. He presupposes, without any justificatory argument, the very egalitarianism he seeks to establish. A believer in basic human inequality, such as Nietzsche, would deny that all men are equal with regard to the special rights. Hence, Hart's argument does not establish the egalitarian universalism he upholds.[19]

Hart's argument, then, falls far short of satisfying the conditions necessary for justifying human rights.

Having demonstrated these shortcomings, Gewirth turns to the famous argument put forward by John Rawls in *A Theory of Justice*. Rawls, he notes, argues

> that if the constitutional structure of a society were to be chosen by persons who are "in an initial position of equality" and who choose from behind a "veil of ignorance" of all their particular qualities, the

principles of justice they would choose would provide that each person must have certain basic, equal rights.[20]

A debate has been raging for more than thirty years about these key features of Rawls' theory, and Gewirth joins philosophers like Michael Sandel and Robert Nozick in the anti-Rawls camp. Ultimately, he argues that Rawls' premise is both a false and circular one. He agrees, first, with Nozick's critique of the concept of an original position, writing that:

> persons are not in fact equal in power and ability, nor are they ignorant of all their particular qualities. Hence, to assume that they are ... and to base on this equality and ignorance one's ascription of equal rights, is to argue from a false premise.[21]

He goes on to also agree with Sandel's critique, arguing that:

> the total ignorance of particulars that Rawls ascribes to his equal persons has no independent rational justification. Hence, no reason is given as to why actual rational persons, who know their particular characteristics, should accept the equality of rights that is based on their assumed ignorance.[22]

Finally, Gewirth maintains that these problems with the idea of the original position highlight the circularity of Rawls' argument, as its ultimately egalitarian result can only be attained by building false conditions of equality into his original position.

Having dispensed with Rawls' theory of justice, equality, and rights, Gewirth turns to the argument put forward by the drafters of the Universal Declaration of Human Rights. He argues that there are a number of problems with the assertion of human dignity upon which the Declaration bases its rights. The first problem, he notes, is that there is simply no way to empirically assess the claim that all men have inherent dignity. A second problem, to which he devotes considerably more time, "is that the two expressions, 'A has human rights' and 'A has inherent dignity' may seem to be equivalent, so that the latter simply reduplicates the former."[23] But, he continues, if "the two expressions are thus equivalent in meaning, the attribution of dignity adds nothing substantial to the attribution of rights, and someone who is doubtful about the latter attribution will be equally doubtful about the former."[24] On this point, I will state a simple disagreement with Gewirth, for he makes the same sort of argument for which he critiques Hart above. The claim that the expressions "A has human rights" and "A has inherent dignity" are equivalent in meaning is presented – by Gewirth – not as being true but as seeming to be true. Further, he puts forward the presuppositional argument that *if* they are equivalent, *then* the idea of inherent dignity adds nothing to the claim of human rights.

Nowhere, though, does Gewirth actually suggest that the two statements are, in fact, equivalent.

While I do not find Gewirth's appraisal of the Universal Declaration to be as compelling as his other critiques – a number of which are also a bit problematic – I remain impressed by and indebted to him for his examination of such a wide variety of contemporary non-religious theories of human rights. Having considered them all in some detail and found them lacking in one respect or another, it remains to Gewirth to construct his own argument for a non-religious basis for the idea of human rights. Indeed, he goes to great lengths to outline what he sees as the most compelling affirmative answer "to the problem of whether some supreme moral principle can be rationally justified."[25] His answer, the Principle of Generic Consistency, is a fascinating attempt to ground the idea of human rights in what he refers to as the generic features of action, namely voluntariness and purposiveness (or, more simply, freedom and intentionality). The theory begins, Gewirth tells us, with a difficult question: "How, then, can it be shown that from such morally neutral premises there follow determinate, normatively moral conclusions about the necessary content of the supreme principle of morality?"[26] Perry contends that:

> there is something about each and every human being, simply as a human being, such that certain choices should be made and certain other choices rejected; in particular, certain things ought not to be done to any human being and certain other things ought to be done for every human being.[27]

While Gewirth does not disagree with Perry on this point, his problem is that "it is not the case that humans are born having rights in the sense in which they are born having legs. At least, their having legs is empirically verifiable, but this is not the case with their having moral rights."[28] What is required, for Gewirth, is some manner in which we might verify that we have these rights and it is to that task that he turns.

The Principle of Generic Consistency

While it might not be immediately clear where our rights come from just from looking at us, Gewirth is confident that there is a distinctive feature of all human beings from which human rights stem. While Perry argues that it is our sacredness, our connection to God, that grounds our human rights, Gewirth would undoubtedly note that this theory runs into one of the problems he recognized with the Universal Declaration. That is, it is not possible to empirically assess Perry's claim; human sacredness is simply not observable. For Gewirth, an observable feature upon which we can ground the supreme moral principle is the distinctly human ability to plan and execute an action. Upon this bedrock is founded his theory of human

rights, one which is thoroughly non-religious and can be critically assessed. In his own words:

> because of its generic features, action has what I shall call a "normative structure," in that evaluative and deontic judgments on the part of agents are logically implicit in all action; and when these judgments are subjected to certain rational requirements, a certain normative moral principle logically follows from them. To put it otherwise: Any agent, simply by virtue of being an agent, must admit, on pain of self-contradiction, that he ought to act in certain determinate ways.[29]

From this beginning, Gewirth proceeds to lay out the logic of his theory. At the outset, I mentioned that this chapter would treat Gewirth's argument as though it consisted of two main parts even though Gewirth himself puts forward some fifteen steps, each of which is carefully connected to its predecessor as well as its successor. In what follows, I will look at each of these steps before arguing for the importance of the two steps upon which my critique – in the next section – will be based. At the outset, Gewirth claims, as noted above, that every action is characterized by two generic features, voluntariness and purposiveness. He elaborates instructively on this point:

> By an action's being voluntary or free I mean that its performance is under the agent's control in that he unforcedly chooses to act as he does, knowing the relevant proximate circumstances of his action. By an action's being purposive or intentional I mean that the agent acts for some end or purpose that constitutes his reason for acting; this purpose may consist in the action itself or in something to be achieved by the action.[30]

There are, of course, a number of arguments against both of these generic features of action and Gewirth proceeds to tackle the most demanding of them in turn. With regard to the feature of voluntariness, he considers the problems of both direct and indirect compulsion, as well as of determinism. In the first two situations, Gewirth maintains that when one acts under compulsion, one cannot properly be said to have made a choice and so voluntary action precludes forced choice. His argument against determinism is that:

> Choices may indeed be extensively affected by previous psychological conditioning. But such conditioning may take a variety of forms. Even when strong emotional factors are invoked, these and other conditioning influences need not be exhaustive determinants of a person's choices; he may still reflectively consider various reasons for alternative actions and choose among them on the basis of such

consideration. It is when a person controls his behavior by such unforced choices based on his own informed reasons that his action is fully voluntary.[31]

Having discussed voluntary action, he proceeds to purposiveness and the objection that one might act solely out of a sense of obligation, without trying to fulfill any desire or purpose of one's own. Gewirth's response is that the idea of a desire implicit in the objection is not as robust as his own. He says:

> It is important to remember that "wanting" has not only an inclinational or hedonic sense, but also an intentional sense. In the inclinational sense, to want to do X is to take pleasure in doing X or to like doing X; but in the intentional sense, to want to do X is simply to intend to do X, to regard one's doing X as having some point or purpose even if one doesn't like doing it.[32]

One might very well take pleasure in doing X, but for Gewirth's argument the most important feature of purposive action is that one simply intends to do X. That said, Gewirth takes care to note that one ultimately engages in X because one feels positively about the end to which X is directed: "For even if he regards his action as morally indifferent or as not making any difference on some other specific criterion, by the very fact that he aims to do the action he has a pro-attitude toward doing it and hence a positive or favorable interest in doing it."[33]

In laying out these generic features of action, Gewirth has accomplished the first two steps in his argument for voluntary and purposive action as the foundation of human rights. In order to make sense of these two steps, as well as to see how they relate to the generic features of action explicated above, Gewirth carefully describes his agent:

> When he performs an action, he can be described as saying or thinking:
>
> (1) "I do X for end or purpose E."
>
> Since E is something he unforcedly chooses to attain, he thinks E has sufficient value to merit his moving from quiescence to action in order to attain it. Hence, from his standpoint, (1) entails
>
> (2) "E is good."

Note that (2) is here presented in quotation marks, as something said or thought by the agent A. The kind of goodness he here attributes to E need not be moral goodness; its criterion varies with whatever

purpose E the agent may have in doing X. But what it shows already is that, in the context of action, the 'Fact–Value gap' is already bridged, for by the very *fact* of engaging in action, every agent must implicitly accept for himself a certain *value*-judgment about the value or goodness of the purposes for which he acts.[34]

With these two steps carefully explained, Gewirth moves forward with his argument. As we have seen, (1) and (2) are not presented as being free from controversy; however, their articulation is far simpler than (3) through (12), which contain positive arguments and counterfactuals, and which I will fold into the first of what I consider the two main components of Gewirth's theory.

Having established that agent A always acts for a purpose that she regards as good, Gewirth makes the claim that – in order to do so – she must accept "(3) 'My freedom and well-being are necessary goods.'"[35] This follows, he argues, from (2) because "freedom and well-being are the necessary conditions of action and of successful action in general."[36] The reasoning behind this step in his argument is that every action is characterized, as we recall, by the generic features of voluntariness (or freedom) and purposiveness; when extended to include successful action rather than simply action-as-such, purposiveness "becomes a more extensive condition which I shall call *well-being*."[37] He explains this move from the general condition of purposiveness to the more specific notion of well-being in a bit more detail as follows: "freedom and well-being are the most general and proximate necessary conditions of all his purpose-fulfilling actions, so that without his having these conditions his engaging in purposive action would be futile or impossible."[38] If one is performing any action at all, in other words, one must have freedom and well-being. Put another way, "well-being consists in having the various substantive conditions and abilities, ranging from life and physical integrity to self-esteem and education, that are required if a person is to act either at all or with general chances of success in achieving the purposes for which he acts."[39] Therefore, he writes, "Every agent must regard these capabilities of action not only as goods but also, because they are required for all purposive action, as necessary goods."[40] And, as Gewirth tells us, (3) "may also be put as (4) 'I must have freedom and well-being,' where this 'must' is a practical-prescriptive requirement, expressed by the agent, as to his having the necessary conditions of his action."[41] From (3) and (4), he argues, comes "(5) 'I have rights to freedom and well-being,'"[42] which, for our purposes, is the most important step that Gewirth makes to this point.

It is this fifth step, where Gewirth introduces the idea of rights, that causes a good deal of controversy; it will, consequently, be examined in far greater detail in the third section. For the present, it will suffice to explain how Gewirth moves from (4) to (5), as well as how he proceeds from (5) onward to the rest of his argument. First, Gewirth argues that "Since the

agent regards as necessary goods the freedom and well-being that constitute the generic features of his successful action, he logically must also
hold that he has rights to these generic features, and he implicitly makes a
corresponding right-claim."[43] In claiming these rights to freedom and well-
being,

> The agent holds that other persons owe him at least noninterference
> with his freedom and well-being, not because of any specific transac-
> tion or agreement they have made with him, but on the basis of his
> own prudential criteria, because such noninterference is necessary to
> his being a purposive agent.[44]

Having put forward these rights and explained the correlative duty that
arises from claiming them, Gewirth must demonstrate that an agent must
make such a claim. This is demonstrated by examining what it would
mean to deny (5). For if one were to deny (5), he maintains, one must also
deny "(6) 'All other persons ought at least to refrain from removing or
interfering with my freedom and well-being.'"[45] Of course, "By denying
(6), he must accept (7) 'It is not the case that all other persons ought at
least to refrain from removing or interfering with my freedom and well-
being.'"[46] One ought not accept (7), clearly, because it necessitates acceptance of "(8) 'Other persons may (i.e. It is permissible that other persons)
remove or interfere with my freedom and well-being.'"[47] Accepting (7) and
(8) causes the greatest amount of trouble for any agent who sought to
avoid claiming the rights laid out in (5). For, in accepting (8), "he must
accept (9) 'I may not (i.e. It is permissible that I not) have freedom and
well-being."[48] The trouble is immediately obvious: it was previously established by Gewirth and accepted by the agent in (4) that freedom and well-
being were necessary goods for agency in general. To be an agent at all,
one must have the goods of freedom and well-being; therefore, one cannot
accept that there may be a time when one may not have those goods. It is
necessary, then, that others refrain from interfering with one's freedom
and well-being.[49] As Gewirth explains:

> Since every agent must accept (4), he must reject (9). And since (9)
> follows from the denial of (5), 'I have rights to freedom and well-
> being,' every agent must also reject that denial. Hence, every agent
> logically must accept (5) 'I have rights to freedom and well-being.'[50]

In this manner, then, Gewirth puts forward the first major component of
his theory of human rights, namely the idea that all agents have rights.

The hard-won rights to freedom and well-being, however, are only
what Gewirth calls generic rights, "in that they are rights to have the
generic features of successful action characterize one's behavior."[51] In
addition, he notes that these rights are prudential rather than moral:

in that the criterion consists for each agent in his own needs of agency in pursuit of his own purposes. Even though the right-claim is addressed to all other persons as a correlative 'ought'-judgment, still its justifying criterion for each agent consists in the necessary conditions of his own action.[52]

At this point, then, our rights have been established, but they belong to no one but ourselves. In order to establish the rights to freedom and well-being as moral rights, Gewirth undertakes a number of additional steps and these form the second of the two main components of Gewirth's argument, namely that our rights are universal. As with the above argument for generic rights, I will simply outline Gewirth's argument for their universalizability in what immediately follows and will offer a critique in the next section of the chapter.

In order to make our rights to freedom and well-being universal, Gewirth begins with a further demonstration of the importance of agency to any right-claim in order to highlight the reason behind the rights, as Perry would argue he must. For Perry, "The fundamental challenge to each and every human rights claim is a demand for reasons."[53] And Gewirth is in agreement on this point, noting that:

> Every right-claim or attribution of a right is made on behalf of some person or group under a certain description or for a certain reason that is held to justify the claim.... Without a reason, he would be making not a right-claim but only a peremptory demand akin to that voiced by a gunman.[54]

With the need for such a reason in mind, Gewirth puts forward his argument for the universalizability of his generic rights. The structure of this point is relatively simple and Gewirth provides a clear explication:

> Now whatever the description under which or the sufficient reason for which it is claimed that a person has some right, the claimant must admit, on pain of contradiction, that this right also belongs to any other person to whom that description or sufficient reason applies. This necessity is an exemplification of the formal principle of universalizability in its moral application, which says that whatever is right for one person must be right for any similar person in similar circumstances.[55]

In the structure of Gewirth's argument, this principle of universalizability occupies steps (10) through (13).

The first step, (10), serves as a reminder of the nine steps that brought us to this point and established our generic rights. With all of those steps completed, Gewirth argues, the agent "must accept (10) 'I have rights to freedom and well-being because I am a prospective purposive agent,'

where this 'because' signifies a sufficient as well as a necessary justifying condition."[56] It is immediately obvious that our terms have changed a bit, as Gewirth has made the purposive agent into one who is also prospective. He has done so, he argues, because:

> the agent claims these rights not only in his present action with its particular purpose but in all his actions. To restrict to his present purpose his reason for claiming the rights of freedom and well-being would be to overlook the fact that he regards these as goods in respect of all his actions and purposes, not only his present one. To be a prospective agent, then, is not necessarily to be an actual agent; it is rather to have desires or goals one wants or would want to fulfill through action.[57]

In this way, the experience of agency has been expanded a great deal, for it is not necessary to actually engage in action or even to have excellent prospects for doing so in order to have rights to freedom and well-being. All that is necessary is "his occurrently or dispositionally looking ahead in some way to acting for purposes he regards as good."[58]

Having thus established the importance of adding this notion of prospecting, Gewirth then turns to demonstrating that being a prospective purposive agent (PPA) is both a necessary and sufficient reason for having rights to freedom and well-being, which he accomplishes through what he calls "the Argument from the Sufficiency of Agency (*ASA*)."[59] The argument runs as follows:

> Suppose some agent were to reject (10), and were to insist, instead, that the only reason he has the generic rights is that he has some more restrictive characteristic R. Examples of R would include: being an American, being a professor, being an *übermensch*, being male, being a capitalist or a proletarian, being white, being named "Wordsworth Donisthorpe," and so forth. Thus, the agent would be saying:
>
> (11) "I have rights to freedom and well-being *only* because I am R,"
>
> where "R" is something more restrictive than being a prospective purposive agent.
>
> Such an agent, however, would contradict himself. For he would then be in the position of saying that if he did *not* have R, he would *not* have the generic rights, so that he would have to accept
>
> (12) "I do not have the rights to freedom and well-being."

But, we saw before that, as an agent, he *must* hold that he has rights to freedom and well-being. Hence, he must drop his view that R alone

is the sufficient justifying condition of his having the generic rights, so that he must accept that simply being a prospective purposive agent is a sufficient as well as a necessary justifying condition of his having rights to freedom and well-being.[60]

If the agent accepts that he has rights to freedom and well-being for no other reason than because he is a prospective purposive agent – and, as we have just seen, he must – it follows that "the agent must also accept (13) 'All prospective purposive agents have rights to freedom and well-being.'"[61] With the acceptance of (13), Gewirth has made our generic rights universal, as it "is a direct application of the principle of universalizability; and if the agent denies the generalization, then, as we have seen, he contradicts himself."[62]

It is also at this point that the generic rights change from merely prudential to moral ones. As Gewirth argues:

> When the original agent now says that *all* prospective purposive agents have rights to freedom and well-being, he is logically committed to respecting and hence taking favorable account of the interests of all other persons with regard to their also having the necessary goods or conditions of action.[63]

With that in mind, and "Since all other persons are actual or potential recipients of his action, every agent is logically committed to accepting (14) 'I ought to act in accord with the generic rights of my recipients as well as of myself.'"[64] Expressed somewhat differently, this statement can be rendered as (15), what Gewirth calls the Principle of Generic Consistency: "Act in accord with the generic rights of your recipients as well as of yourself."[65] In articulating the PGC, Gewirth, it seems, has succeeded in setting forth a non-religious foundation for the idea of human rights: human agency. Carefully taking us through these fifteen steps, he has demonstrated how the PGC is both rationally derived and how its acceptance is rationally required by every agent. The final section of this chapter will explore my critique of the PGC and argue that Gewirth's foundation, while compelling, is ultimately inadequate when it comes to the task of grounding the idea of human rights.

A critique of Generic Consistency

In the twenty-five years since *Reason and Morality* was first published, the Principle of Generic Consistency has undergone nearly as much and as careful scrutiny as has John Rawls' *A Theory of Justice*. Gewirth has done us a great service in responding to many of his critics himself and he has also received considerable assistance from Deryck Beyleveld, whose own work examines and refutes sixty-six well-crafted objections to the PGC. It

should be noted that it is not my intention, here, to rehearse all of these critiques, primarily because Beyleveld has done a fine job of collecting ten years of this scholarship but also because such a rehearsal does not serve the interests of this chapter.[66] I will, instead, focus on making three inter-related arguments that highlight what I consider the inadequacy of the PGC as a foundation for the idea of human rights. These arguments are by no means original and each has been examined in some detail by Gewirth and Beyleveld; however, I will argue that these important objections are not persuasively refuted, unlike the majority of the objections they consider. First, I will critique the notion that self-contradiction represents the most compelling argument against violating human rights; Gewirth's theory assumes both that all agents have the meta-desire to avoid contradiction and that contradiction is painful enough to prevent agents from violating human rights. Second, I will dispute Gewirth's argument about universalizability and contradiction by suggesting that an agent might accept the first part of Gewirth's theory about his own generic rights and reject without contradiction the second part about universalizing those rights. My final objection combines the first two, applying Michael Sandel's critique of Rawls' original position and veil of ignorance to Gewirth's PGC to argue that Gewirth's prospective purposive agents are too far removed from the real world in which human rights are actually in play.

To begin, then, let us consider the argument that engaging in a self-contradictory action would be impossibly problematic for any agent. It is important to note that the problem of contradiction seems to be simply implied, for nowhere does Gewirth actually make a case for why we may not engage quite comfortably in self-contradiction. In fact, in a footnote dealing with Millard Schumaker's multiple objections to the PGC, Beyleveld points out that quite the opposite is the case:

> The error lies in Schumaker's reading of "incurring the pain of self-contradiction." We are to understand that Gewirth argues that PPAs will be motivated to be moral by the fact that to act immorally is to suffer some form of emotional distress. But to say that X does Y on "pain of self-contradiction" is to say only that if X does Y then X contradicts itself. It is not to say that if X does Y then X contradicts itself *and that* this state of affairs causes X to suffer anguish.[67]

It seems, then, that self-contradiction is not necessarily painful for the agent. If it is not, we might wonder, what reason is there for avoiding it, particularly if engaging in it could be in an agent's self-interest or if avoiding it turns out to be costly? The only answer that Gewirth seems to provide comes at the very beginning of his argument for the PGC, in the following statement about his rational agent: "It is to be noted that the criterion of 'rational' here is a minimal deductive one, involving consistency

or the avoidance of self-contradiction in ascertaining or accepting what is logically involved in one's acting for purposes and in the associated concepts."[68] The assumption, here, is that all agents have a meta-desire for consistency upon which all of their rational decisions are built. And yet, it seems important to question whether we can assume that human beings are necessarily rational actors who behave as Gewirth outlines or, instead, a bundle of desires engaged in continual struggle, especially after looking at the psychoanalytic theory of Jacques Lacan.

Lacan's response to the sort of theory put forward by Gewirth would be, Malcolm Bowie notes, something to this effect: "How wrong we have all been until now, and how deluded; what a lesson we all need on the vanity of our wholeness-talk, our selfhood-talk and our integrity-talk."[69] Like Nietzsche before him, Lacan insists that desire is insatiable and will always go unfulfilled. Further, he argues that:

> the essential day-to-day facts about human beings are these: they address each other and affect each other by what they say; they say what they mean and what they don't mean simultaneously; whatever they get they always want more, or something different; and at any one moment they are consciously aware of only some of what they want.[70]

Lacan's vision of humanity, we can safely say, is both more complex and enigmatic than the one envisioned by Gewirth. The PGC, as we have seen, seeks to provide both a prudential and a moral explanation for respecting human rights. Lacan would most likely respond that Gewirth's agent is neither completely aware of his preferences nor certain of the language he uses to express his rights to freedom and well-being. For Gewirth, an agent's choices are predicated on an evaluation and ordering of desires, the most important of which is the meta-desire for rational action. For Lacan, this concept of ordering is itself mistaken because human beings are fundamentally broken rather than the unified agents that Gewirth assumes; perhaps the best we can do, he suggests, is to come to an understanding of death and live with it.[71] Ultimately, he is far less willing than Gewirth to take anything as given – save the fundamental disunity of the world on which he bases his theory.

While this Lacanian critique is an interesting one, it is not the strongest argument against Gewirth on the question of contradiction. It might be the case that people are unable to rationally order their preferences, as Lacan argues, or that some people do not have the sort of meta-desire for rational consistency that Gewirth assumes for the purposes of his theory, but it certainly seems to be more often the case that people can and do. What Gewirth fails to properly consider, however, is the ability that people have to rationalize their actions in an effort to avoid the cognitive dissonance that comes with self-contradiction. He clearly recognizes the problem, pointing out that "some person may without inconsistency claim the right

to inflict various harms on other persons on the ground that he possesses qualities that are had only by himself or by some group he favors."[72] By way of a response, as noted above, he puts forward the ASA – that being a PPA is both the necessary and sufficient justificatory reason for having the generic rights. This answer seems not to have placated Gewirth's detractors, nor has it gone far enough to suit me. Of course, Beyleveld deals with multiple versions of this objection in the fortieth through forty-fifth objections to the PGC. One such objection is that of Donald E. Geels, who "alleges that '[i]t is trivial to claim that whatever is right for one person must be right for any relevantly similar person in any relevantly similar circumstances,' because there is no determinate criterion of relevant similarity."[73] This sounds remarkably similar to Gewirth's own objection to the formal principle, described above. As Beyleveld points out, however, Gewirth has quite clearly specified the criterion of relevant similarities:

> a PPA must claim that it has the generic rights (according to the argument for the sufficiency of agency [ASA]) for the sufficient reason that it is a PPA. Because a PPA logically must claim the generic rights, it is the property of being a PPA that is logically required to be the criterion of relevant similarities.[74]

More interesting, in my estimation, are arguments like the one made by N. Fotion, that "a 'fanatic' (read 'elitist') can grant itself rights on the grounds that it is a superior PPA, yet refuse to grant these rights to other PPAs, who are not superior PPAs, without contradiction."[75] While Fotion has taken an important first step, namely recognizing that some PPAs will view themselves as somehow different or better than other PPAs, he has not truly challenged Gewirth's PGC. Summarizing Gewirth's own response to Fotion's argument, Beyleveld says:

> In effect, what Fotion fails to see is that agency, independent of the *content* of a PPA's particular occurrent purposes or its SPR ["Subjective viewpoint on practical reasonableness"] for its purposes (represented here by the fanatic's principle), has a normative structure. Since this normative structure reflects judgments that a PPA must accept on pain of contradicting that it is a PPA independently of the *content* of its purposes (because these judgments are functions of the necessary conditions of its pursuit/achievement of any purposes), a PPA *might* reason from its SPR, but can only do so consistently with the assumption that it is a PPA *if* these reasonings are consistent with the judgments contained in the necessary normative structure of agency.[76]

Gewirth is correct in this refutation of the idea of a fanatic's special status as a PPA, as is Beyleveld. But Fotion's argument presents only part of the problem and, I believe, not its most difficult elucidation.

More challenging for Gewirth is the claim not that a PPA is in some way special and thereby deserving of rights, but instead that some other PPA is somehow damaged and thereby not worthy of them. Such an argument, however, seems neither to have been made directly against Gewirth nor is it carefully considered by him or by Beyleveld. Gewirth seems to recognize the existence of this problem – indeed, he seems to put it forward himself – but fails to really grapple with it in any meaningful way. He says:

> To be P, that is, a prospective purposive agent, requires having the practical abilities of the generic features of action: the abilities to control one's behavior by one's unforced choice, to have knowledge of relevant circumstances, and to reflect on one's purposes. These abilities are gradually developed in children, who will eventually have them in full; the abilities are had in varying impaired ways by mentally deficient persons; and they are largely lacking among animals.... Since the quality that determines whether one has the generic rights is that of being P, it follows from these variations in degree, according to the Principle of Proportionality, that although children, mentally deficient persons, and animals do not have the generic rights in the full-fledged way normal human adults have them, members of these groups approach having the generic rights in varying degrees, depending on the degree to which they have the requisite abilities.[77]

Of course, in reading these remarks, one must wonder whether it is acceptable to infringe upon the rights of those who fall within the categories Gewirth lays out. If one is like a child, then perhaps it is acceptable for society to take away one's rights to freedom and well-being. Surely that must be the case if one is like an animal for, as Gewirth says, "the lesser the abilities, the less one is able to fulfill one's purposes without endangering oneself and other persons."[78] There is something rather troubling about making these sorts of statements, but Gewirth seems not to see it. For him, it is sufficient to argue that one ought to have the generic rights to the degree to which one approaches being a PPA. Beyleveld's response to this objection, unlike his many others, is surprisingly lacking and is confined to a footnote. By doing so, he seems to have made things worse for Gewirth, as he points out that five theorists have taken issue with the PGC on this important point but then offers no substantive rejoinder. He says:

> It seems to me that Gewirth's theory is essentially a theory of the rights of PPAs, and not a theory of human rights as such.... From this it follows that there are some human beings (those who are not even marginal agents) who do not have the generic rights, and that nonhuman beings might have the generic rights.... The question of the rights of "marginal agents" is, however, a more complex one. I do not

discuss this, because I view its importance as being for the argument *from* the PGC, rather than the argument *to* the PGC, with which this book is solely concerned; so I shall not discuss any of the above claims in detail.[79]

Having sidestepped the issue entirely, he makes a few general points that deal with other issues raised by the objection and then offers some final words that are meant to provide consolation to the concerned:

> A question might be raised about the extent to which the practical import of the PGC is narrowed by conative normality's being a definitional requirement of being a PPA. The answer is, Not very much! Conative normality is, after all, something that is characteristic of most adult human beings. In practice, we are required to treat human beings as conatively normal (as PPAs) unless we have compelling evidence that they are not PPAs.[80]

The trouble with this response is pointed out by Richard Rorty, who offers the rejoinder, made by an agent who wants to infringe upon the rights of another, that philosophers like Gewirth "seem oblivious to blatantly obvious moral distinctions, distinctions any decent person would draw."[81] For Rorty, the problem cannot be solved by sitting down with a chalkboard and diagramming how the agent and his potential victim are both PPAs. It is, he argues, a problem that will not be solved by demonstrating that the agent violates his victim on pain of self-contradiction because, for this agent, the victim is not properly a PPA, despite looking very much like one. The old adage about looking, swimming, and quacking like a duck comes to mind here; no amount of quacking will convince the agent that his victim is, in fact, a duck. As Rorty points out:

> This rejoinder is not just a rhetorical device, nor is it in any way irrational. It is heartfelt. The *identity* of these people, the people whom we should like to convince to join our Eurocentric human rights culture, is bound up with their sense of who they are *not*.... What is crucial for their sense of who they are is that they are *not* an infidel, *not* a queer, *not* a woman, *not* an untouchable.... Since the days when the term "human being" was synonymous with "member of our tribe," we have always thought of human beings in terms of *paradigm* members of the species. We have contrasted *us*, the *real* humans, with rudimentary or perverted or deformed examples of humanity.[82]

There are, I believe, two problems for Gewirth's theory here. The first is that an agent can quite clearly sidestep rational inconsistency by believing that his victim is somehow less of an agent (and, in the case presented by Rorty, less of a human being) than he is himself. The agent, here, might

recognize that his victim is a PPA, but other factors (being an infidel, a queer, a woman, or an untouchable) have far greater resonance and preclude her having the same rights as the agent. He might also recognize his victim as a potential PPA, but not one in the fullest sense of that term or one who has actually achieved that status; as Gewirth himself notes, "there are degrees of approach to being prospective purposive agents."[83] It seems to me that the Nazis knew quite well that their Jewish victims could be PPAs in some sense; the Nuremberg Laws of 1935 confirm their awareness that Jews could plan and execute the same sorts of actions they could (voting and working, for example). The rights of the Jews could be restricted, however, because Jews were quite different from Germans; rather than PPAs in the fullest sense, they were, in the eyes of the Nazis, what Rorty calls "pseudo-humans."[84] On this point, Rorty's point is both clear and compelling:

> Resentful young Nazi toughs were quite aware that many Jews were clever and learned, but this only added to the pleasure they took in beating such Jews. Nor does it do much good to get such people to read Kant and agree that one should not treat rational agents simply as means. For everything turns on who counts as a fellow human being, as a rational agent in the only relevant sense – the sense in which rational agency is synonymous with membership in *our* moral community.[85]

The second problem for the PGC pointed out by Rorty is that it is overly academic and insufficiently pragmatic. In other words, its fifteen steps might be logically compelling to those in a philosophy department, but not to those who are actually making these decisions on inclusion and exclusion. "This is not," Rorty tells us, "because they are insufficiently rational. It is, typically, because they live in a world in which it would be just too risky – indeed, would often be insanely dangerous – to let one's sense of moral community stretch beyond one's family, clan, or tribe."[86] This second point leads to the final critique of Gewirth's argument for the PGC.

In reviewing Gewirth's argument to this point I have clearly been assisted by the very structure that he employs, for he is the consummate analytic philosopher. Each step he takes is clearly articulated and then defended against several possible criticisms. Further, there is, as we have seen throughout this chapter, something exceedingly logical in the organization he employs and, more than that, in his theory itself. In what might be a bit of a surprising turn, then, I will argue that this logic ultimately serves as Gewirth's undoing. The problem, interestingly, is very similar to that which Gewirth himself notes of John Rawls' *A Theory of Justice* and it is one he seems to anticipate. Indeed, he goes so far as to quote Friedrich Engels' critique of theories that take too abstract a view of humanity. As Engels argues in the *Anti-Dühring*:

> In order to establish the fundamental axiom that two people and their
> wills are absolutely equal to each other and that neither lords it over
> the other, we cannot use any couple of people at random. They must
> be two persons who are so thoroughly detached from all reality, from
> all national, economic, political, and religious relations which are
> found in the world, from all sex and personal differences, that nothing
> is left of either person beyond the mere idea: person – and then of
> course they are "entirely equal." They are therefore two complete
> phantoms conjured up.[87]

Gewirth recognizes that he must work through this objection and proposes
that the way to do so is to offer an abstraction from our differences that
does not completely ignore them and that is also "able to subject the differences or their alleged moral implications to moral evaluation."[88] He has
done so, he believes, by offering "the standpoint of the agent,"[89] or what
Beyleveld calls "the internal viewpoint of PPAs *as PPAs*."[90] Just because
the ideas of agency and rights have been discussed in the abstract,
Beyleveld argues, "does not mean that they are not of 'real' concern to real
people."[91] This seems not to be a particularly compelling argument, in my
estimation, nor does Beyleveld's second attempt.

In responding to Virginia Held's objection to the PGC – "If we require
that in acting we are all so similar that we all claim the same thing, then
Gewirth's theory is a theory of the ideal agent rather than of real agents"[92]
– Beyleveld attempts to show that Gewirth is speaking of real rather than
ideal agents. According to Beyleveld:

> The only sense in which the generic features of agency are "abstract"
> is that they are universally and necessarily applicable to all PPAs *amid*
> their enormously varying particular occurrent purposes. In attending
> to the generic features, it is not assumed that PPAs are so similar that
> it will be in their particular occurrent interests for them all to make
> (wish to make) the same rights-claims. It is assumed only that PPAs,
> whatever their particular occurrent purposes, are PPAs (that they have
> purposes). It follows *logically* from *the fact that PPAs have purposes*
> that they must accept the PGC. It, therefore, follows logically, *for
> PPAs with varying particular occurrent purposes and characteristics*,
> that they must accept the PGC. For, whatever their particular occur-
> rent characteristics, to deny the PGC is to deny that they have pur-
> poses, and this is to deny that they have *any* particular occurrent
> purposes (which, of course, includes the ones they have)."[93]

Despite his best efforts to demonstrate the way in which the PGC applies
to real agents, Beyleveld has simply restated Gewirth's argument and, in
my estimation, added additional jargon that seems to encourage rather
than refute Held's objection. The biggest difficulty with this defense –

apart from the way it is worded, which lends credence to our belief that there is something not quite human about these PPAs – is that Beyleveld seems to have conflated characteristics and purposes. It is correct that a PPA must accept the PGC regardless of the nature of his purposes, for having any purposes at all entails that he is a PPA and being a PPA necessitates his acceptance of the PGC. However, it does not follow that he must accept the PGC regardless of the nature of his (or others') characteristics, for these characteristics might invalidate some aspect of the PGC. He might be, for example, one of the unfortunate marginal agents discussed above; alternately, he might be acting upon one of those marginal agents, in which case he need not worry about granting the generic rights that he claims for himself. Beyleveld's response to this concern seems lackluster:

> a PPA, regardless of its particular occurrent characteristics, is logically required to concentrate attention on the generic features as the basis of its rights-claims, and must restrict its *categorically binding* rights-claims to these features, because it is not logically required to attend to any other features.[94]

Leaving aside the fact that Beyleveld refers to PPAs as neither "him" nor "her," but rather "it," at the same time that he is attempting to humanize them, the argument he makes here does not stand up to scrutiny.[95] All he claims is that PPAs are required to base their rights-claims on the generic features of action (which everyone, except for marginal agents, must possess) because they are not required to base those claims on other features. This does not mean that a PPA cannot base his claim on characteristics other than the generic features of action; it simply means he must also include the generic features of action in his claim, as they – unlike the other characteristics – are necessarily connected with agency.

By and large, then, it seems that Gewirth has not gone a great distance toward refuting this critique, nor has Beyleveld offered much assistance. In fact, Gewirth seems to recognize his shortcoming even as he attempts to offer his response to Engels:

> Hence, while not entirely exempt from Engels's criticism, the present approach in terms of the generic features of action has an important justification. For it sets up a morally neutral starting point that does not accept persons' actual power relations and other differences as a moral datum.[96]

This, though, seems to be the point of Engels' critique and of more recent critiques of analytical theories that attempt to abstract away from the world in order to discuss it. Indeed, Michael Sandel's objections to Rawls' well-known ideas of the original position and veil of ignorance are equally

apt in looking at the greatest weakness of Gewirth's theory. Although Sandel stands quite close to Rawls on the question of what a liberal society's principles of justice ought to be, he contends that Rawls' assumptions about the populace of that society provide a poor foundation for his principles. The presuppositions that Sandel accuses Rawls of making are four-fold. First, the Rawlsian self is seen as one that possesses its assets. In other words, the self and its assets are separable from one another. One must wonder, though, what actually constitutes each individual human being if not all the things that make up those particular selves. Next, Rawls suggests that the self is prior to and independent of its ends; put another way, the self is seen as the selector of its ends. If each self chooses its own ends, there can be no ultimate conception of the good, and Rawlsian societies must not choose a particular conception of the good in order to avoid impinging on the many and various choices of the selves in these societies. Third, selves are perfectly indifferent to one another in the original position; they are radically and fully separate from one another. Finally, the Rawlsian self has nothing to reflect upon about itself. It cannot ask, "Who am I?" because it has no identity beyond being an abstract possessor and selector. The problem, for Sandel, is that human beings are not constituted in this way: "To imagine a person incapable of constitutive attachments . . . is not to conceive an ideally free and rational agent, but to imagine a person wholly without character, without moral depth."[97] If these selves actually existed, Sandel asserts that they likely would not adopt the Rawlsian principles of justice. They are, after all, not bound by common identity, by sympathy, or by mutual agreement on a common good, so they would be more likely to choose the market-driven society that someone like Robert Nozick describes. As Sandel argues:

> We cannot regard ourselves as independent in this way without great cost to those loyalties and convictions whose moral force consists partly in the fact that living by them is inseparable from understanding ourselves as the particular person we are – as members of this family or community or nation or people, as bearers of this history, as sons and daughters of that revolution, as citizens of this republic. Allegiances such as these are more than values I happen to have or aims I "espouse at any given time". They go beyond the obligations I voluntarily incur and the "natural duties" I owe to human beings as such. They allow that to some I owe more than justice requires or even permits, not by reason of agreements I have made but instead in virtue of those more or less enduring attachments and commitments which taken together partly define the person I am.[98]

Sandel claims, then, that we must invoke a much richer notion of selfhood and a deep sense of community if we hope to achieve Rawls' conclusions. There exists, of course, a great deal of debate about the value of Sandel's

critique, especially on the question of whether Rawls intended his original position to be an accurate description of the world around us. As mentioned in note twenty-one, it seems clear that Rawls is conducting a thought experiment and that the parties in the original position are not meant to constitute human beings who exist in society. Sandel, however, does not seem to take this into account at all in his critique of Rawls and, for that, his argument loses a great deal of its force. The same seems not to be true, I believe, of Gewirth's PGC for, while Gewirth is also engaged in a thought experiment, his has to do with establishing the generic rights and the relevant features of action, not with the construction of the PPAs themselves. Indeed, as noted above, both Gewirth and Beyleveld go to great lengths to establish that their PPAs are, in fact, real rather than ideal agents and that the problems that people face in the world are the problems faced by PPAs. In this way, I believe Sandel's critique to be more applicable to the PGC than it is to Rawls' conclusions.

Conclusion

In order to offer a truly compelling non-religious foundation for the idea of human rights, one must do more than Gewirth has done in demonstrating the logical necessity of accepting a principle that entails the universalization of the generic rights of freedom and well-being. As we have seen, Gewirth crafts an interesting argument for human rights in theory, but runs into considerable trouble when his theory is put into practice. As critics like Rorty and Sandel point out, there is something about the Principle of Generic Consistency that rings a bit hollow. For Rorty, the problem lies in Gewirth's failure to appreciate the fierce partiality that often drives human rights violations; it is a confusion to point out contradictions to those who either refuse to recognize them or are not terribly troubled by them. For Sandel, the PGC must fail for the same reason that Rawls' original position fails; there is simply no getting around the fact that human beings are more complex than abstract possessors of goods or prospective purposive agents. Any examination of human life that abstracts in these ways removes the discussion too far from the real world in which human rights are actually violated. These violations cannot be said to be the same thing as the simple removal of freedom and well-being from a PPA, for this sort of language is hopelessly sterile. Human rights violations happen, instead, to men like Aleksandr Solzhenitsyn and Primo Levi, who struggle desperately to survive and, if successful, carry the scars of their experiences with them for the rest of their lives. This is a mistake of the highest order, one that Gewirth and Beyleveld cannot possibly intend to make, but that creeps up on them as the abstractions with which they deal multiply.

In abstracting away so many characteristics from human beings in order to create the prospective purposive agent, something has clearly been lost from Gewirth's account of the justification for human inviolability. It

might be philosophically interesting to consider whether the generic features of action can logically provide a non-religious grounding for the idea of human rights, and it might provide a response to Perry, but what is at stake seems overly academic. Human rights, conversely, are not simply academic – as both Perry and Gewirth recognize, with their talk about the importance of persuasiveness – and their justification is far more than a philosophical puzzle; they are terribly serious, often a matter of life and death. For this reason, human rights cannot be considered in a vacuum and any attempt at their justification must be firmly entrenched in the real world. While I have quibbled with the PGC on its own terms and argued that (15) does not necessarily follow from (1), and while I have noted that a great many other theorists have done likewise, my deepest critique is that the PGC's assumptions cause a great deal of trouble whether or not Gewirth's theory ultimately makes logical sense. As Rorty argues, Gewirth's theory removes the discussion of human rights from the realm of the actual and concentrates on the purely theoretical. In doing so, it calls to mind Arthur Koestler's point that "Statistics don't bleed; it is the detail which counts."[99] Neither, it seems to me, do PPAs bleed. And the terrible reality is that human beings do, often at the hands of others. This grim reality is not surprising to anyone, but it is not often expressed in the way that Samantha Power does, for example. In writing about the 1994 genocide in Rwanda, Power offers a quotation from a UN official on the ground during the worst of the violence:

> When we arrived, I looked at the school across the street, and there were children, I don't know how many, forty, sixty, eighty children stacked up outside who had all been chopped up with machetes. Some of their mothers had heard them screaming and had come running, and the militia had killed them, too. We got out of the vehicle and entered the church. There we found 150 people, dead mostly, though some were still groaning, who had been attacked the night before.... The Rwandan army had cleared out the area, the gendarmerie had rounded up all the Tutsi, and the militia had hacked them to death.[100]

This sort of thick description stands in marked contrast to the kind of language that Gewirth employs in his discussion of the PGC's applications. Consider the following example, one of the few in which Gewirth departs from talking about PPAs and assigns names:

> Suppose Ames physically assaults Blake, who defends himself by physically assaulting Ames. In a purely formal view, Ames and Blake are each disobeying the moral principle that requires persons to respect and not infringe one another's well-being. On the PGC's substantive view, however, these two infractions are not on a par as being both unjustified. Since Ames inflicted or acted to inflict basic harm on

Blake, and hence intended to violate a generic right of Blake while acting in accord with his own generic rights, Ames's intention was inconsistent and his action morally wrong.[101]

Because they are not real and no attempt has been made to make them real for us, we do not – we cannot – become emotionally attached to Ames and Blake, and we do not care, therefore, what happens to either of them. Our eyes trip lightly over the words "physically assaults" in Gewirth's example in a way that they cannot move past the words "who had all been chopped up with machetes" in Power's.

We have no conception, of course, of what it would be like to die at the hands of a man wielding a machete or to wield that machete ourselves. By and large, we cannot even conceive of watching such a terrible spectacle. But we react to the idea of this crime in a far more immediate way than we do to the abstract physical assaults of Ames and Blake. The difference is two-fold for William F. Schulz, the former Executive Director of Amnesty International USA. First:

> I am stricken at heart because I have the imagination to know at least in proximate form what the experience, the pain, must have felt like. I am stricken at heart because on some level I identify with the victims; I know what it is to bleed.[102]

Second:

> when I heard of cases of cruelty, I responded with revulsion. . . . It is a revulsion grounded in part in recognition. Recognition not that I am capable of inflicting exactly that kind of pain, I trust, but recognition that the capacity to inflict suffering, like the capacity to feel compassion, is a familiar one.[103]

Because we can imagine, at least in some small way, what it must have been like to be a victim in that situation, we recognize the importance of defending the idea of human rights around the world. And because we are all too familiar with the deepest and darkest part of ourselves, we can contribute to the conversation about how best to prevent violations of human rights. I have argued throughout this chapter, for a variety of reasons, that men who butcher women and children like animals will not be dissuaded by Gewirth's argument that they are acting inconsistently. The claim that we are all rational agents simply cannot bear the weight of the idea of human rights. If we want to argue, as Gewirth does, that there are certain features or qualities about human beings that preclude their wanton destruction, they must be far more persuasive than the generic features of action and they must be grounded in the world as it is rather than only in the world of theory.

3 The problem of secular sacredness
Ronald Dworkin, Michael Perry, and human rights foundationalism

As the first two chapters have made abundantly clear, human beings seem to have the unique ability to devise cruel ways in which to harm one another. In one sense, this is the very reason why the project of justifying human rights is such an important and topical one. At the same time, however, it is not far-fetched to wonder if there actually exist any qualities that make us worthy of special protection or whether Thomas Hobbes was right when he said that our equality stemmed from the ability of one individual to kill any other.[1] If human history is, in fact, little more than a lengthy tale of misery and violence, then we ought to hope for a way to protect, for example, the right to life, but we ought not be overly naive in thinking that its foundation can be found within us. In his discussion of the myth of the noble savage, Steven Pinker quotes William James on this point:

> We, the lineal representatives of the successful enactors of one scene of slaughter after another, must, whatever more pacific virtues we may also possess, still carry around with us, ready at any moment to burst into flame, the smoldering and sinister traits of character by means of which they lived through so many massacres, harming others, but themselves unharmed.[2]

This ominous view of humanity, espoused forcefully by Friedrich Nietzsche and considered in the first chapter, is rather unpopular today; I suspect that it is, to a great extent, why so many people are unwilling even to consider the conclusions about human nature offered by Pinker and other evolutionary biologists (and considered in greater detail in the next chapter). And yet, Pinker argues:

> The prevalence of violence in the kinds of environments in which we evolved does not mean that our species has a death wish, an innate thirst for blood, or a territorial imperative. There are good evolutionary reasons for the members of an intelligent species to try to live in peace. . . . Thus while conflict is a human universal, so is conflict

resolution. Together with all their nasty and brutish motives, all people display a host of kinder, gentler ones: a sense of morality, justice, and community, an ability to anticipate consequences when choosing how to act, and a love of children, spouses, and friends.[3]

Even amongst those who believe – in Michael Perry's words – "that the world is nothing but a great cosmic process utterly bereft of ultimate meaning and therefore, from a human point of view, absurd,"[4] there is a sense of hopefulness about the possibility of finding some redeeming quality of humanity upon which the idea of human rights might be based.

To this point, we have examined Perry's claim that this hopefulness can only be fulfilled by adopting a religious cosmology of one sort or another and I have argued that religion – or, at least, organized religion – does not necessarily provide a groundwork for the sort of robust understanding of egalitarian rights that the international community outlined in the Universal Declaration of Human Rights. Further, we have seen the impact of a theory like Nietzsche's that is antithetical to the concept of rights itself. We also began the attempt to locate a non-religious justification for the idea of human rights, focusing in the preceding chapter on Alan Gewirth's argument for the Principle of Generic Consistency (PGC) and my objection that such a principle is too far removed from our world, the one in which rights are really at issue. This chapter picks up, in a sense, where the previous one left off; in it, I examine another response to Perry's argument, one that attempts to provide a more compelling defense of rights than Gewirth's PGC could offer. In the first section, the discussion focuses on a non-religious conception of human rights, as outlined by Ronald Dworkin. The second section considers Perry's objections to Dworkin's theory of secular sacredness, while the final section presents my rebuttal to Perry's question, quoted earlier, about the idea of human rights being a fundamentally religious one. I argue that human dignity actually provides the foundation, and that – contrary to existing theoretical work on this subject – sacredness and dignity should not be treated as synonyms.

Toward a secular conception of "sacred"

In writing about the debates surrounding abortion and euthanasia, Ronald Dworkin asserts that "there is a secular as well as a religious interpretation of the idea that human life is sacred."[5] The religious version of human sacredness, Dworkin notes, is easy enough to understand, as it is based on the notion that all livings things are "imaginative designs produced by God's inspired genius, to be honored as such."[6] His secular vision, however, is considerably more complicated and will be evaluated in greater detail below. Dworkin's core claim is that "most people who are not religious also have general, instinctive convictions about whether, why, and how any human life has intrinsic value."[7] Irrespective of the chain of

reasoning behind it, Dworkin argues, most people acknowledge the intrinsic value of human life.[8] At bottom, we feel that "it is *intrinsically* regrettable when human life, once begun, ends prematurely. We believe, in other words, that a premature death is bad in itself, even when it is not bad for any particular person."[9] While he admits that there is a powerful critique of the idea of intrinsic value – simply put, that "objects or events can be valuable *only* when and because they serve someone's or something's interests"[10] – he believes that he can provide a persuasive answer. "Something is intrinsically valuable," Dworkin suggests, "if its value is *independent* of what people happen to enjoy or want or need or what is good for them."[11] He notes that we often regard events and objects as being valuable in themselves and that, therefore, the idea is a familiar one to us; examples include "knowledge, experience, art, and nature."[12] However, he takes care to distinguish between these sorts of things, which are valuable incrementally, and things – like human life itself – which he suggests are "*sacred* or *inviolable* values."[13] In other words, while we believe that the more knowledge or experience we have the better, we feel differently about simply creating as much human life as possible: "It is not important that there be more people. But once a human life has begun, it is very important that it flourish and not be wasted."[14]

Some people may intuitively understand Dworkin's claim that certain things are valuable in themselves, regardless of whether this encourages us to increase our inventory of them or simply value those that are already in existence.[15] Perry concludes, however, that "The notion that something is valuable independently of a beneficial relation to anyone or anything – whether a human being, a nonhuman but living entity, or God – is perfectly opaque."[16] It is, he notes, illogical to claim that something might be valuable in itself and, at the same time, have no value for anyone, as Dworkin seems to suggest. Instead, Perry argues that something is intrinsically valuable when it "has value for someone (or something) *not merely as a means to an end but as an end in itself*."[17] Strangely, the italicized portion of this quotation is less important to this discussion than the words that precede it, for the main difference between his and Dworkin's definitions of intrinsic value is that Perry maintains that things can only be intrinsically valuable if they have value for someone or something. Dworkin, he suggests, might have wanted to say that human life is objectively valuable, which would be

> to say that something has value for someone (for example, that it is good for her, that it is conducive to or perhaps even constitutive of her flourishing) *even if she is unaware that it has value for her – indeed, even if she believes that it has disvalue for her.*[18]

On my reading, Dworkin has indeed substituted intrinsic for objective value, setting the former in opposition to subjective value and omitting the

latter entirely, but he has done so without equating value with benefit in the way that Perry insists he must. To do so, Dworkin seems to suggest, would require yet another type of value: "Something is *instrumentally* important if its value depends on its usefulness."[19] He notes,

> David Hume and many other philosophers insisted that objects or events can be valuable only when and because they serve someone's or something's interests. On this view, nothing is valuable unless someone wants it or unless it helps someone get what he does want.[20]

But, as Perry argues:

> The second sentence here is a glaring non sequitur. It does not follow, from the Humean view, that nothing is valuable unless someone wants it or unless it helps someone get what he does want. It follows only that nothing is valuable unless it serves someone's or something's interests. That something serves my interests does not entail that I want it (or that it helps me get what I do want). After all, I may not know that something serves my interests, or I may not know what my real interests are. Indeed, that I want something (or that it helps me get what I do want) does not entail that it serves my interests: I may want things that are not good for me – indeed, that are bad for me.[21]

This trouble over the definition of intrinsic value is only the beginning of the disagreement between the two theorists. And the burden seems to fall on Dworkin, who says he will provide an answer to questions like, "How can it be important that a life continue unless that life is important for or to someone?"[22]

To answer this question, we must turn to Dworkin's suggestion that the current controversies over abortion and euthanasia can be traced to the fact that most people hold human life sacred. While we generally associate "sacred" with the religious idea of holiness, Dworkin argues that the sacredness of human beings can be held as a "secular but deep philosophical belief,"[23] rather than one that is necessarily religious in origin. Something might be held sacred when we attach a certain value to it, when we hold it in very high esteem. Perry's initial rebuttal of this notion of secular sacredness is that intrinsic value, using his definition of the term, is necessary but not sufficient to establish sacredness: "An end to my itch has both objective and intrinsic value for me, but it is not thereby sacred."[24] The reply that remains to Dworkin is that Perry's definition of intrinsic value is simply not as strenuous as his own. Under his own definition, intrinsic value is both a necessary and sufficient condition for sacredness, while Perry deliberately weakens his definition in order to leave room for the very problem he then demonstrates. The further challenge that Perry presents to Dworkin, however, is a more difficult and engaging one:

> For some persons who count themselves religious, to say that every human being is sacred is to say (speaking analogically) that every human being is the beloved child of God (God who is love). For persons who do not count themselves religious, what does it mean to say that every human being is sacred?[25]

Unlike its predecessor, this challenge goes a great distance in pressing Dworkin's conclusions and will provide a platform for this chapter's inquiry into the relation of human rights and human sacredness.

For Dworkin, "something is sacred or inviolable when its deliberate destruction would dishonor what ought to be honored."[26] While this definition is not particularly helpful, the expansion that he undertakes is instructive. There are, Dworkin asserts, two ways in which something might be considered sacred. The first, sacredness by association, is explained through the example of flags and other national symbols: "Many Americans consider the flag sacred because of its conventional association with the life of the nation; the respect they believe they owe their country is transferred to the flag."[27] The second, sacredness based on creation, can be demonstrated by looking at our attitude toward endangered species or cultures.[28] It is this second understanding of sacredness that Dworkin suggests is behind the feeling most people have about not wasting human life. This language of creation, he acknowledges, immediately brings to mind the notion that human beings are sacred because each is a child of God. He argues, however, that the same conservationist result can be obtained by secular means:

> For most Americans, and for many people in other countries, the evolutionary process is quite literally creative, for they believe that God is the author of nature. On that assumption, causing a species to disappear, wholly to be lost, is destroying a creative design of the most exalted artist of all. But even people who do not take that view, but who accept instead the Darwinian thesis that the evolution of species is a matter of accidental mutation rather than divine design, nevertheless often use artistic metaphors of creation. They describe discrete animal species as not just accidents but as achievements of adaptation, as something that nature has not just produced but wrought.[29]

There is an unmistakable connection drawn here between art and life. Indeed, the crux of Dworkin's argument is that "each developed human being is the product not just of natural [divine or evolutionary] creation, but also of the kind of deliberative human creative force that we honor in honoring art."[30] The first part of this claim is straightforward enough; human beings, he suggests, are considered sacred because they are the highest biological form of life. The second, however, requires some unpacking. What does it mean to say that each individual life results from

deliberately-applied human creativity? Here, Dworkin moves beyond the idea of sacredness as given to human beings by virtue of their biology (whether influenced directly by God or through natural processes) and focuses on sacredness as produced by human beings.

It is this move, from created to creating, that provides Dworkin with the most interesting component of his secular claim. He argues that both the decision to have a child and the child's life itself are creative endeavors. He notes that "a deliberate decision of parents to have and bear a child is of course a creative one. Any surviving child is shaped in character and capacity by the decisions of parents and by the cultural background of community."[31] It is not immediately clear, though, why Dworkin believes that the sacredness of persons flows from the decision of parents to have a child or from their shaping of its character. In order to provide a more thorough explanation of his word choice, Dworkin returns to the idea of life as artwork: "As that child matures, in all but pathological cases, his own creative choices progressively determine his thoughts, personality, ambitions, emotions, connections, and achievements. He creates his life just as much as an artist creates a painting or a poem."[32] This idea – that human beings shape their lives and, in a sense, create themselves – is the grounding of Dworkin's secular usage of sacredness. Of course, because his multi-part definition contains both religious and secular elements, Dworkin is confident that it is sufficiently inclusive to command the respect of the religious and non-religious alike. He is certainly correct in his assumption that those who believe that each human being is a child of God will agree with his claims about the sacredness of persons. Dworkin's non-religious claim may not perform its function as effectively, however. Indeed, the process as outlined is certainly a creative one, but we might be justified in wondering whether it makes human life sacred or simply beautiful, unique, or important.

Michael Perry's objection

The crux of Perry's complaint about Dworkin's secular sacredness proceeds from the assertion that a human life is a work of art made valuable as a result of natural and human investments. Summarizing the problem, he says

> Let us agree that every human being is a creative masterpiece and, as such, inspires (or should inspire) awe in us. That something justifiably inspires awe in us, however – James Joyce's *Ulysses*, for example – entails neither that we believe it to be sacred nor that it is sacred.[33]

For Perry, a sacred thing is one which – due to its sacredness – inspires awe in us and which, consequently, we value highly.[34] Dworkin, however, reverses the order, suggesting that something is held sacred in response to

its inherent value, to the awe it inspires in us. The problem with this reversal, according to Perry, is that it makes secular sacredness entirely subjective. Dworkin, he suggests, appeals to no objective standard in his argument for secular sacredness and thus leaves himself open to the possibility that others simply will not feel as he does about the value of mankind. He argues that:

> Dworkin seems to be using "sacred" in what we can call a weak, or "subjective", sense – something (e.g., a human life) is sacred *because*, or *in the sense that*, it inspires awe in us and we attach great value to it – rather than in the strong, or "objective", sense – something is sacred and *therefore* it inspires awe in us and we attach great value to it.[35]

To add specificity, Perry asks that we imagine using Dworkin's secular concept of human sacredness to change someone's mind about the human rights violation he is about to commit. He hopes that, in thinking through the discussion we might have with a Bosnian Serb intent on raping a Bosnian Muslim, we will come to the conclusion that an appeal to some objective standard carries more weight:

> If "sacred" is meant in the subjective sense, the Bosnian Serb can reply: "Sacred to you and yours, perhaps, but not to me and mine. In the scheme of things, we happen not to attach much value to her life." By contrast, "sacred" in the objective sense is not fundamentally a matter of "sacred to you" or "sacred to me"; it is, rather, a matter of how things really are .... If every human being is sacred in the objective sense, then, in violating the Bosnian Muslim, the Bosnian Serb does not merely violate what some of us attach great value to; he violates the very order of creation.[36]

While Perry's point is a compelling one, and one that Dworkin does not address, I am not entirely convinced that he has presented the knock-down argument to Dworkin's secular claim. Instead, Perry has raised three interesting and interrelated problems for himself with this example.

First, we might ask whether Perry is actually responding to Dworkin on his own terms. Because Perry questioned the definition of intrinsic value that Dworkin put forward and then simply proceeded with his own instead, he now misses an important component of Dworkin's argument. In failing to show conclusively that intrinsically valuable things must have value *for* someone or something, Perry leaves Dworkin free to argue that human life is valuable in itself and, in that respect, to provide an answer to the imagined Bosnian Serb. Nowhere, after all, does Dworkin suggest that skeptical people ought to be convinced that human life is sacred simply because it is valuable to him (or to us). Instead, Dworkin claims that human life is

intrinsically valuable – valuable in itself – and, in doing so, he manages to side-step Perry's charge of subjectivity. Indeed, Dworkin's entire argument that human lives be considered creative masterpieces is his attempt to show that it is, in fact, possible for something to be valuable without its having value for anyone in particular. We are entitled, of course, to question whether Dworkin actually succeeds in demonstrating the intrinsic value of human life. And, indeed, a compelling case can be made against Dworkin on this question of intrinsic value. He has not, in fact, shown anywhere that events or objects *should* be considered valuable in and of themselves.[37] He has, however, asserted that we believe some events or objects *are* valuable in this way. But is this sufficient to convince those who do not?

This question spills directly into the second problem, namely that, in adding the concrete example of ethnic cleansing in Bosnia, Perry has altered his project in an important way. Rather than seeking to demonstrate that the only intelligible version of human rights is one that has its roots in religion, Perry now entertains the hope of convincing others of the virtues of the contemporary international human rights regime. That these are two very different projects is demonstrated nicely by Christopher Eberle in his discussion of moral obligation stemming from the Divine Command Theory (DCT). He notes that:

> Even if the Divine Command theorist can't justify the DCT to anyone else, it's *possible* that she's justified in adhering to the DCT: given the particularities of her epistemic condition, and in particular, given the other theistic claims she affirms, it's possible that her perspective on the world entitles her to believe that the DCT is true.[38]

This is very much in line with an argument that Perry makes in a recent essay about the religious nature of the notion of human inviolability. He sketches out the belief system of a woman whose faith helps her to love even those who are the most unfamiliar or remote, as well as those who harm her: "Sarah loves even those from whom she is most estranged and towards whom she feels most antagonistic: those whose ideologies and projects and acts she judges to be not merely morally objectionable, but morally abominable."[39] In agreement with Eberle, Perry notes that:

> Sarah's religious position is embedded in – and it has whatever plausibility or implausibility it has because of its embeddedness in – a broader family of religious claims, especially the claims that (a) every human being is a beloved child of God and a sister or brother to one's self and (b) human beings are created by God to love one another.[40]

The heart of the matter, then, is that Sarah and the Divine Command theorist are free to believe whatever it is that they would like to believe – just as I may justify my own beliefs in any way I might like – but they

ought not assume that anyone else will be convinced by the same reasoning that convinces them. In our attempts to justify our beliefs to others, we ultimately reach a point beyond which we can rationally argue no further. This is true whether our beliefs are based in religion, nature, or reason. Even Immanuel Kant, upon completing his *Grounding for the Metaphysics of Morals*, recognized this problem:

> Now it is an essential principle of all use of our reason to push its knowledge to a consciousness of its necessity (for without necessity there would be no rational knowledge). But there is an equally essential restriction of the same reason that it cannot have insight into the necessity either of what is or what does happen or of what should happen, unless there is presupposed a condition under which it is or does happen or should happen. In this way, however, the satisfaction of reason is only further and further postponed by the continual inquiry after the condition. Reason, therefore, restlessly seeks the unconditionally necessary and sees itself compelled to assume this without having any means of making such necessity conceivable; reason is happy enough if only it can find a concept which is compatible with this assumption.... And so even though we do not indeed grasp the practical unconditioned necessity of the moral imperative, we do nevertheless grasp its inconceivability. This is all that can be fairly asked of a philosophy which strives in its principles to reach the very limit of human reason.[41]

Sarah, the Divine Command theorist, and Kant must all eventually say, with Wittgenstein, "If I have exhausted the justifications I have reached bedrock, and my spade is turned. Then I am inclined to say: 'This is simply what I do.' "[42]

Perry, however, is critical of those – like Dworkin – who would attempt to convince others of the rightness of human sacredness either without first successfully specifying their source of normativity or whose source of normativity "doesn't withstand scrutiny even on its own (secular) terms."[43] On this point, that there is something incomplete about the non-religious argument, Perry notes that the assertion that all human beings are sacred and, as a result, inviolable, is simply a statement of the theorist's own preference for a world in which these beliefs are honored. The problem, however, is that this preference for a world that respects human rights does not necessarily line up with non-religious beliefs about the way the world works. In agreement with Perry on this point is Jeffrie Murphy, who notes that:

> Liberal theorists have a self-destructive tendency to be charmed by views that undermine their own central doctrines – for example, a failure to realize that the liberal virtues of value pluralism and value

tolerance may undermine the absolutism about human rights upon which liberalism ultimately depends.[44]

According to Perry, the problem is not simply one of competing liberal virtues; instead, it goes as deep as these theorists' core beliefs:

> It is a presupposition of the nonreligious position that the universe is just what Clarence Darrow and Steven Weinberg (among others) have proclaimed it to be: a cosmic process bereft of ultimate meaning.... Far from being created "in the image of God," human beings are merely the unplanned, unintended yield of random mutation and natural selection. But, lo and behold, it just happens that the evolved nature of human beings is such that being a person who "loves one another just as I have loved you" is the most deeply satisfying way of life of which human beings are capable. This free floating nonreligious position seems so ad hoc, as if those who espouse the position were determined to cleave to a consoling belief about human nature long after the religious vision in which the belief has traditionally been embedded has ceased to have, for them, credibility.[45]

Perry charges, in other words, that nonreligious thinkers have embraced a cosmology that looks upon human existence as the product of random chance, but hope to maintain a foundation for the idea of human rights. The problem is that such a contingent picture of human nature does not provide a solid enough grounding for human rights; this view, he argues, cannot possibly prove effective in the face of counterclaims by human rights abusers. This is a valid critique, but the religious position – despite specifying a source of normativity – also offers no assistance when the task is persuading those with different beliefs. Sarah believes that:

> By becoming [people who love one another as God loves us], we fulfill – we perfect – our created nature and thereby achieve our truest, deepest, and most enduring happiness. That fact, coupled with our commitment to our own authentic well being, is, according to Sarah, the source of normativity.[46]

The problem, of course, is that Sarah's source of normativity is the result of her own deep, yet personal, religious commitment, a commitment that she cannot really justify to others in a convincing manner. As Perry notes, "Sarah specifies the source of normativity – though, of course, if one is a nonbeliever, or a believer of the 'wrong' sort, the source Sarah specifies will not move one."[47]

This yields the third – and, in my opinion, most interesting – problem that Perry's critique raises. Indeed, it offers us an entrée into the central argument that underlies *The Idea of Human Rights*. In his critique of

Dworkin, Perry insists that "The premise that every human being is sacred-in-the-subjective-sense cannot begin to bear the weight of the premise that every human being is sacred-in-the-objective-sense."[48] By stating his objection in this manner, he alludes to the problem discussed above: that Dworkin's argument for secular sacredness is not convincing in the same way as the religious argument (or not convincing at all). Put succinctly, Perry contends that at the center of every human rights claim is the notion of the sacredness of persons, which is, contra Dworkin, a fundamentally religious concept. His project is to examine some of the existing non-religious understandings of "the conviction that every human being is sacred – *sacred in the strong/objective sense, sacred because of how the world really is, and not because of what we attach value to in the world.*"[49] But, in framing the search in this way, Perry sets an impossible task for others to accomplish. The closest that Dworkin comes to succeeding is in his discussion of intrinsic value, where he poses a question that is notable for its conditional wording: "If it is a horrible desecration to destroy a painting, for example, even though a painting is not a person, why should it not be a much greater desecration to destroy something whose intrinsic value may be vastly greater?"[50] Were he to remove the conditional wording and answer this question, which he does not, he would still fail in his project of suggesting a secular understanding of human sacredness. The best answer Dworkin can give is one he gave earlier: destroying a person would be a much greater desecration than destroying a painting based on the fact that we believe human lives to be intrinsically valuable or sacred, which is itself based on our belief that human beings are the most creative species in existence. But this is not the same as arguing that human beings actually *are* valuable in and of themselves, nor will it convince those with radically opposing beliefs to change their minds. How, after all, can we talk about something having intrinsic value in the absence of some external and unchanging measuring tool? As Perry asks, "How do we get from 'the universe is (or might be) nothing but a cosmic process bereft of ultimate meaning' to 'every human being is nonetheless sacred (in the strong or objective sense)'?"[51] How, in other words, might a human life be both sacred *and* low-level nuclear waste? In order to show that something is objective, non-religious, and sacred in the sense that Perry wants, one must actually show that it is *religiously* non-religious, which would – of course – defeat the purpose.

The idea that Perry is looking for something that is both religious and non-religious at once is a difficult one to grasp and requires some investigation. The most fruitful way to do so is to continue our detailed examination of Perry's argument to see how he creates this puzzle. Both Perry and Dworkin attempt to draw political conclusions from the notion of the sacredness of persons. Just as Dworkin hopes to find a grounding for the debate about abortion and euthanasia, Perry wants to highlight the foundation of universal human rights. Dworkin, according to Perry, has failed

to show "that either a secular cosmology or cosmological atheism can yield the requisite conviction about *how things really are.*"[52] While we can certainly question whether this was ever Dworkin's intent, we must also consider the reasonableness of Perry's demand. Is it possible, in the end, for those who are not religious – people like Clarence Darrow or Steven Weinberg – to give to us a definitive answer about the nature of the universe and our place in it? It seems unlikely that either could provide the sort of answer that Perry desires. Their inability to do so, however, threatens to leave the contemporary human rights regime with a severely eroded foundation, for Perry insists on the intimate connection between human sacredness and human rights. In his own words: "The conviction that every human being is sacred is, in my view, inescapably religious – and the idea of human rights is, therefore, ineliminably religious."[53] But what exactly is the connection between the sacredness of persons and the idea of human rights?

The question of whether there is something inherent in human beings from which our rights spring is fundamental to any attempt at understanding human rights claims. As Perry says, "The fundamental challenge to each and every human rights claim ... is a demand for reasons."[54] Indeed, this book began with an effort to trace the notion of grounding our rights and noted that one can look at least as far back as the Stoics in doing so. The importance of this search is nicely elucidated by Perry, who contends that:

> there is something about each and every human being, simply as a human being, such that certain choices should be made and certain other choices rejected; in particular, certain things ought not to be done to any human being and certain other things ought to be done for every human being.[55]

Despite overwhelming agreement that something about us is surely responsible for our having rights, theorists have not often been in agreement about what exactly that something might be. Enlightenment thinkers conclude that it is our ability to use reason; theologians suggest that it is our status as children of God, made in His image. And, of course, international human rights documents contend that it is our dignity that sets us apart from all of the other species.

For Perry, the foundational component of the idea of human rights is the conviction that every human being is sacred; it clearly relies, he argues, on a spiritual belief of one kind or another in order to be intelligible. Regardless of whether he is correct on that score, Perry is surely correct in saying:

> The fundamental challenge to human rights claims is a real-world challenge: Many to whom such claims are addressed have conspicuously not adopted anything like "the moral (impartial, universal) point

of view". The moral point of view is not a justificatory basis for human rights claims – at least not a fundamental basis. The moral point of view is itself in dire need of justification, especially in a world – *our* world, the *real* world – that is often fiercely partial/local rather than impartial/universal.[56]

His religious understanding of the sacredness of persons is an attempt at providing just such a justification. It represents, in his view, the only intelligible way to answer "what David Tracy has called the 'limit-question' of morality: 'Why be moral at all?' "[57]

As we have seen, Dworkin's secular conception of sacredness fails to provide a satisfactory answer to this question. Robert Grant concludes a bit more forcefully that, "In *Life's Dominion*, Professor Dworkin makes considerable play with, indeed frankly exploits, the idea of the sacred, but shows no understanding of it."[58] Indeed, considerable difficulties arise over his unconventional definition of intrinsic value and over his idea that each of us holds in higher esteem one of the two investments that make something sacred. In addition, and perhaps most importantly, there is the problem of subjectivity to which Dworkin's secular sacredness falls prey. That said, it is important to avoid tossing away Dworkin's contribution entirely. Though somewhat the worse for wear on the question of sacredness, there is a very valuable point that *Life's Dominion* raises, namely the idea of self-creation. As discussed earlier, Dworkin argues that human life is valuable because of the creative contributions of both nature and humanity. The key component of this argument is the latter notion, the idea that each human being is created by her culture and community, as well as her own thoughts. On this point, Dworkin's ideas are very well-articulated:

> The life of a single human organism commands respect and protection, then, no matter in what form or shape, because of the complex creative investment it represents and because of our wonder at the ... processes of nation and community and language through which a human being will come to absorb and continue hundreds of generations of culture and forms of life and value, and, finally, when mental life has begun and flourishes, at the process of internal personal creation and judgment by which a person will make and remake himself, a mysterious, inescapable process in which we each participate, and which is therefore the most powerful and inevitable source of empathy and communion we have with every other creature who faces the same frightening challenge.[59]

Put succinctly, each human life is inherently valuable because human beings are self-creating; they are, in Dworkin's view, a source of value in the way that God or nature might be for others. Dworkin, then, offers an

interesting contribution about the possibilities of human creativity and his work is valuable to our discussion if only for that.[60] More than that, though, the task that Perry assigns to non-religious theorists (and that Dworkin sets for himself) – of providing a coherent secular understanding of a deeply religious concept – may very well be an impossible one and Dworkin's failure in this respect should not be emphasized excessively.

While we have already looked, in detail, at these challenges to Dworkin's theory and at the problem of secularizing the concept of sacredness, we have not dealt with Perry's understanding of sacredness in its entirety. A crucial point left for us to consider is that Perry's conception of human sacredness can be said to encompass a number of the aforementioned "somethings" on which our rights rely. More specifically, Perry suggests that rights claims all rely on the notion that human beings are sacred, which is – in turn – based on the idea that we are the children of God. In addition, Perry contends that the sacredness of persons can be equated with the concept of inherent dignity that is highlighted in the Universal Declaration of Human Rights. His contention, however, is merely implied, for Perry puts the two together only once – in a question – at the very beginning of his argument:

> Or must we conclude that the idea of human rights is indeed inelimi-inably religious, that a fundamental constituent of the idea, namely, *the conviction that every human being is sacred – that every human being is "inviolable", has "inherent dignity", is "an end in himself", or the like* – is inescapably religious?[61]

Perry seems to suggest that dignity and sacredness are, in fact, synonyms for one another. But this is too large an assumption, in my estimation, and too much hinges on it. Put succinctly, Perry wants to demonstrate that the sacredness of persons can only be understood religiously. Doing so, he claims, will mean that the idea of human rights is ineliminably religious. He fails to show, however, how it is that sacredness is necessarily connected to the idea of human rights; it is, instead, one of many possible foundations. Simply putting all of these possibilities together and implying that they are derivative of human sacredness does not properly constitute an argument.

In a later chapter of his book, Perry is more forthcoming about his view of the connection between international law and the sacredness of persons. Indeed, he argues that the former is clearly derived from the latter:

> Why is the good of every human being an end worth pursuing in its own right? .... One answer – the answer that informs the international law of human rights – is that the good of every human being is an end worth pursuing in its own right *because every human being is sacred.*[62]

The problem, however, is that none of the international human rights documents actually use this term. In fact, the language he examines from the International Bill of Human Rights does not contain the word "sacred" anywhere. As Perry himself notes:

> The ... Universal Declaration of Human Rights (1948), speaks, in the Preamble, of "the inherent dignity ... of all members of the human family" and of "the dignity and worth of the human person". In Article 1, the Declaration proclaims: "All human beings ... should act towards one another in a spirit of brotherhood".... The preamble common to both [the International Covenant on Civil and Political Rights (1976) and the International Covenant on Economic, Social, and Cultural Rights (1976)] echoes the Universal Declaration in speaking of "the inherent dignity ... of all members of the human family". The preamble then states: "[T]hese rights derive from the inherent dignity of the human person ...."[63]

It is obvious that the idea of human rights, as understood in contemporary international documents, is based on the inherent dignity of persons. It is not immediately clear, however, where sacredness comes into the picture. Indeed, there is no mention of the sacredness of human beings in any international human rights document, and it is not necessarily the case that dignity and sacredness can be equated in the way that Perry assumes them to be.

In addition to suggesting that dignity and sacredness are intimately connected, Perry further implies that dignity is a religious concept. "What are we to make of such talk," he asks, "talk about 'the inherent dignity' of all human beings ... and about the importance, therefore, of all human beings acting toward one another 'in a spirit of brotherhood'? It is easy enough to understand such talk as *religious* talk."[64] And Perry is not alone in conflating these terms and assigning the same religious origin to both. Murphy makes the same connection and, like Perry, does not offer an explanation for doing so: "The rich moral doctrine of the sacredness, the preciousness, the dignity of persons cannot in fact be utterly detached from the theological context in which it arose and of which it for so long formed an essential part."[65] But should we assume that human dignity has the same theological foundation as human sacredness? In other words, are Perry and Murphy correct? Is the inherent dignity of persons just as religious (or religious in the same way) as the sacredness of persons? Perry goes to great lengths to suggest that sacredness is a fundamentally religious concept, but he has done nothing to conclusively show that dignity is similarly religious. If sacredness and dignity are not synonymous with one another, then Perry has not demonstrated that the idea of human rights is ineliminably religious. A brief glance at the language of the International Bill of Rights shows that dignity is clearly bound up with the concept of

international human rights, but not necessarily sacredness; the latter, according to Perry, is an inextricably religious concept, but the former has not been similarly evaluated.

Indeed, Australian philosopher Raimond Gaita suggests that these concepts cannot be used interchangeably and do not carry the same weight. He does, however, agree with Perry that sacredness is a fundamentally religious concept and far more powerful than dignity. He notes:

> Only someone who is religious can speak seriously of the sacred, but such talk informs the thoughts of most of us whether or not we are religious.... If we are not religious, we will often search for one of the inadequate expressions which are available to us to say what we hope will be a secular equivalent of it. We may say that all human beings are inestimably precious, that they are ends in themselves, that they are owed unconditional respect, that they possess inalienable rights, and, of course, that they possess inalienable dignity. In my judgment these are ways of trying to say what we feel a need to say when we are estranged from the conceptual resources we need to say it.[66]

While I am quite sympathetic to Gaita's position throughout *A Common Humanity*, there is a problem that arises from the way in which he stakes out this particular argument, namely that the five examples of secular – and weak – versions of sacredness are not themselves synonyms. On my reading, Gaita seems to be lumping together actions and reasons for those actions. There is, for example, a clear discrepancy between the notion that "all human beings are inestimably precious" and the idea "that they are owed unconditional respect." Inestimable preciousness and inalienable dignity are similar, possibly secular, versions of the idea that people are sacred; the notion that people are owed unconditional respect and possess inalienable rights belong to an entirely different category. The difference is that the former concepts are the reasoning behind our believing the latter concepts. Indeed, the notions of sacredness and dignity are so vitally important precisely because of this difference; they provide the justification for our believing in the idea of human rights and the reason for our insistence that others act toward every human being as we do. While this is problematic, however, a more pressing issue is whether Gaita or Perry is correct about the separation of dignity from sacredness. To untangle that question, it is necessary to gain a deeper understanding of both terms and it is to their etymological roots that we now turn.

The etymology of rights

The Oxford English Dictionary lists seven definitions of "sacred," ranging from those that typically come to mind ("Secured by religious sentiment,

reverence, sense of justice, or the like, against violation, infringement, or encroachment" and "Regarded with or entitled to respect or reverence similar to that which attaches to holy things") to those that are a bit more obscure ("Of the Eucharistic elements: Consecrated" and "Applied as a specific defining adj. to various animals and plants that are or have been considered sacred to certain deities").[67] Indeed, there are only two definitions that do not make reference to religion or a deity: first, "Accursed [After L. *sacer*; freq. translating or in allusion to Virgil's *auri saca fames* (Æn. III. 57)]" and, second, "Dedicated, set apart, exclusively appropriated to some person or some special purpose."[68] The former provides us an opportunity to look into the Latin root, *sacer*, which – depending on context – could mean either "dedicated, consecrated, devoted, sacred," "Accursed, execrable, detestable, horrible, infamous," or "Regarded with reverence, holy, awful, venerable."[69] There is, to be sure, something strange about using the same word to mean both accursed and holy, but solving that mystery is not our present purpose. Instead, it is sufficient to note that the Latin root of a non-religious definition returns us to religious language. Having done so, we can turn to the second of the two non-religious definitions. While it is not explicitly clear, with this definition, what might make "some person or some special purpose" sacred, a look at all of the other definitions of "sacred" seems to suggest that a relationship with a deity is most likely the source.

Having looked at the term "sacred" and noted the clear connection to "holy" and "religious" words in both English and Latin, it remains to us to consider "dignity" in the same manner. *The Oxford English Dictionary* contains eight possible definitions, ranging once again from the very obvious ("The quality of being worthy or honourable; worthiness, worth, nobleness, excellence" and "Nobility or befitting elevation of aspect, manner, or style; becoming or fit stateliness, gravity") to the very obscure ("A situation of a planet in which its influence is heightened, either by its position in the zodiac, or by its aspects with other planets" and "The term for a 'company' of canons").[70] None of the definitions makes reference to the concepts of sacredness, holiness, or religion. Similarly, exploring the Latin root, *dignus*, does not help to connect sacredness and dignity; it is defined as "worthy, deserving (in a good or ill sense), of things, suitable, fitting, becoming, proper."[71] The Latin, in turn, can be traced back to the Greek δόξα, which is defined as "expectation, notion, judgement, whether well grounded or not" or "the opinion which others have of one, estimation, repute."[72] The only connection between "dignity" and "sacred" can be found in an obscure definition of "dignified," which usually is defined as "Invested with dignity; exalted" or "Marked by dignity of manner, style, or appearance; characterized by lofty self-respect without haughtiness; stately, noble, majestic."[73] The obscure definition, "Holding a position of dignity; ranking as a dignitary (esp. ecclesiastical),"[74] does provide a connection, albeit a very tenuous one, to a religious understanding of dignity.

Despite the fact that "dignified" once suggested that the clergy were highly ranked in society, the concept of dignity seems, on the whole, not to be related to the idea of human sacredness. Something is held sacred in virtue of a clear connection to some other holy thing. Sacredness can apply to objects as well as to people, and it provides the foundation for inviolability. In other words, human beings ought not to be violated because of their connection to the divine; likewise, human beings ought to be respected in much the same way that God is respected. The value of the object – in this case, a person – is fixed because of its unchanging relationship to the source of all value, God. The concept of dignity, conversely, applies only to people and, traditionally, only to a certain sort of person. It is, traditionally understood, an aristocratic concept. Unlike sacredness, which applies to all of the objects that are related to God, one must be worthy, noble, or honorable in order to be considered a bearer of dignity. One's dignity is, it seems, based on what others think; in that sense, it is very much a subjective concept, as it is open to interpretation by definition. That said, it is important to note that our understanding of dignity has changed considerably in the last 200 years. Prior to the revolutions in America and France in the eighteenth century, dignity and its attending esteem were strictly reserved for members of the nobility. With the collapse of the belief that a fraction of the populace was born into a position of greater worth, the concept of dignity underwent a considerable expansion. The Glorious Revolution of 1688–1689 provided a great deal of support to the idea that people might rightfully oppose a tyrannical government, but the American and French revolutionaries were the first to draw up a list of specific rights that applied, they said, to all men.[75]

While the United States Declaration of Independence states that "all men are created equal"[76] and the French Declaration of the Rights of Man and Citizen declares that "Men are born and remain free and equal in rights,"[77] neither makes mention of human dignity as the basis for this belief. And, perhaps not surprisingly, neither Declaration went to great lengths to ensure that the equality of rights applied equally to everyone. Clearly, the problem of slavery was not dealt with at the time of the signing of the United States Declaration, nor would it be dealt with in the lifetimes of the men who signed it. And, of course, the promulgation of the French Declaration was followed almost immediately by Robespierre's Terror and the execution of thousands by guillotine (including, eventually, Robespierre himself). Only ten years after proclaiming the Rights of Man and Citizen, political control over France was seized by Napoleon Bonaparte.

Despite what can graciously be termed serious problems of implementation, both the American and French Declarations are unequivocal in the principles that serve as their guide. In addition, the French revolutionaries provide support for the connection between human rights and sacredness, stating that they "have resolved to set forth in a solemn declaration the

natural, inalienable, and sacred rights of man."[78] And yet, despite the use of Perry's terminology, it is important to note that it is the *rights* that are sacred and not the *people*. Indeed, it is a bit of a mystery as to the reason behind the sacredness of the rights, which seems not to reside in the inherent equality of the people; this second concept, after all, requires a foundation of its own. It makes the most sense to assume that all men possess equally the sacred rights of "liberty, property, security, and resistance to oppression" because of their (unstated) connection to "the Supreme Being" "in the presence and under the auspices of [whom]" the rights were affirmed by the French National Assembly.[79] A similarly nondescript "Creator" appears in the American Declaration as well, and is very clearly the source of man's "certain unalienable rights."[80] Of primary importance to both the American and French Declarations, though, are the rights themselves, not their ultimate guarantor, because their infringement provided a rallying cry for the revolutions and their protection was at the heart of the radical democratic experiment that the revolutionaries proposed. And, in fact, both revolutions promised to usher in an era of hitherto unimagined civil peace and religious tolerance, based on the complete absence of a state-sanctioned religion.[81]

Still the questions remain, how and why the change from "natural, inalienable, and sacred rights" protected by a Supreme Being to the contemporary notion of the inviolability of persons based on their inherent dignity? I submit that a primary reason for the change is that, historically, the rights have not been held in practice to be particularly sacred. The United Nations Charter seems to bear this idea out:

> We the peoples of the United Nations determined
> to save succeeding generations from the scourge of war, which twice in our lifetime has brought untold sorrow to mankind, and
> to reaffirm faith in fundamental human rights, in the dignity and worth of the human person . . .
> Have resolved to combine our efforts to accomplish these aims.[82]

Likewise, the Universal Declaration of Human Rights begins by noting that "disregard and contempt for human rights have resulted in barbarous acts which have outraged the conscience of mankind."[83] Given the propensity that human beings have had, especially in the last century, for violating the rights enshrined in the American and French Declarations, the United Nations proposed a new way of understanding the duties that governments had to their citizens and, conversely, the rights those citizens could claim.[84] According to William Schulz, "What the Universal Declaration supplies all of us are rights in the form of norms to which every person can appeal, rights that . . . are designed to depict the best way we know of at the moment to counter cruelty and build a decent society."[85] Indeed, a statement by Eleanor Roosevelt, who chaired

the Human Rights Commission that drafted the Universal Declaration, does much to confirm that its drafters appreciated the Declaration's revolutionary character:

> We stand today at the threshold of a great event both in the life of the United Nations and in the life of mankind.... This Declaration may well become the international Magna Carta of all men everywhere. We hope its proclamation by the General Assembly will be an event comparable to the proclamation of the Declaration of the Rights of Man by the French people in 1789, the adoption of the Bill of Rights by the people of the United States, and adoption of comparable declarations at different times in other countries.[86]

In addition to this statement by Roosevelt, Charles Malik – the Lebanese philosopher and politician who ultimately shepherded the Declaration through the General Assembly – lends support to the idea that the community of nations stood on entirely new ground as it considered a rights instrument with the support of the entire world behind it. According to Malik:

> Thousands of minds and hands have helped in its formation. Every member of the United Nations has solemnly pledged itself to achieve respect for and observance of human rights. But, precisely what these rights are we were never told before, either in the Charter or in any other international instrument. This is the first time the principles of human rights and fundamental freedoms are spelled out authoritatively and in precise detail. I now know what my government pledged itself to promote, achieve and observe when I had the honor to sign the [UN Charter]. I can agitate against my government, and if she does not fulfil her pledge, I shall have and feel the moral support of the entire world.[87]

Proposing such a list, however, is not the same as suggesting that the enumerated rights and the human dignity underlying them are objectively true. As Schulz argues:

> The question to ask about rights is not, Are they true? The question is, Do they work? Do they work to spread empathy, combat cruelty, and protect the weak from their oppressors? The experience of the international human rights community is that these do.[88]

Such an argument, though, seems to leave the idea of human rights on shaky ground; it is akin to admitting that, in fact, human rights might be a fad that could just as well not be in fashion tomorrow. Indeed, Schulz recognizes this problem:

Such a concept of rights does not lend them the kind of irrefragable authority that God's will or Nature's command might. Theoretically, the Universal Declaration could be rescinded or amended. Human concepts of rights *do* change and there is no reason to believe that today's notions and norms will be identical to those of the twenty-second century any more than our norms are identical to those of the nineteenth.[89]

This argument – that the idea of human rights and the human dignity that grounds it is constructed and, therefore, changeable – is one that is anathema to both Michael Perry and Ronald Dworkin, as both argue for the importance of a transcendent foundation for rights, one that is ultimately grounded in some feature or quality of humanity. The non-religious foundation that Dworkin proposes, however, is flawed for a variety of reasons, not the least of which is that it misunderstands the concept of sacredness on which it is based. But the task that he sets for himself and that Perry argues he fails to complete seems to me to be one that is both impossible and unnecessary. It is impossible, I have argued, because the idea of secular sacredness is one that cannot be made sense of; it is unnecessary, I believe, because the concept of sacredness is not required to ground the idea of human rights in the way that Perry suggests. It is, instead, human dignity upon which the International Bill of Rights stands and it is possible that the concept of dignity for all humanity is a very recent development. Schulz, who is both a theorist and a practitioner of human rights, embraces the idea that we have recently established the ground upon which our rights stand and contends that this seemingly tenuous position need not dull the luster of human rights. While this theory might not provide the sort of objectively strong defense that Perry requires, it is clear that no truly non-religious theory will be able to do so because any such theory seems to lack the objectivity that religious theories claim.

4 Human dignity without teleology
Human rights and evolutionary biology

There has been no shortage, in recent years, of debate on the subject of human dignity. In particular, much ink has been spilled – and much legislative wrangling has taken place – in an attempt to clarify what it means to die with dignity. Behind this puzzle lies one that is more fundamental, namely what it means to have dignity at all. This, it seems to me, has as much to do with life as it does with death. And, I want to suggest, piecing together this puzzle will yield a great deal of information on what we mean when we talk about human persons and human rights. For bound up with the question of human dignity is the question of what constitutes the human person who is the subject of the dignity and, consequently, the rights. The recent dispute surrounding Terri Schiavo, a Florida woman in a persistent vegetative state (PVS) whose husband sought to remove the feeding tube that kept her alive and whose parents were opposed to doing so, is a good indicator that these issues remain very much unresolved. The Schiavo case received an amazing amount of attention from the media, politicians, and the populace – far more, for example, than the humanitarian crisis taking place in the Darfur region of Sudan at the same time. While few people in the USA could find Darfur on a map, it would be nearly impossible to find someone without an opinion on Schiavo's medical care. And the reason for all the attention is quite clearly that there were two opposing camps with the exact opposite opinion about what ought to be done: either keep her alive with the assistance of a feeding tube or remove the tube and wait for her to die. The Schiavo case prompted people to ask themselves whether they would want to remain alive with the aid of machines and it reopened the national debate that swirled around the similar cases of Karen Ann Quinlan in the 1970s and Nancy Cruzan in the late 1980s.

This debate about the end of life mirrors the one about the beginning of life. Just as we remain uncertain about Terri Schiavo's rights, we remain sharply divided on the question of whether fetuses may be aborted and, if so, at what stage of pregnancy it becomes impermissible to do so. In other words, we have not – as yet – conclusively decided when a person becomes a person or when a person stops being a person. Consider, for example,

this description of a PVS patient from a recent *New York Times* op-ed piece:

> In a persistent vegetative state, the cerebral cortex has been destroyed, leaving the person incapable of thought or memory, but the brainstem remains intact and functional. A person in a persistent vegetative state can live for years without a mechanical ventilator or other technological support.[1]

The question to be addressed, one which the authors, Gary Kalkut and Nancy Neveloff Dubler, do not consider, is in what sense the PVS patient is a person. How can we speak of a person if the PVS patient is lacking a functional cerebral cortex? In the same op-ed, Kalkut and Dubler point to Schiavo's situation and note that "There was no question that she was alive. Her heart and lungs received signals from her brainstem – they didn't need machines to sustain their activity."[2] But, again, this begs the question with which we are concerned; without thought or memory, without a functioning cerebrum, what is it about the patient that makes her a person? Specifically, in this case, in what sense should the patient who was alive, whose heart and lungs were functioning, be considered Terri Schiavo? It seems to me of fundamental importance to address this problem because, I want to argue, Terri Schiavo and the PVS patient who was Terri Schiavo are not the same.

But what makes Terri Schiavo – or Karen Ann Quinlan or Nancy Cruzan or any of us – different from a PVS patient? Asking this question is not the same as asking whether we are alive, for PVS patients are obviously alive in the sense that they have cardiopulmonary function and brainstem activity. What it asks, instead, is what makes us *us*? Answering this question requires creating a distinction, one to which I will return later in this chapter, between human animals and human persons.[3] The former, I want to suggest, are lacking in some important respect and the latter are not; to be a pre- or post-person is to be not quite all that one can be. The PVS patient is very much a post-person, just as some fetuses are pre-persons, and we make a mistake in failing to recognize what they lack in comparison, for example, to the coma patient or the infant. But what accounts for this difference? What makes someone specifically a person rather than merely an animal? In this chapter, I turn to evolutionary biology to make an argument about the primacy of dignity in differentiating between human animals and human persons.

Such a suggestion about deriving dignity from an argument about human nature raises at least two concerns. First, my argument runs headlong into a heated debate about whether there is any such thing as human nature in the first place. There are those who believe that an understanding of evolutionary biology undermines many – if not all – of the traditional philosophical and theological arguments about human nature. While I

believe I can answer this objection without a great deal of difficulty, I will have a bit more trouble with the second concern, a philosophical puzzle that Michael J. Perry highlights in a recent article: "For one who believes that the universe is utterly bereft of transcendent meaning, why, in virtue of what, does every human being have inherent dignity?"[4] This is a particularly challenging question, I think, and it clearly lies at the center of this chapter. Perry's disbelief in the prospects of successfully navigating this terrain notwithstanding, I believe that a compelling answer to this problem can be arrived at by looking outside the fields of philosophy, political science, or public policy in which these sorts of arguments are typically concentrated.

That the concept of human dignity might be derived from evolutionary principles undoubtedly invites a great deal of skepticism from a great many sources on both sides of the political divide. Clearly, there will be some strong resistance to this sort of theory from those who believe evolutionary biology wrongheaded in the first place. But any perceived connection to an argument grounded in what might be termed sociobiology is enough to get me into some trouble with even those who claim to be non-religious, as evolutionary biologists and psychologists have been the well-used whipping-boys of the academy for a couple of decades now precisely because of their adherence to a theory of human nature. As Steven Pinker notes:

> For invoking nurture *and* nature, not nurture alone, these authors have been picketed, shouted down, subjected to searing invectives in the press, even denounced in Congress. Others expressing such opinions have been censored, assaulted, or threatened with criminal prosecution.[5]

There is something about such an argument that does not sit well with many of those in the Humanities and Social Sciences; in particular, I think, an argument that makes claims about human nature and that attempts to sort out what people might have been like in some sort of "ancestral environment" sends many in the academy into fits. Listen, again, to Pinker on this point:

> When it comes to explaining human thought and behavior, the possibility that heredity plays any role at all still has the power to shock. To acknowledge human nature, many think, is to endorse racism, sexism, war, greed, genocide, nihilism, reactionary politics, and neglect of children and the disadvantaged. Any claim that the mind has an innate organization strikes people not as a hypothesis that might be incorrect but as a thought it is immoral to think.[6]

I well understand this reaction, however; sociobiology has, after all, been put to nefarious use in the past and it would not be overly difficult to do

so again. And yet, I want to argue that a discussion of human universals or a detailed account of the way the mind works will not yield the sort of problem that many of my colleagues might assume. Rather than highlighting the differences between races or sexes, then, I think we might be able to tell a plausible story about our common humanity that draws out an argument about dignity from the principles of evolutionary biology.

Human beings are complex animals, to be sure. And while we do not yet have a full appreciation of all our internal workings, we are making significant progress in many areas. Consider, for example, the project of mapping the human genome and the many recent advances in neuroscience, like neuropharmacology. Though our knowledge remains incomplete at present, I want to argue that the information we have begun to compile about the human mind can yield some interesting conclusions about the idea of human dignity. In the first section of this chapter, I briefly construct an argument for a human nature that is rooted in evolutionary biology. Having done so, the second section will make a case for locating personhood in the human mind; in particular, I consider arguments in favor of and against linking personal identity with either higher- and whole-brain activity. In the third section, I return to this brief discussion of PVS patients, fetuses, and persons with a view to sorting through some possible sources of personhood. The final section will offer a resolution to these controversies – which David DeGrazia calls "the boundaries of our existence"[7] – and, in so doing, will demonstrate the priority of dignity to personhood. Ultimately, I will argue that an intelligible grounding for human dignity – itself a foundational component of human rights – can be arrived at through an argument about the way our minds function; more specifically, I contend that dignity is a feature of higher-brain activity and, in making this case, I provide one possible answer to Perry's question, quoted earlier, about how a non-religious person – one who embraces evolutionary theory – might arrive at the concept of human dignity.

The evolution of human nature

For many people in the United States, there is no question that humans have a distinct nature; by and large, ours is a nation of believers and one of the most fundamental beliefs is that humanity was created in the image of God. This position holds that our special status among the created beings derives from our relationship with God; the intricacies of the human mind – with which this chapter is concerned – are instilled in us by Him, largely to assist us in contemplating and serving Him. All of this is relatively unproblematic – unless one puts more weight on the discoveries of modern science, which are often directly at odds with the biblical account of creation and, consequently, human nature. As science seemed to put the lie to the Bible on things like the age of the Earth or its position in the universe, many began to wonder what it meant to be human absent a special rela-

tionship with God. For the faithful, an acceptance of evolutionary biology and a rejection of the Bible yields a universe without design, one in which the rise of *homo sapiens* occurred by chance and to no particular end. In such a world, there is nothing special about humanity, it is an absurdity to talk about morality, and, as a result, any action is permitted.[8]

I want to suggest that one reaches this conclusion only through a mistaken understanding of evolutionary biology; indeed, few non-religious people today have jettisoned the idea of human nature entirely and, interestingly, evolutionary biologists and psychologists are today championing a more meaningful understanding of human nature.[9] Their struggle against the theory of human nature that has been the most popular amongst non-religious intellectuals – the Blank Slate – is the topic of this section, as it is my goal to highlight the possibility of a robust non-religious theory of human nature. To begin, a simple definition is in order; the Blank Slate, following Pinker, is "the idea that the human mind has no inherent structure and can be inscribed at will by society or ourselves."[10] Though it gained most of its ground in the twentieth century, the idea can be traced back to John Locke, who argued against "theories of innate ideas in which people were thought to be born with mathematical ideals, eternal truths, and a notion of God."[11] Then, as now, the doctrine of the Blank Slate was a progressive one; its more recent adherents were responding to social and political philosophies that saw racism and sexism as inevitable consequences of accepting evolutionary biology. By way of response, American intellectuals argued that behavior was shaped by a person's surroundings – by culture – rather than by natural forces. Arguments about the genetic inferiority of women or Jews or blacks – or any other targeted group – were dismissed and, in their places, adherents of the Blank Slate agreed with Margaret Mead "that human nature is almost unbelievably malleable, responding accurately and contrastingly to contrasting cultural conditions."[12] And so the argument raged – back and forth – between those who argued in favor of human nature, based on our understanding of genetics, and those who claimed that the only feature of humanity's nature was its plasticity. Francis Fukuyama nicely sums up this nature/nurture warfare, saying:

> The dubious pedigree of hereditarian arguments cast a pall over most discussions of genetics during the second half of the twentieth century. Progressive intellectuals were particularly intent on beating back arguments about nature. This was not only because natural differences between groups of people implied social hierarchy, but also because natural characteristics, even when universally shared, implied limits to human plasticity, and hence to human hopes and aspirations.[13]

Lest anyone infer from this quotation that one of my goals is to maintain or strengthen societal hierarchies, let me clearly state my opposition to the

misuses to which evolutionary theories have been put. That said, I don't think one should embrace a theory like the Blank Slate when it seems obviously wrong. Nor should one ignore the study of genetics simply because it might lend weight to the idea that there are natural differences between people. Indeed, a more careful reading of the literature suggests that we have much more in common – our human nature – than the obvious differences (like gender, religion, or skin color) would suggest.

None of this – or what follows – should be read as solving the nature/nurture debate in favor of nature alone, for that is not at all my intention. Indeed, all of this talk about human nature does not invalidate the obvious importance of environmental factors to human behavior; it only suggests that the Blank Slate – the idea that humans are entirely cultural beings whose only nature is a malleable one – does not make the most sense, especially in the face of modern genetics and neuroscience. As Pinker notes:

> In some cases, an extreme environmentalist explanation is correct: which language you speak is an obvious example, and differences among races and ethnic groups in test scores may be another. In other cases, such as certain inherited neurological disorders, an extreme hereditarian explanation is correct. In most cases the correct explanation will invoke a complex interaction between heredity and environment: culture is crucial, but culture could not exist without mental faculties that allow humans to create and learn culture to begin with.[14]

In short, culture still counts for a lot and there is variation among cultures – but the existence of culture requires a common human nature that stems from our brains and the genes that make them.

That caveat out of the way, one thing that still remains to be considered is exactly what about the Blank Slate is so wrong. There are myriad problems with the doctrine of the Blank Slate, but I will limit my critique to only two of the most obvious.[15] The first is that *"The mind cannot be a blank slate, because blank slates don't do anything."*[16] While it remains unclear exactly how much software comes with our mental hardware, it is obvious that some software is needed in order for us to perform the complex functions of which we are capable. As Pinker notes:

> Cognitive modelers have found that mundane challenges like walking around furniture, understanding a sentence, recalling a fact, or guessing someone's intentions are formidable engineering problems.... The suggestion that they can be solved by a lump of Silly Putty that is passively molded by something called "culture" just doesn't cut the mustard.[17]

We know that humans learn a great deal over the course of a lifetime, but clearly "there can be no learning without the innate circuitry to do the

learning."[18] This is not a particularly new idea; it dates back at least as far as Leibniz, whose critique of Locke's theory of human understanding was that "There is nothing in the intellect that was not first in the senses ... except the intellect itself."[19]

The second problem is based on the idea of natural selection and points out that "The mind was forged in Darwinian competition, and an inert medium would have been outperformed by rivals outfitted with high technology."[20] If the human mind were simply a Blank Slate, we would have fallen victim to all sorts of problems and likely would not have made it very far. There are a great many challenges in the world, not the least of which involve maintaining ourselves, and we desperately need our big, complex brains to accomplish tasks like locating sustenance, fashioning shelter, and avoiding predators. That is, of course, to say nothing of our need to find a suitable mate and successfully produce offspring. An inability to do so spells disaster, not only for ourselves but for our genes – and so the evolutionary importance of a brain that is hard-wired to do these things becomes immediately apparent.

While all of this suggests that the doctrine of the Blank Slate fails to properly explain the human mind, very little has been said about human nature. How do genetics and neuroscience help make that case? Precisely because "the mind no longer looks like a formless lump pounded into shape by culture,"[21] there is more space opened up for an argument about human universals and for the human mind as the ultimate grounding for all that is common to humanity. Indeed, as the arguments against the Blank Slate have implied, the going scientific hypothesis is that "the mind evolved with a universal complex design."[22] Such a mind accounts far better for our ability to learn, as well as our ability to survive (and even thrive) in a quite hostile ancestral environment. Lending weight to this theory, "Child psychologists no longer believe that the world of an infant is a blooming, buzzing confusion, because they have found signs of the basic categories of mind (such as those for objects, people, and tools) in young babies."[23] The mind, it seems, comes equipped with quite a lot of software because waiting for much of it to get loaded – through the learning process – would have unsatisfactory evolutionary consequences. Further, "Archaeologists and paleontologists have found that prehistoric humans were not brutish troglodytes but exercised their minds with art, ritual, trade, violence, cooperation, technology, and symbols."[24]

And while this knowledge is helpful in constructing a picture of the mental hardware that is common to us all, anthropological work on diverse cultures has provided even more evidence to suggest a common human nature that arose as a result of the complex human mind. As Pinker points out, "Hundreds of traits, from fear of snakes to logical operators, from romantic love to humorous insults, from poetry to food taboos, from exchange of goods to mourning the dead, can be found in every society ever documented."[25] Given this information, what sort of

nature are we actually talking about? Quite clearly, it is not one that does the same sort of work as the religious account; it does not suggest that all human life is sacred because each individual bears the divine imprint. Nor is it "a nature that is rigidly programmed, impervious to the input, free of culture, or endowed with the minutiae of every concept and feeling."[26] Instead, it is one that is built on the human mind and, consequently, it cannot even suggest that all humans will always be equipped with it. But that, of course, does not make it any less correct nor does it make it any less a human nature. Indeed, Pinker argues that "it is a nature that is rich enough to take on the demands of seeing, moving, planning, talking, staying alive, making sense of the environment, and negotiating the world of other people."[27] And, as I will argue in the next section, it is rich enough to provide us with a way to talk about the concept of human dignity upon which our contemporary understanding of human rights might stand.

Personal identity and the mind's "I"

I have thus far tried to make a case for deriving human nature from the evolution of the universal complex human mind. Much more needs to be said, however, to demonstrate that the concept of human dignity is part of our hard-wiring. While it would likely be simple enough to suggest that humans – across cultures – understand the concept of dignity, I want to argue that humans have more than an understanding of the concept; we actually *have* the dignity. Since I have been suggesting to this point that, put succinctly, what you see is what you get when it comes to humanity, the challenge is to locate dignity somewhere within us. Bound up with this problem is one that I alluded to very briefly at the end of the previous section, one that a religious vision of human nature does not face. When we ground human nature – and human dignity – in the mind, we might be suggesting that only some human lives – those with properly functioning minds – have our nature and our dignity. Those whose minds have either stopped or haven't begun working might not be included. This will clearly be a troubling conclusion for many and it is one that must be examined fully. Doing so, I believe, will shed a great deal of light on what it means to have dignity and, therefore, what it means to be a person. Perhaps the most useful tool for examining the distinction between those human lives with dignity and those in which dignity is lacking is personal identity theory, about which much has been said in the philosophical literature. I will offer a brief rehearsal of the main approaches to the question of personal identity – psychological and biological – with a view to sorting out what we mean by personhood. My argument, ultimately, is that a variant of the biological approach is more compelling than any of the various psychological approaches to personhood precisely because it affords a place for the concept of dignity in making its case.

As might be expected with such a basic and fundamental question as

what constitutes personhood, there is great deal of disagreement on the answer. By and large, though, the psychological approach has enjoyed pride of place in much of the literature. In describing this mainstream approach, David DeGrazia says that it "comprises various theories that assert that our identity – or continuing existence over time – is (at least partly) a function of psychological continuity."[28] Although there is a good deal of variation within the psychological approach, I will confine my discussion to the standard version here. The standard account of personal identity begins from a very unusual premise: what would happen, theorists ask, if your cerebrum were somehow transplanted into someone else's body? Would you go with your cerebrum into the new body, would you stay in your old body, or would you cease to exist entirely? And what, of course, would happen to your old body once your cerebrum was removed?[29] While all of this is obviously a bit fanciful, there are much more realistic thought experiments that have developed along this line: what would happen to you, for example, if you had a brain injury and, as a result, entered PVS? Would you, in that case, still be yourself or would you cease to exist, despite your body's continued existence? The intuition that drives the psychological approach to personal identity "is the hunch or feeling, the *pull* towards saying, that one survives in the transplant story as the offshoot who gets one's cerebrum."[30] Similarly, in the more practical account, the intuition would be that one's identity does not survive PVS. As Jeff McMahan correctly notes, "a person ceases to exist when it ceases to be the case that there will be someone existing in the future with whom he will be psychologically continuous."[31] While this conclusion seems right to me, I take issue with the reasoning used by adherents of the psychological approach to arrive at it. This reasoning is based on two arguments: "Our identity is a function of psychological continuity and we are essentially persons."[32] The first argument is clear enough from the transplant and PVS thought experiments; this continuity is based either on "*experiential connections*, such as having an experience and later remembering it, or forming an intention and later fulfilling it" or "on the continuation of *basic psychological capacities*."[33] The second argument, DeGrazia explains, is based on "the thesis that we, who are now human persons, are *essentially* persons – beings with the capacity for complex forms of consciousness – and therefore cannot exist at any time without being persons at that time."[34]

There are, in my estimation, many problems that arise from holding these two arguments; in what follows, I will consider two of the most serious. The first problem is that, on the psychological account, none of us was ever a newborn infant, given the argument about psychological continuity and personhood. Clearly, there are times in a human life when psychological continuity does not hold; in thinking about my identity, in other words, the person I am today is not strongly connected to the infant I was. I do not have experiential connections with the infant and the infant does not have the capacity for complex consciousness.[35] From these premises:

> It follows that the two-day-old infant cannot be strongly psychologically connected with itself the day before, that there is therefore no psychological continuity in early infancy, that none of us now is psychologically continuous with a newborn infant, and thus that none of us is now numerically the same individual as a newborn infant.[36]

But, quite obviously, each of us was – at one time – a newborn infant, despite the absence of any strong psychological connections to that infant. Of course, the infant has the capacity to become a person and, in my case, this is the happy story I will tell about my development. But this is quite different from saying that I share some sort of psychological connectedness with this infant – just as it would be odd to say that I am the same person as the fetus from whence I came – and it implies that when I began to exist, in the psychologically continuous manner in which I do, the infant ceased to exist. To get around this difficulty, one might argue that "perhaps the fetus your mother bore did not cease to exist when you came into being, but simply came to share its space and its matter with you."[37] But this yields the second problem with the psychological account.

If one were to argue that the fetus – or the infant – did not cease to exist, one would be committed to the idea that there are two beings existing at the same time within the same body, the human person that is me and the human animal that is not. This second problem with the psychological account, as DeGrazia points out, is that it "has yet to produce a plausible account of the relationship between a person and the human animal associated with her."[38] There is no doubt, I think, that humans are animals; whether we have divine or evolutionary origins, we tend to think of ourselves as either particularly special or clever animals – but animals just the same. On the psychological account, however, we cannot be animals because we are persons. In thinking about the possibility that the infant (the pre-person) shares its matter with me (the person), one necessarily runs into the following problem: "if you are essentially a person, you cannot *be* (identical with) the animal that precedes and may succeed you, as nothing can precede or outlast itself."[39] In other words, if I am essentially a person, then there cannot be a time when I exist and am not a person. If we return to the earlier transplant story, moreover, we see the problem in even sharper focus. When we remove the cerebrum, the animal stays in place but the person is transferred to another body; in this account, the person and the animal are separable and thus the person "could not be that animal: a thing and itself cannot go their separate ways."[40] The argument for separating persons and animals is, in my estimation, the greatest weakness of the psychological account of personal identity.

The biological account, conversely, does not face similar pitfalls and it is, I believe, a far more plausible understanding of human personhood than the psychological account. Put succinctly, the theory states that:

we human persons are essentially living human animals and the criteria for our identity are biological: Human person X at one time and any Y at another time are one and the same being if and only if X's (biological) life is Y's (biological) life.[41]

On this account, we avoid the problems described above because we are human animals – not something that shares space with them – and we can determine when the human animal both came into being and when it ceases to be. Unlike the psychological approach, all of this is grounded in the science of human biology rather than in abstract thought experiments. There are good reasons, after all, to think of ourselves as human animals – not the least of which is that, biologically, we actually are – and Olson argues that this line of thinking does not reduce us to the status of "*mere* animals."[42] Humans are a particular kind of animal, one that is capable of consciousness rather than one that exists because it is conscious. Even though we are not anything more special than that – not, for example, the rational animal or the thoughtful animal – this is nothing about which to feel ashamed. My personal identity is bound up with my being this sort of animal and I remain who I am so long as that animal lives. For Olson, then:

> A human vegetable that can be kept alive with a feeding tube is still a living human animal, even though it no longer has any mental functions. A four-week-old human embryo is also a living human animal: it has its own DNA, its own closed circulatory system, its own blood type, its own immune system, and the primitive beginnings of its own nervous system.[43]

It is a mistake, on this account, to think that I am somehow different from the animals described in these situations.

And yet, in my estimation, Olson does not spend nearly enough time discussing how consciousness fits into his theory. He does make the argument that a consequence of the biological view is that we are nothing but our bodies, but – contrary to those who suggest, for example, that it is me and not my body that is happy or sad – this does not mean we are incapable of rational thought or feelings. On this point, Olson is exactly right: our bodies *are* doing the thinking, despite the awkwardness of language that arises from saying something like, "My brain thought about your question from the other day." The trouble for Olson arises when all of this theorizing is put into practice. Because Olson is making an argument about the priority of the whole body to personhood, I want to argue that his biological account fails to properly negotiate the difficult terrain that arises at the beginning and end of human lives. All it tell us, as DeGrazia points out, is that:

> We were all mindless fetuses before we became persons, and we might again exist as nonpersons in severe dementia or even as nonsentient

beings in PVS. Thus, like childhood and adulthood, personhood represents a *phase* of our existence rather than an essential property.[44]

What we need to know, at this point, is what it means to be a person because, on my reading, there is a fundamental difference between human persons and human animals even though the two are nearly the same biologically. In other words, I want to argue that the fetus that I once was and the person I now am are different in some important respect – even though they are biologically the same animal at two different stages of development. For Olson, though, this difference simply does not exist – or it exists entirely in our heads. It will be helpful to quote Olson at some length on this point:

> Some find it strange to say that *I* was once an unthinking embryo. "I" is a personal pronoun, they point out, and calling something by a personal pronoun, unless we are speaking loosely, as we do with ships and pets, implies that it is a person, that is, a rational, self-conscious being. The embryo is not an "I", but an "it". So we cannot sensibly ask *who* a fetus is, since that is to ask which person it is, and a fetus is not a person . . . . The problem of how to talk about the way I was or may come to be when not a person is no more serious than the problem of how to talk about someone who has had or is planning a sex change operation. When a man has such an operation, we refer to him afterwards as "she", and talk about the things she did when she was a man. While this may be grammatically awkward, it is hardly reason to think that it is impossible to change one's gender. And what goes for "he" and "she", I think, goes for "I" and "it" as well.[45]

While Olson is right to point out the grammatical difficulty, doing so highlights the category mistake he is making. Unless by "woman" we mean a human being with a vagina instead of a penis, a man who undergoes a sex change operation does not actually *become* a woman; he has simply altered his sexual characteristics through surgery and hormone therapy. Similarly, a human fetus is one thing and a human person quite another, even though the former can (and quite often does) become the latter.

It is a mistake, then, to claim – as Olson does – that *we* were embryos, despite my agreement with his argument that we are the same biological animals that began as our embryos. He is right to note that:

> a genuine human embryo – the multicellular organism that later becomes a fetus, an infant, and an adult – comes into being about sixteen days after fertilization, when the cells that develop into the fetus (as opposed to the placenta) become specialized and begin to grow and function in a coordinated manner.[46]

He is wrong, however, to suggest that "you are the organism that comes into being then."[47] You and the embryo are the same biological animal, but *you* will not come into being until much later in the process of fetal development. I want to depart from Olson's biological account here, deny that personhood is bound up with whole-brain function (cerebrum and brainstem), and claim instead that identity is a direct result of higher-brain function.[48] The "you" that we've been talking about is, after all, entirely dependent on higher-brain function and, therefore, you and the embryo that will become you cannot be the same thing. In attempting this argument, haven't I fallen back into the trouble, discussed earlier, of thinking that I am not my animal? Happily, I think I can avoid this problem because I don't want to dispute the connection between myself as an adult and the embryo that became that adult. I am not suggesting that I – the human animal – was never an embryo; quite clearly, I was. Instead, I am arguing that the key distinguishing characteristic about the human animal that I am, namely the "I," was not present at that early stage of development. But when and how does the "I" arise? The remaining sections of this chapter will consider these two questions; although there are a great many possible answers, I find only one to be particularly compelling. I will look closely at some of the possible avenues to personhood – language, autonomous agency, and basic needs – and argue that each is a necessary characteristic, but that they are insufficient without one another. Indeed, I ultimately argue for the primacy of dignity in differentiating between human animals and human persons precisely because it serves to unite these various components of personhood.

Human animals and human persons

To return to the example with which we began, it seems to me that the PVS patient and the person who became that patient are different in many ways; similarly, I want to argue that a fetus at, say, twelve weeks of gestation is quite different from the born human person that began life as that fetus. In both cases – the fetus and the PVS patient – personhood either hasn't yet been attained or has been lost. That is all well and good, so long as a compelling case can be made for what constitutes personhood. In what ways then are PVS patients and fetuses so different from persons? Turning to the first possible source of personhood, we might say that human persons are able to use language to communicate with one another (and with themselves) and human animals are not. Might it be the case, then, that the use of language accounts for personhood? This is a plausible possibility, for as Pinker suggests, "Of all the faculties that go into the piece of work called man, language may be the most awe-inspiring."[49] The ability to communicate, to express thoughts and feelings, is of obvious importance not just to personhood but also to the evolution of human society. Robert Wright argues, for example, that "Learning by observing,

teaching by threatening, and using sticks and stones can do a lot for a culture, but if your species hopes to get to the point of attending operas and anthropology lectures, the biological infrastructure for language is a must."[50]

Clearly, human persons make great use of language – but doing so relies on much more than just the ability to string words together. Language, ultimately, is only as useful as the human mind behind it. Pinker points out that:

> we know how to interpret ambiguous headlines such as "Kids Make Nutritious Snacks," "Prostitutes Appeal to Pope," and "British Left Waffles on Falkland Islands," because we effortlessly apply our background knowledge about the kinds of things that people are likely to convey in newspapers. Indeed, the very existence of ambiguous sentences, in which one string of words expresses two thoughts, proves that thoughts are not the same thing as strings of words.[51]

Behind our ability to speak are a host of mental processes that we typically take for granted.[52] And, of course, if our brains stop working properly we lose – among many other things – our ability to use language. That said, it seems to me impossible that the use of language can mark the distinction between human animals and human persons. For while almost all of the avenues under consideration also rely on the human mind, the use of language is itself not distinctly human. Basic language skills abound in other species:

> Bees convey the location of flowers with their famous waggle dance. Ground squirrels emit a warning call on sighting a predator, as do many birds. Ants send out chemicals that mean everything from "Invaders!" to "Food!" ... East African vervet monkeys have several warning calls, depending on the predator; one means "snake," one means "eagle," one means "leopard," and each elicits an apt response."[53]

On the whole, then, it seems that the use of language cannot properly account for the separation that exists between Terri Schiavo and the PVS patient that once was Terri Schiavo. For if it were sufficient we might conclude that East African vervet monkeys should also properly be recognized as human persons, given their ability to use "a symbolic code by which information is transmitted from one organism to another."[54] The monkeys, after all, are better able to communicate with one another than are the PVS patients. While it might make sense at some point to make this case, for the moment there are very few who go so far as to suggest that these monkeys are persons like us. But this is really only half of the issue; far more important is that there are human persons who are unable to use

language. Consider the case of Helen Keller, who grew up both blind and deaf, and whose education, portrayed in William Gibson's *The Miracle Worker*, illustrates clearly the problem with using language skills to delineate personhood. Prior to her introduction to sign language, Keller was almost completely in her own world, unable to communicate:

> As a result of their intense frustrations at not being able to communicate, deaf-blind children ... throw temper tantrums, scratching, biting, hitting, and pinching other people. Helen Keller was no exception. No one had the heart to discipline her. She was willful and quick-tempered by nature and tyrannized the household.[55]

Despite her inability to use language until painstakingly taught, Keller – and others in her position – are quite clearly human persons, with the full complement of emotions, thoughts, feelings, and needs. Like any other person, those without language are very different from, say, a fetus or PVS patient. Their inability to communicate has little to do with their desire to do so, and this separates them from human animals, who lack desires altogether. This brings us, then, to the second possibility described above, namely that the distinguishing feature of personhood is autonomous human agency.

The notion that personhood is contingent on autonomous agency has been a prominent feature of the philosophical landscape at least since Kant, who argued that the key feature of autonomy was the ability to act in conformity to duty. In obeying laws that we legislate for ourselves – that we arrive at through the use of reason – we are able to master our inclinations, passions, and, needs. Only in doing so are we able to demonstrate a freedom of will.[56] Since Kant, the literature on autonomous agency has grown extensively and a great deal of liberal democratic theory today is concerned with how the political community ought to respect the various choices of the autonomous agent and when those choices might be constrained. In the main, then, we all understand the basic principle of autonomy and we all see ourselves as autonomous agents. Peter Singer puts the point succinctly:

> By "autonomy" is meant the capacity to choose, to make and act on one's own decisions. Rational and self-conscious beings presumably have this ability, whereas beings who cannot consider the alternatives open to them are not capable of choosing in the required sense and hence cannot be autonomous.[57]

There is no doubt that an important feature of personhood is agency, and that PVS patients and fetuses are fundamentally not autonomous agents. I weigh various options and then make choices for myself; this – in large part – makes me the person I am. Were I no longer capable of autonomous agency, you might safely say that I was no longer the same person.

Having said that, I want to argue that – in fact – autonomous agency is not the distinguishing feature of personhood. Indeed, I will go so far as to say that, despite our sense of the importance of autonomy, we are simply not the autonomous agents we think we are. Pinker suggests that:

> Agents are recognized by their ability to violate intuitive physics by starting, stopping, swerving, or speeding up without an external nudge, especially when they persistently approach or avoid some other object. The agents are thought to have an internal and renewable source of energy, force, impetus, or oomph, which they use to propel themselves, usually in service of a goal.... Some self-propelled things, like cars and windup dolls, are artifacts. And many agents do not merely approach and avoid goals but act out of beliefs and desires; that is, they have minds.[58]

I have no problem with this description of agency, nor do I want to suggest that there is any mistake in concluding that agents are goal-directed because they have minds. My problem with the concept of autonomous agency, in fact, is the same as Pinker's and I draw much of my critique of agency from his treatment in *The Blank Slate*. That is, it seems to me that the entire enterprise is a mistaken one: in thinking of ourselves as autonomous agents, we ignore a great deal of information about human biology and posit a creative fiction instead. While it is tempting to think of ourselves as autonomous choosers, doing so seems to me to be an error; there is, in fact, much evidence to the contrary.

To say that *homo sapiens* have minds, as Pinker does, is not the same as saying that *homo sapiens* are autonomous agents. Indeed, the mind does an incredible amount of work, but we go too far in saying that we make choices and the mind puts those choices into action. The reason for my hesitation is that doing so implies a self, a chooser, and there is no evidence that such a thing exists within the human body. What we know, instead, is not far from the Hobbesian argument "that 'reasoning is but reckoning'.... Perception, memory, imagery, reasoning, decision making, language, and motor control are being studied in the lab and successfully modeled as computational paraphernalia such as rules, strings, matrices, pointers, lists, files, trees, arrays, loops, propositions, and networks."[59] Of course, there remains an incredible amount of resistance to arguments of this sort. Dispatching with the tried and true notions of the self or the soul is not an easy task; what happens, after all, when one accepts that Cartesian mind/body dualism is mistaken, that there is no ghost in the machine, that the machine is running itself? Pinker is right when he says that:

> It can indeed be upsetting to think of ourselves as glorified gears and springs. Machines are insensate, built to be used, and disposable; humans are sentient, possessing of dignity and rights, and infinitely

precious. A machine has some workaday purpose, such as grinding grain or sharpening pencils; a human being has higher purposes, such as love, worship, good works, and the creation of knowledge and beauty. The behavior of machines is determined by the ineluctable laws of physics and chemistry; the behavior of people is freely chosen. With choice comes freedom, and therefore optimism about our possibilities for the future. With choice also comes responsibility, which allows us to hold people accountable for their actions. And of course if the mind is separate from the body, it can continue to exist when the body breaks down, and our thoughts and pleasures will not someday be snuffed out forever.[60]

We want very much to suggest that we are more than the sum of our parts, that what counts about us are our souls, or that we are rational choosers. "It is still tempting to think of the brain as it was shown in old educational cartoons, as a control panel with gauges and levers operated by a user – the self, the soul, the ghost, the person, the 'me,'" as Pinker says. "But cognitive neuroscience is showing that the self, too, is just another network of brain systems."[61]

In the end, the argument is that the brain is put together in a certain way, that its being put together in that manner is the result of genetic programming, and that – having been put together in such a manner – "every aspect of our mental lives depends entirely on the physiological events in the tissues of the brain."[62] This is not the same as suggesting that human behavior is wholly determined by our genes, that we are incapable of learning, or that we have no choices to make for ourselves. As Pinker argues:

> The idea from the cognitive revolution that the mind is a system of universal, generative computational modules obliterates the way that debates on human nature have been framed for centuries. It is now simply misguided to ask whether humans are flexible or programmed.... Humans behave flexibly *because* they are programmed: their minds are packed with combinational software that can generate an unlimited set of thoughts and behavior.[63]

What all of this means is not always entirely clear. Many people – even respected scientists – have suggested that subscribing to this view is akin to choosing Nazism over liberal democracy. For example, in response to E.O. Wilson's *Sociobiology*, which included "the hypothesis that some universals (including the moral sense) may come from a human nature shaped by natural selection,"[64] renowned experts on evolution like paleontologist Stephen Jay Gould and geneticist Richard Lewontin attached their signatures to a letter in the *New York Review of Books* denouncing Wilson's book. According to the letter:

> The reason for the survival of these recurrent determinist theories is that they consistently tend to provide a genetic justification of the *status quo* and of existing privileges for certain groups according to class, race, or sex.... These theories provided an important basis for the enactment of sterilization laws and restrictive immigration laws by the United States between 1910 and 1930 and also for the eugenics policies which led to the establishment of gas chambers in Nazi Germany.[65]

Of course, *Sociobiology* did not include the suggestion that anyone be sterilized or that genocide be committed; instead, scientists like Gould and Lewontin argued that this sort of thinking was uncomfortably deterministic and that "its adherents claim ... that the details of present and past social arrangements are the inevitable manifestations of the specific action of genes."[66]

The fact that we might feel a bit unnerved to know so much about ourselves, however, is not the same as arguing that what we now know is wrong. To take two examples:

> Gay men are likely to have a smaller third interstitial nucleus in the anterior hypothalamus, a nucleus known to have a role in sex differences. And convicted murderers and other violent, antisocial people are likely to have a smaller and less active prefrontal cortex, the part of the brain that governs decision making and inhibits impulses.[67]

Knowing these things does not mean that we should murder gay men or lock up everyone with a smaller prefrontal cortex; in fact, thinking carefully about them might encourage us to stop thinking of homosexuals as having made a bad lifestyle choice and to seek new ways of understanding violence (and the violent) in our society. Indeed, I think Pinker is most persuasive on this score, arguing that "The megalomania of the genes does not mean that benevolence and cooperation cannot evolve, any more than the law of gravity proves that flight cannot evolve. It means only that benevolence, like flight, is a special state of affairs in need of an explanation, not something that just happens."[68] Charges of determinism and racism aside, the evidence against the existence of a ghost in the machine seems clear. And with the ghost gone, it becomes increasingly difficult to argue that autonomous agency accounts for the difference between persons and non-persons.

That said, there are many who will argue that the differences between the PVS patient, the fetus, and myself are minimal in comparison to the relevant similarities, or that making distinctions of the kind I want to make will lead inexorably down a slippery slope that ignores "the moral and spiritual worth of individuals within the human species."[69] By and large, those who oppose my proposed distinction do so on the grounds

that all human life is sacred and that assigning more or less value to some life will yield public policy outcomes that generally disrespect human life. In response to the Schiavo case, for example, George W. Bush labeled himself an adherent of this more respectful position, saying "we should be on the side of defending life at all stages, and that includes people that are incapacitated or people with disabilities."[70] Perhaps one of the clearest and most thoughtful representatives of this viewpoint within the academy is Timothy P. Jackson.

According to Jackson, the problem with creating a distinction between human animals and human persons is that the dichotomy is a false one. Following the Judeo-Christian tradition, he argues that all human life is sacred and that elevating personhood ignores what is most important about humans. Indeed, it is simply a mistake to sort out, as I have here, when some humans start or stop using language or making autonomous choices because doing so ignores the sanctity of all human life. As Jackson points out, "Sanctity, what the Christian tradition calls 'being made in the Image of God,' is most fundamentally the ability to give or receive loving care (*agape*). As such, sanctity is both pre- and post-personal, something coextensive with humanity itself."[71] On this reading, human lives are honored or valued for a far more basic reason, one that has much less to do with any human capabilities and much more to do with an external source of value. Rather than focusing on achieving personhood, Jackson argues that humans need not do anything or reach any particular platform – like language usage or autonomy – in order to warrant a high standard of respect. Because "sanctity is closely allied with agapic love, construed as willing the good for someone independently of merit," it inheres in every human irrespective of traditional benchmarks of personhood.[72] The reason for this is that humanity is defined by needs, most importantly the need for loving care. The ultimate consequence of this way of thinking about humanity, of course, is that there is nothing particularly special about personhood. And Jackson says as much:

> Personhood does not spontaneously generate ... nor, by Christian lights, is individual personhood an end in itself (certainly not the highest). The rational agency associated with autonomous persons is to be used for the sake of ends outside of and larger than the self.[73]

Instead of focusing on the individual freedom that arises from rationality or autonomy, the hallmark of liberal democracy since its inception, this sort of argument centers around the basic neediness of all humans, those who we see as agents and those who we do not. For Jackson, "Even rational individuals making autonomous choices are not without profound dependencies on one another and on God."[74] We need one another – and God, on this reading – to successfully make our way in this world and this is the central feature of who *we* are.

The trouble for Jackson, on my reading, is two-fold. First, I am not convinced that he has done enough work to demonstrate that our need for loving care – and our ability to benefit from it – is what defines us. Second, I remain unconvinced that human animals – fetuses and PVS patients – are the beneficiaries of loving care in the way that Jackson suggests. He argues:

> Because it makes sense to talk of non-voluntary development and noncognitive well-being, fetuses, babes in arms, the frail elderly, as well as the permanently demented may all be said to benefit from loving care. Although they are not "rational persons," ... these human beings have needs and capabilities that can be addressed constructively by others and/or by God.[75]

Clearly, it seems impossible to comment on whether their needs and capabilities can be or are being addressed by God. But in what sense do human animals benefit from our care? The only possible answer is the one that Jackson mentions. They are capable of noncognitive well-being, which might mean, for example, that their bodies benefit from the nourishment we provide, even though – since they are no longer persons – they have no understanding or recognition that they are benefiting. Insofar as the body remains alive, however, Jackson might argue that "They can be served as fellow creatures, and this service redounds to both their and others' good."[76] My argument is that to benefit from loving care, to have needs and capabilities, is to be a human person; it is, in short, to recognize one's own needs and to understand that one is the recipient of loving care. Put another way, only persons are properly capable of benefiting from loving care – though all beings can obviously be cared for – because non-persons lack an understanding of their needs, which attend brain function. Plants, for example, need water and we care for them by watering them; it is a mistake, however, to suggest that a plant suffers without water in the same way that a person suffers without water. While the plant will likely die if we fail to water it, there is no awareness of death for the plant. The biggest difficulty with substituting the PVS patient for the plant in this example is that the PVS patient *was once* a person. As Kalkut and Dubler correctly state, "For a family who has lost a loved one, often from an acute illness or terrible accident, it is unspeakably difficult to accept that this warm body with a heartbeat is lifeless."[77] It remains for me to address the complications implied by this quotation, namely how the PVS patient can be both clearly alive – as mentioned above – but also lifeless. The answer, I argue, can be found in considering the definitions of life and death; looking at these definitions will yield the distinctive feature that makes only some of us persons: dignity.

Dignity and "the boundaries of our existence"

As anyone who keeps abreast of the news knows, there is an on-going and impassioned debate about euthanasia, physician-assisted suicide, and the end of life. While it is markedly less heated than the debate about abortion and the beginning of life, the two are directly related and considering one sheds a great deal of light on the other. In order to reach some sort of conclusion, we need to know at what point someone dies. Two schools of thought exist when it comes to this question: one that argues that living is properly associated with whole-brain activity and one that affords pride of place to higher-brain function. The former, to which Olson belongs, suggests that we are human animals and our continued existence is quite clear: so long as we are breathing and our heart is pumping, we are living. These functions are regulated by the brainstem, rather than the cerebrum, and so the PVS patient – whose cerebrum is fundamentally injured – remains alive. I agree with this assessment; the patient is still clearly alive, if we define life in the way that whole-brain adherents do. The trouble, though, is that the person who went into the hospital is no longer in existence. And that is why death seems to actually occur with higher-brain death: "The patient whose upper brain is lost has, after all, a life just as low in quality as that of the patient whose whole brain is gone."[78] All the things that made Terri Schiavo, for example, the person she was have left the body of the PVS patient that was Terri Schiavo. These things are far more integral to our conception of personhood – and of life itself – than the mere animal functioning of brainstem, heart, and lungs (all of which can be duplicated by machine).[79] What cannot be duplicated or replaced, however, is the sense of self, the "I" that I want to argue makes us persons and from which human dignity is derived.

The "I" is, in my estimation, the most important factor in determining personhood because it is at the heart of identity; without a sense of self, we would be incapable of using language self-reflexively, of thinking of ourselves as autonomous, or of having basic needs. As Jackson notes, "*The Oxford English Dictionary* observes [that] combining 'self-' with another word often means 'expressing reflexive action, automatic or independent action.' The self both thinks and acts, both in relations to others and reflexively."[80] In positing such a self – and arguing for its central role in personhood – haven't I simply aligned myself with the psychological approach to identity that I dismissed earlier as incorrect? My sense is that I have not. My solution to the problem of personal identity is a biological one, rather than a psychological one, because my argument is that the self arises from the way the brain works; it is a higher brain function, rather than a psychological feature of the way the mind works. But how do we derive dignity from a sense of self?

I do not want to suggest that we achieve dignity through rational thought or action, i.e., that we earn our dignity in the way that Kant

suggests; instead, my argument is that dignity arises from a different sort of higher-brain function. In particular, dignity is a function of our self-consciousness, our ability to talk and think about ourselves. As noted in the previous chapter, the Greek δόξα, from which dignity is derived, is defined as "the opinion which others have of one, estimation, repute."[81] While this ancient concept was thought to rely on the way we were perceived by others, I want to argue that of far greater importance is the opinion we have of ourselves and, in particular, the stories we tell about ourselves. My dignity is bound up with my answer to the most fundamental identity question, "Who am I? [which] will normally address what is most salient in one's sense of self."[82] This narrative identity, DeGrazia notes, "involves our self-conceptions, our sense of what is most important to who we are."[83] Bound up with my narrative identity is the sense that I can make something of myself; this ability to posit a future that I have a hand in shaping can be traced back at least as far as Nietzsche and has been updated by contemporary theorists like Ronald Dworkin – discussed in the previous chapter – and Richard Rorty, the subject of the next chapter. DeGrazia puts this especially cogently: "Much of what matters (to most of us, anyway) is our continuing existence *as persons* – beings with the capacity for complex forms of consciousness – with unfolding self-narratives and, if possible, success in self-creation."[84]

On this understanding, it is clear that the PVS patient is not Terri Schiavo, though the two are the same biological animal. The person who was Terri Schiavo, so this argument goes, died when her cerebral cortex, the self-creating part of her brain, stopped functioning. Peter Singer explains:

> we can tell in which sections of the brain that blood is still flowing, and in which it is not flowing. If blood is not flowing to the cortex, then – even though the brain stem might still be functioning and so the patient would not be brain dead – the patient would be 'cortically dead' and would never recover consciousness.[85]

The huge row that surrounded Michael Schiavo's decision to remove the life-sustaining feeding tube from the PVS patient was, then, misguided on this reading because Terri Schiavo was no longer alive and, absent personhood, the PVS patient has no interests and is not the bearer of dignity. Of course, the uproar makes a great deal of sense under the assumption that – regardless of consciousness – the PVS patient is still a human animal and, consequently, is worthy of respect and care. Similarly, it makes a great deal of sense if one argues that the PVS patient is a beloved child of God and, therefore, is sacred. These positions are coherent ones, but they are very different from arguing – as many did – that *Terri* was alive and had rights.[86]

On the opposite end of the spectrum, the fetus we have been discussing throughout this chapter presents another puzzle to be solved. At what

point, one might justifiably wonder, does a fetus gain a right to life: conception, viability, birth, or some other time? Famously, Peter Singer has argued "that since no fetus is a person no fetus has the same claim to life as a person."[87] On this point, he and I are in agreement: fetuses are not self-conscious, cannot engage in self-creation, and are not bearers of dignity. But Singer goes much further:

> Now it must be admitted that these arguments apply to the newborn baby as much as to the fetus. A week-old baby is not a rational and self-conscious being, and there are many nonhuman animals whose rationality, self-consciousness, awareness, capacity to feel, and so on, exceed that of a human baby a week or a month old. If the fetus does not have the same claim to life as a person, it appears that the newborn baby does not either.[88]

The reason, on my reading, that Singer goes too far with his suggestion about the permissibility of infanticide is that he puts too much weight on the psychological aspect of the human mind and not enough on the biological. It might well be the case, as argued above, that we who are persons do not have strong psychological connections to the infants we were, but – as yet – we aren't certain. We know, however, that healthy infants' brains display organized cortical brain activity (OCBA) and we can measure both the beginning and ending of this "electrical activity in the cerebral cortex of the sort that produces recognizable EEG readings."[89] Given that, David Boonin's argument for using OCBA as the standard by which to judge whether a fetus is a person makes a good deal of sense. If OCBA is not present, we would be hard pressed to make a case for the self-creative feature of the human mind. For the cerebral cortex must be working in an organized manner before anyone can claim that the brain has created the sense of self that is the key feature of personhood.

If we are drawing lines – and with questions of birth and death it often appears that we must – then the line should be drawn at the earliest stage possible as a precaution. With regard to self-consciousness and dignity, it seems to me that Boonin's line allows much less room for error than Singer's. Although it might very well be the case that selfhood (as we understand it) begins in infancy – and with it, dignity and personhood – Boonin suggests that we draw the line at the twenty-fifth week of pregnancy; the reason is that there is "ample evidence to suggest that [OCBA begins] to occur sometime between the 25th and 32nd week."[90] We might push the line back a bit, however, and adopt an even more conservative estimate about OCBA by drawing the line at twenty weeks; as Boonin concedes:

> Burgess and Tawia identify 20 weeks of gestation as "the most conservative location we could plausibly advocate" as the beginning of

what they call "cortical birth," because it is at this point that "the first 'puddle' of cortical electrical activity" of an "extremely rudimentary nature" begins to appear in brief spurts.[91]

Adopting this position – rather than Singer's – would be to argue for a fetal right to life at the twentieth week of pregnancy (the earliest time at which it is possible for OCBA to occur) and, of course, to prohibit things like infanticide. This is, of course, a somewhat radical position, as it suggests that the ruling in *Roe* v. *Wade* – already controversial enough – needs to be reconsidered in favor of limiting some abortions. While many would argue that redrawing this line is wildly problematic, those who would most feel the effect of doing so are those who suggest that fetuses are persons with rights from the moment of conception, for Boonin notes that "even if we push back the gray area from 25 weeks to 20 weeks, it will still turn out that 99 percent of abortions take place before the fetus acquires a right to life."[92] In the end, tying the permissibility of abortion to the absence of organized cortical brain activity seems to have a limited effect on public policy and squares a difficult issue with the non-religious understanding of personhood I have been advancing.

Of course, none of this should be read as suggesting that there is some "I" inside my head, for that would be to fall back onto the untenable position, discussed earlier, of the ghost in the machine. It is often difficult to talk about the "I" without sounding like I am referring to the self that is hard at work inside me, but this is not what I have in mind when I refer to self-consciousness as the source of human dignity. As Pinker suggests:

> Cognitive neuroscientists have not only exorcised the ghost [in the machine] but have shown that the brain does not even have a part that does exactly what the ghost is supposed to do: review all the facts and make a decision for the rest of the brain to carry out. Each of us feels that there is a single "I" in control. But that is an illusion that the brain works hard to produce. . . . The brain does have supervisory systems in the prefrontal lobes and anterior cingulated cortex, which can push the buttons of behavior and override habits and urges. But those systems are gadgets with specific quirks and limitations; they are not implementations of the rational free agent traditionally identified with the soul or the self.[93]

I want to argue, with Pinker, that the existence of the "I" is an evolutionary strategy developed by my genes to make my brain a better, more clever one. But knowing that there is no "I" in the center of my brain, pulling levers and adjusting dials, does not alter or invalidate my feeling of selfhood. And, as I have argued, it is this feeling that accounts for my having dignity and being a person. It is, in my estimation, the feature that separates human persons from human animals and, so far as we know, from all other animals.

5 Does might make human rights?

Sympathy, solidarity, and subjectivity in Richard Rorty's final vocabulary

The question of whether there is some feature or quality inherent in human beings from which our rights spring is central to any attempt at understanding human rights claims. As Michael Perry notes:

> The fundamental challenge to each and every human rights claim – in particular, to each and every claim about what ought not to be done to any human being or what ought to be done for every human being – is a demand for reasons.[1]

For Richard Rorty, however, this demand for reasons is symptomatic of a deep desire, one that is at the heart of the Enlightenment project and can be traced back as far as the earliest priests and philosophers:

> They were going to explain to us the ultimate locus of power, the nature of reality, the conditions of the possibility of experience. They would thereby inform us what we really are, what we are compelled to be by powers not ourselves. They would exhibit the stamp which had been impressed on *all* of us. This impress would not be blind, because it would not be a matter of chance, a mere contingency. It would be necessary, essential, telic, constitutive of what it is to be a human.[2]

Today, Rorty argues, this desire is an outmoded – but firmly entrenched – one;[3] despite Nietzsche's suggestion that we give up "the idea of finding a single context for all human lives,"[4] most people are not anxious to abandon the possibility of an objective truth and many philosophers are nervous about what might result should they do so.[5] That said, Rorty believes that because such a foundation does not necessarily exist, philosophy ought not be tasked with its discovery.

Despite these assertions, however, he also notes that in "abandoning the traditional notion of truth, Nietzsche does not abandon the idea of discovering the causes of our being what we are."[6] Rather than "coming to know a truth which was out there (or in here) all the time," Nietzsche "saw self-knowledge as self-creation" and suggests that "coming to know oneself,

confronting one's contingency, tracking one's causes home, is identical with the process of inventing a new language – that is, of thinking up some new metaphors."[7] Indeed, Rorty argues that Nietzsche bases his philosophy on the idea that certain people, those who embrace "mere contingent circumstance"[8] and exert their will nonetheless, could create their own truths about the world they inhabit:

> He hoped that once we realized that Plato's 'true world' was just a fable, we would seek consolation, at the moment of death, not in having transcended the animal condition but in being that peculiar sort of dying animal who, by describing himself in his own terms, had created himself.[9]

Rorty argues that, like Nietzsche, Sigmund Freud believes that there are far more important tasks for individuals to undertake than a search for a single truth. For Freud, the objective is "to sketch a narrative of our development, our idiosyncratic moral struggle, which is far more finely textured, far more custom-tailored to our individual case, than the moral vocabulary which the philosophical tradition offered us."[10] In the end, Rorty argues, "He leaves us with a self which is a tissue of contingencies rather than an at least potentially well-ordered system of faculties."[11]

Like both Nietzsche and Freud, Rorty attempts to enter into an existing debate on his own terms; rather than arguing with Plato and Locke about metaphysics, Rorty insists that the entire discipline is now outdated. For Rorty, "the vocabulary of Enlightenment rationalism, although it was essential to the beginnings of liberal democracy, has become an impediment to the preservation and progress of democratic societies."[12] While this claim is an engaging one, it is also troubling for a great many human rights theorists. Perry, for example, argues that the only intelligible understanding of the idea of human rights is a religious one and that the Nietzschean undermining of religion has serious repercussions for any defense of human rights. He takes clear aim at the nonchalance with which Rorty "has recommended that we simply stop trying to defend the idea of 'human rights.'"[13] Doing as Rorty recommends, Perry (and others) argue, could open the door to any number of illiberal possibilities. That said, it might instead suggest a plausible non-religious grounding for the idea of human rights of the sort that Perry denies.[14] With these stakes in mind, the first section of this chapter will take a detailed look at the Rortyan ideal of liberal irony and the question of whether this sort of irony is a desirable, or even psychologically possible, character trait. The second section brings the disagreement between Rorty and those he refers to as metaphysicians into sharper focus by examining the figure of the illiberal ironist, who is armed with the same tools as his liberal counterpart but reaches the opposite conclusion about human suffering. Finally, the chapter considers the

place of sympathy and solidarity in what I take to be Rorty's answer to his detractors. I ultimately argue that Rorty has been unsuccessful in abandoning metaphysical claims, as he relies on the foundational idea that sympathy and solidarity are natural and universal characteristics of humanity; in doing so, however, Rorty has succeeded in providing an answer to Perry's assertion that "the idea of human rights is ... ineliminably religious"[15] by suggesting a plausible non-religious foundation.[16]

The trouble with irony

Despite his disdain for metaphysics and his embracing of contingency, Rorty should not be thought of as a complete relativist. In fact, he has a very clear formulation of the goods that liberal societies should secure for their citizens; perhaps the two most important items on this list are a guarantee of private self-creation and a general lessening of cruelty. But why should a society of people engage themselves in private self-creation and a public campaign against cruelty, particularly if there can be no recourse to metaphysical concepts like human nature or the common good? Herein lies the problem with philosophers of the Nietzschean tradition: "This is the view that liberal institutions and culture either should not or cannot survive the collapse of the philosophical justification that the Enlightenment provided for them."[17] Steven Kautz, for example, is appalled "that 'there is no *neutral*, noncircular way to defend' liberal ways ... against 'Nazi and Marxist enemies of liberalism'"[18] in Rorty's system. For Rorty, however, the only possible defense of liberalism – and indeed of anything at all – is a revolving, contestable one. Even Rorty's own assertions about the contingency of language, selfhood, and community, he maintains, are circular; this inability to offer irrefutable proof for his own position is nicely internally consistent. For Kautz, the main problem is that it seems impossible for "this new species of liberalism ... [to] sustain the practice of the humane liberal virtues."[19] As Perry noted earlier, the Nietzschean assertion "'thus I willed it,'"[20] so dear to Rorty's process of individual self-creation, leaves open an avenue for "a nasty, illiberal rebellion ... against gentle liberal virtues."[21]

Indeed, for Perry and Kautz, this is the most dangerous aspect of Rorty's theory and also the most difficult to understand. It is dangerous for two reasons; first, it leaves us without a reason for sustaining our own beliefs about the virtues of the contemporary human rights regime. The question becomes:

> why shouldn't those of us who have acquired a fondness for human rights try to disabuse ourselves of that fondness ... at least, why shouldn't we try to moderate that fondness – once it becomes clear that indulging a fondness for human rights can be, politically, economically, militarily, and so forth, a rather costly proposition?[22]

Second – as Kautz notes – it provides no defense against those who do not hold the same beliefs we do about the value of human life. Perry wonders, for example, whether it is

> really enough, when confronted by intellectual or, worse, existential repudiations of human rights, to retreat, *pace* Rorty, into a kind of ethnocentrism – at one point Rorty refers to "our Eurocentric human rights culture" – proclaiming proudly and loudly that although among us late-twentieth-century North Americans and Western Europeans (and perhaps a few others), a great fondness for human rights, or for "the moral point of view", is nothing more [than] a culturally acquired taste, it is *our* acquired taste and we are willing, if necessary, to fight and even die for it?[23]

It is not entirely clear how Rorty would respond to this question but there is certainly something very troubling, however, about saying – with Rorty:

> that when the secret police come, when the torturers violate the innocent, there is nothing to be said to them of the form "There is something within you which you are betraying. Though you embody the practices of a totalitarian society which will endure forever, there is something beyond those practices which condemns you."[24]

This point may emphasize Rorty's greatest weakness: there is little (or nothing) a liberal ironist can do to contest the type of self-creation that leads some people to a life of extreme cruelty.[25] As Perry notes:

> if the fondness for human rights some of us have is, at bottom, nothing more than an acquired taste, what is there to say to those who have not acquired the taste – and who might even have acquired a taste for violating (what we call) human rights – other than, perhaps, "Try it, you'll like it (maybe)"?[26]

While this ironist can certainly assert in a liberal society, as Rorty does, that "cruelty is the worst thing we do,"[27] she has no recourse to stop any potential offender that is an "other" and, consequently, outside of that liberal society.[28] It would seem that only when the people in that "other" society deems cruelty to be the worst thing *they* do as well can Rorty's liberal ironist take action to stop offenses. But what of those proponents of liberalism who live within an "other" society and risk extrajudicial execution, torture, or disappearance at the hands of their fellows (and their government) who disagree about cruelty being the worst thing they do? In these "other" societies around the world, the waiting game played by targeted groups (that of anticipating a time when Western liberals will provide assistance to their cause) seems both interminable and deadly serious.

On the surface, then, Rorty's theory does not seem to be very exportable. Rather, he seems content to work at resolving inequalities within American liberalism while quietly ignoring the various atrocities that occur with frighteningly high frequency elsewhere. I do not think that this is the extent of Rorty's answer, however. His response, bound up with the notion of solidarity, will be considered in greater detail below. To arrive at that argument, we must begin by recognizing the importance, for Rorty, not only of the fact that "contemporary liberal society already contains the institutions for its own improvement,"[29] but also that "more and more people ... are able to recognize the contingency of the vocabulary in which they state their highest hopes – the contingency of their own consciences – and yet have remained faithful to these consciences."[30] Traditional liberals generally balk at the Rortyan notion that:

> what justifies a conception of justice is not its being true to an order antecedent to and given to us, but its congruence with our deeper understanding of ourselves and our aspirations, and our realization that, *given our history and the traditions embedded in our public life,* it is the most reasonable doctrine *for us.*[31]

This position, according to Kautz, leaves liberals with no good reason why people should make "reason, not force, their rule of right,"[32] since it is necessary under Rorty's version of liberalism to "repudiate any appeal to our common human natures, rather than providing a response or to our 'essential humanity,' as a ground of principles of right conduct."[33] Rorty requires individuals to think about whether there exists, for them, a "social good more important than avoiding cruelty," but this begs the question rather than providing a response as to why a society should refrain from using force or being cruel.[34] Indeed, Rorty does not seem to have an adequate response to Kautz on this point.[35] He avoids entirely the language that I have employed here, choosing to take "should" and "ought" out of the pragmatist's vocabulary entirely. Despite removing these two words, however, Rorty's plan for an ironist liberal society is filled with what sound like thinly-veiled moral imperatives. In other words, we might substitute every "is" for an "ought" without doing violence to the position that Rorty advocates. With this in mind, I believe that Rorty provides an answer to Kautz; he wants to prohibit liberals from using force in order to avoid a particular form of cruelty, one that infringes on individual self-creation. And his argument is that liberals ought to refrain from being cruel because that, ultimately, is what stands at the core of liberalism.

Indeed, Rorty asserts that "The social glue holding together the ideal liberal society ... consists in little more than a consensus that the point of social organization is to let everybody have a chance at self-creation to the best of his or her abilities."[36] As I have previously noted, Rorty is unwilling

to base this type of assertion on the foundation of "a view about universally shared human ends, human rights, the nature of rationality, the Good
for Man, nor anything else."[37] Instead, Rorty's distinctly Western (indeed,
American) response to Kautz's argument for the necessity of classical
liberal foundations is simply that:

> without the protection of something like the institutions of bourgeois
> liberal society, people will be less able to work out their private salva-
> tions, create their private self-images, reweave their webs of belief and
> desire in the light of whatever new people and books they happen to
> encounter.[38]

The liberal ironist, however, should not be deterred by the obvious frustration of having to work within a Rortyan, and thus anti-foundationalist,
system to achieve her ends.[39] For Rorty, there is simply no need for the universalistic principles put forward by Plato or Kant, and reiterated by Perry
and Kautz; it is adequate to use our common history as proof of the practical advantage of individual self-creation and "bourgeois" freedoms rather
than demand that all people are born with this type of entitlement.[40]

This important point is not presented as being free of controversy; as
usual, Rorty attempts to anticipate the arguments of his detractors. The
task at hand is to persuade those who question him that Western liberal
human rights are no less defensible simply because they are useful and
because they are ours than they would be if it could be determined that they
were aligned with *"how the world really is."*[41] I submit that he is less successful in this than he is in providing a useful framework from which we
can construct a non-religious defense of these same rights. For Rorty, there
are two main objections to his idea of the "social glue" that holds together
the ideal liberal society: first, "that the ... metaphysical rhetoric of public
life in the democracies is essential to the continuation of free institutions,"
and second "that it is psychologically impossible to be a liberal ironist – to
be someone for whom 'cruelty is the worst thing we do,' and to have no
metaphysical beliefs about what all human beings have in common."[42]

To dispel the suggestion that our society will most likely collapse with
the emergence of liberal irony, "the general adoption of antimetaphysical,
antiessentialist views about the nature of morality and rationality and
human beings,"[43] Rorty looks to the decline of religious faith amongst liberals. Interestingly, contra Nietzsche, a weakening of the belief in an afterlife
has not contributed to the destruction of moral fiber, "social glue," or the
liberal societies that thought themselves hinged on the concept of future
rewards.[44] Indeed, liberalism seems to have benefited from this change, as
an individual postmortem good has transferred easily to a social one:

> whereas belief in an immortal soul kept being buffeted by scientific
> discoveries and by philosophers' attempts to keep pace with natural

science, it is not clear that any shift in scientific or philosophical opinion could hurt the sort of social hope ... that life will eventually be freer, less cruel, more leisured, richer in goods and experiences, not just for our descendants but for everybody's descendants.[45]

This defense is a plausible one and offers nothing surprising to those who have begun to accept the Rortyan ideas of contingency and irony.[46] The interesting twist here, however, is Rorty's final assertion that irony is a necessarily private activity:

> I cannot go on to claim that there could or ought to be a culture whose public rhetoric is *ironist*. I cannot imagine a culture which socialized its youth in such a way as to make them continually dubious about their own process of socialization.[47]

The entire concept of irony necessitates a contrast between public and private.

The manner in which Rorty deals with the first objection to his "social glue" formulation, then, necessitates a convincing answer to the second objection, the "suggestion that the public–private split I am advocating will not work: that no one can divide herself up into a private self-creator and public liberal, that the same person cannot be, in alternate moments, Nietzsche and J.S. Mill."[48] Clearly, the claim of a tension, potentially unresolvable, between liberalism and ironism is a very serious one and it seems to me that Rorty does not provide the answer we need. Recall that liberals, in Rorty's formulation, are "the people who think that cruelty is the worst thing we do"[49] and that ironism "results from awareness of the power of redescription."[50] One cannot, on this reading, be a good liberal and a good ironist all at once. For to be an ironist is to consistently engage in redescriptive projects. But, as "Redescription often humiliates,"[51] good liberals ought not practice such redescription publicly. Indeed, we should be skeptical, at least to some degree, when it comes to those with a penchant for redescription and deconstruction.

Cleverly, Rorty puts forward the possibility that humiliation is not necessarily tied to ironism, despite the potential that exists for humiliation when a final vocabulary is threatened. Indeed, Rorty claims that irony is no more inclined to humiliate than is metaphysics: "The metaphysician also redescribes, even though he does it in the name of reason rather than in the name of the imagination."[52] The difference between the two, however, is that metaphysics gives the impression of empowerment through redescription by offering to show the objective truth to those whose final vocabularies did not previously include it. The ironist, rather than humiliating others through the process of redescription, is simply unable to "offer the same sort of social hope as metaphysicians offer."[53] I remarked that Rorty is clever in this maneuver; indeed, he momentarily

diverts our attention from the original problem: some people may not wish to have their final vocabularies redescribed and it is, therefore, cruel to do so. One cannot be a good liberal and a good ironist all at once. This scenario, then, offers to us a reason for the importance of a split between public and private. The ironist may describe anyone or anything in whatever way she sees fit *privately*, but must – as she is also a liberal – "become aware of all the various ways in which other human beings whom I might act upon can be humiliated."[54] Rorty does a nice job of pointing out the distinction here. Public life need not be distinguished from private life for the metaphysician because he is convinced that he knows, and can share, the truth "about how things really are."[55] For the ironist, who does not have access to the concept of objective truth, public life is characterized by "a certain kind of know-how,"[56] which necessitates learning all she can about what humiliates other people and avoiding these particular actions or redescriptions in public.[57]

While this is a fine, eloquently explained position, I would be remiss if I did not point out that Rorty's reformulation of the second opposition to his concept of "social glue" allows him to duck that opposition entirely. He has not actually defended the notion that ironism and liberalism can co-exist thanks to a split between the public and private realms, but rather that such a split is absolutely necessary *if* the two were ever to co-exist. Indeed, two chapters of *Contingency, Irony, and Solidarity* are devoted to detailing two famous literary creations who embody irony but not liberalism: Nabokov's Humbert Humbert and Orwell's O'Brien.[58] But Rorty is not without an answer – both to the original opposition and also to his reason for including literary examples of famous illiberal ironists. After leveling the playing field by sketching the possibility that metaphysicians could easily face the same charge of humiliation that ironists currently face, Rorty returns to the definition of liberals as "the people who think that cruelty is the worst thing we do."[59] If liberalism can indeed be boiled down to this statement,[60] it seems obvious that liberals would seek to end (or, at the very least, lessen) the cruelty they do. Rorty notes, however, that metaphysicians – particularly those pointing accusatory fingers at liberal ironists who they claim are not doing enough – are concerned only with "answering questions like 'Why not be cruel?' or 'Why be kind?'"[61] Liberal ironists, who face charges of anti-liberal sentiment because of their refusal to answer these questions, are actually better liberals than their accusers. As Rorty explains:

> For public purposes, it does not matter if everybody's final vocabulary is different, as long as there is enough overlap so that everybody has some words with which to express the desirability of entering into other people's fantasies as well as into one's own. But those overlapping words – words like "kindness" or "decency" or "dignity" – do not form a vocabulary which all human beings can reach by reflection

on their natures. Such reflection will not produce anything except a heightened awareness of the possibility of suffering. It will not produce a *reason to care* about suffering. What matters for the liberal ironist is not finding such a reason but making sure that she *notices* suffering when it occurs.[62]

These distinctions between ironists and metaphysicians help to explain why irony should not be called on to further the causes of freedom, equality, or justice. The failure of ironist philosophy to do so, as noted earlier, is a direct result of the expectations, grounded in a metaphysical upbringing, that liberals have of philosophy in general: "If we could get rid of the expectation, liberals would not ask ironist philosophy to do a job which it cannot do, and which it defines itself as unable to do."[63] Rorty's answer, then, is a fairly straightforward one:

I conclude that what the ironist is being blamed for is not an inclination to humiliate but an inability to empower. There is no reason the ironist cannot be a liberal, but she cannot be a "progressive" and "dynamic" liberal in the sense in which liberal metaphysicians sometimes claim to be.[64]

Self-creation and humiliation

While Rorty makes an interesting point with regard to the expectations placed on ironist philosophy, he has only suggested that nothing *prevents* a liberal from also being an ironist. He does give an example, that of "the typical modern intellectual,"[65] and he goes on to argue "that ironist philosophers are private philosophers ... [whose] work is ill-suited to public purposes, of no use to liberals qua liberals."[66] Rorty has in mind, here, "the young Hegel, Nietzsche, Heidegger, and Derrida."[67] This list is a bit unusual, as this group does not immediately call to mind the idea of liberalism; for Rorty, however, Nietzsche and Heidegger present the most compelling picture of the importance of private philosophy:

They are figures whom the rest of us can use as examples and as material in our own attempts to create a new self by writing a bildungsroman about our old self. But as soon as either tries to put forward a view about modern society, or the destiny of Europe, or contemporary politics, he becomes at best vapid, and at worst sadistic.[68]

With that in mind, Rorty goes on to argue that

We should stop trying to combine self-creation and politics, especially if we are liberals.... [L]iberal political discourse would do well to

remain as untheoretical and simpleminded as it looks ..., no matter how sophisticated the discourse of self-creation becomes.[69]

And this prescription can be seen as a sort of prelude to Rorty's decision to dedicate two chapters of *Contingency, Irony, and Solidarity* to illiberal ironist characters, for in an area where philosophy does little – giving voice to those who suffer – literature is capable of doing a great deal. The liberal ironist, as we noted above, needs to gather as much information as possible about humiliation and other existing final vocabularies in order to avoid causing the former through a public redescription of the latter. Literature is the key that grants access to this information:

> Fiction like that of Dickens, Olive Schreiner, or Richard Wright gives us the details about kinds of suffering being endured by people to whom we had previously not attended. Fiction like that of Choderlos de Laclos, Henry James, or Nabokov gives us the details about what sorts of cruelty we ourselves are capable of, and thereby lets us redescribe ourselves.[70]

Is there anything, however, that prevents people from rejecting outright Rorty's claim that "cruelty is the worst thing we do"?[71] Might it not be said, in some societies, that cruelty is actually the *best* thing that people do, that it is the only thing they have in common with one another, or that it is necessary in order to accomplish a desired communal end? Keeping in mind that there is no concept of humanity or universal truth to appeal to, Rorty cannot deny this possibility, nor can he make the claim that all humans qua humans have a certain set of rights which are guaranteed to them. All he can assert is that a small group of people, citizens in liberal societies, have these particular liberties and rights. This, undoubtedly, is the most worrisome aspect of Rorty's theory. It enables foundationalist philosophers to suggest how Rorty might discuss the Holocaust: while it is not something "we" would ever do because of our societal history, perhaps it is something that Germans are inclined to do; we cannot intervene if it were to happen again because it might simply be something useful for them in their society. I do not believe that this would be Rorty's response, if we read him correctly.

Rorty's response to a society that takes cruelty to be its standard relies heavily on the idea of redescription. But would it be possible for a liberal ironist to effectively redescribe Nazism, for example, to persuade practitioners of extreme cruelty and of genocide to embrace liberalism? Or, on the other hand, might a particularly clever, eloquent, imaginative – in short, ironist – Nazi succeed at redescribing liberalism to show that cruelty, as we have already stated, might be the *best* thing for some people to do to others? These questions are taken up by Eric Gander in a particularly interesting response to Rorty's theory. As the illiberal ironist is cer-

tainly the most frightening aspect of Rorty's philosophical system to foundationalist and anti-foundationalist critics alike, Gander focuses on how Rorty would imagine a liberal ironist capable of stopping such a Nazi from constructing a persuasive redescription of liberalism. From the outset, Rorty is engaged in a reformulation of his assignment; rather than 'prove' to the Nazi that being cruel is wrong, he will attempt to change his mind about some of the choices he makes. In Rorty's words:

> If I were assigned the task not of refuting or answering but of *converting* a Nazi ... I could show him how nice things can be in free societies, how horrible things are in the Nazi camps, how the Führer can plausibly be redescribed as an ignorant paranoid rather than as an inspired prophet, how the Treaty of Versailles can be resdescribed as a reasonable compromise rather than a vendetta, and so on.[72]

This reformulation is the basis of one of Gander's two main critiques of Rorty. In his view, "Just as soon as the conversation begins, *Rorty excludes reason*"[73] from his discussion with the Nazi.

Reason, Gander insists, is capable of "showing" the Nazi that some of his most important beliefs contradict other important beliefs. This, though, is simply one more example of a metaphysical conviction and Rorty has always maintained that "There is no *neutral*, noncircular way"[74] for the liberal ironist to demonstrate that one position is right and the other wrong. If he could now 'show' us such a way, he would place himself in a very difficult – even contradictory – position. Instead, Rorty explains that describing various contradictions within Nazism will yield poor results: "attempts at showing the philosophically sophisticated Nazi that he is caught in a logical or pragmatic self-contradiction will simply impel him to construct invidious redescriptions of the presuppositions of the charge of contradiction."[75] So what is there for a liberal ironist to do? In attempting to proceed through this philosophical mess, Rorty might employ a clever maneuver that has worked for him previously: he can point out, against Gander, that metaphysics is no more useful in this case than is liberal irony. The metaphysical hope at stopping Nazi atrocities would be based on some appeal to reason or our common humanity. If, for example, the Nazis could only be made to see the truth of the human condition, they would cease their brutality.[76] Unfortunately, those who are intent on committing genocide are not much interested in listening to sermons about why cruelty against other human beings is wrong, and these types of appeal are easily silenced by a single gunshot. Force quickly wins out over persuasion – even when the truth is involved. This might be why Rorty rejects any attempt to use reason against the ironist Nazi. In the end, Gander finds Rorty's response unconvincing because he believes "we must maintain a minimalist foundationalist political rhetoric that centers on reason."[77] I am also not convinced, but for a very different, distinctly Rortyan, reason.

When Rorty sets out to "convert" the Nazi rather than "refuting" him, we are reminded that much of his writing on liberalism focuses on avoiding cruelty. As I noted earlier, Rorty takes great care to avoid the particular type of cruelty (humiliation) that arises from the redescription of a person's final vocabulary. Unless the redescription of Nazism is a metaphysical one and results in an empowering conversion, the liberal ironist engaging the Nazi runs the risk of humiliating him. If we recall Rorty's original answer to this problem – to learn all we can about ways to avoid this type of humiliation – we are faced with the realization that we must avoid any attempt to convert those who would rather not be converted. What Gander notices about this Rortyan conundrum is quite valuable: "the avoidance of humiliation requires more than simple restraint, more than mere tolerance. It requires *active acceptance*, at some level, of another's final vocabulary."[78] While the liberal ironist is not required to reform her own final vocabulary in order to avoid humiliating others, she must understand what humiliates others and avoid those actions. Based on his own argument, then, Rorty ought not attempt to convert the Nazi at all.

There is a tension here which we must try to resolve based on the seeming necessity of finding a way to deal with the problem of Nazism in Rorty's system. Although it might be important to avoid humiliating the Nazi by redescribing his final vocabulary in order to convert him, we must recall Rorty's belief that liberals attempt, always, to alleviate suffering. What about the suffering they experience when unable to make public their own final vocabularies in the same way the Nazi can? As Gander notes, "all sorts of groups ... *do not want to (or feel they cannot) keep their private vocabularies private*. Indeed, quite a few groups would argue that forcing them to keep their private vocabularies private is both humiliating and oppressive."[79] We have returned, here, to our earlier discussion about the public/private split necessitated by Rorty's ideas concerning cruelty and liberalism. In this case of conflicting final vocabularies, Rorty seems to have an answer ready:

> A lot of things that some of the powerful believe in their hearts – e.g., that men have the right to beat up on women whenever they need to bolster their own self-confidence – are things they can no longer say in public, and can barely admit to themselves. We have a long way to go in this direction, obviously, but I see no better political rhetoric available than the kind that pretends "we" have a virtue even when we do not have it yet. That sort of pretense and rhetoric is just how new and better "we's" get constructed. For what people cannot say in public becomes, eventually, what they cannot say even in private, and then, still later, what they cannot even believe in their hearts.[80]

If we continue to highlight the tension between liberalism and Nazism, the objectionable one of the two vocabularies will become outmoded and

unacceptable publicly and, eventually, privately as well. But what about all of the suffering that might have been alleviated by simply killing the Nazi rather than engaging him in conversation? And, if we persist with our attempt at conversion, what guarantee do we have that the vocabulary we oppose will become passé and not our own? Not only are we without such a guarantee, but we can only hope that the powerful decide not to use force to assure the success of their final vocabularies.

Rorty, however, understands this vocabulary manipulation as good (or, at least, decent) advice on the way to maintain a public/private split and also to fend off the claim that a conversation with our ironist Nazi always results in a lose–lose situation for our liberal ironist. I am not convinced, however, that he has established anything other than a situation wherein proponents of liberalism and Nazism butt heads for a while before they simply part ways, each hopeful that the other will give up his policy of conversational engagement. Both parties have, by this time, experienced the humiliation of having their final vocabularies redescribed in the hope that one will eventually become unpopular and outmoded, but neither has achieved this outcome. Liberals have always liked to imagine themselves incapable of waking one morning as good Party members. Rorty would agree; our particular history and system of values enables us to resist a fascistic redescription of society. The same, however, should also be true of the Nazi – he is as well-equipped to resist redescription as we are. The problem with this scenario is that we can imagine the liberal ironist and the ironist Nazi presenting each other with a list of the various reasons the other is insufferable. Neither seems likely to succeed in converting the other, however, and the suffering of Europe's Jews would continue unabated.

This discussion puts a finer point on a problem presented earlier by Perry and Kautz. Gander correctly points out the potentiality of Weimar's citizens also imagining themselves incapable of succumbing to Hitler's redescription. If they fell victim to Nazism, what will prevent us from following suit when we adopt this policy of engagement with the Nazi? In Rorty's system, the liberal ironist is armed with nothing more than the power of her mind and *chance*, as a liberal society can "make life harder for others only by words, and not deeds."[81] As Gander notes, "If we leave it entirely up to redescriptive chance, we have no more reason for believing we will finally end up a liberal society than for believing we will finally end up a Nazi society."[82] This is as insufficient and desperately frightening of a response for Gander as it was for Kautz and Perry. Because we might be converted by the illiberal ironist's resdescription, Gander quickly attempts to convince us that Rorty has – by allowing us to even engage in conversation with the Nazi – taken us to the very brink of the abyss and that the only way to bring us back is by relying on the foundationalist notion of objective truth. Indeed, he goes so far as to suggest that "If Rorty is correct in what he says, then we liberals should act now to eliminate forcefully the possibility that antiliberals could engage in conversation *with us*."[83]

Further, since Rorty's own conception of liberalism will never allow this type of behavior, Gander concludes that Rorty must, finally, "have *some* faith in Jefferson's claim that 'Truth is...the proper *and sufficient* antagonist to error' and has nothing to fear in a free and open encounter."[84]

Replacing "why" with "how"

I disagree with the avenue by which Gander arrives at his conclusion about Rorty's own version of foundationalism, but I do not dispute that conclusion. Positing that the first answer to the ironist Nazi has not alleviated any suffering whatsoever, I will hypothesize a second way in which Rorty might respond to the Nazi threat. It is, in my opinion, presupposed by Rorty's position throughout *Contingency, Irony, and Solidarity*, and it is explicitly laid out in a more recent article, "Human Rights, Rationality, and Sentimentality." In order to proceed with it, however, we must recognize an important component of Rorty's own final vocabulary, one that has been implicitly understood throughout this chapter: human beings are unique, as compared to other animals, in their ability to engage in self-creation and to experience humiliation.[85] There is, of course, a distinctly universalistic flavor to this statement, but it seems to me that Rorty must ultimately be willing to reject his anti-universalist stance if he wants to proceed from evolutionary principles, as he frequently suggests he does.[86] In this case, the conclusion that Rorty has been implicitly suggesting has to do with the way the human mind works and – as the previous chapter highlighted – scientists who study the brain have been arguing for some time that there is a good deal of evidence suggesting the existence of human universals and a human nature. Rather than adopt a speciesist line here, let me add that it is not impossible – though it might be a bit far-fetched at this point in time – to imagine a time when people will also speak of the ability of dolphins or chimps to imagine entirely new descriptions of the world. Until that time, it seems quite plausible to imagine Rorty speaking of a single, indivisible unit of human rights: the mind.[87]

Rorty utilizes the writing of George Orwell to sketch the ability of those in power to violate our two human rights. With regard to our right to be free from humiliation, he notes:

> O'Brien [in *1984*] reminds us that human beings who have been socialized – socialized in any language, any culture – do share a capacity which other animals lack. They can all be given a special kind of pain: They can all be humiliated by the forcible tearing down of the particular structures of language and belief in which they were socialized (or which they pride themselves on having formed for themselves).[88]

Orwell also provides an example of what happens when our right to self-creation is violated, which highlights its close relationship to humiliation:

Making Winston briefly believe that two plus two equals five serves the same "breaking" function as making him briefly desire that the rats chew through Julia's face rather than his own. But the latter episode differs from the former in being a final, irreversible unmaking. Winston might be able to include the belief that he had once, under odd conditions, believed that two plus two equals five within a coherent story about his character and his life. Temporary irrationality is something around which one can weave a story. But the belief that he once wanted them to *do it to Julia* is not one he can weave a story around. That was why O'Brien saved the rats for the best part, the part in which Winston had to watch himself go to pieces and simultaneously know that he could never pick up those pieces again.[89]

While we may still be unable, in a Rortyan world, to intervene on behalf of those suffering under Nazi oppression with a sweeping appeal to the objective truth about the sacredness of persons, Rorty ought to suggest that we insist on every human being's right to self-creation. This statement, however, may seem a lower bar than any appeal to our common humanity embraced by foundationalist philosophers. Kautz points out an interesting problem, here, when he says that "It does no moral good to abolish the floor of our moral world (our 'humanity') simply because we fear that some foolish individualists may mistake the floor for the ceiling."[90] There *is* something valuable in recognizing our common humanity, but that will only take us so far. As Rorty notes:

> To get whites to be nicer to blacks, males to females, Serbs to Muslims, or straights to gays ... it is of no use whatever to say, with Kant: notice that what you have in common, your humanity, is more important than these trivial differences. For the people we are trying to convince ... are offended by the suggestion that they treat people whom they do not think of as human as if they were human.[91]

Indeed, atrocities are most often committed by those who "take themselves to be acting in the interests of true humanity by purifying the world of pseudo-humanity."[92] William F. Schulz expresses this nicely: "In Shakespeare's *The Merchant of Venice*, Shylock cries out, 'I am a Jew, Hath not a Jew eyes?'.... What do we say to the killer who responds to Shylock, 'Yes, a Jew has eyes but so does a pig'?"[93]

With that in mind, Rorty's bar might actually be a bit higher than the traditional one, for he insists that each individual mind must be free to construct the story of itself. By recognizing even "the private poem of the pervert, the sadist, or the lunatic,"[94] we ensure that no one can make a claim against the self-creative ability of even those who seem the most unworthy citizens. The position that Rorty adopts is this: we can make an argument for human rights by raising the bar from our common humanity

– the existence of which we should be skeptical of – to the power of the individual mind which, if we recognize all minds regardless of the type of self-creation they embark on, is indisputable.[95] With this, Rorty has, perhaps unwittingly, stepped into the same trap that snared Nietzsche. Ironically, Rorty himself calls our attention to

> that side of Nietzsche which Heidegger rightly condemned as one more example of inverted Platonism – the romantic attempt to exalt the flesh over the spirit, the heart over the head, a mythical faculty called "will" over an equally mythical one called "reason."[96]

It is impossible not to notice that the power of the mind (both its self-creative ability and susceptibility to humiliation) is a foundation like any other Rorty consistently criticizes. We should, if Rorty is to be consistently applied, be as skeptical of his claim as we are of any other.

It seems to me, though, that this particular foundation ought to be embraced even (or especially) by Rortyans because it tells us a great deal about ourselves without also necessitating a belief in some transcendent or teleological worldview. The similarities of humanity, far more numerous than our surface differences, are – on this reading – the result of the blind evolutionary process alone. Such a foundation offers us a non-religious story we can tell about ourselves that includes the universal complex brain that Rorty implicitly endorses – even though he tries, strangely, to reject the human nature built upon that brain.[97] Eventually, though, it seems necessary that Rorty fully come to terms with the position he is advocating. Rorty, of course, refuses to admit that he – like Perry, Kautz, and Gander – is some kind of foundationalist. And worse still, his thoughts on how to deal with cruelty and suffering haven't, to this point, met his own test of making a practical difference. After all, if liberal ironists believe that "cruelty is the worst thing we do"[98] and have the "desire to prevent, the actual and possible humiliation of others,"[99] their goal must be to minimize cruelty and suffering.[100] Despite being "able to recognize the contingency of the vocabulary in which they state their highest hopes,"[101] ironist liberals must also remain faithful to that vocabulary or face humiliation. The same is true of the ironist Nazi; he must always refuse our liberal redescriptions of his world. After all, a successful, ironist conversion of "a sophisticated, consistent, passionate, psychopath – for example, a Nazi who would favor his own elimination if he himself turned out to be a Jew,"[102] would necessarily result in the humiliation of that Nazi. Following such a thoroughly wrenching, torturous conversion, he could only say to himself – like *1984*'s Winston Smith – of Nazism: "'Now that I have believed or desired *this*, I can never be what I hoped to be, what I thought I was.'"[103] But Rorty insists that liberals must only persuade or convert – they ought not to force – those who hold illiberal beliefs to give up their cruelty.[104] If the ironist Nazi refuses to accept the various redescriptions we

put forward in favor of minimizing cruelty, as it seems likely he will, what other options do we have? Rorty seems to have bound our hands: there are times when we must either act cruelly ourselves by humiliating others or sanction cruelty against innocents by refusing to commit cruel acts against perpetrators (and thereby humiliate ourselves). In the end, it seems that there are times when force cannot be avoided in order to both alleviate great suffering and ensure the success of our final vocabulary, even if we privately recognize the contingent nature of the liberal commitments we publicly espouse.

That said, his answer at the end of *Contingency, Irony, and Solidarity* is quite different and more hopeful for those who eschew the use of violence in the service of human rights. It is correct that Rorty will not suggest that "the guards at Auschwitz, and the Belgians who watched the Gestapo drag their Jewish neighbors away were 'inhuman' "[105] because doing so necessitates a belief in our common humanity (despite his implied acceptance of just such a foundation). Likewise, he insists that there is no "moral obligation to feel a sense of solidarity with all other human beings."[106] Rorty insists that victims of persecution, rather than making an appeal to our common humanity, have traditionally been better served by appealing to a more powerful, more immediate, commonality. Pushing the example of the Holocaust further, he notes:

> Did they [non-Jewish Danes and Italians] say, about their Jewish neighbors, that they deserved to be saved because they were fellow human beings? Perhaps sometimes they did, but surely they would usually, if queried, have used more parochial terms to explain why they were taking risks to protect a given Jew – for example, that this particular Jew was a fellow Milanese, or a fellow Jutlander, or a fellow member of the same union or profession, or a fellow bocce player, or a fellow parent of small children.[107]

For Rorty, solidarity and sympathy are directly resultant from personal identifications.[108] When those who are suffering "are thought of as 'one of us,' where 'us' means something smaller and more local than the human race,"[109] the sense of solidarity with them is strongest. Indeed, he suggests that human rights promotion is best served by "[concentrating] our energies on manipulating sentiments, on sentimental education. That sort of education gets people of different kinds sufficiently well acquainted with one another that they are less tempted to think of those different from themselves as only quasi-human."[110] Following Annette Baier, he refers to this plan as "a progress of sentiments."[111]

In agreement with Rorty on this point is Schulz, the former Executive Director of Amnesty International USA, whose argument is very much based on a Rortyan final vocabulary.[112] After detailing human rights abuses in Nigeria, Afghanistan, and El Salvador, he notes,

I am stricken at heart because I have the imagination to know at least in proximate form what the experience, the pain, must have felt like. I am stricken at heart because on some level I identify with the victims; I know what it is to bleed. Although I have never been bitten by a horde of red ants or had a thumb amputated or been crushed by a wall, I have enough acquaintance with human suffering, either my own or that of those I love, that my memory of that acquaintance stokes my recognition.[113]

Not everyone, however, finds Rorty's argument compelling. Norman Geras is surprised by

how abstract ... how obviously speculative, Rorty's thesis about the rescuers is. "Perhaps", he suggests, they occasionally said something like this; but "surely" they more often said something like that. These rescuers were real people and there is a body of writing about them.[114]

On first blush, Geras' detailed examination of the reasons these men and women give for their heroic actions seems damning. After more careful consideration, however, the picture is a bit less clear, as many of those interviewed ascribe their actions to their own religious faith.[115] Those who do not – like Eva Anielska, a Polish woman who saved Jews who were strangers to her – took action because each one was "a persecuted human being, desperately struggling for life and in need of help ... a persecuted, humiliated human being."[116] Did she save these Jews because she identified with their humanity or with their persecution and humiliation? While this example might support the claims of either Rorty or Geras, there is also the example of Bill Bouwma, who helped Jews "because he knew what it felt like to be the underdog"[117] and of Louise Steenstra, who said, "'we felt so sorry for those Jewish people with their kids screaming when the Nazis came in the night to pick them up'; '[w]hen you are the mother of one child, you are mother to them all.'"[118] We might continue on with additional examples, but at bottom, Rorty's concern is not with creating more heroes like Anielska, Bouwma, and Steenstra; his goal, instead, is to expand everyone's sense of solidarity in order to prevent the human rights violations that require their heroic behavior.

Conclusion

Rorty's theory – as we have seen thus far – seems to deal primarily with attempting to persuade ourselves that someone we identify with is suffering, rather than providing a basis by which we could stop cruelty in those societies (though he implicitly endorses one such basis). The example of the Holocaust is useful once again: Danes and Italians *did* rescue many Jews that they could sympathize with, but little – if anything – was done to

persuade Germans to abandon their genocidal plans. It would seem that a good liberal would be actively practicing the former while also attempting the latter. If not, cruelty toward Jews could continue indefinitely and only those Jews "we" identify with at the time might be saved. The answer is a troubling one to us, but Rorty argues that it is also our only available option. First, it is a troubling solution because "We shall have to accept the fact that the fate of the women of Bosnia depends on whether television journalists manage to do for them what Harriet Beecher Stowe did for black slaves – whether these journalists can make us, the audience back in the safe countries, feel that these women are more like us, more like real human beings, than we had realized."[119] Second, it is disturbing because of the length of time required to make progress. As he notes, "We *resent* the idea that we shall have to wait for the strong to turn their piggy little eyes to the suffering of the weak, slowly open their dried-up little hearts."[120] But this, Rorty tells us, is the best we can hope for and, he argues, might achieve its end more quickly than we anticipate: "These two centuries are most easily understood ... as a period ... in which there occurred an astonishingly rapid progress of sentiments."[121]

How has the progress of sentiments occurred and what can we do to extend its reach? On this, it will be helpful to quote Rorty at some length:

> The right way to take the slogan "We have obligations to human beings simply as such" is as a means of reminding ourselves to keep trying to expand our sense of "us" as far as we can. That slogan urges us to extrapolate further in the direction set by certain events in the past – the inclusion among "us" of the family in the next cave, then of the tribe across the river, then of the tribal confederation beyond the mountains, then of the unbelievers beyond the seas (and, perhaps last of all, of the menials who, all this time, have been doing our dirty work). This is a process which we should try to keep going. We should stay on the lookout for marginalized people – people who we still instinctively think of as "they" rather than "us." We should try to notice our similarities with them. The right way to construe the slogan is as urging us to *create* a more expansive sense of solidarity than we presently have. The wrong way is to think of it as urging us to *recognize* such a solidarity, as something that exists antecedently to our recognition of it. For then we leave ourselves open to the pointlessly skeptical question 'Is this solidarity *real*?' We leave ourselves open to Nietzsche's insinuation that the end of religion and metaphysics should mean the end of our attempts not to be cruel.[122]

Most important to note, first, is Rorty's notion that our sense of who "we" are can be continually expanded to include more and more people. Indeed, Robert Wright notes that Rorty's argument lines up nicely with Charles Darwin's thinking in *The Descent of Man*:

As man advances in civilization, and small tribes are united into larger communities, the simplest reason would tell each individual that he ought to extend his social instincts and sympathies to all the members of the same nation, though personally unknown to him. This point being once reached, there is only an artificial barrier to prevent his sympathies extending to the men of all nations and races.[123]

In the end, then, our sense of solidarity could encompass everyone on Earth because of the similarities we all share. Rorty anticipates the charge of universalism, here, and responds by noting that these similarities are not found so much as they are created by telling

the sort of long, sad, sentimental story that begins, "Because this is what it is like to be in her situation – to be far from home, among strangers," or "Because she might become your daughter-in-law," or "Because her mother would grieve for her."[124]

Telling these sorts of stories, he argues, is the most practical method for increasing our sense of solidarity with those we once considered "others." My sense is that Rorty is correct that focusing on our common humanity will ultimately prove less successful than telling these stories about those who are suffering. Even though we might argue that both their suffering and their right not to suffer actually stem from what we know about the human mind and human nature, human rights advocates are likely to be more successful by increasing our sense of solidarity than by appealing to human universals. Consider, by way of an example, the work of Amnesty International, the world's largest grassroots human rights organization that, since 1961, has encouraged its members to get involved by telling personal stories about individual prisoners of conscience. In addition to this obvious example, Rorty's theory receives a great deal of support from a very unlikely source, a Nazi:

Because there were children among the Jews we had brought and at the time I myself was a father with a family of three children, I told the lieutenant something to the effect that I was unable to shoot and asked if he couldn't assign me to something else.[125]

Given these examples, and notably, this particular testimonial, it makes sense to try out Rorty's proposal – even though the anti-foundationalism upon which it is built ultimately fails – and to recognize that Rorty has provided us with a compelling non-religious understanding of the idea of human rights against Michael Perry. In addition, his theory – and my extrapolation from it – puts forward a reasonable, distinctly Rortyan defense of our liberal desire to bring about an end to cruelty against those who might favor "a nasty, illiberal rebellion . . . against gentle liberal virtues."[126]

6   Rights and wrongs without God

A non-religious grounding for human rights in a pluralistic world

In this concluding chapter, I hope to offer a final persuasive refutation of one of the central claims in Michael J. Perry's *The Idea of Human Rights: Four Inquiries*. He argues, in the first chapter of that book, that:

> There is no intelligible (much less persuasive) secular version of the conviction that every human being is sacred; the only intelligible versions are religious. . . . The conviction that every human being is sacred is, in my view, inescapably religious – and the idea of human rights is, therefore, ineliminably religious.[1]

Conversely, in his most recent book, *Rights From Wrongs: a Secular Theory of the Origins of Rights*, Alan Dershowitz shrugs off Perry's claim and argues that:

> It is more realistic to try to build a theory of rights on the agreed-upon wrongs of the past that we want to avoid repeating, than to try to build a theory of rights on idealized conceptions of the perfect society about which we will never agree.[2]

While I am generally sympathetic with Dershowitz on this point – indeed, I will ultimately argue for what I take to be a more persuasive variant of this claim – he seems to have quite clearly failed to specify how one might determine whether some action is right or wrong. Consider the following paragraphs:

> In one important respect . . . this theory of rights is a theory of wrongs. It begins with the worst injustices: the Crusades, the Inquisition, slavery, the Stalinist starvation and purges, the Holocaust, the Cambodian slaughter, and other abuses that reasonable people now recognize to have been wrongs.
>
> The ongoing nature of the righting process – and the fact that there is no consensus with regard to perfect justice – does not require that we ignore the wrongs of obvious injustice or allow those who

advocate or inflict them to fall back on moral relativism as a justification for immorality.[3]

We would be remiss, I think, if we failed to push Dershowitz on the question of how he *knows* that the Holocaust or slavery are actually wrongs.
The only answer he provides is that "every reasonable person now recognizes that slavery was a grave injustice."[4] But this is obviously not the case,
as can be attested to by the continued need for non-governmental organizations like Anti-Slavery International, the existence of contemporary first-
person slave narratives, and – of course – the fact of slavery as a persistent
violation of human rights around the world today.[5]

While Dershowitz might argue that those who continue to enslave
others are both behaving unreasonably and committing an injustice, he has
done very little to explain why that is necessarily the case beyond simply
asserting it. Further, he states that "We have seen injustice and we now
know it, even if some did not know it at the time it was being perpetrated."[6] While it might very well be the case that his list of injustices is
correct, the trouble with this argument is two-fold: first, it means human
rights can only be reactive and, second, it means that the victors determine
rights and wrongs. The Holocaust, on this reading, was not objectively
wrong and it was not necessarily wrong while it was being perpetrated; it
is considered a wrong today because the Nazis lost World War II to those
who believed it to be a wrong and at the time it was an open question
about which reasonable people might have disagreed. As Dershowitz
notes, "What constitutes perfect justice remains debatable among decent
and intelligent people today, but no such people would debate the injustice
of the Holocaust or other instances of deliberate, mass genocide."[7] This
suggests that "decent and intelligent people" debated whether or not the
Holocaust was just while it was occurring – and they did.[8] More than that,
though, it is clear that people continue to debate – and, worse, to commit
– genocide. Labeling such people indecent or unintelligent does precious
little to convince them to give up their genocidal plans because it fails to
specify *why* genocide is an obvious wrong.

This problem is by no means a new one; it has been puzzled over at
least since the time of Herodotus. In *The Histories*, he gives the quintessen-
tial example of the many differences that exist in people's traditions and
customs:

> When Darius was king, he summoned the Greeks who were with him
> and asked them for what price they would eat their fathers' dead
> bodies. They answered that they wouldn't do it for any amount of
> money. Then Darius summoned those Indians who are called Calla-
> tiae, who eat their parents, and asked them (the Greeks being present
> and understanding through interpreters what was said) what would
> make them willing to burn their fathers at death. The Indians cried

aloud, that he should not speak of so horrible an act. So firmly rooted are these beliefs; and it is, I think, rightly said in Pindar's poem that custom is king of all.[9]

Does this mean that cross-cultural dialogue is an impossibility, that we will necessarily remain at odds when it comes to determining a list of rights and wrongs? Presumably, both the Greeks and the Indians would have responded – if questioned further – that their decision to either burn or eat their dead was based on what they took to be a sacred obligation, to use Perry's terminology. While there might very well be no clear way to determine whether one of these groups was right and the other wrong, it seems to me that we need not reach Herodotus' (and Pindar's) conclusion that "custom is king of all." Although Dershowitz's secular theory of rights does not offer us a reason to think that slavery or the Holocaust are wrongs and Perry's religious theory does, I believe that a refutation of Perry's argument is needed for two reasons. First, there are many non-religious people with firm convictions about human rights and it is strange to think they might not hold an intelligible view. Second, a compelling non-religious foundation would make it easier for an ever-widening group of individuals around the world to reach a consensus on the manner in which they ought to treat one another, even if – with Herodotus in mind – they are unable to reach any other agreement. Prior to any such attempt, however, it is necessary to engage in a discussion of what it would take to provide a persuasive justification for the idea of human rights generally. Here, I argue for the necessity of inclusivity, persuasiveness, and practicality to any foundation of human rights.

Earlier, I examined Perry's line of reasoning in detail, arguing that in a pluralistic world – one in which most people do not hold the same religious worldview and many hold worldviews that would not fit within Perry's definition of religion[10] – a wider framework is needed to ground the idea of human rights. This is, of course, quite different from showing that Perry is incorrect about religion providing a compelling grounding for human rights and I do not think he is. The language of human dignity, upon which the concept of human rights rests, can certainly find a solid foundation in many of the world's great religious texts, especially – as Perry notes – the Christian Gospels. The Christian language of love and respect for the other, as well as of the equality of persons, provides a strong justification for the belief that people ought to be treated with respect and compassion, and that they ought not be abused or otherwise harmed. That said, this appeal to Christian love will not necessarily be persuasive or compelling to those who do not share the Christian worldview, despite Perry's desire for his religious foundation for human rights to be persuasive to others. Moreover, his claim that religious worldviews provide the only intelligible foundation for the idea of human rights seems to fly in the face of ample evidence that such worldviews can also be

compatible with beliefs and behavior completely antithetical to the idea of human rights. While this argument does not invalidate Perry's claim, it is important to note, first, that religious people may violate others' human rights on the basis of their interpretation of a final reconciliation and of ultimate meaning and, second, that Perry's definition of religion is expansive enough to include worldviews that are opposed to the idea of human rights. From this account of Perry's theory come two important facets of providing an adequate justification for the idea of human rights, those of *inclusivity* and *persuasiveness*, which I believe he fails to provide. In other words, a compelling foundation for the idea of human rights must speak to the largest possible number of people from the greatest number of different traditions and must also provide reasons for its account that are persuasive to those people. As Jürgen Habermas argues, "Just those action norms are valid to which all possibly affected persons could agree as participants in rational discourses."[11] Failing to satisfy these conditions leaves us with human rights that are partial and local, as opposed to universal; on my reading, this failure also prohibits me from making any claims that go beyond my own subjective understanding of how human beings ought to treat one another.

In an attempt to locate a non-religious grounding for human rights that fulfills these conditions, we must also be careful not to minimize or overlook entirely the indignity, injustice, and cruelty that are central to the human rights discourse. Any examination of human life that discusses only theoretical harms or abstracts away from abuses removes the discussion too far from the real world in which human rights are actually violated. And, indeed, this problem of excessive abstraction can also be found in Perry's argument, for his stated goal is to argue against the existence of an intelligible secular foundation for the idea of human rights. In framing his argument this way, he seems primarily concerned with theoretical or metaphysical argumentation, divorced from the real world. This highly abstract argument, one in which the validity of the claims behind Perry's religious foundation are not even considered, is almost immediately tempered by Perry's decision to turn to the real-world problem of refuting a genocidal Serb. While this task might well set the bar for any theory of human rights impossibly high, Perry makes use of it to refute Ronald Dworkin's interesting non-religious idea about the source of human dignity and human rights. While I ultimately agree with Perry's conclusion that Dworkin's argument is unsatisfying for a variety of reasons, I also argued in the third chapter that Perry's most damning critique changes the terms of the debate entirely and opens up some space for us to consider the importance of including the concept of *practicality* in this discussion. For Perry argues that Dworkin's theory fails because it is entirely subjective and thus cannot be used to persuade those who abuse human rights. It seems to me, however, that Perry's own argument for religion as the foundation of human rights is ultimately likely to meet the same fate; it finally must run

up against Wittgenstein's claim, "If I have exhausted the justifications I have reached bedrock, and my spade is turned. Then I am inclined to say: 'This is simply what I do.'"[12] While the religious believer is free to claim that the concept of human sacredness is, in fact, objectively true, this truth claim is not verifiable and Perry even suggests that he has no intention of trying to prove the "claim that every human being is sacred and therefore one attacks the normative order of the world – including one's own deepest nature – when one violates human rights."[13] This discussion reveals what I take to be the justificatory limits of metaphysical argumentation, namely that it makes claims about objective truth that are persuasive only to those who either already share or can be convinced of the validity of the core beliefs upon which the claims in question rest. Perry and Dworkin are free to believe whatever it is that they would like to believe – just as I may justify my own beliefs in any way I might like – but they ought not assume that anyone else will be convinced by the same reasoning that convinces them. In our attempts to justify our foundational beliefs to others, we ultimately reach a point beyond which we can rationally argue no further. This is true whether our beliefs are based in religion, nature, or reason. In Perry's case, one must be convinced not simply that all human beings are sacred; one must already hold the belief or be convinced that God exists to guarantee that human sacredness.

At this point, my project turns from a metaphysical to a practical, political one. No longer are we concerned with providing an intelligible non-religious foundation for the idea of human rights *for its own sake*; instead, our goal has become to provide a foundation that can be said to speak to the problem of human rights as it exists in the world, to consider what Jürgen Habermas terms the "basic questions" of practical philosophy: " 'What ought I do?' or 'What is good for us in the long run and on the whole?' "[14] These questions, he notes, have been taken "from everyday life in an unmediated way [and treated] without the objectivating filter of social science."[15] In this chapter, I put forward what I take to be a non-religious foundation for human rights that goes a long way toward fulfilling the necessary justificatory conditions of inclusivity, persuasiveness, and practicality that I have outlined above. In contrast to the theories of both Michael Perry and Ronald Dworkin, I argue that there might not actually be a feature or quality inherent in human beings from which our rights spring. Indeed, I believe that searching for rights-grounding aspects of human nature has led many non-religious rights theorists astray. Following Richard Rorty, I contend that these features or qualities are not found so much as they are created. While I believe that Rorty's theory – that telling sentimental stories is the most practical method for increasing our sense of solidarity with those we once considered "others"[16] – is an interesting response to Michael Perry, I will depart from it here because I think Rorty is unsuccessful in abandoning the idea of universal truths about human nature. Though I agree with Rorty – indeed, I fleshed out and made

explicit his implicit argument in the previous chapter – I instead make a procedural and practical argument here, one that steps back from arguments about a universal human nature. To do so, I claim that human rights represent a political consensus of overlapping ideas from cultures and communities around the world. In the end, I argue that the Universal Declaration of Human Rights (UDHR) provides us with all we need to defend human rights; in particular, I contend that the process by which it was drafted and the deliberations surrounding the subsequent human rights instruments represent the best possible proof of the universal applicability of the rights that they espouse.

Constructing the foundation: a reply to cultural relativism

There is something about the idea of social construction that is at once exciting and unsettling. As Ian Hacking argues, "Social construction has in many contexts been a truly liberating idea, but that which on first hearing has liberated some has made all too many others smug, comfortable, and trendy in ways that have become merely orthodox."[17] The lion's share of the trouble, it seems, stems from the fact that no one is really sure what social construction actually means and many feel that someone out there sees the overused phrase as an all-or-nothing concept; it either applies to quarks in the same way as it does to ideas or it doesn't apply at all. On this point, Hacking notes that:

> We require someone who claims that every object whatsoever – the earth, your feet, quarks, the aroma of coffee, grief, polar bears in the Arctic – is in some nontrivial sense socially constructed. Not just our experience of them, our classifications of them, our interests in them, but these things themselves.[18]

Quite clearly, however, he argues that this view of social construction is mistaken, that no one is actually arguing for the social construction of *everything*.

To make his point, he examines Andrew Pickering's argument in the controversially-titled book *Constructing Quarks*, and notes that "Pickering does not claim that quarks, the objects, are constructed."[19] Instead, the upshot of the book is that the *idea* of a quark is constructed and, along Rortyan lines, that scientists' arrival at the quark is a story about contingency. "Pickering," he says, "never denies that there are quarks. He maintains only that physics did not have to take a quarky route."[20] While this view remains contentious, especially amongst physicists, it is instructive for this project because human rights and the idea of human dignity upon which they are based are quite dissimilar from quarks. While a quark is an object, like a polar bear or your feet, a human right is not. Rights are theoretical; in some very real sense, they do not exist in the world until we say

they do. As Arthur C. Danto argues, "This is the way it is with rights. You want'em, so you say you got'em, and if nobody says you don't, then you do."[21] The trouble with this formulation, as Alan Gewirth rebuts, is that it

> ignores such questions as these: what if someone, like, say, Brezhnev or Pinochet, says you *don't* have the rights? Does this, therefore, go any way toward *establishing* that you don't?.... To make rights dependent entirely on declaration and recognition would mean that slaves and other oppressed groups would have no rights even in the sense of moral justification.[22]

I intend to demonstrate that Danto is right about rights, in a sense, while also answering Gewirth's concern as best I can, making use of the concept of social construction in arguing for a non-religious foundation for the idea of human rights. Following Hacking, I take social construction to mean a contingent process that applies to the development of ideas rather than objects in the world. In making this argument, I am mindful of the problem articulated above by Gewirth and reiterated by William F. Schulz:

> Such a concept of rights does not lend them the kind of irrefragable authority that God's will or Nature's command might. Theoretically, the Universal Declaration could be rescinded or amended. Human concepts of rights *do* change and there is no reason to believe that today's notions and norms will be identical to those of the twenty-second century any more than our norms are identical to those of the nineteenth.[23]

If both the idea of human rights and its foundation, human dignity, are socially constructed and thus open to reinterpretation – by advocates as well as by those who do not respect them – how can they be said to be *grounded* in any real sense?

To begin, let us consider the particular episode of social construction in question. Unlike the theories I briefly considered above, which attempted to construct free-standing justifications for the idea of human rights, the remainder of this chapter looks at the manner in which people actually came to argue for and agree upon the human rights norms of the post-World War II era. It is well-known that the Universal Declaration of Human Rights is a product of one of the United Nations' earliest established committees, the Economic and Social Council's Commission on Human Rights. The Declaration was drafted and edited under the chairmanship of Eleanor Roosevelt, though she did not remain at the Commission's helm during the push for its passage by the General Assembly. That task fell to Charles Malik of Lebanon, who had served as the Commission's rapporteur and one of the Declaration's chief framers from the beginning. Members of the Commission came from eighteen different

nations, thirteen of whom alternated at three-year intervals and five of whom – the United States, the Soviet Union, the United Kingdom, France, and China – were permanent. In addition to these permanent members, about whom much will be said, the first members of the Commission represented a diverse body of nations: Australia, Belgium, Byelorussia, Chile, Egypt, India, Iran, Lebanon, Panama, Philippines, Ukraine, Uruguay, and Yugoslavia.[24] And, as can be imagined, the route by which people from such divergent political, religious, economic, and moral backgrounds came together to form a document of such importance was circuitous, challenging, and quite often contentious.

It is often argued that the Declaration is a document enshrining not human but Western rights and that, consequently, the claim to universality in its title is wishful thinking at best and cultural imperialism at worst. An excellent summation of a variety of these arguments is undertaken by Heiner Bielefeldt, and it is worthwhile to quote him at some length:

> "Human Rights: A Western Construction with Limited Applicability" is the polemical title of an article by Pollis and Schwab, two representatives of cultural relativism and most outspoken critics of universal human rights. Pollis and Schwab argue that since human rights originated historically in Western Europe and North America, they are essentially connected – and indeed confined – to the cultural and philosophical concepts of the Occidental tradition.... Fikentscher, a German lawyer and historian, locates the historic origin of human rights in the sixteenth-century Netherlands, that is, in the context of the Dutch Protestant liberation movement against the Spanish Catholic occupation. With regard to the originally Christian motives underneath the Dutch struggle for rights and liberties, Fikentscher asserts ironically that "the mainly secular-minded 'Western' reformers" in Third World countries unconsciously propagate Christian values: "not knowing what they are doing, they actually continue Christian missionary work." The most prominent contemporary representative of an essentialist "Western" understanding of human rights, however, is Huntington, the prophet of the danger of a "clash of civilizations." In his global political map, human rights – as well as democracy, liberalism, and political secularism – belong exclusively to Western civilization. Huntington is convinced that universalism of human rights is bound to fail. For people from other civilizations, he says, the only way to have full access to human rights is to adopt essentially "Western" values and hence to implicitly "convert" to Western civilization.[25]

Having laid out these arguments, Bielefeldt attempts to provide a refutation by noting that, while "Human rights certainly did not develop in a vacuum,"[26] there are very similar conceptions to be found in a variety of non-Western philosophical and religious traditions. While this is certainly

correct, I believe that an even more direct refutation of cultural relativism is offered by an examination of the Universal Declaration's drafting process itself.

The beginning of such a refutation can be found in the decision of the UN's Educational, Scientific and Cultural Organization (UNESCO) to create a Committee on the Theoretical Bases of Human Rights. "This blue-ribbon panel, chaired by Cambridge political historian E.H. Carr, [and including] University of Chicago philosopher Richard McKeon as rapporteur and French social philosopher Jacques Maritain,"[27] began its work, in March 1947, by drafting and sending out a "questionnaire asking for reflections on human rights from Chinese, Islamic, Hindu, and customary law perspectives, as well as from American, European, and socialist points of view."[28] By June, they had received some seventy responses from experts across the globe.[29] Philosophers, political scientists, poets, and novelists from India to Italy confirmed the Committee's suspicions: "the sources of human rights were present in their traditions, even though the language of rights was a relatively modern European development."[30] To cite just two examples, consider the responses of Indian political scientist, S.V. Puntambekar, and Humayin Kabir, the Bengali Muslim poet and philosopher. The former notes

> that great Hindu thinkers had 'propounded a code, as it were, of ten essential human freedoms and controls or virtues necessary for good life': five social freedoms ('freedom from violence, freedom from want, freedom from exploitation, freedom from violation and dishonor and freedom from early death and disease') and five individual virtues ('absence of intolerance, compassion or fellow-feeling, knowledge, freedom of thought and conscience, and freedom from fear, frustration or despair').[31]

The latter writes of the importance of making the concept of human rights both universal and egalitarian:

> The "fundamental flaw in the Western conception of human rights' was not in the idea, but in the frequent failure to live up to it. "In practice," … human rights "often applied only to Europeans and sometimes to only some among Europeans.'[32]

Many of the responses – including those of Chung-Shu Lo, Teilhard de Chardin, Salvador de Madariaga, and Mohandas Gandhi – mentioned the importance of considering what Chinese diplomat Peng-chun Chang explained to his fellow Human Rights Commissioners "as two-man mindedness: 'a sympathetic attitude of regarding all one's fellow men as having the same desires, and therefore the same rights, as one would like to enjoy oneself.'"[33]

The similarities that could be identified in responses from such divergent traditions proved quite helpful to the fledgling project of drafting a universal human rights document. As Glendon notes, "Finding that several practical concepts constituted 'a sort of common denominator' among widely separated ideologies, the philosophers pronounced themselves 'convinced that the members of the United Nations share common convictions on which human rights depend.'"[34] The Committee's report itself ties these findings together nicely:

> Varied in cultures and built upon different institutions, the members of the United Nations have, nevertheless, certain great principles in common. They believe that men and women all over the world have the right to live a life that is free from the haunting fear of poverty and insecurity. They believe that they should have a more complete access to the heritage, in all its aspects and dimensions, of the civilization so painfully built by human effort. They believe that science and the arts should combine to serve alike peace and the well-being, spiritual as well as material, of all men and women without discrimination of any kind.[35]

These endorsements, from some of the world's leading men of letters, did more than simply confirm the suspicions of UNESCO's philosophers; they lent a great deal of weight to the project that Roosevelt and her Commission colleagues had undertaken. Today, they are able to play another prominent role, though very little time is currently spent examining them. In my estimation, they do a good deal of damage to the claim, outlined above, that the Universal Declaration of Human Rights is nothing more than a tool of Western imperialism in the guise of universalism. For these responses show that there is substantial cross-cultural agreement on the idea of human rights upon which the UDHR could be built.

In addition to this interesting and important work by UNESCO, the claim that the idea of human rights is limited by its Western origin fails to take into account the active participation of Human Rights Commissioners like Hansa Mehta of India, Carlos Romulo of the Philippines, and Hernán Santa Cruz of Chile in drafting the Universal Declaration. In addition, two of the most prominent and vocal members of the Commission were not Westerners: Charles Malik of Lebanon and China's P.C. Chang. The two became quite well-known for both their ability to work together and their heated arguments about the theory of rights that would buttress the Declaration; each wanted to ensure that the final document represented a vision embraced by their particular culture, but both were also able, to a degree, to transcend those cultures to theorize on a more global scale. As Mary Ann Glendon describes them:

> The occasional skirmishes between Chang and Malik in the Human Rights Commission had been partly clashes between two strong

personalities, partly a confrontation between religious and secular worldviews, and partly disagreements about how far one could go in the direction of pragmatic compromises without putting truth, and therefore universality, up for grabs. Malik believed the Declaration should be anchored more explicitly in "nature," Chang thought it better to leave it up to each culture to supply its own account of the philosophical underpinnings of human rights. Both men's ideas had been unsettled by the "transvaluation of values" in the post-Nietzschean, postwar world, but neither was ready to give up on values altogether.[36]

Of course, a common rejoinder is that the two diplomats were capable of this sort of work on the Declaration precisely because both had, in some sense, left the experience of the non-Western world behind them. After all, Chang and Malik had both been educated in the West – the former earning his doctorate from Columbia University and the latter from Oxford – and both spent a great deal of their adult lives away from home. To this critique about a possible Western influence on Chang and Malik, Glendon responds that "their performance in the Human Rights Commission suggests something rather different. Not only did each contribute significant insights from his own culture, but each possessed an exceptional ability to understand other cultures and to 'translate' concepts from one frame of reference to another."[37]

If we accept, as I believe we should, that the multiculturalism of the Declaration's drafters themselves serves as the beginnings of an argument for its universality, we have taken a significant step toward the completion of a non-religious foundation for the idea of human rights that is based on the UDHR itself. That said, there remain several significant challenges unanswered. First, not everyone was invited to the table to help create the Universal Declaration and second, even if they had been or have contributed to the dialogue since, what justificatory weight does their agreement actually hold? The first argument is, as Glendon notes, "that much of the world's population was not represented in the UN in 1948: large parts of Africa and some Asian countries remained under colonial rule; and the defeated Axis powers – Japan, Germany, Italy, and their allies – were excluded as well."[38] Glendon's response to this challenge is that:

> Not every country in the world had its say, but many did, and their response supported the UNESCO philosophers' conclusion that a few basic practical concepts of human rights are so widely shared that they 'may be viewed as implicit in man's nature as a member of society'.[39]

Bielefeldt reaches a similar conclusion, arguing that:

> It is especially the idea of human dignity that can connect human rights with different religious, philosophical, and cultural traditions

because the insight into the unalienable dignity of every human being constitutes both the basic ethical principle of human rights and a central element of the teachings of various religions and philosophies. The "Project on Religion and Human Rights," based in New York, has come to the conclusion that "there are elements in virtually all religious traditions that support peace, tolerance, freedom of conscience, dignity and equality of persons, and social justice."[40]

Of course, this important point about dignity as a universal concept remains somewhat contentious. Rhoda Howard and Jack Donnelly, for example, argue

> that internationally recognized human rights require a liberal regime. Other types of regimes, and the conceptions of human dignity on which they rest, may be defensible on other moral or political grounds, but they will not stand up to scrutiny under the standard of human rights.[41]

Apart from being surprisingly ethnocentric, Howard and Donnelly's argument seems rather incomplete. They assert, for example, that traditional societies – defined as "communal, status-based societies, governed according to principles and practices held to be fixed by tradition"[42] – do not share the Western conception of dignity upon which human rights are based:

> One's dignity – which usually is conceived primarily as an attribute of one's kinship, age, sex, or occupational group – is obtained or validated by discharging the (traditionally defined) duties of one's station, rather than by autonomously creating or unfolding a unique individual existence. In traditional society, there are neither human beings, in the relevant moral sense, nor equal, inalienable, and universal rights.[43]

This seems to be far from a complete picture of the concept of dignity in traditional societies (which include, but seem not to be limited to, all of Africa and every sort of Islamic society),[44] and Howard and Donnelly offer only one reference for their assertions.[45]

A far more thorough examination of the problem is undertaken by Abdullahi Ahmed An-Na'im, who offers a middle ground between Glendon and Bielefeldt, on the one hand, and Howard and Donnelly on the other. In discussing the problem of cruel, unusual, and degrading treatment with reference to Qur'anic punishments, he notes that "On the one hand, it is necessary to safeguard the personal integrity and human dignity of the individual against excessive or harsh punishments. . . . On the other hand, it is extremely important to be sensitive to the dangers of cultural

imperialism."[46] It is not that Islamic societies do not understand the idea of human rights or have a different conception of dignity; instead, An-Na'im argues that the benefits to both the individual and society seem to outweigh the costs. In addition to the deterrent effect of the punishment, for example:

> In the next *eternal* life, every human being will stand judgment and suffer the consequences of his or her actions in this life. A religiously sanctioned punishment, however, will absolve an offender from punishment in the next life because God does not punish twice for the same offence.[47]

An-Na'im's reasoned response to this dilemma is an interesting one because it recognizes the challenge that traditional societies can present to the idea of human rights but also highlights the possibility for societal change based on cross-cultural dialogue about commonalities with the West. In his own words:

> there is room for agreement on a wide range of substantive and procedural matters even in relation to an apparently inflexible position, such as the Islamic position on Qur'anic punishments. Provided such agreement is sought with sufficient sensitivity, the general status of human rights will be improved, and wider agreement can be achieved in relation to other human rights.[48]

Rights by committee and the idea of an overlapping consensus

This notion of cross-cultural dialogue is, in some sense, precisely what took place when the Human Rights Commission began the work of enumerating, revising, and then defending its list of rights. As the Commissioners represented a great many different cultures, religious traditions, and political systems, there were heated debates about the wording of nearly every one of the thirty articles, as well as of the introductory clauses. Much of the trouble, however, was not cultural, coming instead in the form of a series of alternating Soviet representatives. They had been instructed to dig in their heels on what Moscow viewed as potential threats to the concept of national sovereignty: "the right to freedom of movement, the right to a nationality, a nation's right to accord asylum to political refugees, and protections against arbitrary expulsion from a country."[49] Other arguments arose around the difficult question of how implementation of the rights in the UDHR would be achieved[50] and the charge, again from the Soviets, "that the United States wanted a Declaration that was as 'short and empty as possible.'"[51] From the beginning, though, the greatest point of contention centered around the idea of

grounding the rights that the Declaration set out. After having arrived at what seemed to be some agreement on the text as drafted first by Canada's John Humphrey, revised by France's René Cassin, and finally amended by a working group, the Commission revisited the draft as a whole and focused on the language of each article:

> The full Commission once again consumed much precious time arguing over Article 1's general statement concerning the human person. Cassin and [the Phillipines' Carlos] Romulo, in the working group, had slightly revised the first article to read: "All men are brothers. They are endowed by nature with reason and conscience. They are born equal in dignity and rights." [Lebanon's Charles] Malik ... now proposed substituting the words "by their Creator" for "by nature." He cited the American Declaration of Independence ("endowed by their Creator with certain unalienable rights"). That amendment was opposed by Cassin on the grounds that references to God would undermine the universality of the document. [The Soviet representative, Alexander] Bogomolov moved to drop the entire article, saying that it made no sense to clutter up the document with vacuous assertions, whether they were drawn from eighteenth-century French philosophy or from the Bible.[52]

This discussion demonstrates the challenge inherent in any cross-cultural attempt to ground the idea of human rights. Malik, for example, felt that it was important to assign the source of our rights to a Creator, while this sort of focus, for Cassin, could damage the document's acceptability for a great many people.

Though Cassin ultimately persuaded his fellow Commissioners of the importance of leaving the document – and, in particular, its first article – free of any statements that might take away from its claim to universality, the question of grounding the Declaration's rights was far from settled. In the point-by-point discussion of each of the Universal Declaration's thirty articles that took place in committee before it could move to the General Assembly for a vote, the drafters were called upon to defend their decisions with respect both to the language used and the rights that were chosen. The first article remained one of the most contentious, not the least because it is a statement about human nature rather than an enumeration of a right. After this fire had been quelled by Roosevelt, who explained that "Article 1 did not refer to specific rights because it was meant to explain why human beings have rights to begin with,"[53] the discussion shifted to an amendment by the Brazilians to include the words, "all human beings are created in the image of and likeness of God."[54] This proposal was ultimately defeated, but only after Chang stepped in to defend the universal applicability of the article as it stood:

His own country, he pointed out, comprised a large proportion of humanity, and its people had ideals and traditions different from those of the Christian West. Chinese ideals included good manners, decorum, propriety, and consideration for others. Yet he, as the Chinese representative on the Human Rights Commission, had refrained from proposing those ideals for inclusion in the Declaration. . . . Article 1 as it stood, Chang said, struck just the right note by calling upon all men to act toward one another in a spirit of brotherhood. That was consistent with the Chinese belief in the importance of considerate treatment of others – and also with the ideals of eighteenth-century Western thought. The first line of the article, therefore, should refer neither to nature nor to God. Those who believed in God, he suggested, could still find the idea of God in the strong assertions that all human beings are born free and equal and endowed with reason and conscience.[55]

Chang's argument is an important one, as it outlines how each culture might find their own particular vision within even the most controversial articles. " 'As only he can do,' wrote Humphrey, Chang reminded his fellow delegates that each culture's contributions had to be made with a view toward producing a document 'meant for all men everywhere.'"[56] This did not mean, as some were afraid, that one culture or another would have to compromise values or traditions; instead, it meant that the document had to represent what John Rawls would term, years later, an overlapping consensus.[57]

The idea of an overlapping consensus is the backbone of the sort of liberalism that Rawls envisions, one in which the principles of justice outlined in *A Theory of Justice* can be established and flourish.[58] On this point, he says:

> Our exercise of political power is fully proper only when it is exercised in accordance with a constitution the essentials of which all citizens as free and equal may reasonably be expected to endorse in the light of principles and ideals acceptable to their common human reason. This is the liberal principle of legitimacy. . . . Only a political conception of justice that all citizens might be reasonably expected to endorse can serve as a basis of public reason and justification.[59]

Seeking that endorsement on the evening of December 9, 1948, Malik took the podium to introduce the Universal Declaration to the General Assembly. In doing so, he recognized the unusual nature of the document before him: "Unlike previous declarations of rights that had sprung from particular cultures, he said, the Universal Declaration was something new in the world."[60] Its uniqueness, clearly, stemmed from the agreement it represented between so many divergent cultures and traditions on an issue,

the grounding of human rights, that was vastly contentious. And, indeed, Malik points out exactly this fact in his speech. As Glendon highlights:

> Malik pointed each country to places in the Declaration where it could either find its own contribution or the influence of the culture to which it belonged.... Due to the immense variety of its sources, the Declaration had been constructed on a "firm international basis wherein no regional philosophy or way of life was permitted to prevail."[61]

This quotation from Malik's speech begins to lead us down the wrong path through its assertion that no single philosophical or religious tradition – what Rawls calls a comprehensive doctrine – won out over any other, for I want to argue that the Universal Declaration represents a much greater achievement. It is not simply that no single tradition was victorious in setting out the foundation of human rights that others could accept, though it is true that none was; instead, the Declaration's virtue is that everyone was able to agree upon and endorse a *common* foundation: the dignity of the human person. This is true of the General Assembly in 1948 – the Declaration was approved without a single vote cast against it – and it holds true to an even greater extent more than fifty years later.[62] As Donnelly points out, in an argument similar to mine, "The increasing political prominence of human rights over the past few decades has led more and more adherents of a growing range of comprehensive doctrines to endorse human rights – but (only) as a political conception of justice."[63] This caveat, important for Donnelly's argument that there remain some comprehensive doctrines anathema to the idea of human rights, is noteworthy here for a different reason. The distinction between comprehensive doctrines and political conceptions of justice is a vitally important one for Rawls' argument about achieving an overlapping consensus. As Donnelly notes: "Because the latter address only the political structure of society, defined (as far as possible) independent of any particular comprehensive doctrine, adherents of different comprehensive doctrines may reach an 'overlapping consensus' on a political conception of justice."[64] In other words, we may be unable to come to any agreement where our religious or philosophical traditions and beliefs are concerned, but this need not prevent us from coming to consensus on a political conception of justice. Indeed, we may find our comprehensive doctrines quite at odds, but this is precisely why Rawls counsels us to leave them out of our political deliberations. In his own words, "we do not put forward more of our comprehensive view than we think needed or useful for the political aim of consensus."[65]

This argument, that the Universal Declaration represents a Rawlsian overlapping consensus, is not a new one; it is put forward persuasively by Jack Donnelly. I agree with Donnelly's assessment that:

Even where citizens do not have a particularly sophisticated sense of what a commitment to human rights means, they respond to the general idea that they and their fellow citizens are equally entitled to certain basic goods, services, protections, and opportunities. The Universal Declaration, I would suggest, offers a good first approximation of the list that they would accept, largely irrespective of civilization, after considerable reflection.[66]

But I take the argument a step further, as I do not believe that Donnelly's conception of the overlapping consensus represented by the UDHR speaks to the problem posed throughout this chapter. In other words, we differ in the *substance* of that consensus, as he believes that it centers around the rights that the Commission enumerated rather than the foundation of those rights. On that question, Rawls recommends silence and Donnelly seems to be in agreement with him, noting only that the consensus has formed around "something very much like Ronald Dworkin's idea that the state is required to treat each citizen with equal concern and respect."[67] In my estimation, Donnelly is not saying much more, here, than the state is required to respect citizens' human rights, which – clearly – is the consensus established by the UDHR. More importantly, though, I want to argue that its drafters arrived at a consensus on the *reason* behind the requirement that the state respect human rights; this, I argue, is the idea that human beings have dignity and it is this consensus that makes the Declaration unique in comparison to all of the previous rights instruments that human beings have drafted.

And yet, I also want to argue that it is more than this cross-cultural understanding that human beings have dignity that grounds the contemporary human rights regime. For the notion that human beings possess dignity seems to open the door to yet another question; that is, one must wonder from where we have acquired this dignity. And, in so wondering, we are back at the problem first outlined by Michael Perry, namely whether the concept of dignity – like its religious coeval, sacredness – can be understood in the absence of a religious cosmology. This is the sort of problem that Rawls wants to help us to avoid by telling us to keep quiet about our comprehensive doctrines when we enter into deliberations over political conceptions of justice. It seems to me, though, that we do not need to flinch from this sort of discussion because the international community has already agreed on the answer to Perry's questions; indeed, I want to argue that it is the experience of coming to consensus on the question of a foundation for human rights that provides the concept's grounding. Human dignity and the human rights that stem from it, on my reading, are socially constructed ideas in the way that, for example, quarks and polar bears are not. But this, I think, is necessarily going to be true simply because dignity and rights are ideas rather than objects. As such, it seems to me that they must be constructed; ideas, after all, do not exist in

the world independently of human experience in the way that polar bears do. I am confident that polar bears would exist in the absence of human beings; human dignity, however, would not. It might be the case, then, that human beings actually have inherent dignity and it might not be; the matter is, as Gewirth notes, not empirically verifiable.[68] That said, whether or not our dignity is something real, something that actually exists in the world, it is incumbent upon all of us to act as though it is, as though it does, because we have agreed to do so.

Can consensus have justificatory force?

This entire discussion raises the interesting, controversial, and related problems of whether consensus itself can have morally justificatory force and whether agreement is a sufficient guide on questions of right action.[69] As Habermas correctly points out, "Communicative reason ... does not itself supply any substantive orientation for managing practical tasks – it is neither informative nor immediately practical."[70] While I have been implicitly arguing that the overlapping consensus on the idea of human rights has justificatory power and obligates us to act in accordance with the rights enshrined in the Universal Declaration, I must also note the powerful counterexamples presented by Nazi Germany and American slavery, both of which established a consensus that defenders of human rights consider obviously immoral and criminal. While it is clear that Germans reached a consensus on (or at least majority support for) the anti-Semitic Nazi regime and the American South reached a consensus on slavery, those agreements are notably different from the one described in this chapter. In what sense, though, is this consensus different? How is it possible for one sort of consensus to have justificatory weight while others do not? There are, I maintain, a number of conditions that must be met for any given consensus to have justificatory power and I will argue that this particular consensus meets those conditions. Following Habermas, I argue first that "the claim to legitimacy on the part of a legal order built on rights can be redeemed only through the socially integrative force of the 'concurring and united will of all' free and equal citizens."[71] A chief difference, then, is that the consensus on human dignity and human rights – unlike those of Nazism or the antebellum American South – is the result of a highly participatory process, one that accepted input from a more diverse group than had ever been assembled. As we have seen, both the UNESCO philosophers' committee and the Human Rights Commission included members of newly-independent nations, representatives from socialist and capitalist countries, spokespersons from the powerful and the weaker states alike, and officials from both the East and West. Discussions on the foundations of human rights and on the content of the UDHR engaged a politically, culturally, religiously, economically, and geographically diverse group, one that was representative of the fledgling

United Nations itself. By contrast, any potential consensus on genocide or slavery quite clearly fails to take into account the dissenting voices of the groups targeted by those policies and their allies. While the agreement on human dignity and human rights might not have been unanimous, it was certainly overwhelming. The same cannot be said of a less-participatory consensus.

Of course, as noted earlier, there were a great many groups not represented in these deliberations. Indeed, a wide array of the nations and groups recognized today were not acknowledged at the time of the UDHR's drafting. Examples are easy to come by and certainly include the myriad African states granted independence in the decades succeeding World War II, indigenous peoples around the globe, and groups – like lesbians, gays, bisexuals, and transgendered people – that are still unrecognized in some parts of the world today. That said, I want to argue that this seeming weakness actually helps to demonstrate a strength of this particular consensus. Once again following Habermas, I argue that a second necessary component of a legitimate consensus is that "the decisions of the legislature . . . are both contingent and revisable."[72] In the case of this particular consensus, it is clear that the process did not end with the drafting and passage of the Universal Declaration. For although the UDHR itself has not been amended and has achieved, many argue, the status of customary international law, an entire group of increasingly inclusive institutions has arisen from this auspicious beginning. The process that began with the drafting of the Declaration has evolved to include such diverse entities as the United Nations Convention on the Elimination of all forms of Discrimination Against Women, the draft Declaration on the Rights of Indigenous Peoples, and the Convention on the Rights of the Child. In addition, it is notable that the newly independent states of the Organization of African Unity went on to draft their own declaration of rights – the African [Banjul] Charter on Human and Peoples' Rights – that recognizes their desire "to co-ordinate and intensify their co-operation and efforts to achieve a better life for the peoples of Africa and to promote international co-operation having due regard to the Charter of the United Nations and the Universal Declaration of Human Rights."[73] While some critics suggest that the revisable nature of the Universal Declaration might leave it open to radical change or outright reversal, I argue instead that its revisability has directly contributed to a deeper, more lasting, and more legitimate set of institutions. As Habermas notes:

> Without religious or metaphysical support, the coercive law tailored for the self-interested use of individual rights can preserve its socially integrating force only insofar as the addressees of legal norms may at the same time understand themselves, taken as a whole, as the rational *authors* of those norms.[74]

And, indeed, these various human rights conventions and declarations have achieved the force of law, as embodied in a variety of regional courts and the newly established International Criminal Court.

Finally, the above quotation from Habermas brings us to a third important condition for consensus to achieve justificatory weight. In addition to its inclusive and participatory nature and its contingency and revisability, a consensus must also be achieved through a democratic and deliberative process. According to Habermas, "modern law lives off a solidarity concentrated in the value orientations of citizens and ultimately issuing from communicative action and deliberation."[75] As discussed in detail above, the drafting and adoption of the Universal Declaration were quite clearly democratic and deliberative processes in which the participants carefully considered, discussed, and voted upon not only the language to employ in each of the Declaration's thirty articles but also on the philosophical underpinnings of the document itself.[76] As Habermas points out:

> the binding energies of language can be mobilized to coordinate action plans only if the participants suspend the objectivating attitude of an observer, along with the immediate orientation to personal success, in favor of the performative attitude of a speaker who wants to *reach an understanding* with a second person about something in the world.[77]

And, indeed, one of the truly unique features of the consensus arrived at by the Commission is the record of discussion and deliberation of such a diverse group upon a wide range of opinion not only about the human good – about what enables us to flourish – but also about what brings us to grief.[78] The opening clauses of the Universal Declaration speak to this point, especially in recognizing that:

> disregard and contempt for human rights have resulted in barbarous acts which have outraged the conscience of mankind, and the advent of a world in which human beings shall enjoy freedom of speech and belief and freedom from fear and want has been proclaimed as the highest aspiration of the common people.[79]

The limits of language

Having considered the necessary conditions under which consensus can have justificatory force, it is important to recognize that challenges remain. As Habermas asks:

> how can disenchanted, internally differentiated and pluralized life-worlds be socially integrated if, at the same time, the risk of dissention is growing, particularly in the spheres of communicative action that

have been cut loose from the ties of sacred authorities and released from the bonds of archaic institutions?[80]

While I have argued that the process of drafting the Universal Declaration provides an answer to this question, it is important to recognize that controversy exists on whether discussion, deliberation, and consensus themselves can have any justificatory force or impel action. Habermas notes, on this point, that:

> The ideal character of semantic generality shapes communicative action inasmuch as the participants could not even intend to reach an understanding with one another about something in the world if they did not *presuppose*, on the basis of a common (or translatable) language, that they conferred identical meanings on the expressions they employed.... The presupposition that linguistic expressions are used with identical meanings can often turn out to be false from an observer's perspective, and perhaps this is always the case under the ethnomethodologist's microscope.[81]

Put more simply, there are problems inherent in the use of language that can trip up even the best attempts to open dialogue and reach consensus. I can best make this point by returning to an example that Perry offers to highlight the weakness of Dworkin's theory of secular sacredness. Perry's challenge is to

> Imagine someone saying to a Bosnian Serb: "The Bosnian Muslim, too, no less than you, is sacred. It is wrong for you to rape her." If "sacred" is meant in the subjective sense, the Bosnian Serb can reply: "Sacred to you and yours, perhaps, but not to me and mine. In the scheme of things, we happen not to attach much value to her life." By contrast, "sacred" in the objective sense is not fundamentally a matter of "sacred to you" or "sacred to me"; it is, rather, a matter of how things really are.... If every human being is sacred in the objective sense, then, in violating the Bosnian Muslim, the Bosnian Serb does not merely violate what some of us attach great value to; he violates the very order of creation.[82]

Perry wants to give the Serb a reason why he ought not violate the Muslim. For both he and Dworkin, the reason is their belief that the Muslim is sacred; in this case, the reason is our belief that the Muslim is a bearer of human dignity. When further challenged and asked to provide a compelling reason for our belief, Perry would undoubtedly argue that its social construction hamstrings us. The larger challenge, however, is the one pointed out by Habermas, namely that we might be unable to speak with the Serb on this point at all. In this case – and in any situation where

human rights are under fire – we can respond by explaining that there is an international consensus about the ideas of human dignity and human rights. While this might not change the Serb's mind – and, indeed, it might be the case that *nothing* will change the mind of a genocidal person – we can further note the existence of international human rights conventions and the emergence of the International Criminal Court, which now serve to back up our consensus. While this is certainly not the strong sort of theoretical defense that Perry desires, and while it does little more than sidestep Habermas' concern about the limits of language, it is also not such a weak one. For, while Rorty points out that this truth, like any other, "is made rather than found,"[83] he also argues that the importance of its defense should shake us from our complacency and encourage us to offer compelling reasons for our holding it that stem from *our* having made it. In addition, and perhaps more practically, the consensus on at least a basic set of human rights enjoys widespread, if not universal, approval and the institutions that are extensions of that consensus have achieved the force of law.

Although there are clearly limits to the use of language that create some serious difficulties for the idea that the process of drafting the Universal Declaration can have justificatory force, I submit that it remains a strong beginning in responding to Perry. In addition, it also goes a long way toward fulfilling the conditions for a persuasive justification that I set out above: inclusivity, persuasiveness, and practicality. As discussed throughout this chapter, the drafting process was (and continues to be) a highly inclusive one. It is also, in my estimation, persuasive and its persuasiveness arises in no small part from its having met the conditions set out above for achieving justificatory force. Finally, the consensus on human rights and human dignity is sufficiently grounded in the real world to meet the condition of practicality; it is able to embrace many divergent viewpoints with a view toward involving the widest array of peoples in this vital discussion. And, indeed, Eleanor Roosevelt made this point herself about the substance of the consensus:

> Now, I happen to believe that we are born free and equal in dignity and rights because there is a divine Creator, and there is a divine spark in men. But, there were other people around the table who wanted it expressed in such a way that they could think in their particular way about this question, and finally, these words were agreed upon because they ... left it to each of us to put in our own reason, as we say, for that end.[84]

The subtext of this statement also speaks to my point, for Roosevelt argues that this particular consensus, reached on such an important philosophical question as the nature of man, allows everyone to come to the table and discuss the idea of human rights regardless of *why* they hold this belief.

Rawls makes the same point, noting that "The idea of an overlapping consensus leaves this step to be taken by citizens individually in line with their own comprehensive views."[85] The nations of the world may disagree on a great many things – philosophical as well as practical – but they have all agreed on this important point: every human being is entitled to the rights enshrined in the Universal Declaration by virtue of the inherent dignity that is common to us all.

This conclusion was also reached by Jacques Maritain and his colleagues on the UNESCO Committee, who noted that the cross-cultural agreement of the world's leading men of letters was broad but shallow:

> Maritain liked to tell the story of how a visitor at one meeting expressed astonishment that champions of violently opposed ideologies had been able to agree on a list of fundamental rights. The man was told: "Yes, we agree about the rights but on condition no one asks us why."[86]

On my reading, Maritain's answer is a bit too self-effacing; the members of his committee were able to reach an agreement not only about the rights but also about human dignity, the reason why. Perhaps what Maritain meant to say was that everyone disagreed on the source of that dignity, on the reason behind the reason. Either way, we can learn much from Maritain and his overly modest comment, as well as his argument that

> If there are some things so terrible in practice that virtually no one will publicly approve them, and some things so good in practice that virtually no one will oppose them, a common project can move forward without agreement on the reasons for those positions.[87]

While we might not all agree on the reason behind the reason, at bottom, we have all agreed that human beings possess dignity and that, by virtue of this fact, they are inviolable; this idea can be embraced by those who subscribe to what Perry calls a religious cosmology and also by those who do not. In constructing this consensus, then, we have succeeded in establishing a practical non-religious foundation upon which the idea of human rights can rest.

Notes

Prologue: Starvin' for Justice

1 The Abolitionist Action Committee explains: "June 29 is the anniversary of the 1972 *Furman* v. *Georgia* decision in which the U.S. Supreme Court found the death penalty to be applied in an arbitrary and capricious manner. At that time, more then 600 condemned inmates had their death sentences reduced to terms of life imprisonment, and all states were forced to rewrite their death penalty laws. July 2 is the anniversary of the 1976 *Gregg* v. *Georgia* decision, which allowed executions to resume in the United States" based on the constitutionality of the states' new death penalty statutes (www.abolition.org/starvin13.FV history.html).

2 Consider the very different stories of two participants in the most recent Fast & Vigil, Bill Pelke and Juan Melendez. Pelke's seventy-eight-year-old grandmother Ruth was murdered by four ninth-grade girls she invited into her home for Bible lessons. One of the girls, Paula Cooper, was sentenced to death for the crime. She had been fifteen when the murder occurred, and at sixteen became the youngest female on death row in America. Originally supportive of Paula's death sentence, Bill eventually forgave Paula, began corresponding and visiting with her, and worked to overturn her sentence. She is now serving sixty years in prison (see Bill Pelke, *Journey of Hope ... From Violence to Healing* (Philadelphia: Xlibris, 2003)). Second:

> Juan Roberto Melendez Colon became the 24th person exonerated and released from Florida's death row when he was freed on January 3, 2002 after spending almost 18 years facing execution for a crime he had nothing to do with. Melendez was convicted in 1984 at the age of 33 with no physical evidence linking him to the crime and testimony from questionable witnesses. In fact, prosecutors hid evidence and lied to the court in order to protect the real killer, a police informant. Melendez's conviction fell apart when the police informant's confession came to light in 1999 – a confession that prosecutors knew about before they took Melendez to trial.
>
> (www.journeyofhope.org/pages/juan_melendez.htm)

3 Abolitionist Action Committee website: www.abolition.org/starvin13fasting.html.

4 Ronald Dworkin, *Life's Dominion: an Argument About Abortion, Euthanasia, and Individual Freedom* (New York: Vintage Books, 1994), 4.

5 Michael J. Perry, *The Idea of Human Rights: Four Inquiries* (Oxford: Oxford University Press, 1998), 30–31.

6 Ibid., 39–40, citation omitted.

7 For Alan M. Dershowitz, the question of whether or not it is permissible to

torture a captured terrorist seems not at all to turn on the relationship between men and God. In *Why Terrorism Works: Understanding the Threat, Responding to the Challenge* (New Haven: Yale University Press, 2002), he argues that a government wishing to protect its citizens from terror ought to consider the use of torture so long as enough information is known about the "ticking bomb suspect" so that a "torture warrant" can be obtained by the authorities (pp. 131–163). Apart from what are obvious problems of implementation that Dershowitz's argument clearly raises, there exists a familiar philosophical dilemma in this "ticking bomb suspect" example whose origin is the scene in Fyodor Dostoevsky's *The Brothers Karamazov* where Ivan tempts his virtuous brother, Alyosha, with the possibility of eternal happiness for all mankind at the cost of the torture and death of one innocent child. In an article in the *Guardian*, "Are there times when we have to accept torture?" (May 8, 2004), Ariel Dorfman comments on the torture of Iraqi prisoners by American and British soldiers, and reflects on Alyosha's choice. His argument, which echoes much of what follows, notes that:

> What Alyosha is telling Ivan, in the name of humanity, is that he will not accept responsibility for someone else torturing in his name. He is telling us that torture is not a crime committed only against a body, but also a crime committed against the imagination. It presupposes, it requires, it craves the abrogation of our capacity to imagine someone else's suffering, to dehumanise him or her so much that their pain is not our pain. It demands this of the torturer, placing the victim outside and beyond any form of compassion or empathy, but also demands of everyone else the same distancing, the same numbness, those who know and close their eyes, those who do not want to know and close their eyes, those who close their eyes and ears and hearts.

8 Amy Gutmann, "Introduction" in Michael Ignatieff, *Human Rights as Politics and Idolatry*, ed. Amy Gutmann (Princeton: Princeton University Press, 2001), xvii.
9 Ibid.

Introduction: the first day of class

1 In most cases, the obligation clearly lies with governments, but there are some human rights that are considerably less clear about where the duty lies. For example, Article Nine of the United Nations Universal Declaration of Human Rights in *The Human Rights Reader: Major Political Writings, Essays, Speeches, and Documents from the Bible to the Present*, ed. Micheline R. Ishay (New York: Routledge, 1997) – "No one shall be subjected to arbitrary arrest, detention or exile" (p. 409) – clearly implies an obligation on the part of national governments to refrain from arbitrarily arresting, detaining, or exiling their citizens. The same, however, cannot be said of Article Twenty-Eight – "Everyone is entitled to a social and international order in which the rights and freedoms set forth in this Declaration can be fully realized" (ibid., 411–412) – for it is not at all clear who is obliged to ensure that such a social and international order is established. Undoubtedly, we are all responsible for ensuring this right, but this makes a violation of such a right far more difficult to address.
2 William F. Schulz, *In Our Own Best Interest: How Defending Human Rights Benefits Us All* (Boston: Beacon Press, 2002), 24.
3 Ibid., 18.

4 Michael J. Perry, *The Idea of Human Rights: Four Inquiries* (Oxford: Oxford University Press, 1998), 11–12.
5 As K. Anthony Appiah notes, in "Grounding Human Rights" in Michael Ignatieff, *Human Rights as Politics and Idolatry*, ed. Amy Gutmann. (Princeton: Princeton University Press, 2001): The wide diversity of people who call upon [human rights] includes ... a substantial diversity of opinion on matters metaphysical – on religion in particular – and even if there is a single truth to be had about these matters, it is not one that we shall all come to soon (p. 105).
6 Perry, 15.
7 David DeGrazia, "Identity, Killing, and the Boundaries of Our Existence," *Philosophy & Public Affairs* 31(4) (Fall 2003), 413.
8 Perry, 37.
9 Ibid., 12.
10 Richard Rorty, *Truth and Progress: Philosophical Papers, Volume 3* (Cambridge: Cambridge University Press, 1998), 184–185.

1 Michael Perry and the religious cosmology: foundations and critiques of human rights

1 United Nations Universal Declaration of Human Rights in *The Human Rights Reader: Major Political Writings, Essays, Speeches, and Documents from the Bible to the Present*, ed. Micheline R. Ishay (New York: Routledge, 1997), 407.
2 According to Burns H. Weston, in "Human Rights" in *The New Encyclopædia Britannica, Volume 20* (Chicago: Encyclopædia Britannica, 2002):

> Most students of human rights trace the historical origins of the concept back to ancient Greece and Rome, where it was closely tied to the premodern natural law doctrines of Greek Stoicism (the school of philosophy founded by Zeno of Citium, which held that a universal working force pervades all creation and that human conduct therefore should be judged according to, and brought into harmony with, the law of nature).
>
> (p. 656)

3 There are a wide variety of quotations from Eastern thinkers to support this point. Among my favorites are those pointed out by William F. Schulz in *In Our Own Best Interest: How Defending Human Rights Benefits Us All* (Boston: Beacon Press, 2002), that "Confucius himself asserted that 'an oppressive government is worse than a tiger' " (p. 183, citation omitted) and Mary Ann Glendon in *A World Made New: Eleanor Roosevelt and the Universal Declaration of Human Rights* (New York: Random House, 2001), that:

> The Bengali Muslim poet and philosopher Humayin Kabir sounded a universalist note in writing about human rights and the Islamic tradition. Kabir proudly recalled that early Islam had 'succeeded in overcoming distinction of race and colour to an extent experienced neither before nor since.
>
> (p. 74, citation omitted)

Of course, Schulz goes on to point out the so-called "Asian values" critique of human rights, "has a certain logical ring to it," namely that:

> to advance human rights around the globe is to try to impose American values on other people and hence should be avoided ... Mao was raised

in the Chinese tradition. The Chinese tradition has no concept of human rights. To expect Mao to abide by them, therefore, is not only unfair but reflects an attempt to foist Western values on a different culture. The Chinese Communist Party may decree, as indeed it has, that Mao's merits outweigh his mistakes by a proportion of 7 to 3, but making judgments like that is not up to outsiders.

(p. 183)

While Schulz clearly disagrees with this sort of logic, Glendon offers a more powerful disagreement with those, like Singapore's Lee Kuan Yew, who argue that the idea of human rights is a Western construct that does not apply to Asian cultures:

The absence of formal declarations of rights in China, said Confucian philosopher Chung-Shu Lo, did not signify "that the Chinese never claimed human rights or enjoyed the basic rights of man." He explained: "[T]he problem of human rights was seldom discussed by Chinese thinkers of the past, at least in the same way as it was in the West. There was no open declaration of human rights in China, either by individual thinkers or by political constitutions, until this conception was introduced from the West .... [However], the idea of human rights developed very early in China, and the right of the people to revolt against oppressive rulers was very early established .... A great Confucianist, Mencius (372–289 B.C.), strongly maintained that a government should work for the will of the people. He said: "People are of primary importance. The State is of less importance. The sovereign is of least importance."

(pp. 73–74, citation omitted)

In addition, and perhaps even more pragmatic, are the words of Xiao Quiang, a Chinese dissident, at a 1998 Harvard symposium on the fiftieth anniversary of the Universal Declaration of Human Rights: "If you were to voice dissent from the prevailing view in China, you would end up in jail, and there you would soon be asking for your rights, without worrying about whether they were 'American' or 'Chinese'" (ibid., 232, citation omitted).

4 In the Confucian *Analects*, "Tse-kung asked, 'Is there one word that can serve as a principle of conduct for life?' Confucius replied, 'It is the word 'shu' – reciprocity. Do not impose on others what you yourself do not desire'" (15:23). The Islamic *Forty Hadiths of an-Nawawi* contends that "Not one of you is a believer until he desires for his brother what he desires for himself" (No. 13). In the *Mahabharata* of Hinduism, it is said, "Do naught to others which, if done to thee, would cause thee pain: this is the sum of duty" (5.1517). The Buddhist *Majjhima Nikaya* declares: "Is there a deed, Rahula, thou dost wish to do? Then bethink thee thus: Is this deed conducive to my own harm, or to others harm, or to that of both? Then is this a bad deed entailing suffering. Such a deed must thou surely not do" (1.415). This is by no means an exhaustive list, as it leaves out similar statements from Taoism, Sikhism, Shintoism, Zoroastrianism, and many others (see Ontario Consultants on Religious Tolerance: www.religioustolerance.org/reciproc.htm).

5 By way of an example, consider this passage about the freeing of slaves from Deuteronomy 15:12–15:

If a fellow Hebrew, a man or a woman, sells himself to you and serves you six years, in the seventh year you must let him go free. And when you release him, do not send him away empty-handed. Supply him liberally

from your flock, your threshing floor and your winepress. Give to him as the Lord your God has blessed you. Remember that you were slaves in Egypt and the Lord your God redeemed you. That is why I give you this command today.

(*The Holy Bible: New International Version.* Grand Rapids: Zondervan Publishing House, 1986, 142)

It is interesting to note, of course, that this commandment applies to Jewish slaves only, but more important for our present purpose is that there is no manner by which the slave can protest if his owner chooses to disobey God's commandment and keep him in bondage for more than seven years. Any violation of the commandment is between God and the slave-owner; the owner clearly has a duty (to God) to release the slave, but the slave seems not to have an explicit right to his freedom.

6 Michael J. Perry, *The Idea of Human Rights: Four Inquiries* (Oxford: Oxford University Press, 1998), 13, citations omitted.

7 Ibid., 15.

8 Ibid., 30–31.

9 Ibid., 11.

10 Ibid., citation omitted. This quotation, Perry tells us in his citation, is from a diary entry on August 11, 1913. It is of some interest to note another quotation from Tawney's diary that Perry includes in the citation, this one from three days earlier: "Unless a man believes in spiritual things – in God – altruism is absurd. What is the sense of it? Why shld [sic] a man recognize any obligation to his neighbor, unless he believes that he has been put in the world for a special purpose and has a special work to perform in it?" A great deal of recent work in the field of evolutionary psychology now stands against Tawney's invalidation of the idea of non-religious altruism. As early as 1976, in *The Selfish Gene* (New York: Oxford University Press, 1989), Richard Dawkins – very much *not* a religious thinker – suggested that:

A long memory and a capacity for individual recognition are well developed in man. We might therefore expect reciprocal altruism to have played an important part in human evolution. [Robert] Trivers goes so far as to suggest that many of our psychological characteristics – envy, guilt, gratitude, sympathy, etc. – have been shaped by natural selection for improved ability to cheat, to detect cheats, and to avoid being thought to be a cheat.... It is even possible that man's swollen brain, and his predisposition to reason mathematically, evolved as a mechanism of ever more devious cheating, and ever more penetrating detection of cheating in others.

(pp. 187–188)

Altruism, on this reading, has nothing at all to do with a belief in God; instead, the existence of altruistic behavior is explained through Darwinian natural selection. One acts altruistically not because one loves one's neighbors and values them as children of God, but because one's genes "know" the value of altruism, namely that one's neighbors will reciprocate in the future and that, therefore, everyone's altruistic genes will be passed on to the next generation. While this argument against Tawney's connection of altruism and religion does not necessarily invalidate his argument, three days later, about the connection between human rights and religion, it is interesting nonetheless.

11 Perry, 11.

12 Ibid., 39–40, citation omitted.
13 Ibid., 21. Perry also notes that differences exist within as well as across religious traditions, but that these differences "ought not to obscure the fact that the experience of all human beings as sacred is widely shared among different sects and religions" (Ibid.).
14 Perry, 17, citation omitted.
15 Michael J. Perry, "The Morality of Human Rights: a Nonreligious Ground?," *Emory Law Journal* 54 (2005), 112.
16 Ibid., 112–113.
17 Raimond Gaita, *A Common Humanity: Thinking about Love and Truth and Justice* (New York: Routledge, 2002), xxiii.
18 E-mail message from Michael J. Perry to Ari Kohen, April 28, 2003.
19 Perry, *Idea*, 19.
20 Ibid.
21 Perry, "Morality," 115.
22 Ibid., 115–117, citations omitted.
23 Ibid., 116n.
24 Harry G. Frankfurt, "Freedom of the Will and the Concept of a Person," *Journal of Philosophy* 68(1) (January 14, 1971), 7.
25 Ibid.
26 Perry, *Idea*, 19, citation omitted.
27 Matthew 25:31–46 in *The Holy Bible*, 739. Perry quotes a slightly different translation of the same passage in *Idea*, 20, but the ideas expressed are identical.
28 Perry, *Idea*, 20–21.
29 Ibid., 21–22.
30 In what follows, I will consider some problems that exist for the idea of human rights in Judaism and Christianity, as they are the two religious traditions with which I am most familiar. This should *not* be read as a condemnation of these traditions nor as an affirmation of other traditions – Islam, Buddhism, or Hinduism, for example – that I do not consider.
31 Genesis 6:11–13 in *The Pentateuch and Haftorahs*, ed. J.H. Hertz (London: Soncino Press, 1993), 26.
32 There are a number of other stories of murder and destruction from Genesis, ranging from the very well-known to the obscure. The most famous is undoubtedly the wholesale extermination of Sodom and Gomorrah ("Then the Lord caused to rain upon Sodom and upon Gomorrah brimstone and fire from the Lord out of heaven; and he overthrew those cities, and all the Plain, and all the inhabitants of the cities and that which grew upon the ground" (19:24–25 in Ibid., 68)). Perhaps the least famous, but a personal favorite, is the triumphal ode to violence ascribed to Lamech, to whom rabbinic commentary gives the dubious distinction of killing Cain ("And Lamech said unto his wives: Adah and Zillah, hear my voice; Ye wives of Lamech, hearken unto my speech; For I have slain a man for wounding me, And a young man for bruising me; If Cain shall be avenged sevenfold, Truly Lamech seventy and sevenfold" (4:23–24 in Ibid., 16)).
33 Genesis 22:10–12 in Ibid., 75.
34 I Samuel 15:2–33 in Ibid., 996–998.
35 Ibid., 995.
36 Ibid.
37 Perry, *Idea*, 31.
38 To cite just two examples, first Jesus famously prevents the stoning death of a woman brought before him:

> At dawn he appeared again in the temple courts, where all the people gathered around him, and he sat down to teach them. The teachers of the law and the Pharisees brought in a woman caught in adultery. They made her stand before the group and said to Jesus, "Teacher, this woman was caught in the act of adultery. In the Law Moses commanded us to stone such women. Now what do you say?" .... When they kept on questioning him, he straightened up and said to them, "If any one of you is without sin, let him be the first to throw a stone at her."
>
> (John 8:2–7 in *The Holy Bible*, 796)

Second, and perhaps more famously, Judas receives thirty pieces of silver for his part in the arrest and eventual execution of Jesus:

> Then one of the Twelve – the one called Judas Iscariot – went to the chief priests and asked, 'What are you willing to give me if I hand him over to you?' So they counted out for him thirty silver coins. From then on Judas watched for an opportunity to hand him over.
>
> (Matthew 26:14–16 in ibid., 740)

39 William Edward Hartpole Lecky, *History of European Morals From Augustus to Charlemagne* (New York: George Braziller, 1955), ii, 195–196, citations omitted.

40 William Schulz provides just such an example of minor differences within a singular religious tradition in *Tainted Legacy: 9/11 and the Ruin of Human Rights* (New York: Nation Books, 2003):

> One of the factions in the early Christian Church, followers of the charismatic preacher Montanus, believed that only those who ate a steady diet of radishes would be saved. The women in the community, who played an inordinately powerful role in the life of the movement, especially promoted this healthy regimen. Had Montanism prevailed, Christians might eat vegetables at Holy Communion rather than wafers, and the Roman Catholic church might suffer today no shortage of priests.
>
> (p. 109)

Rather than prevailing, however, the Montanists were condemned as heretics, their churches were destroyed, and the movement sharply declined into obscurity.

41 Karen Armstrong, *Holy War: the Crusades and Their Impact on Today's World* (New York: Doubleday, 1991), 178–179.

42 Aleksandr I. Solzhenitsyn, *The Gulag Archipelago 1918–1956: an Experiment in Literary Investigation, Parts I–II* trans. Thomas P. Whitney (New York: Harper & Row, 1974), 173–174.

43 Raymond Aron, *The Opium of the Intellectuals* (New Brunswick: Transaction Publishers, 2001), 323.

44 Perry, *Idea*, 14. Interestingly, Perry's citation of Heschel on this point also includes a similar quotation taken from Dostoevsky's *The Brothers Karamazov*:

> For the secret of man's being is not only to live but to have something to live for. Without a stable conception of the object of life, man would not consent to go on living, and would rather destroy himself than remain on earth, though he had bread in abundance.

As Perry notes, this is one of the Grand Inquisitor's statements.

45 Aron, 323.

46 Perry, *Idea*, 22, citation omitted.

47 Leo Strauss, *Natural Right and History* (Chicago: University of Chicago Press, 1971), 42–43.

48 Perry, *Idea*, 14.

49 Ibid.

50 Ibid., 14–15.

51 Ibid., 15.

52 Ibid.

53 Aron, 84–85.

54 Karen Armstrong, *A History of God: The 4,000-Year Quest of Judaism, Christianity and Islam* (New York: Ballantine Books, 1993), 354.

55 Ibid.

56 Karl Marx, *Economic and Philosophic Manuscripts of 1844* in *The Marx–Engels Reader*, ed. Robert C. Tucker (New York: W.W. Norton & Company, 1978), 84.

57 Armstrong, *History of God*, 83–84.

58 Ibid., 129.

59 Ibid.

60 Perry, *Idea*, 16.

61 Martin Heidegger, *An Introduction to Metaphysics*, trans. Ralph Manheim (New Haven: Yale University Press, 1987), 1–2.

62 Martin Heidegger, *Nietzsche, Volume IV: Nihilism*, trans. Frank A. Capuzzi in *Nietzsche, Volumes Three and Four* ed. David Farrell Krell (New York: HarperCollins Publishers, 1991), 22.

63 Ibid., 162–164, 168–172.

64 Friedrich Nietzsche, *The Gay Science* in *The Portable Nietzsche*, ed. and trans. Walter Kaufmann (New York: Penguin Books, 1982), 95.

65 Heidegger, *Nietzsche*, 203.

66 Ibid., 19.

67 Perry, *Idea*, 16.

68 Friedrich Nietzsche, *The Will to Power*, trans. Walter Kaufmann and R.J. Hollingdale, and ed. Walter Kaufmann (New York: Vintage Books, 1968), 142.

69 Perry, *Idea*, 24, citation omitted.

70 Samantha Power, *"A Problem from Hell": America and the Age of Genocide* (New York: Perennial, 2003), 196–197.

71 Perry, *Idea*, 17, citation omitted.

72 Ibid., 19, citation omitted.

73 Walter Kaufmann, "Editor's Introduction" in Nietzsche, *Will to Power*, xv–xvi.

74 Friedrich Nietzsche, *On the Advantage and Disadvantage of History for Life*, trans. Peter Preuss (Indianapolis: Hackett Publishing Company, 1980), 18.

75 Ibid., 20.

76 Ibid., 10.

77 Ibid.

78 Ibid., 30.

79 Friedrich Nietzsche, *On the Genealogy of Morals: a Polemic* in *Basic Writings*, 485, citation omitted. In his footnote, Kaufmann translates the Latin: "The blessed in the kingdom of heaven will see the punishments of the damned, *in order that their bliss be more delightful for them.*" He notes, also, that this is not quite what one finds in Aquinas' *Summa Theologiae*; to be exact, Aquinas writes, "*Ut beatitude sanctorum eis magis complaceat, et de ea uberiores*

gratias Deo agant, datur eis ut poenam impiorum perfecte intueantur." In English: "In order that the bliss of the saints may be more delightful for them and that they may render more copious thanks to God for it, it is given to them to see perfectly the punishment of the damned." While the original differs from Nietzsche's rendering of it, the spirit is clearly unchanged. The lengthy quotation that Nietzsche employs following Aquinas, while also in Latin, is even more faithful to its author, Tertullian. Here is a short sample, in English:

> Yes, and there are other sights: that last day of judgment, with its everlasting issues; that day unlooked for by the nations, the theme of their derision, when the world hoary with age, and all its many products, shall be consumed in one great flame! How vast a spectacle then bursts upon the eye! *What there excites my admiration? What my derision? Which sights gives me joy? Which rouses me to exultation?* – as I see so many illustrious monarchs, whose reception into the heavens was publicly announced, groaning now in the lowest darkness with great Jove himself, and those, too, who bore witness of their exultation; governors of provinces, too, who persecuted the Christian name, in fires more fierce than those with which in the days of their pride they raged against the followers of Christ.

80 Friedrich Nietzsche, *Beyond Good and Evil: Prelude to a Philosophy of the Future* in *Basic Writings*, 251.
81 Ibid., 393.
82 Ibid., 395.
83 Ibid., 243.
84 Ibid.
85 Friedrich Nietzsche, *The Birth of Tragedy: Out of the Spirit of Music* in *Basic Writings of Nietzsche*, ed. and trans. Walter Kaufmann (New York: The Modern Library, 1992), 42.
86 Nietzsche, *Beyond Good and Evil*, 416.
87 Thomas Hobbes, *Leviathan*, ed. Richard Tuck (Cambridge: Cambridge University Press, 1996), 89.
88 Werner J. Dannhauser, "Friedrich Nietzsche" in *History of Political Philosophy*, ed. Leo Strauss and Joseph Cropsey (Chicago: University of Chicago Press, 1987), 848–849.
89 Ibid., 849.
90 Ibid.
91 Perry, *Idea*, 13, citations omitted.

2 The possibility of non-religious human rights: Alan Gewirth and the Principle of Generic Consistency

1 Aleksandr I. Solzhenitsyn, *The Gulag Archipelago 1918–1956: an Experiment in Literary Investigation, Parts I–II*, trans. Thomas P. Whitney (New York: Harper & Row, 1974), 168.
2 Primo Levi, *The Drowned and the Saved*, trans. Raymond Rosenthal (New York: Vintage International, 1989), 48–49.
3 Jonathan Glover, *Humanity: a Moral History of the Twentieth Century* (New Haven: Yale University Press, 2001), 401.
4 Ibid., 406.
5 Alan Gewirth, *Reason and Morality* (Chicago: University of Chicago Press, 1981), ix.

6 Michael J. Perry, *The Idea of Human Rights: Four Inquiries* (Oxford: Oxford University Press, 1998), 13, citations omitted.

7 Alan Gewirth, "The Epistemology of Human Rights," 1 *Social Philosophy & Policy* 1(2) (Spring 1984), 14–17.

8 Ibid., 18.

9 Ibid.

10 Ibid., 5, citations omitted.

11 Ibid. While Gewirth is correct in arguing that it is insufficient to simply assert that individuals have rights and expect those rights to be respected, he is wrong to think that he has properly dismissed Nozick's claim. In fact, Nozick spends a good deal more time on the question of the origin of rights than Gewirth seems to recognize. While it is correct to say that Nozick does not provide a complete argument, closing instead with a lengthy series of questions, he certainly goes beyond peremptory assertion on this point. For Nozick's discussion of the source of our rights and his grappling with the question of how the meaning we give our lives might provide such an origin, see his *Anarchy, State, and Utopia* (New York: Basic Books, 1974), 48–51.

12 Gewirth, "Epistemology," 6.

13 Ibid.

14 Ibid.

15 This critique of Feinberg is one that should not be presented as free from difficulty, as Gewirth seems not to be engaging with Feinberg's core argument about rights in "The Nature and Value of Rights." Instead, he quotes from the next essay, "The Rights of Animals and Unborn Generations." While the latter deals with interests, the former contains a detailed discussion of the origin of rights that focuses on the importance of claiming them rather than their derivation from our having interests:

> Having rights enables us to "stand up like men," to look others in the eye, and to feel in some fundamental way the equal of anyone. To think of oneself as the holder of rights is not to be unduly but properly proud, to have that minimal self-respect that is necessary to be worthy of the love and esteem of others. Indeed, respect for persons . . . may simply be respect for their rights, so that there cannot be the one without the other; and what is called "human dignity" may simply be the recognizable capacity to assert claims. To respect a person then, or to think of him as possessed of human dignity, simply is to think of him as a potential maker of claims.
> (Joel Feinberg, *Rights, Justice, and the Bounds of Liberty: Essays in Social Philosophy* (Princeton: Princeton University Press, 1980), 151)

16 Gewirth, "Epistemology," 6, citation omitted.

17 Ibid., 7, citation omitted.

18 Ibid., 8, citation omitted.

19 Ibid., 8–9.

20 Ibid., 9, citation omitted. For Rawls' formulation of the original position and veil of ignorance, see his *A Theory of Justice*, Revised Edition (Cambridge: The Belknap Press of Harvard University Press, 1999), 15–19, 109–112, and 118–123.

21 Gewirth, "Epistemology," 9. The argument employed by Gewirth against Rawls is somewhat problematic for at least two reasons. The first is that Rawls, clearly, does not imagine the original position to be the truth about the world; it is, instead, a thought experiment that Rawls employs in an

attempt to derive a version of justice that would be justifiable to all from very modest premises. The second problem for Gewirth is that, in all that follows, he does something very similar to Rawls in constructing his own argument about the generic rights of prospective purposive agents.

22 Ibid.
23 Ibid., 10.
24 Ibid.
25 Gewirth, *Reason*, 7.
26 Ibid., 25.
27 Perry, 13, citation omitted.
28 Gewirth, "Epistemology," 3.
29 Gewirth, *Reason*, 25–26.
30 Ibid., 27.
31 Ibid., 37. This argument against determinism might not pass muster with thoughtful contemporary determinists, who could argue that being the sort of person who can "reflectively consider various reasons for alternative actions and choose among them on the basis of such consideration" is itself determined by a host of factors over which one has no control.
32 Ibid., 39, citation omitted.
33 Ibid., 40.
34 Gewirth, "Epistemology," 14–15.
35 Ibid., 15.
36 Ibid.
37 Ibid.
38 Gewirth, *Reason*, 65.
39 Gewirth, "Epistemology," 15.
40 Gewirth, *Reason*, 59–60.
41 Gewirth, "Epistemology," 15.
42 Ibid.
43 Gewirth, *Reason*, 63.
44 Ibid., 66.
45 Gewirth, "Epistemology," 15.
46 Ibid.
47 Ibid., 16.
48 Ibid.
49 This point raises the issue of criminal justice, as punishing a criminal obviously interferes with his freedom and well-being. On this point, Gewirth argues that punishment acts as a mechanism for restoring the equality of freedom and well-being that exists between agents: "If the agent inflicts a basic or other serious harm on some recipient, he violates this equality in a quite specific way, and the punishment prescribed by the criminal law is justified as a way of restoring the equality by redressing the previously disturbed balance" (*Reason*, 297). By way of example, he considers the case of A and B, and the problem that arises when A harms B: "A not only removes X units from B; he also adds a comparable number of units to his own stock of well-being. . . . The punishment prescribed by the criminal law, in accordance with the Principle of Proportionality, removes from A this additional satisfaction" (ibid.). This is, of course, quite different from the Kantian argument about punishment in *The Metaphysics of Morals*, namely that:

> Judicial punishment can never be merely a means of furthering some extraneous good for the criminal himself or for civil society, but must always be imposed on the criminal simply *because he has committed a crime*. For a

human being can never be manipulated just as a means of realising someone else's intentions, and is not to be confused with the objects of the law of kind. He is protected against this by his inherent personality, although he may well be sentenced to forfeit his civil personality.

(In Immanuel Kant, *Political Writings*, ed. Hans Reiss and trans. H.B. Nisbet (Cambridge: Cambridge University Press, 1996), 154–155)

50 Gewirth, "Epistemology," 16.
51 Gewirth, *Reason*, 64.
52 Gewirth, "Epistemology," 16.
53 Perry, *Idea*, 30–31.
54 Gewirth, *Reason*, 104.
55 Ibid., 104–105.
56 Gewirth, "Epistemology," 16.
57 Gewirth, *Reason*, 111–112.
58 Ibid., 112.
59 Ibid., 110.
60 Gewirth, "Epistemology," 16–17.
61 Ibid., 17.
62 Gewirth, *Reason*, 112.
63 Gewirth, "Epistemology," 17.
64 Ibid.
65 Ibid. For a great deal more discussion of the PGC, including its derivation, its formal necessity, and a number of objections and responses, see Gewirth, *Reason*, 129–198. Some of these points will also be discussed in the third section of this chapter. For a shorter restatement of the PGC, see Alan Gewirth, *The Community of Rights* (Chicago: University of Chicago Press, 1996), 13–30; the remainder of that book concerns itself with applying the PGC to the idea of social solidarity or community, arguing that rights to freedom and well-being "are also positive, in that in certain circumstances they require active assistance whereby one helps other persons to have freedom and well-being" (p. 31). Beyond Gewirth's own writings on the PGC, Deryck Beyleveld has undertaken two painstakingly detailed summaries of the PGC in *The Dialectical Necessity of Morality: an Analysis and Defense of Alan Gewirth's Argument to the Principle of Generic Consistency* (Chicago: University of Chicago Press, 1991). Beyleveld also examines more than sixty objections to Gewirth's argument (from the publication of Gewirth's *Reason and Morality* in 1978 to 1989, when Beyleveld prepared his own manuscript for publication) and I will turn to his exhaustive defense of the PGC in the third section of this chapter.
66 In a series of footnotes to his introduction, Beyleveld provides a comprehensive list of the arguments to which he responds in his book and to which Gewirth has already responded (p. 398–400). He also notes:

I cannot, of course, guarantee that I have located all items.... If I have overlooked items, then these are most likely to be reviews, comments in books, comments in articles that are not specifically on Gewirth, or articles in foreign languages. After February 1990, I did not attempt to locate further items.

(p. 400)

Although Beyleveld's catalog of critiques is now sixteen years old, I have chosen not to conduct my own search for more recent arguments against the

PGC because I am confident that those included in Beyleveld's book offer a complete picture of the problems theorists have identified with Gewirth's theory. A quick search reveals, for example, a 1992 article by Louis P. Pojman that includes a short critique of Gewirth, but it seems to me to have been dealt with by Gewirth himself as early as his first articulation of the theory in *Reason and Morality* and again by Beyleveld. In "Are Human Rights Based on Equal Human Worth?," *Philosophy and Phenomenological Research* 52(3) (September 1992), Pojman offers this critique:

> I don't see why the PGC doesn't apply to animals as well as humans, thus making them equal recipients of our attention. Cats and rats implicitly act on the principles of needing freedom and well-being, even if they cannot articulate them or bring them consciously to mind.
>
> (pp. 616–617)

Gewirth, though, tells us in his first explication of his theory why the PGC doesn't apply to animals:

> it must be noted that not all entities that pursue or seem to pursue purposes are agents in the sense used here. Animals other than humans lack for the most part the ability to control their behavior by their unforced choice, to have knowledge of relevant circumstances beyond what is present to immediate awareness, and especially to reflect rationally on their purposes.
>
> (*Reason*, 120)

67 Beyleveld, 402.
68 Gewirth, *Reason*, 46.
69 Malcolm Bowie, *Lacan* (Cambridge: Harvard University Press, 1991), 10.
70 Ibid., 15–16.
71 Lacan's attempt to offer a solution to his own nihilistic conclusion is based on the idea of self-knowledge, which he argues can be attained by acquiring a certain level of understanding of Lacanian theory and submitting to psychoanalysis. Crucial to the notion of self-knowledge, however, is that its acquisition does not leave an agent with the same ends he had prior to its acquisition. In other words, what the agent thought he was aiming at turns out not at all to be what he truly had as an end. In this way, self-knowledge cannot be seen as a goal on the path to achieving one's ends. Rather than hoping to make better decisions or find out an ultimate end, Lacan seems only to suggest that arriving at the truth about ourselves will – in some way – help us to understand the various conflicts that arise in our lives. He does not even go so far as to put forward the idea that self-knowledge will necessarily help us in our effort not to run afoul of them. For more on this important point, see Jacques Lacan, *The Seminar of Jacques Lacan: Book VII, The Ethics of Psychoanalysis 1959–1960*, ed. Jacques-Alain Miller and trans. Dennis Porter (New York: W.W. Norton & Company, 1997), 291–301. See also, Bowie, 197–203.
72 Gewirth, *Reason*, 106.
73 Beyleveld, 243, citation omitted.
74 Ibid. For Gewirth's own, very thorough account of the criterion of relevant similarities, see *Reason*, 104–128.
75 Beyleveld, 247.
76 Ibid., 248.

77 Gewirth, *Reason*, 122.

78 Ibid.

79 Beyleveld, 447.

80 Ibid., 448. Beyleveld and Shaun Pattinson return to this problem in "Precautionary Reason as a Link to Moral Action" in *Medical Ethics*, ed. Michael Boylan (Upper Saddle River: Prentice Hall, 2000) and their conclusion is essentially that we ought to assume human beings are PPAs (pp. 43–45). Failure to do so, they argue, might lead us to violate an agent's rights and precautionary reasoning dictates that we should err on the side of caution in these cases: "even where an other being is apparently only a partial agent there remains a risk that – if I suppose that it is not an agent, and act accordingly – it is an agent, and I will have deprived it of the protection of the Principle of Generic Consistency to which it is entitled" (ibid., 43). This is all well and good as long as we are uncomfortable taking these risks with possible PPAs and, Beyleveld and Pattinson point out, as long as we have some reason to believe that these beings might be agents in the fullest sense. When it comes to those who are obviously partial agents – and to those who are possibly partial agents – another problem arises. As Beyleveld and Pattinson note, "the moral status of beings who are more probably agents is greater than that of beings who are less probably agents. In other words, the moral status of beings is *proportional* to the probability that they are agents" (p. 44). The only duties that Beyleveld and Pattinson recognize as being owed to partial agents "are unavoidably paternalistic" and even the duty not to harm the partial agent can be overcome if failing to observe that duty allows us to observe a duty to an agent or a being suspected of greater agency than the partial agent (ibid.).

81 Richard Rorty, *Truth and Progress: Philosophical Papers, Volume 3* (Cambridge: Cambridge University Press, 1998), 178.

82 Ibid., 178–179.

83 Gewirth, *Reason*, 122.

84 Rorty, 177, citation omitted.

85 Ibid.

86 Ibid., 178.

87 Friedrich Engels, *Anti-Dühring: Herr Eugen Dühring's Revolution in Science* (New York: International Publishers, 1966), 108–109. Gewirth's quotation of Engels can be found in *Reason*, 127–128; another copy of the quotation and a defense of Gewirth on this point can be found in Beyleveld, 309–310.

88 Gewirth, *Reason*, 128.

89 Ibid.

90 Beyleveld, 310.

91 Ibid.

92 Virginia Held, "Reason and Economic Justice" in *Economic Justice: Private Rights and Public Responsibilities* ed. Kenneth Kipnis and Diana T. Meyers (Totowa: Rowman and Allanheld, 1985), 38. The quotation can also be found in Beyleveld, 311.

93 Beyleveld, 314–315.

94 Ibid., 314.

95 Beyleveld and Pattinson point out that they "use 'it' to avoid implying that all agents are human or are necessarily gendered" (p. 41n). While there is likely some value in avoiding this assumption about agents, I want to argue that a discussion of rights loses a great deal of its precision and force when it achieves this degree of abstraction.

96 Gewirth, *Reason*, 128.

97   Michael Sandel, *Liberalism and the Limits of Justice*, Second Edition (Cambridge: Cambridge University Press, 1998), 179.
98   Ibid.
99   Arthur Koestler, *The Yogi and the Commissar: and Other Essays* (New York: The Macmillan Company: 1946), 91.
100 Samantha Power, *"A Problem from Hell": America and the Age of Genocide* (New York: Perennial, 2003), 349. In addition to its frank discussion of Rwanda, Power's book looks closely at the genocidal campaigns carried out in the twentieth century in Turkey, Germany, Cambodia, Iraq, and Bosnia. Each chapter is well-stocked with stories about violence as gruesome as this one, as is the entirety of Philip Gourevitch's account of the Rwandan genocide, *We Wish to Inform You That Tomorrow we Will be Killed with our Families: Stories from Rwanda* (New York: Picador USA, 1998). It is possible, quite literally, to open Gourevitch's book to any page and find descriptions of violence the likes of which are unknown to Western readers and seem too horrible to be true. Power offers an interesting quotation to this effect in her discussion of Bosnia:

> "They were talking about women being put in rape camps. They were talking about all these killings – some they said they'd seen, others they'd only heard about. They talked about people being thrown off cliffs, men being held and tortured and starved in camps.... No matter how much I heard, I just found it hard to believe. I couldn't believe. In fact, I didn't believe.
>
> (p. 270)

101 Gewirth, *Reason*, 213.
102 William F. Schulz, *In Our Own Best Interest: How Defending Human Rights Benefits Us All* (Boston: Beacon Press, 2002), 23.
103 Ibid., 25.

3 The problem of secular sacredness: Ronald Dworkin, Michael Perry, and human rights foundationalism

1   Hobbes says, in *Leviathan*, ed. Richard Tuck (Cambridge: Cambridge University Press, 1996), "the weakest has strength enough to kill the strongest, either by secret machination, or by confederacy with others, that are in the same danger with himselfe" (p. 87).
2   Steven Pinker, *The Blank Slate: the Modern Denial of Human Nature* (New York: Viking, 2002), 56, citation omitted.
3   Ibid., 58, citation omitted.
4   Michael J. Perry, *The Idea of Human Rights: Four Inquiries* (Oxford: Oxford University Press, 1998), 24, citation omitted. As the first chapter made clear, Perry's understanding of a meaningful universe is quite distinct: it is one that is "hospitable to our deepest yearnings for what [Abraham] Heschel called 'ultimate relationship, ultimate belonging'" (ibid., citation omitted). For Pinker, of course, the world might very well be meaningless in the sense that Perry has in mind, but it is not necessarily absurd. If we were to consider the world from the point of view of our genes, the future has quite a long shadow indeed, far longer than the span of any one individual life. That said, Pinker would likely dispute the use of words like meaningless and absurd to describe the world and our place in it. Simply because human beings are, in a sense, well-oiled machines whose function is to deliver their genes into the next generation does

not entail that their existence is absurd or meaningless. We are quite capable of making plans, forming attachments, and living full lives – and these are no less real if our purpose for doing them is to propel our genetic material into the future.

5 Ronald Dworkin, *Life's Dominion: an Argument about Abortion, Euthanasia, and Individual Freedom* (New York: Vintage Books, 1994), 195.

6 Ibid., 79.

7 Ibid., 155.

8 I will alternate between "human being" and "human life" throughout this chapter, as Perry writes of the former and Dworkin the latter. While I recognize that these terms are charged, particularly within the literature on reproductive rights, I will not take a position on whether the concept of sacredness best applies to one or the other. It seems sufficient to note, for the purposes of this chapter, that it does not seem odd to refer to either the sacredness of all human life or every human being. It might, however, be a bit of a stretch to refer to the inherent dignity of all human life, as opposed to every human being, for reasons which will be discussed in greater length later in this chapter and the next.

9 Dworkin, 68–69.

10 Ibid., 69, italics mine.

11 Ibid., 71.

12 Ibid.

13 Ibid., 70.

14 Ibid., 74.

15 There are, however, some things that tend to blur the distinction for Dworkin. While art is intrinsically valuable, *great* art is sacred and might also – on occasion – be incrementally valuable. The same, he suggests, might be true of great lives: "even those who are most in favor of controlling population growth would not want fewer Leonardo da Vincis or Martin Luther Kings" (p. 74). It seems, though, that the question of incremental value is ultimately a personal one; as Dworkin tells us, "I do not myself wish that there were more paintings by Tintoretto than there are. But I would nevertheless be appalled by the deliberate destruction of even one of those he did paint" (p. 74). It is not terribly difficult to imagine someone who yearned for more Tintorettos and fewer da Vincis, and it is not immediately obvious from Dworkin's argument how this dispute might be adjudicated.

16 Perry, 26.

17 Ibid.

18 Ibid.

19 Dworkin, 71.

20 Ibid., 69.

21 Michael J. Perry, "The Gospel According to Dworkin," *Constitutional Commentary* 11(1) (Winter 1994), 178n.

22 Dworkin, 69.

23 Ronald Dworkin, "Life is Sacred. That's the Easy Part," *The New York Times Magazine* (May 16, 1993), 36.

24 Perry, *Idea*, 26.

25 Ibid.

26 Dworkin, *Life's Dominion*, 74.

27 Ibid.

28 As John Tomasi correctly notes, in "Liberalism, Sanctity, and the Prohibition of Abortion," *Journal of Philosophy* 94(10) (October 1997), "The crucial move, according to Dworkin, is to think of the creative inputs in people's lives,

whether from nature (natural selection or, on some views, God's work) or from humans (culture and training), not simply as contributions but as *investments*" (p. 493). We can clearly understand what the investment is toward when considering a purely human investment, but it is considerably murkier with natural investments. The puzzle is that, despite this difficulty, most people seem quite confident about whether or not their actions are respectful of natural investment:

> When human projects, directly or indirectly, threaten an entire species of animal (consider the ivory hunting of the African elephant, or the eradication of the snail darter by the Tellico Dam) most people are quite sure that this is a terrible thing, an act of desecration.
>
> (Ibid., 495)

The puzzle is solved by what Tomasi terms the investment connection (IC) and, specifically, by the notion that IC is severed by what he calls a *crossbasal violation* when one closes an investment account opened by someone else. To flesh this idea out somewhat, consider the following example:

> When a species of tree or animal naturally goes extinct, there seems to be a great subtraction of nature's creative investment. Yet people do not feel here ... that such an event is a violation of the sacred.... Since nature (theistic/secular) opened the account embodied in the tree species, when nature closes the account, IC has been preserved.... Imagine a different case whereby a community of young lumberjacks had developed a (to them) richly rewarding and meaningful life project centrally committed to the project of efficiently cutting down trees. Unfortunately, the remaining stand of some ... tree species gets in their way and is destroyed.... In both cases, the eradication of an entire tree species involves a great subtraction from what is wonderful in the world.... But, faced with uncertainty about what nature intends ... people feel the loss in the lumberjack case is worse because of the way the loss comes about: that loss involves what we might call a *sacred violation*.
>
> (Ibid., 497–498)

Despite all of this talk about avoiding sacred violations, Tomasi might not be entirely correct, as two important examples help to highlight. While it is true that most people worry about the extinction of beautiful, exotic, or helpful animals, the same cannot be said about the possibility of killing off nature's peskier creations. For example, mosquitoes are deliberately destroyed every minute of every day, and people do not so much as pause to consider that these creatures are a product of a great deal of natural investment. Mosquitoes are not on the verge of extinction, of course, but I am not confident that our decision to slap at them would change a great deal if they were. Similarly, few homeowners would be terribly upset if mankind found a way to exterminate crabgrass from the face of the planet. The distinctly human project of cultivating attractive lawns, especially when it involves strong chemicals to destroy weeds, is clearly disrespectful of nature's creative investment in crabgrass. These two examples call attention to the fact that not all of Tomasi's sacred violations are extremely troubling to most people; in fact, most people seem not to be concerned in the least about *these* sorts of crossbasal violations. Few people, if any, would suggest that human beings and mosquitoes represent equivalent creative investments, of course, which might account for

the confidence that Dworkin has in our ability to figure out how much respect we owe to each.

29 Dworkin, *Life's Dominion*, 76.
30 Ibid., 82.
31 Ibid., 83.
32 Ibid.
33 Perry, *Idea*, 27.
34 There are, of course, other ways of in which people are awestruck that have no connection at all to sacredness. It is entirely possible for one to be filled with awe and find no value at all in the awesome object or event. Consider this famous description from Niccolò Machiavelli, *The Prince*, trans. Harvey C. Mansfield, Jr. (Chicago: University of Chicago Press, 1985):

> And because this point is deserving of notice and of being imitated by others, I do not want to leave it out. Once the duke had taken over Romagna, he found it had been commanded by impotent lords who had been readier to despoil their subjects than to correct them.... So he put there Messer Remirro de Orco, a cruel and ready man, to whom he gave the fullest power. In a short time Remirro reduced it to peace and unity, with the very greatest reputation for himself. Then the duke judged that such excessive authority was not necessary.... And because he knew that past rigors had generated some hatred for Remirro, to purge the spirits of that people and to gain them entirely to himself, he wished to show that if any cruelty had been committed, this had not come from him but from the harsh nature of his minister. And having seized this opportunity, he had him placed one morning in the piazza at Cesena in two pieces, with a piece of wood and a bloody knife beside him. The ferocity of this spectacle left the people at once satisfied and stupefied.
>
> (pp. 29–30, citation omitted)

35 Perry, *Idea*, 28.
36 Ibid.
37 At times, Dworkin seems uncertain as to his *own* position on whether something can possess value independently of anyone valuing it:

> I do not mean to take any position on a further, very abstract philosophical issue not pertinent to this discussion: whether great paintings would still be valuable if intelligent life were altogether destroyed forever so that no one could ever have the experience of regarding paintings again. There is no inconsistency in denying that they would have value then, because the value of a painting lies in the kind of experience it makes available, while still insisting that this value is intrinsic because it does not depend on any creatures' actually wanting that kind of experience.
>
> (*Life's Dominion*, 248n)

38 Christopher J. Eberle, "Unnatural Sacrifice" (unpublished manuscript, 2003), 4, citation omitted.
39 Michael J. Perry, "The Morality of Human Rights: a Nonreligious Ground?," *Emory Law Journal* 54 (2005), 112–113.
40 Ibid., 141.
41 Immanuel Kant, *Grounding for the Metaphysics of Morals*, trans. James W. Ellington (Indianapolis: Hackett Publishing Company, 1993), 61–62.
42 Ludwig Wittgenstein, *Philosophical Investigations*, trans. G.E.M. Anscombe (Oxford: Basil Blackwell, 1968), 85.

43 E-mail message from Michael J. Perry to Ari Kohen, May 12, 2003.
44 Jeffrie G. Murphy, "Afterword: Constitutionalism, Moral Skepticism, and Religious Belief" in *Constitutionalism: The Philosophical Dimension*, ed. Alan S. Rosenbaum (New York: Greenwood Press, 1988), 247–248.
45 Perry, "Morality," 141–142, citations omitted.
46 Ibid., 140.
47 E-mail message from Michael J. Perry to Ari Kohen, May 12, 2003.
48 Perry, *Idea*, 28.
49 Ibid., 29.
50 Dworkin, *Life's Dominion*, 73.
51 Perry, *Idea*, 28.
52 Ibid., 28, italics mine.
53 Ibid., 12.
54 Ibid., 30–31.
55 Ibid., 13, citation omitted.
56 Ibid., 31, citation omitted.
57 Ibid., 30, citation omitted.
58 Robert Grant, "Abortion and the Idea of the Sacred," *Times Literary Supplement* (June 18, 1993), 11.
59 Dworkin, *Life's Dominion*, 84.
60 The next two chapters will examine the concept of self-creation in greater detail and I will argue for its centrality to non-religious understandings of human dignity and human rights. Richard Rorty, the subject of the penultimate chapter, offers what is, in my mind, a more complete – or more robust – discussion of the self-creation that human beings underake than Dworkin does.
61 Perry, *Idea*, 13, citations omitted.
62 Ibid., 60.
63 Ibid., 12.
64 Perry, *Idea*, 13, citations omitted.
65 Murphy, 245.
66 Raimond Gaita, *A Common Humanity: Thinking about Love and Truth and Justice* (New York: Routledge, 2002), 23.
67 *The Oxford English Dictionary, Volume 14*, ed. J.A. Simpson and E.S.C. Weiner (Oxford: Oxford University Press, 1989), 338–339.
68 Ibid.
69 Charlton T. Lewis and Charles Short, *A Latin Dictionary* (Oxford: Oxford University Press, 1969), 1610–1611.
70 *The Oxford English Dictionary, Volume 4*, 656–657.
71 Lewis and Short, 578.
72 Henry George Liddell and Robert Scott, *A Greek–English Lexicon*, revised and augmented by Sir Henry Stuart Jones with the assistance of Roderick McKenzie (Oxford: Oxford University Press, 1969), 444.
73 *The Oxford English Dictionary, Volume 4*, 656.
74 Ibid.
75 In 1689, the English Bill of Rights recognized that "the late King James the Second, by the assistance of divers evil counselors, judges, and ministers employed by him, did endeavour to subvert and extirpate the protestant religion, and the laws and liberties of this kingdom" (in *The Human Rights Reader: Major Political Writings, Essays, Speeches, and Documents from the Bible to the Present*, ed. Micheline R. Ishay (New York: Routledge, 1997), 91). While the Bill recognized that considerable violations of the citizens' rights had occurred under James, it concluded "that his said highness the prince of Orange will ... still preserve them from the violation of their rights, which they have here asserted, and

from all other attempts upon their religion, rights, and liberties" (in Ibid., 93). Although the English had successfully challenged the notion that kings ruled by divine right, the Bill perpetuates the idea that a small subset of the population ought to rule over the commoners, provided they do so benevolently.

76 The United States Declaration of Independence in ibid., 127.
77 The French Declaration of the Rights of Man and Citizen in ibid., 138.
78 Ibid.
79 Ibid.
80 The United States Declaration of Independence in ibid., 127.
81 Whereas the English Bill of Rights recognized the necessity for Protestants to "have arms for their defense suitable to their conditions" (in ibid., 92), the first two amendments to the Constitution of the United States of America hoped that weapons would only be "necessary to the security of a free state," since Congress could "make no law respecting an establishment of religion, or prohibiting the free exercise thereof" (in Alexander Hamilton, James Madison, and John Jay, *The Federalist Papers*, ed. Clinton Rossiter (New York: New American Library, 1992, 542).
82 United Nations Charter in Ishay, 406.
83 United Nations Universal Declaration of Human Rights in ibid., 407.
84 As Jonathan Glover points out, in *Humanity: a Moral History of the Twentieth Century* (New Haven: Yale University Press, 2001):

> To talk of the twentieth-century atrocities is in one way misleading. It is a myth that barbarism is unique to the twentieth century: the whole of human history includes wars, massacres, and every kind of torture and cruelty: there are grounds for thinking that over much of the world the changes of the last hundred years or so have been towards a psychological climate more humane than at any previous time. But it is still right that much of twentieth-century history has been a very unpleasant surprise. Technology has made a difference. The decisions of a few people can mean horror and death for hundreds of thousands, even millions, of other people. These events shock us not only by their scale. They also contrast with the expectations, at least in Europe, with which the twentieth century began.
>
> (p. 3)

85 William F. Schulz, *In Our Own Best Interest: How Defending Human Rights Benefits Us All* (Boston: Beacon Press, 2002), 26.
86 Mary Ann Glendon, *A World Made New: Eleanor Roosevelt and the Universal Declaration of Human Rights* (New York: Random House, 2001), 166.
87 ibid., 164.
88 Schulz, 27.
89 Ibid., 26.

4 Human dignity without teleology: human rights and human biology

1 Gary Kalkut and Nancy Neveloff Dubler, "The Line Between Life and Death," *New York Times* (May 10, 2005).
2 Ibid.
3 I will utilize the distinction of human animals and human persons, found in the literature on personhood, despite some discomfort with the former term. While "human beings" seems more appropriate and might better convey my personal feelings of respect and care for pre- and post-persons than "human animals," maintaining the same language throughout the chapter will ease the discussion.

4 Michael J. Perry, "The Morality of Human Rights: a Non-Religious Ground?," *Emory Law Journal* 54 (2005), 128. Perry understands proponents of evolution to be proceeding from what he terms – in *The Idea of Human Rights: Four Inquiries* (Oxford: Oxford University Press, 1998) – an absurd universe (p. 14) and, although I think this is a problematic assumption, I won't challenge it here because a) it ultimately makes little difference to my central argument in this chapter and b) he is likely correct that few evolutionary theorists think about the meaning of the universe or of human life in the sense that he has in mind.

5 Steven Pinker, *The Blank Slate: the Modern Denial of Human Nature* (New York: Viking, 2002), viii, citation omitted.

6 Ibid.

7 David DeGrazia, "Identity, Killing, and the Boundaries of Our Existence," *Philosophy & Public Affairs* 31(4) (Fall 2003), 413.

8 See Perry, *Idea*, 14.

9 While much of what follows will draw on Steven Pinker's accounts of the human mind and human nature, he is by no means the only one to write on these subjects. Interested readers should also see Robert Wright, *The Moral Animal: Evolutionary Psychology and Everyday Life* (New York: Vintage Books, 1995); Gary Marcus, *The Birth of the Mind: How a Tiny Number of Genes Creates the Complexities of Human Thought* (New York: Basic Books, 2004); Richard Dawkins, *The Selfish Gene* (Oxford: Oxford University Press, 1989); Owen Flanagan, *The Problem of the Soul: Two Visions of Mind and How to Reconcile Them* (New York: Basic Books, 2003); and two books by Matt Ridley: *The Origins of Virtue: Human Instincts and the Evolution of Cooperation* (New York: Penguin Books, 1996) and *Genome: the Autobiography of a Species in 23 Chapters* (New York: Perennial, 2000). This list is by no means an exhaustive one, but these books are excellent resources in no small part because of their eloquent presentations of challenging material.

10 Pinker, 2.

11 Ibid., 5.

12 Margaret Mead, *Sex and Temperament in Three Primitive Societies* (New York: William Morrow, 1963), 280.

13 Francis Fukuyama, *Our Posthuman Future: Consequences of the Biotechnology Revolution* (New York: Picador, 2002), 20–21.

14 Pinker, viii–ix.

15 See Ibid., 5–102.

16 Ibid., 34.

17 Ibid., 35.

18 Ibid.

19 Gottfried Wilhelm Leibniz, *New Essays on Human Understanding* (New York: Cambridge University Press, 1996), 111.

20 Pinker, 54.

21 Ibid., 55.

22 Ibid.

23 Ibid., citation omitted.

24 Ibid., citation omitted.

25 Ibid.

26 Ibid., 100.

27 Ibid., 100–101.

28 DeGrazia, 417.

29 In transplanting only the cerebrum, rather than the whole brain, I follow Eric T. Olson's account of this thought experiment in *The Human Animal: Personal*

Identity Without Psychology (Oxford: Oxford University Press, 1999) because, as he notes,

> the whole-brain-transplant story does not clearly distinguish between the Psychological and Biological Approaches. The result of removing and transplanting your cerebrum ... is a living human animal without a cerebrum, in which your life-sustaining functions continue on, and a human being with your cerebrum and your psychology who nevertheless doesn't seem to be the living animal that was once associated with you.
>
> (p. 45)

30 Ibid., 43.
31 Jeff McMahan, *The Ethics of Killing: Problems at the Margins of Life* (Oxford: Oxford University Press, 2002), 43.
32 DeGrazia, 418, citation omitted.
33 Ibid., 417
34 Ibid.
35 As McMahan points out

> in infancy the degree of psychological connectedness from day to day is not clearly strong, and in very early infancy and during fetal gestation, what connectedness there is is clearly not strong – that is, there are far fewer psychological connections from day to day than half the number that hold over a day in the life of a normal adult.
>
> (p. 44)

On this point, Olson notes that:

> According to Piaget, clear signs of intentional or goal-directed behavior appear four to eight months after birth, and infants do not acquire the capacity for symbolic representation – reasoning – until one and a half to two years. Many psychologists now think that Piaget's timetable is a bit late for most children; still it seems clear that you could not have come into existence until at least a year after your birth, if rationality is essential to you.
>
> (p. 75)

36 McMahan, 45.
37 Olson, 88.
38 DeGrazia, 418.
39 Ibid.
40 Olson, 95.
41 DeGrazia, 421.
42 Olson, 124.
43 Ibid., 89.
44 DeGrazia, 421.
45 Olson, 89–90.
46 Ibid., 91.
47 Ibid.
48 The distinction, which arose during debates about death and about which more will be said in the next section, is captured nicely by DeGrazia. In talking about death, then, the whole-brain approach is defined "as the irreversible cessation of all functions of the entire brain, including the brainstem (the functioning of

which is necessary for *spontaneous* cardiopulmonary function," while the higher brain approach sees "human death as *the irreversible cessation of the capacity for consciousness*" (p. 436).

49 Pinker, 207.
50 Robert Wright, *Nonzero: the Logic of Human Destiny* (New York: Vintage Books, 2001), 287–288.
51 Pinker, 211.
52 For another example, consider the following point about language and representation that Steven Pinker makes in *How the Mind Works* (New York: W.W. Norton & Company, 1999):

> If you learned that *wapiti* was another name for an elk, you could take all the facts connected to the word *elk* and instantly transfer them to *wapiti*, without having to solder new connections to the word one at a time. Of course, only your zoological knowledge would transfer; you would not expect *wapiti* to be *pronounced* like *elk*. That suggests you have a level of representation specific to the concepts behind the words, not just the words themselves. Your knowledge of facts about elks hangs off the concept; the words *elk* and *wapiti* also hang off the concept; and the spelling *e-l-k* and pronunciation [ɛlk] hang off the word *elk*.
>
> (p. 86)

53 Wright, *Nonzero*, 288.
54 Ibid.
55 Dorothy Hermann, *Helen Keller: a Life* (New York: Alfred A. Knopf, 1998), 11.
56 Immanuel Kant, *Grounding for the Metaphysics of Morals*, trans. James W. Ellington (Indianapolis: Hackett Publishing Company, 1993), 43.
57 Peter Singer, *Writings on an Ethical Life* (New York: Ecco, 2001), 137.
58 Pinker, *Mind Works*, 322–323.
59 Pinker, *Blank Slate*, 33.
60 Ibid., 10.
61 Ibid., 42.
62 Ibid., 41.
63 Ibid., 40–41.
64 Ibid., 108.
65 Elizabeth Allen, Barbara Beckwith, Jon Beckwith, Steven Chorover, David Culver, Margaret Duncan, Stephen Jay Gould, Ruth Hubbard, Hiroshi Inouye, Anthony Leeds, Richard C. Lewontin, Chuck Madansky, Larry Miller, Reed Pyeritz, Miriam Rosenthal, and Herb Schreier, "Against 'Sociobiology'" in *New York Review of Books* 22(18) (November 13, 1975), 43.
66 Richard C. Lewontin, Steven Rose, and Leon J. Kamin, *Not in our Genes* (New York: Pantheon, 1984), 236.
67 Pinker, *Blank Slate*, 44.
68 Ibid., 53.
69 Robert P. Kraynak, "Defending Human Dignity: The Challenge of Our Times" in *In Defense of Human Dignity: Essays for Our Times*, ed. Robert P. Kraynak and Glenn Tinder (Notre Dame: University of Notre Dame Press, 2003), 4.
70 CNN.com Inside Politics, "Schiavo Ruling Disappoints White House, DeLay" (March 22, 2005). Online available at: www.cnn.com/2005/ALLPOLITICS/03/22/schiavo.reaction/index.html.
71 Timothy P. Jackson, "A House Divided, Again: Sanctity vs. Dignity in the Induced Death Debates" in *In Defense of Human Dignity: Essays for Our*

Times, ed. Robert P. Kraynak and Glenn Tinder (Notre Dame: University of Notre Dame Press, 2003), 144.

72 Timothy P. Jackson, "The Image of God and the Soul of Humanity: Reflections on Dignity, Sanctity, and Democracy" in *Religion in the Liberal Polity,* ed. Terence Cuneo (Notre Dame: University of Notre Dame Press, 2005), 46.

73 Jackson, "House Divided," 157.

74 Jackson, "Image of God," 48.

75 Jackson, "House Divided," 144.

76 Ibid., 144–145.

77 Kalkut and Dubler.

78 Michael B. Green and Daniel Wikler, "Brain Death and Personal Identity," *Philosophy and Public Affairs* 9(2) (Winter 1980), 116n21.

79 Consider DeGrazia on this point about the problem with the whole-brain standard:

> brain-dead bodies can, with mechanical support, maintain integrated functioning. For example, pregnant brain-dead women have maintained bodily functions for months, carrying fetuses to term; and a brain-dead boy has over several years grown, overcome infections, and healed wounds.
>
> (p. 438)

80 Jackson, "Image of God," 51, citation omitted.

81 Henry George Liddell and Robert Scott, *A Greek–English Lexicon,* revised and augmented by Sir Henry Stuart Jones with the assistance of Roderick McKenzie (Oxford: Oxford University Press, 1969), 444.

82 DeGrazia, 423.

83 Ibid., 424.

84 DeGrazia, 424.

85 Peter Singer, *Rethinking Life and Death: the Collapse of our Traditional Ethics* (New York: St. Martin's Griffin, 1994), 43.

86 Incidentally, it seems to me that human animals *do* warrant our respect and care. But nothing about that statement entails that they be thought of as persons with dignity and rights. It makes sense to care for those animals who might become – or who once were – human persons, but it is a mistake to conclude that these animals have a right to life.

87 Singer, *Writings,* 160.

88 Ibid.

89 David Boonin, *A Defense of Abortion* (Cambridge: Cambridge University Press, 2003), 115.

90 Ibid.

91 Ibid., 128, citation omitted.

92 Ibid. This does, however, affect that notion – drawn from the ruling in *Planned Parenthood of Pennsylvania* v. *Casey* – that viability is an important moment to consider in the life of a fetus. As William Cooney suggests – in "The Fallacy of All Person-Denying Arguments for Abortion," *Journal of Applied Philosophy* 8(2) (1991) – it is not: "Does a 5–month-old fetus then *become* a person when that stage of technology exists? Can personhood be a condition relative to and dependent on technology?" (p. 161). If technology were to allow for earlier viability, this would not change the facts about personhood because a viable pre-OCBA fetus lacks a sense of self and, consequently, dignity and rights.

93 Pinker, *Blank Slate,* 42–43.

5 Does might make human rights? Sympathy, solidarity, and subjectivity in Richard Rorty's final vocabulary

1 Michael J. Perry, *The Idea of Human Rights: Four Inquiries* (Oxford: Oxford University Press, 1998), 30–31.
2 Richard Rorty, *Contingency, Irony, and Solidarity* (Cambridge: Cambridge University Press, 1989), 26.
3 It should be noted that Rorty is not opposed to the idea of providing reasons for our actions. He argues, however, that our reasons can only take us so far. As we will see, Rorty has an answer – a reason – to give to those who ask, "Why not act cruelly toward others?": "Because we believe that cruelty is the worst thing we do; we think of ourselves as the sort of people who seek to minimize suffering, rather than expand it." If pressed further – "Why are we this sort of people and not another?" – Rorty would have another reason: "We feel as we do because we were socialized in a particular time and place by people who either held this belief themselves or thought that the next generation ought to." Rorty could continue in this vein for a very long time; the problem is that answers of this sort cannot possibly do what Perry insists is necessary, namely back up on an unchanging, objective reason for respecting the rights of others. The type of reason that Perry is looking for – and that Rorty opposes – is one that transcends the subjectivity that Rorty embraces.
4 Rorty, 27.
5 Perry quotes Glenn Tinder on the particular danger of rehabilitating Nietzsche in the way that Rorty does:

> Many would like to think that there are no consequences – that we can continue treasuring the life and welfare, the civil rights and political authority, of every person without believing in a God who renders such attitudes and conduct compelling. Nietzsche shows that we cannot.
>
> (p. 23)

6 Rorty, 27.
7 Ibid.
8 Ibid., 26.
9 Ibid., 27.
10 Ibid., 32.
11 Ibid. The word "contingency" has been bandied about quite a bit thus far, but it will be helpful to see what exactly Rorty has in mind. He does a particularly nice job of describing the idea of the contingency of selfhood:

> Anything from the sound of a word through the color of a leaf to the feel of a piece of skin can, as Freud showed us, serve to dramatize and crystallize a human being's sense of self-identity. For any such thing can play the role in an individual life which philosophers have thought could, or at least should, be played only by things which were universal, common to us all. It can symbolize the blind impress all our behavings bear. Any seemingly random constellation of such things can set the tone of a life. Any such constellation can set up an unconditional commandment to whose service a life may be devoted – a commandment no less unconditional because it may be intelligible to, at most, only one person.
>
> (p. 37)

12 Ibid., 44.
13 Perry, 37.

14   There is no intelligible (much less persuasive) secular version of the conviction that every human being is sacred; the only intelligible versions are religious. . . . The conviction that every human being is sacred is, in my view, inescapably religious – and the idea of human rights is, therefore, ineliminably religious.

(ibid., 11–12)

15 Ibid., 12.

16 Before we go too far, it is clearly important to define what Rorty means when he talks about two closely related terms, metaphysics and foundations. Rorty is a bit hard to pin down on these terms, but he does say the following in *Philosophy and Social Hope* (New York: Penguin, 1999):

The distinction between the found and the made is a version of that between the absolute and the relative, between something which is what it is apart from its relations to other things, and something whose nature depends upon those relations. In the course of the centuries, this distinction has become central to what Derrida calls "the metaphysics of presence" – the search for a "full presence beyond the reach of play", an absolute beyond the reach of relationality. So if we wish to abandon metaphysics we must stop distinguishing between the absolute and the relative.

(p. xviii)

Eric M. Gander, in *The Last Conceptual Revolution: a Critique of Richard Rorty's Political Philosophy* (Albany: State University of New York Press, 1999), does an excellent job of succinctly elucidating Rorty's meaning:

The metaphysician is one who believes that humans are ultimately accountable to some higher, non-human reality – God, or Reason, or Natural Law, or some analogous "Truth." This belief is what allows, in fact, compels the metaphysician to adopt the vocabulary of grounding.

(p. 40)

The relationship between metaphysics and foundationalism is a clear one that Rorty highlights later in *Philosophy*:

A foundationalist need only claim that every belief occupies a place in a natural, transcultural, transhistorical order of reasons – an order which eventually leads the inquirer back to one or another "ultimate source of evidence". Different foundationalists offer different candidates for such sources: for example, Scripture, tradition, clear and distinct ideas, sense-experience, common sense.

(p. 151, citation omitted)

Metaphysicians, then, embrace foundations and suggest that their particular foundations are objective rather than subjective. James Conant, in "Freedom, Cruelty, and Truth: Rorty versus Orwell" in *Rorty and His Critics*, ed. Robert B. Brandom (Oxford: Blackwell Publishers, 2000), argues, as I do, that Rorty has not been successful in his attempt to abandon metaphysics, noting eight characteristically "Rortian theses" that demonstrate "Rorty's own substantial metaphysical commitments" (p. 275). These theses, working to jettison

particular Realist theses to which Conant sets them in opposition, are: "the thesis that solidarity ought to replace objectivity"; "the thesis of linguistic idealism"; "the thesis of instrumentalism concerning linguistic norms"; "the thesis of the conversational basis of moral belief"; "the thesis of historicism"; "the thesis that public and private goods are incommensurable"; "the thesis of Rortian liberalism"; and "the thesis of ironism" (ibid., 275–277). I think Conant makes a compelling point, here, though Rorty's response, in his "Response to James Conant" in *Rorty and His Critics*, ed. Robert B. Brandom (Oxford: Blackwell Publishers, 2000), is unsurprising:

> I think of all the "Rortian" theses he lists as suggestions about how to redescribe familiar situations in order to achieve various practical goals. I think of both archetypal metaphysicians like Plato, Spizona and Hegel and archetypal anti-metaphysicians like Dewey, Wittgenstein and Heidegger as having made similar suggestions. I see the difference between the metaphysicians and anti-metaphysicians as consisting mainly in the anti-Realism of the latter. In my jargon, "metaphysical" and "Realist" are pretty well co-extensive terms.
>
> (p. 344)

Rorty seeks to avoid the charge of being a metaphysician himself by suggesting that "Conant obviously attaches a very different meaning to the term 'metaphysical' than I do, and I wish that he had explained his use of the term in more detail." My argument in this chapter, generally sympathetic with Conant's, is more specific in substance – particularly on the question of Rorty's own metaphysical foundations – and offers a further challenge to Rorty's claim, just above, that he is simply offering "suggestions about how to redescribe familiar situations in order to achieve various practical goals" (ibid.).

17 Richard Rorty, *Objectivity, Relativism, and Truth: Philosophical Papers, Volume 1* (Cambridge: Cambridge University Press, 1991), 177.

18 Steven Kautz, *Liberalism and Community* (Ithaca, NY: Cornell University Press, 1995), 77, citation omitted.

19 Ibid., 78–79.

20 Rorty, *Contingency*, 29.

21 Kautz, 79.

22 Perry, 38. However, this argument about cost might not hold. The central premise of William F. Schulz's compelling book, *In Our Own Best Interest: How Defending Human Rights Benefits Us All* (Boston: Beacon Press, 2002), is that:

> respect for human rights both in the United States and abroad has implications for our welfare far beyond the maintenance of our ethical integrity. Ignoring the fates of human rights victims anywhere almost invariably makes the world – *our* world – a more dangerous place. If we learned nothing else from the horrific events of September 11, perhaps we learned that.
>
> (p. xix)

23 Perry, 37–38, citations omitted.

24 Richard Rorty, *Consequences of Pragmatism: Essays, 1972–1980* (Minneapolis: University of Minnesota Press, 1982), xlii.

25 Rorty defines a liberal ironist, in *Contingency*, as

> the sort of person who faces up to the contingency of his or her own most central beliefs and desires – someone sufficiently historicist and nominalist to have abandoned the idea that those central beliefs and desires refer back to something beyond the reach of time and chance. Liberal ironists are people who include among these ungroundable desires their own hope that suffering will be diminished, that the humiliation of human beings by other human beings may cease.
>
> (p. xv)

26 Perry, 38.
27 Rorty, *Contingency*, xv.
28 Kautz seems to agree with Rorty on this point; he argues that "we may not deny [other human beings] their natural rights," but also – strangely – that "liberals are under no obligation to concern themselves with the preservation of the ways of life of those who are not members of our community" (p. 106). He goes on to suggest that "The liberal American would perhaps be willing to fight in a war to preserve our American way of life," but "perhaps" is not a particularly strong word and it is not clear if our protection should be extended to include fledgling versions of our way of life in non-American communities. My sense is that Kautz's version of liberalism would not come to the aid of the 'other' in this situation, especially given his footnote about Michael Walzer's discussion of this problem in *Spheres of Justice*: "Walzer's account is in certain respects too humane, it seems to me; Walzer sometimes emphasizes duties to humanity at the expense of the duties and rights of consenting liberal individuals" (p. 106n).
29 Rorty, *Contingency*, 63.
30 Ibid., 46. This is what Rorty has in mind when he discusses the concept of a final vocabulary. He says

> All human beings carry about a set of words which they employ to justify their actions, their beliefs, and their lives. These are the words in which we formulate praise of our friends and contempt for our enemies, our long-term projects, our deepest self-doubts and our highest hopes. They are the words in which we tell, sometimes prospectively and sometimes retrospectively, the story of our lives.... [T]heir user has no noncircular argumentative recourse. Those words are as far as he can go with language; beyond them there is only helpless passivity or a resort to force.
>
> (p. 73)

31 Rorty, *Objectivity*, 185.
32 Kautz, 102.
33 Ibid., 103.
34 Rorty, *Contingency*, 65.
35 Of course, Rorty would undoubtedly argue that – once again – his theory is being upbraided for its failure to adequately take into account the metaphysical needs of others and provide reasons to calm their fears, tasks for which it is specifically not designed.
36 Rorty, *Contingency*, 84.
37 Ibid.
38 Ibid., 84–85.
39 In what sense is Rorty's theory an obviously frustrating one? Jonathan Glover points out, in a section of *Humanity: a Moral History of the Twentieth Century* (New Haven: Yale University Press, 2001) entitled "The Soul and the

Hunger for Belief" (in the midst of his discussion of Nazism, interestingly), that "People want their lives to add up to something, to contribute to something larger than themselves.... There is a need for transcendence: for something that reaches to the soul.

(p. 362)

40 That said, a compelling argument can be made against Rorty here, namely that our common history is actually one of considerable inhumanity. As Glover notes:

> At the start of the century there was optimism, coming from the Enlightenment, that the spread of a humane and scientific outlook would lead to the fading away, not only of war, but also of other forms of cruelty and barbarism. They would fill the chamber of horrors in the museum of our primitive past. In the light of these expectations, the century of Hitler, Stalin, Pol Pot and Saddam Hussein was likely to be a surprise. Volcanoes thought extinct turned out not to be.

(p. 6)

Of course, Rorty would likely suggest that these examples are precisely the sort of historical proof we can use to suggest that the human rights regime is one with great practical advantages over a global order that permits regimes like these to act with impunity.

41 Perry, 29.
42 Rorty, *Contingency*, 85.
43 Ibid.
44 Recall Nietzsche's assertion, in *The Will to Power*, trans. Walter Kaufmann and R.J. Hollingdale and ed. Walter Kaufmann (New York: Vintage Books, 1968), that the death of God would result in the destruction of morality: "Naiveté: as if morality could survive when the *God* who sanctions it is missing! The 'beyond' absolutely necessary if faith in morality is to be maintained" (p. 147).
45 Rorty, *Contingency*, 86.
46 It seems important to note, here, that it is not entirely so clear that the United States is seeing a decline in religious belief. More than most liberal countries, America remains by and large a nation of believers. As Steven Pinker points out, in *The Blank Slate: the Modern Denial of Human Nature* (New York: Viking, 2002)

> According to recent polls, 76 percent of Americans believe in the biblical account of creation, 79 percent believe that the miracles in the Bible actually took place, 76 percent believe in angels, the devil, and other immaterial souls, 67 percent believe they will exist in some form after their death, and only 15 percent believe that Darwin's theory of evolution is the best explanation for the origin of human life on Earth.

(p. 2, citation omitted)

And, to the extent that there has been any decline in religious belief amongst American liberals, we must also note a clearly expressed discontent about the decay of morality and the traditional family structure. That said, the same discontent is not nearly as pronounced in Europe, where the level of religious belief is markedly lower. In further defense of Rorty's position, Europeans

generally seem to have a much more pronounced commitment to the contemporary international human rights regime than do Americans.

47 Rorty, *Contingency*, 87.
48 Ibid., 85.
49 Ibid., xv.
50 Ibid., 89.
51 Ibid., 90.
52 Ibid.
53 Ibid., 91.
54 Ibid., 92.
55 Perry, 28.
56 Rorty, *Contingency*, 93.
57 It is interesting to note, of course, that Rorty's project is itself in violation of this dictate. Good liberal ironists ought to avoid public redescriptions of others' final vocabularies, but Rorty's work is well-known precisely because of his very public critiques of Enlightenment metaphysics.
58 Conant challenges Rorty about O'Brien's motivation for torturing Winston in Orwell's *1984*, noting that:

> Rorty's reading threatens to leave O'Brien appearing peculiarly obsessed with getting Winston to assent to falsehoods for no particular reason. Rorty sees the problem this poses for his reading and draws the only conclusion he consistently can in light of his interpretive claim: the obsession with getting Winston to assent to falsehoods is simply O'Brien's obsession and has nothing to do with O'Brien's own attachment to the beliefs of whose truth he tries to convince Winston.
>
> (p. 290)

What Conant suggests, here, is a very different reading of O'Brien from Rorty's, namely that O'Brien might actually be a firm believer in the Party and not at all an ironist.

59 Rorty, *Contingency*, xv.
60 Rorty and Judith Shklar (from whom he borrows this basic definition of liberalism) believe it can be thus boiled down. For more of Shklar's discussion of humiliation, see her *Ordinary Vices* (Cambridge, MA: Belknap Press of Harvard University Press, 1984).
61 Rorty, *Contingency*, 94.
62 Ibid., 92–93.
63 Ibid., 94.
64 Ibid., 91.
65 Ibid., 89.
66 Ibid., 94–95.
67 Ibid., 96.
68 Ibid., 119–120.
69 Ibid., 120–121.
70 Ibid., xvi.
71 Ibid., xv.
72 Richard Rorty, "Truth and Freedom: a Reply to Thomas McCarthy," *Critical Inquiry* 16 (Spring 1990), 636–637.
73 Gander, 164.
74 Rorty, *Contingency*, 197.
75 Rorty, "Truth and Freedom," 636–637.
76 Perry makes a strikingly similar claim in his discussion of subjectivity and objectivity:

"Imagine someone saying to a Bosnian Serb: "The Bosnian Muslim, too, no less than you, is sacred. It is wrong for you to rape her." If "sacred" is meant in the subjective sense, the Bosnian Serb can reply: "Sacred to you and yours, perhaps, but not to me and mine. In the scheme of things, we happen not to attach much value to her life." By contrast, 'sacred' in the objective sense is not fundamentally a matter of 'sacred to you' or "sacred to me"; it is, rather, a matter of how things really are. . . . If every human being is sacred in the objective sense, then, in violating the Bosnian Muslim, the Bosnian Serb does not merely violate what some of us attach great value to; he violates the very order of creation.

(p. 28)

The problem with this sort of thinking, Rorty would undoubtedly note, is that the Bosnian Muslim is violated whether one speaks of the subjective or the objective truth about her to the Serb. Rorty suggests that it might be more practical to concern ourselves with preventing that violation rather than with attempting to discover the truth about the world.

77 Gander, 145–146.
78 Ibid., 82.
79 Ibid., 89.
80 Richard Rorty, "What Can You Expect From Anti-Foundationalist Philosophers? A Reply to Lynn Baker," 78 *Virginia Law Review* 78 (April 1992), 725–726.
81 Rorty, *Contingency*, 61.
82 Gander, 168.
83 Ibid. This suggestion brings to mind Tracy B. Strong's description of Carl Schmitt in "Foreword: Dimensions of the New Debate Around Carl Schmitt" in Carl Schmitt, *The Concept of the Political*, trans. George Schwab (Chicago: University of Chicago Press, 1996). Schmitt argued "that politics cannot be made safe and that the attempts to make politics safe will result in the abandonment of the state to private interests and to 'society'" (p. xv). He is an unusual character because of his decision to join the Nazi Party in 1933 and because, before doing so, he "was among those who sought to strengthen the Weimar regime by trying to persuade Hindenburg to invoke the temporary dictatorial powers of article 48 against the extremes on the Right and the Left" (p. xv, citation omitted).
84 Gander, 168.
85 Norman Geras reaches a similar conclusion in *Solidarity in the Conversation of Humankind: the Ungroundable Liberalism of Richard Rorty* (New York: Verso, 1995). He wonders "why Rorty should sometimes . . . deny that people share a common nature composed of characteristics specific to them as humans, when he also affirms precisely such common human characteristics" (p. 53). See also Jean Bethke Elshtain, "Don't Be Cruel: Reflections on Rortyian Liberalism" in *The Politics of Irony: Essays in Self-Betrayal*, ed. Daniel W. Conway and John E. Seery (New York: St. Martin's Press, 1992), though her discussion of this point is brief and mentioned only in passing: "All that matters is a brotherhood and sisterhood of pain and humiliation. This smuggles universalism back in, of course, but that isn't the most important point" (p. 202).
86 See Richard Rorty, *Essays on Heidegger and Others: Philosophical Papers, Volume 2* (Cambridge: Cambridge University Press, 1991), 143–145; Richard Rorty, *Truth and Progress: Philosophical Papers, Volume 3* (Cambridge: Cambridge University Press, 1998), 299–306; and Rorty, *Philosophy*, 81–88.

Rorty will not, of course, suggest that Darwin was right or that evolutionary biology is the truth about the way the world works. He does, however, proceed quite clearly from Darwinian assumptions in everything he writes. Consider the following examples: "My criticisms of Heidegger ... and of Derrida ... center around their failure to take a relaxed, naturalistic, Darwinian view of language" (Rorty, *Essays*, 3); "The antinaturalist self-images suggested to us by, among others, Plato and Kant have served us well, but they are hard to reconcile with Darwin's account of our origins" (Rorty, *Truth*, 48); and – most clearly:

> After Darwin ... it became possible to believe that nature is not leading up to anything – that nature has nothing in mind. This idea, in turn, suggested that the difference between animals and humans is not evidence for the existence of an immaterial deity. It suggested further that humans have to dream up the point of human life, and cannot appeal to a nonhuman standard to determine whether they have chosen wisely.
>
> (Rorty, *Philosophy*, 266)

87 This argument draws a great deal on the work of Steven Pinker. Though Pinker does not actually go so far as to make this claim, the previous chapter expanded on his cogent explanations of how our minds work with a view to suggesting a connection between self-creation and dignity, a cornerstone of the idea of human rights. I want to build on that idea here by suggesting that – although it runs counter to his claims against human nature – Rorty ought to adopt this distinctly universalistic position, as it is a clear consequence of his theory of human rights.

88 Rorty, *Contingency*, 177.

89 Ibid., 178.

90 Kautz, 106.

91 Richard Rorty, *Truth*, 178.

92 Ibid., 168.

93 Schulz, 24.

94 Rorty, *Contingency*, 38.

95 As the previous chapter showed, a problem arises in thinking about those humans whose brains are incapable of self-creation. Do they too have rights? This is a difficult spot to be in, as it seems that the pervert and the sadist have rights, but not – for example – the innocent fetus whose brain remains incompletely formed. There is, of course, an extensive body of literature on this subject, but it seems to me that there are only two plausible answers: either humans have rights because they have the potential for self-creation (whether they achieve it or not) or else only those whose brains are actually able to engage in self-creation can claim the rights.

96 Rorty, *Contingency*, 33.

97 In "Ironist Theory as a Vocation: a Response to Rorty's Reply," *Critical Inquiry* 16(3) (Spring 1990), Thomas McCarthy points out, convincingly I think, why this is a strange move for Rorty to make:

> he consistently equates the *contingency* of individual existence ... with the absence of universal conditions or features of human life. But contingency is opposed to necessity, not universality, and so one might well ask whether there are any contingent universals relevant to thinking about morality and politics.
>
> (p. 649, citation omitted)

The contingent story of the evolution of the universal complex human mind is, I think, relevant.

98 Rorty, *Contingency*, xv.

99 Ibid., 93.

100 This raises the question – left unanswered above – about *why* we ought to eschew cruelty and encourage self-creation, especially as both are natural characteristics. Beyond Rorty's response that we avoid cruelty because it is the worst thing we do, we can also turn back to evolutionary psychology for an answer. Using game theory, Robert Wright – in *The Moral Animal: Evolutionary Psychology and Everyday Life* (New York: Vintage Books, 1995) – offers a very helpful summary of this line of thinking about the evolutionary value of compassion and disutility of antagonism. A quotation from biologist George Williams on the strategy of expanding altruism beyond kinship barriers makes the point most clearly: "an individual who maximizes his friendships and minimizes his antagonisms will have an evolutionary advantage, and selection should favor those characters that promote the optimization of personal relationships" (Wright, 190). Why not be cruel, then? Simply stated, in the long run it is in our best interests not to be. Of course, Wright also points out the trouble with this sort of thing:

> Some people worry that the new Darwinian paradigm will strip their lives of all nobility. If love of children is just defense of our DNA, if helping a friend is just payment for services rendered, if compassion for the downtrodden is just bargain-hunting – then what is there to be proud of?
>
> (ibid., 376)

Although this sort of argument might very well leave us feeling a bit cold, it nonetheless provides a clear and compelling answer to the question about why we ought not privilege the cruelty of which we are capable. Further, Wright argues that we are not forced to act this way *simply* because it's in our best interest; we can, in some sense, transcend our nature and act morally: "Go above and beyond the call of a smoothly functioning conscience; help those who aren't likely to help you in return, and do so when nobody's watching. This is one way to be a truly moral animal (ibid., 377).

101 Ibid., 46.

102 Rorty, "Truth and Freedom," 636–637.

103 Rorty, *Contingency*, 179.

104 One might well ask whether Rorty is as thorough-going a pacifist as I suggest; indeed, it is possible to read his words, here, as nothing more than the prescription for an ideal society, one that makes the world safe for pacifists. That said, consider his argument, in "Fighting Terrorism with Democracy," *The Nation* (October 21, 2002).

> We may have the strength to keep our democratic institutions intact even after realizing that our cities may never again be invulnerable. We may be able to keep the moral gains – the increases in political freedom and in social justice – made by the West in the past two centuries even if 9/11 is repeated year after year. But we shall only do so if the voters of the democracies stop their governments from putting their countries on a permanent war footing – from creating a situation in which neither the judges nor the newspapers can restrain organizations like the FBI from doing whatever they please, and in which the military absorbs most of the nation's resources.
>
> (pp. 13–14)

105 Rorty, *Contingency*, 189.
106 Ibid., 190.
107 Ibid., 190–191.
108 Glover is much more forthcoming than Rorty about the foundations of sympathy and solidarity that he too employs. He recognizes, as Perry and Kautz do, the dangers of Nietzschean philosophy, but argues that:

> Fortunately, there are also the "moral resources", certain human needs and psychological tendencies which work against narrowly selfish behaviour. These tendencies make it natural for people to display self-restraint, and to respect and care for others. They make it unlikely that "morality" in a broad sense will perish, despite the fading of belief in a moral law.
>
> (p. 22)

109 Rorty, *Contingency*, 191.
110 Rorty, *Truth*, 176.
111 Ibid., 181, citation omitted. Perry has an interesting critique of this language: "in what sense is it a *progress*, and not merely a *change*, of sentiments, if the new sentiments don't more accurately reflect a *truth* about the Other" (p. 38). Perry is right on this score, it seems to me, although the "truth about the Other" is that the way her brain works affords her with rights to live a self-creative life that is free of humiliation, rather than something more transcendent like that she is sacred or the beloved child of God.
112 Schulz also adopts Rorty's pragmatism:

> The question to ask about rights is not, Are they true? The question is, Do they work? Do they work to spread empathy, combat cruelty, and protect the weak from their oppressors? The experience of the international human rights community is that these do.
>
> (p. 27)

113 Ibid., 23.
114 Geras, 11. In addition, Elshtain offers five examples of Holocaust rescuers that, like Geras' examples, suggest problems with Rorty's theory about personal identification (p. 212–214).
115 This remark is not meant to imply that people with religious commitments would obviously act heroically, as most did not; instead, I want to subtract those who did so based on religious faith from both theorists' totals. Rather than saving Jews because they identified with them personally or simply as human beings as such, the people who based their actions on religious dictates are more appropriately placed in a third category. According to Christopher J. Eberle, in "Unnatural Sacrifice" (unpublished manuscript, 2003):

> Irrespective of whether the existence of people intent on pursuing genocidal policies is suprising on the theistic hypothesis, theists who adhere to the [Divine Command Theory] should surely expect that, if the world *does* contain people with such evil intentions, then God will obligate them to do what they can to come to the aid of those targeted for destruction.
>
> (p. 22)

This fits in nicely with Geras' examination of

> A young French Catholic, Germaine Ribière ... [who] speaks to a rabbi, saying she will help in any way she can. Another entry by her reads, "Humanity is the body of Christ. One part of that humanity is being tortured. ... And we look on in silence as the crime is being perpetrated."
>
> (p. 27)

116 Geras, 24.
117 Ibid., 25.
118 Ibid., 33.
119 Rorty, *Truth*, 181. Consider, however, the argument of Seble Dawit and Salem Mekuria about female genital mutilation in Africa in "The West Just Doesn't Get It," *New York Times* (December 7, 1993):

> Instead of being an issue worthy of attention in itself, it has become a powerfully emotive lens through which to view personal pain – a gauge by which to measure distance between the West and the rest of humanity. ... Superior Western attitudes do not enhance dialogue or equal exchange of ideas .... A media campaign in the West will not stop genital mutilation.
>
> (p. A27)

120 Rorty, *Truth*, 182.
121 Ibid., 185.
122 Rorty, *Contingency*, 196.
123 Wright, 372.
124 Rorty, *Truth*, 185.
125 Glover, 347, citation omitted.
126 Kautz, 79.

6 Rights and wrongs without God: a non-religious grounding for human rights in a pluralistic world

1 Michael J. Perry, *The Idea of Human Rights: Four Inquiries* (Oxford: Oxford University Press, 1998), 11–12.
2 Alan Dershowitz, *Rights from Wrongs: a Secular Theory of the Origins of Rights* (New York: Basic Books, 2004), 7.
3 Ibid., 81.
4 Ibid., 82.
5 See, for example, Mende Nazer and Damien Lewis, *Slave: My True Story* (New York: PublicAffairs, 2003) and Francis Bok, *Escape From Slavery: the True Story of My Ten Years in Captivity – and My Journey to Freedom in America* with Edward Tivnan (New York: St Martin's Griffin, 2004).
6 Dershowitz, 84.
7 Ibid.
8 This raises the unresolved – and potentially impossible to resolve – question of whether Germans were aware of the genocidal program upon which their leaders embarked. Even if we assume – and I believe we should not – that Germans were generally unaware of the mass murder undertaken by their government, it is clear that Germans were generally supportive of Hitler's regime. Indeed, even two of Germany's most well-respected philosophers, Martin Heidegger and Carl Schmitt, were members of the Nazi Party (with

varying degrees of ardor in different years of the Nazi era). And as Claudia Koonz points out, in *The Nazi Conscience* (Cambridge: Belknap Press of Harvard University Press, 2003):

> In 1933 Carl Schmitt, a distinguished political theorist and avid Hitler supporter, paraphrased a slogan used often in Nazi circles when he denounced the idea of universal human rights, saying: Not every being with a human face is human. This belief expressed the bedrock of Nazi morality.
>
> (p. 2)

9 Herodotus, *The Histories*, trans. Robin Waterfield (Oxford: Oxford University Press, 1998), 3.38.
10 As discussed in the first chapter, Perry's definition of a religious worldview is one that is "grounded or embedded in a vision of the finally or ultimately meaningful nature of the world and of our place in it" (p. 15).
11 Jürgen Habermas, *Between Facts and Norms: Contributions to a Discourse Theory of Law and Democracy*, trans. William Rehg (Cambridge: MIT Press, 1999), 107.
12 Ludwig Wittgenstein, *Philosophical Investigations*, trans. G.E.M. Anscombe (Oxford: Basil Blackwell, 1968), 85.
13 Perry, 39.
14 Habermas, 9.
15 Ibid.
16 Richard Rorty, *Truth and Progress: Philosophical Papers, Volume 3* (Cambridge: Cambridge University Press, 1998), 184–185.
17 Ian Hacking, *The Social Construction of What?* (Cambridge: Harvard University Press, 2001), vii.
18 Ibid., 24.
19 Ibid., 68.
20 Ibid., 70.
21 Arthur C. Danto, "Comment on Gewirth: Constructing an Epistemology of Human Rights: a Pseudo Problem?," *Social Philosophy & Policy* 1(2) (Spring 1984), 30.
22 Alan Gewirth, "Reply to Danto," *Social Philosophy & Policy* 1(2) (Spring 1984), 34.
23 William F. Schulz, *In Our Own Best Interest: How Defending Human Rights Benefits Us All* (Boston: Beacon Press, 2002), 26.
24 For more on the establishment and first session of the Human Rights Commission, see Mary Ann Glendon, *A World Made New: Eleanor Roosevelt and the Universal Declaration of Human Rights* (New York: Random House, 2001), 30–50.
25 Heiner Bielefeldt, "'Western' versus 'Islamic' Human Rights Conceptions? A Critique of Cultural Essentialism in the Discussion on Human Rights," *Political Theory* 28(1) (February 2000), 90–91, citations omitted.
26 Ibid., 92.
27 Glendon, 51.
28 Ibid., 73.
29 Several of these responses are quoted in Glendon, 73–78; others are collected, along with the Committee's report and its questionnaire, in *Human Rights: Comments and Interpretations*, ed. UNESCO (New York: Columbia University Press, 1949).
30 Glendon, 73.

31 Ibid., 74, citation omitted.
32 Ibid.
33 Ibid., 75–76, citation omitted.
34 Ibid., 77, citation omitted.
35 Ibid., citation omitted.
36 Ibid., 134.
37 Ibid., 225–226. In addition to Glendon's response, I want to take issue with the criticism that a Western education somehow removes the distinct cultural imprint from people like Chang and Malik or that it makes them more Western than – and no longer representative of – their countrymen. This argument seems to regularly surface only when universal concepts like human rights are at issue; no one suggests, after all, that the movement for Indian independence was a Western one, despite the fact that both Gandhi and Nehru were educated in the West. While I want to argue, then, that Malik and Chang can be considered representatives of their respective cultures, it is also important to note the particular problem that Malik raises. I am grateful to Islamic human rights scholar Recep Senturk for raising the point that Malik, a Lebanese Christian, cannot be said to have represented the thoughts, feelings, ideas, and concerns of the Muslim world in the drafting process. Although Muslims were represented in the UNESCO survey and in the Human Rights Commission, they were notably absent on the drafting committee. As Senturk notes, "it would have been wiser to include a Muslim who is well-versed in the universalistic branch of Islamic law ... to forestall the later complications which we still face ... in the Muslim world regarding the UDHR" (e-mail message from Recep Senturk to Ari Kohen, April 4, 2005). I think this is clearly right and obviously problematic, though it is also important to note that the UDHR is perfectly in keeping with the tenets of Islam, as many Islamic scholars argued at the time and as others – including Senturk – have since pointed out. As he notes:

> Turkish scholars of Islamic law put their full support behind [the] UDHR even before it was declared.... For instance, Huseyin Kazim Kadri wrote a commentary ... demonstrating how each article is in conformity with Islamic law and therefore should be supported by Muslims.
> (E-mail message from Recep Senturk to Ari Kohen, April 6, 2005)

38 Glendon, 225.
39 Ibid., 226, citation omitted.
40 Bielefeldt, 116, citation omitted. For more on the "Project on Religion and Human Rights," see *Religion and Human Rights*, ed. John Kelsay and Sumner B. Twiss (New York: Project on Religion and Human Rights, 1994).
41 Rhoda E. Howard and Jack Donnelly, "Human Dignity, Human Rights, and Political Regimes," *American Political Science Review* 80(3) (September 1986), 802.
42 Ibid., 808.
43 Ibid.
44 In the first chapter of her recent book, *The History of Human Rights: From Ancient Times to the Globalization Era* (Berkeley: University of California Press, 2004), Micheline R. Ishay details the contributions of traditional societies to the contemporary notions of human rights and human dignity (pp. 16–61). Looking to their ancient historical documents, she demonstrates that these societies (traditionally as well as today) "urge protection for the poor, the disabled, the sick, and the powerless, praise good and impartial rulings,

encourage some forms of social and economic justice, condemn arbitrary killing, offer moral prescriptions for wartime, and so forth" (p. 60).

45 The reference is to Asmarom Legesse, "Human Rights in African Political Culture" in *The Moral Imperatives of Human Rights: a World Survey*, ed. Kenneth W. Thompson (Washington, DC: University Press of America, 1980). Donnelly offers a far more thorough explication of the argument that human rights are Western in origin and cannot be said to have existed in Islamic, Confucian Chinese, traditional African, or Hindu Indian societies prior to their establishment in the West in "Human Rights and Human Dignity: an Analytic Critique of Non-Western Conceptions of Human Rights," *American Political Science Review* 76(2) (June 1982). He revises this argument, by removing his discussion of the Soviet Union, and also expands it, by including a discussion of the dearth of rights in the premodern West, in his *Universal Human Rights in Theory and Practice*, Second Edition (Ithaca: Cornell University Press, 2003), 71–88. It is important to note, however, that Donnelly does not dispute the point that I have been making about the universality of human dignity; in fact, his argument seems to support that conclusion even as he contends that the contemporary conception of rights did not proceed from those societies' recognition of inherent dignity (ibid., 71–72).

46 Abdullahi Ahmed An-Na'im, "Toward a Cross-Cultural Approach to Defining International Standards of Human Rights: the Meaning of Cruel, Inhuman, or Degrading Treatment or Punishment" in *Human Rights in Cross-Cultural Perspectives: a Quest for Consensus*, ed. Abdullahi Ahmed An-Na'im (Philadelphia: University of Pennsylvania Press, 1995), 37–38.

47 Ibid., 35.

48 Ibid., 39.

49 Glendon, 59.

50 Ibid., 84–86.

51 Ibid., 88.

52 Ibid., 89, citation omitted.

53 Ibid., 146.

54 Ibid.

55 Ibid., citation omitted.

56 Ibid., 142, citation omitted.

57 While the notion is first developed in his *A Theory of Justice*, Revised Edition (Cambridge: The Belknap Press of Harvard University Press, 1999), Rawls spends considerably more time explicating its principles in *Political Liberalism* (New York: Columbia University Press, 1996), 133–172. More recently, the idea of an overlapping consensus is internationalized in Rawls' *The Law of Peoples* (Cambridge: Harvard University Press, 2001). In order for diverse cultures to reach consensus on principles of justice and human rights, Rawls suggests a trimming of the rights articulated in the Universal Declaration. As Evan Charney notes, in "Cultural Interpretation and Universal Human Rights: a Response to Daniel A. Bell," *Political Theory* 27(6) (December 1999), "Rawls presents an absolute minimum list of basic human rights that any society must uphold in order to be what he terms a 'member in good standing' of the 'society of peoples'" (p. 842). I argue, in this chapter, that Rawls' trimming of the UDHR might not be necessary in order to achieve the international consensus on human rights that he seeks.

58 There is, of course, considerable controversy in Rawls scholarship on the question of whether the principles of justice articulated in *A Theory of Justice* survive in *Political Liberalism* or whether the former proves to be an example

of a comprehensive doctrine that might be compatible with, but is not fully realized in, all forms of political liberalism.

59 Rawls, *Political Liberalism*, 137.
60 Glendon, 164.
61 Ibid., 165.
62 Glendon offers a description of the voting that took place that night:

> When the speeches were over, the General Assembly polled the members on each article separately, with an impressive result: twenty-three of thirty articles gained unanimous approval. A few scattered abstentions were recorded on Articles 1 and 2 – as well as on the articles dealing with freedom of movement, freedom of religion, freedom of opinion and expression, the right to education, and the article stating that everyone has a right to a social and international order in which the Declaration's rights can be fully realized. There were no nays except on the nondiscrimination article (one vote); the article on the family (six votes); and the article on freedom of opinion and expression (seven votes). With the Declaration certain of adoption at that point, the president called the roll and drew by lot the name of the county to vote first, Burma. After Burma voted yes, Byelorussia, next in order, abstained, as did the other members of the Soviet bloc when their turns came up – Czechoslovakia, Poland, the Ukraine, the USSR, and Yugoslavia. It had been clear from the beginning that South Africa would be unable to accept the Declaration, but she too abstained rather than voting against it. So did Saudi Arabia, breaking ranks with the other Muslim nations that had voted yes. The final tally was forty-eight in favor, eight abstentions, and none opposed. Two countries, Honduras and Yemen, were absent.
>
> (pp. 169–170)

To this, David P. Forsythe – in "Human Rights Fifty Years after the Universal Declaration: Reconciling American Political Science and the Study of Human Rights," *PS: Political Science and Politics* 31(3) (September 1998) – adds:

> No state has ever sought to join the United Nations but reserve against Articles 55 and 56 of the UN Charter, which mandate cooperation on human rights. Of the eight states that abstained from the General Assembly vote in 1948 approving the Universal Declaration, all but Saudi Arabia have publicly renounced their abstentions.
>
> (p. 508)

63 Donnelly, *Human Rights*, 41.
64 Ibid., 40, citation omitted.
65 Rawls, *Political Liberalism*, 153.
66 Donnelly, *Human Rights*, 39.
67 Ibid., 43.
68 Alan Gewirth, "The Epistemology of Human Rights," *Social Philosophy & Policy* 1(2) (Spring 1984), 3.
69 There is significant disagreement on this subject that dates back at least as far as Hanna Pitkin's influential 1965–1966 *American Political Science Review* articles. In "Obligation and Consent," Pitkin ultimately argues that people must decide for themselves whether their actions are right, that anyone else can have a say in whether they judged correctly, and that there might very well be no "last word" on the matter of right and wrong action.

70 Habermas, 5.
71 Ibid., 32.
72 Ibid., 33.
73 African [Banjul] Charter on Human and Peoples' Rights in *The Human Rights Reader: Major Political Writings, Essays, Speeches, and Documents from the Bible to the Present*, ed. Micheline R. Ishay (New York: Routledge, 1997), 473.
74 Habermas, 33.
75 Ibid.
76 I want to argue, here, only that the process of drafting and adopting the Universal Declaration was a democratic one, rather than that those who participated in that process were somehow democratic themselves or were the representatives of democratic governments. As this chapter has demonstrated, many of the countries represented in these deliberations were not themselves democratic and this could certainly constitute a challenge to the claim that the millions of people represented by these individuals at the United Nations participated in any meaningful way in the drafting and adoption of the UDHR. That said, the intervening years have seen the end of many of these non-democratic governments – the Soviet Union, for example – and the adoption, by the new and more democratic regimes, of the principles enshrined in the Universal Declaration.
77 Habermas, 18.
78 Dershowitz makes much of this point – indeed, he bases his entire argument on it – and, I believe, rightly so. Yet, as I have argued above, I see his conclusion as lacking the sort of specificity that I am attempting to reach, here, on the question of the foundation for human rights, which – contra Dershowitz – I take to be human dignity rather than human wrongs.
79 United Nations Universal Declaration of Human Rights in Ishay, *Human Rights Reader*, 407.
80 Habermas, 26.
81 Ibid., 19.
82 Perry, 28.
83 Richard Rorty, *Contingency, Irony, and Solidarity* (Cambridge: Cambridge University Press, 1989), 53.
84 Glendon, 147, citation omitted.
85 Rawls, *Political Liberalism*, 153, citation omitted.
86 Glendon, 77, citation omitted.
87 Ibid., 78, citation omitted.

Bibliography

Abolitionist Action Committee. Online, available at: www.abolition.org/starvin13. FVhistory.html and www.abolition.org/starvin13fasting.html.

Allen, Elizabeth, Barbara Beckwith, Jon Beckwith *et al.*, "Against 'Sociobiology'," *New York Review of Books* 22(18) (November 13, 1975).

An-Na'im, Abdullahi Ahmed, "Toward a Cross-Cultural Approach to Defining International Standards of Human Rights: the Meaning of Cruel, Inhuman, or Degrading Treatment or Punishment," *Human Rights in Cross-Cultural Perspectives: a Quest for Consensus*, ed. Abdullahi Ahmed An-Na'im (Philadelphia: University of Pennsylvania Press, 1995).

Appiah, K. Anthony, "Grounding Human Rights," in Ignatieff, Michael, *Human Rights as Politics and Idolatry*, ed. Amy Gutmann (Princeton: Princeton University Press, 2001).

Armstrong, Karen, *Holy War: the Crusades and Their Impact on Today's World* (New York: Doubleday, 1991).

——, *A History of God: The 4,000-Year Quest of Judaism, Christianity and Islam* (New York: Ballantine Books, 1993).

Aron, Raymond, *The Opium of the Intellectuals* (New Brunswick: Transaction Publishers, 2001).

Beyleveld, Deryck, *The Dialectical Necessity of Morality: An Analysis and Defense of Alan Gewirth's Argument to the Principle of Generic Consistency* (Chicago: University of Chicago Press, 1991).

Beyleveld, Deryck and Shaun Pattinson, "Precautionary Reason as a Link to Moral Action," *Medical Ethics*, ed. Michael Boylan (Upper Saddle River: Prentice Hall, 2000).

Bielefeldt, Heiner, "'Western' versus 'Islamic' Human Rights Conceptions? A Critique of Cultural Essentialism in the Discussion on Human Rights," *Political Theory* 28(1) (February 2000).

Bok, Francis, *Escape From Slavery: the True Story of My Ten Years in Captivity – and My Journey to Freedom in America*, with Edward Tivnan (New York: St Martin's Griffin, 2004).

Boonin, David, *A Defense of Abortion* (Cambridge: Cambridge University Press, 2003).

Bowie, Malcolm, *Lacan* (Cambridge: Harvard University Press, 1991).

Charney, Evan, "Cultural Interpretation and Universal Human Rights: a Response to Daniel A. Bell," *Political Theory* 27(6) (December 1999).

CNN.com Inside Politics, "Schiavo Ruling Disappoints White House, DeLay"

(March 22, 2005). Online, available at: www.cnn.com/2005/ALLPOLITICS/03/22/schiavo.reaction/index.html.

Conant, James, "Freedom, Cruelty, and Truth: Rorty versus Orwell," *Rorty and His Critics* ed. Robert B. Brandom (Oxford: Blackwell Publishers, 2000).

Cooney, William, "The Fallacy of All Person-Denying Arguments for Abortion," *Journal of Applied Philosophy* 8(2) (1991).

Dannhauser, Werner J., "Friedrich Nietzsche," *History of Political Philosophy*, ed. Leo Strauss and Joseph Cropsey (Chicago: University of Chicago Press, 1987).

Danto, Arthur C., "Comment on Gewirth: Constructing an Epistemology of Human Rights: a Pseudo Problem?," *Social Philosophy & Policy* 1(2) (Spring 1984).

Dawit, Seble and Salem Mekuria, "The West Just Doesn't Get It," *New York Times* (December 7, 1993).

Dawkins, Richard, *The Selfish Gene* (Oxford: Oxford University Press, 1989).

DeGrazia, David, "Identity, Killing, and the Boundaries of Our Existence," *Philosophy & Public Affairs* 31(4) (Fall 2003).

Dershowitz, Alan M., *Why Terrorism Works: Understanding the Threat, Responding to the Challenge* (New Haven: Yale University Press, 2002).

——, *Rights from Wrongs: a Secular Theory of the Origins of Rights* (New York: Basic Books, 2004).

Donnelly, Jack, "Human Rights and Human Dignity: an Analytic Critique of Non-Western Conceptions of Human Rights," *American Political Science Review* 76(2) (June 1982).

——, *Human Rights in Theory and Practice*, Second Edition (Ithaca: Cornell University Press, 2003).

Dorfman, Ariel, "Are There Times When We Have to Accept Torture?," *Guardian* (May 8, 2004).

Dworkin, Ronald, "Life is Sacred. That's the Easy Part," *New York Times Magazine* (May 16, 1993).

——, *Life's Dominion: an Argument About Abortion, Euthanasia, and Individual Freedom* (New York: Vintage Books, 1994).

Eberle, Christopher J., "Unnatural Sacrifice" (unpublished manuscript, 2003).

Elshtain, Jean Bethke, "Don't Be Cruel: Reflections on Rortyian Liberalism," *The Politics of Irony: Essays in Self-Betrayal*, ed. Daniel W. Conway and John E. Seery (New York: St Martin's Press, 1992).

Engels, Friedrich, *Anti-Dühring: Herr Eugen Dühring's Revolution in Science* (New York: International Publishers, 1966).

Feinberg, Joel, *Rights, Justice, and the Bounds of Liberty: Essays in Social Philosophy* (Princeton: Princeton University Press, 1980).

Flanagan, Owen, *The Problem of the Soul: Two Visions of Mind and How to Reconcile Them* (New York: Basic Books, 2003).

Forsythe, David P., "Human Rights Fifty Years after the Universal Declaration: Reconciling American Political Science and the Study of Human Rights," *PS: Political Science and Politics* 31(3) (September 1998).

Frankfurt, Harry G., "Freedom of the Will and the Concept of a Person," *Journal of Philosophy* 68(1) (January 14, 1971).

Fukuyama, Francis, *Our Posthuman Future: Consequences of the Biotechnology Revolution* (New York: Picador, 2002).

Gaita, Raimond, *A Common Humanity: Thinking About Love and Truth and Justice* (New York: Routledge, 2002).

Gander, Eric M., *The Last Conceptual Revolution: a Critique of Richard Rorty's Political Philosophy* (Albany: State University of New York Press, 1999).

Geras, Norman, *Solidarity in the Conversation of Humankind* (New York: Verso, 1995).

Gewirth, Alan, *Reason and Morality* (Chicago: University of Chicago Press, 1981).

——, "The Epistemology of Human Rights," *Social Philosophy & Policy* 1(2) (Spring 1984).

——, "Reply to Danto," *Social Philosophy & Policy* 1(2) (Spring 1984).

——, *The Community of Rights* (Chicago: University of Chicago Press, 1996).

Glendon, Mary Ann, *A World Made New: Eleanor Roosevelt and the Universal Declaration of Human Rights* (New York: Random House, 2001).

Glover, Jonathan, *Humanity: a Moral History of the Twentieth Century* (New Haven: Yale University Press, 2001).

Gourevitch, Philip, *We Wish to Inform You That Tomorrow We Will Be Killed With Our Families: Stories from Rwanda* (New York: Picador USA, 1998).

Grant, Robert, "Abortion and the Idea of the Sacred," *Times Literary Supplement* (June 18, 1993).

Green, Michael B. and Daniel Wikler, "Brain Death and Personal Identity," *Philosophy and Public Affairs* 9(2) (Winter 1980).

Gutmann, Amy, "Introduction," Ignatieff, Michael, *Human Rights as Politics and Idolatry*, ed. Amy Gutmann (Princeton: Princeton University Press, 2001).

Habermas, Jürgen, *Between Facts and Norms: Contributions to a Discourse Theory of Law and Democracy*, trans. William Rehg (Cambridge: MIT Press, 1999).

Hacking, Ian, *The Social Construction of What?* (Cambridge: Harvard University Press, 2001).

Hamilton, Alexander, James Madison, and John Jay, *The Federalist Papers*, ed. Clinton Rossiter (New York: Penguin Books, 1961).

Heidegger, Martin, *An Introduction to Metaphysics*, trans. Ralph Manheim (New Haven: Yale University Press, 1987).

——, *Nietzsche, Volume IV: Nihilism*, trans. Frank A. Capuzzi, in *Nietzsche, Volumes Three and Four*, ed. David Farrell Krell (New York: HarperCollins Publishers, 1991).

Held, Virginia, "Reason and Economic Justice," *Economic Justice: Private Rights and Public Responsibilities*, ed. Kenneth Kipnis and Diana T. Meyers (Totowa: Rowman and Allanheld, 1985).

Hermann, Dorothy, *Helen Keller: A Life* (New York: Alfred A. Knopf, 1998).

Herodotus, *The Histories*, trans. Robin Waterfield (Oxford: Oxford University Press, 1998).

Hertz, J.H., ed., *The Pentateuch and Haftorahs* (London: Soncino Press, 1993).

Hobbes, Thomas, *Leviathan*, ed. Richard Tuck (Cambridge: Cambridge University Press, 1996).

The Holy Bible: New International Version (Grand Rapids: Zondervan Publishing House, 1986).

Howard, Rhoda E. and Jack Donnelly, "Human Dignity, Human Rights, and Political Regimes," *American Political Science Review* 80(3) (September 1986).

Ishay, Micheline R., ed., *The Human Rights Reader: Major Political Writings,*

Essays, Speeches, and Documents from the Bible to the Present (New York: Routledge, 1997).

——, *The History of Human Rights: From Ancient Times to the Globalization Era* (Berkeley: University of California Press, 2004).

Jackson, Timothy P., "A House Divided, Again: Sanctity vs. Dignity in the Induced Death Debates," *In Defense of Human Dignity: Essays for Our Times*, ed. Robert P. Kraynak and Glenn Tinder (Notre Dame: University of Notre Dame Press, 2003).

——, "The Image of God and the Soul of Humanity: Reflections on Dignity, Sanctity, and Democracy," *Religion in the Liberal Polity*, ed. Terence Cuneo (Notre Dame: University of Notre Dame Press, 2005).

Journey of Hope . . . From Violence to Healing. Online, available at: www.journeyofhope.org/pages/juan_melendez.htm.

Kalkut, Gary and Nancy Neveloff Dubler, "The Line Between Life and Death," *New York Times* (May 10, 2005).

Kant, Immanuel, *Grounding for the Metaphysics of Morals*, trans. James W. Ellington (Indianapolis: Hackett Publishing Company, 1993).

——, *The Metaphysics of Morals* in *Political Writings*, ed. Hans Reiss and trans. H.B. Nisbet (Cambridge: Cambridge University Press, 1996).

Kaufmann, Walter, "Editor's Introduction," Nietzsche, Friedrich, *The Will to Power*, trans. Walter Kaufmann and R.J. Hollingdale and ed. Walter Kaufmann (New York: Vintage Books, 1968).

Kautz, Steven, *Liberalism and Community* (Ithaca: Cornell University Press, 1995).

Kelsay, John and Sumner B. Twiss, eds, *Religion and Human Rights* (New York: Project on Religion and Human Rights, 1994).

Koestler, Arthur, *The Yogi and the Commissar: and Other Essays* (New York: The Macmillan Company, 1946).

Koonz, Claudia, *The Nazi Conscience* (Cambridge: Belknap Press of Harvard University Press, 2003).

Kraynak, Robert P., "Defending Human Dignity: the Challenge of Our Times," *In Defense of Human Dignity: Essays for Our Times*, ed. Robert P. Kraynak and Glenn Tinder (Notre Dame: University of Notre Dame Press, 2003).

Lacan, Jacques, *The Seminar of Jacques Lacan: Book VII, The Ethics of Psychoanalysis 1959–1960*, ed. Jacques-Alain Miller and trans. Dennis Porter (New York: W.W. Norton & Company, 1997).

Lecky, William Edward Hartpole, *History of European Morals From Augustus to Charlemagne* (New York: G. Braziller, 1955).

Legesse, Asmarom, "Human Rights in African Political Culture," *The Moral Imperatives of Human Rights: a World Survey*, ed. Kenneth W. Thompson (Washington: University Press of America, 1980).

Leibniz, Gottfried Wilhelm, *New Essays on Human Understanding* (New York: Cambridge University Press, 1996).

Levi, Primo, *The Drowned and the Saved*, trans. Raymond Rosenthal (London: Simon & Schuster, 1988).

Lewis, Charlton T. and Charles Short, *A Latin Dictionary* (Oxford: Oxford University Press, 1969).

Lewontin, Richard C., Steven Rose, and Leon J. Kamin, *Not in our Genes* (New York: Pantheon, 1984).

Liddell, Henry George and Robert Scott, *A Greek–English Lexicon*, revised and

augmented by Sir Henry Stuart Jones with the assistance of Roderick McKenzie (Oxford: Oxford University Press, 1959).

McMahan, Jeff, *The Ethics of Killing: Problems at the Margins of Life* (Oxford: Oxford University Press, 2002).

Machiavelli, Niccolò, *The Prince*, trans. Harvey C. Mansfield, Jr. (Chicago: University of Chicago Press, 1985).

McCarthy, Thomas, "Ironist Theory as a Vocation: a Response to Rorty's Reply," *Critical Inquiry* 16(3) (Spring 1990).

Marcus, Gary, *The Birth of the Mind: How a Tiny Number of Genes Creates the Complexities of Human Thought* (New York: Basic Books, 2004).

Marx, Karl, *Economic and Philosophic Manuscripts of 1844*, in *The Marx–Engels Reader*, ed. Robert C. Tucker (New York: W.W. Norton & Company, 1978).

Mead, Margaret, *Sex and Temperament in Three Primitive Societies* (New York: William Morrow, 1963).

Murphy, Jeffrie G., "Afterword: Constitutionalism, Moral Skepticism, and Religious Belief," *Constitutionalism: the Philosophical Dimension*, ed. Alan S. Rosenbaum (New York: Greenwood Press, 1988).

Nazer, Mende and Damien Lewis, *Slave: My True Story* (New York: PublicAffairs, 2003).

Nietzsche, Friedrich, *The Will to Power*, trans. Walter Kaufmann and R.J. Hollingdale and ed. Walter Kaufmann (New York: Vintage Books, 1968).

——, *On the Advantage and Disadvantage of History for Life*, trans. Peter Preuss (Indianapolis: Hackett Publishing Company, 1980).

——, *The Gay Science*, in *The Portable Nietzsche*, ed. and trans. Walter Kaufmann (New York: Penguin Books, 1982).

——, *Beyond Good and Evil: Prelude to a Philosophy of the Future*, in *Basic Writings of Nietzsche*, ed. and trans. Walter Kaufmann (New York: The Modern Library, 1992).

——, *On The Genealogy of Morals: a Polemic*, in *Basic Writings of Nietzsche*, ed. and trans. Walter Kaufmann (New York: The Modern Library, 1992).

——, *The Birth of Tragedy: Out of the Spirit of Music*, in *Basic Writings of Nietzsche*, ed. and trans. Walter Kaufmann (New York: The Modern Library, 1992).

Nozick, Robert, *Anarchy, State, and Utopia* (New York: Basic Books, 1974).

Olson, Eric T., *The Human Animal: Personal Identity Without Psychology* (Oxford: Oxford University Press, 1999).

Ontario Consultants on Religious Tolerance. Online, available at: www.religioustolerance.org/reciproc.htm.

Pelke, Bill, *Journey of Hope ... From Violence to Healing* (Philadelphia: Xlibris Corporation, 2003).

Perry, Michael J., "The Gospel According to Dworkin," *Constitutional Commentary* 11(1) (Winter 1994).

——, *The Idea of Human Rights: Four Inquiries* (Oxford: Oxford University Press, 1998).

——, E-mail messages to Ari Kohen (April 28 and May 12, 2003).

——, "The Morality of Human Rights: a Nonreligious Ground?" *Emory Law Journal* 54 (2005).

Pinker, Steven, *How the Mind Works* (New York: W.W. Norton & Company, 1999).

——, *The Blank Slate: The Modern Denial of Human Nature* (New York: Viking, 2002).

Pojman, Louis P., "Are Human Rights Based on Equal Human Worth?," *Philosophy and Phenomenological Research* 52(3) (September 1992).

Power, Samantha, *"A Problem from Hell": America and the Age of Genocide* (New York: Perennial, 2003).

Rawls, John, *Political Liberalism* (New York: Columbia University Press, 1996).

——, *A Theory of Justice,* Revised Edition (Cambridge: The Belknap Press of Harvard University Press, 1999).

——, *The Law of Peoples* (Cambridge: Harvard University Press, 2001).

Ridley, Matt, *The Origins of Virtue: Human Instincts and the Evolution of Cooperation* (New York: Penguin Books, 1996).

——, *Genome: the Autobiography of a Species in 23 Chapters* (New York: Perennial, 2000).

Rorty, Richard, *Consequences of Pragmatism: Essays, 1972–1980* (Minneapolis: University of Minnesota Press, 1982).

——, *Contingency, Irony, and Solidarity* (Cambridge: Cambridge University Press, 1989).

——, "Truth and Freedom: a Reply to Thomas McCarthy," *Critical Inquiry* 16 (Spring 1990).

——, *Objectivity, Relativism, and Truth: Philosophical Papers, Volume 1* (Cambridge: Cambridge University Press, 1991).

——, *Essays on Heidegger and Others: Philosophical Papers, Volume 2* (Cambridge: Cambridge University Press, 1991).

——, "What Can You Expect From Anti-Foundationalist Philosophers? A Reply to Lynn Baker," *Virginia Law Review* 78 (April 1992).

——, *Truth and Progress: Philosophical Papers, Volume 3* (Cambridge, Cambridge University Press, 1998).

——, *Philosophy and Social Hope* (New York: Penguin, 1999).

——, "Response to James Conant," *Rorty and His Critics*, ed. Robert B. Brandom (Oxford: Blackwell Publishers, 2000).

——, "Fighting Terrorism with Democracy," *The Nation* (October 21, 2002).

Sandel, Michael J., *Liberalism and the Limits of Justice*, Second Edition (Cambridge: Cambridge University Press, 1998).

Schulz, William F., *In Our Own Best Interest: How Defending Human Rights Benefits Us All* (Boston: Beacon Press, 2001).

——, *Tainted Legacy: 9/11 and the Ruin of Human Rights* (New York: Nation Books, 2003).

Senturk, Recep, E-mail messages to Ari Kohen (April 4 and April 6, 2005).

Shklar, Judith N., *Ordinary Vices* (Cambridge: The Belknap Press of Harvard University Press, 1984).

Simpson, J.A. and E.S.C. Weiner, eds, *The Oxford English Dictionary* (Oxford: Oxford University Press, 1989).

Singer, Peter, *Rethinking Life and Death: the Collapse of Our Traditional Ethics* (New York: St. Martin's Griffin, 1994).

——, *Writings on an Ethical Life* (New York: Ecco, 2001).

Solzhenitsyn, Aleksandr I., *The Gulag Archipelago 1918–1956: an Experiment in Literary Investigation, Parts I–II*, trans. Thomas P. Whitney (New York: Harper & Row, 1974).

Strauss, Leo, *Natural Right and History* (Chicago: University of Chicago Press, 1971).

Strong, Tracy B., "Foreword: Dimensions of the New Debate Around Carl Schmitt," Carl Schmitt, *The Concept of the Political*, trans. George Schwab (Chicago: University of Chicago Press, 1996).

Tomasi, John, "Liberalism, Sanctity, and the Prohibition of Abortion," *Journal of Philosophy* 94(10) (October 1997).

UNESCO, ed., *Human Rights: Comments and Interpretations* (New York: Columbia University Press, 1949).

Weston, Burns H., "Human Rights," *The New Encyclopædia Britannica* (Chicago: Encyclopædia Britannica, 2002).

Wittgenstein, Ludwig, *Philosophical Investigations* trans. G.E.M. Anscombe (Oxford: Basil Blackwell, 1968).

Wright, Robert, *The Moral Animal: Evolutionary Psychology and Everyday Life* (New York: Vintage Books, 1995).

——, *Nonzero: The Logic of Human Destiny* (New York: Vintage Books, 2001).

Index

Photo Credits

Photograph of Gerald Ledlow on page xv courtesy of Silke Ledlow.

Chapter 4
4-1 Courtesy of MyOliveTrees [www.myolivetrees.com]; **4-2** Courtesy of Santiago Soto Borreiros; **4-3** © Victorian Traditions/ShutterStock, Inc.

Chapter 8
8-1 © AP Photos; **8-2** Courtesy of Prints & Photographs Division, Library of Congress [LC-ppmsca-04598]; **8-4** © Fred Prouser/Reuters

Chapter 16
16-1 © rgaf72/Dreamstime.com

Unless otherwise indicated, all photographs and illustrations are under copyright of Jones & Bartlett Learning, LLC, or have been provided by the author(s).